CCIE Routing and Switching Exam Certification Guide

A. Anthony Bruno, CCIE #2738

Cisco Press

Cisco Press
201 West 103rd Street
Indianapolis, IN 46290 USA

CCIE Routing and Switching Exam Certification Guide

A. Anthony Bruno

Published by:
Cisco Press
201 West 103rd Street
Indianapolis, IN 46290 USA

Printed in the United States of America 1 2 3 4 5 6 7 8 9 0

First Printing July 2002

Library of Congress Cataloging-in-Publication Number: 20-01092525

ISBN: 1-58720-053-8

Warning and Disclaimer

This book is designed to provide information about the CCIE Routing and Switching written exam. Every effort has been made to make this book as complete and as accurate as possible, but no warranty or fitness is implied.

The information is provided on an "as is" basis. The author, Cisco Press, and Cisco Systems, Inc. shall have neither liability nor responsibility to any person or entity with respect to any loss or damages arising from the information contained in this book or from the use of the discs or programs that may accompany it.

The opinions expressed in this book belong to the author and are not necessarily those of Cisco Systems, Inc.

Trademark Acknowledgments

All terms mentioned in this book that are known to be trademarks or service marks have been appropriately capitalized. Cisco Press or Cisco Systems, Inc. cannot attest to the accuracy of this information. Use of a term in this book should not be regarded as affecting the validity of any trademark or service mark.

Feedback Information

At Cisco Press, our goal is to create in-depth technical books of the highest quality and value. Each book is crafted with care and precision, undergoing rigorous development that involves the unique expertise of members from the professional technical community.

Readers' feedback is a natural continuation of this process. If you have any comments regarding how we could improve the quality of this book, or otherwise alter it to better suit your needs, you can contact us through e-mail at feedback@ciscopress.com. Please make sure to include the book title and ISBN in your message.

We greatly appreciate your assistance.

Publisher	John Wait
Editor-in-Chief	John Kane
Executive Editor	Brett Bartow
Cisco Systems Management	Michael Hakkert
	Tom Geitner
Production Manager	Patrick Kanouse
Acquisitions Editor	Michelle Grandin
Development Editor	Andrew Cupp
Project Editor	San Dee Phillips
Copy Editor	Christopher Mattison
Contributing Author	Roy Spencer
Technical Editors	Jennifer Carroll
	Galina Pildush
Team Coordinator	Tammi Ross
Book Designer	Gina Rexrode
Cover Designer	Louisa Klucznik
Production Team	Octal Publishing, Inc.
Indexer	Tim Wright

Corporate Headquarters
Cisco Systems, Inc.
170 West Tasman Drive
San Jose, CA 95134-1706
USA
http://www.cisco.com
Tel: 408 526-4000
800 553-NETS (6387)
Fax: 408 526-4100

European Headquarters
Cisco Systems Europe
11 Rue Camille Desmoulins
92782 Issy-les-Moulineaux
Cedex 9
France
http://www-europe.cisco.com
Tel: 33 1 58 04 60 00
Fax: 33 1 58 04 61 00

Americas Headquarters
Cisco Systems, Inc.
170 West Tasman Drive
San Jose, CA 95134-1706
USA
http://www.cisco.com
Tel: 408 526-7660
Fax: 408 527-0883

Asia Pacific Headquarters
Cisco Systems Australia,
Pty., Ltd
Level 17, 99 Walker Street
North Sydney
NSW 2059 Australia
http://www.cisco.com
Tel: +61 2 8448 7100
Fax: +61 2 9957 4350

Cisco Systems has more than 200 offices in the following countries. Addresses, phone numbers, and fax numbers are listed on the Cisco Web site at www.cisco.com/go/offices

Argentina • Australia • Austria • Belgium • Brazil • Bulgaria • Canada • Chile • China • Colombia • Costa Rica • Croatia • Czech Republic • Denmark • Dubai, UAE • Finland • France • Germany • Greece • Hong Kong Hungary • India • Indonesia • Ireland • Israel • Italy • Japan • Korea • Luxembourg • Malaysia • Mexico The Netherlands • New Zealand • Norway • Peru • Philippines • Poland • Portugal • Puerto Rico • Romania Russia • Saudi Arabia • Scotland • Singapore • Slovakia • Slovenia • South Africa • Spain • Sweden Switzerland • Taiwan • Thailand • Turkey • Ukraine • United Kingdom • United States • Venezuela • Vietnam Zimbabwe

About the Author

A. Anthony Bruno is a Principal Consultant with International Network services and has over 11 years of experience in the internetworking field. His network certifications include CCIE, CWNA, CCDP, CCNA-WAN, Microsoft MCSE, Nortel NNCSS, Checkpoint CCSE, and Certified Network Expert (CNX) in Ethernet. As a consultant, he has worked with many enterprise and service provider customers in the design, implementation, and optimization of large-scale multiprotocol networks. Anthony has worked on the design of large company network mergers, wireless LANs, Voice over IP, and Internet access. He formerly worked as an Air Force Captain in network operations and management. He completed his B.S. degree in electrical engineering from the University of Missouri-Rolla in 1994 and his M.S. degree in electrical engineering from the University of Puerto Rico-Mayaguez in 1990. Anthony is also a part-time instructor for the University of Phoenix-Online, teaching networking courses.

Anthony is the co-author for the Cisco Press release *CCDA Exam Certification Guide* and a contributor and the lead technical reviewer for the Cisco Press release *Cisco CCIE Fundamentals: Network Design and Case Studies,* Second Edition. Anthony contributed a chapter to a Syngress publication titled *Designing Wireless Networks*. He has also performed technical reviews of Cisco Press titles *CID Exam Certification Guide* and *Internetworking Troubleshooting Handbook*.

About the Contributing Author

Roy Spencer is a Cisco Certified Network Associate for WAN switching and a Certified Cisco Systems Instructor with over fifteen years experience in the education segment of the networking industry. He has worked as a course developer for Cisco Systems, Inc., 3Com Corporation, and Nortel Networks Limited. Roy has written and taught classes on ATM switch configuration, network management, router configuration, LAN switch configuration, SONET multiplexers, Ethernet, and TCP/IP. He is currently employed as a course developer for a leading SONET optical switch manufacturer. Roy was the contributing author for the ATM material in Chapter 5 of this book.

About the Technical Reviewers

Jennifer DeHaven Carroll, CCIE #1402, has planned, designed, and implemented many large networks over the past thirteen years. She has also developed and taught network technology theory and implementation classes. Jennifer has a bachelor of science degree in computer science from the University of California, Santa Barbara.

Galina Diker Pildush, CCIE #3176, JNCIE #18, is with Juniper Networks, Inc. She provides training and course development for Juniper Networks, the leading provider of Internet systems. After earning her master of science degree in computer science, she worked for nineteen years for major, worldwide corporations in the areas of internetwork design, architecture, network optimization, implementation, and project management and training.

Galina has been an academic teacher at York University, teaching computer science, data communications, and computer network courses. Gaining extensive technical experience in internetworking and the Cisco line of products, she received her Routing and Switching CCIE certification in 1997. Upon achieving her CCIE, Galina dedicated a majority of her professional career to training and mentoring CCIE candidates by taking on the role of technical director for Netgun Academy CCIE preparation program at Global Knowledge Network, Inc. Deploying her passion for teaching, Galina taught a variety of Cisco courses. Upon joining Juniper Networks, Galina received one of the industry's toughest certifications—Juniper Networks Certified Internet Expert (JNCIE). Galina continues to teach at Juniper, enjoying state-of-the-art technology. Her areas of interest and specialization are ATM, internetwork design and optimization, VoIP, VPNs, MPLS, and Wireless technologies. One of Galina's most recent publications is *Cisco ATM Solutions* from Cisco Press. In addition to the demanding professional work, Galina, her husband, their two children, and their dog, who is a Canadian Champion, enjoy spending those rare moments together traveling, skiing, and cycling.

Dedications

This book is dedicated to my parents, Augustus Anthony Bruno, Sr. and Iris Belia Bruno. Thanks for your guidance and teaching during my "growing up" years. Dad: Thanks for the VIC20 computer. Also, I wish to dedicate this book to my sister, Anjanette.

Acknowledgments

This book would not have been possible without the efforts of many dedicated people. First, thanks to Andrew Cupp, Development Editor, whose guidance and expertise has improved this book, making it a better test guide for the readers. Thanks to Michelle Grandin, Acquisitions Editor, for giving me the opportunity to write this book. Thanks to Brett Bartow, Executive Editor, for your guidance. And special thanks to John Kane, Editor-in-Chief, for getting me started with Cisco Press in 1999.

Thanks to Roy Spencer for contributing the ATM material in the WAN chapter.

Thanks to the technical reviewers, Galina Pildush and Jennifer Carroll. Your advice and careful attention to detail significantly improved this book.

I also want to thank my boss of four years, Randy Kunkel, Managing Principal. Thanks for your support during this time.

Finally, I wish to thank my loving wife, Ivonne, and our daughters, Joanne Nichole and Dianne Christine, for their support during the development of this book.

Foreword

"The will to succeed is useless without the will to prepare"...Henry David Thoreau

The CCIE program is designed to help individuals, companies, industries, and countries succeed in an era of increasing network reliance by distinguishing the top echelon of internetworking experts. If that sounds like a lofty mission, then our standards for excellence are equally high.

To achieve the CCIE certification is to ascend the pinnacle of technical excellence in the IT profession. While CCIEs inevitably gain extensive product knowledge on their way to certification, product training is not the program objective. Rather, the focus is on identifying those experts capable of understanding and navigating the intricacies and potential pitfalls inherent in end-to-end networking, regardless of technology or product brand.

The first step along the CCIE path is for individuals to take a challenging written exam designed to assess their knowledge across a range of technologies and topologies relevant today. If their scores indicate expert-level knowledge, candidates then proceed to the performance-based CCIE Certification Lab Exam. Administered only by Cisco Systems, this hands-on exam truly distinguishes the CCIE program from all others. Candidates must demonstrate true mastery of internetworking through a series of timed exercises under intense conditions simulating today's mission-critical IT world.

Becoming CCIE Certified requires significant investment in education and preparation by each candidate. Moreover, a rigorous and mandatory biyearly recertification process ensures the commitment is long lasting and helps guarantee program integrity. These rigid requirements ensure that CCIEs are leaders with a proven and enduring commitment to their career, the industry, and the process of ongoing learning.

Cisco does not require candidates to complete specific training in preparation for either the written exam or the performance-based component of the CCIE certification process. The program is intended to identify hands-on experience and acquired expertise rather than the completion of specified course work. If you have committed yourself to beginning the journey toward achieving CCIE certification, *CCIE Routing and Switching Exam Certification Guide* can help ensure that your valuable preparation time is invested wisely. By providing candidates with typical exam subject matter, topic summaries, and practice and review questions that test the comprehensive networking knowledge expected, the *CCIE Routing and Switching Exam Certification Guide* can greatly assist in certification preparation. It offers you complete, late-stage exam preparation guidance that will enable you to assess your strengths and weaknesses and focus your study where you need the most help.

Lorne Braddock
Director, CCIE Program Group
Cisco Systems, Inc.

Contents at a Glance

Table of Contents

CHAPTER 1

CCIE Certification, Test Preparation, and Using This Book

Cisco Certifications

So you have worked on Cisco routers and switches for a while and now want to get your CCIE? There are several good reasons to do so. Cisco's certification program allows network analysts and engineers to demonstrate competence in different areas and levels of internetworking. Cisco certification can help you land a job or increase your pay because clients, peers, and superiors recognize you as a networking expert. CCIE certification is regarded as the most difficult and rewarding of the internetworking industry.

This book covers all exam objectives for the CCIE Routing and Switching (R&S) written test. The CCIE R&S Exam objectives are listed later in this chapter. You can find more information on the CCIE R&S test by visiting the following web site and selecting CCIE from the pull-down menu:

www.cisco.com/warp/public/10/wwtraining/

This book also covers the general networking objectives of the CCIE Communications and Services (C&S) written test. The general networking objectives of the CCIE C&S test are 50 percent of the total objectives for that test. The CCIE C&S general networking objectives are listed later in this chapter. You can find more information on the CCIE C&S test at the following web site:

www.cisco.com/warp/public/625/ccie/certifications/services.html

Cisco Certification Areas

Cisco divides its certification program into three major areas and provides specialist certifications. Each area usually includes a certification at the associate, professional, and expert level; the associate level certification is the lowest level and the expert level is the highest. The areas and certifications are as follows:

- **Network Installation and Support**—According to Cisco's web site, this path is for "professionals who install and support Cisco technology-based networks in which LAN and WAN routers and switches reside." This book helps prepare you for the CCIE R&S written exam. The certifications available in this track are as follows:

  — CCIE Routing and Switching (CCIE R&S)

  — Cisco Certified Network Professional (CCNP)

  — Cisco Certified Network Associate (CCNA)

CCIE C&S Written Exam General Knowledge Blueprint

Half of each C&S written test contains questions from the general knowledge blueprint. The general knowledge blueprint is a subset of the CCIE R&S blueprint. The CCIE C&S general knowledge blueprint includes the following: Cisco device operation, general networking theory, bridging and LAN switching, WAN media, IP theory, IP routing protocols, and performance management. This book helps prepare you for the general knowledge portion of the CCIE C&S exam. The CCIE C&S general knowledge blueprint is described in the next section.

CCIE Written Exam Objectives

This section provides tables that cover the CCIE written exam objectives from the published blueprint and the corresponding chapters in this book that cover those objectives. Two tables are included: one for the CCIE R&S written exam and one for the general knowledge portion of the CCIE C&S exam.

CCIE R&S Written Exam Objectives

Table 1-1 lists the CCIE R&S exam objectives and the corresponding chapters in this book that cover those objectives.

Table 1-1 *CCIE R&S Written Exam Objectives*

Exam Objective	Chapter
I. Cisco Device Operation	
Commands—**show**, **debug**	3
Infrastructure—NVRAM, Flash, memory and CPU, file system, configuration register	3
Operations—File transfers, password recovery, Simple Network Management Protocol (SNMP), accessing devices, security (passwords)	3
II. General Networking Theory	
OSI model—Layer comparisons, functions	2
General routing concepts—Split horizon, link-state, difference between switching and routing, summarization, link-state versus distance vector, loops, tunneling	2
Standards—802.x, protocol limitations	4
Protocol mechanics—Windowing/Acknowledgments (ACK), fragmentation, maximum transmission unit (MTU), handshaking, termination	6

Table 1-1 *CCIE R&S Written Exam Objectives (Continued)*

Exam Objective	Chapter
III. Bridging and LAN Switching	
Transparent Bridging—IEEE/DEC spanning tree, translational, integrated routed and bridging (IRB), concurrent routing and bridging (CRB), access lists, Multiple Instances of Spanning Tree (MISTP)	4
Source-route bridging (SRB)—Source-route translational bridging (SR/TLB), source-route transparent bridging (SRT), data-link switching (DLSw), remote source-route bridging (RSRB), access lists	4
LAN switching—Trunking, VLAN Trunk Protocol (VTP), virtual LANs (VLANs), Fast Ether Channel (FEC), Cisco Discovery Protocol (CDP)	4
LANE—LAN Emulation Client (LEC), LAN Emulation Server (LES), broadcast and unknown server (BUS), LAN Emulation Configuration Server (LECS), Simple Server Redundancy Protocol (SSRP)	4
Security—Private VLANs	4
IV. Internet Protocol	
Addressing—Classless interdomain routing (CIDR), subnetting, Address Resolution Protocol (ARP), Network Address Translation (NAT), Hot Standby Router Protocol (HSRP)	6
Services—Domain Name System (DNS), Bootstrap Protocol (BOOTP), Dynamic Host Configuration Protocol (DHCP), Internet Control Message Protocol (ICMP)	6
Applications—Telnet, File Transfer Protocol (FTP), Trivial File Transfer Protocol (TFTP)	6
Transport—IP fragmentation, sockets, ports	6
IP access lists	10
IPv6	6
V. IP Routing Protocols	
Open Shortest Path First (OSPF): Design—Areas, virtual links, stub areas, not-so-stubby areas (NSSA), area border router (ABR)/autonomous system boundary router (ASBR) redistributions, media dependencies, external versus internal, summarization Operation—Designated router (DR), backup designated router (BDR), adjacencies, link-state advertisement (LSA) types, link-state database, shortest path first (SPF) algorithm, authentication	8

continues

Table 1-1 *CCIE R&S Written Exam Objectives (Continued)*

Exam Objective	Chapter
Border Gateway Protocol (BGP): Design—peer groups, route reflectors, confederations, clusters, attributes, autonomous systems Operation—route maps, filters, neighbors, decision algorithm, Interior Border Gateway Protocol (IBGP), Exterior Border Gateway Protocol (EBGP)	9
Enhanced Interior Gateway Routing Protocol (EIGRP)—Metrics, mechanics, and design	7
Intermediate System-to-Intermediate System (IS-IS)—Metrics, mechanics, and design	8
Routing Information Protocol version 1 (RIPv1) and Routing Information Protocol version 2 (RIPv2)—Metrics, mechanics, and design	7
Access lists—distribute lists, route maps, policy routing, redistribution, route tagging	10
Dial-on-demand routing (DDR)—Dial backup	5
VI. Desktop Protocols	
Internetwork Packet Exchange (IPX)—Netware Link Services Protocol (NLSP), IPX-Routing Information Protocol/Services Advertisement Protocol, IPX-EIGRP, Sequenced Packet Exchange (SPX), Network Control Protocol (NCP), IPXWAN, IPX addressing, Get Nearest Server (GNS), Novell Directory Services (NDS) (routing and mechanisms), access control lists	12
Windows/NT—NetBIOS, browsing, domain controller (e.g. WINS), access control lists	12
VII. Quality of Service (QoS)	
Fancy queuing, Packet over Sonet (PoS) and IP Precedence, class of service (CoS), Weighted Round Robin/queue scheduling, shaping versus policing (rate limiting)/Committed Access Rate (CAR), Network-Based Application Recognition (NBAR), 802.1x, Differentiated Services Code Point (DSCP)	11
VIII. WAN (Addressing, Signaling, Framing)	
Integrated Services Digital Network (ISDN)—Link Access Procedure on the D channel (LAPD), Basic Rate Interface (BRI)/Primary Rate Interface (PRI) framing, signaling, mapping, Network Termination type 1 (NT1), dialer map, interface types, B/D channels, channel bonding	5
Frame Relay—Local Management Interface (LMI), data link connection identifier (DLCI), permanent virtual circuit (PVC), framing, traffic shaping, forward explicit congestion notification (FECN), backward explicit congestion notification (BECN), CIR, discard eligible (DE), mapping, compression	5
X.25—Addressing, routing, Link Access Procedure Balanced (LAPB), error control/recovery, windowing, signaling, mapping, switched virtual circuit (SVC)/permanent virtual circuit (PVC), protocol translation	5

Table 1-1 *CCIE R&S Written Exam Objectives (Continued)*

Exam Objective	Chapter
ATM—SVC/ PVC, ATM adaptation layer (AAL), Service Specific Connection Oriented Protocol (SSCOP), User-Network Interface (UNI)/Network-Network Interface (NNI), Interim Local Management Interface (ILMI), cell format, QoS, RFC 1483 and 1577, Private Network-Network Interface (PNNI), mapping	5
Physical Layer—Synchronization, Synchronous Optical Network (SONET), T1, E1, encoding	5
Leased Line Protocols—High-level data link control (HDLC), Point-to-Point Protocol (PPP), asynchronous lines and modems, compression	5
PoS (Packet over SONET/SDH)	5
Dynamic Packet Transport (DPT)/spatial reuse protocol (SRP)	5
IX. LAN	
Data-link layer—Addressing, 802.2	4
Ethernet/Fast Ethernet/Gigabit Ethernet—Encapsulation, carrier sense multiple access collision detect (CSMA/CD), topology, speed, controller errors, limitations	4
Token Ring—Token passing, beaconing, active monitor, ring insertion, soft and hard errors, encapsulation, topology, MTU, speed, limitations	4
Wireless/802.11b	4
X. Security	
Authentication, authorization, and accounting (AAA), Terminal Access Controller Access Control System (TACACS), and RADIUS—General concepts, usage, comparisons	12
Firewalls—PIX, access lists, Demilitarized Zones (DMZ)	12
Encryption—Public/private key, Data Encryption Standard (DES)	12
XI. Multiservice	
Voice/Video—H.323, codecs, Signaling System 7 (SS7), Real-Time Transport Protocol (RTP), RTP Control Protocol (RTCP), Session Initiation Protocol (SIP)	12
Multiprotocol Label Switching (MPLS)	11
XII. IP Multicast	
Internet Group Management Protocol (IGMP)/Cisco Group Management Protocol (CGMP)—IGMPv1, IGMPv2, designated querier	10
Addressing—Group addresses, admin group, link-local L3-to-L2 mapping	10
Distribution Trees—Shared trees, source trees	10
Protocol Independent Multicast-Sparse Mode (PIM-SM) Mechanisms—Joining, pruning PIM state, Mroute table	10
Rendezvous Points (RP)—Auto-RP, Bootstrap Router (BSR)	10

CCIE C&S Written Exam General Knowledge Objectives

Table 1-2 lists the CCIE C&S general knowledge objectives from the published blueprint and the corresponding chapters in this book that cover those objectives.

Table 1-2 *CCIE C&S Written Exam General Knowledge Objectives*

C&S General Knowledge Objective	Chapter
I. Cisco Device Operation	
Commands—**show**, **debug**	3
Infrastructure—NVRAM, Flash, memory and CPU, file system, configuration register	3
Operations—File transfers, password recovery, Simple Network Management Protocol (SNMP), accessing devices, security (passwords)	3
II. General Networking Theory	
OSI model—Layer comparisons, functions	2
General Routing Concepts—Split horizon, difference between switching and routing, summarization, link-state versus distance vector, loops, tunneling	2
Protocol Comparisons—Internet Protocol (IP) versus Internetwork Packet Exchange (IPX), Transmission Control Protocol (TCP), User Datagram Protocol (UDP)	6
Standards—802.x, protocol limitations	4
Protocol Mechanics—Windowing/Acknowledgments (ACK), fragmentation, maximum transmission unit (MTU), handshaking, termination	6
III. Bridging and LAN Switching	
Transparent Bridging—IEEE/DEC spanning tree, translational, Configuration Bridging Protocol Data Unit (BPDU), integrated routing and bridging (IRB), Concurrent Routing and Bridging (CRB), access lists	4
LAN Switching—Trunking, VLAN Trunk Protocol (VTP), Inter-Switch Link (ISL), virtual LANs (VLANS), Fast Ether Channel (FEC), Cisco Discovery Protocol (CDP)	4
IV. Internet Protocol	
Addressing—Classless interdomain routing (CIDR), subnetting, Address Resolution Protocol (ARP), Network Address Translation (NAT), Hot Standby Router Protocol (HSRP)	6
Services—Domain Name System (DNS), Bootstrap Protocol (BOOTP), Dynamic Host Configuration Protocol (DHCP), Internet Control Message Protocol (ICMP)	6
Applications—Telnet, File Transfer Protocol (FTP), Trivial File Transfer Protocol (TFTP)	6
Transport—IP fragmentation, sockets, ports	6
IP access lists	10

Examples of data-link layer technologies are the following:

- Frame Relay
- Asynchronous Transport Mode (ATM)
- Synchronous Data Link Control (SDLC)
- High-level data-link control (HDLC)
- IEEE 802.3z and IEEE 802.3ab (Gigabit Ethernet)
- IEEE 802.3u (Fast Ethernet)
- Ethernet version 2
- Integrated Services Digital Network (ISDN)
- Point-to-Point Protocol (PPP)
- Token Ring
- Spanning-Tree Protocol (STP)

Network Layer (OSI Layer 3)

The network layer is concerned with the routing of information and methods to determine paths to a destination. Information at this layer is called packets. Specifications include routing protocols, logical network addressing, and packet fragmentation. Routers operate in this layer. The CCIE lives and dies in this layer.

Examples of network layer specifications are the following:

- Internet Protocol (IP)
- Routing Information Protocol (RIP)
- Open Shortest Path First (OSPF)
- Enhanced Interior Gateway Routing Protocol (EIGRP)
- Internetwork Packet Exchange (IPX)
- Connectionless Network Protocol (CLNP)

Transport Layer (OSI Layer 4)

The transport layer provides reliable, transparent transport of data segments from upper layers. It provides end-to-end error checking and recovery, multiplexing, virtual circuit management, and flow control. Messages are assigned a sequence number at the transmission end. At the receiving end the packets are reassembled, checked for errors, and acknowledged. Flow control

manages the data transmission to ensure that the transmitting device does not send more data than the receiving device can process.

Examples of transport layer specifications are the following:

- Transmission Control Protocol (TCP)
- Real-Time Transport Protocol (RTP)
- Sequenced Packet Exchange (SPX)
- AppleTalk's Transaction Protocol (ATP)
- User Datagram Protocol (UDP) (provides unreliable transport at this layer with less overhead than TCP)

Session Layer (OSI Layer 5)

The session layer provides a control structure for communication between applications. It establishes, manages, and terminates communication connections called sessions. Communication sessions consist of service requests and responses that occur between applications on different devices. The management of sessions involves the synchronization of dialog control by using checkpoints in the data stream.

Examples of specifications that operate at the session layer are the following:

- NetBIOS
- Real-Time Control Protocol (RTCP)
- Session Control Protocol (SCP)
- AppleTalk's Zone Information Protocol (ZIP)
- DECnet's Session Control Protocol (SCP)
- H.323, H.245, H.225
- Real-Time Control Protocol (RTCP)

Presentation Layer (OSI Layer 6)

The presentation layer provides data representation with a variety of coding and conversion functions. These functions ensure that data sent from a sending application on one system is readable by the application layer on another system. This layer provides the conversion of character representation formats, data compression schemes, and encryption schemes. Voice coding schemes are specified at this layer.

Examples of specifications that operate at the presentation layer are the following:

- Abstract Syntax Notation 1 (ASN.1)
- ASCII
- EBCDIC
- Motion Picture Experts Group (MPEG)
- Graphics Interchange Format (GIF)
- Joint Photographic Experts Group (JPEG)
- Tagged Image File Format (TIFF)
- G.711, G.729a, G.726, G.728

Application Layer (OSI Layer 7)

The application layer provides the user or operating system access to the network services. It interacts with software applications by identifying communication resources, determining network availability, and distributing information services. It also provides synchronization between the peer applications that reside on separate systems.

Examples of application layer specifications are the following:

- Telnet
- File Transfer Protocol (FTP)
- Simple Mail Transfer Protocol (SMTP)
- Simple Network Management Protocol (SNMP)
- Network File System (NFS)
- Association Control Service Element (ACSE)
- Remote Operations Service Element (ROSE)

Example of Layered Communication

If you use a Telnet application, Telnet maps into the top three layers of the OSI model. Figure 2-3 shows that a user on Host 1 enables the Telnet application to access a remote host (Host 2). The Telnet application provides a user interface (application layer) to network services. As defined in Request For Comments (RFC) 854, ASCII is the default code format used (presentation layer). There is no session layer defined for Telnet; it is not an OSI protocol. Per the RFC, Telnet uses TCP for connectivity (transport layer). The TCP segment gets placed into an IP packet (network layer) with a destination IP address of Host 2. The IP packet gets placed into an Ethernet frame (data-link layer), which is converted into bits, and sent onto the wire (physical layer).

Figure 2-3 *Telnet Example*

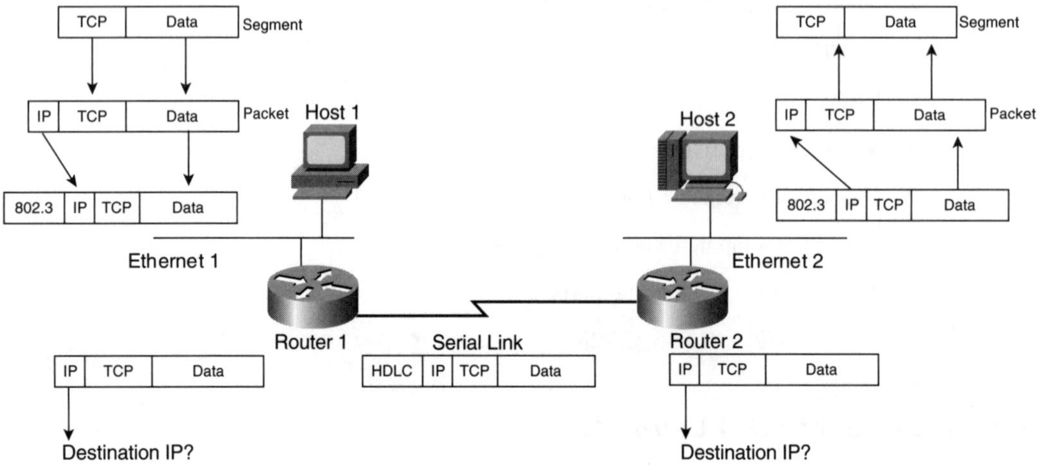

When the frame arrives to Router 1, it converts the bits into a frame, removes the frame headers (data link), checks the destination IP address (network), places a serial link header to the packet, which makes it a serial frame, and forwards the frame to the serial link (data link), which sends it as bits.

Router 2 receives the bits, converts to a frame, removes the serial encapsulation headers, checks the destination IP address (network), adds an Ethernet header to the packet, which makes it a frame, and places a frame on Ethernet 2 (data link). Host 2 receives bits (physical) from the Ethernet cable and converts the bits into a frame (data link). Then, the IP protocol is examined and the packet data is forwarded to TCP, which checks the segment number for errors and forwards the segment to TCP port 23 (Telnet), which is the application.

Numeric Conversion

This section focuses on the techniques used to convert between decimal, binary, and hexadecimal numbers. Although there might not be a specific question on the exam that asks you to convert a binary number to decimal, you need to know how to convert these numbers to complete problems on the test. A diagram might show a Token Ring with a decimal number but the RIF might be shown as hexadecimal. An IP address might be shown as binary or in dotted decimal format. Some **show** commands have output information in hexadecimal or binary formats. As a CCIE candidate, you must be prepared.

Hexadecimal Numbers

The decimal numeric system that is commonly used has 10 numeric digits, 0 through 9. After 9, you use 2 digits starting at 10 and then cycle the right-most digits from 0 through 9 again. The hexadecimal numeric system follows this same concept, but instead of 10 digits, there are 16 digits. Table 2-1 shows the hexadecimal digits and their decimal equivalent.

Table 2-1 *Hexadecimal Digits*

Hexadecimal Digits	Decimal Value
0	0
1	1
2	2
3	3
4	4
5	5
6	6
7	7
8	8
9	9
A	10
B	11
C	12
D	13
E	14
F	15
10	16

Hexadecimal Representation

It is common to represent a hexadecimal number with 0x before the number so that it is not confused with a decimal number. The hexadecimal number of decimal 16 is written as 0x10, not 10. Another method is to use an h subscript to the right of the number, such as 10_h. It is also common to use the term hex when speaking of hexadecimal. You will use hex in much of the text that follows.

Converting Decimal to Hexadecimal

First things first, memorize Table 2-1. For larger numbers, there are two methods. The first method is to convert decimal to binary and then from binary to hex. The second method is to divide the decimal number by 16; the residual is the right-most bit. Then keep dividing until the number is not divisible. For the first method, use the schemes described in later sections. For the second method, follow the examples described here.

First, divide the decimal number by 16. The residual is the first digit. If the result is not divisible by 16, you are done; the result and the residual are the hex number. If the division result is still divisible by 16, follow the procedure again. This becomes clearer with the following examples.

Conversion Example 1: *Convert 26 to Its Hex Equivalent*

Divide by 16:

```
      1
16 | 26
    -16
     10 = Ah
```

Answer: **$1A_h$**

Conversion Example 2: *Convert 96 to Its Hex Equivalent*

Not divisible by 256; divide by 16:

```
      6
16 | 96
    -96
      0 = 0h
```

Answer: **60_h**

Conversion Example 3: *Convert 375 to Its Hex Equivalent*

Divide by 16 first:

```
      23
16 | 375
    -32
     55
    -48
      7
```

Now divide 23 by 16:

```
      1
16 | 23
    -16
      7
```

Now take the residual from the first division (7) and concatentate it with the residual from the second division (7), plus the result of the second division (1), and the answer is 177_h.

Conversion Example 4: *Convert 218 to Its Hex Equivalent*

Divide by 16:

```
      13 = Dh
16 | 218
    -16
     58
    -48
     10 = Ah
```

Answer: **DA_h**

Converting Hexadecimal to Decimal

To convert a hex number to decimal, take the right-most digit and convert it to decimal (i.e., 0xC=12). Then add this number to the second right-most digit × 16 and the third rightmost digit × 256. Don't expect to convert numbers larger than 255 on the CCIE written exam because the upper limit of IP addresses in dotted decimal format is 255, although Token Ring numbers do reach 4096. Some examples follow.

Conversion Example 5: *Convert 177_h to Decimal*

```
1 x 256 = 256
7 x  16 = 112
7 x   1 =   7
          375d
```

Conversion Example 6: *Convert* 60_h *to Decimal*

$$
\begin{array}{r}
6 \times 16 = 96 \\
0 \times 1 = \underline{\ \ 0} \\
\mathbf{96_d}
\end{array}
$$

Conversion Example 7: *Convert* 100_h *to Decimal*

$$
\begin{array}{r}
1 \times 256 = 256 \\
0 \times 16 = 0 \\
0 \times 1 = \underline{\ \ 0} \\
\mathbf{256_d}
\end{array}
$$

Conversion Example 8: *Convert* $1DA_h$ *to Decimal*

$$
\begin{array}{r}
1 \times 256 = 256 \\
13 \times 16 = 208 \\
10 \times 1 = \underline{\ \ 10} \\
\mathbf{474_d}
\end{array}
$$

An Alternate Method to Convert from Hex to Decimal

Another way to convert is to go from hex to binary and then binary to decimal.

Binary Numbers

The binary number system uses two digits: 1 and 0. Binary numbers are primarily used by computer systems. IP addresses and MAC addresses are represented by binary numbers. The number of binary 1s or 0s is the number of bits. For example, 01101010 is a binary number with 8 bits. An IP address has 32 bits and a MAC address has 48 bits. Table 2-2 shows that IP addresses are usually represented in dotted decimal format; therefore, it is helpful to know how to covert between binary and decimal numbers. MAC addresses are usually represented in hexadecimal numbers; therefore, it is helpful to know how to covert between binary and hexadecimal numbers.

Table 2-2 *Binary Representation of IP and MAC Addresses*

	Binary	Dotted Decimal	Hexadecimal
IP Address	00101000 10001010 01010101 10101010	40.138.85.170	
Mac Address	00001100 10100001 10010111 01010001 00000001 10010001		0C:A1:97:51:01:91

The CCIE candidate needs to memorize Table 2-3, which shows numbers from 0 to 16 in decimal, binary, and hexadecimal formats.

Table 2-3 *Decimal, Binary, and Hexadecimal Numbers*

Decimal Value	Hexadecimal	Binary
0	0	0000
1	1	0001
2	2	0010
3	3	0011
4	4	0100
5	5	0101
6	6	0110
7	7	0111
8	8	1000
9	9	1001
10	A	1010
11	B	1011
12	C	1100
13	D	1101
14	E	1110
15	F	1111
16	10	10000

Converting Binary to Hexadecimal

To convert binary numbers to hex, group the bits into groups of four, starting with the right-justified bits. Groups of four bits are usually called nibbles. Each nibble has a hex equivalent. The following are some examples.

Conversion Example 9: *Convert 0010011101 to Hex*

Group the bits:
00 1001 1101
Answer: **$09D_h$**

Conversion Example 10: *Convert 001010100101100100001011 0001 to Hex*

Group the bits:
0010 1010 0101 1001 0000 1011 0001
Answer: **$2A590B1_h$**

Converting Hexadecimal to Binary

This procedure is also easy—Just change the hex digits into their four-bit equivalent. The following are some examples.

Conversion Example 11: *Convert 0DEAD0 into Binary*

Hex:	0	D	E	A	D	0
Binary:	0000	1101	1110	1010	1101	0000

Answer: **000011011110101011010000**

Conversion Example 12: *Convert AA0101 into Binary*

Hex:	A	A	0	1	0	1
Binary:	1010	1010	0000	0001	0000	0001

Answer: **101010100000000100000001**

Converting Binary to Decimal

To convert a binary number to decimal, multiply each instance of 1 by the power of 2. Table 2-4 shows that each bit in the binary number 11111111 has a decimal equivalent from 1 to 128, which is based on the location of the bit in the binary. This is similar to decimal numbers where the numbers are based on 1s, 10s, 100s, and so on. In decimal format, the number 111 is 100+10+1. In binary format, the number 11111111 is the sum of 128+64+32+16+8+4+2+1 = 255. For 10101010, this results in 128+0+32+0+8+0+2+0 = 170. This is similar to decimal numbers where the numbers are based on 1s, 10s, 100s, and so on. The following are some examples.

Table 2-4 *Decimal Values of Bits in a Binary Number*

Power of 2	$2^7 = 128$	$2^6 = 64$	$2^5 = 32$	$2^4 = 16$	$2^3 = 8$	$2^2 = 4$	$2^1 = 2$	$2^0 = 1$
Binary	1	1	1	1	1	1	1	1

NOTE Memorize 1, 2, 4, 8, 16, 32, 64, and 128. Use this as you read a binary number from right to left. This should be helpful in converting faster.

Conversion Example 13: *Convert 10110111 to Decimal*

Sum: 128 + 0 + 32 + 16 + 0 + 4 + 2 + 1
Answer = **183**

Conversion Example 14: *Convert 11011 to Decimal*

Sum: 16 + 8 + 0 + 2 + 1
Answer = **27**

Conversion Example 15: *Convert 11111111 to Decimal*

Sum: 128 + 64 + 32 + 16 + 8 + 4 + 2 + 1
Answer = **255**

Converting Decimal to Binary Numbers

This procedure is similar to converting from hex to decimal (by dividing), but now you divide the decimal number by 2. You use each residual to build the binary number. Each residual bit is prepended to the previous bit starting with the right. Repeat the procedure until you cannot divide anymore. The only problem is that for large numbers you might have to divide many times. An alternate method follows the next example.

Conversion Example 16: *Convert 26 to Binary*

```
     13
2 | 26
   -26
     0
```

The first bit is 0; now divide 13 by 2. [0]

```
      6
2 | 13
   -12
     1
```

The second bit is 1; now divide 6 by 2. [10]

```
     3
2 | 6
   -6
    0
```

The third bit is 0; now divide 3 by 2. [010]

```
     1
2 | 3
   -2
    1
```

The fourth bit is 1; the leftmost bit is the division result at the top, which is one. [11010]

Answer: **11010**

An Alternate Method

The dividing procedure described previously works, but it takes a lot of time. Another method is to remember the bit position values within a byte: 128, 64, 32, 16, 8, 4, 2, 1, and play with the bits until the sum adds up to the desired number. Table 2-5 shows these binary numbers and their decimal value.

Table 2-5 *Bit Values*

Binary Number	Decimal Value
10000000	128
01000000	64
00100000	32
00010000	16

Table 2-5 *Bit Values (Continued)*

Binary Number	Decimal Value
00001000	8
00000100	4
00000010	2
00000001	1

To convert 26, you know that it is a number smaller than 128, 64, and 32, so those three bits are 0 [000?????]. Now, you need to find a combination from 16, 8, 4, 2, and 1 that adds up to 26. This method involves using subtraction to compute the remaining number. Start with the largest number. Make the bit at 16 a 1 [0001????]. The difference between 26 and 16 is 10, so what combination of 8, 4, 2, and 1 gives you ten? [1010]. The answer is 00011010. You might think this method involves too much guess work, but it becomes second nature after some practice.

Conversion Example 17: *Convert 137 to Binary*

The number is larger than 128; enable that bit. [1???????]

How far is 137 from 128: 9; enable the remaining bits for a value of 9 [1???1001].

The answer is 10001001.

Conversion Example 18: *Convert 211 to Binary*

The number is larger than 128; enable that bit. [1???????]

Because 211–128 is greater than 64, enable that bit. [11??????] (Remember that 11000000 = 192.)

Because 211–192=19, enable bits 16, 2, and 1. [11?1??11]

The answer is 11010011.

It helps to remember both the bit position values (128, 64, 32, 16, 8, 4, 2, 1) and the network subnet masks values. This makes it easier to figure out if a bit needs to be enabled. Table 2-6 summarizes the binary subnet mask numbers and their decimal values.

Table 2-6 *Binary Masks and Their Decimal Values*

Binary Mask	Decimal
10000000	128
11000000	192
11100000	224
11110000	240

continues

Table 2-6 *Binary Masks and Their Decimal Values (Continued)*

Binary Mask	Decimal
11111000	248
11111100	252
11111110	254

General Routing Concepts

This section reviews the hierarchical network architecture model, routing protocol characteristics and metrics, broadcast and collision domains, and default routing. The concepts discussed in this section prepare you for topics in following chapters. Bridging is discussed in Chapter 4. Routing protocols are discussed in detail in Chapter 7, "Static Routing and Distance Vector Routing Protocols," Chapter 8, "IP Link-State Routing Protocols," and Chapter 9, "Border Gateway Protocol."

Hierarchical Model for Networks

The use of a hierarchical design for networks facilitates the operation and management of the internetwork. With a hierarchical design, the network is easier to understand, the network can scale up as size requirements grow, it is easier to implement service policies, and troubleshooting network problems are simplified. The IP addressing assignment is accomplished by following a hierarchy that maximizes route summarization. Routing protocols can aggregate addresses into summary routes, which provide increased stability and less overhead on the network. This is a model for network design. In smaller networks, some layers might merge; in larger networks, there can be a larger hierarchy.

Figure 2-4 shows the hierarchical model for network design, which consists of three layers:

- Core
- Distribution
- Access

First, the core layer provides high-speed transport between sites. The core has optimal transport, low latency, high availability, and redundancy. You use high-speed switches in this layer. No compression, access lists, or encryption are done in this layer.

Second, the distribution layer provides route policies and filtering. Typically implemented in this layer are the following: access lists, distribution lists, route summarization, VLAN routing, security policy, address aggregation, address filters, encryption, compression, and quality of service (QoS). You use high-speed routers and Layer-3 switches in this layer.

Figure 2-4 *Hierarchical Model*

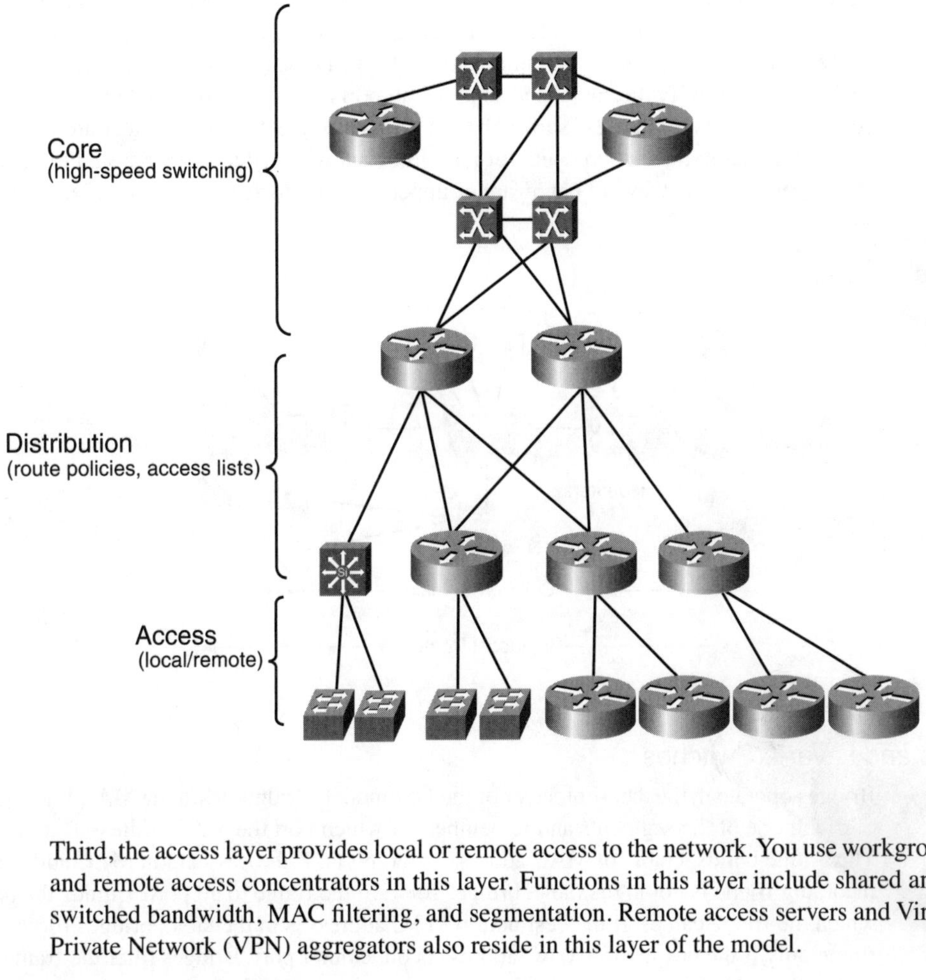

Third, the access layer provides local or remote access to the network. You use workgroup hubs and remote access concentrators in this layer. Functions in this layer include shared and switched bandwidth, MAC filtering, and segmentation. Remote access servers and Virtual Private Network (VPN) aggregators also reside in this layer of the model.

Basic Internetworking Devices

Network devices can be categorized based on their function relative to the OSI model. The main devices are the following:

- Hubs and repeaters
- Bridges and Layer-2 switches
- Routers and Layer-3 switches

Hubs and Repeaters

Repeaters operate in the physical layer of the OSI model. They basically repeat the data (bits) from one port to all other ports. Hubs are repeaters with many ports that were created to concentrate the wiring into a communication closet. These devices are not aware of frames or packets; they amplify the signal and send out all ports. Repeaters do not delineate broadcast or collision domains. Figure 2-5 shows that all devices connected to a repeater are in the same collision domain; they all compete for the same bandwidth. Repeaters are said to be protocol transparent because they are not aware of upper-layer protocols, such as IP, IPX, DECnet, and so on.

Figure 2-5 *Repeaters*

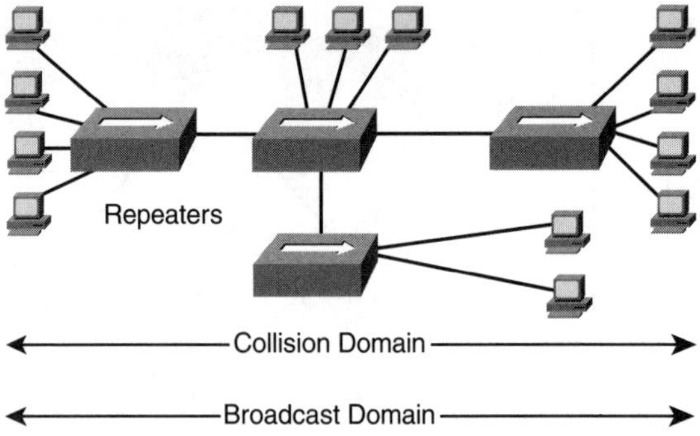

Bridges and Layer-2 Switches

Bridges operate in the data-link layer of the OSI model. Bridges learn the MAC layer addresses of each node of the segments and remember off which port the MAC addresses are located. The bridge builds a table of MAC addresses and ports. If the destination MAC address of an incoming frame is not in the table, bridges forward the frame to all ports (minus the port from which the frame came). If the destination MAC address is in the table, bridges forward the frame only if the destination MAC address is on another port. Bridges filter the frame if the destination MAC address is located on the same port on which the frame arrived.

Bridges are store-and-forward devices. They store the entire incoming frame and verify the checksum before forwarding the frame. If a checksum error is detected, the frame is discarded.

Figure 2-6 shows that bridges define the collision domains; each port off a bridge is a separate collision domain. Collision domains are also referred to as bandwidth domains because all devices in the collision domain share the same bandwidth. Bridges do not control broadcasts. Bridges flood broadcasts out all ports. Bridges are protocol transparent; they are not aware of upper-layer protocols, such as IP and IPX. Bridges are designed to flood all unknown and broadcast traffic.

Figure 2-6 *Bridges Control Collision Domains*

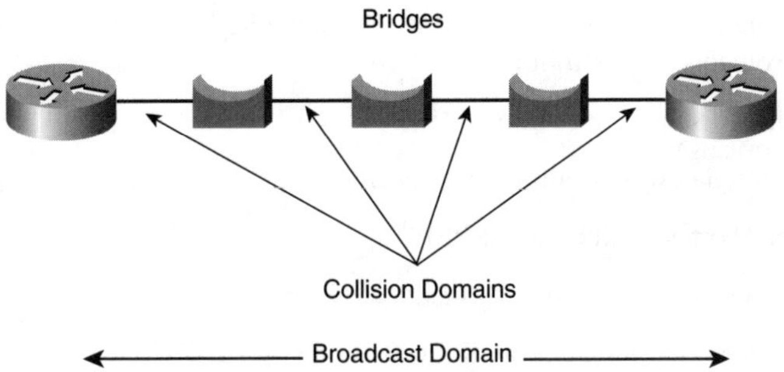

Switches use fast integrated circuits that reduce the latency common to regular bridges. Switches are the evolution of bridges. Some switches have the capability to run in cut-through mode where the switch does not wait for the entire frame to enter its buffer; instead, it begins to forward the frame as soon as it finishes reading the destination MAC address. Cut-through operation increases the probability that error frames are propagated on the network because the frame is forwarded before the entire frame is buffered and checked for errors. Because of these problems, most switches today perform store-and-forward operations as bridges do. Switches are exactly the same as bridges with respect to collision domain and broadcast domain characteristics. Each port on a switch is a separate collision domain. All ports in a switch are in the same broadcast domain.

Various types of bridges exist, including transparent, translational, source-route, and so on. These bridging types are covered in Chapter 4.

Routers and Layer-3 Switches

Routers operate in the network layer of the OSI model. They make forwarding decisions based on network layer addresses (e.g., an IP address). Figure 2-7 shows that routers define both collision (bandwidth) and broadcast domains. Each router interface is a separate broadcast domain that is defined by a separate sub-network. Routers are protocol aware, which means that they are capable of forwarding packets of routable protocols such as IP, IPX, DECnet, and AppleTalk.

Figure 2-7 *Routers Define Collision and Broadcast Domains*

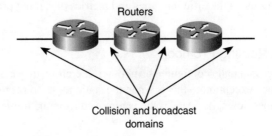

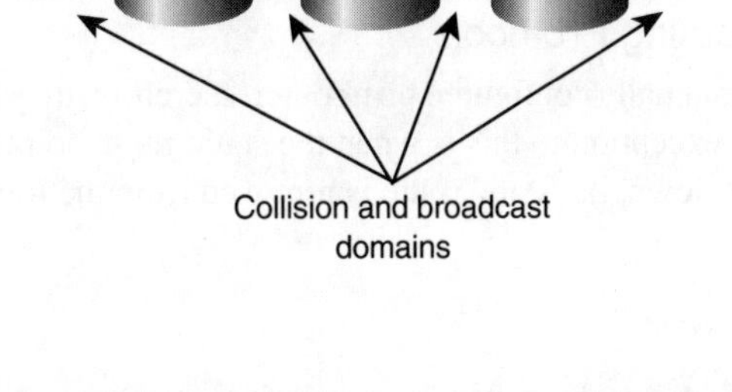

Routers are configured to run routing protocols to determine the best paths to a destination. Routers exchange information about destination networks and their interface status by using these routing protocols. Routers can also be configured manually with static routes. Some IP routing protocols are the following:

- Routing Information Protocol (RIP)
- Interior Gateway Routing Protocol (IGRP)
- Open shortest Path First (OSPF)
- Intermediate System-to-Intermediate System (IS-IS)
- Enhanced Interior Gateway Routing Protocol (EIGRP)
- Border Gateway Protocol (BGP)

These protocols are discussed in Chapter 7, Chapter 8, and Chapter 9.

LAN switches that are capable of running routing protocols are called Layer-3 switches. They run the full routing protocols and can communicate with routers as peers. Layer-3 switches off-load local traffic from wide-area network (WAN) routers by performing network-layer forwarding within the local-area networks (LANs). Both routers and Layer-3 switches make forwarding decisions based on IP addresses and not MAC addresses. Both participate in the exchange of route information based on the dynamic routing protocol they participate in.

The Difference Between Layer-2 Switching and Routing

The most obvious difference between Layer-2 switching and routing is that switching occurs at Layer 2 of the OSI reference model and routing occurs at Layer 3. Switches forward frames based on MAC address information. Routers forward packets based on logical addresses (IP address).

NOTE Throughout this book, switching means bridging, unless you see the term Layer-3 switching.

Routing Protocol Characteristics

This section discusses the different types and metrics of routing protocols.

Static Versus Dynamic Routing Protocols

Static routes are manually configured on a router; therefore, they cannot react based on network outages. The one exception to this is when the static route points to the outbound interface: If the interface goes down, the static route is removed from the routing table. The size of today's networks prohibits the manual configuration of every router. This is why there are dynamic protocols that use algorithms that can react to network changes.

The main benefit of static routing is that the router generates no routing protocol overhead. Static routing is recommended for hub-and-spoke topologies with low bandwidth links.

Dynamic routing protocols can determine the best routes to a destination automatically. If the network topology changes, the routing protocol can adjust the routes without user intervention. Dynamic routing protocols use metrics to determine the best path. Some use one metric and other protocols use a combination of metrics. Routing metrics are discussed later in this section.

Interior Versus Exterior Routing Protocols

Routing protocols can be labeled as Interior Gateway Protocols (IGPs) or exterior gateway protocols (EGPs). IGPs are meant for routing within a company's administrative domain. EGPs are routing protocols that communicate with exterior domains. One of the first EGPs was called exactly that, exterior gateway protocol. Today, Border Gateway Protocol (BGP) is the defacto EGP. All other IP routing protocols are IGPs: RIP, OSPF, IS-IS, IGRP, and EIGRP.

Link-State Versus Distance Vector Routing Protocols

The first routing protocols were distance vector routing protocols, which are occasionally referred to as Bellman-Ford algorithms. In distance vector routing protocols, routes are advertised as vectors of distance and direction. The distance metric is usually the router hop count. The direction is the next-hop router to which the packet is forwarded. For RIP, the maximum number of hops is 15, which is a serious limitation especially in nonhierarchical networks.

Distance vector algorithms call for each router to send all or some portion of its routing table only to its neighbors. The table is sent periodically (every 30 or 60 seconds). The router builds a new table and sends it to its neighbors, and so on. In today's networks, waiting half a minute for a new routing table with new routes is too long. Some distance vector protocols send triggered updates (a full routing table update sent before the update timer has expired), but a router can receive a routing table with 500 routes with only one route change. This creates serious overhead on the network, which is another drawback. Distance vector protocols are discussed in Chapter 7.

Another protocol, Enhanced Interior Gateway Routing Protocol (EIGRP), is considered a hybrid routing protocol. EIGRP is a distance vector protocol that implements some link-state routing protocol characteristics. Although using similar metrics as its predecessor, IGRP and EIGRP sends partial updates and maintains neighbor state information, similar to link-state protocols. EIGRP does not send periodic updates. The important thing to remember for the test is that EIGRP can be presented as a hybrid protocol. EIGRP is discussed in Chapter 7.

The following is a list of distance vector routing protocols (including non-IP routing protocols):

- Routing Information Protocol (RIPv1 and RIPv2)
- Interior Gateway Routing Protocol (IGRP)
- Enhanced Interior Gateway Routing Protocol (EIGRP) (could be considered a hybrid)
- IPX Routing Information Protocol (IPX RIP)
- AppleTalk Routing Table Maintenance Protocol (RTMP)
- DEC DNA Phase IV
- Xerox's XNS Routing Information Protocol (XNS RIP)

Link-state routing protocols were developed to address some limitations of distance vector protocols. When running a link-state routing protocol, routers originate information about themselves (IP addresses), their connected links (number and type of links), and the state of those links (up/down). The information is forwarded to all routers in the network. Each router makes a copy of the information and does not change it. Each router independently calculates the best paths to destinations and maintains a map of the network. Link-state routing protocols are discussed in Chapter 8.

The following is a list of link-state routing protocols (including non-IP routing protocols):

- Open Shortest Path First (OSPF)
- Intermediate System-to-Intermediate System (IS-IS)
- IPX NetWare Link-Services Protocol (NLSP)
- DECnet Phase V

Hierarchical Versus Flat Routing Protocols

Some routing protocols require a network topology where some routers are assigned to a backbone network. Routes from nonbackbone routers are fed into the backbone. Some of these protocols support a two- or three-layer hierarchy. Some routers are assigned the role of forwarding routes into the backbone. OSPF and IS-IS are examples of hierarchical routing protocols.

Flat routing protocols do not require a hierarchical network topology, although they work a lot better in a hierarchical network. Any router can be a peer of any other router in flat routing protocols. No router is assigned a special role in the internetwork. RIP is an example of a flat routing protocol.

Classless Versus Classful Routing Protocols

Routing protocols can be classified based on their support for classful or classless routing. Classful routing protocols do not advertise subnet masks in their routing updates; therefore, the entire internetwork uses the configured subnet mask for the IP network. For example, if you use a classful routing protocol for network 130.170.0.0, the chosen mask (i.e., 255.255.255.0) has to be used on all router interfaces using the 130.170.0.0 network. Serial links and local-area networks are configured with the same mask of 255.255.255.0. RIPv1 and IGRP are classful routing protocols.

Classless routing protocols advertise the subnet mask with each route. Subnetworks of a given IP network number can be configured with different subnet masks. Large LANs can be configured with a smaller subnet mask, and serial links can be configured with larger subnet mask, thereby conserving IP address space. Classless routing protocols also allow flexible route summarization and superneting. Supernets are created by the aggregation of classful networks. For example, 200.100.100.0/23 is a supernet of 200.100.100.0/24 and 200.100.101.0/24. RIPv2, OSPF, EIGRP, IS-IS, and BGP are classless routing protocols.

NOTE The use of the **ip classless** command does not make routing protocol classless or classful. The command permits packets destined for an unrecognized subnet to be forwarded to the best supernet possible. If it is not enabled, the packets are discarded.

Routing Metrics

Routing protocols use one or more metrics to determine the best routes to a destination. Some routing metrics are

- Hop count
- Bandwidth
- Cost
- Load
- Delay
- Reliability

Hop Count

The hop count metric counts only the number of routers that the packet must take to reach a destination. If links are the same bandwidth, this metric works well. The problem with routing protocols that use only this metric is that the shortest hop count isn't always the quickest path. For example, if there are two paths to a destination, one with two 56 k links and another with four T1 links, the first path is selected because of the lower number of hops (see Figure 2-8). However, this is not necessarily the fastest path. If you have a 20 MB file, you want to transfer it through T1 links rather than 56 k links.

Figure 2-8 *Hop Count Metric Prefers Fewer Hops*

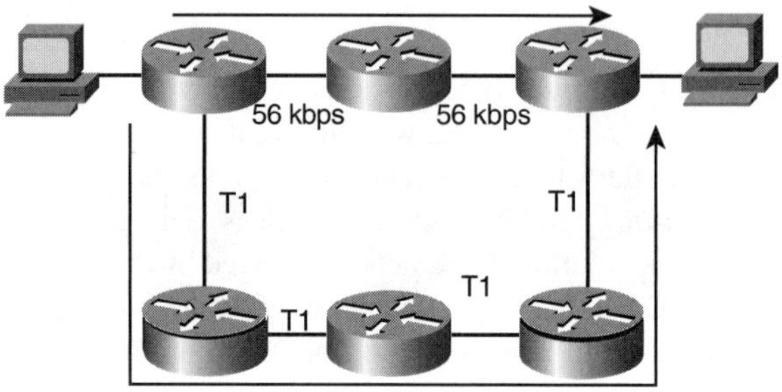

Bandwidth

The bandwidth metric uses the default or configured interface bandwidth. With this metric, Fast Ethernet (100 Mbps) is preferred over DS-3 (45 Mbps). You can alter the metric by using the interface command **bandwidth** *speed*, where the speed is entered in kbps. To configure a serial interface for 128 kbps, use the following commands:

```
router3(config)#interface serial 0
router3(config-if)#bandwidth 128
  router3(config-if)#
```

Use the **show interface** command to verify the configured bandwidth:

```
router3>show interface serial 0
Serial0 is up, line protocol is up
  Hardware is PQUICC Serial
  MTU 1500 bytes, BW 128 Kbit, DLY 20000 usec, rely 254/255, load 1/255
    Encapsulation HDLC, crc 16, loopback not set, keepalive set (10 sec)
```

Cost

OSPF and IS-IS use the cost metric, which is can be derived from the bandwidth of the interface. IS-IS assigns a default cost of 10 for all interfaces. It does not use the auto cost determination that OSPF uses.

To calculate cost in OSPF, use the following formula:

10^8 / BW, where BW is the default or configured bandwidth of the interface.

For Ethernet, calculate the cost as follows:

$$BW = 10\ Mbps = 10 \times 10^6 = 10^7$$
$$Cost\ (Ethernet) = 10^8 / 10^7 = 10$$

The sum of all the costs to reach a destination is the metric for that route. The lowest cost is the preferred path.

Load

The load metric refers to the degree to which the interface link is busy. The router keeps track of the interface utilization. Routing protocols can use this metric in the calculation of a best route. If you have 512 k and 256 k links to reach a destination, but the 512 k circuit is 99 percent busy, and the 256 k is only 5 percent busy, the 256 k link is the preferred path. The load can be verified with the **show interface** command. Lower load numbers are better. Example 2-1 shows that the load is 1/255.

Example 2-1 **show interface** *Command Used to Check the Current Load of the Interface*

```
router3>show interface serial 1
Serial1 is up, line protocol is up
  Hardware is PQUICC Serial
  Internet address is 10.100.1.1/24
  MTU 1500 bytes, BW 1544 Kbit, DLY 20000 usec, rely 255/255, load 1/255
```

Delay

The delay metric refers to the length in time to move a packet to the destination. Delay depends on many factors, such as link bandwidth, utilization, port queues, and physical distance traveled. The delay of an interface can be configured with the **delay** *tens-of-microseconds* command, where *tens-of-microseconds* specifies the delay in tens of microseconds for an interface or network segment. Example 2-2 shows that the delay of the interface is 20000 microseconds.

Example 2-2 **show interface** *Command to Check the Delay of an Interface*

```
router3>show interface serial 1
Serial1 is up, line protocol is up
  Hardware is PQUICC Serial
  Internet address is 10.100.1.1/24
  MTU 1500 bytes, BW 1544 Kbit, DLY 20000 usec, rely 255/255, load 1/255
```

Reliability

The reliability metric is the dependability of a network link. There might be WAN links that tend to go up and down throughout the day. These links receive a small reliability rating.

Reliability is measured by the expected, received keepalives of a link. If the ratio is high, the line is reliable. The best rating is 255/255, which is 100 percent reliability. Example 2-3 shows that the reliability of an interface can be verified using the **show interface** command.

Example 2-3 **show interface** *Command to Check the Reliability of an Interface*

```
router4#show interface serial 0
Serial0 is up, line protocol is up
  Hardware is PQUICC Serial
  MTU 1500 bytes, BW 1544 Kbit, DLY 20000 usec, rely 255/255, load 1/255
```

Loop Prevention Schemes

Some routing protocols employ schemes to prevent the creation of routing loops in the network. These schemes are the following:

- Simple split horizon
- Split horizon with poison reverse
- Counting to infinity

These schemes are discussed in the following sections.

Simple Split Horizon

Distance vector routing protocols use the split horizon technique to prevent routing loops. Routes that are learned from a neighboring router are not sent back to that neighboring router, thus suppressing the route. If the neighbor is already closer to the destination, it already has a better path.

In Figure 2-9, Routers 1, 2, and 3 learn about Networks A, B, C, and D. Router 2 learns about A from Router 1 and also has Network B and C in its routing table. Router 3 advertises Network D to Router 2. Now, Router 2 knows about all the networks. Router 2 sends its routing table to Router 3 without the route for Network D because it learned that route from Router 3.

Figure 2-9 *Simple Split Horizon Example*

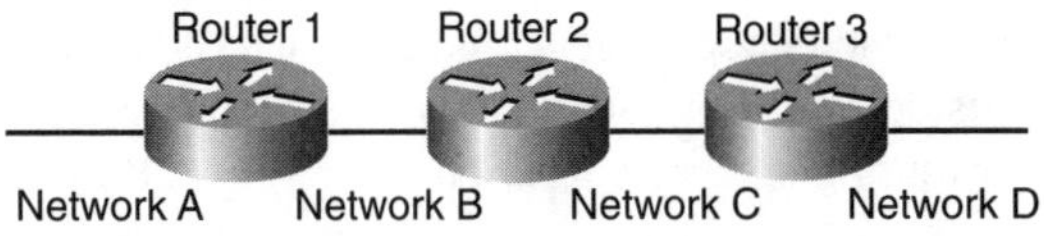

With split horizon, Router 2 sends Network A and Network B routes to Router 3. No route for Network D is sent to Router 3.

With poison reverse, Router 2 sends Network A and Network B routes to Router 3. Also, it sends a route for Network D with an infinite metric.

Split Horizon with Poison Reverse

Split horizon with poison reverse is a route update sent out an interface with an infinite metric for routes learned (received) from the same interface. Poison reverse is a technique that enables split horizon to say that the learned route is unreachable. Poison reverse is more reliable than simple split horizon. Refer to the example in Figure 2-9. Instead of suppressing the route for Network D, Router 2 sends that route in the routing table but it is marked as unreachable. In RIP, the poison reverse route is marked with a metric of 16 (infinite).

Counting to Infinity

Some routing protocols keep track of router hops as the packet travels through the network. If the maximum limit is reached, the packet is discarded. It is assumed that the network diameter is smaller than the maximum allowed hops.

Triggered Updates

Another loop prevention and fast convergence technique that routing protocols use is triggered updates. When a router interface changes state (up or down), the router is required to send an update message, even if it is not time for the periodic update message. An immediate notification about a network outage is key to maintaining valid routing entries within all routers in the network. Some distance vector protocols, including RIP, specify a small time delay to avoid triggered updates generating excessive network traffic.

Summarization

Another characteristic of routing protocols is the capability to summarize routes. Protocols that support CIDR and variable length subnet masks (VLSMs) have the capability to perform summarization outside of IP class boundaries. By summarizing, the routing table size is reduced and fewer routing updates appear on the network. Refer to the network in Figure 2-10.

Figure 2-10 *Route Summarization*

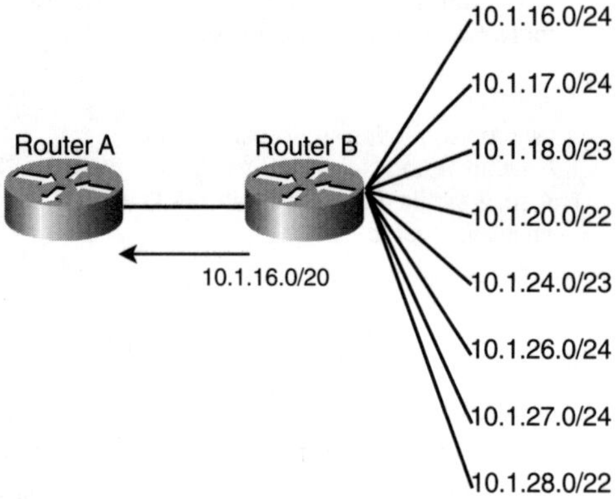

Router B has the following networks:

- 10.1.16.0/24
- 10.1.17.0/24
- 10.1.18.0/23
- 10.1.20.0/22
- 10.1.24.0/23
- 10.1.26.0/24
- 10.1.27.0/24
- 10.1.28.0/22

Router B generates eight route entries from these networks and forwards the routes to Router A. Router B can summarize all these routes with a single route: 10.1.16.0/20. Protocol specifics on how to summarize are discussed in the applicable chapters in this book.

Default Routing

Another routing concept you must understand is the default route for the network. This route becomes the gateway of last resort for packets with destination IP addresses that are not in the routing table. Usually, you use these for access to the Internet. Because external networks are not usually advertised into the user's internetwork, you use the default route to route those Internet bound packets to a default router, firewall, or gateway.

Routing protocols handle default route configuration differently. The default route is usually configured by using a static route command, such as the following:

```
ip route 0.0.0.0 0.0.0.0 x.x.x.x
```

x.x.x.x is the IP address of the next hop.

Or the destination can be an output interface, as follows:

```
ip route 0.0.0.0 0.0.0.0 serial 0
```

Another way to configure the default route is to use the **ip default-network** command. You use this command when IP routing is enabled. The configured network becomes the gateway of last resort if it is the routing table.

The router in the following example does not have the default network configured.

Listing the routes in Example 2-4 shows that the gateway of last resort is not set.

Example 2-4 *Gateway of Last Resort Is Not Set*

```
router4#show ip route
Codes: C - connected, S - static, I - IGRP, R - RIP, M - mobile, B - BGP
       D - EIGRP, EX - EIGRP external, O - OSPF, IA - OSPF inter area
       N1 - OSPF NSSA external type 1, N2 - OSPF NSSA external type 2
       E1 - OSPF external type 1, E2 - OSPF external type 2, E - EGP
       i - IS-IS, L1 - IS-IS level-1, L2 - IS-IS level-2, * - candidate default
       U - per-user static route, o - ODR

Gateway of last resort is not set

     10.0.0.0/8 is variably subnetted, 4 subnets, 2 masks
D       10.1.3.0/24 [90/2195456] via 10.100.1.1, 00:02:45, Serial1
S       10.0.0.0/8 [1/0] via 10.1.3.0
C       10.1.4.0/24 is directly connected, Ethernet0
C       10.100.1.0/24 is directly connected, Serial1
D    192.168.1.0/24 [90/2297856] via 10.100.1.1, 00:02:45, Serial1
router4#
```

Now, configure the default gateway(see Example 2-5).

Example 2-5 *Configuration of the IP Default Network*

```
router4#config terminal
Enter configuration commands, one per line. End with CNTL/Z.
router4(config)#ip default-network 192.168.1.0
router4(config)#^Z
router4#
```

If the network is in the routing table, it is assigned as the gateway of last resort. Network 192.168.1.0 is in the routing table and is assigned as the gateway of last resort (refer to Example 2-6).

Example 2-6 *Gateway of Last Resort Set*

```
router4#show ip route
Codes: C - connected, S - static, I - IGRP, R - RIP, M - mobile, B - BGP
       D - EIGRP, EX - EIGRP external, O - OSPF, IA - OSPF inter area
       N1 - OSPF NSSA external type 1, N2 - OSPF NSSA external type 2
       E1 - OSPF external type 1, E2 - OSPF external type 2, E - EGP
       i - IS-IS, L1 - IS-IS level-1, L2 - IS-IS level-2, * - candidate default
       U - per-user static route, o - ODR

Gateway of last resort is 10.100.1.1 to network 192.168.1.0

     10.0.0.0/8 is variably subnetted, 4 subnets, 2 masks
D       10.1.3.0/24 [90/2195456] via 10.100.1.1, 00:01:00, Serial1
S       10.0.0.0/8 [1/0] via 10.1.3.0
C       10.1.4.0/24 is directly connected, Ethernet0
C       10.100.1.0/24 is directly connected, Serial1
D*   192.168.1.0/24 [90/2297856] via 10.100.1.1, 00:01:00, Serial1
```

NOTE Do not confuse the **ip default-network** command with the **ip default-gateway** command. You use the **ip default-gateway** command only when IP routing is disabled (**no ip routing**). Use the **ip default-gateway** command when configuring an interface with an IP address and accessing a remote TFTP server to load up configuration or IOS files. The **ip default-gateway** command points to an IP address, not a network. The router when in boot mode also uses the **ip default-gateway** command, when no routing processes are running.

Use the **ip default-network** command when IP routing is enabled. Any routing protocol can be enabled.

References Used

The following resources were used to create this chapter:

www.cisco.com/univercd/cc/td/doc/cisintwk/ito_doc/introint.htm

www.cisco.com/univercd/cc/td/doc/cisintwk/ito_doc/multiacc.htm

www.cisco.com/univercd/cc/td/doc/cisintwk/ito_doc/routing.htm#xtocid8

Foundation Summary

The Foundation Summary is a condensed collection of material that provides a convenient review of key concepts in this chapter. If you are already comfortable with the topics in this chapter, this summary will help you recall a few details. If you just read the Foundation Topics section, this review should help solidify some key facts. If you are doing your final preparation before the exam, these materials are a convenient way to review the day before the exam.

Table 2-7 *OSI Reference Model*

Layer Number	OSI Layer Name	Description
7	Application	Provides the user or operating system access to the network services.
6	Presentation	Data representation, compression, encryption, voice coding.
5	Session	Establishes, manages, and terminates communication connections called sessions.
4	Transport	Provides reliable, transparent transport of data segments from upper layers. It provides end-to-end error checking and recovery, multiplexing, virtual circuit management, and flow control.
3	Network	Concerned with routing of packets and methods to determine paths to a destination.
2	Data-link	Reliable transport of data frames across a physical link. Data-link specifications include the following: sequencing of frames, flow control, synchronization, error notification, network topology, and physical addressing.
1	Physical	Bits and interfaces. Concerned with the electrical, mechanical, functional, and procedural specifications for physical links.

Table 2-8 *Decimal, Binary, and Hexadecimal Numbers*

Decimal Value	Hexadecimal	Binary
0	0	0000
1	1	0001
2	2	0010
3	3	0011
4	4	0100
5	5	0101

continues

Table 2-8 *Decimal, Binary, and Hexadecimal Numbers (Continued)*

Decimal Value	Hexadecimal	Binary
6	6	0110
7	7	0111
8	8	1000
9	9	1001
10	A	1010
11	B	1011
12	C	1100
13	D	1101
14	E	1110
15	F	1111
16	10	10000

Table 2-9 *Hierarchical Model*

Layer	Description
Core	High-speed transport, high reliability, and low latency
Distribution	Access lists, distribution lists, route summarization, VLAN routing, security policy, address aggregation, address filters, encryption, compression, and quality of service
Access	Remote Access Servers, shared and switched bandwidth, MAC filtering, and segmentation

Table 2-10 *Networking Devices*

Device	OSI Layer	Function
Hub/ repeater	Physical	Forwards bits out all interfaces. Protocol transparent.
Bridge/ switch	Data-link	Forwards frames based on MAC table. Protocol transparent. Controls collision (bandwidth) domain.
Router/ L3 switch	Network	Forwards packets based on learned routing table. Protocol aware. Controls broadcast domain.

Table 2-11 *IGP and EGP Routing Protocols*

Type	Routing Protocols
EGP	BGP, EGP
IGP	RIPv1, IGRP, OSPF, EIGRP, RIPv2, IS-IS

Table 2-12 *Classless and Classful Routing Protocols*

Type	Routing Protocols
Classful	RIPv1, IGRP
Classless	OSPF, EIGRP, IS-IS, RIPv2, BGP

Table 2-13 *Routing Metrics*

Metric	Description
Hop count	Counts the number of routers that the packet must cross to reach a destination.
Bandwidth	Uses the default or configured interface bandwidth.
Cost	Derived from the bandwidth of the interface. The formula to calculate cost is as follows: 10^8 / BW, where BW is the default or configured bandwidth of the interface.
Delay	Length in time to move a packet to the destination.
Reliability	Dependability of a network link. Measured with the expected keepalives.
Load	Refers to the degree to which the interface link is busy.

Table 2-14 *Loop Prevention Techniques*

Technique	Description
Simple split horizon	Routes that are learned from a neighboring router are not sent back to that neighboring router, thus suppressing the route.
Split horizon with poison reverse	Routes that are learned from a neighboring router are announced back to that router with an infinite metric.
Triggered updates	Update message sent immediately for a route for which the metric has changed, sent before the periodic update timer expires.
Counting to infinity	Keeps track of router hops as the packet travels through the network. If the maximum limit is reached, the packet is discarded.

Q & A

The Q & A questions are more difficult than what you can expect on the actual exam. The questions do not attempt to cover more breadth or depth than the exam; however, they are designed to make sure that you retain the material. Rather than allowing you to derive the answer from clues hidden inside the question itself, these questions challenge your understanding and recall of the subject. Questions from the "Do I Know This Already?" quiz are repeated here to ensure that you have mastered the chapter's topic areas. A strong understanding of the answers to these questions will help you on the CCIE written exam. As an additional study aide, use the CD-ROM provided with this book to take simulated exams.

Select the best answer. Answers to these questions are in the Appendix, "Answers to Quiz Questions."

1 Routers limit network traffic by controlling what?

a. DNS domain

b. Broadcast domain

c. Microsoft broadcast domains

d. Novell SAP broadcasts

2 Which layer of the OSI model is responsible for converting frames into bits and bits into frames?

a. Network layer

b. Physical layer

c. Data-link layer

d. LLC layer

3 Which scheme suppresses a route announcement out an interface from which the route was learned?

a. Holddowns

b. Split horizon

c. Poison reverse

d. Passive interface

4 Convert the following IP address into dotted decimal format:

10100010001011010001100111000000

a. 162.46.24.128

b. 162.45.25.92

c. 161.45.25.192

d. 162.45.25.192

5 List the routing protocols that support VLSM.

a. IGRP, EIGRP, OSPF, IS-IS

b. RIPv2, EIGRP, OSPF, IS-IS

c. EIGRP, OSPF, IS-IS, IGRP

d. EIGRP, OSPF, RIPv2, IGRP

6 When you have configured your router for EIGRP routing, how do you configure the gateway of last resort?

a. Use the **ip default-gateway** command.

b. Use the **ip-default gateway** command.

c. Use the **ip default-network** command.

d. Use the **ip default-gateway-network** command.

7 If a Token Ring has been configured with ring number 24, what is its hexadecimal equivalent?

a. 0x18

b. 0x24

c. 0x16

d. 0x10

8 Which layer of the hierarchical design model implements access lists, distribution lists, route summarization, VLAN routing, security policy, and address aggregation?

a. Session layer

b. Distribution layer

c. Transport layer

d. Core layer

9 Which routing protocol periodically sends its routing table to its neighbors?

a. A hierarchical routing protocol

b. A hybrid routing protocol

c. A link-state routing protocol

d. A distance vector routing protocol

10 The switch functions of blocking and forwarding, which are based on a MAC address, operates in which layer of the OSI model?

a. Layer 3

b. Network layer

c. Data-link layer

d. Layer 1

11 Which is the best measurement of reliability and load of an interface?

a. Rely 255/255, load 1/255

b. Rely 255/255, load 255/255

c. Rely 1/255, load 1/255

d. Rely 1/255, load 255/255

12 Which OSI layer deals with frames?

a. Physical layer

b. Layer 4

c. Network layer

d. Data-link layer

13 Which type of routing protocol do you use between autonomous systems?

a. Interior Gateway Protocol

b. Exterior gateway protocol

c. Interior Gateway Routing Protocol

d. Nonrouting exterior gateway protocol

14 Which layer of the OSI model is concerned with data representation, data compression schemes, encryption, and voice coding?

a. Session layer

b. Presentation layer

c. Data-link layer

d. Physical layer

15 Which metric is concerned with the time a packet takes to travel from one end to another in the internetwork?

a. Cost

b. Reliability

c. Delay

d. Load

16 Which summary route aggregates the following networks: 192.168.33.0/24, 192.168.32.0/25, 192.168.32.128/25, 192.168.34.0/23?

a. 192.168.33.0/22

b. 192.168.32.0/22

c. 192.168.30.0/22

d. 192.168.32.0/21

17 Which device controls collision domains but does not control broadcast domains?

a. Bridges

b. Hubs with Ethernet ports

c. Routers

d. Forwarding gateways

18 Which routing protocol requires a hierarchical topology?

a. IGRP

b. RIP

c. EIGRP

d. OSPF

19 Which layer of the OSI model does TCP operate in?

a. Layer 3

b. Layer 4

c. Layer 5

d. Layer 6

20 Convert 11011011 to decimal.

a. 199

b. 215

c. 219

d. 217

21 Which OSI layer operates with packets?

a. Physical layer

b. Core layer

c. Network layer

d. Distribution layer

22 For what metric is the value for a 10 Mbps Ethernet interface calculated as $10^8 / 10^7 = 10$?

a. Cost

b. Hop count

c. Bandwidth

d. Load

23 In which type of routing protocol does each router advertise its status to all routers in the network, and each router calculates the best routes in the network.

a. Hop count

b. Link-state

c. Distance vector

d. Hybrid state

24 Which command can be used to configure the default route out interface serial 0?

a. **ip default-gateway serial0**

b. **ip default 0.0.0.0 0.0.0.0 serial 0**

c. **ip default-network serial 0**

d. **ip route 0.0.0.0 0.0.0.0 serial 0**

25 What is 0xFC in decimal?

a. 240

b. 248

c. 253

d. 252

26 A routing protocol that sends out routes with an unreachable metric is using what?

a. Metric holddowns

b. Poison reverse

c. Route updates

d. Simple split horizon

27 Which hierarchical design model layer has high-speed backbone ATM switches with redundant connections?

a. Data-link layer

b. Core layer

c. Network layer

d. Transport layer

28 Convert the mask 255.255.255.224 into binary.

a. 11111111 11111111 11111111 11000000

b. 11111111 11111111 11111111 11110000

c. 11111111 11111111 11111111 11100000

d. 00000000 00000000 00000000 00111111

29 What does OSI stand for?

a. Operation System Interconnection

b. Open System Interconnection

c. Open Systems Interconnect

d. Operation Systems Interconnect

30 Which of the following routing protocols is classful?

a. IGRP

b. RIPv2

c. EIGRP

d. OSPF

Scenario

Answer the following questions based on Figure 2-11. Each question tests your knowledge of how different metrics affect the chosen route to a destination. Answers to these questions are in the Appendix, "Answers to Quiz Questions."

Figure 2-11 *Scenario Diagram*

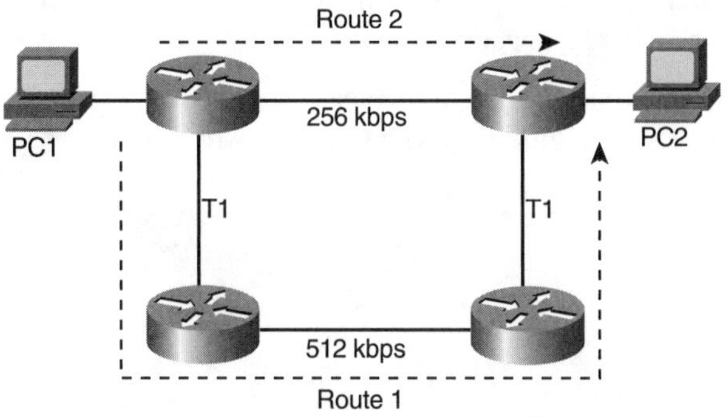

1 A user performs a Telnet from PC 1 to PC 2. If the metric that the configured routing protocol uses is bandwidth, which route will the packets take?

a. Route 1.

b. Route 2.

c. Neither, there is not sufficient information.

d. One packet takes Route 1, the following packet takes Route 2, and so on.

2 A user performs a Telnet from PC 1 to PC 2. If the metric that the configured routing protocol uses is hop count, which route will the packets take?

a. Route 1.

b. Route 2.

c. Neither, there is not sufficient information.

d. One packet takes Route 1, the following packet takes Route 2, and so on.

3 A user performs a Telnet from PC 1 to PC 2. If the metric that the configured routing protocol uses is cost, which route will the packets take?

a. Route 1.

b. Route 2.

c. Neither, there is not sufficient information.

d. One packet takes Route 1, the following packet takes Route 2, and so on.

This chapter covers the following topics needed to master the CCIE Routing and Switching (R&S) written exam:

- **Infrastructure**—Review device CPU, configuration register, and memory components, such as dynamic random-access memory (DRAM), nonvolatile (NVRAM), and flash memory
- **Router modes**—Review the user exec, privileged exec, and read-only memory (ROM) monitor router environments
- **Router operations**—Review image and configuration file transfers, router access, and password management
- **Router command-line interface**—Review router **show** and **debug** commands and look at some similarities with Catalyst **switch** commands

CHAPTER 3

Cisco Equipment Operations

This chapter covers the memory types, router operations, router modes, and the command-line interface (CLI) of Cisco routers.

"Do I Know This Already?" Quiz

The purpose of this assessment quiz is to help you determine how to spend your limited study time. If you can answer most or all of these questions, you might want to skim the Foundation Topics section and return to it later as necessary. Review the Foundation Summary section and answer the questions at the end of the chapter to ensure that you have a strong grasp of the material covered. If you intend to read the entire chapter, you do not necessarily need to answer these questions now. If you find these assessment questions difficult, read through the entire Foundation Topics section and review it until you feel comfortable with your ability to answer all of the Q & A questions at the end of the chapter. The following questions are repeated at the end of the chapter in the Q & A section with additional questions to test your mastery of the material.

Select the best answer. Answers to these questions are in the Appendix, "Answers to Quiz Questions."

1 If the configuration register is set to 0x2101, where is the IOS image booted from?

a. Flash

b. Slot0:

c. ROM

d. NVRAM

2 Which command copies the IOS image file from a UNIX server into flash?

a. **config net**

b. **copy tftp flash**

c. **copy unix flash**

d. **copy tftp startup-config**

3 Which switch command's output is similar to the output of the router **show ip interface brief** command?

a. **show vlan interface brief**

b. **show port status**

c. **show port interface**

d. **show ip vlan**

4 When booting a router, you reach the following message:

```
          --- System Configuration Dialog ---
Would you like to enter the initial configuration dialog? [yes/no]:
```

What might have caused this to occur?

a. The router's configuration register was set to 0x2142.

b. A **write erase** command was performed prior to reboot.

c. The running configuration was deleted from NVRAM.

d. Answer a or b.

5 After entering the **debug ip rip** command, no messages appear on your Telnet screen. What is one likely cause?

a. OSPF is also running.

b. The console port is disabled.

c. The **terminal monitor** command needs to be configured.

d. RIP broadcasts every 30 seconds.

6 Which command can be used to verify the configuration register setting for the next reload?

a. **show hardw**

b. **show version**

c. **show config-reg**

d. Answer a or b

7 Where is the startup configuration usually stored?

a. slot0 of the flash card

b. NVRAM

c. Active RAM after bootup

d. ROM

8 Which statement is correct?

a. The **enable secret** command overrides the **password** *password* command.

b. The **enable secret** command overrides the **enable password** command.

c. The **enable secret** command overrides the **service password-encryption** command.

d. The **enable secret** command sets the console password.

9 What does the **o/r 0x2142** command do?

a. Configures the router to ignore the contents in flash

b. Configures the router to ignore the boot system commands

c. Configures the router to enter into rommon mode

d. Configures the router to ignore the contents in NVRAM

10 Which command configures the enable password on a Catalyst switch?

a. **set enablepass**

b. **set password**

c. **set enable secret**

d. **set pass**

Foundation Topics

Infrastructure

This section reviews router CPU and memory components, such as NVRAM, flash, and RAM memory. For the test, you need to be familiar with the location of configuration files and IOS images.

Central Processing Unit (CPU)

Most Cisco routers have the Motorola 68000 series or Orion RISC (R4700) microprocessors. The CPU is the brain of the system. It runs route algorithms, exec processes, route filtering, network management, and so on. Some processes, such as Open Shortest Path First(OSPF), task the CPU with large computations.

The CPU type can be checked with the **show version** command. Example 3-1 shows a Cisco MC3810 using the Motorola MPC860 processor.

Example 3-1 **show version** *Command Used to Check Processor Type*

```
Router>show version
Cisco Internetwork Operating System Software
IOS (tm) MC3810 Software (MC3810-A2ISV5-M), Version 12.0(7)XK1, EARLY DEPLOYMENT
 RELEASE SOFTWARE (fc1)
TAC:Home:SW:IOS:Specials for info
Copyright (c) 1986-2000 by cisco Systems, Inc.
Compiled Wed 15-Mar-00 11:49 by phanguye
Image text-base: 0x00023000, data-base: 0x00B97D30

ROM: System Bootstrap, Version 11.3(1)MA1, MAINTENANCE INTERIM SOFTWARE
ROM: MC3810 Software (MC3810-WBOOT-M), Version 11.3(1)MA1,  MAINTENANCE INTERIM
SOFTWARE

Router uptime is 1 week, 4 days, 23 hours, 1 minute
System returned to ROM by power-on
System image file is "flash:mc3810-a2isv5-mz.120-7.XK1.bin"

Cisco MC3810 (MPC860) processor (revision 04.06) with 28672K/4096K bytes of memory.
Processor board ID 07548638
PPC860 PowerQUICC, partnum 0x0000, version A03(0x0013)
Channelized E1, Version 1.0.
Bridging software.
X.25 software, Version 3.0.0.
```

CPU use is verified by the **show process** or **show process cpu** commands, as shown in Example 3-2. Both of these commands provide a list of the router's CPU use in the last five seconds, one minute, and five minutes. The **show process cpu** command also shows the processes.

Example 3-2 *CPU Use Verified*

```
R2#show process
CPU utilization for five seconds: 16%/14%; one minute: 17%; five minutes: 16%
 PID QTy       PC Runtime (ms)    Invoked    uSecs    Stacks TTY Process
   1 Csp   25F66C            0        171        0 2640/3000   0 Load Meter
   2 M*         0         3000        336    892810072/12000   0 Exec
   3 Lst   24880C        20694       1083    19108 5740/6000   0 Check heaps
   4 Cwe   23FC10            4          1     4000 5604/6000   0 Chunk Manager
...
...
R2#sh process cpu
CPU utilization for five seconds: 21%/14%; one minute: 18%; five minutes: 16%
 PID  Runtime(ms)  Invoked  uSecs    5Sec   1Min   5Min TTY Process
   1          0       163      0   0.00%  0.00%  0.00%   0 Load Meter
   2       2908       311   9350   0.00%  1.58%  0.57%   0 Exec
   3      20357      1064  19132   6.47%  1.71%  1.83%   0 Check heaps
   4          4         1   4000   0.00%  0.00%  0.00%   0 Chunk Manager
...
...
```

Primary Memory

Primary memory is also referred to as main memory. DRAM chipsets store primary memory. DRAM is volatile, which means that if the router is turned off, all contents stored in system DRAM are erased. Primary memory stores data, such as routing tables, Address Resolution Protocol (ARP) caches, and operating code (in most models). Many IOS functions, such as OSPF, use a lot of memory, and you need to make sure that you have enough memory or the router might crash. With over 118,000 BGP routes so far, routers connected to the Internet require 256 megabytes or more of RAM. Different code versions and feature sets require different amounts of system RAM.

Nonvolatile RAM (NVRAM)

NVRAM stores the router configuration files. NVRAM is nonvolatile because it does not lose its contents when powered off, which makes it analogous to a floppy disk on a PC. Because NVRAM stores a text configuration file, it is approximately 256 KB in size.

Read-Only Memory (ROM)

Some routers might have a ROM chip that contains a version of the IOS that supports minimum functionality. The ROM chip also contains the power-on diagnostics and ROM monitor program. The only way to upgrade the code in the ROM is by replacing the ROM chip.

Boot Flash

The Boot Flash, similar to boot ROM, stores the ROM monitor program and power-up diagnostics. Newer routers contain the boot program in Boot Flash rather than in a ROM chip. The ROM monitor performs important functions, such as system diagnostics, hardware initialization, and booting the operating system. The ROM monitor can also be used to recover passwords, change the configuration register, and download IOS images. The ROM monitor has a user interface that is recognized by the following ROM monitor prompt:

```
rommon >
```

Flash Memory

Flash memory allows you to store and delete IOS images without having to change a ROM chip. The file is stored even if the router is turned off. If capacity allows, multiple images can be stored in flash. The image that gets loaded during the boot process is the one identified in the **boot system** configuration commands.

Flash memory can be internal or external. The external flash system uses Personal Computer Memory Card International Association (PCMCIA) cards inserted into slots on the router.

Flash File System

IOS images stored in the flash system can be copied, erased, transferred, and so on.

To show the contents in flash, enter the **show flash** command, as shown in Example 3-3. Example 3-3 shows system flash with a capacity of 8192 KB. An IOS image called mc3810-a2isv5-mz.120-7.XK1.bin uses 6,697,836 bytes; 1,428,992 bytes are free in the flash file system.

Example 3-3 **show flash** *Command*

```
r4>show flash
8192K bytes of processor board System flash (INTEL28F016)

Directory of flash:/

  2  -rwx     6697836   Mar 27 1993 02:53:08  mc3810-a2isv5-mz.120-7.XK1.bin

8128000 bytes total (1428992 bytes free)
```

The **dir** command lists the contents in the current directory, as shown in Example 3-4. Example 3-4 shows the same information as Example 3-2. Use the **dir** command to list the files in the current system when there are several flash file systems.

Example 3-4 **dir** *command*

```
r4#dir
Directory of flash:/

  2  -rwx     6697836   Mar 27 1993 02:53:08  mc3810-a2isv5-mz.120-7.XK1.bin

8128000 bytes total (1428992 bytes free)
```

If the router has two PCMCIA flash cards, you can move from one card to another by changing directories with the **cd** (change directory) command:

- **cd slot1**—changes the second PCMCIA flash card in slot1:.
- **cd slot0**—changes the first PCMCIA flash card in slot0:.

When you delete a file from flash, it is not necessarily removed from the flash card directory. After the **delete** command, the files appear with a D to mark them as deleted. Example 3-5 shows a list of files that are deleted. The **dir deleted** command lists all deleted files in flash.

Example 3-5 **dir deleted** *Command Lists Deleted Files*

```
router#dir deleted

-#- ED --type-- --crc--- -seek-- nlen -length- -----date/time------ name
  1 .D ffffffff 81a027ca   41bdc   22     7004 Apr 01 1998 15:27:45 5002.config.
4.1.98.cfg
  2 .D ffffffff ccce97a3   43644   23     6630 Apr 01 1998 15:36:47 5002.default
.config.cfg

1213952 bytes available (6388224 bytes used)
```

At this point, the deleted files can be restored with the **undelete** command.

Use the **squeeze** command to remove the files from the flash. The **squeeze** command removes all files that are marked with a D, as shown in Example 3-6.

Example 3-6 **squeeze** *Command*

```
router# squeeze slot0:
All deleted files will be removed, proceed (y/n) [n]? y

Squeeze operation may take a while, proceed (y/n) [n]? y

Erasing squeeze log
```

Configuration Register

The configuration register is a 16-bit virtual register that specifies boot sequence and break parameters and sets the console baud rate. The register is usually represented in hexadecimal. Figure 3-1 shows one of the common values for the configuration register, 0x2102. Another common value is 0x0101. The significance of each bit in the configuration register is described in this section.

Figure 3-1 *Configuration Register*

Bit:	15	14	13	12	11	10	9	8	7	6	5	4	3	2	1	0
0x2102	0	0	1	0	0	0	0	1	0	0	0	0	0	0	1	0

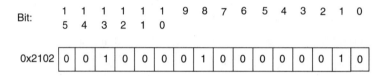

You can change the configuration register by using the global configuration command **config-register**. The following changes the configuration register to 0x10e:

```
Router(config)#config-register 0x10e
```

Boot Sequence

The last four bits (bits 3 to 0) of the configuration register specify the location of the boot file that the router must use when booting up:

- 0x0000 specifies to go to ROM monitor mode.
- 0x0001 specifies to boot from ROM.
- 0x0002 to 0x000F specify to examine the configuration file in NVRAM for **boot system** commands.

If no **boot system** commands are in the configuration file, the router attempts to boot the first file in system flash memory. If no file is found in system flash memory, the router attempts to boot a default file from the network whose name is derived from the value of the boot field (e.g., cisco2-4500) by using Trivial File Transfer Protocol (TFTP). If the attempt to boot from a network server fails, the boot helper image in boot Flash boots up.

The default filename is constructed by the word cisco, the value of the boot bits, and the router model or processor name. The format is **cisco***n-processor_name*, where *n* is a value between 2 and 15 and equal to the value of the boot field. If the boot field is set to 3 (0011 binary) on a Cisco 4500, the default boot name is cisco3-4500.

If several **boot system** commands are in the configuration, they are attempted in the order that they appear. Example 3-7 shows the configuration for a router where it first attempts to boot an image from flash, and if that fails, to boot from a TFTP server, and if that fails, to boot from ROM. The IP address of the TFTP server is specified in the **boot system tftp** command.

Example 3-7 *The Order of* **boot system** *Commands Determines Which IOS Is Loaded*

```
boot system flash mc3810-a2isv5-mz.120-7.XK1.bin
boot system tftp mc3810-a2isv5-mz.120-7.XK1.bin 1.1.1.1
boot system rom
```

Sample Boot Sequence

This section covers a sample boot sequence for a MC3810 router. For the test, you must have a high level of familiarity with the boot sequence of a router. Following are the four stages:

- System bootstrap
- Bootloader
- Booting of the system IOS image
- Initialization of interfaces/System Restart

The first stage of the boot sequence is the loading of bootstrap software. The bootstrap software initializes the CPU and launches the bootloader:

```
System Bootstrap, Version 11.3(1)MA1, MAINTENANCE INTERIM SOFTWARE
Copyright (c) 1998 by cisco Systems, Inc.
Compiled Sat 24-Jan-98 14:55 by krunyan
PPC860 PowerQUICC, partnum 0x0000, version A03(0x0013)
  MC3810 platform with 32768 Kbytes of main memory
```

The second stage of the boot sequence is the bootloader. The bootloader is not a full router image. It contains minimal functionality for reading the configuration and accessing the flash file system (highlighted). The router at this point can act as an end host with no routing functionality. If the bootloader is not present, the router attempts to load the first file present in the flash file system. The system identifies which messages are from the bootloader:

```
program load complete, entry point: 0x23000, size: 0x11437c
Self decompressing the image : ####################################################
################################################################## [OK]
Slot 3 OK. Configured as T1 TEB CSU  Serial #08076360 Version 4.70

Initialize Flash file system.....
total size = 8388608

flashfs[4]: 1 files, 1 directories
flashfs[4]: 1 orphaned files, 1 orphaned directories
flashfs[4]: Total bytes: 8128000
flashfs[4]: Bytes used: 6757888
flashfs[4]: Bytes available: 1370112flashfs[4]: flashfs fsck took 18 seconds.
flashfs[4]: Initialization complete.

Readfile
(flash:mc3810-a2isv5-mz.120-7.XK1.bin) into ram (0x41E0E0) ...

flashfs[4]: dostat, unable to lookup filemap for fileid 0!!!!!!!!!!!!!!!!!!!!!!!!

!!!!!!!!!!!!!
Finished - 6697836 bytes

  %SYS-6-BOOT_MESSAGES: Messages above this line are from the boot loader.
```

The third stage of the boot sequence is the booting of the system IOS image. The IOS image can be contained in the flash file system or booted from a TFTP server. After the image is loaded, the router lists the IOS version and the recognized interfaces:

```
UART re-init OK (disable AUX port)
program load complete, entry point: 0x23000, size: 0x663250
Self decompressing the image : #################################################
################################################################################

################################################################################
################################################################################
################################################################################
###################################################### [OK]

              Restricted Rights Legend

Use, duplication, or disclosure by the Government is
subject to restrictions as set forth in subparagraph
(c) of the Commercial Computer Software - Restricted
Rights clause at FAR sec. 52.227-19 and subparagraph
(c) (1) (ii) of the Rights in Technical Data and Computer
Software clause at DFARS sec. 252.227-7013.

           cisco Systems, Inc.
           170 West Tasman Drive
           San Jose, California 95134-1706


Cisco Internetwork Operating System Software
IOS (tm) MC3810 Software (MC3810-A2ISV5-M), Version 12.0(7)XK1, EARLY DEPLOYMENT
 RELEASE SOFTWARE (fc1)
TAC:Home:SW:IOS:Specials for info
Copyright (c) 1986-2000 by cisco Systems, Inc.
Compiled Wed 15-Mar-00 11:49 by phanguye
Image text-base: 0x00023000, data-base: 0x00B97D30

Slot 3 OK. Configured as T1 TEB CSU  Serial #08076360 Version 4.70
Cisco MC3810 (MPC860) processor (revision 04.06) with 28672K/4096K bytes of memory
Processor board ID 07548638
PPC860 PowerQUICC, partnum 0x0000, version A03(0x0013)
Channelized E1, Version 1.0.
Bridging software.
X.25 software, Version 3.0.0.
Primary Rate ISDN software, Version 1.1.
MC3810 SCB board (v04.K0)
1 Multiflex T1(slot 3) RJ45 interface(v01.K0)
1 Six-Slot Analog Voice Module (v07.B0)
1    Analog FXS voice interface (v05.A0) port 1/1
1    Analog FXS voice interface (v05.A0) port 1/2
1 6-DSP(slot2) Voice Compression Module(v01.K0)
1 Ethernet/IEEE 802.3 interface(s)
1 Serial network interface(s)
2 Serial(sync/async) network interface(s)
1 Channelized E1/PRI port(s)
1 Channelized T1/PRI port(s)
256K bytes of non-volatile configuration memory.
8192K bytes of processor board System flash (INTEL28F016)
Press RETURN to get started!
```

The fourth and final stage of the boot sequence is the initialization of the interfaces. The %SYS-5-RESTART: System restarted message is shown by the router in this stage. Several UPDOWN interface and port messages are shown in this stage:

```
Initialize Flash file system.....

total size = 8388608

../src-m860-mc3810/mc3810_avm.c, 2105, AVM PIM present
Serial # 201205538
Version # 8.1
avm system bus fpga init pass:
:FPGA program OK.
 avm fpga programming successful
:avm qslac fpga init pass:
:
00:00:03: 1/1 circuit type voice
00:00:03: 1/2 circuit type voice
00:00:16: %ATM-5-UPDOWN: Changing VC 0/16 VC-state to PVC activated.
00:00:16: %ATM-5-UPDOWN: Changing VC 0/16 VC-state to PVC created.
00:00:18: %SYS-5-CONFIG_I: Configured from memory by console
00:00:18: %LINK-3-UPDOWN: Interface Ethernet0, changed state to up
00:00:18: %LINK-3-UPDOWN: Interface Serial1, changed state to down
00:00:18: %LINK-3-UPDOWN: Interface Serial0, changed state to up
00:00:18: %LINEPROTO-5-UPDOWN: Line protocol on Interface ATM0, changed state to
 down
00:00:18: %LINK-5-CHANGED: Interface ATM0, changed state to reset
00:00:18: %SYS-5-RESTART: System restarted --
Cisco Internetwork Operating System Software
IOS (tm) MC3810 Software (MC3810-A2ISV5-M), Version 12.0(7)XK1, EARLY DEPLOYMENT
 RELEASE SOFTWARE (fc1)
TAC:Home:SW:IOS:Specials for info
Copyright (c) 1986-2000 by cisco Systems, Inc.
Compiled Wed 15-Mar-00 11:49 by phanguye
00:00:19: %LINK-5-CHANGED: Interface FR-ATM20, changed state to administratively
 down
00:00:20: %LINEPROTO-5-UPDOWN: Line protocol on Interface Ethernet0, changed state
 to up
00:00:20: %LINEPROTO-5-UPDOWN: Line protocol on Interface Serial1, changed state
 to down
00:00:20: %LINEPROTO-5-UPDOWN: Line protocol on Interface Serial0, changed state
 to up
00:00:20: %LINEPROTO-5-UPDOWN: Line protocol on Interface FR-ATM20, changed state
 to down
flashfs[9]: 1 files, 1 directories
flashfs[9]: 0 orphaned files, 0 orphaned directories
flashfs[9]: Total bytes: 8128000
flashfs[9]: Bytes used: 6699008
flashfs[9]: Bytes available: 1428992
flashfs[9]: flashfs fsck took 20 seconds.
flashfs[9]: Initialization complete.
00:00:39: %Voice-port 1/1 is up.
00:00:39: %Voice-port 1/2 is up.
00:00:39: %LINK-3-UPDOWN: Interface FXS 1/2, changed state to up
00:00:39: %LINK-3-UPDOWN: Interface FXS 1/1, changed state to up
```

Configuration Register Bit Meanings

Table 3-1 shows a description of each bit in the configuration register. Bits 0 to 3 are the boot field, which select the boot characteristics for the router. You use bit 6 to perform password recovery. When set, the configuration register has the number 4, as in 0x2142. Bit 8 is commonly set to permit a user to halt the router while operating. Bit 10 changes the broadcast type, but it is not commonly used. Bits 11 and 12 change the console line speed; by default, these bits are set to 00 for 9600 speed. Bit 13 is set to use the image on ROM if a network boot fails. Bit 15 enables diagnostic messages.

Table 3-1 describes the meaning of each bit of the virtual configuration register.

Table 3-1 *Configuration Register Bit Meanings*

Bit Number	Hex Value	Description
0-3 (boot field)	0x0000 to 0x000f	Selects boot characteristics. Boot field: 0000—Stay at bootstrap prompt 0001—Boot image on EPROM 0002 to 1111—Use the **boot system** commands in the configuration; selects default network boot filenames.
4	-	Unused.
5	-	Unused.
6	0x0040	Causes system to ignore the configuration stored in NVRAM.
7	0x0080	OEM bit enabled.
8	0x0100	When set, the Break key is disabled when system is operating. If not set, the system enters the bootstrap monitor, halting normal operation.
9	-	Unused.
10	0x0400	IP broadcast with all zeros.
11-12	0x0800 to 0x1800	Console line speed: [12/11] Hex Baud 00 0x0000 9600 01 0x0800 4800 10 0x1000 1200 11 0x1800 2400
13	0x2000	Boots default ROM software if network boot fails.
14	0x4000	IP broadcasts do have network numbers.
15	0x8000	Enables diagnostics messages and ignores NVRAM contents.

The most common configuration register settings are 0x102 and 0x2102. When the configuration register is set to 0x0102, it has the Break key disabled when the router is operating, and it looks into the configuration to determine the boot sequence. With 0x2102, the settings are the same as in 0x0102, but the system also boots the default ROM software if the system attempts to boot from the network and fails.

Another common configuration register setting is 0x2142, which is for password recovery. It ignores the configuration in NVRAM when booting and prompts the user with the Initial Configuration Dialog.

Router Modes

This section reviews the different router modes and how the CLI prompt changes in these different modes. You must be familiar with the router modes—especially what the router prompt looks like in each mode.

ROM Monitor

If the router boots but does not load an IOS image, it enters into ROM monitor mode. The ROM monitor prompt is the following:

```
>
```

or

```
rommon >
```

Boot Mode

If the boot flash contains a bootloader with minimal functional IOS, the router prompt is the following:

```
router(boot)>
```

The router is in boot mode. In this mode, the router bootstrap program does not load the full IOS image. The bootloader permits viewing of the configuration and can act as an end host with no routing functionality. A default gateway can be configured to load an IOS image by using the TFTP protocol.

User Exec Mode

If there is a successful boot of the full IOS code, the first level of access into the router is the user exec mode. At this level, the user is allowed to display system information, perform basic tests, and change terminal settings. Viewing the configuration file and configuration changes and using **debug** commands are not allowed. The command prompt in the user mode is the router's name followed by the greater than symbol:

```
Router>
```

Privileged Exec Mode

The second level of full access is the privileged exec level—more commonly known as enable mode. At this level, the user is allowed to show system settings and status, enter into configuration mode, and run **debug** commands. The command prompt in enable mode is the router's name followed by a # symbol:

```
Router#
```

Configuration Mode

In enable mode, you can enter configuration mode with the **configure terminal** command. You use configuration mode for interface, router, and line configuration:

```
routerlab#configure terminal
Enter configuration commands, one per line. End with CNTL/Z.
routerlab(config)#
```

If an interface is configured, the prompt changes as follows:

```
router1(config)#interface ethernet 0
router1(config-if)#
```

If a routing protocol is configured, the prompt changes as follows:

```
router1(config)#router rip
router1(config-router)#exit
router1(config)#router eigrp 100
router1(config-router)#
```

If a console or virtual type terminal (vty) line is configured, the prompt changes as follows:

```
router1(config)#line con 0
router1(config-line)#exit
router1(config)#line vty 2
router1(config-line)#
```

If a route map is configured, the prompt changes as follows:

```
router1(config)#route-map ccie
router1(config-route-map)#
```

Be familiar with how the router prompt changes when in configuration mode. There might be test questions where the correct answer depends on the router prompt presented.

Initial Configuration Dialog

At bootup, the router prompts the user to enter into the system configuration dialog if the router has no configuration (because it is new or because the configuration file was erased [by the **write erase** command]). In Example 3-8, the router output shows a sample of the configuration dialog. If you enter the dialog, a series of questions walk you through the configuration of the router. In Example 3-8, you enter the basic network management configuration. The first level of configuration is global configuration of the hostname, the exec password, and the enable password. Then, the network management interface is configured with an IP address and mask. A configuration file is created that is saved into NVRAM.

Example 3-8 *System Configuration Dialog*

```
Notice: NVRAM invalid, possibly due to write erase.
        --- System Configuration Dialog ---

Would you like to enter the initial configuration dialog? [yes/no]: yes

At any point you may enter a question mark '?' for help.
Use ctrl-c to abort configuration dialog at any prompt.
Default settings are in square brackets '[]'.

Basic management setup configures only enough connectivity
for management of the system, extended setup will ask you
to configure each interface on the system

Would you like to enter basic management setup? [yes/no]: yes

Configuring global parameters:

  Enter host name [Router]: router1

  The enable secret is a password used to protect access to
  privileged EXEC and configuration modes. This password, after
  entered, becomes encrypted in the configuration.
  Enter enable secret:
% No defaulting allowed
  Enter enable secret: cisco

  The enable password is used when you do not specify an
  enable secret password, with some older software versions, and
  some boot images.
  Enter enable password: ins

  The virtual terminal password is used to protect
  access to the router over a network interface.
  Enter virtual terminal password: cisco
  Configure SNMP Network Management? [yes]: n

Current interface summary

Any interface listed with OK? value "NO" does not have a valid configuration

Interface      IP-Address      OK? Method Status              Protocol
Ethernet0      unassigned      NO  unset  up                  up

FR-ATM20       unassigned      NO  unset  initializing        down

Serial0        unassigned      NO  unset  up                  up

Serial1        unassigned      NO  unset  up                  up
```

continues

Example 3-8 *System Configuration Dialog (Continued)*

```
Enter interface name used to connect to the
management network from the above interface summary: ethernet0
Configuring interface Ethernet0:
  Configure IP on this interface? [yes]:
    IP address for this interface: 10.1.1.1
    Subnet mask for this interface [255.0.0.0] : 255.255.255.0
    Class A network is 10.0.0.0, 24 subnet bits; mask is /24

The following configuration command script was created:

hostname router1
enable secret 5 $1$ZM99$H3tEBLCFKozELMV54MPfi1
enable password ins
line vty 0 4
password cisco
no snmp-server
!
no ip routing

!
interface Ethernet0
no shutdown
ip address 10.1.1.1 255.255.255.0
!
interface FR-ATM20
shutdown
no ip address
!
interface Serial0
shutdown
no ip address
!
interface Serial1
shutdown
no ip address
!
end


[0] Go to the IOS command prompt without saving this config.
[1] Return back to the setup without saving this config.
[2] Save this configuration to nvram and exit.

Enter your selection [2]: 2
Building configuration...
Use the enabled mode 'configure' command to modify this configuration.
```

Router Operations

This section reviews the line and enable passwords, password recovery, and the different methods to access the routers.

Password Security

Passwords can be set for the console, auxiliary port, terminal controller (TTY), and virtual terminal (VTY) lines. The **login** command tells the router to prompt for the password. The **password** command sets the password. The **login** command can also authenticate with locally configured usernames and passwords or use TACACS for authentication. You use the **login local** command when using locally configured users. You use the **login tacacs** command when using authentication. A series of commands must be configured when using these advanced features, which are not covered in this book. You use the **login** command with no options to use the configured line password.

The console is configured with the **line console 0** command. The following commands configure the console to prompt for the password and to set the password:

```
router1(config)#line console 0
router1(config-line)#login
router1(config-line)#password cisco
```

The auxiliary port is configured with the **line aux 0** command. The following commands configure the auxiliary port to prompt for the password and to set the password:

```
router1(config)#line aux 0
router1(config-line)#login
router1(config-line)#password cisco
```

Most routers have five terminal lines, from line 0 to line 4. All terminal lines are configured with the **line vty 0 4** command. The following commands configure the virtual terminal lines to prompt for a password and to set the password:

```
router1(config)#line vty 0 4
router1(config-line)#login
router1(config-line)#password cisco
```

NOTE If you use the **login** command, but the password is not set for vty lines, Telnet access is not granted. The router returns a **password not set** message and disconnects the Telnet session. If you do not use the **login** command, users are granted access without prompting for passwords.

There are two methods to set the enable (privileged mode) password. The first is the **enable password** command. This method was superceded by the **enable secret** command, which was introduced to provide the additional security of password encryption. If you use both commands, the **enable secret** command overrides the **enable password** command.

One of the following commands sets the enable password:

```
enable password password
```

or

```
enable secret password
```

TFTP

The IOS images and configuration files can be transferred to and from the routers by using the TFTP protocol.

The **write network** or **copy running-config tftp** command saves the configuration file on a TFTP server. These commands perform the same function. You must then enter the IP address of the TFTP server and the filename, as shown in Example 3-9. The **configure network** or **copy tftp running-config** command copies the configuration file from the TFTP server. The file is copied into active RAM memory.

Example 3-9 The **copy tftp running-config** *Command*

```
R2#copy tftp running-config
Address or name of remote host []? 1.1.1.1
Source filename []? router-config1
Destination filename [running-config]?
```

IOS image files can also be transferred to and from a TFTP server. You must enter the IP address and filenames when using the **copy flash tftp** command, as shown in Example 3-10. The **copy flash tftp** command copies from the flash file system to the TFTP server. The **copy tftp flash** command copies the IOS image from the TFTP server and places it in the flash file system.

Example 3-10 copy *Commands Used to Copy IOS from Flash to the TFTP Server or Vice Versa*

```
r4#copy flash tftp
Source filename []? mc3810
Address or name of remote host []? 1.1.1.1
Destination filename [mc3810]?

r4#copy tftp flash
Address or name of remote host []? 1.1.1.1
Source filename []? mc3810
Destination filename [mc3810]?
```

Configuration File Manipulation

The router configuration can reside in several locations: NVRAM, DRAM, terminal, or on a TFTP server. When the router is booted, the configuration stored in NVRAM is the startup configuration. After the router is booted, the configuration is placed in DRAM. When users attaches to the console or telnets to the router, they view the active configuration on the terminal. The configuration file can also be transferred to or from a TFTP server.

Figure 3-2 shows the commands that manipulate the configuration file. Each command is described in Table 3-2. Older commands, such as **write terminal**, **configure terminal**, **configure memory**, **write memory**, **write network**, and **configure network**, are confusing. The functions of these commands are accomplished with the showing or copying of the startup configuration (startup-config) and the running configuration (running-config). The startup-config is the configuration in NVRAM. The running-config is the configuration in active memory.

Figure 3-2 *Configuration Commands*

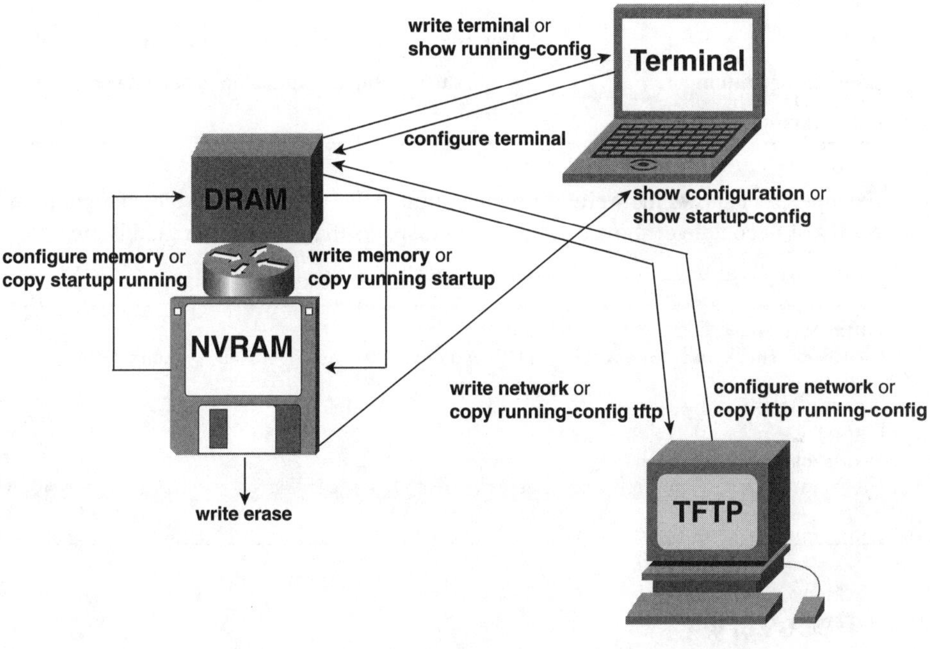

Table 3-2 *Configuration File Manipulation*

Command	Description
write terminal **show running-config**	Copies the running configuration into the terminal screen.
configure terminal	Enters configuration mode; in this mode, the router copies any **terminal configuration** commands into the running configuration.

continues

Table 3-2 *Configuration File Manipulation (Continued)*

configure memory **copy startup-config running-config**	Copies the configuration in NVRAM into active memory (running configuration).
write memory **copy running-config startup-config**	Copies the active configuration into NVRAM.
copy tftp running-config **configure network**	Copies the configuration file from a TFTP server into active memory.
copy running-config tftp **write network**	Copies the active configuration to a TFTP server.
write erase	Erases the configuration file in NVRAM.
show configuration **show startup-config**	Copies the startup configuration in NVRAM to the terminal screen.

Example 3-11 shows the **write erase** operation. After the erasure of the configuration in NVRAM is complete, **show configuration** displays that no configuration is present.

Example 3-11 **write erase** *Command Used to Erase the Startup Configuration*

```
R1#write erase
Erasing the nvram filesystem will remove all files! Continue? [confirm]y
[OK]
Erase of nvram: complete
R1#
R1#show configuration
%% Non-volatile configuration memory is not present
R1#
```

Password Recovery

Router password recovery is accomplished by rebooting the router and breaking into ROM monitor mode, setting the device to ignore the configuration file, rebooting, canceling the Initial Configuration Dialog, configuring memory, and then reading or resetting the password. You must be familiar with the password recovery steps for the test.

The following procedure is from Cisco's web site. This is the procedure for routers using Reduced Instruction Set Computer (RISC)-based processors:

Step 1 Turn the power switch off and back on to recycle the power.

Step 2 Press the **Break** key or key sequence to put the router into ROM monitor mode. The Break key varies by computer or terminal software. The sequence might be **CTRL-D**, **CTRL-Break**, **CTRL-]**, or another combination.

Step 3 At the rommon > prompt, type **confreg 0x2142** to boot from flash without loading the startup configuration in NVRAM at the next reload.

Step 4 Type **reset**. The router reboots but ignores the configuration in NVRAM.

Step 5 The router runs the Setup Dialog. Type **no** or press **Ctrl-C** to skip the Initial Setup Dialog.

Step 6 Type **enable** at the Router> prompt to go to privileged exec mode.

Step 7 Copy the startup configuration to the running configuration by using the **configure memory** or **copy startup-config running-config** commands. Do not type **configure terminal**. If you use the **configure terminal** command, you overwrite the configuration stored in NVRAM.

Step 8 View the configuration by typing **write terminal** or **show running-config**. View the configured line, vty, and enable passwords. Any encrypted passwords need to be changed.

Step 9 Enter configuration mode by typing **configure terminal**. Change the line or enable passwords as necessary.

Step 10 All interfaces are in a shutdown state. Issue the **no shutdown** command on every interface that is to be used.

Step 11 Type **config-register 0x2102** to return the router to normal operation at the next reload.

Step 12 Exit configuration mode by pressing **Ctrl-z** or **End**.

Step 13 Save your changes by typing **write memory** or **copy running-config startup-config**.

Step 14 Reload the router and verify the passwords.

The following is the procedure for non-RISC based routers. This procedure is from Cisco's web site at www.cisco.com/warp/public/474/.

NOTE Non-RISC based routers include Cisco models 2000, 2500, 3000, 4000, 7000(RP), AGS, and IGS.

Step 1 Turn the power switch off and back on to recycle the power.

Step 2 Press the **Break** key or key sequence to put the router into ROM Monitor mode. The Break key varies by computer or terminal software. The sequence might be **CTRL-D**, **CTRL-Break**, **CTRL-]**, or another combination.

Step 3 At the > prompt, type **o** to record the current value of the configuration register (usually 0x2102, or 0x102):

```
>o
Configuration register = 0x2102 at last boot
Bit#    Configuration register option settings:
15      Diagnostic mode disabled
...
```

Step 4 Type **o/r 0x2142** to tell the router to boot from flash without loading the configuration in NVRAM at the next reload.

Step 5 Type **i** to have the router reboot. The router ignores the configuration in NVRAM.

Step 6 The router runs the Setup Dialog. Type **no** or press **Ctrl-C** to skip the Initial Setup Dialog.

Step 7 Type **enable** at the Router> prompt to go to privileged exec mode.

Step 8 Copy the startup configuration to the running configuration by using the **configure memory** or **copy startup-config running-config** commands. Do not type **configure terminal**. If you use the **configure terminal** command, you overwrite the configuration stored in NVRAM.

Step 9 View the configuration by typing **write terminal** or **show running-config**. View the configured line, vty, and enable passwords. Any encrypted passwords need to be changed.

Step 10 Enter configuration mode by typing **configure terminal**. Change the line or enable passwords as necessary.

Step 11 All interfaces are in a shutdown state. Issue the **no shutdown** command on every interface that is to be used.

Step 12 Type **config-register 0x2102** to return the router to normal operation at the next reload.

Step 13 Exit configuration mode by pressing **Ctrl-z.**

Step 14 Save your changes by typing **write memory** or **copy running-config startup-config**.

Step 15 Reload the router and verify the passwords.

The index for password recovery procedures for all Cisco devices can be found at the following web site: www.cisco.com/warp/public/474/.

Accessing Devices

Routers can be accessed and managed by the console through modem dial-up into the auxiliary port, through a virtual terminal (i.e., Telnet), through asynchronous interfaces, or through Simple Network Management Protocol (SNMP).

Console

When accessing router consoles, the terminal emulation is set as follows:

- 9600 baud rate
- No parity
- 8 data bits
- 1 stop bit
- No flow control

The console is configured as follows:

```
line con 0
 password password
 login
```

Auxiliary Port

This port is usually connected to a modem for remote access as follows:

```
line aux 0
 password password
 login
 transport input all
 modem autoconfigure discovery
 exec-timeout 30 0
```

Telnet

You can reach a configured router through a virtual terminal (i.e., Telnet). Virtual terminal lines are configured as follows:

```
line vty 0 4
 password password
 login
```

Asynchronous Interfaces

Terminal servers can access routers. A router with asynchronous interfaces can act as a terminal server. Asynchronous lines are connected to the console interfaces of the routers. You can access the terminal server through Telnet and then access all routers by using reverse Telnet. A loopback

IP address is configured on the terminal server for reverse Telnet. If the terminal server's loopback IP address is 1.1.1.1, the **telnet 1.1.1.1 2001** command connects to the router through the first asynchronous line. The second router is accessed through the second asynchronous line by using the **telnet 1.1.1.1 2002** command. You can switch between the routers and the terminal server by using the **CTRL-SHIFT-6 x** key sequence.

SNMP

To access the router from a SNMP server, the SNMP read and read-write community strings need to be configured. The router can also be configured to send SNMP traps to the network management server.

To set the SNMP read-only community string, use the **snmp community** command. The following sets the read-only string to ccie-read:

```
R1(config)#snmp community ccie-read ro
```

The read-write community string is also set with the **snmp community** command. The following is set to ccie-write:

```
R1(config)#snmp community ccie-write rw
```

To send all traps to the SNMP server (1.1.1.1) with the SNMP community string of ccie-trap, enter the following **global configuration** command:

```
R1(config)#snmp host 1.1.1.1 ccie-trap
```

Router CLI

This section reviews the router CLI by reviewing **show** and **debug** commands. In the user exec or privileged exec mode, you can use **show** commands to display the status of routing protocols, interfaces, and the system.

You can check many keywords. Use the **show ?** command to go through the available options. Example 3-12 shows how you can bring up the various **show** command options (the list has been reduced) by typing **show ?**. The **show access-list** command displays all configured access lists on the router. The **show accounting** command shows active sessions and statistics. The **show flash** command displays the contents of the flash file system. Frame Relay information is displayed with the **show frame-relay** command. Interface information is displayed with the **show interfaces** command. The **show running-config** displays the active configuration. The **show startup-config** displays the configuration in NVRAM. The important **show** commands for each topic are covered in the corresponding sections throughout this book.

Example 3-12 *Some Options of the* **show** *Command*

```
R2#show ?
  access-lists              List access lists
  accounting                Accounting data for active sessions
  flash:                    display information about flash: file system
```

Example 3-12 *Some Options of the* **show** *Command (Continued)*

```
  frame-relay               Frame-Relay information
  interfaces                Interface status and configuration
  ip                        IP information
  logging                   Show the contents of logging buffers
  running-config            Current operating configuration
  spanning-tree             Spanning tree topology
  standby                   Hot standby protocol information
  startup-config            Contents of startup configuration
```

The **show ip** *keywords* command is one of the most common options. Example 3-13 displays some items that can be inspected. The **show ip arp** command displays the IP ARP table. The **show ip bgp** command displays the Border Gateway Protocol (BGP) table. The **show ip eigrp** command displays options to check the status of the Enhanced Interior Gateway Routing Protocol (EIGRP). The **show ip route** command displays the router's full routing table. The important **show** commands for each topic are in the corresponding sections throughout this book.

Example 3-13 *Some Options of the* **show ip** *Command*

```
R2#show ip ?
  arp                       IP ARP table
  bgp                       BGP information
  eigrp                     IP-EIGRP show commands
  interface                 IP interface status and configuration
  ospf                      OSPF information
  pim                       PIM information
  policy                    Policy routing
  protocols                 IP routing protocol process parameters and statistics
  rip                       IP RIP show commands
  route                     IP routing table
```

In Example 3-14, to quickly verify the status of all IP-enabled interfaces, you use the **show ip interface brief** command. This command displays all interfaces, the configured IP address, and the up/down status of the interface and protocol.

Example 3-14 *IP Interface Summary Displayed with the* **show ip interface brief** *Command*

```
R2#show ip interface brief
Interface              IP-Address      OK? Method Status                Protocol
Ethernet0              136.2.30.3      YES manual up                       up

FR-ATM20               unassigned      YES unset  administratively down down

Loopback0              unassigned      YES unset  up                       up

Serial0                unassigned      YES unset  administratively down down

Serial1                136.2.19.2      YES manual up                       up
```

Another frequently used command is **show version**. This command checks the booted IOS version, system uptime, amount of RAM, flash, NVRAM, CPU type, interfaces, and the setting of the configuration register. The way that the system was powered on (power on, reload, bug error) can also be checked. The **show hardware** command displays the same information as the **show version** command.

Example 3-15 displays the **show version** command's router output. From the output, you can gather that this router is a MC3810 multiservice concentrator that is running IOS 12.0(7)XK1 early deployment release software. The system bootstrap software is version 12.0(1)XA4. The router has been up for 1 day, 7 hours, and 28 minutes. The router has 32 MB of DRAM. Several Ethernet and serial interfaces are listed. There are two voice FXS and two voice E&M interfaces. The router has 256 KB of NVRAM and 16,384 KB of flash memory.

Example 3-15 **show version** *Command*

```
R2#show version
Cisco Internetwork Operating System Software
IOS (tm) MC3810 Software (MC3810-A2ISV5-M), Version 12.0(7)XK1, EARLY DEPLOYMENT
 RELEASE SOFTWARE (fc1)
TAC:Home:SW:IOS:Specials for info
Copyright (c) 1986-2000 by cisco Systems, Inc.
Compiled Wed 15-Mar-00 11:49 by phanguye
Image text-base: 0x00023000, data-base: 0x00B97D30

ROM: System Bootstrap, Version 12.0(1)XA4, EARLY DEPLOYMENT RELEASE SOFTWARE (fc
1)
ROM: MC3810 Software (MC3810-WBOOT-M), Version 12.0(1)XA4, EARLY DEPLOYMENT RELE
ASE SOFTWARE (fc1)

R2 uptime is 1 day, 7 hours, 28 minutes
System returned to ROM by reload
System image file is "flash:mc3810-a2isv5-mz.120-7.XK1.bin"

Cisco MC3810 (MPC860) processor (revision 16.00) with 28672K/4096K bytes of memory.
Processor board ID 09461375
PPC860 PowerQUICC, partnum 0x0000, version A03(0x0013)
Channelized E1, Version 1.0.
Bridging software.
X.25 software, Version 3.0.0.
Primary Rate ISDN software, Version 1.1.
MC3810 SCB board (v16.A0)
1 Multiflex T1(slot 3) RJ45 interface(v02.C0)
1 Six-Slot Analog Voice Module (v03.K0)
1    Analog E&M voice interface (v03.K0) port 1/1
1    Analog E&M voice interface (v03.K0) port 1/2
1    Analog FXS voice interface (v05.A0) port 1/3
1    Analog FXS voice interface (v05.A0) port 1/4
1 6-DSP(slot2) Voice Compression Module(v02.A0)
1 Ethernet/IEEE 802.3 interface(s)
1 Serial network interface(s)
```

Example 3-15 **show version** *Command (Continued)*

```
2 Serial(sync/async) network interface(s)
1 Channelized E1/PRI port(s)
1 Channelized T1/PRI port(s)
256K bytes of non-volatile configuration memory.
16384K bytes of processor board System flash (AMD29F016)

Configuration register is 0x2102
```

Other chapters in this book contain more detailed discussions of the **show** commands relevant to the topic at hand. As a CCIE candidate, you must be familiar with the available **show** commands.

Debug

The **debug** commands are available only in privileged exec (enable) mode. If you attempt to use **debug** in user exec mode, the command is not recognized. You must use **debug** commands with caution because the router's CPU use significantly increases when debugging is enabled.

NOTE If you access the router through a virtual terminal, such as Telnet, you need to enter the **terminal monitor** command to have debug output show on your screen. This command is not necessary if you access the router from the console.

Use the **debug ?** command to check the available debugging options, as shown in Example 3-16.

Example 3-16 **debug** *Command Options*

```
R2#debug ?
  MC3810                      MC3810 related debug flag
  aaa                         AAA Authentication, Authorization and Accounting
  access-expression           Boolean access expression
  all                         Enable all debugging
  alps                        ALPS debug information
  arp                         IP ARP and HP Probe transactions
  ...
```

To debug routing protocols, you can use **debug ip routing** or one of the more specific commands displayed in Table 3-3.

Table 3-3 **debug** *Commands for OSPF, EIGRP, and Routing Information Protocol (RIP)*

Debug Command	Description
OSPF	
debug ip ospf adj	Provides OSPF adjacency events
debug ip ospf events	Provides OSPF event information
debug ip ospf packet	Provides OSPF packet information
debug ip ospf spf	Provides OSPF Shortest Path First algorithm information
debug ip ospf tree	Provides OSPF database tree information
EIGRP	
debug ip eigrp neighbors	Provides EIGRP neighbor information
debug ip eigrp packets	Provides EIGRP packet information
debug ip eigrp transmit	Provides EIGRP transmission events
RIP	
debug ip rip database	Provides RIP database event information
debug ip rip events	Provides RIP protocol events
debug ip rip trigger	Provides RIP triggered packet events

Use the **show debug** command to verify the enabled debugging options, as shown in Example 3-17. This example shows debugging enabled for Internet Control Message Protocol (ICMP) packets. OSPF intra-area, interarea, and external events debugging are also enabled. RIP protocol and Frame Relay event debugging are also enabled.

Example 3-17 **show debug** *Command Displays All Active Debugging*

```
R2#show debug
Generic IP:
  ICMP packet debugging is on
IP routing:
  OSPF spf intra events debugging is on
  OSPF spf inter events debugging is on
  OSPF spf external events debugging is on
  RIP protocol debugging is on
Frame Relay:
  Frame Relay events debugging is on
```

Use the **undebug all** command to disable all debugging, as shown in Example 3-18. All possible debugging is disabled.

Example 3-18 *Disable Debugging with the* **undebug all** *Command*

```
R2#undebug all
All possible debugging has been turned off
```

Switch Commands

On the CCIE Routing and Switching (R & S) written exam, you need to know general **switch** commands and their functions, which are similar to **router** commands. This section covers commands of the Catalyst operating system (CatOS). The **switch** command that is similar to the **router** command **write erase** is **clear config all**. Example 3-19 shows a sample of this command. The CatOS **clear config all** command erases the configuration stored in NVRAM. On routers, **write erase** is the command that erases the configuration in NVRAM.

Example 3-19 *CatOS* **clear config all** *Command*

```
Console> (enable) clear config all
This command will clear all configuration in NVRAM.
This command will cause ifIndex to be reassigned on the next system startup.
Do you want to continue (y/n) [n]? y
........
.............................

System configuration cleared.
Console> (enable)
```

Passwords are configured in the Catalyst with the **set password** and **set enablepass** commands:

```
set password password
set enablepass password
```

Use the command **set interface sc0** *ip address mask broadcast* to configure an IP address for sc0, as shown in Example 3-20. The message returned by the switch tells you which parameters changed. The sc0 interface is an in-band management interface that handles SNMP, Telnet, Cisco Discovery Protocol (CDP), Virtual Terminal Protocol (VTP), and the Spanning-Tree Protocol (STP).

Example 3-20 *Configuration of Interface sc0*

```
Switch-A> (enable) set interface sc0 172.16.19.5 255.255.255.0 172.16.19.255
Interface sc0 IP address, netmask, and broadcast set.
Switch-A> (enable)
```

Use **show interface** to check the interfaces, as shown in Example 3-21. The **show interface** command displays the configured sc0 interface and its status.

Example 3-21 *The Catalyst* **show interface** *Command*

```
cat5000: (enable) show interface
sl0: flags=51<UP,POINTOPOINT,RUNNING>
        slip 0.0.0.0 dest 0.0.0.0
sc0: flags=63<UP,BROADCAST,RUNNING>
        vlan 1 inet 172.16.19.5 netmask 255.255.255.0 broadcast 172.16.19.255
```

The default gateway is configured with the **set ip default** command:

set ip default *gateway*

A CatOS **switch** command that is similar to the **router** command **show ip interface brief** is **show port status**, as shown in Example 3-22. This command provides a summary table of switch ports, their status, configured virtual local-area network (VLAN), and type. Example 3-22 shows that switch ports 2/4 and 2/9 are in VLAN 24.

Example 3-22 *CatOS* **show port status** *Command*

```
cat5000: (enable) show port status
Port  Name               Status     Vlan       Level  Duplex Speed Type
----- ------------------ ---------- ---------- ------ ------ ----- ----------
 1/1                     notconnect 1          normal   half   100 100BaseTX
 1/2                     notconnect 1          normal   half   100 100BaseTX
 2/1                     connected  1          normal   half    10 10BaseT
 2/2                     notconnect 1          normal   half    10 10BaseT
 2/3                     connected  1          normal   half    10 10BaseT
 2/4                     connected  24         normal   half    10 10BaseT
 2/5                     connected  1          normal   half    10 10BaseT
 2/6                     notconnect 1          normal   half    10 10BaseT
 2/7                     connected  1          normal   half    10 10BaseT
 2/8                     notconnect 1          normal   half    10 10BaseT
 2/9                     connected  24         normal   half    10 10BaseT
 2/10                    connected  1          normal   half    10 10BaseT
 2/11                    connected  1          normal   half    10 10BaseT
 2/12                    connected  1          normal   half    10 10BaseT
 2/13                    notconnect 1          normal   half    10 10BaseT
 2/14                    notconnect 1          normal   half    10 10BaseT
 2/15                    notconnect 1          normal   half    10 10BaseT
 2/16                    notconnect 1          normal   half    10 10BaseT
 2/17                    notconnect 1          normal   half    10 10BaseT
 2/18                    notconnect 1          normal   half    10 10BaseT
```

Configuring a VLAN

VLANs are configured with the **set vlan** command. Example 3-23 shows the command structure for the **set vlan** command. Ports 2/20-24 are assigned to Ethernet VLAN 101. The configuration is verified with the **show vlan** command. The **set vlan 101 name ccie said 10 type enet** command configures VLAN 101 with the name ccie and a unique SAID of 10; the type is Ethernet. The **set vlan 2/20-24** command assigns ports 2/20 to 2/24 to VLAN 101. The **show vlan** command verifies that ports 2/20-24 are assigned to VLAN 101.

Example 3-23 *CatOS* **set vlan** *Command*

```
cat5000: (enable) set vlan ?
Usage: set vlan <vlan_num> <mod/ports...>
       (An example of mod/ports is 1/1,2/1-12,3/1-2,4/1-12)
Usage: set vlan <vlan_num> [name <name>] [type <type>] [state <state>]
                           [said <said>] [mtu <mtu>] [ring <hex_ring_number>]
                           [decring <decimal_ring_number>]
                           [bridge <bridge_number>] [parent <vlan_num>]
                           [mode <bridge_mode>] [stp <stp_type>]
                           [translation <vlan_num>] [backupcrf <off¦on>]
                           [aremaxhop <hopcount>] [stemaxhop <hopcount>]
       (name = 1..32 characters, state = (active, suspend)
        type = (ethernet, fddi, fddinet, trcrf, trbrf)
        said = 1..4294967294, mtu = 576..18190
        hex_ring_number = 0x1..0xfff, decimal_ring_number = 1..4095
        bridge_number = 0x1..0xf, parent = 2..1005, mode = (srt, srb)
        stp = (ieee, ibm, auto), translation = 1..1005
        hopcount = 1..13)
cat5000: (enable)
cat5000: (enable) set vlan 101 name ccie said 10 type enet
Vlan 101 configuration successful
cat5000: (enable) set vlan 101 2/20-24
VLAN 101 modified.
VLAN 1 modified.
VLAN  Mod/Ports
---- -----------------------
101   2/20-24
cat5000: (enable) show vlan
VLAN Name                             Status    IfIndex Mod/Ports, Vlans
---- -------------------------------- --------- ------- ------------------------
1    default                          active    5       1/1-2
                                                        2/1-3,2/5-8,2/10-19
2    banzai                           active    38
3    VLAN0003                         active    35
24   VLAN0024                         active    39      2/4,2/9
56   VLAN0056                         active    36
79   VLAN0079                         active    37
101  ccie                             active    40      2/20-24
1002 fddi-default                     active    6
1003 trcrf-default                    active    9
1004 fddinet-default                  active    7
1005 trbrf-default                    active    8       1003
```

Some switches might be equipped with a routing engine or Multilayer Switch Feature Card (MSFC). You use the **session** *slot-number* command to reach the card from the CatOS.

The CCIE candidate must be familiar with the basic configuration commands for Catalyst OS switches.

References Used

The following resources were used to create this chapter:

www.cisco.com/warp/public/474/

www.cisco.com/univercd/cc/td/doc/product/access/acs_fix/cis2500/2509/acsvrug/techovr.htm

www.cisco.com/univercd/cc/td/doc/product/access/acs_mod/cis3600/hw_inst/3600hig/3600appb.htm

www.cisco.com/warp/public/63/arch_4000.shtml

www.cisco.com/univercd/cc/td/doc/product/access/acs_fix/827/827swcfg/basskls.htm#16914

www.cisco.com/univercd/cc/td/doc/product/core/cis7505/cicg7500/cicg75bc.htm

Foundation Summary

The Foundation Summary is a condensed collection of material that provides a convenient review of key concepts in this chapter. If you are already comfortable with the topics in this chapter, this summary will help you recall a few details. If you just read the Foundation Topics section, this review should help solidify some key facts. If you are doing your final preparation before the exam, these materials are a convenient way to review the day before the exam.

Table 3-4 *Configuration Register Bit Meanings*

Bit Number	Hex Value	Description
0–3 (boot field)	0x0000 to 0x000f	Select boot characteristics. Boot field is as follows: 0000—Stay at bootstrap prompt. 0001—Boot image on EPROM. 0002 to 1111—Use the **boot system** commands in the configuration; select default network boot filenames.
4	—	Unused.
5	—	Unused.
6	0x0040	Causes system to ignore the configuration stored in NVRAM.
7	0x0080	OEM bit enabled.
8	0x0100	When set, the Break key is disabled when system is operating. If not set, the system enters the bootstrap monitor, halting normal operation.
9	—	Unused.
10	0x0400	IP broadcast with all zeros.
11–12	0x0800 to 0x1800	Console line speed. [12/11] Hex Baud 00 0x0000 9600 01 0x0800 4800 10 0x1000 1200 11 0x1800 2400
13	0x2000	Boots default ROM software if network boot fails.
14	0x4000	IP broadcasts do have network numbers.
15	0x8000	Enables diagnostics messages and ignores NVRAM contents.

Table 3-5 *Router Modes*

Router Mode	Description
rommon	ROM monitor mode; the prompt is as follows: > or rommon >
User exec	To perform **show** commands, the prompt is as follows: router>
Privileged exec	Enable mode, can enter configuration mode and run **debug** commands; the prompt is as follows: router#
Configuration	Configuration commands are entered; the prompt is as follows: router(config)#

Table 3-6 *Configuration File Manipulation*

Command	Description
write terminal **show running-config**	Copies the running configuration into the terminal screen.
configure terminal	Enters configuration mode; in this mode, the router copies any terminal configuration commands into the running configuration.
configure memory **copy startup-config running-config**	Copies the configuration in NVRAM into active memory (running configuration).
write memory **copy running-config startup-config**	Copies the active configuration into NVRAM.
copy tftp running-config **configure network**	Copies the configuration file from a TFTP server into active memory.
copy running-config tftp **write network**	Copies the active configuration to a TFTP server.
write erase	Erases the configuration file in NVRAM.
show configuration **show startup-config**	Copies the startup configuration in NVRAM to the terminal screen.

Routers can be accessed by the following methods:

- Direct console port
- Through dialup modem using the auxiliary port
- Virtual terminal (Telnet)
- Terminal server using asynchronous lines
- Network Management Server (NMS) using SNMP

Q & A

The Q & A questions are more difficult than what you can expect on the actual exam. The questions do not attempt to cover more breadth or depth than the exam; however, they are designed to make sure that you retain the material. Rather than allowing you to derive the answer from clues hidden inside the question itself, these questions challenge your understanding and recall of the subject. Questions from the "Do I Know This Already?" quiz are repeated here to ensure that you have mastered the chapter's topic areas. A strong understanding of the answers to these questions will help you on the CCIE written exam. As an additional study aide, use the CD-ROM provided with this book to take simulated exams.

Select the best answer. Answers to these questions are in the Appendix, "Answers to Quiz Questions."

1 If the configuration register is set to 0x2101, where is the IOS image booted from?

a. Flash

b. Slot0:

c. ROM

d. NVRAM

2 Which command copies the IOS image file from a UNIX server into flash?

a. **config net**

b. **copy tftp flash**

c. **copy unix flash**

d. **copy tftp startup-config**

3 Which switch command's output is similar to the output of the router **show ip interface brief** command?

a. **show vlan interface brief**

b. **show port status**

c. **show port interface**

d. **show ip vlan**

4 When booting a router, you reach the following message:

```
            --- System Configuration Dialog ---
Would you like to enter the initial configuration dialog? [yes/no]:
```

What could have caused this to occur?

a. The router's configuration register was set to 0x2142.

b. A **write erase** command was performed prior to reboot.

c. The running configuration was deleted from NVRAM.

d. Answer a or b.

5 After entering the **debug ip rip** command, no messages appear on your Telnet screen. What is one likely cause?

a. OSPF is also running.

b. The console port is disabled.

c. The **terminal monitor** command needs to be configured.

d. RIP broadcasts every 30 seconds.

6 Which command verifies the configuration register setting for the next reload?

a. **show hardw**

b. **show version**

c. **show config-reg**

d. Answer a or b

7 Where is the startup configuration usually stored?

a. slot0 of the flash card

b. NVRAM

c. Active RAM after bootup

d. ROM

8 Which statement is correct?

a. The **enable secret** command overrides the **password** *password* command.

b. The **enable secret** command overrides the **enable password** command.

c. The **enable secret** command overrides the **service password-encryption** command.

d. The **enable secret** command sets the console password.

9 What does the **o/r 0x2142** command do?

a. Configures the router to ignore the contents in flash

b. Configures the router to ignore the boot system commands

c. Configures the router to enter into rommon mode

d. Configures the router to ignore the contents in NVRAM

10 Which command configures the enable password on a Catalyst switch?

a. **set enablepass**

b. **set password**

c. **set enable secret**

d. **set pass**

11 The configuration register is set to 0x2101 and the **boot** commands are as follows:

```
boot system tftp mc3810-a2isv5-mz.120-7.XK1.bin 1.1.1.1
boot system flash
```

Which IOS is used?

a. IOS on the TFTP server

b. IOS in flash

c. IOS in ROM

d. IOS in NVRAM

12 What is the purpose of the bootstrap?

a. Initializes the CPU and starts the bootloader

b. Links the IOS in flash to the boot ROM

c. Initializes the CPU and starts the routing processes

d. Copies the startup configuration to the running configuration

13 Which command configures the router from the network?

a. **copy startup-config running-config**

b. **copy tftp running**

c. **copy running-config tftp**

d. **write network**

14 Which command allows the NMS server to make changes on the router?

a. **snmp enable ccie rw**

b. **snmp community ccie ro**

c. **snmp community ccie rw**

d. **enable snmp-secret ccie rw**

15 If you Telnet to a router that has the **login** command configured for all vtys but cannot log in, what is missing?

a. The enable password

b. The **password** command

c. The **login** command

d. The auxiliary port configuration

16 Which command sets the configuration register to 0x2102?

a. router(config-in)**#configure-register 0x2102**

b. router(config)**#configure-register 0x2102**

c. router(config)**#conf-reg 0x2102**

d. router(config)**#config-register 0x2102**

17 Which command shows the five second, one minute, and five minute CPU use time for each process on the router?

a. **show process**

b. **show process cpu**

c. **show process memory**

d. **show cpu**

18 Which command shows the memory (allocated/freed/holding) used per process?

a. **show process**

b. **show process cpu**

c. **show process memory**

d. **show ram**

19 Where is the IOS image stored?

a. Flash

b. NVRAM

c. ROM

d. Answers a and c

20 A user telnets to a router that has the **password** command configured for all vty lines. If the user is granted access with no password, what is missing?

a. The console password

b. The enable password

c. The **login** command

d. The **enable secret** command

21 Which prompt indicates that the router is in ROM monitor mode?

a. >

b. router>

c. router#

d. router(config)#

22 What is the procedure for password recovery?

a. Break, reboot, set ignore NVRAM, copy password

b. Reboot, break, set 0x2142, reboot, copy password, disable ignore NVRAM, reboot

c. Reboot, break, set 0x2142, reboot, copy password, ignore NVRAM, reboot, enter password

d. Set 0x2142, reboot, copy password

23 You have deleted two files in the flash, but when you try to copy a new image into flash, an error occurs. What is the reason for the error?

a. You deleted the files but did not format the flash card.

b. If the files still show when a **dir** command is issued, it means that you have not deleted the files.

c. When the **dir** command is issued, the files show up with a "D"; perform a squeeze.

d. Reboot the router; that fixes everything.

Scenario

This scenario tests your understanding of the configuration register, **boot system** commands, and passwords used in Cisco routers. Use the following configuration to answer the Scenario questions:

```
hostname router1
!
boot system flash mc3810-a2isv5-mz.120-7.XK1.bin
boot system tftp mc3810-a2isv5-mz.120-6.XK1.bin 1.1.1.1
boot system rom
!
enable secret 5 1$yfrZ$TWjcS4u2GVh/FbH3zK  (encrypted ccie2)
enable password ccie1
!
interface ethernet 0
 ip address 1.1.1.2 255.255.255.0
!
line con 0
 password ccie3
 login
!
line vty 0 4
 password ccie4
!
```

1 If the configuration register is set to 0x2102, which IOS is loaded?

a. mc3810-a2isv5-mz.120-7.XK1.bin

b. mc3810-a2isv5-mz.120-6.XK1.bin

c. IOS in ROM

d. ROM monitor

2 If the configuration register is set to 0x2100, which IOS is loaded?

a. mc3810-a2isv5-mz.120-7.XK1.bin

b. mc3810-a2isv5-mz.120-6.XK1.bin

c. IOS in ROM

d. ROM monitor

3 If the configuration register is set to 0x2101, which IOS is loaded?

a. mc3810-a2isv5-mz.120-7.XK1.bin

b. mc3810-a2isv5-mz.120-6.XK1.bin

c. IOS in ROM

d. ROM monitor

4 If the configuration register is set to 0x2102, and there is no IOS image file in flash, which IOS is loaded?

a. mc3810-a2isv5-mz.120-7.XK1.bin

b. mc3810-a2isv5-mz.120-6.XK1.bin

c. IOS in ROM

d. ROM monitor

5 If the configuration register is set to 0x2102, and there is no IOS image file in flash and the TFTP server is down, which IOS is loaded?

a. mc3810-a2isv5-mz.120-7.XK1.bin

b. mc3810-a2isv5-mz.120-6.XK1.bin

c. IOS in ROM

d. ROM monitor

6 If the configuration register is set to 0x2142, which IOS is loaded?

a. 3810-a2isv5-mz.120-7.XK1.bin

b. 3810-a2isv5-mz.120-6.XK1.bin

c. IOS in ROM

d. ROM monitor

7 What password is entered to reach privileged exec mode?

a. ccie1

b. ccie2

c. ccie3

d. ccie4

8 What password accesses the router through Telnet to the router?

a. ccie2

b. ccie3

c. ccie4

d. No password is used

This chapter covers the following topics needed to master the CCIE exam:

- **Local-area network (LAN) media review**—Data-link protocols and media topology requirements for Ethernet, Fast Ethernet (FE), Gigabit Ethernet (GE), Token Ring, and wireless LANs (WLANs)
- **Transparent bridging (TB)**—Reviews bridging functions such as shielded twisted-pair (STP), integrated routing and bridging (IRB), and concurrent routing and bridging (CRB)
- **Source-route bridging (SRB)**—Reviews bridging protocols that involve Token Ring networks, such as SRB, source-route transparent bridging (SRT), source-route translational bridging (SR/TLB), remote source-route bridging (RSRB), and data-link switching (DLSw), and Routing Information Field (RIF)
- **LAN switching Topics**—Reviews virtual LAN (VLAN) trunking, Fast EtherChannel (FEC), and Cisco Discovery Protocol (CDP); VLAN trunking topics, which include Inter-Switch Link (ISL), Institute of Electrical and Electronics Engineers (IEEE) 802.1q, and Virtual Terminal Protocol (VTP); and Security topics, which include access lists, Private VLANs, and IEEE 802.1x port-based authentication
- **Asynchronous Transfer Mode (ATM) LAN emulation (LANE)**—Reviews ATM LANE components and the Simple Server Redundancy Protocol (SSRP)

CHAPTER 4

Local-Area Networks and LAN Switching

This chapter covers the CCIE Written blueprint objectives related to bridging, local-area networks, and LAN switching. Other blueprint topics covered in this chapter include ATM LANE and LAN security.

"Do I Know This Already?" Quiz

The purpose of this assessment quiz is to help you determine how to spend your limited study time. If you can answer most or all of these questions, you might want to skim the Foundation Topics section and return to it later as necessary. Review the Foundation Summary section and answer the questions at the end of the chapter to ensure that you have a strong grasp of the material covered. If you intend to read the entire chapter, you do not necessarily need to answer these questions now. If you find these assessment questions difficult, read through the entire "Foundation Topics" section and review it until you feel comfortable with your ability to answer all of the Q&A questions at the end of the chapter. The following questions are repeated at the end of the chapter in the Q & A section with additional questions to test your mastery of the material.

Select the best answer. Answers to these questions are in the Appendix, "Answers to Quiz Questions."

1 What bit of each byte does an Ethernet NIC expect to read first off the wire?

a. The least significant bit first; this is the noncanonical format.

b. The most significant bit first; this is the noncanonical format.

c. The least significant bit first; this is the canonical format.

d. The most significant bit first; this is the canonical format.

2 Which access method listens to the wire before transmitting?

a. Token access

b. CSMA/CD

c. Token bus

d. 4B/5B

3 Which IEEE frame format includes a type field?

a. IEEE 802.3

b. IEEE 802.5

c. IEEE 802.3 SNAP

d. IEEE 802.1q

4 Which bridging method associates a MAC address with its ports?

a. Transparent

b. SRB

c. SR/TLB

d. RSRB

5 What does the following command do?

```
source-bridge transparent 10 5 1 6
```

a. Configures DLSw

b. Configures transparent bridging

c. Configures source-route bridging

d. Configures translational bridging from an Ethernet bridge group

6 What is the RIF in hexadecimal for a source route frame if it is to route from Token Ring 4, through bridge 12, ending on Token Ring 15?

a. 0630.004c.0015

b. 0630.0412.0015

c. 0630.040c.0150

d. 0630.004c.00f0

7 Which access list denies 00c0.00a0.0010 but permits other MAC addresses?

a.

```
access-list 700 deny 00c0.00a0.0010 ffff.ffff.ffff
access-list 700 permit 0000.0000.0000 ffff.ffff.ffff
```

b.

```
access-list 700 deny 00c0.00a0.0010 0000.0000.0000
access-list 700 permit 0000.0000.0000 ffff.ffff.ffff
```

c.

```
access-list 200 deny 00c0.00a0.0010 ffff.ffff.ffff
access-list 200 permit 0000.0000.0000 ffff.ffff.ffff
```

d.

```
access-list 200 deny 00c0.00a0.0010 0000.0000.0000
access-list 200 permit 0000.0000.0000 ffff.ffff.ffff
```

8 Which trunking method places an internal tag to identify the VLAN number?

a. ISL

b. 802.1q

c. 802.1p

d. VTP pruning

9 Which answer best describes the VTP client?

a. Stores VLAN information in NVRAM

b. Adds and deletes VLANs in the VTP domain

c. Maintains a full list of VLANs

d. Does not participate in VTP

10 What is the BID?

a. BLAN ID number

b. Bridge identifier in STP

c. Border identifier in SRB

d. Bridged identifier in VTP

11 What is the transparent bridge port state sequence from a disabled port to a forwarding port?

a. Disabled, listening, learning, forwarding, blocked

b. Disabled, enabled, listening, learning, forwarding

c. Disabled, blocking, listening, learning, forwarding

d. Disabled, blocking, learning, listening, forwarding

12 What is a BVI?

a. Bridged VLAN identifier

b. Bridge virtual interface, used in IRB

c. Bridge ID, in RIFs

d. When set, indicates to use SRB

13 Which type of bridge removes the RIF, checks the MTU, and reorders bits before sending the frame on?

a. Transparent

b. DLSw

c. SRT

d. SR/TLB

e. SRB

f. RSRB

14 What is the RIF in the following?

```
source-bridge ring-group 5
!
dlsw local-peer peer-id 1.1.1.1 promiscuous
dlsw remote-peer 0 tcp 2.2.2.1
!
interface tokenring 0
 source-bridge 1 2 5
```

a. 0630.0012.0050.

b. 0830.0125.

c. 0830.0012.0051.

d. Not enough information is given.

15 What is the maximum segment length of 10Base2 media?

a. 100 m

b. 185 m

c. 200 feet

d. 500 feet

16 At what speed does Gigabit Ethernet transmit data?

a. 1000 kbps

b. 100 Mbps

c. 1000 Mbps

d. 1250 kbps

17 What is the IEEE standard for Fast Ethernet?

a. IEEE 802.3a

b. IEEE 802.3ab

c. IEEE 802.3u

d. IEEE 802.3z

18 What is a BPDU?

a. Bridge packet descriptor unit

b. Bridge protocol data unit

c. Basic protocol descriptor unit

d. None of the above

Foundation Topics

LAN Media Review

This section covers Media Access Control (MAC) addresses, the Ethernet family of data-link layer technologies, Token Ring, and wireless LANs (WLANs).

MAC Address Format

Ethernet or Token Ring router interfaces and all device *network interface cards (NICs)* are identified with a unique *burned-in address (BIA)*. This is the *MAC address*, which is also called the *physical address*. It is an implementation of Layer 2 of the OSI reference model—or more specifically, the MAC layer of the IEEE model to identify the station. The MAC address is 48 bits in length (6 octets) and is represented in hexadecimal.

The router output in Example 4-1 shows the MAC address (00-10-7b-3a-92-3c) of an Ethernet interface.

Example 4-1 *Router Interface MAC Address*

```
router> show interface
  Ethernet0 is up, line protocol is up
  Hardware is Lance, address is 0010.7b3a.923c (bia 0010.7b3a.923c)
  Internet address is 135.119.110.30/24
  MTU 1500 bytes, BW 10000 Kbit, DLY 1000 usec,
     reliability 255/255, txload 1/255, rxload 1/255
  Encapsulation ARPA, loopback not set
  Keepalive set (10 sec)
  ARP type: ARPA, ARP Timeout 04:00:00
  Last input 00:00:00, output 00:00:00, output hang never
  Last clearing of "show interface" counters never
  Input queue: 1/75/0/0 (size/max/drops/flushes); Total output drops: 0
  Queueing strategy: fifo
  Output queue :0/40 (size/max)
  5 minute input rate 1000 bits/sec, 2 packets/sec
  5 minute output rate 1000 bits/sec, 2 packets/sec
     1999164 packets input, 379657585 bytes, 0 no buffer
     Received 1785091 broadcasts, 0 runts, 0 giants, 0 throttles
     1 input errors, 0 CRC, 0 frame, 0 overrun, 1 ignored
     0 input packets with dribble condition detected
     745208 packets output, 82211652 bytes, 0 underruns
     0 output errors, 63 collisions, 16 interface resets
     0 babbles, 0 late collision, 345 deferred
     0 lost carrier, 0 no carrier
     0 output buffer failures, 0 output buffers swapped out
```

The first three bytes of a MAC address form the Organizational Unique Identifier (OUI), which identifies the manufacturer/vendor. The last three octets are administered by the manufacturer and assigned in sequence.

Canonical Transmission

When converting hexadecimal MAC addresses to binary, each hexadecimal number is represented in its 4-bit binary equivalent. For example, ac-10-7b-3a-92-3c is converted normally to binary as the following:

10101100 00010000 01101011 00111010 01010010 00111100

For Token Ring networks, each octet of this MAC address is transmitted from left to right, from the *most significant bit (MSB)* to the *least significant bit (LSB)*. This *noncanonical* transmission is also known as *MSB first*.

For Ethernet networks, each octet of the previous MAC address is transmitted from left to right, but LSB to MSB. The difference is that for each octet, the LSB is transmitted first and the MSB is transmitted last. This *canonical* transmission is also known as *LSB first*. The MAC address AC-10-7b-3a-92-3c is transmitted as the following:

00110101 00001000 11010110 01011100 01001010 00111100

The octet AC is transmitted from left to right as 00110101, the second octet (10) is transmitted from left to right as 000010000, and so on.

For both Ethernet and Token Ring networks, the order of each octet is transmitted the same: from Most Significant Octet to Least Significant Octet. The difference is in the transmission order of the bits of each octet. For Ethernet networks, the LSB of the first octet is transmitted first. This bit is the Individual/Group (I/G) Address Bit. If the I/G is set to 0, it indicates an individual MAC address. If the I/G bit is set to 1, it indicates that the address is a group address. The I/G is set to 1 for broadcast and multicast MAC addresses.

The first (leftmost) bit in the binary representation is the I/G Address Bit. If set to 0, it indicates an individual address. It can be set to 1 in an address allocated by the vendor to indicate that the address is a group address. The second leftmost bit is the U/L bit. If set to 0, it indicates a universally administered address. If set to 1, it indicates that the address is locally administered.

Ethernet

Today's Ethernet networks are based on the Ethernet development by Digital, Intel, and Xerox (DIX). Version 1 of the standard was created in 1980. It used unbalanced signaling, meaning that a 0 is represented by 0 voltage, and a 1 is represented by a positive voltage. In 1982, version 2 of Ethernet was introduced. It added the heartbeat signal to transceivers and moved to balanced signaling. Balanced signaling uses positive and negative voltages, which allow more speed. The heartbeat signal is used as a link test pulse. Ethernet version 2 is the basis of today's

Ethernet networks. Ethernet uses carrier-sense multiple access with collision detection (CSMA/CD) as the access method.

CSMA/CD Media Access Method

CSMA/CD is the media access method on Ethernet networks. In this scheme, hosts listen to the network for activity. If there is no network activity, hosts can transmit a frame onto the network, while transmitting hosts listen to the network for any collisions with other transmitting nodes.

If no collision is detected, the host assumes that the frame transmitted successfully. If a collision is detected, the node waits a random amount of time and listens for traffic on the segment. If there is no traffic, it attempts to send the frame again. It attempts 16 times before sending an error message to the upper-layer protocol (ULP).

NOTE You only use CSMA/CD in shared networks or hubs. If an Ethernet or FE interface is configured for full-duplex operation, it does not use CSMA/CD. Because no collisions are in full-duplex mode, CSMA/CD is not required.

Ethernet Encoding

Manchester encoding was selected to code signals on the wire on Ethernet. In Manchester encoding, a 0 is represented as a transition from high to low in the middle of the clocking time interval. A 1 is represented as a transition from low to high in the middle of the time interval. Figure 4-1 shows a sample of Manchester encoding.

Figure 4-1 *Manchester encoding*

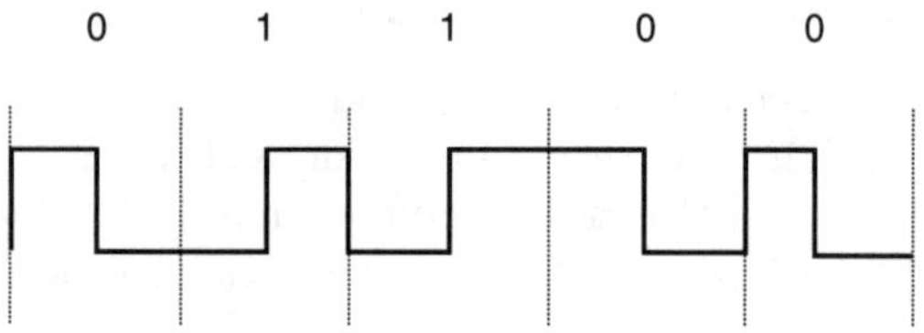

Ethernet Frame Formats

After the Ethernet V2 standard was published, an effort went into producing an IEEE standard for Ethernet. The IEEE 802 committee produced their 802.3 and 802.3 SNAP frame formats, with the 802.2 Logical Link Control (LLC). Novell also produced a frame format for its network operating system. These different groups produced different frame formats for the Ethernet wire, but the signaling, encoding, and frame maximum and minimum sizes remain the same.

Therefore, these four frame formats can reside on the same segment. A few differences exist, which are explained.

The four frame formats are as follows:

- Ethernet version 2
- Novell 802.3 Raw
- IEEE 802.3
- IEEE 802.3 Subnetwork Access Protocol (SNAP)

Ethernet Version 2 Frame Format

Figure 4-2 shows the Ethernet version 2 frame format. The frame fields are described in Table 4-1.

Figure 4-2 *Ethernet V2 Frame Format*

Preamble	DA	SA	Type	Data + pad	FCS
8 bytes	6 bytes	6 bytes	2 bytes	46-1500 bytes	4 bytes

Table 4-1 *Ethernet V2 Frame Fields Descriptions*

Field	Description
Preamble	String of binary 1s and 0s ending with 11 to indicate the beginning of the destination address (DA) field: 10101010 10101010 10101010 10101010 10101010 10101010 10101010 10101011
Destination Address (DA)	48-bit MAC layer Ethernet address of the destination host.
Source Address (SA)	48-bit MAC layer Ethernet address of the host that sent the frame (source host).
Type	Contains the Ethernet Type number that indicates the ULP that this frame should be sent to. This number is greater than 1500 (05DC hex). Examples of EtherTypes are 0x0800 for the IP protocol and 0x6004 for Dec LAT. A list of Ethernet types can be viewed at www.standards.ieee.org/regauth/ethertype/type-pub.html.
Data	Contains ULP information.
Frame Check Sequence (FCS)	The FCS uses a 32-bit cyclic redundancy check (CRC) for error detection.

The minimum frame size on Ethernet is 64 bytes, and the maximum is 1518 bytes. When calculating the frame size, do not include the preamble in the summation. The Ethernet V2 frame format conforms to the following specification:

- The minimum frame size is 6 + 6 + 2 + 46 + 4 = 64 bytes
- The maximum frame size is 6 + 6 + 2 + 1500 + 4 = 1518 bytes

Novell 802.3 Raw Frame Format

Prior to the IEEE 802.3 specification, Novell needed a frame format for their NetWare Internetwork Packet Exchange (IPX) network operating system. Novell produced their own frame format to run on CSMA/CD networks.

Figure 4-3 shows the Novell 802.3 raw frame format. The frame field descriptions are displayed in Table 4-2.

Figure 4-3 *Novell 802.3 Raw Frame Format*

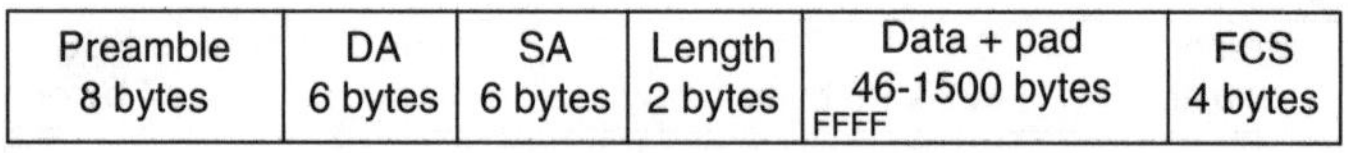

Table 4-2 *Novell 802.3 Raw Frame Fields Descriptions*

Field	Description
Preamble	Same as with Ethernet V2; a string of binary 1s and 0s ending with 11
Destination Address (DA)	48-bit MAC address of the destination host
Source Address (SA)	48-bit MAC address of the host that sent the frame (source host)
Length	Contains the length of the data field in binary; indicated values are from 3 to 1500 bytes
Data	Contains ULP IPX information
Frame Check Sequence (FCS)	Contains the 32-bit cyclic redundancy check (CRC) for error detection

Novell frames are unique in that the data field begins with an FFFF hex (at the beginning of the IPX protocol header).

IEEE 802.3 Frame Format

The IEEE produced its Ethernet standard in June 1983. The type field changed to a length field and the IEEE 802.2 LLC layer was added.

Figure 4-4 shows the IEEE 802.3 frame format. Table 4-3 displays the IEEE 802.3 frame fields.

Figure 4-4 *IEEE 802.3 Frame Format*

Preamble 7 bytes	SFD 1 byte	DA 6 bytes	SA 6 bytes	Length 2 bytes	LLC 3 bytes	Data + pad 43-1497 bytes	FCS 4 bytes

Table 4-3 *IEEE 802.3 Frame Fields Descriptions*

Field	Description
Preamble	The IEEE defined the *preamble* as a string of 1s and 0s that is 7 bytes long.
Start Frame Delimiter (SFD)	1 byte set to 10101011 to indicate the start of the destination address.
Destination Address (DA)	48-bit MAC address of the destination host.
Source Address (SA)	48-bit MAC address of the host that sent the frame (source host).
Length	Contains the length of the LLC and the data field in binary. Indicated values are from 3 to 1500 bytes.
Logical Link Control (LLC)	Identifies the ULP.
Data+Pad	Contains ULP information.
Frame Check Sequence (FCS)	Contains the 32-bit cyclic redundancy check (CRC) for error detection.

The LLC is specified by IEEE 802.2. The LLC provides connectionless (LLC type 1) and connection-oriented (LLC type 2) services. You use LLC1 with Ethernet networks and LLC2 in IBM SNA environments. The LLC is divided into three fields, as shown in Figure 4-5.

Figure 4-5 *LLC Fields*

DSAP 1 byte	SSAP 1 byte	Control 1 or 2 bytes

The destination service access point (DSAP) indicates the destination ULP. The source service access point (SSAP) indicates the source ULP. Examples of SAP values are as follows:

- NetBIOS = 0xF0
- Bridge PDU = 0x42
- SNA = 0x04, 0x05, 0x0C

- SNAP = 0xAA
- X.25 = 0x7E
- IP = 0x06

In Ethernet networks, the control field is set to 0x03 to indicate an 802.2 unnumbered format for connectionless service.

IEEE 802.3 SNAP Frame Format

The SNAP field was created to help transition protocols from Ethernet V2 to an IEEE 802.3 compliant frame. It uses the same type values as Ethernet V2, but the EtherType field is preceded by a 3-byte field for protocol family identification (protocol ID).

The SNAP field includes the Ethernet type information in Ethernet V2. Figure 4-6 shows the IEEE 802.3 SNAP frame format. The remainder of this section discusses the fields in this format.

Figure 4-6 *IEEE 802.3 SNAP Frame Format*

Preamble 7 bytes	SFD 1 byte	DA 6 bytes	SA 6 bytes	Length 2 bytes	LLC 3 bytes	SNAP 5 bytes	Data + pad 38-1492 bytes	FCS

All fields are the same as in the IEEE 802.3 frame format. The SSAP and DSAP of the LLC are set to 0xAA. The SNAP field is added. The SNAP field contains two fields, including a 3-byte vendor code field. This 3-byte vendor code is unique to different vendors. The next field in the SNAP is the 2-byte Ethernet type field in Ethernet V2. The SNAP fields are displayed in Figure 4-7.

Figure 4-7 *IEEE SNAP Fields*

Vendor Code 3 bytes	Type 2 bytes

In the years that followed these standards, there has been a mix of frame formats in the network. IP and DEC protocols use Ethernet V2, Novell's IPX (3.x) uses its 802.3 raw format, and SNA uses 802.3. As most networks migrate to the IP protocol, Ethernet V2 frames are more common on the network.

The remainder of this section covers Ethernet physical specifications.

Ethernet Media Specifications

This section lists the physical media specifications, including range limitations for Ethernet, FE, and GE.

10Base5 Thick Ethernet

Commonly referred to as Thick Ethernet or Thicknet, this specification uses 0.4 inch, 50-ohm coaxial cable. The specifications for Thicknet are as follows:

- 0.4 inch, 50 ohm coax cable.
- Maximum segment length is 500 m.
- Maximum number of attachments per segment is 100.
- Maximum AUI cable length is 50 m.
- Minimum separation between attachments (MAU) is 2.5 m.
- Cable ends terminate with 50 ohm terminators.
- MAU attach workstations.
- Maximum network length is 5 segments and 2500 m.
- Maximum number of stations on the network is 1024.

Figure 4-8 shows a sample 10Base5 Ethernet network.

Figure 4-8 *Sample 10Base5 Network*

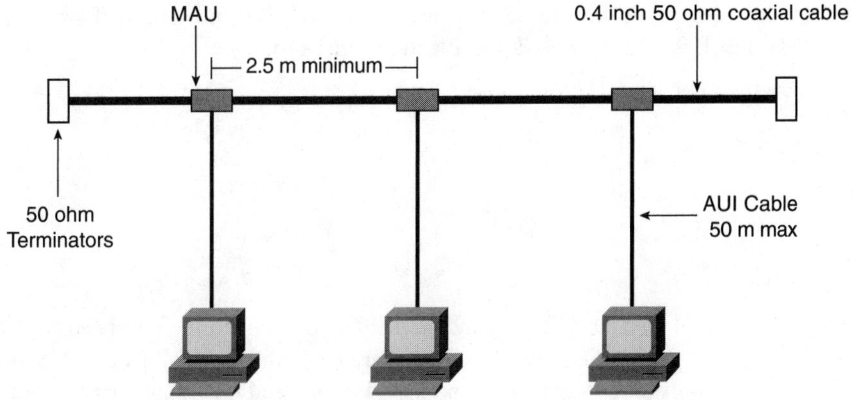

10Base2 Thinnet

Commonly referred to as Thinnet, this specification uses 0.2 inch, 50 ohm coaxial cable. Thinnet specifications are as follows:

- 0.2 inch, RG58-U, 50 ohm coax cable.
- Maximum segment length is 185 m.
- Maximum number of attachments per segment is 30.
- Minimum separation per segment is 0.5 m.
- T-connectors attach workstations.

Figure 4-9 shows a sample 10Base2 Ethernet network.

Figure 4-9 *Sample 10Base2 Network*

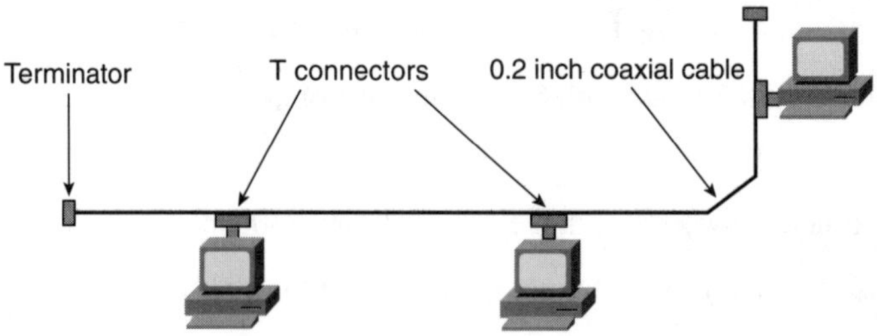

10BaseT Ethernet

UTP has become the defacto standard media for LAN systems. 10BaseT was made an IEEE standard in 1990. The 10BaseT specifications are as follows:

- 24 AWG UTP .4/.6 mm cable.
- Maximum segment length is 100 m.
- 1 device per cable.

Fast Ethernet

The IEEE developed the 802.3U standard in 1995 to provide Ethernet speeds of 100 Mbps over UTP and fiber cabling. The 100BaseT standard is similar to 10 Mbps Ethernet in that it uses CSMA/CD, runs on Category 3, 4, and 5 UTP cable, and the frame formats are preserved. Connectivity still uses hubs, repeaters, and bridges.

The encoding for 100BaseT is 4B/5B with nonreturn to zero (NRZ), the new speed is 100 Mbps, and the media independent interface (MII) was introduced as a replacement to the attachment unit interface (AUI).

The 4B/5B coding takes 4 bits of data and expands it into a 5-bit code for transmission on the physical channel. Because of the 20 percent overhead, pulses run at 125 MHz on the wire to achieve 100 Mbps. Table 4-4 shows how some data numbers are converted to 4B/5B code.

Table 4-4 *FE 4B/5B Code*

Data	Binary	4B/5B Code
0	0000	11110
1	0001	01001
2	0010	10100
...	...	...
D	1101	11011
E	1110	11100
F	1111	11101

The following specifications are covered in this section:

- 100BaseTX
- 100BaseT4
- 100BaseFX

100BaseTX FE

The 100BaseTX specification uses Category 5 UTP wiring. Similar to 10BaseT, FE uses only two pairs of the 4-pair UTP wiring. If Category 5 cabling is already in place, upgrading to FE only requires a hub or switch and NIC upgrades. Because of the low cost, most of today's installations use switches. The specifications are as follows:

- Transmission over Cat 5 UTP or Cat 1 STP wire.
- RJ-45 connector (same as in 10BaseT).
- Punchdown blocks in the wiring closet must be Category 5 certified.
- 4B5B coding.

100BaseT4 FE

The 100BaseT4 specification was developed to support UTP wiring at the Category 3 level. This specification takes advantage of higher speed Ethernet without recabling to Category 5 UTP. This implementation is not widely deployed. The specifications are as follows:

- Transmission over Cat 3, 4, or 5 UTP wiring.
- Three pairs are for transmission, and the fourth pair is for collision detection.

- No separate transmit and receive pairs are present, so full-duplex operation is not possible.
- 8B6T coding.

100BaseFX

The 100BaseFX specifications for fiber are as follows:

- Operates over two strands of multimode or single-mode fiber cabling
- Can transmit over greater distances than copper media
- Uses media interface connector (MIC), ST, or SC fiber connectors defined for FDDI and 10BaseFX networks
- 4B5B coding

1000 Mbps GE

Gigabit Ethernet is specified by two standards: IEEE 802.3z and 802.3ab. The 802.3z standard specifies the operation of GE over fiber and coaxial cable and introduces the Gigabit MII (GMII). The 802.3z standard was approved in July 1998. The 802.3ab standard specifies the operation of GE over Category 5 UTP, as approved in June 1999. GE still retains the frame formats and frame sizes of 10 Mbps Ethernet, along with the use of CSMA/CD in shared segments. Similar to Ethernet and FE, full-duplex operation is possible. Differences can be found in the encoding; GE uses 8B/10B coding with simple NRZ. Because of the 20 percent overhead, pulses run at 1250 MHz to achieve 1000 Mbps. GE includes the following methods to achieve 1 Gbps speed:

- 8B/10B Coding.
- Bytes are encoded as 10-bit symbols.
- Run-length limited (no long sequences of 1s or 0s).
- Pulses on the wire run at 1250 MHz to achieve 1000 Mbps speed.

Table 4-5 shows how data is converted into 8B/10B code for transmission.

Table 4-5 *8B/10B Encoding*

Data	Binary (8B)	10B Code
00	00000000	0110001011
01	00000001	1000101011
02	00000010	0100101011
03	00000011	1100010100
04	00000100	0010101011

The following specifications are covered in this section:

- 1000BaseLX
- 1000BaseSX
- 1000BaseCX
- 1000BaseT

1000BaseLX Long Wavelength GE

The IEEE 1000BaseLX uses long wavelength optics over a pair of fiber strands. The specifications are as follows:

- Uses long wave (1300 nm).
- Use on multimode or single-mode fiber.
- Maximum lengths for multimode fiber are as follows:
  - — 62.5 um fiber: 440 m
  - — 50 um fiber: 550 m
- Maximum length for single-mode fiber is 9 um: 5 km.
- Uses 8B/10B encoding with simple NRZ.

1000BaseSX Short Wave GE

- The IEEE 1000BaseSX uses short wavelength optics over a pair of multimode fiber stands. The specifications are as follows:
- Uses short wave (850 nm).
- Use on multimode fiber.
- Maximum lengths are as follows:
  - — 62.5 um: 260 m
  - — 50 um: 550 m
- Uses 8B/10B encoding with simple NRZ.

1000BaseCX GE over Coaxial Cable

- The IEEE 1000Base-CX standard is intended for short copper runs between servers. The specification is as follows:

- Used on short run copper.
- Runs over a pair of 150 ohm balanced coaxial cable (twinax).
- Maximum length is 25 m.
- Mainly for server connections.
- Uses 8B/10B encoding with simple NRZ.

1000BaseT GE over UTP

The IEEE standard for 1000 Mbps Ethernet over Category 5 UTP is IEEE 802.3ab; it was approved in June 1999. This standard uses the 4 pairs in the cable. (100BaseTX and 10BaseT Ethernet only use 2 pairs.) The specifications are as follows:

- Category 5, 4-pair UTP.
- Maximum length is 100m.
- Encoding defined is a 5-level coding scheme.
- 1 byte is sent over the 4 pairs at 1250 MHz.

10 GE

Although not a test topic, the CCIE candidate should be familiar with the developing IEEE 802.3ae 10 GE technology. The draft standard mentions that it only functions on optical fiber and operates in full-duplex mode. It can provide media solutions for metropolitan-area networks (MANS) and wide-area networks (WANS). The standard is to be adopted in mid 2002. More information is at the 10 Gigabit Alliance web site at www.10gea.org.

Token Ring

Token Ring was developed by IBM for the forwarding of data on a logical unidirectional ring. Token Ring is implemented in the data-link layer. Token Ring networks move a small frame, called a *token*, around the network. Possession of the token grants the right to transmit data. After a station has the token, it modifies it into a data frame, appends the data for transmission, and sends the frame to the next station. No token is on the ring until the data frame is received by the source station marked as read and copied, and releases a token back into the ring.

The IEEE standard for Token Ring is IEEE 802.5; the differences with IBM's specification are minor. Table 4-6 shows the similarity and difference between the specifications.

Table 4-6 *IBM and IEEE 802.5 Token Ring Specification Similarities*

Specification	IBM Token Ring	IEEE 802.5
Data Rate	4 or 16 Mbps	4 or 16 Mbps 4 Mbps only, on UTP
Stations per segment	260 (on STP) 72 (on UTP)	250 (on STP) 72 (on UTP)
Physical Topology	Star	Not specified
Media	Twisted pair	Not specified
Signaling	Baseband	Baseband
Access Method	Token passing	Token passing
Encoding	Differential Manchester	Differential Manchester

The physical implementation topology can be a ring or more commonly a star. When connected as a ring, devices connect to a multistation access unit (MSAU). MSAUs can be connected together with patch cables to form a ring. The MSAU can also bypass stations that are defective on the ring. Figure 4-10 shows the connectivity in the Token Ring network. The MSAUs are connected in a physical ring.

Figure 4-10 *Token Ring MSAU*

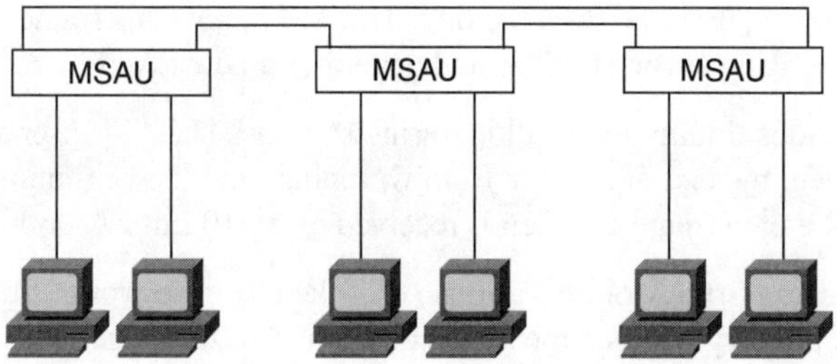

Token Ring Coding

Token Ring uses differential Manchester as the encoding scheme. In differential Manchester, a 0 is represented as a transition at the beginning of the clock time interval. A 1 is indicated as an absence of a transition.

Token Ring Operation

Access is controlled by using a token. A token is passed along the network from station to station. Stations with no data to transmit forward the token to the next station. If the station wants to transmit data, it seizes the token, produces a data frame by appending data, and sends it to the destination. The receiving station reads the frame and forwards it along the ring back to the source station. The receiving station also sets the address-recognized and framed-copied bits on the forwarded frame. The source station verifies that the data frame was read and releases a token back onto the network. The default operation permits the use of the Token in round-robin fashion.

Token Ring Priority

Token Ring includes an optional priority system that permits stations configured with a higher priority value to use the network more frequently than permitted by the default round-robin operation. Eight levels of priority are provided using a 3-bit reservation field and a 3-bit priority field. As an information frame passes, a station sets a higher priority in the reservation field, which reserves the token. The transmitting station then sends a token out with the higher priority set. After the high priority station completes sending its frame, it releases a token with the normal or previous priority.

Active Monitor (AM)

One station on the Token Ring is selected to be the AM. This station performs a variety of ring-maintenance functions. The AM removes continuously circulating frames that are not removed by a failed transmitting station. As a frame passes the AM, the monitor count bit is set. If a frame passes with the monitor count bit set, the AM assumes that the original sender of the frame was unable to remove the frame from the ring. The AM purges this frame, sends a Token Soft Error message to the Ring Error Monitor, and generates a new token.

The AM provides timing information to ring stations. The AM inserts a 24-bit propagation delay to prevent the end of a frame from wrapping onto the beginning of the frame, and also confirms that a data frame or token is received every 10 milliseconds.

Standby and Ring Error Monitors are also on Token Ring networks. Standby Monitors take over as AM if the primary AM is removed from the ring or no longer performs its functions. Ring Error Monitors can also be present on the ring to collect ring status and error information.

Beaconing

A beacon frame is sent by a station that does not receive any more frames—either a data frame or a token—from its upstream neighbor. An adapter keeps beaconing until it begins to receive frames again. A beacon MAC frame includes the beaconing station's MAC address and the address of the station's nearest active upstream neighbor (NAUN), indicating that the problem lies between the two stations.

Early Token Release (ETR)

In a normal token ring operation, the station that transmitted the data frame removes it and then generates a free token.

With ETR, a token is released immediately after the sending station transmits its frame. The sending station does not wait for the data frame to circle the ring. ETR is only available on 16 Mbps rings. Stations running ETR can coexist with stations not running ETR. With ETR, a free token can circulate the ring with multiple data frames.

On supported router platforms, early token release is configured as follows:

```
interface token 0
 early-token-release
```

Ring Insertion

The process for a station to insert into the token ring follows five phases:

- Phase 0—Lobe media test
- Phase 1—Physical insertion
- Phase 2—Address verification
- Phase 3—Participation in ring poll
- Phase 4—Request initialization

Phase 0: Lobe Media Test

The first step when a token ring device is inserted is the lobe media test. The transmitter and receiver of the adapter and the cable between the adapter and the MSAU are tested in this phase.

Phase 1: Physical Insertion

In phase 1, the adapter opens a relay on the MSAU. After the MSAU opens, the adapter determines an AM is present on the ring, which indicates successful completion of phase 1.

Phase 2: Address Verification

This phase verifies that the MAC address is unique to the ring. This phase can detect if two Locally Administered Addresses (LAAs) are configured with the same MAC address. This phase is also called the *duplicate address test*.

Phase 3: Participation in Ring Poll

In this phase, the station learns its upstream neighbor's address and informs its downstream neighbor of the inserting adapter's address and produces a station list. If the adapter successfully participates in a ring poll, it proceeds into the final phase of insertion.

Phase 4: Request Initialization

Phase 4 is the final phase of ring insertion. The adapter sends request initialization MAC frames to the functional address of the Ring Parameter Server (RPS). The RPS responds with information such as the ring number and speed. The adapter uses its own default values and reports successful completion of the insertion process if no RPS is present.

Token Ring Frame Format

The two types of frame formats are tokens and data/command frames, as displayed in Figure 4-11 and Figure 4-12, respectively. Tokens are 3 bytes in length and consist of a start delimiter, an access control byte, and an end delimiter. Data/command frames vary in size, depending on the size of the Information field. Command frames contain control information and do not carry upper-layer protocols.

Figure 4-11 *Token Frame (No Data)*

SD	AC	ED
1 byte	1 byte	1 byte

Figure 4-12 *Data/Command Frame*

SD	AC	FC	DA	SA	Data	FCS	ED	FS
1 byte	1 byte	1 byte	6 bytes	6 bytes		4 bytes	1 byte	1 byte

Table 4-7 contains an explanation of the fields in Figures 4-11 and 4-12.

Table 4-7 *Token Ring Frame Fields Descriptions*

Field	Description
Start Delimiter (SD)	Alerts a station of the arrival of a frame.
Access Control (AC)	Its format is PPPTMRRR; contains the token bit that you use to differentiate a token from a data/command frame. If T=0, it is a token, if T=1, it is a frame. AC also contains priority and reservation fields.
Frame Control (FC)	Indicates if the frame contains data or if it is a command frame with control information.
Destination Address (DA)	48-bit Token Ring MAC address of the destination host.
Source Address (SA)	48-bit Token Ring MAC address of the source host.

Table 4-7 *Token Ring Frame Fields Descriptions (Continued)*

Field	Description
Data	Contains the ULP information; this field is of variable size.
Frame Check Sequence (FCS)	Contains the 32-bit cyclic redundancy check (CRC) for error detection.
End-delimiter (ED)	Indicates the end of the Token Ring frame.
Frame Status	Terminates a data/command frame. Included in the frame status are the address-recognized and frame-copied bits.

Token Ring Interface

As shown in Example 4-2, the Token ring interface maximum transmission unit (MTU), speed, MAC, and other information can be checked with the **show interface tokenring 0** command. From the router output, you can see that the encapsulation is SNAP, the ring speed is 16 Mbps, and the interface MTU is 4464 bytes.

Example 4-2 *Token Ring Interface*

```
router> show interface tokenring 0
TokenRing0 is up, line protocol is up
  Hardware is TMS380, address is 0007.0d26.7612 (bia 0007.0d26.7612)
  Internet address is 133.5.88.8/24
  MTU 4464 bytes, BW 16000 Kbit, DLY 630 usec,
     reliability 255/255, txload 1/255, rxload 1/255
  Encapsulation SNAP, loopback not set
  Keepalive set (10 sec)
  ARP type: SNAP, ARP Timeout 04:00:00
  Ring speed: 16 Mbps
  Duplex: half
  Mode: Classic token ring station
  Group Address: 0x00000000, Functional Address: 0x08000000
  Ethernet Transit OUI: 0x000000
  Last input 00:00:00, output 00:00:00, output hang never
  Last clearing of "show interface" counters never
  Input queue: 0/75/0/0 (size/max/drops/flushes); Total output drops: 0
  Queueing strategy: fifo
  Output queue :0/40 (size/max)
  5 minute input rate 0 bits/sec, 0 packets/sec
  5 minute output rate 0 bits/sec, 0 packets/sec
     1278 packets input, 55402 bytes, 0 no buffer
     Received 1007 broadcasts, 0 runts, 0 giants, 0 throttles
     0 input errors, 0 CRC, 0 frame, 0 overrun, 0 ignored, 0 abort
     331 packets output, 26189 bytes, 0 underruns
     0 output errors, 0 collisions, 1 interface resets
     0 output buffer failures, 0 output buffers swapped out
     3 transitions
```

Wireless LANs

WLANs provide the capability to access internetworking resources without having to be wired to the network. WLAN applications include inside-building access, LAN extension, outside building-to-building communications, public access, and small-office home-office (SOHO) communications. For the CCIE written test, focus on the IEEE 802.11b standard.

The first standard for WLANs is IEEE 802.11, approved by the IEEE in 1997. IEEE 802.11 implemented WLANs at speeds of 1 Mbps and 2 Mbps using Direct Sequence Spread Spectrum (DSSS) and Frequency Hopping Spread Spectrum (FHSS) on the physical layer of the OSI model. DSSS divides data into separate sections, and each section is sent over different frequencies at the same time. FHSS uses a frequency hopping sequence to send data in bursts. With FHSS, some data is transmitted at frequency 1; then the system hops to frequency 2 to send more data, and so on, returning to transmit more data at frequency 1.

Current implementations use the IEEE 802.11b standard. The IEEE 802.11b standard is referred to as *high-rate* and provides speeds of 11, 5.5, 2, and 1 Mbps. An interoperability certification exists for IEEE 802.11b WLANs called Wireless Fidelity (Wi-Fi). The Wi-Fi certification is governed by the Wireless Ethernet Compatibility Alliance (WECA). IEEE 802.11b uses DSSS and is backward-compatible with 802.11 systems that use DSSS. The modulation techniques used by IEEE 802.11b are as follows:

- Complementary Code Keying (CCK) at 5.5 and 11 Mbps
- Differential Quadrature Phase Shift Keying (DQPSK) at 2 Mbps
- Differential Binary Phase Shift Keying (DBPSK) at 1 Mbps

A description of each modulation technique is outside the scope of the CCIE written test and is not covered in this book.

Service Set Identifier (SSID)

WLANs use a SSID to identify the network name of the WLAN. The SSID can be 2 to 32 characters in length. All devices in the WLAN must have the same configured SSID to communicate.

WLAN Access Method

The IEEE 802.11 MAC layer implements carrier sense multiple access with collision avoidance (CSMA/CA) as an access method. With CSMA/CA, each WLAN station listens to see if a station is transmitting. If there is no activity, the station transmits. If there is activity, the station uses a random countdown timer. When the timer expires the station transmits.

WLAN Modes

WLAN architecture has three modes of operation. The first mode is the *Basic Service Set (BSS)*. In BSS mode, all stations communicate with the Access Point (AP). The AP provides communication between clients and connects the WLAN network with the wired LAN. As shown in Figure 4-13, in BSS mode, clients do not communicate directly with each other; all communication is through the AP. BSS is also referred to as *infrastructure mode*.

Figure 4-13 *BSS (Infrastructure) Mode*

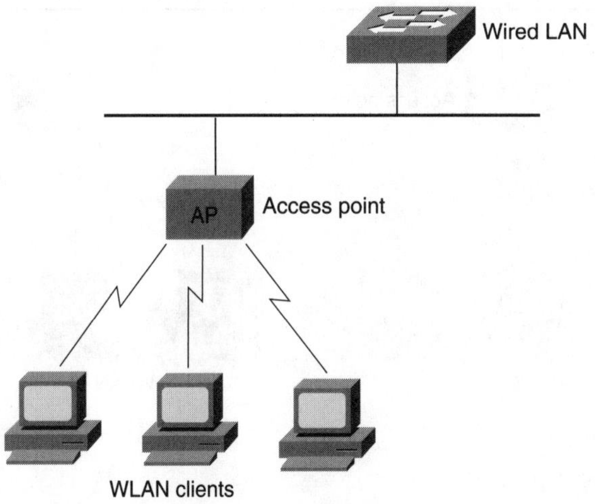

The second mode is the *Independent Basic Service Set (IBSS)*. In IBSS mode, stations communicate directly with each other without using an AP. IBSS is also known as *Ad hoc mode*. Figure 4-14 displays IBSS (Ad-hoc) mode.

Figure 4-14 *IBSS (Ad-hoc) Mode*

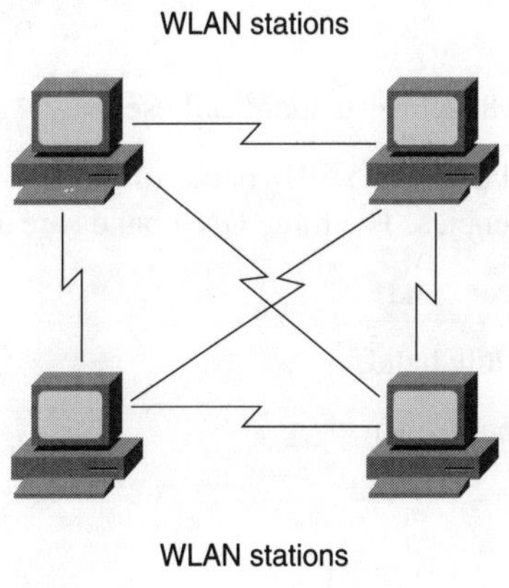

The third mode is the *Extended Service Set (ESS)*. As shown in Figure 4-15, ESS is a set of BSS where APs have connectivity in the WLAN, which provides a distribution system for roaming capabilities.

Figure 4-15 *Wireless ESS Mode*

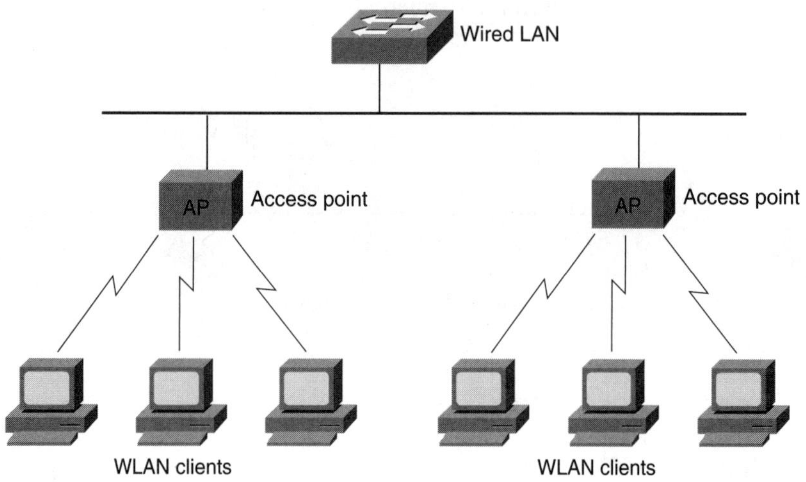

Frequencies Used by WLANs

The IEEE 802.11b standard uses the 2.4 GHz band of the Industrial, Scientific, and Medical (ISM) frequencies. The Federal Communication Commission (FCC) authorizes ISM frequencies for unlicensed use in the United States. The three ISM frequency bands are as follows:

- 902 to 928 MHz
- 2.4000 to 2.5000 GHz
- 5.725 to 5.875 GHz

IEEE 802.11, 802.11b, and 802.11g standards all use the 2.4 ISM band.

The IEEE 802.11a standard uses the 5 GHz bands of the Unlicensed National Information Infrastructure (UNII) frequencies. The three UNII bands are as follows:

- 5.15 to 5.25 GHz (lower band)
- 5.25 to 5.35 GHz (middle band)
- 5.75 to 5.85 GHz (upper band)

WLAN Security

WLANs without any encryption present a security risk because the SSIDs can be snooped by using publicly available software. The IEEE 802.11 standard specifies the use of the Wired Equivalency Privacy (WEP) for encryption. WLANs use two types of WEP keys: 64-bit and 128-bit. Although WEP provides additional security, it has some weaknesses that provide security risks. By gathering (snooping) traffic, hackers can obtain the WEP keys by using freeware software.

Some APs can implement MAC address and protocol filtering to enhance security or limit the protocols over the WLAN. Again, MAC address filtering can be hacked.

To enhance security, WLANs can be implemented with Virtual Private Network (VPN) software or use the IEEE 802.1x port-based access control protocol. IEEE 802.1x is covered in the LAN security section in this chapter.

Cisco also provides dynamic per-user, per-session WEP keys to provide additional security over statically configured WEP keys, which are not unique per user. For centralized user-based authentication, Cisco developed the Cisco Extensible Authentication Protocol (LEAP), which uses mutual authentication between the client and the network server and uses IEEE 802.1x for 802.11 authentication messaging. LEAP uses a RADIUS server to manage user information.

New and Future WLAN Standards

The IEEE 802.11a standard provides an increase of throughput from 802.11b with speeds up to 54 Mbps. IEEE 802.11a uses the 5 GHz bands of the UNII frequencies. For this reason, it is not backward-compatible with 802.11b WLANs.

IEEE 802.11g is an emerging standard that provides faster WLAN speeds in the ISM 2.4 GHz band. IEEE 802.11g is backward-compatible with 802.11b WLANs.

IEEE 802.11d provides specifications for WLANs in markets not served by the current 802.11, 802.11b, and 802.11a standards.

IEEE 802.11i provides enhancements to the security and authentication protocols for WLANS.

The emerging IEEE 802.15 standard provides specifications for Wireless Personal Area Networks (WPANs). The emerging IEEE 802.16 standard provides specifications for fixed Broadband Wireless Access.

Transparent Bridging (TB)

This section covers bridging between Ethernet networks, STP, CRB, and IRB.

Bridges and STP

Ethernet bridging occurs in the data-link layer of the OSI model. Switches perform the same function as bridges. For the rest of the chapter, the term *switches* refers to bridges. Bridges (and switches) forward frames from one interface to another based on the destination MAC address. For any incoming frame, bridges forward the frame out a specific port, if the destination MAC address is known, or it is flooded out all ports if the MAC address is unknown. If the destination MAC is unknown, the bridges forward the frame out all ports. This is known as *flooding*. Bridges have three primary functions:

- To learn the MAC addresses of all nodes and their associated port
- To filter incoming frames whose destination MAC addresses are located on the same incoming port
- To forward incoming frames to the destination MAC through their associated port

Bridges keep a bridge table to track the MAC addresses available out each port.

An example of the table on a Catalyst switch is shown in Example 4-3. The switch creates a table that lists the MAC address and port for the stations. For example, the station with MAC address 00-10-7b-80-ba-d5 is located out port 2/10. This MAC table was created dynamically.

Example 4-3 *Bridge MAC Table*

```
cat5000: show cam dynamic
VLAN  Dest MAC/Route Des   Destination Ports or VCs / [Protocol Type]
----  -----------------   ------------------------------------------
710   00-10-7b-80-ba-d5   2/10 [ALL]
34    00-10-7b-1b-6f-9c   2/3 [ALL]
59    00-10-7b-7e-cc-c3   2/5 [ALL]
59    00-e0-b0-64-6e-47   2/9 [ALL]
1     00-e0-b0-64-6e-49   2/12 [ALL]
1     00-10-7b-7e-cc-cd   2/11 [ALL]
710   00-e0-b0-64-6e-07   2/7 [ALL]
34    00-50-3e-e4-58-59   2/4 [ALL]
Total Matching CAM Entries Displayed = 8
```

Routers can also be configured to bridge protocols. By default, if bridging is configured on an interface, the router bridges any protocol that is not routed on that interface.

The configuration in Example 4-4 bridges between Ethernet 1 and Ethernet 0. Bridge group 1 is configured for the IEEE STP with the **bridge 1 protocol ieee** command. Each interface is configured to bridge with the **bridge-group 1** command.

Example 4-4 *Configuration of Bridge Between Ethernet 0 and Ethernet 1*

```
bridge 1 protocol ieee
!
interface ethernet 0
```

Example 4-4 *Configuration of Bridge Between Ethernet 0 and Ethernet 1 (Continued)*

```
  bridge-group 1
!
interface ethernet 1
 bridge-group 1
```

Transparent Bridge Modes

Bridges and switches can operate in two basic modes: *store-and-forward* and *cut-through*. The legacy mode is store-and-forward. The bridge stores the entire frame and verifies the CRC before forwarding the frame. If a CRC error is detected, the frame is discarded.

With the evolution of bridges and switches with fast integrated circuits, a new mode of operation is usually available: cut-through. In this mode, the switch does not wait for the entire frame to enter its buffer; instead, it forwards the frame just after it reads the destination MAC address. The advantage is that the switching operation is faster. The disadvantage is that the cut-through operation does not check for CRC errors, which increases the amount of runt and error frames on the network. Because of this problem, most switches provide the option to switch the mode back to store-and-forward if an error threshold is met. Switches in cut-through can track the CRC errors of forwarded frames to determine if there are too many errors. Other switches implement modified cut-through, which waits to receive 64 bytes before it begins transmission, which prevents the switch from sending runt frames.

STP

When multiple bridges connect the same LAN segments, bridge loops can occur. The STP is a Layer-2 link management protocol that discovers a loop free topology for connectivity between LANs. As shown in Figure 4-16, STP might place some redundant bridged interfaces in a blocked state. STP provides recovery from bridge failures by changing blocked interfaces to a forwarding state, if a primary link fails. Although a DEC and IBM version are available, the IEEE 802.1d standard is the default protocol.

Root Bridge Election

A root bridge is elected as the root of the spanning-tree topology. All ports that are not needed to reach the root bridge are placed in blocking mode. The selection of the root bridge is based on the lowest numerical bridge priority. The bridge priority ranges from 0 to 65535. If all bridges have the same bridge priority, the bridge with the lowest MAC address is selected as the root. Physical changes of the network force spanning-tree recalculation.

Figure 4-16 *STP*

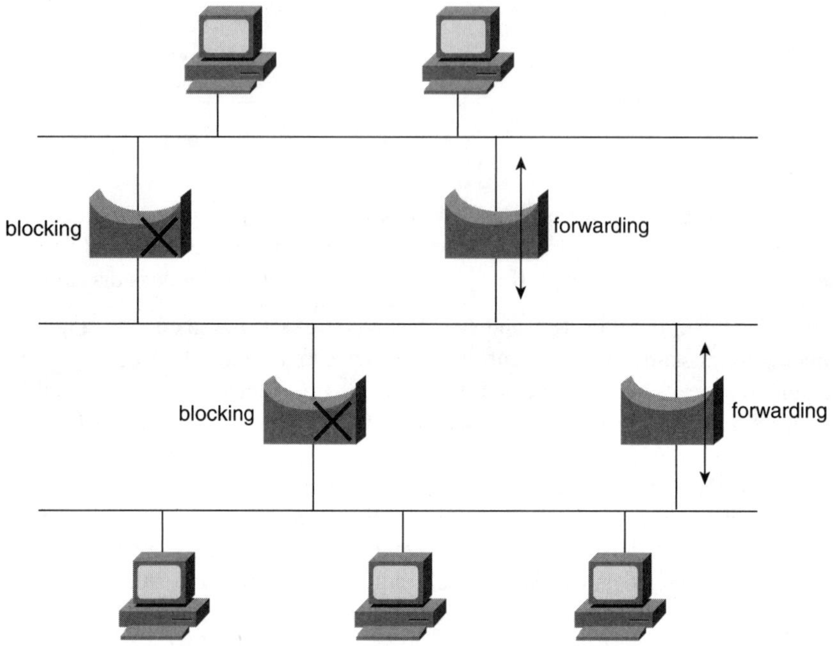

The router interface priority can be changed with the **priority** keyword, with priority values ranging from 1 to 255:

```
R4(config-if)#bridge-group 1 priority ?
  <0-255>
```

Bridge Identifier (BID) and Path Costs

As shown in Figure 4-17, the BID is 8 bytes long and contains a bridge priority (2 bytes), along with one of the bridge's MAC addresses (6 bytes). With 2 bytes, the priority values range from 0 to 65,535. The default priority is 32,768.

Figure 4-17 *BID Format*

Bridge Priority	MAC Address
2 bytes	6 bytes

Each port is assigned a Port ID. Port IDs are 16 bits long and consist of two parts: a 6-bit priority setting and a 10-bit port number.

A path cost value is assigned to each port. The costs are accumulated to determine the total cost to reach the root. According to the original specification in 802.1d, cost is calculated by dividing 1000 Mbps (1 gigabit per second) by the bandwidth (in megabits per second) of the segment connected to the port. Using this formula, a 100 Mbps connection has a cost of 10 (1000 / 100 = 10). To accommodate higher speeds, such as GE, the IEEE adopted new values. Table 4-8 shows the revised path costs for STP.

Table 4-8 *STP Path Costs*

Bandwidth	STP Cost Value
4 Mbps	250
10 Mbps	100
16 Mbps	62
45 Mbps	39
100 Mbps	19
155 Mbps	14
622 Mbps	6
1 Gbps	4
10 Gbps	2

Bridge Protocol Data Unit (BPDU)

Transparent bridges performing STP communicate by exchanging BPDUs. BPDU packets contain information on ports, addresses, priorities and costs. Bridges do not forward received BPDUs, instead the information generates new BPDUs.

The BPDU contains the following information:

- **Root BID**—The BID of the bridge that the transmitting bridge believes to be the root bridge.
- **Path Cost**—The cost of the path to reach the root bridge. If the segment is attached to the root bridge, it has a cost of 0. For example, if the data has to travel over three 10 Mbps segments to reach the root bridge, the cost is 200 (100 + 100 + 0).
- **Sender BID**—The BID of the bridge that sent this BPDU.
- **Port ID**—The port ID on the bridge that sent this BPDU.

NOTE BPDU destination addresses use the bridge group multicast MAC address 01-80-C2-00-00-00. These frames are copied by bridges but ignored by all other stations.

BPDU Types

The two types of a BPDU follow:

- Configuration BPDU
- Topology Change Notification (TCN) BPDU

Configuration BPDUs are sent from the root bridge with the root BID. The configuration BPDUs flow through all active paths, which provides the root BID and path cost information. The TCN BPDUs flow upstream to the root bridge to alert it of a topology change. The spanning-tree algorithm is recalculated by the bridges to determine any necessary changes in the path. After the network converges, no TCN BPDUs are present in the network.

Bridge Port States

Each port of a transparent bridge exists in the following states:

- **Disabled**—The port is inactive and does not participate in STP.
- **Blocking**—When a port is enabled, it first moves to the blocked state before listening to the network. In this state, it does not participate in frame forwarding. It receives bridge PDUs and sends them to the STP algorithm for processing.
- **Listening**—When the bridge determines that the port should participate in frame forwarding, it changes to the listening state. In this state, the bridge does not forward frames and does not learn of network MAC addresses. The bridge does receive and process BPDUs and network management frames, but it does not send BPDUs.
- **Learning**—The bridge port discards incoming frames. The bridge begins to add MAC addresses associated with this port into the table. BPDU and network management messages are processed. The bridge processes, generates, and sends BPDUs in this state.
- **Forwarding**—The full functional state for a bridged port. In this state, the bridge does not discard incoming frames. The bridge forwards frames to other ports; the bridge also forwards frames out this port. BPDUs and network management frames are processed.

Designated Ports

If connected with more than one port to the same segment, bridges select a designated port. The designated port is the port that sends and receives frames on the segment; other ports are placed in the blocking state (nondesignated ports).

Multi-Instance Spanning-Tree Protocol (MISTP)

Each VLAN configured in a switch runs an independent instance of the STP. MISTP is a proprietary spanning-tree mode in Cisco switches, which allows the grouping of multiple VLANs under a single instance of the STP. The MISTP instance has its own root switch and forwarding ports. When VLANs are mapped into a MISTP instance, it reduces the number of BPDUs because only MISTP BPDUs are sent between the switches configured for MISTP, which allows STP to scale to larger networks such as MANs.

CRB

CRB, introduced in IOS 11.0, enables the administrator to both route and bridge the same protocol on separate interfaces. With CRB, the routed traffic is confined to the routed interfaces, and bridged traffic is confined to the interfaces configured with bridge groups. Prior to CRB, routers could only bridge or route the same protocol—but not both.

As shown in Figure 4-18, IP traffic is routed on Ethernet interfaces 0 and 1 and concurrently bridged between Ethernet interfaces 2 and 3.

Figure 4-18 *CRB*

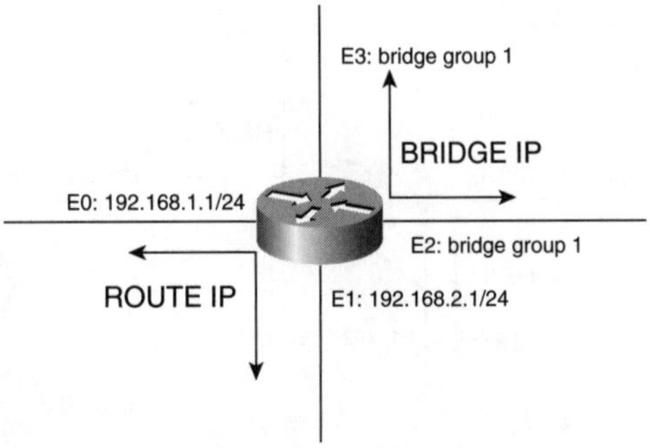

The router configuration is displayed in Example 4-5.

Example 4-5 *Configuration Example of CRB*

```
bridge 1 protocol ieee
bridge crb
!
interface ethernet 0
 ip address 192.168.1.1 255.255.255.0
!
interface ethernet 1
 ip address 192.168.2.1 255.255.255.0
!
interface ethernet 2
 bridge-group 1
 no ip address
!
interface ethernet 3
 bridge-group 1
 no ip address
```

CRB is enabled with the **bridge crb** global command. The decision to route or bridge is in the hands of the transparent bridge group, with the **bridge** *number* **route ip** command, which configures IP to be routed in a bridge group.

The **show interfaces crb** command shows information about which protocols are routed and which are bridged.

IRB

IRB was introduced in IOS 11.2 as an enhancement to CRB. With IRB, a protocol can be routed between routed interfaces, bridged interfaces, or different bridge groups. As shown in Figure 4-19, this permits routing of IP from routed interfaces to bridged interfaces.

Figure 4-19 *IRB*

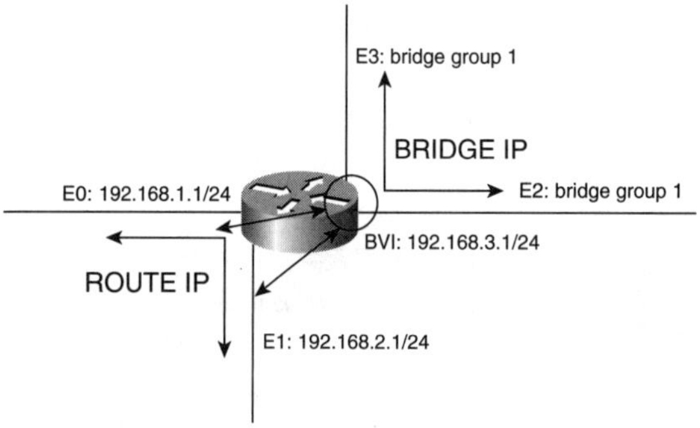

IRB is enabled with the **bridge irb** global configuration command. A virtual IRB interface is created to have packets from the routed interfaces reach hosts in the bridge interfaces. The command to create the virtual bridge interface is **interface bvi** *bridge-group*.

The router configuration is shown in Example 4-6. In this example, the virtual bridge interface is created for Bridge group 1 with the **interface bvi 1** command. IRB is enabled with the **bridge irb** command. With the **bridge 1 route ip** command, IP is routed between Ethernet 0, Ethernet 1, and the BVI interface; IP is bridged between Ethernet 2 and Ethernet 3.

Example 4-6 *Configuration of IRB*

```
bridge 1 protocol ieee
bridge irb
bridge 1 route ip
!
interface ethernet 0
 ip address 192.168.1.1 255.255.255.0
!
interface ethernet 1
 ip address 192.168.2.1 255.255.255.0
```

Example 4-6 *Configuration of IRB (Continued)*

```
!
interface ethernet 2
 bridge-group 1
 no ip address
!
interface ethernet 3
 bridge-group 1
 no ip address
!
interface bvi 1
 ip address 192.168.3.1 255.255.255.0
```

The **show interface irb** displays information about the IRB interface.

SRB

This section covers SRB explorer frames, SRT, SR/TLB, RSRB, and DLSw Plus (DLSw+).

SRB Operation

IBM developed SRB in the mid-80s as a way to bridge between Token Ring LANs. The IEEE adopted most of IBM's proposal into the IEEE 802.5 standard. As shown in Figure 4-20, in SRB, the source determines the route to the destination node by sending an explorer frame to it. SRB bridges do not keep a MAC table of hosts and do not worry about bridge loops. This is different to Ethernet transparent bridging where the bridges have the smarts of MAC layer destinations and determine the path by creating a spanning-tree. SRB networks are limited to a 7-bridge hop count. (Some implementations can extend to 13 hops.) In SRB, the source node obtains the knowledge of routes to destinations on the network. This is accomplished using explorer frames.

Figure 4-20 *SRB Network*

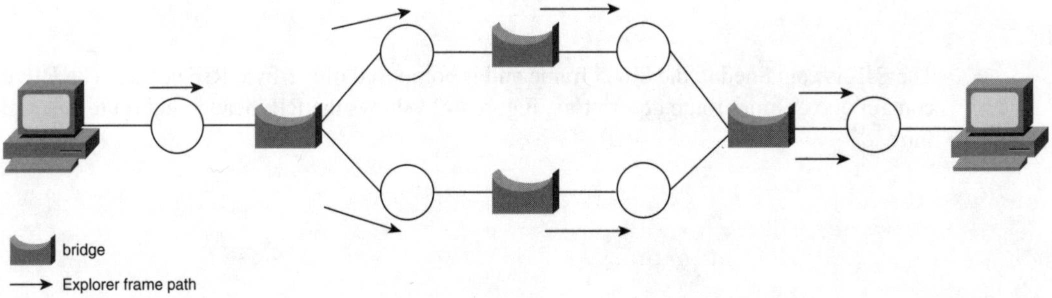

Explorer Frames

When a source node wants to send information to a destination that is not on the local LAN, it sends out an explorer frame. Bridges pick up the explorer frames and forward them out the other interfaces. The bridges add route information to the frames as they travel through the network. The route information includes a Token Ring number and bridge number pair that the explorer frame travels on. As seen in Figure 4-21, when the explorer frame reaches Bridge 6, a route descriptor is added to the frame that includes Ring 7/Bridge 6. At Bridge 4, another route descriptor with Ring 3/Bridge 4 is added. Finally, Ring 2 is added at the destination node with the bridge value set to 0 to indicate that the destination has been reached.

Figure 4-21 *SRB Ring/Bridge Routing Information*

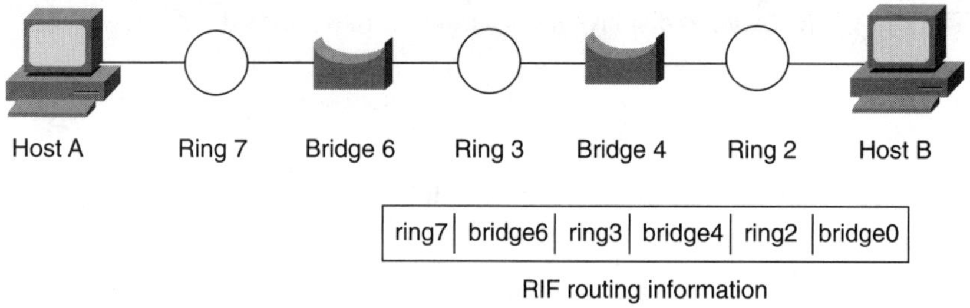

When the explorer frames arrive at the destination, the destination frame sets the direction bit (also known as the D-bit) to 1 and sends the frame back to the source node through the same route that was used to arrive to the destination. When multiple frames reach back to the source node, it usually uses the route of the first frame received. Other decision metrics include the minimum number of hops and the path with the largest MTU allowed.

There are two types of explorer frames. The first is the all-routes explorer (ARE) frame. This explorer takes all possible paths to the destination. The second type is the spanning-tree explorer (STE) frame; these explorer frames use a spanning tree to reach a destination to prevent loops.

RIF

The RIF is contained in the 802.5 frame and is composed of a 2-byte RIF header. The RIF can contain one or more route descriptors. Figure 4-22 shows the RIF header and route descriptor format.

Figure 4-22 *RIF*

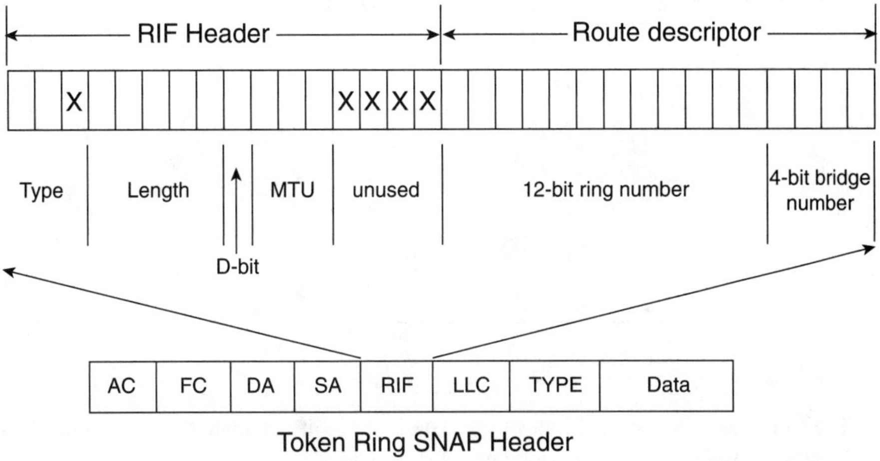

The first two most significant bits indicate the type of frame:

- **00**—Non Broadcast (specific route). Indicates that this is a regular frame that should be routed to the destination following the information in the route descriptors.
- **10**—All-routes broadcast. Indicates this is an All-rings explorer packet that should take all possible routes to the destination.
- **11**—Single-route broadcast. Indicates that this is a limited broadcast that should take one path to the destination.

The next bit is unused.

The 5 least significant bits in the first byte indicate the total length of the RIF field including the 2-byte header. A RIF with only one bridge hop is 6-bytes long.

The most significant bit in the second byte is the D-bit (direction bit). A value of 0 indicates forward direction, which means the source to the destination. The route descriptors are read from left to right when the D-bit equals 0. A value of 1 indicates reverse direction, meaning the destination station has seen it and the frame travels from the destination to the source. The route descriptors are read right to left when the D-bit equals 1.

The next 3 bits indicate the maximum transmission frame size for the 802.5 frame. This is the maximum frame size that this station is willing to accept. A value of 011 indicates 4136 bytes, and a value of 100 indicates 8232 bytes. (Some references might say the values are 4472 and 8144, respectively.) Table 4-9 shows possible maximum frame size values.

Table 4-9 *RIF Max Frame Size Values*

RIF MTU Bit Value	Max Frame Size (bytes)
000	512
001	1500
010	2052
011	4472
100	8144
101	11407
110	17800

The lower 4 bits are not used.

The route descriptors are 2 bytes long. The first 12 bits indicate the ring number. The 4 least-significant bits indicate the bridge number.

Figure 4-23 shows Token Ring and bridge numbers between Hosts A and B. Some numbers are in decimal and others are in hexadecimal format.

Figure 4-23 *RIF Example*

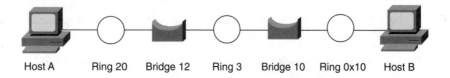

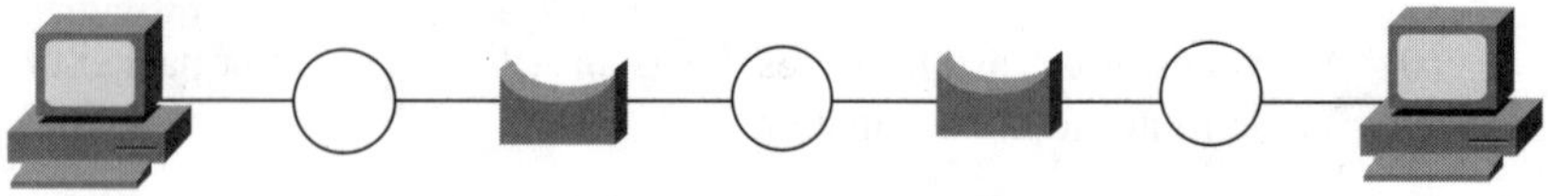

The RIF header from Host A to Host B is constructed as follows:

00001000 00110000 = 0x0830

From the bits, you can determine the following:

- This is a regular frame (type = 00).
- It is 8 bytes in length (length = 01000).
- The maximum frame size is 4472 (MTU = 011).
- The direction bit is set to 0.

The route descriptors are constructed as follows. The last bridge number is set to 0x0:

Ring 20 (0x014) to Bridge 12 (0xC) to Ring 0x003 to Bridge 10 (0xA) to Ring (0x010) = 014c.003A.0100

The RIF field in hex is 0830.014c.003a.0100.

The CCIE candidate should know how to read and construct the RIF field for regular SRB and in other scenarios, such as RSRB and DLSw. RIF examples are included in each corresponding section.

SRB Configuration with Cisco Routers

SRB is limited in that it is a flat network topology in the data-link layer. Another limitation is the maximum hop limitation of 7 bridges. Routers can be introduced into the network to help limit the number of hops on the network. Remote Token Ring networks can be attached to routers to reduce bridge hops. This is accomplished with the concept of the virtual ring, as seen in Figure 4-24. Consider each router interface a minibridge that connects the external ring to the internal virtual ring. You use the ring number in the RIF field just like any other physical ring.

Figure 4-24 *SRB Configuration*

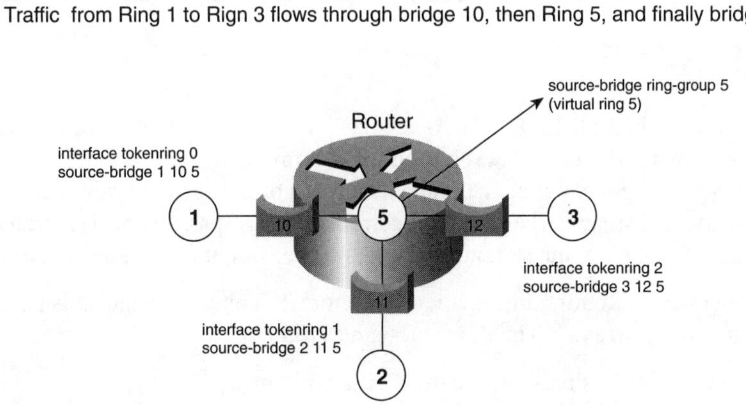

To configure the virtual ring group, use the global command **source-bridge ring-group** *virtual-ring-group-number.* Each Token Ring LAN is bridged to the virtual ring by using the interface command **source-bridge** *ring-number bridge-number virtual-ring-group-number.* The bridge number can be from 1 to 15. The ring number is from 1 to 4095.

The configuration for the router in Figure 4-24 is displayed in Example 4-7.

Example 4-7 *Configuration Example of Source Route Bridging*

```
source-bridge ring-group 5
!
interface tokenring 0
 source-bridge 1 10 5
 source-bridge spanning
```

continues

Example 4-7 *Configuration Example of Source Route Bridging (Continued)*

```
!
interface tokenring 1
 source-bridge 2 11 5
 source-bridge spanning
!
interface tokenring 2
 source-bridge 3 12 5
 source-bridge spanning
```

The frame in this example from Token Ring 1 to Token Ring 2 is source routed as follows: Ring 1 to Bridge 0xA to Ring 5 to Bridge 0xB to Ring 2. The RIF is 0830.001a.005b.0020.

NOTE The CCIE candidate must master how the RIF is built. At the end of some of the following sections, there is a paragraph on how the RIF looks.

SRT

SRT is specified in the IEEE 802.1d Appendix C standard. SRT bridges can forward traffic from both transparent and source-route end nodes and form a common spanning tree with transparent bridges. SRT bridges combine the implementations of transparent bridges and source-route bridges and can distinguish between source-route and transparently bridged frames. SRT allows transparent or source-route stations to communicate with other stations of the same type.

SRT bridges use a Routing Information Indicator (RII) bit to distinguish between SRB and transparent bridge frames. The RII values are as follows:

- 0, means a RIF is present; use the SRB algorithm.
- 1, means a RIF is not present; the frame is transparently bridged.

SR/TLB

SR/TLB bridges provide bridging between Ethernet and Token Ring networks. The difference between SR/TLB and SRT bridges is that SR/TLB bridges can forward frames between source-route and transparently bridged networks. Considering the differences between these two technologies, SR/TLB has many challenges to overcome so that transparent Ethernet networks can communicate with SRB token ring networks and vice versa.

As shown in Figure 4-25, source-route translational bridges overcome the following issues:

- **Bit ordering of MAC addresses**—As explained in an earlier section, Ethernet NICs expect to receive the least-significant bit first for each octet; Token Ring considers the first bit to be the most significant bit of each octet. Translational bridges reorder source and destination addresses when translating between Token Ring and Ethernet.
- **MTU size**—Ethernet's MTU is 1500 bytes; Token Ring has a MTU of 4472 bytes on 4 Mbps networks and 17,800 on 16 Mbps networks. Translational bridges usually set the MTU on the Token Ring networks to 1500 to facilitate the transfer of frames to Ethernet. They check the MTU of every frame.
- **Frame Status**—Ethernet does not use frame status bits that are used in Token Ring. Some bridges set the C (copied) bit to 1 when a frame is transferred from Token Ring to Ethernet.
- **Explorer Frames**—Ethernet does not use explorer frames. These frames are dropped when converting from Token Ring to Ethernet segments.
- **RIF**—Ethernet does not understand the concept of source-routed frames.
- **Spanning-tree algorithm**—Token Ring bridges do not understand Ethernet's STP.
- **Frame Conversion**—Ethernet V2 frames are converted to Token Ring SNAP frames, and vice versa.

Figure 4-25 *SR/TLB*

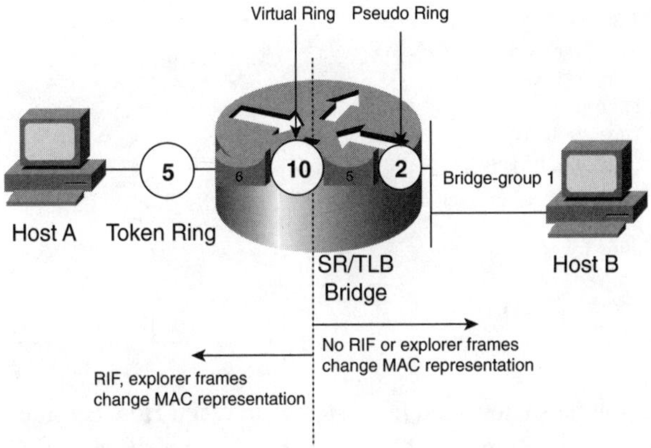

SR/TLBRouter Configuration

Configuring SR/TLB involves the configuration of SRB and transparent bridging as described in earlier sections. An additional command ties in the SRB domain with the transparent bridged domain:

source-bridge transparent *ring-group pseudo-ring bridge-number tb-group*

The arguments are as follows:

- *ring-group*—The virtual ring group number created with the **source-bridge ring-group** command.
- *pseudo-ring*:—A virtual ring group number created for the transparent bridge group. The Token Ring side sends frames to this ring number to reach the host in the transparent bridge side.
- *bridge-number*:—A bridge number is assigned for the bridge between the virtual ring group and the pseudo ring.
- *tb-group*:—The transparent bridge group number configured with the **bridge-group** command.

To perform SR/TLB the router configuration of the network in Figure 4-25 is displayed in Example 4-8. The virtual ring group number is 10. From the **source-bridge transparent 10 2 5 1** command, you can determine that transparent bridge group 1 uses pseudo ring 2, which is bridged to virtual ring 10. Bridge number 5 bridges between pseudo ring 2 and virtual ring 10.

Example 4-8 *Example of SR/TLB*

```
source-bridge ring-group 10
source-bridge transparent 10 2 5 1
!
interface tokenring 0
 source-bridge 5 6 10
 source-bridge spanning
!
interface ethernet 0
 bridge-group 1
!
bridge 1 protocol ieee
```

The RIF of a source route frame from Host A to reach Host B routes from Ring 5, Bridge 6, Ring 10, Bridge 5, to Ring 2. In hex, the RIF is 0830.0056.00a5.0020.

RSRB

RSRB permits the bridging of Token Rings that are located on separate routers across non-Token Ring media. The routers are remotely connected through serial lines, Ethernet, or other methods. RSRB routers create the same virtual ring number that is a logical ring that encompasses both routers. There are four methods of transport:

- Direct
- Frame Relay
- Fast Sequenced Transport (FST)
- TCP

If you use direct encapsulation over serial lines, they need to have high-level data-link control (HDLC) encapsulation. Direct encapsulation can run over Ethernet, Frame Relay-ATM Interworking, or serial interfaces. If you use TCP encapsulation, RSRB traffic can be prioritized over WAN links.

RSRB Configuration

The configuration of RSRB involves the regular SRB configuration with virtual rings. All routers in RSRB need to have the same virtual ring number configured. The additional configuration command is the configuration of **source-route remote-peer** statements. The configuration of every RSRB encapsulation is not presented in this subsection. Example configurations follow for direct and TCP RSRB encapsulation. More information on RSRB is at the site www.cisco.com/warp/public/701/2.html.

RSRB with Direct Encapsulation

Looking at Figure 4-26, Router A connects to Router B through a serial line. The RSRB configuration is shown in Example 4-9. The **source-bridge remote-peer 10 interface serial 0** command defines the RSRB remote peer as being available through serial 0.

Figure 4-26 *RSRB with Direct Encapsulation*

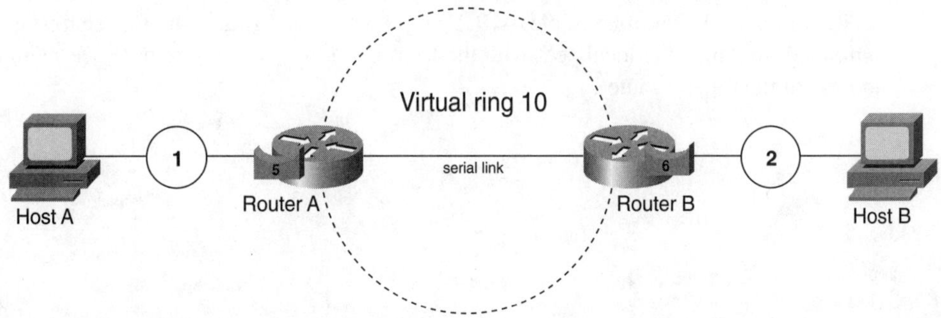

Example 4-9 *RSRB Configuration with Direct Encapsulation*

```
!Router A
source-bridge ring-group 10
source-bridge remote-peer 10 interface serial 0
!
interface tokenring 0
 source-bridge 1 5 10
 source-bridge spanning
!
interface serial 0
 encapsulation hdlc

!Router B
source-bridge ring-group 10
source-bridge remote-peer 10 interface serial 0
!
interface tokenring 0
 source-bridge 2 6 10
 source-bridge spanning
!
interface serial 0
 encapsulation hdlc
```

The RIF of a source route frame from Host A to reach Host B routes from Ring 1, Bridge 5, Ring 10, Bridge 6, to Ring 2. In hex, the RIF is 0830.0015.00a6.0020.

RSRB with TCP Encapsulation

Looking at Figure 4-27, Router A reaches Router B through an IP network. With TCP, the local peer IP address is configured with one **remote-peer** statement, and the remote peer IP address is also configured with another **remote-peer** statement. The router can also be configured to acknowledge sessions destined for the remote peer by using the *local-ack* argument. The RSRB configuration is shown in Example 4-10. You use the shaded **source-bridge remote-peer** commands to define the local peer with the local IP address, and the remote peer with the IP address of the remote router.

Figure 4-27 *RSRB with TCP Encapsulation*

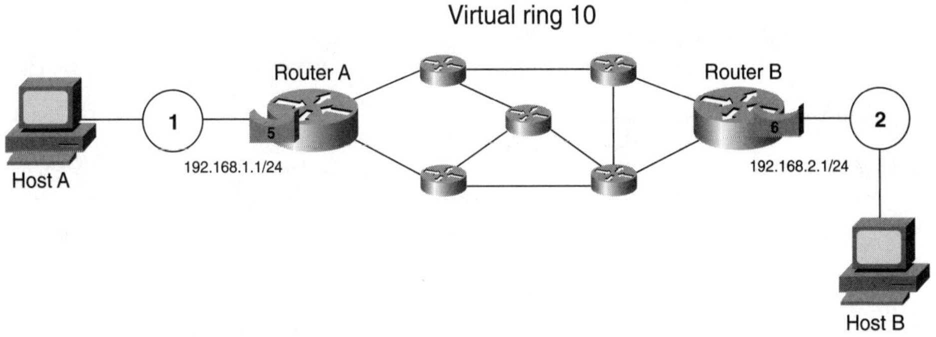

Example 4-10 *Configuration of RSRB with TCP Encapsulation*

```
!Router A
source-bridge ring-group 10
source-bridge remote-peer 10 tcp 192.168.1.1
source-bridge remote-peer 10 tcp 192.168.2.1 local-ack
!
interface tokenring 0
 ip address 192.168.1.1 255.255.255.0
 source-bridge 1 5 10
 source-bridge spanning


!Router B
source-bridge ring-group 10
source-bridge remote-peer 10 tcp 192.168.2.1
source-bridge remote-peer 10 tcp 192.168.1.1 local-ack
!
interface tokenring 0
 ip address 192.168.2.1 255.255.255.0
 source-bridge 2 6 10
 source-bridge spanning
```

The RIF of a source route frame from Host A to reach Host B routes from Ring 1, Bridge 5, Ring 10, Bridge 6, to Ring 2. In hex, the RIF is 0830.0015.00a6.0020.

DLSw+

DLSw version 2 is documented in RFC 2166 and DLSw version 1 is documented in RFC 1795. It was originally submitted by IBM to the IETF as RFC 1434 to overcome some of the limitations of SRB networks, especially in WAN networks. DLSw serves as a replacement of SRB and serves SNA data-link connections (DLC) and NetBIOS traffic.

Cisco's implementation of DLSw is called DLSw+. Some of the benefits of implementing DLSw+ are that link-layer acknowledgments and keepalive messages of SNA and NetBIOS traffic do not have to travel through the WAN. Also DLSw+ traffic can reroute around link failures and can be prioritized on WAN links, whereas SRB does not provide this capability. Cisco routers can be configured to communicate with devices running standards-based DLSw.

Figure 4-28 displays a sample DLSw network.

Figure 4-28 *DLSw Network*

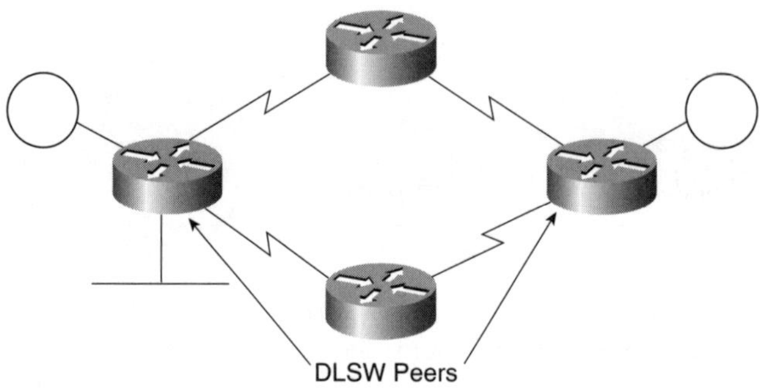

End systems can attach to the DLSw network from the Token Ring, Ethernet, Fiber Distributed Data Interface (FDDI), Qualified Logical Link Control (QLLC) (X.25), and SDLC networks. Although there are other methods, the preferred method for establishing peer connections is by using TCP. After a connection is established, the peer routers can exchange capabilities. Circuits are established between end-systems (SNA and NetBIOS). NetBIOS names can be configured to prevent NetBIOS Name Queries to traverse the DLSw network; MAC addresses can be configured in the same manner to reduce SRB explorer frames.

DLSw uses the Layer-2 Switch-to-Switch Protocol (SSP) between DLSw peer routers. SSP switches frame at the SNA layer. DLSw also encapsulates frames into TCP/IP for transport over IP networks.

DLSw supports termination of RIFs at the local virtual ring, which is the default mode. DLSw local termination eliminates the requirement for link-layer acknowledgments and keepalive messages to flow across a WAN. With RIF termination, the virtual rings do not have to be the same between the peers, and all remote hosts appear to be connected to the local router's virtual ring. DLSw also supports RIF Passthru, which does not terminate the RIF at the local end. With RIF Passthru, the virtual ring numbers of the DLSw peer routers must match, and the **rif-passthru** keyword must be in the **remote-peer** statement.

SNA devices on a LAN find other SNA devices by sending an explorer frame with the MAC address of the target SNA device. When a DLSw router receives an explorer frame, the router sends a *canureach* frame to each of the DLSw partners. If one of its DLSw partners can reach the specified MAC address, the partner replies with an *icanreach* frame. The specific sequence includes a *canureach ex* (explore) to find the resource and a *canureach cs* (circuit setup) that triggers the peering routers to establish a circuit.

NetBIOS circuit establishment is similar, but instead of forwarding a *canureach* frame that specifies a MAC address, DLSw routers send a name query (NetBIOS NAME-QUERY) frame that specifies a NetBIOS name. Instead of an *icanreach* frame, there is a name recognized (NetBIOS NAME-RECOGNIZED) frame.

Most DLSw implementations cache information learned as part of the explorer processing (from the *icanreach* responses) so that subsequent searches for the same resource do not result in the sending of additional explorer frames. This is also true with DLSw+.

DLSw Configuration

The basic configuration of DLSw is quite simple. Each router with attached networks is configured with a **local -peer** command. Remote peers are configured to remote routers. It is preferred to use the loopback IP addresses to configure the peers because the DLSw peers stay connected regardless of the state of local or remote LAN interfaces. For designs with multiple branches connecting to a hub site, the **promiscuous** keyword can be used on the hub router's **local-peer** command to permit remote peers to connect without having to explicitly configure each remote peer on the hub router. The configurations of the routers in Figure 4-29 are shown in this section.

Figure 4-29 *DLSw Example Network*

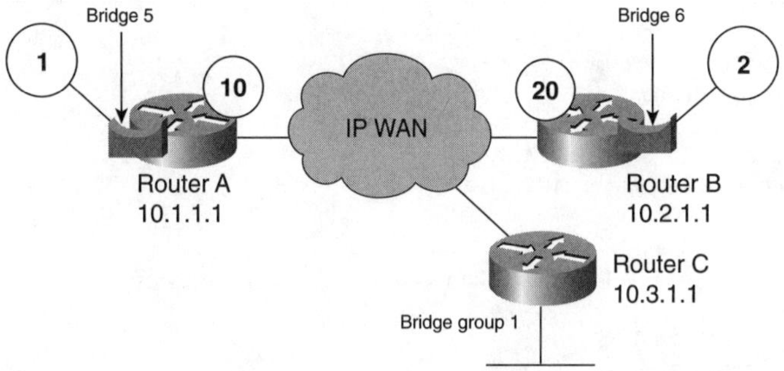

The configuration for Router A is displayed in Example 4-11.

Example 4-11 *DLSw Configuration of Router A*

```
source-bridge ring-group 10
!
dlsw local-peer peer-id 10.1.1.1 promiscuous
```

continues

Example 4-11 *DLSw Configuration of Router A (Continued)*

```
dlsw remote-peer 0 tcp 10.2.1.1
!
interface loopback 0
 ip address 10.1.1.1 255.255.255.255
!
interface tokenring 0
 source-bridge 1 5 10
```

The configuration for Router B is displayed in Example 4-12.

Example 4-12 *DLSw Configuration of Router B*

```
source-bridge ring-group 20
!
dlsw local-peer peer-id 10.2.1.1
dlsw remote-peer 0 tcp 10.1.1.1
!
interface loopback 0
 ip address 10.2.1.1 255.255.255.255
!
interface tokenring 0
 source-bridge 2 6 20
```

The configuration for Router C is displayed in Example 4-13.

Example 4-13 *DLSw Configuration of Router C*

```
bridge-group 1 protocol ieee
!
dlsw bridge-group 1
!
dlsw local-peer peer-id 10.3.1.1
dlsw remote-peer 0 tcp 10.1.1.1
!
interface loopback 0
 ip address 10.3.1.1 255.255.255.255
!
interface Ethernet 0
 bridge-group 1
```

Router A only defines a remote peer for Router B. It does not need to define Router C as a peer because the **promiscuous** keyword accepts connections from remote peers without having to define them. Router C defines Router A as a remote peer.

The RIF for a host on Router A to reach a host on Router B takes the path from Ring 1 to Bridge 5 to Ring 10. Because the virtual ring numbers are different, the RIF is terminated on virtual ring 10 on Router A. The RIF in hex is 0630.0015.00a0.

If the router configuration on Router B is changed to virtual ring 10 and DLSw is configured for RIF Passthru, the RIF reaches the far end ring. The RIF from the host on Router A to Router B takes the path from Ring 1 to Bridge 5 to Ring 10 to Bridge 6 to Ring 2. The RIF in hex is 0830.0015.00a6.0020.

LAN Switching Topics

Following the CCIE written exam blueprint, this section covers VLAN trunking, CDP, and forward error correction (FEC). The VLAN trunking methods covered are Inter-Switch Link (ISL), 802.1q, and Cisco's Virtual Terminal Protocol (VTP).

VLAN Trunking

A VLAN is an association of ports within a switch that serves a group of end stations with a common set of requirements. All stations in a VLAN share the same IP subnet; therefore, traffic between VLANs must be routed by an external router or a route-switch module in a Catalyst. Each VLAN is a logical broadcast domain.

Stations with the same VLAN do not necessarily need to be in the same physical location. You use trucking schemes to span VLANs throughout LAN switches. Each VLAN runs an instance of the STP. Figure 4-30 shows logical connectivity between LAN switches and a router. Because attached stations can be connected to any VLAN, all trunks must include the configured VLANs. The following sections discuss trunking schemes.

Figure 4-30 *VLAN Trunks*

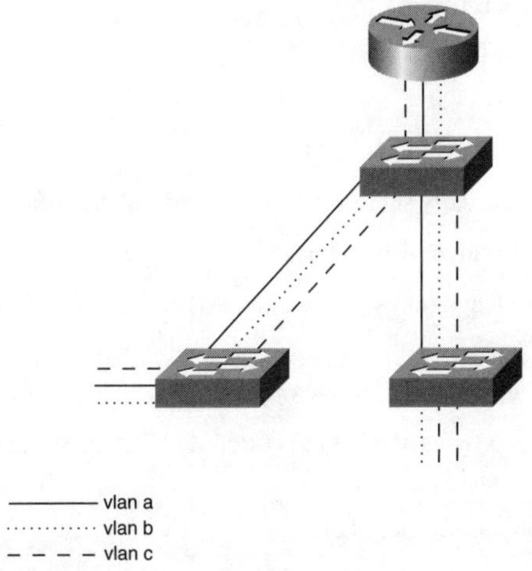

ISL

Cisco's ISL is a proprietary trunk encapsulation method for carrying VLANs over FE or GE interfaces.

ISL tags each frame to identify the VLAN it belongs to. The tag is a 30-byte header and CRC that is added around the FE frame. This includes a 26-byte header and 4-byte CRC. The header includes a 15-bit VLAN ID that identifies each VLAN. Although ISL is a point-to-point protocol (over FE and GE) between two Cisco devices, it can carry FDDI, Token Ring, and ATM in its payload.

ISL Frame Format

As shown in Figure 4-31, ISL adds a 26-byte header and 4-byte trailer to a frame when it is sent through a trunk.

Figure 4-31 *ISP Frame Format*

ISL Header (26 bytes)	Original Frame (variable)	ISL CRC (4 bytes)

The ISL frame with header, data, and trailer includes the following fields listed in Table 4-10.

Table 4-10 *ISL Frame Fields*

ISL Field	Description
DA	40-bit destination address set to multicast address 0x01 00 c0 00 00.
Type	4-bit value that indicates the source frame type with the following values: 0000 = Ethernet 0001 = Token Ring 0010 = FDDI 0011 = ATM
User	4-bits, usually set to zero, but can extend the meaning of the Type field.
SA	48-bit source MAC address.
LEN	16-bit length of user data and ISL header, excluding DA, T, U, SA, LEN, and CRC fields.
SNAP	3-byte field set to 0xAAAA03.
HSA	Upper 3 bytes, the manufactured ID portion, of the SA field; it must contain the value 0x00_00_0C.
VLAN ID	15-bit VLAN identifier.
BPDU	1-bit set for all BPDUs that are encapsulated by ISL.
INDX	16-bit index indicates the port index of the source of the packet as it exits the switch.

Table 4-10 *ISL Frame Fields (Continued)*

ISL Field	Description
RES	16-bit reserved field, set to zero for Ethernet.
Encapsulated Frame	Encapsulated Ethernet, Token Ring, FDDI, or ATM frame, including its own CRC, completely unmodified.
CRC	32-bit CRC value calculated on the entire encapsulated frame from the DA field to the encapsulated frame field.

ISL Configuration

On router interfaces, subinterfaces are created for each VLAN. On each subinterface, the encapsulation is set to ISL to enable ISL trunking to the switches. As shown in Example 4-14, each subinterface is configured with a different VLAN number with the **encapsulation isl** *vlan-number* command.

Example 4-14 *ISL Configuration*

```
interface fastethernet 1/1.1
 encapsulation isl 1
 ip address 192.168.1.1 255.255.255.0
!
interface fastethernet 1/1.2
 encapsulation isl 2
 ip address 192.168.2.1 255.255.255.0
!
interface fastethernet 1/1.3
 encapsulation isl 3
 ip address 192.168.3.1 255.255.255.0
```

On Catalyst, use the **set trunk** command. Because ISL is the default, you do not use the **isl** keyword:

```
set trunk mod/port [on | desirable | auto | negotiate] isl
```

IEEE 802.1q

The IEEE 802.1q standard trunks VLANs over FE and GE interfaces and can be used in a multivendor environment. IEEE 802.1q uses one instance of STP for each VLAN allowed in the trunk. Similar to ISL, 802.1q uses a tag on each frame with a VLAN identifier. Unlike ISL, 802.1q uses an internal tag.

IEEE 802.1q also provides support for the IEEE 802.1p priority standard. A priority field is included in the 802.1q frame.

IEEE 802.1q Frame Format

As shown in Figure 4-32, IEEE 802.1q inserts a 4-byte tag after the Source Address field (before the Type/Length field) of Ethernet frames.

Figure 4-32 *IEEE 802.1q Frame Format*

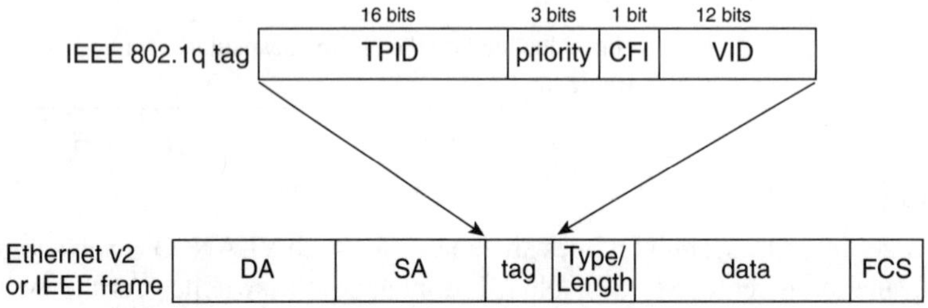

The tag fields are described in Table 4-11.

Table 4-11 *IEEE 802.1q Tag Fields*

IEEE 802.1q Field	Description
TPID	16-bit Tag Protocol Identifier, which indicates that an 802.1q tag follows.
Priority	3-bit IEEE 802.1p priority, which provides 8 levels of prioritization.
CFI	Canonical Format Indicator, which indicates whether the MAC addresses are in canonical (0) or noncanonical (1) format.
VID	12-bit VLAN identifier that allows 4096 unique VLAN values; VLAN numbers 0, 1, and 4095 are reserved.

IEEE 802.1q Configuration

On router interfaces, subinterfaces are created for each VLAN. On each subinterface, the encapsulation is set to IEEE 802.1q to enable trunking to the switches. As shown in Example 4-15, each subinterface is configured with a different VLAN number with the **encapsulation dot1q** *vlan-number* command.

Example 4-15 *IEEE 802.1q Configuration Example*

```
interface fastethernet 1/1.1
 encapsulation dot1q 10
 ip address 192.168.1.1 255.255.255.0
!
interface fastethernet 1/1.2
 encapsulation dot1q 20
 ip address 192.168.2.1 255.255.255.0
```

Example 4-15 *IEEE 802.1q Configuration Example (Continued)*

```
!
interface fastethernet 1/1.3
 encapsulation dot1q 30
 ip address 192.168.3.1 255.255.255.0
```

On Catalyst, use the **set trunk** command. Because ISL is the default, the **dot1q** keyword is necessary.

```
set trunk mod/port [on | desirable | auto | negotiate] dot1q
```

VLAN Trunk Protocol (VTP)

VTP is a Cisco proprietary protocol that distributes VLAN information among Catalyst switches. VTP uses ISL or 802.1q encapsulated links to communicate. VTP's purpose is to ease the administrative burden of managing VLANs, by managing the addition, deletion, and renaming of VLANs.

With VTP, a VTP domain is created for all Catalyst switches that are to be in an administrative domain. VTP operates through VTP messages (multicast messages) that are sent to a particular MAC address (01-00-0C-CC-CC-CC). VTP advertisements only travel through trunk ports and are carried only through VLAN 1.

VTP Switch Modes

Catalyst switches can be configured for one of three different VTP modes. The configuration command is as follows:

```
set vtp mode [server | client | transparent]
```

The VTP server maintains a full list of all VLANs within the VTP domain. Information is stored in NVRAM. The server can add, delete, and rename VLANs. The VTP client also maintains a full list of all VLANs. However, it does not store in NVRAM. The client cannot add, delete, or rename VLANs. Any changes made must be received from a VTP server advertisement. The VTP transparent does not participate in VTP. However, it does pass on a VTP advertisement. VLAN, as defined, is only local to the switch and is stored in NVRAM.

VTP Pruning

A major feature of VTP is VTP pruning, which limits the distribution of broadcasts throughout the VTP domain. As shown in Figure 4-33, a VTP domain has VLANs 1, 2, and 3. If switch S3 does not have users in VLAN 1, no broadcasts are sent to switch S3.

Figure 4-33 *VTP Pruning*

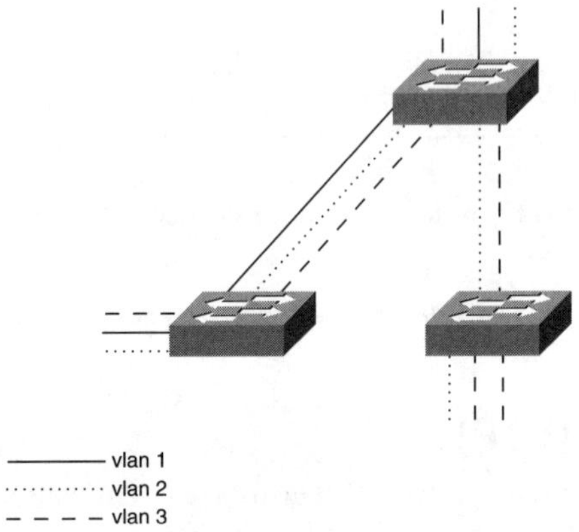

VTP Configuration

To configure Catalysts for VTP, a VTP domain name is created, and the VTP mode is configured. Options such as VTP pruning can be configured for all or a range of VLANs. Example 4-16 configures VTP domain CCIE with pruning on all eligible ports. Enabling VTP pruning on the server only enables pruning in the VTP management domain. All other devices need to be configured for pruning.

Example 4-16 *VTP Configuration*

```
cat5000: (enable) set vtp domain ccie
VTP domain ccie modified
cat5000: (enable) set vtp mode server
VTP domain ccie modified
cat5000: (enable)
cat5000: (enable) set vtp pruning enable
This command will enable the pruning function in the entire management domain.
All devices in the management domain should be pruning-capable before enabling.
Do you want to continue (y/n) [n]? y
VTP domain ccie modified
```

Fast EtherChannel (FEC)

Cisco's FEC provides a method to increase the bandwidth between two systems by bundling FE links. FEC also provides load sharing and redundancy capabilities. If a link fails in the FEC bundle, the other links take on the rest of the traffic load. Although this discussion focuses on FE, EtherChannel works for 10 Mbps Ethernet links and for GE links.

The requirements for EtherChannel are that all ports must be of the same speed, be in duplex mode, and belong to the same VLAN. Up to four ports are permitted in a bundle.

FEC Configuration

On a router, FEC is configured by assigning interfaces to a port-channel with the **channel-group** *number* **mode on** command. The virtual interface is created with the **interface port-channel** *number* command. Example 4-17 shows the FEC configuration of two FE interfaces assigned to channel 1.

Example 4-17 *FEC Configuration on a Router*

```
ag1.hstttx.lab(config)#int fast 2/25
ag1.hstttx.lab(config-if)#channel-group ?
  <1-256>  Channel group number

ag1.hstttx.lab(config-if)#channel-group 1 mode on
Creating a port-channel interface Port-channel1
ag1.hstttx.lab(config-if)#int fast 2/26
ag1.hstttx.lab(config-if)#channel-group 1 mode on
ag1.hstttx.lab(config-if)#exit
ag1.hstttx.lab(config)#interface port-channel ?
  <1-256>  Port-channel interface number

ag1.hstttx.lab(config)#interface port-channel 1
```

On the Catalyst switch, the configuration command is **set port channel**:

```
cat5000: (enable) set port channel ?
Usage: set port channel <port_list> [on|off|desirable|auto]
       (example of port_list: 2/1-4 or 2/1-2 or 2/5,2/6)
```

CDP

CDP is a Cisco proprietary protocol that you use to obtain hardware platforms and addresses of neighboring Cisco devices. CDP is media and protocol independent, and it runs over any Layer-2 protocol that supports SNAP frames including Ethernet, Frame Relay, and ATM. CDP allows network management stations to retrieve the device type and SNMP IP address of neighboring routers.

CDP is enabled by default. To disable CDP, use the **no cdp run** global command. CDP can be disabled per interface with the **no cdp enable** interface command. In Catalyst OS (CatOS), the command to globally disable CDP is **set cdp disable**. In CatOS, to disable CDP on a port, use the **set cdp disable** [*mod/port*] command.

The router output in Example 4-18 shows the information that can be gathered from **show cdp**.

Example 4-18 *Router* **show cdp** *Command Output*

```
R8#show cdp ?
  entry      Information for specific neighbor entry
  interface  CDP interface status and configuration
  neighbors  CDP neighbor entries
  traffic    CDP statistics
  |         Output modifiers
  <cr>
```

To find out about neighboring Cisco routers or switches, use the **show cdp neighbors** command, which gives summary information of each router. Example 4-19 shows the output of the **show cdp neighbors** command. The router has two neighbors, called R7 and R9, which are Cisco 2500 routers.

Example 4-19 *Router* **show cdp neighbors** *Command Output*

```
R8#show cdp neighbors
Capability Codes: R - Router, T - Trans Bridge, B - Source Route Bridge
                  S - Switch, H - Host, I - IGMP, r - Repeater

Device ID        Local Intrfce     Holdtme    Capability  Platform  Port ID
R7               Ser 1              133          R        2500      Ser 1
R9               Tok 0              176          R        2500      Tok 0
```

You use the same command on a Catalyst switch. Example 4-20 shows the output of the **show cdp neighbor** command of a switch. This switch has six neighboring routers (one MC3810 and five Cisco 2500s), which are marked with an R that describes router capabilities.

Example 4-20 *Switch* **show cdp neighbor** *Command Output*

```
cat5000: (enable) show cdp neighbor
Capability Codes: R - Router, T - Trans Bridge, B - Source Route Bridge
                  S - Switch, H - Host, I - IGMP, r - Repeater

Port     Device-ID                Port-ID          Platform      Capability
-------- ------------------------ ---------------- ------------------ --
 2/4     R3                       Ethernet0        Cisco MC3810        R
 2/5     R5                       Ethernet0        cisco 2500          R
 2/7     R7                       Ethernet0        cisco 2500          R
 2/9     R9                       Ethernet0        cisco 2500          R
 2/10    R10                      Ethernet0        cisco 2500          R
 2/11    R6                       Ethernet0        cisco 2500          R
```

To get more detailed information about neighboring routers, use the **show cdp neighbors detail** command, as shown in Example 4-21. From the output, you can gather neighbor information such as name, IP address, platform type, and IOS version.

Example 4-21 *Router* **show cdp neighbors detail** *Command Output*

```
R8#show cdp neighbors detail
-------------------------
Device ID: R7
Entry address(es):
  IP address: 133.5.78.1
Platform: cisco 2500,  Capabilities: Router
Interface: Serial1,  Port ID (outgoing port): Serial1
Holdtime : 148 sec

Version :
Cisco Internetwork Operating System Software
IOS (tm) 2500 Software (C2500-JOS56I-L), Version 12.1(7), RELEASE SOFTWARE (fc1)
Copyright (c) 1986-2001 by cisco Systems, Inc.
Compiled Fri 23-Feb-01 01:30 by kellythw

advertisement version: 2

-------------------------
Device ID: R9
Entry address(es):
  IP address: 150.100.1.9
Platform: cisco 2500,  Capabilities: Router
Interface: TokenRing0,  Port ID (outgoing port): TokenRing0
Holdtime : 131 sec

Version :
Cisco Internetwork Operating System Software
IOS (tm) 2500 Software (C2500-JOS56I-L), Version 12.1(7), RELEASE SOFTWARE (fc1)
Copyright (c) 1986-2001 by cisco Systems, Inc.
Compiled Fri 23-Feb-01 01:30 by kellythw

advertisement version: 2
```

LAN Security

This section covers bridging access lists, IEEE 802.1x port-based access protocol, and private VLANs.

Bridging Access Lists

Cisco provides two types of bridging access lists. The first is based on MAC addresses, the second on Ethernet types. The access list numbers for MAC address filters are from 700 to 799. The access list numbers for ethertype filters are from 200 to 299.

MAC Address Filter Configuration

MAC addresses can be filtered at the interface level, inbound or outbound. You use the **input-access-list** or **output-access-list** keywords in the **bridge-group** command to filter. Example 4-22 filters MAC 00c0.0404.091a inbound. Access list 700 specifically denies MAC address 00c0.0404.091a and permits all other MAC addresses. The access list is applied to Ethernet 0 as an inbound filter with the **bridge-group 1 input-access-list 700** command.

Example 4-22 *MAC Address Filtering*

```
 interface ethernet 0
  bridge-group 1
  bridge-group 1 input-access-list 700
!
access-list 700 deny 00c0.0404.091a 0000.0000.0000
access-list 700 permit 0000.0000.0000 ffff.ffff.ffff
```

Ethernet Type Filter Configuration

Ethernet frames can be filtered by type code at the interface level, inbound or outbound. Use the **input-type-list** or **output-type-list** keywords in the **bridge-group** command. Example 4-23 filters (denies) DEC LAT (Type=6004) outbound. Access list 200 specifically denies Ethernet type 0x6004 and permits all other Ethernet types. The access list is applied as an outbound filter on Ethernet 0 with the **bridge-group 1 output-type-list 200** command.

Example 4-23 *Ethernet Type Filtering*

```
interface ethernet 0
 bridge-group 1
 bridge-group 1 output-type-list 200
!
access-list 200 deny 0x6004 0x0000
access-list 200 permit 0x0000 0xffff
```

IEEE 802.1x Port-Based Authentication

IEEE 802.1x is a port-based authentication standard for LANs. Use the standard to authenticate a user before allowing services on Ethernet, FE, and WLANs.

With 802.1x, client workstations run 802.1x client software to request services. Clients use the Extensible Authentication Protocol (EAP) to communicate with the LAN switch. The LAN switch verifies client information with the authentication server and relays the response to the client. LAN switches use a Remote Authentication Dial-In User Service (RADIUS) client to communicate with the server. The RADIUS authentication server validates the identity of the client and authorizes the client. The server uses RADIUS with EAP extensions to make the authorization.

IEEE 802.1x Configuration

IEEE 802.1x port-based authentication is configured by enabling AAA authentication, configuring the RADIUS server parameters, and enabling 802.1x on the interface. Example 4-24 enables 802.1x authentication on an FE interface. The **aaa authentication dot1x default group radius** command enables IEEE 802.1x authentication on the switch. In Example 4-24, the RADIUS server has an IP address of 1.1.1.1, and the RADIUS key is ccie-key. The interface is configured to use 802.1x authentication with the **dot1x port-control auto** command.

Example 4-24 *802.1x Configuration Example*

```
aaa new-model
aaa authentication dot1x default group radius
!
radius-server host 1.1.1.1 auth-port 1812 key ccie-key
!
interface fastethernet 1/1
 dot1x port-control auto
```

Private VLANs

Private VLANs provide isolation for ports that are configured within the private VLAN structure. You can use private LANs when hosts on the same segment do not need to communicate with each other but do need to communicate with the same router or firewall. Private VLANs provide isolation at Layer 2 of the OSI model.

Private VLANs consist of the following VLANs:

- Primary VLAN—Receives frames from the promiscuous port and forwards it to ports in the primary, isolated, and community VLANs.
- Isolated VLAN—All ports in this VLAN can communicate only with the promiscuous port. Isolated ports cannot communicate with other isolated ports. Isolated VLANs are secondary VLANs.
- Community VLAN—All ports in this VLAN can communicate with each other and with the promiscuous port. Community VLANs are secondary VLANs.

Private VLAN Configuration

To configure private VLANs, create the primary and secondary VLANs, bind secondary VLANs to the primary VLAN, and assign ports. Then, the secondary VLANs are mapped to the promiscuous port.

Example 4-25 shows a simple configuration of private VLANs. The **set vlan** command creates the primary and secondary VLANs. Use the **set pvlan** *primary secondary mod/port* command to bind secondary VLANs to the Primary VLAN and to associate ports. Finally, use the **set**

pvlan mapping command to map the secondary VLANs to the promiscuous port of the primary VLAN.

Example 4-25 *Private VLAN Configuration Example*

```
set vlan 10 pvlan-type primary
set vlan 101 pvlan-type community
set vlan 102 pvlan-type isolated
set vlan 103 pvlan-type isolated
set pvlan 10 101 3/2-12
set pvlan 10 102 3/13
set pvlan 10 103 3/14
set pvlan mapping 10 101 3/1
set pvlan mapping 10 102 3/1
set pvlan mapping 10 103 3/1
```

ATM LANE

Cisco removed ATM LANE as a CCIE Routing and Switching lab exam topic but has retained it in the CCIE written blueprint, but with less emphasis. Know the LANE components and the SSRP that are used for redundancy. This section only covers LANE. Other ATM topics are covered in Chapter 5, "Wide-Area Networks."

LANE provides connectivity between Ethernet or Token Ring stations and ATM connected stations. LANE also provides connectivity for Ethernet or Token Ring stations across an ATM network. LANE creates an emulated LAN (ELAN) for each LAN segment it connects to.

ATM LANE Components

The components of ATM LANE are shown in Table 4-12.

Table 4-12 *ATM LANE Components*

ATM LANE Component	Description
LANE Client (LEC)	There is a LEC for each member of the ELAN. LECs implement LE-ARP address resolution and emulate a LAN for higher-level protocols. LEC builds a table to map MAC addresses to ATM addresses. Each LEC has an ATM address. LECs can be a computer station, switch, or router.
LANE Server (LES)	The LES is the central resource for the ELAN. It provides management of all stations in the ELAN by providing address registration and resolution, and handling LE-ARP requests.
LANE Configuration Server (LECS)	A LEC consults the LECS when first joining the ELAN. The LECS provides the ATM address of the LES to the LEC.

Table 4-12 *ATM LANE Components (Continued)*

ATM LANE Component	Description
Broadcast and Unknown Server (BUS)	The BUS handles all broadcast, multicast packets, and unicasts sent to unknown destinations. Because broadcasts do not exist in ATM, the BUS processes the broadcasts to create virtual circuits to all stations in the ELAN. The LES and BUS functions are commonly implemented in the same device.

LANE Join and Circuit Establishment Operation

When a new station joins the ELAN, the following procedure occurs:

1. The LEC requests the ATM address of the LES from the LECS. The LECS provides the address.
2. The LEC contacts the LES to join the ELAN.
3. The LES adds the LEC to the ELAN and sends a response to the LEC.
4. The LEC sends an LE-ARP to the LES to obtain the ATM address of the BUS. The LES provides the address.
5. The LEC contacts the BUS, which adds the LEC to the Multicast Send Virtual Circuit Connection.

After the LEC is ready to communicate with a destination station but does not have the destination ATM address, it sends an LE-ARP request to the LES. If the LES knows the destination ATM address, it provides it to the LEC. If the LES does not know the ATM destination address, it sends an LE-ARP to all LECs, the destination LEC responds to the LES, and the ATM address is forwarded to the sending LEC. Then, the sending LEC sets up a virtual circuit to the destination LEC.

SSRP

SSRP is a Cisco proprietary protocol that provides replication for LECS or LES/BUS services. With SSRP, if the active LES and BUS device fails, another device assumes the roles of LES and BUS. Also, if the active LECS fails, another device assumes the role of the LECS. The active and secondary services do not run concurrently on the ELAN.

A sample configuration of SSRP can be found at the following site:

www.cisco.com/warp/public/121/ssrpconfig.html

References Used

The following resources were used to create this chapter:

- *Internetworking Technologies Handbook*, Second Edition, 1998, Cisco Press
- www.cisco.com/univercd/cc/td/doc/cisintwk/ito_doc/ethernet.htm#xtocid3
- www.cisco.com/warp/public/100/45.html#control
- www.cisco.com/univercd/cc/td/doc/product/lan/cat5000/rel_5_2/config/spantree.htm#xtocid287967
- www.cisco.com/univercd/cc/td/doc/cisintwk/ito_doc/mmbridge.htm
- www.cisco.com/univercd/cc/td/doc/product/lan/c3550/1218ea1/3550scg/sw8021x.htm
- www.cisco.com/univercd/cc/td/doc/product/lan/cat6000/121_8aex/swconfig/pvlans.htm

Foundation Summary

The Foundation Summary is a condensed collection of material that provides a convenient review of key concepts in this chapter. If you are already comfortable with the topics in this chapter, this summary will help you recall a few details. If you just read the Foundation Topics section, this review should help solidify some key facts. If you are doing your final preparation before the exam, these materials are a convenient way to review the day before the exam.

Table 4-13 *Ethernet Frame Formats*

Frame	Description
Ethernet V2	Uses 2-byte Type field.
IEEE 802.3	Uses 2-byte Length field and 3-byte LLC.
IEEE 802.3 SNAP	Uses 2-byte length field, 3-byte LLC, and 5-byte SNAP; the SNAP values are 0xAA.
Novell Raw	Uses 2-byte length field; data begins with 0xFFFF.

Media Specifications

The specifications for Thicknet (10Base5) are as follows:

- 0.4 inch, 50 ohm coax cable.
- Maximum segment length is 500 m.
- Maximum number of attachments per segment is 100.
- Maximum AUI cable length is 50 m.
- Minimum separation between attachments (MAU) is 2.5 m.
- Cable ends terminate with 50 ohm terminators.
- MAU attach workstations.
- Maximum network length is 5 segments and 2500 m.
- Maximum number of stations on the network is 1024.

The media specifications for 10Base2 are as follows:

- 0.2 inch, RG58-U, 50 ohm coax cable.
- Maximum segment length is 185 m.
- Maximum number of attachments per segment is 30.
- Minimum separation per segment is 0.5 m.
- T-connectors attach workstations.

The 10BaseT specifications are as follows:

- 24 AWG UTP .4/.6 mm cable.
- Maximum segment length is 100 m.
- 1 device per cable.

The media specifications for 100Base-TX are as follows:

- Transmission over Cat 5 UTP or Cat 1 STP wire.
- RJ-45 connector (same as in 10BaseT).
- Punchdown blocks in the wiring closet must be Category 5 certified.
- 4B5B coding.

Table 4-14 *IBM and IEEE 802.5 Token Ring Specification Similarities*

Specification	IBM Token Ring	IEEE 802.5
Data Rate	4 or 16 Mbps	4 or 16 Mbps 4 Mbps only, on UTP
Stations per segment	260 (on STP) 72 (on UTP)	250 (on STP) 72 (on UTP)
Physical Topology	Star	Not specified
Media	Twisted pair	Not specified
Signaling	Baseband	Baseband
Access Method	Token passing	Token passing
Encoding	Differential Manchester	Differential Manchester

Table 4-15 *Token Ring Characteristics*

Token Ring Function	Description
Active Monitor (AM)	Acts as the centralized source of timing information for other ring stations and performs a variety of ring-maintenance functions.
Beaconing	A beacon frame is sent by a station that does not receive any more frames from its upstream neighbor.
Early Token Release (ETR)	A token is released immediately after the sending station transmits its frame.

Process for a Station to Insert into the Token Ring

The process for a station to insert into the Token Ring follows five phases:

- Phase 0—Lobe media check
- Phase 1—Physical insertion
- Phase 2—Address verification
- Phase 3—Participation in ring poll
- Phase 4—Request initialization

Transparent Bridge Functions

Transparent bridges have three primary functions:

- To learn the MAC addresses of all nodes and their associated port
- To filter incoming frames whose destination MAC addresses are located on the same incoming port
- To forward incoming frames to the destination MAC through their associated port

Table 4-16 *WLAN Modes*

WLAN Mode	Description
Basic Service Set (BSS)	Also known as Infrastructure mode; there is one Access Point.
Independent Basic Service Set (IBSS)	Also known as Ad-hoc mode; there is no Access Point.
Extended Service Set	There is more than one Access Point.

Table 4-17 *Transparent Bridge Modes*

Bridge Mode	Description
Store-and-Forward	Stores the entire frame and verifies the CRC before forwarding the frame. If a CRC error is detected, the frame is discarded.
Cut-Through	Forwards the frame just after it reads the destination MAC address without performing a CRC check.

Transparent Bridge Port States

Each port of a transparent bridge exists in the following states:

- **Disabled**—The port is inactive and does not participate in STP.

- **Blocking**—When a port is enabled, it first moves to a blocked state before listening to the network. In this state, it does not participate in frame forwarding. It receives Bridge PDUs and sends them for processing.
- **Listening**—When the bridge determines that the port should participate in frame forwarding, it changes to the listening state. In this state, the bridge still does not forward frames and does not learn of network MAC addresses. The bridge does receive and process BPDUs and network management frames.
- **Learning**—The bridge port still discards incoming frames or frames switched over for forwarding. The bridge begins to incorporate MAC addresses associated with this port. BPDU and network management messages are still processed.
- **Forwarding**—This is the full functional state for a bridged port. In this state, the bridge does not discard incoming frames and forwards them to other ports; the bridge also forwards frames out the port. BPDUs and network management frames are still processed.

STP

- The selection of the root bridge is based on the lowest numerical bridge priority.
- The bridge with the lowest source MAC address breaks a tie.

CRB

CRB enables the router to both route and bridge the same protocol on separate interfaces. With IRB, a protocol can be routed between routed interfaces, bridged interfaces, or different bridge groups.

The access list numbers for MAC address filters are from 700 to 799. The access list for EtherType filters are from 200 to 299.

Table 4-18 *Methods for Using SRBs*

Bridge Type	Function
Source route bridging (SRB)	The source determines the route to use to reach the destination node before sending an information frame to it. The bridge does not store MAC addresses. Limited to 7 bridge hops; explorer frames used by stations.
Source route transparent bridging (SRT)	SRT bridges can forward traffic from both transparent and source-route end nodes and form a common spanning tree with transparent bridges.
Source-route translational bridging (SR/TLB)	Bridge between SRB and transparently bridged networks. Look at MTU, reorder bits, convert frames.

Table 4-18 *Methods for Using SRBs (Continued)*

Bridge Type	Function
Remote source route bridging (RSRB)	Permits the bridging of token rings located on separate routers across non-Token Ring media. The virtual ring spans the peer routers.
Data-link switching (DLSw)	DLSw serves as a replacement of SRB and serves SNA data-link connections (DLC) and NetBIOS traffic. Supports RIF terminations.

RIF

RIF contains a 2-byte RIF header and one or more route descriptors. Each route descriptor contains a 12-bit ring number and a 4-bit bridge number. The values for the Type field contained in the header indicate the following:

- **00**—Nonbroadcast (specific route): Indicates that this is a regular frame that should be routed to the destination following the information in the route descriptors.
- **10**—All-routes broadcast: Indicates that this is an all-rings explorer packet that should take all possible routes to the destination.
- **11**—Single-route: Indicates that this is a limited broadcast that should take one path to the destination.

VLAN Trunking

- ISL—Cisco's proprietary method of trunk encapsulation for carrying VLANs over FE and GE. You use the VLAN header and trailer outside the frame (external tag).
- IEEE 802.1q—IEEE standard for trunk encapsulation for carrying VLANs over FE and GE. Uses internal 4-byte tag that is placed before the Type/Length field of frames.
- VTP—Cisco's method of distributing VLAN information between Catalyst switches.
- VLAN pruning—Limits the flooding of broadcasts to switches that do not require them.

FEC

FEC provides a method to increase the bandwidth between two systems by bundling FE links. FEC also provides load sharing and redundancy capabilities.

CDP

CDP is a Cisco proprietary protocol that you use to obtain hardware platforms and addresses of neighboring Cisco devices. CDP is media and protocol independent.

LANE

Table 4-19 *ATM LANE Components*

ATM LANE Components	Description
LANE Client (LEC)	There is a LEC for each member of the ELAN. LECs implement LE-ARP address resolution and emulate a LAN for higher-level protocols. LEC builds a table to map MAC addresses to ATM addresses. Each LEC has an ATM address. LECs can be a computer station, switch, or router.
LANE Server (LES)	The LES is the central resource for the ELAN. It provides management of all stations in the ELAN by providing address registration and resolution and handling LE-ARP requests.
LANE Configuration Server (LECS)	A LEC consults the LECS when first joining the ELAN. The LECS provides the ATM address of the LES to the LEC.
Broadcast and Unknown Server (BUS)	The BUS handles all broadcast, multicast packets, and unicasts sent to unknown destinations. Because broadcasts do not exist in ATM, the BUS processes the broadcasts to create virtual circuits to all stations in the ELAN. The LES and BUS functions are commonly implemented in the same device.

Q & A

The Q & A questions are more difficult than what you can expect on the actual exam. The questions do not attempt to cover more breadth or depth than the exam; however, they are designed to make sure that you retain the material. Rather than allowing you to derive the answer from clues hidden inside the question itself, these questions challenge your understanding and recall of the subject. Questions from the "Do I Know This Already?" quiz are repeated here to ensure that you have mastered the chapter's topic areas. A strong understanding of the answers to these questions will help you on the CCIE written exam. As an additional study aide, use the CD-ROM provided with this book to take simulated exams.

Select the best answer. Answers to these questions are in Appendix A, "Answers to Quiz Questions."

1 What bit of each byte does an Ethernet NIC expect to read first off the wire?

a. The least significant bit first; this is the noncanonical format.

b. The most significant bit first; this is the noncanonical format.

c. The least significant bit first; this is the canonical format.

d. The most significant bit first; this is the canonical format.

2 Which access method listens to the wire before transmitting?

a. Token access

b. CSMA/CD

c. Token bus

d. 4B/5B

3 Which IEEE frame format includes a type field?

a. IEEE 802.3

b. IEEE 802.5

c. IEEE 802.3 SNAP

d. IEEE 802.1q

4 Which bridging method associates a MAC address with its ports?

a. Transparent

b. SRB

c. SR/TLB

d. RSRB

5 What does the following command do?

```
source-bridge transparent 10 5 1 6
```

a. Configures DLSw

b. Configures transparent bridging

c. Configures source-route bridging

d. Configures translational bridging from an Ethernet bridge group

6 What is the RIF in hexadecimal for a source route frame if it is to route from Token Ring 4, through bridge 12, ending on Token Ring 15?

a. 0630.004c.0015

b. 0630.0412.0015

c. 0630.040c.0150

d. 0630.004c.00f0

7 Which access list denies 00c0.00a0.0010 but permits other MAC addresses?

a.

```
access-list 700 deny 00c0.00a0.0010 ffff.ffff.ffff
access-list 700 permit 0000.0000.0000 ffff.ffff.ffff
```

b.

```
access-list 700 deny 00c0.00a0.0010 0000.0000.0000
access-list 700 permit 0000.0000.0000 ffff.ffff.ffff
```

c.

```
access-list 200 deny 00c0.00a0.0010 ffff.ffff.ffff
access-list 200 permit 0000.0000.0000 ffff.ffff.ffff
```

d.

```
access-list 200 deny 00c0.00a0.0010 0000.0000.0000
access-list 200 permit 0000.0000.0000 ffff.ffff.ffff
```

8 Which trunking method places an internal tag to identify the VLAN number?

a. ISL

b. 802.1q

c. 802.1p

d. VTP pruning

9 Which answer best describes the VTP client?

a. Stores VLAN information in NVRAM

b. Adds and deletes VLANs in the VTP domain

c. Maintains a full list of VLANs

d. Does not participate in VTP

10 What is the BID?

a. BLAN ID number

b. Bridge identifier used in STP

c. Border identifier used in SRB

d. Bridged identifier used in VTP

11 What is the transparent bridge port state sequence from a disabled port to a forwarding port?

a. Disabled, listening, learning, forwarding, blocked

b. Disabled, enabled, listening, learning, forwarding

c. Disabled, blocking, listening, learning, forwarding

d. Disabled, blocking, learning, listening, forwarding

12 What is a BVI?

a. Bridged VLAN identifier

b. Bridge virtual interface, used in IRB

c. Bridge ID, in RIFs

d. When set, indicates to use SRB

13 Which type of bridge removes the RIF, checks the MTU, and reorders bits before sending the frame on?

a. Transparent

b. DLSw

c. SRT

d. SR/TLB

e. SRB

f. RSRB

14 What is the RIF in the following?

```
source-bridge ring-group 5
!
dlsw local-peer peer-id 1.1.1.1 promiscuous
dlsw remote-peer 0 tcp 2.2.2.1
!
interface tokenring 0
 source-bridge 1 2 5
```

a. 0630.0012.0050.

b. 0830.0125.

c. 0830.0012.0051.

d. Not enough information is given.

15 What is the maximum segment length of 10Base2 media?

a. 100 m

b. 185 m

c. 200 feet

d. 500 feet

16 At what speed does Gigabit Ethernet transmit data?

a. 1000 kbps

b. 100 Mbps

c. 1000 Mbps

d. 1250 kbps

17 What is the IEEE standard for Fast Ethernet?

a. IEEE 802.3a

b. IEEE 802.3ab

c. IEEE 802.3u

d. IEEE 802.3z

18 What is a BPDU?

a. Bridge packet descriptor unit

b. Bridge protocol data unit

c. Basic protocol descriptor unit

d. None of the above

19 If the DSAP and SSAP have the value 0xAAAA, what does it indicate?

a. a.That a SNAP field follows

b. That a NSAP field follows

c. That a V2 frame follows

d. That a FDDI frame follows

20 What bit of each byte does a Token Ring NIC expect to read first off the wire?

a. The least significant bit first; this is the noncanonical format.

b. The most significant bit first; this is the noncanonical format.

c. The least significant bit first; this is the canonical format.

d. The most significant bit first; this is the canonical format.

21 Which bridging method permits source-route frames over non-Token Ring media?

a. Transparent

b. SRT

c. SR/TLB

d. RSRB

22 Which bridging method runs STP?

a. Transparent

b. SRT

c. SR/TLB

d. RSRB

23 What is the RIF in hexadecimal for a source-route frame if it is to route from Token Ring 4, through Bridge 12, to Token Ring 0x11, through Bridge 8, ending on Token Ring 22?

a. 0830.4c11.8220

b. 0830.0412.0011.8220

c. 0830.004c.0118.0160

d. 0630.0412.0011.8220

24 Which answer best describes the VTP server?

a. Stores VLAN information in NVRAM

b. Adds and deletes VLANs in the VTP domain

c. Maintains a full list of VLANs

d. Does not participate in VTP

e. Answers a, b, and c

25 Which answer best describes the VTP transparent switch?

a. Stores VTP learned VLAN info in NVRAM

b. Adds and deletes VLANs in the VTP domain

c. Maintains a full list of VLANs

d. Does not participate in VTP

e. Answers b and c

26 What is the sequence for Token Ring insertion?

a. Physical insertion, lobe check, address verification, initialize, ring poll

b. Lobe check, physical insertion, address verification, ring poll, initialize

c. Physical insertion, lobe check, address verification, initialize, ring poll

d. Physical insertion, ring poll, lobe check, initialize, address verification

27 What command is used to enable IEEE 802.1q trunking on port 2/1?

a. set trunk 2/1 on 802.1q

b. set trunk 2/1 on isl1q

c. set trunk 2/1 on dot1q

d. set trunk 2/1 on isl

28 How many instances of STP are running on a Catalyst running 802.1q with 3 VLANs configured?

a. 1

b. 2

c. 3

d. None

29 What are the functions of a transparent bridge?

a. Disabled, listening, learning, filtering, forwarding

b. Learn, filter, and forward

c. Listen, learn, filter, block, and forward

d. Enabled, listen, forward, flood

30 Which Layer-2 protocol changes blocked interfaces to the forwarding state in the case of bridge failure?

a. HSRP

b. VTP

c. STP

d. EIGRP

31 What is the path cost in STP?

a. Sum of segment costs to reach the root bridge

b. OSPF interface costs for the STP algorithm

c. The cost of Gigabit Ethernet is 1000

d. None of the above

32 Which access list denies Ethernet type 0x6006?

a.

```
access-list 101 deny ipv2 any any 0x6006 eq type
access-list 101 permit ip any any
```

b.

```
access-list 700 deny 0x6006 0x0000
access-list 700 permit 0x0000 0xffff
```

c.

```
access-list 200 deny 0x6006 0x0000
access-list 200 permit 0x0000 0xffff
```

d.

```
access-list 200 deny 0x6006 any eq type
access-list 200 permit any any eq type
```

33 What is the default STP priority?

a. 0

b. 1

c. 32,768

d. 56,535

34 From the following configuration, what is the RIF from Ring 1 to Ring 2?

```
source-bridge ring-group 7
!
interface tokenring 0
 source-bridge 1 10 7
 source-bridge spanning
!
interface tokenring 1
 source-bridge 2 11 7
 source-bridge spanning
```

a. 0830.0110.0711.0200

b. 0630.1A7b.0200

c. 0630.1011.0201

d. 0830.001a.007b.0020

35 What is CDP?

a. Control Description Protocol

b. Control data packet

c. Cisco Discovery Protocol

d. Cisco Description Protocol

36 What information can be gathered from neighbors using CDP?

a. Device name, management IP address, platform type, and OS version

b. Device name and IP address only

c. Answer a, plus running routing protocol

d. Device name, management IP address, platform type, and all enabled interface IP addresses

37 Which command produced the following router output?

```
Capability Codes: R - Router, T - Trans Bridge, B - Source Route Bridge
                  S - Switch, H - Host, I - IGMP, r - Repeater

Port     Device-ID                Port-ID           Platform     Capability
-------- ------------------------ ----------------- ------------------ --
 2/14     Router13                Ethernet0         Cisco MC3810        R
 2/15     Router10                Ethernet0         cisco 2500          R
```

a. show ip ospf neighbor

b. show ip bgp neighbor

c. show ip cdp neighbor

d. show cdp neighbor

38 What standard specifies 11 Mbps wireless LANs at a frequency of 2.4 GHz?

a. IEEE 802.11

b. IEEE 802.11a

c. IEEE 802.11b

d. IEEE 802.11g

39 What standard specifies 54 Mbps Wireless LANs at a frequency of 5 GHz?

a. IEEE 802.11

b. IEEE 802.11a

c. IEEE 802.11b

d. IEEE 802.11g

40 Which standard provides port-based authentication?

a. IEEE 802.11x

b. IEEE 802.11i

c. IEEE 802.1x

d. IEEE 802.1u

41 Which Wireless LAN mode uses one Access Point?

a. BSS

b. IBSS

c. ESS

d. Ad-hoc

42 Which ATM LANE component is contacted first by a joining client?

a. LEC

b. LES

c. LECS

d. BUS

43 Which protocol provides LES/BUS replication in an ATM LANE environment?

a. LE-ARP

b. SSRP

c. BUS

d. PNNI

44 What does LE-ARP translates?

a. IP addresses to MAC addresses

b. IP addresses to ATM addresses

c. MAC addresses to ATM addresses

d. Ethernet MAC addresses to Token Ring addresses

Scenarios

Scenario 4-1

This scenario reviews your knowledge of RSRB. Knowledge of RSRB configurations and RIF constructs in RSRB environments is essential for the CCIE written test. Use Figure 4-34 to answer the following questions.

Figure 4-34 *RSRB*

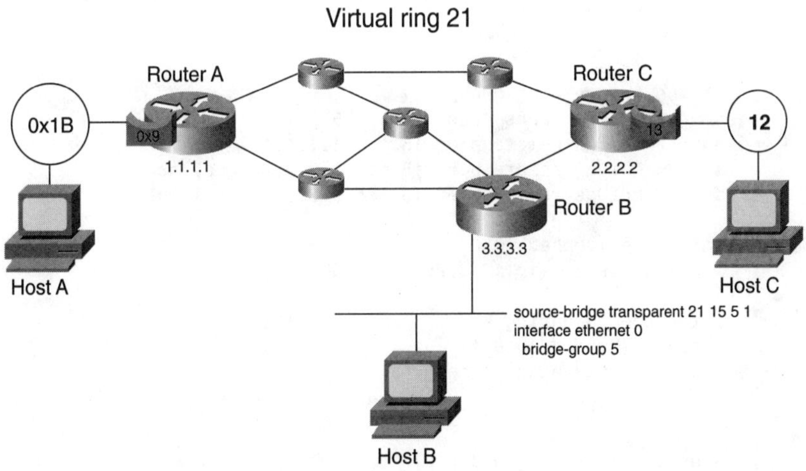

1 What is the RIF from Host A to Host C?

a. 0830.01b9.021d.0120

b. 0830.01b9.015d.00c0

c. 0830.01b9.0151.20c0

d. 0630.01b9.121d.0120

2 What is the RIF from Host A to Host B?

a. 0630.01b9.01f5

b. 0830.01b0.0210

c. 0630.01b9.0150

d. 0830.01b9.0155.00f0

3 What is the correct configuration for Router A?

a.

```
source-bridge ring-group 21
source-bridge remote-peer 21 tcp 1.1.1.1
source-bridge remote-peer 21 tcp 2.2.2.2 local-ack
source-bridge remote-peer 21 tcp 3.3.3.3 local-ack
!
interface loopback 0
 ip address 1.1.1.1 255.255.255.255
!
interface tokenring 0
  source-bridge 1b 9 10
  source-bridge spanning
```

b.

```
source-bridge ring-group 15
source-bridge transparent 15 6 2 5
source-bridge remote-peer 15 tcp 1.1.1.1
source-bridge remote-peer 15 tcp 2.2.2.2 local-ack
source-bridge remote-peer 15 tcp 3.3.3.3 local-ack
!
interface loopback 0
 ip address 1.1.1.1 255.255.255.255
!
interface tokenring 0
  source-bridge 1b 9 15
  source-bridge spanning
```

c.

```
source-bridge ring-group 21
source-bridge remote-peer 21 tcp 1.1.1.1
source-bridge remote-peer 21 tcp 2.2.2.2 local-ack
source-bridge remote-peer 21 tcp 3.3.3.3 local-ack
!
interface loopback 0
 ip address 1.1.1.1 255.255.255.255
!
interface tokenring 0
  source-bridge 27 9 21
  source-bridge spanning
```

d.

```
source-bridge ring-group 15
source-bridge remote-peer 15 tcp 1.1.1.1
source-bridge remote-peer 15 tcp 2.2.2.2 local-ack
source-bridge remote-peer 15 tcp 3.3.3.3 local-ack
!
interface loopback 0
 ip address 1.1.1.1 255.255.255.255
```

```
!
interface tokenring 0
  source-bridge 1b 9 15
  source-bridge spanning
```

4 What is the correct configuration for Router C?

a.

```
source-bridge ring-group 21
source-bridge remote-peer 21 tcp 1.1.1.1 local-ack
source-bridge remote-peer 21 tcp 2.2.2.2
source-bridge remote-peer 21 tcp 3.3.3.3 local-ack
!
interface loopback 0
 ip address 2.2.2.2 255.255.255.255
!
interface tokenring 0
  source-bridge c d f
  source-bridge spanning
```

b.

```
source-bridge ring-group 21
source-bridge remote-peer 21 tcp 2.2.2.2
source-bridge remote-peer 21 tcp 1.1.1.1 local-ack
source-bridge remote-peer 21 tcp 3.3.3.3 local-ack
!
interface loopback 0
 ip address 2.2.2.2 255.255.255.255
!
interface tokenring 0
  source-bridge 12 13 15
  source-bridge spanning
```

c.

```
source-bridge ring-group 15
source-bridge remote-peer 15 tcp 2.2.2.2
source-bridge remote-peer 15 tcp 2.2.2.2 local-ack
source-bridge remote-peer 15 tcp 3.3.3.3 local-ack
!
interface loopback 0
 ip address 2.2.2.2 255.255.255.255
!
interface tokenring 0
  source-bridge 12 13 15
  source-bridge spanning
```

d.

```
source-bridge ring-group 15
source-bridge remote-peer 15 tcp 1.1.1.1
source-bridge remote-peer 15 tcp 2.2.2.2 local-ack
source-bridge remote-peer 15 tcp 3.3.3.3 local-ack
```

```
!
interface loopback 0
 ip address 2.2.2.2 255.255.255.255
!
interface tokenring 0
   source-bridge c d f
  source-bridge spanning
```

5 What is the bridge number of the bridge between the virtual ring and the pseudo-ring on Router B?

a. a. 21

b. b. 0x6

c. c. 0x2

d. d. 0x5

Scenario 4-2

This scenario reviews your knowledge of DLSw. Knowledge of DLSw configuration and RIF construct in DLSw environment is essential for the CCIE written test. Use Figure 4-35 to answer the following questions.

Figure 4-35 *DLSw*

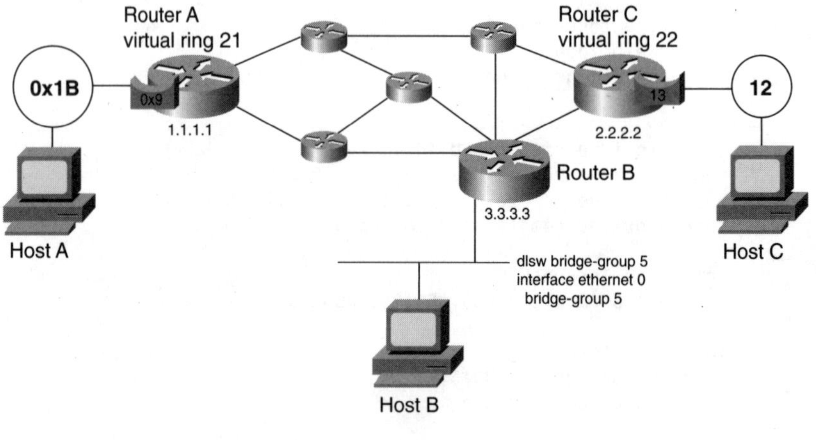

1 What is the RIF from Host A to Host C?

a. 0830.01b9.021d.0120

b. 0830.01b9.015d.00c0

c. 0630.01b9.0210

d. 0630.01b9.0150

2 What is the RIF from Host A to Host B?

a. 0830.01b9.021d.0120

b. 0830.01b9.0152.0060

c. 0630.01b9.0210

d. 0630.01b9.0150

3 What is the correct configuration of Router A?

a.

```
interface loopback 0
 ip address 1.1.1.1 255.255.255.255
!
source-bridge ring-group 21
!
dlsw local-peer peer-id 1.1.1.1
dlsw remote-peer 0 tcp 2.2.2.2
dlsw remote-peer 0 tcp 3.3.3.3
!
interface tokenring 0
 source-bridge 27 9 21
```

b.

```
interface loopback 0
 ip address 1.1.1.1 255.255.255.255
!
source-bridge ring-group 21
!
dlsw local-peer peer-id 1.1.1.1
dlsw remote-peer 0 tcp 2.2.2.2 ring 22
dlsw remote-peer 0 tcp 3.3.3.3 ring 23
!
interface tokenring 0
 source-bridge 27 9 21
```

c.

```
interface loopback 0
 ip address 1.1.1.1 255.255.255.255
!
source-bridge ring-group 21
!
dlsw local-peer peer-id 10.1.1.1
dlsw remote-peer 22 tcp 2.2.2.2
dlsw remote-peer 23 tcp 3.3.3.3
!
interface tokenring 0
 source-bridge 27 9 21
```

d.

```
interface loopback 0
 ip address 1.1.1.1 255.255.255.255
!
source-bridge ring-group 27
!
dlsw local-peer peer-id 11.1.1.1
dlsw remote-peer 0 tcp 2.2.2.2
dlsw remote-peer 0 tcp 3.3.3.3
!
interface tokenring 0
 source-bridge 27 9 21
```

4 What is the pseudo-ring number on Router B?

a. 21.

b. 6.

c. 1.

d. There is no pseudo-ring.

5 Routers A and C are reconfigured as follows:

Router A changes the following:

```
dlsw remote-peer 0 tcp 2.2.2.2 rif-passthru
```

Router C changes the following:

```
source-bridge ring-group 21
dlsw remote-peer 0 tcp 1.1.1.1 rif-passthru
```

What is the RIF from Host A to Host C?

a. 0830.01b9.021d.0120

b. 0830.01b9.015d.00c0

c. 0830.01b9.0151.20c0

d. 0630.01b9.121d.0120

6 What is the correct configuration of Router B?

a.

```
interface loopback 0
 ip address 3.3.3.3 255.255.255.255
!
dlsw bridge-group 1
!
dlsw local-peer peer-id 3.3.3.3
dlsw remote-peer 0 tcp 1.1.1.1
dlsw remote-peer 0 tcp 2.2.2.2
!
interface ethernet 0
 bridge-group 5
```

b.

```
interface loopback 0
 ip address 3.3.3.3 255.255.255.255
!
source-bridge ring-group 21
source-bridge transparent 21 15 6 5
!
dlsw local-peer peer-id 3.3.3.3
dlsw remote-peer 0 tcp 1.1.1.1
dlsw remote-peer 0 tcp 2.2.2.2
!
interface ethernet 0
 bridge-group 5
interface loopback 0
 ip address 3.3.3.3 255.255.255.255
!
source-bridge ring-group 21
source-bridge transparent 21 15 6 1
dlsw transparent bridge-group 1
!
dlsw local-peer peer-id 3.3.3.3
dlsw remote-peer 0 tcp 1.1.1.1
dlsw remote-peer 0 tcp 2.2.2.2
!
interface ethernet 0
 bridge-group 5
```

c.

```
interface loopback 0
 ip address 3.3.3.3 255.255.255.255
!
dlsw transparent bridge-group 5
!
dlsw local-peer peer-id 3.3.3.3
dlsw remote-peer 0 tcp 1.1.1.1
dlsw remote-peer 0 tcp 2.2.2.2
!
interface ethernet 0
 bridge-group 5
```

This chapter covers the following topics needed to master the CCIE Routing and Switching (R&S) written exam:

- **Physical Layer Access**—CCIE blueprint requirements of physical access, such as T1, encoding, digital signal level 3 (DS-3), Synchronous Optical Network (SONET), and Synchronous Digital Hierarchy (SDH)
- **X.25**—CCIE blueprint requirements on X.25 topics, such as addressing, Link Access Procedure, Balanced (LAPB), error recovery, permanent virtual circuits (PVCs), and protocol translation
- **Frame Relay**—CCIE blueprint requirements on Frame Relay, such as Local Management Interface (LMI), data-link connection identifier (DLCI), PVCs, traffic shaping, committed information rate (CIR), forward explicit congestion notification (FECN), backward explicit congestion notification (BECN), and discard eligible (DE) bit
- **Integrated Services Digital Network (ISDN)**—CCIE blueprint requirements on ISDN, such as Link Access Procedure on the D channel (LAPD), Basic Rate Interface (BRI), Primary Rate Interface (PRI), mapping, B and D channel, and Dial backup using ISDN, as well as high-level data link control (HDLC) and Point-to-Point Protocol (PPP)
- **ATM Architecture**—CCIE blueprint requirements on Asynchronous Transfer Mode (ATM), such as PVC/switched virtual circuits (SVCs), ATM adaptation layer (AAL), Service Specific Connection Oriented Protocol (SSCOP), User-Network Interface/ Network-to-Network Interface (UNI/NNI), cell format, Quality of Service (QoS), Request For Comments (RFC) 2684 and 2225, Private Network-Network Interface (PNNI), and Interim-Interswitch Signaling Protocol (IISP)

CHAPTER 5

Wide-Area Networks

"Do I Know This Already?" Quiz

The purpose of this assessment quiz is to help you determine how to spend your limited study time. If you can answer most or all of these questions, you might want to skim the Foundation Topics section and return to it later as necessary. Review the Foundation Summary section and answer the questions at the end of the chapter to ensure that you have a strong grasp of the material covered. If you intend to read the entire chapter, you do not necessarily need to answer these questions now. If you find these assessment questions difficult, read through the entire Foundation Topics section and review it until you feel comfortable with your ability to answer all of the "Q & A" questions at the end of the chapter. The following questions are repeated at the end of the chapter in the Q & A section with additional questions to test your mastery of the material.

Select the best answer. Answers to these questions are in the Appendix, "Answers to Quiz Questions."

1 Which framing standard does X.25 use?

a. HDLC

b. LAPB

c. LAPF

d. LAPD

2 What is the significance of the DE bit?

a. Used in X.25 as a discard error to recover frames

b. Used in ATM to recover from cells with errors

c. Used in Frame Relay to specify discard eligible frames

d. Used in PPP to discard frames

3 What is an NT1 in ISDN architecture?

a. A device that connects the TE2 to the LE

b. Usually lies between the R and S reference points

c. Same as a NT4

d. A device that connects the 4-wire BRI to the 2-wire phone line

4 What is a BECN in Frame Relay?

a. A notification to the destination, indicating congestion in the path from source to destination

b. A notification to the source, indicating congestion in the path from source to destination

c. A notification to the destination, indicating congestion in the path from destination to source

d. A notification to the source, indicating congestion in the path from destination to source

5 Inverse ARP provides what type of address resolution?

a. MAC address to IP address

b. DLCI to IP address

c. X.121 address to IP address

d. ATM address to IP address

6 How many bits are there in a Frame Relay DLCI?

a. 8 bits

b. 10 bits

c. 16 bits

d. 32 bits

7 Which authentication protocol do you use with PPP and encrypted passwords?

a. PPP authentication

b. PAP

c. CHAP

d. SecureID

8 ISDN's D channel uses which framing standard?

a. HDLC

b. LAPB

c. LAPF

d. LAPD

9 For the following configuration, when does the BRI become active?

```
interface serial 0
 ip address 1.1.1.1 255.255.255.252
 backup load 75 10
 backup interface bri 0
```

a. When serial 0 is down for 60 seconds

b. When serial 0 is up for 10 seconds

c. When serial 0 is above 75 percent use

d. When serial 0 is below 10 percent use

10 What does the following command do?

```
x25 map ip 172.18.1.5 12121212 broadcast
```

a. Maps the remote IP address to the remote X.121 address

b. Maps the remote IP address to the local X.121 address

c. Maps the local IP address to the remote X.121 address

d. Maps the local IP address to the local X.121 address

11 Which of the following are layers in the ATM reference model?

a. Physical

b. Data-link

c. ATM

d. Network

e. Transport

f. Presentation

g. Adaptation

h. Session

i. Application

12 How many bytes are in an ATM cell?

a. 21

b. 48

c. 53

d. 128

13 How are ATM payload cells uniquely identified by a switch?

a. By the cell's IP address

b. By the cell's VPI/VCI address

c. By the cell's NSAP address

d. By the cell's AESA address

14 Which ATM class of service is most appropriate for raw video?

a. CBR

b. nrt-VBR

c. ABR

d. UBR

15 In what order does each of the following queues get processed on a DPT ring node?

1. Low-priority transmit queue

2. Low-priority transit queue

3. High-priority transmit queue

4. High-priority transit queue

a. 4,3,2,1

b. 3,4,2,1

c. 4,3,1,2

d. 3,4,1,2

16 Which ATM class of service is most appropriate for Frame Relay data?

a. CBR

b. VBR

c. ABR

d. UBR

17 RFC 2225 provides a method of encapsulating which of the following protocols over ATM?

a. XNS

b. IP

c. IPX

d. SNA

Foundation Topics

Physical Layer Access

This section reviews definitions of physical technologies and the speeds available for each. You need to understand the basic characteristics of synchronization, T1/E1 encoding and line speeds, SONET/SDH, and DTP/SRP.

Synchronous Lines

Most WAN lines run over physical time-division multiplexed (TDM) networks. These circuits are synchronous, meaning that they are dependent on having the same clock so that the receiving side knows exactly when each frame bit is received.

Many synchronous line speeds are available, which are based on the basic digital signal level 0 (DS-0) rate of 64 kbps. In North America, the most common is the T1 carrier. It has a capacity of 1.544 Mbps and can carry 24 DS-0s at 24 × 64 kbps = 1.536 Mbps of bandwidth. Each DS-0 carries data traffic.

In Europe and other countries, the E1 is most common. It has a capacity of 2.048 Mbps and can carry 30 DS-0s at 30 × 64 kbps = 1.920 Mbps.

For both T1s and E1s, less than a full range of individual channels might be used. Fractional T1 or E1 service uses one or more 64 kbps and the DS-0 channel to provide the desired bandwidth.

A T3 is a dedicated phone connection that supports data rates of approximately 45 Mbps. A T3 line actually consists of 672 individual DS-0 channels. The T3 is also commonly called DS-3 and carries 28 T1 lines.

Encoding Schemes of T1s and E1s

Bipolar 8-zero substitution (B8ZS) is a T1 carrier line code in which bipolar violations are deliberately inserted if the data contains a string of 8 or more consecutive 0s. B8ZS ensures a sufficient number of transitions to maintain system synchronization when the user data stream contains an insufficient number of 1s. The European hierarchy uses B8ZS at the T1 rate.

Alternate mark inversion (AMI) is a T1 carrier line code in which 1s are represented by positive or negative voltage, alternatively. A 0 is represented by 0 volts.

SONET and SDH

SONET is an ANSI standard that defines physical interface rates, which allows data streams at different rates to be multiplexed. SONET defines Optical Carrier (OC) levels. North America uses SONET. The rates are as follows:

- OC-1 = 51.85 Mbps
- OC-3 = 155.52 Mbps
- OC-12 = 622.08 Mbps
- OC-24 = 1.244 Gbps
- OC-48 = 2.488 Gbps
- OC-192 = 9.952 Gbps

SONET uses the Synchronous Transport Signal (STS) as its frame format and STS level 1 (STS-1) is the basic signal rate, at 51.84 Mbps. Each SONET frame is constructed of 9 rows by 90 columns of octets for a total of 810 octets (9 rows × 90 columns = 810 octets). These 810 octets are transmitted in 125 μsecs, or 8000 frames/second (8000 × 125 μsec = 1 second). The basic rate for the STS-1 channel is 51.84 Mbps (810 bytes/frame × 8 bits/byte × 8000 frames/second = 51.84 Mbps).

SDH is the international standard defined by the International Telecommunication Union (ITU) for transmission over fiber optics. It defines the hierarchy of rates starting at 155.52 Mbps. The rates are as follows:

- STM-1 = 155.52 Mbps
- STM-4 = 622.08 Mbps
- STM-16 = 2.488 Gbps

One way to transmit network layer packets over a SONET/SDH network is to use ATM to establish connections and provide traffic management over the SONET network.

An alternative is to use Packet over SONET (PoS), which typically adds less overhead from frame headers than ATM does with cells. PoS maps IP directly onto SONET/SDH. PoS has three main components: a link-layer protocol, octet framing to map onto the SONET payload, and data scrambling for data security and reliability. For the link layer, PPP over SONET/SDH is defined in RFC 2615. SONET/SDH links are provisioned as point-to-point circuits, making PPP a suitable choice for the link-layer protocol. As RFC 2615 describes, PPP treats SONET/SDH as octet-oriented synchronous links. Octet-oriented framing (PPP with HDLC-like framing) is defined in RFC 1662. Data scrambling is defined in RFC 2615 and prevents packets with bit patterns that might cause synchronization problems, emulates the SDH set-reset scrambler pattern, and replicates the STS-N frame alignment word.

Both ATM and PPP are discussed in this chapter.

PoS specifies STS-3c/STM-1 (155 Mbps) as the basic data rate, with a usable data bandwidth of 149.760 Mbps.

Dynamic Packet Transport (DPT)/Spatial Reuse Protocol (SRP)

DPT is a Cisco developed, resilient optical packet ring technology that is optimized for data transmission. DPT uses dual, counter-rotating rings that are referred to as inner and outer, which can be used for data and control packet transmission concurrently. DPT operates by sending the data packets in one direction on one fiber ring and the corresponding control packets in the opposite direction on the other fiber ring.

The full capacity of the fiber rings can be utilized for data and control traffic. It is not required to reserve half of the capacity for redundancy.

DPT uses the Spatial Reuse Protocol (SRP) MAC layer protocol, which, according to Cisco, was designed to be scalable and provide optimized IP packet aggregation and transport in local-area networks (LANs), metropolitan-area networks (MANs), and wide-area networks (WANs). It can support up to 128 nodes running at high speeds (OC-48c/STM-16c and OC-192c/STM-64c). The fairness algorithm and packet priority ensures IP packets with bounded end-to-end delay requirements are delivered successfully.

Bandwidth Efficiency

SRP uses destination stripping to increase bandwidth capacity. Other ring technologies, such as Token Ring or Fiber Distributed Data Interface (FDDI), use source stripping—packets traverse the entire ring before being stripped by the source. With SRP, the packet travels on the ring from the source to the destination, and the destination strips the packet, which frees up bandwidth on other segments of the ring for use by other stations.

Fairness

A fairness algorithm is implemented to ensure that all stations on DPT rings can use a fair share of the ring. A distributed copy of the SRP fairness algorithm is run on each DPT station. As defined by Cisco, the fairness algorithm ensures the following:

- **Global fairness**—Each ring node gets its fair share of the ring by controlling the rate at which packets are transmitted onto the ring. When a node is congested, it sends a control message to its upstream neighbor, indicating its own transmit usage. The upstream neighbor adjusts its transmission rate to not exceed the advertised value. This upstream neighbor then propagates the advertised usage to its upstream neighbor. If one of the upstream neighbors is also congested, it propagates the minimum of the advertised usage and its own usage. This procedure ensures that no one node hogs all the bandwidth, creating starvation or excessive delay.

- **Local optimization**—A ring node can transmit more than its fair share of bandwidth to another node on a local segment, as long as nodes on other sections of the ring are not adversely impacted.
- **Scalability**—The fairness algorithm has highly efficient and scalable bandwidth control and can handle up to 128 nodes running at high speeds (OC-48c/STM-16c and OC-192c/STM-64c) over widely distributed geographic areas.

Packet Priority

SRP provides packet priority marking and expedited priority packet handling. SRP provides special handling in the transmit queue and transit buffer. Transmit packets are originated onto the DPT ring by the transmitting node. Transit packets originate in another ring node. A 3-bit priority field is in the SRP MAC header. There is a mapping between these bits and the IP precedence bit values in the type of service (ToS) field in the IP header. The node sourcing the packet onto the ring sets the SRP priority bits. However, only two queues (high priority and low priority) are in SRP for the transmit queue and the transit queue. The SRP node utilizes configurable threshold values to determine into which queue the packets are placed. The packet scheduler in the node utilizes specific packet handling rules to determine which queue is serviced next. The rules are as follows:

1. High-priority transit packets first
2. High-priority transmit packets
3. Low-priority transmit packets
4. Low-priority transit packets

This hierarchy is modified by placing a threshold on the low-priority transit queues to ensure that the transit queue does not overflow while the node is servicing low-priority locally sourced traffic, and the transit queue does not have to wait too long behind locally sourced low-priority traffic.

Ring Resiliency

DPT uses Intelligent Protection Switching (IPS), which uses SRP control packets to proactively monitor ring performance to perform fault isolation and to provide self-healing rings by wrapping around outages within 50 ms. If multiple events occur concurrently, IPS uses event hierarchy rules to determine which events to handle and which events to handle first.

IPS is multilayer aware. It monitors and handles events at Layers 1, 2, and 3 instead of just Layer 1. An event that occurs at Layer 3 is important, but it might not justify a ring wrap. In this case, the node with a Layer-3 problem can automatically or administratively enter SRP pass-through mode. In this state, any packet entering the node is forwarded at the MAC layer to the next node. The problem node is invisible to the ring. It does not perform any address lookup on any received packets, it does not pass packets up to Layer 3, and it does not transmit packets that are received from Layer 3. It does not participate in the SRP fairness algorithm.

X.25

This section covers the X.25 topics that are listed in the blueprint for the CCIE written test. Although newer WAN technologies are popular, networks still use X.25. The CCIE candidate should know that this protocol is used primarily on unreliable links because it implements error correction, unlike Frame Relay, on each link. X.25 is connection-oriented, which provides for error checking and recovery.

X.25 is defined by the ITU. Routers and other devices perform the roles of data terminal equipment (DTE) and data circuit-terminating equipment (DCE). Routers are typically DTEs that are connecting to modems or packet switches, which perform the DCE function.

X.25 is a three-layer protocol, corresponding to the first three layers of the OSI model. At Layer 1, the physical layer, X.25 uses protocols such as RS-232, V.24, V.35 and X.21. The data-link level uses HDLC LAPB. The network layer uses the X.25 Packet Layer Protocol (PLP). The X.25 PLP is concerned with the functions required to move data, such as virtual circuit (VC) initialization and termination, data transfer between two DTEs, flow control on a VC, network level error detection and recovery, and data integrity.

X.25 VCs

X.25 implements VCs as a logical connection between two end devices (DTEs), as shown in Figure 5-1. Physically, the connection can pass through many interconnecting nodes (switches) on the network. X.25 circuits can be switched or permanent. PVCs are always available to transfer data. SVCs are temporary connections for sporadic data transfers. SVCs need to be established before data is transferred. After the data is transferred, the SVC is terminated.

X.121 Addressing

X.25 uses X.121 addresses. The address field includes the International Data Number (IDN). The IDN consists of two fields: the Data Network Identification Code (DNIC) and the National Terminal Number (NTN). Figure 5-2 shows the format for the addresses. The DNIC is an optional field that identifies the exact packet switching node in which the destination DTE is located. The DNIC has Country and PSN subfields.

Figure 5-1 *X.25 Network*

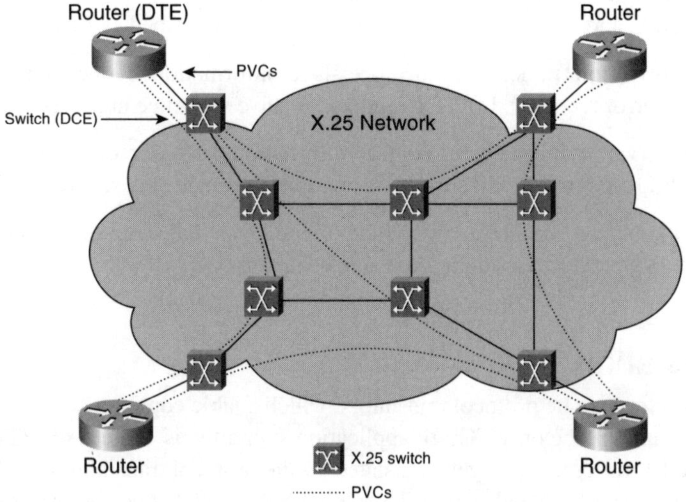

Figure 5-2 *X.121 Address Format*

DNIC		
Country	PSN	NTN

X.25 Framing

X.25 uses HDLC LAPB as the Layer-2 protocol to manage communication between DTE and DCE devices. The LAPB frame has the format, as shown in Figure 5-3.

Figure 5-3 *LAPB Frame Format*

Bytes: 1	1	1	Variable	1	1
Flag	Address	Control	Data	FCS	Flag

Flag is the bit stream 01111110, which indicates the beginning or end of the frame. The address field indicates command or response. The control field indicates if the frame is an information, supervisory, or unnumbered frame. The frame check sequence (FCS) handles error checking. LAPB takes care of error detection and link recovery. In contrast, Frame Relay lets the upper-layer protocol detect the error and handle the retransmission.

LAPB Frame Types

The control field in the LAPB frame indicates one of three frame types: information, supervisory, and unnumbered. The frame types are described as follows:

- Information frames carry the upper-layer information. Sequencing is part of flow control and error recovery. I frames send and receive sequence numbers.
- Supervisory frames carry control information, such as requests for transmissions, acknowledgment, and status information. S frames only receive sequence numbers.
- Unnumbered frames perform functions such as link setup or disconnection and error reporting. U frames do not use sequence numbers.

Protocol Translation

Cisco routers can be protocol translators, which enable communication between X.25 and IP end stations. The only TCP/IP application supported is Telnet. An IP host can Telnet to a specific IP address, which gets translated by the protocol translator to an X.121 address and forwarded to an X.25 end station. The global command that performs this function is **translate tcp** *ip-address* **x25** *x.121*. To translate from X.25 to Telnet, the parameters are reversed: **translate x25** *x.121* **tcp** *ip-address.*

Mapping

IP packets can be encapsulated in X.25 packets for transport over an X.25 network, which is referred to by Cisco as *mapping*. An X.25 **map** statement maps the IP address to the X.121 address associated with the remote IP router. In contrast to frame relay DLCIs, X.121 addresses are globally significant, which results in mapping to the destination X.121 address. Figure 5-4 illustrates the use of mapping.

The **map** command configured on Router A indicates that the next hop IP address, 172.18.1.6, which is on the remote side of the X.25 network, is reachable through the X.121 address 34343434. The **broadcast** keyword informs the router to encapsulate broadcast packets that originate on the IP network and forward them to the remote IP router.

Figure 5-4 *X.25 Configuration*

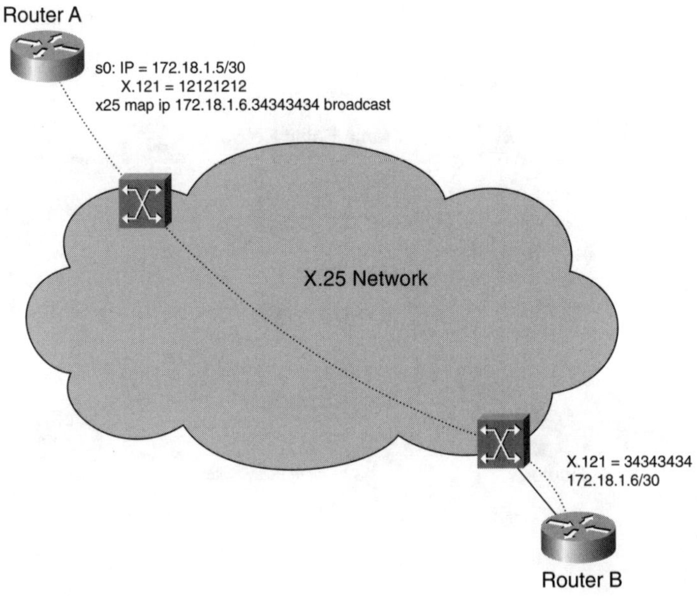

Frame Relay

This section covers the Frame Relay topics that are listed in the blueprint of the CCIE written test.

Frame Relay is a Layer-2 WAN service that sends information in frames. Each frame has an address that the network uses to determine the destination of the frame. Frame Relay was developed when lines became more reliable and the high-overhead link error checking that is found in X.25 was no longer required. This provided more available bandwidth for WAN connectivity. Similar to X.25, Frame Relay uses VCs. Frame Relay leaves the error checking to higher layer protocols. Frame Relay was initially defined by the Frame Relay Forum. More information and implementation agreements are at www.frforum.com.

As shown in Figure 5-5, router and other devices perform the function of DTE by connecting to a Frame Relay switch that has a DCE interface. Although SVCs are possible with Frame Relay, most implementations use PVCs.

Figure 5-5 *Frame Relay Service*

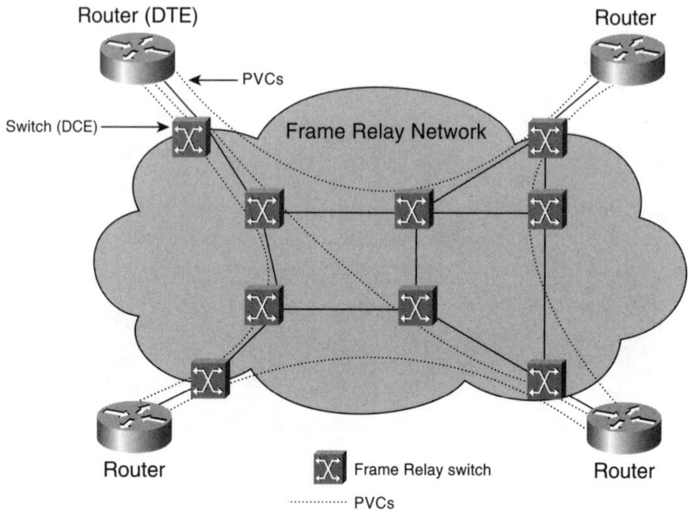

Frame Relay Encapsulation

There are two choices on Cisco routers for the encapsulation of network protocols over Frame Relay. Both support encapsulation of multiple protocols. One method is Cisco proprietary and is the default encapsulation. The other method is defined in RFC 2427, "Multiprotocol Interconnect over Frame Relay". RFC 2427 covers aspects of both bridging and routing and describes the procedure for fragmenting large frames over a Frame Relay network with a smaller MTU.

The encapsulation type must be the same on the two end systems (ESs) that are communicating over the Frame Relay network. If connecting to another vendor's router, unless that vendor supports Cisco encapsulation, you need to configure the ietf standard encapsulation. To configure ietf encapsulation, use the **ietf** keyword in the **encapsulation** command as follows:

```
interface serial 0
 encapsulation frame-relay ietf
```

Committed Information Rate (CIR)

Frame Relay is usually leased by carriers with a contract that bandwidth is guaranteed up to a maximum limit. Although the CIR guarantees the rate, the user traffic can burst to higher rates, if the provider's frame relay network is underutilized. The CIR is defined in two ways, and its use depends on the Frame Relay provider's implementation. The CIR is either the maximum speed that the Frame Relay provider transfers information for each PVC, or it is the average rate (in bps) at which the network guarantees to transfer data over a time T. Traffic can burst at rates above the CIR depending upon use within the carriers network. Traffic can burst above the CIR for an agreed upon amount of time.

Some parameters that define the allowable burst rate and amount of time a burst of traffic can be transmitted are T, B_c, and B_e. T is the time allowed to transmit B_c or B_c+B_e traffic. B_c is the committed burst size; the maximum number of data that can be transmitted during time T. B_e is the maximum number of uncommitted data bits that the network carries during time T.

Local Management Interface (LMI)

LMI is a set of enhancements to the original Frame Relay specification. The LMI extensions include global addressing, virtual-circuit status messages, and multicasting. With LMI, control messages are sent between the DTE and DCE proving status information about the switch and PVCs.

NOTE The LMI type is significant between the local router and connecting Frame Relay switch. The remote router-switch pair can implement a different LMI format.

There are three types of LMI implementations. The LMI type can be set per serial interface with the following command:

```
frame-relay lmi-type {ansi | cisco | q933a}
```

Cisco routers perform autosensing of the LMI type with IOS 11.2 or higher. The **lmi-type** command does not need to be configured on routers running newer code.

Data Link Connection Identifier (DLCI)

Frame Relay uses the DLCI to identify VCs. Each DLCI has local significance. The DLCI number at Router A can be different than the DLCI number at Router B for the same PVC. As shown in Figure 5-6, each router uses the local DLCI number to reach another through the Frame Relay network. Router A uses DLCI 200 to reach Router B, DLCI 300 to reach Router C, and DLCI 400 to reach Router D.

Figure 5-6 *Frame Relay DLCI*

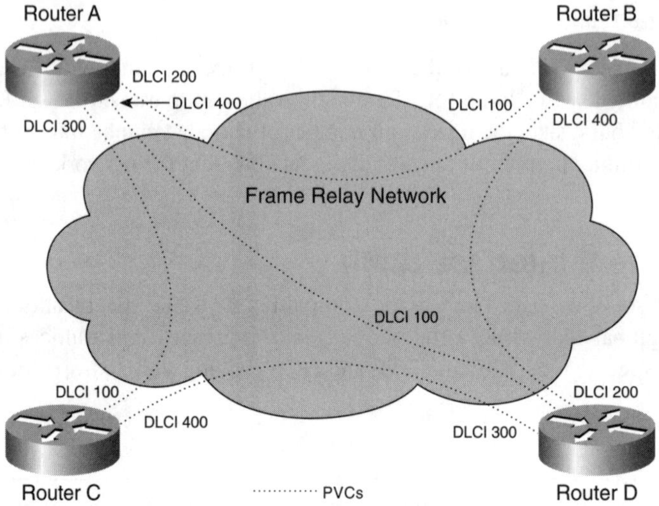

The DLCI is configured for each interface or subinterface to mark the appropriate PVC. For example, the following **frame relay** command configures DLCI 100 on interface serial 0.1:

```
interface serial 0.1 point-to-point
 ip address 192.168.1.5 255.255.255.252
 frame-relay interface-dlci 100
```

Frame Relay Inverse Address Resolution Protocol (InARP)

Frame Relay Inverse ARP maps remote protocol addresses to local DLCI numbers. It is on by default and prevents the need to manually configure DLCI mappings in full mesh topologies (multipoint). Inverse-ARP requests are sent on all VCs when a multipoint interface or VC becomes active.

To configure Inverse ARP, use the **frame-relay inverse-arp** command.

To erase Inverse-ARP mappings, use the **clear frame-relay inarp** command.

Congestion Control

Frame Relay has few control and error mechanisms as compared with X.25, but these have been sufficient, and in fact, contribute to the popularity of the protocol. The following are methods that determine or reduce congestion and errors in the network:

- Forward explicit congestion notification (FECN)
- Backward explicit congestion notification (BECN)

- DE bit
- Frame Relay Error check

When a router sends a frame into the Frame Relay network, it can traverse many switches. If the frame reaches a switch that is experiencing congestion, the switch sets the FECN bit in the frame. The receiving router receives the frame with the FECN bit set. It's up to the upper-layer protocols to determine what to do about the congestion. Sometimes, this bit is just ignored. The BECN functions similar to FECN bits, but the BECN bit is set by the switch on frames heading in the opposite direction of frames experiencing congestion. It is set on frames heading back to the source of the traffic. Depending on the implementation, a flow-control scheme can be used or the BECN can be ignored.

The DE bit marks frames that are eligible to be discarded if the Frame Relay switch becomes congested. The Frame Relay network marks all frames in excess of the CIR as discard eligible. The router can attempt to influence which packets are discarded by marking the frames as discard eligible before they enter the Frame Relay network. The router can be configured to mark frames based on traffic type or other parameters. In Example 5-1, any World Wide Web traffic (on port 80) is marked as discard eligible on the egress of serial 0.1.

Example 5-1 *Configuration Defining Discard Eligible Traffic*

```
frame-relay de-list 1 protocol ip list 150
!
interface serial 0.1 point-to-point
 ip address 192.168.1.5 255.255.255.252
 frame-relay interface-dlci 100
 frame-relay de-group 1 100
!
access-list 150 permit tcp any any eq www
```

Frame Relay also performs a cyclic redundancy check (CRC) to determine errored frames. Frame Relay performs error checking and not error correction. Again, the upper-layer protocol (TCP/IP) is responsible to correct errors or re-send packets.

Frame Relay Frame Format

Frame Relay uses Link Access Procedure for Frame Relay (LAPF) for frame format. LAPF is yet another variation of the HDLC frame format; it supports Frame Relay. There is no control frame, flow control, and error control, and no sequence numbers. Figure 5-7 shows the LAPF frame format.

Figure 5-7 *Frame Relay LAPF Frame Format*

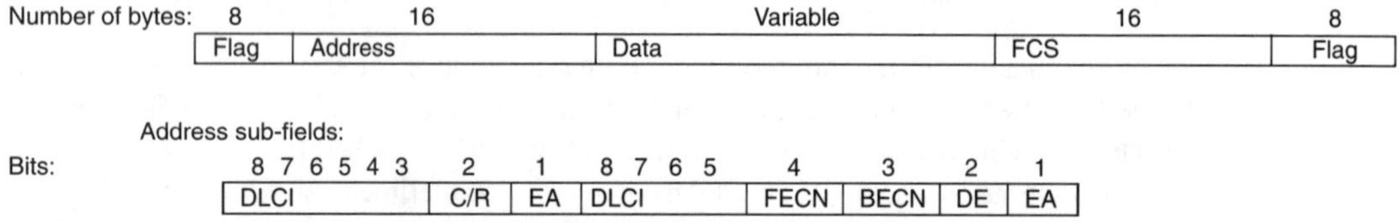

The 10-bit DLCI provides the PVC identifier, which has local significance between the router and the Frame Relay switch. The C/R bit is not used. The EA (extended address) bit is a mechanism that extends the address field an additional 2 bytes. There are two EA bits in a 16-bit address field. The eighth bit of every byte in the address field indicates the extended address. If the bit is set to 0, the containing byte is not the last byte of the address. If the bit is set to 1, the byte is the last byte of the address. Implementations that use the nonextended DLCI addresses set the first EA bit to 0 and the second EA bit to 1.

The control field has the three bits: FECN, BECN, and DE, which were discussed in the previous section.

Table 5-1 displays the Frame Relay LAPF frame address field.

Table 5-1 *Frame Relay LAPF Frame Address Field*

Bit	Description
DLCI	10-bit PVC identifier
C/R	Not used
EA	Extended Address; indicates if the containing byte is the last in the addressing field; a mechanism to extend DLCI length beyond 10 bits
FECN	Bit set in frames traveling to the destination, when congestion is on traffic from source to destination
BECN	Bit set in frames traveling to the source, when congestion is on traffic from source to destination
DE	Bit set to indicate that the frame is eligible for discard

Frame Relay LMI Frame Relay Format

The LMI frame format is shown in Figure 5-8.

Figure 5-8 *LMI Frame Format*

Number of bytes:	1	2	1	1	1	1	Variable	2	1
	Flag	LMI DLCI	UII	PD	Call Ref	Message Type	Info Elements	FCS	Flag

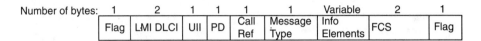

Table 5-2 describes the fields of the LMI frame.

Table 5-2 *LMI Fields*

Field	Description
LMI DLCI	The LMI DLCI is 1023 if you use a cisco-type LMI. It is 0 if you use either ANSI or ITU (q333a).
UII	Unnumbered Information Indicator; sets the poll/final bit to 0.
PD	Protocol Discriminator; contains a value indicating that the frame is an LMI frame.
Call Ref	Call Reference. This field always contains 0s and is not currently used.
Message type	Status-inquiry message—Allows a user device to inquire about the status of the network. Status message—Response to an inquiry message.
IE	Information Elements; contains IE identifiers and data.
FCS	Frame check sequence; verifies the data.
Flags	Delimits the beginning and end of the frame and is always binary 01111110.

Frame Relay Traffic Shaping (FRTS)

FRTS allows for the management of traffic congestion in Frame Relay networks. FRTS-enabled routers use received BECN information as input to manage the outbound traffic. FRTS is enabled on the major interface, and traffic classes are defined in global configuration. A traffic class is applied to each subinterface as it applies.

You can use FRTS in several ways: for rate enforcement on an individual VC by configuring the peak transmission rate, to dynamically throttle traffic on a VC when BECNs are received, or for enhanced queuing support by enabling custom or priority queuing on a VC.

Rate enforcement is shown in Example 5-2. The FRTS class 128 KB is configured for a CIR rate of 128 kbps and a burst rate of 256 kbps. The FRTS 512 KB class is configured with a CIR of 512 kbps and a burst rate (Bc + Be) of 1024 kbps.

Example 5-2 *FRTS Rate Enforcement*

```
interface serial 0
 encapsulation frame-relay
 frame-relay traffic-shaping
!
interface serial 0.1 point-to-point
 ip address 192.168.100.5 255.255.255.252
 frame-relay interface-dlci 100
 frame-relay class 128kb
!
interface serial 0.2 point-to-point
 ip address 192.168.100.9 255.255.255.252
 frame-relay interface-dlci 200
 frame-relay class 512kb
!
map-class frame-relay 128kb
 frame-relay traffic-rate 128000 256000
!
map-class frame-relay 512kb
 frame-relay traffic-rate 512000 1024000
```

The **frame-relay traffic-shaping** command enables traffic shaping for all VCs defined on the interface. The **frame-relay class** *map-class-name* command specifies the map class that is applied to the interface or subinterface. If this command is applied to a main interface, all the VCs on the interface's subinterfaces inherit the map class's properties. The actual properties for the FRTS are defined with the **map-class frame-relay** *map-class-name* command and all the map class subcommands. In Table 5-3, the traffic rate is specified with average and peak values. Other possible traffic shaping commands that are configured under **map-class frame-relay** are described in Table 5-3.

Table 5-3 *FRTS Traffic Shaping Commands*

Command	Description
frame-relay traffic-rate *average* [*peak*]	Defines the traffic rate for the VC.
frame-relay adaptive-shaping {**becn** | **foresight**}}}}	Enables dynamic traffic shaping based on received BECNs or ForeSight. ForeSight is a Cisco proprietary traffic control mechanism. This command replaces **frame-relay becn-response-enable**.
frame-relay custom-queue-list *list-number*	Defines a custom queue list number to apply to the VC.
frame-relay priority-group *list-number*	Defines a priority group number to apply to the VC to enable priority queuing. It applies the priority list that was defined at the global configuration level.

Frame Relay Compression

With Cisco routers, you can configure payload compression on point-to-point or multipoint interfaces. Either the Stacker method or FRF.9 using the Stacker method can be configured. The Stacker method uses an encoded dictionary to replace a stream of characters with codes. The symbols represented by the codes are stored in memory in a dictionary style list. The Stacker method is not discussed in this book; however, the following commands configure the router to use the Stacker method on frame-relay subinterfaces.

For point-to-point subinterfaces use the following command:

```
frame-relay payload-compress packet-by-packet
```

For multipoint subinterfaces, the command is as follows:

```
frame-relay map protocol protocol-address dlci payload-compress packet-by-packet
```

FRF.9 Compression

Implementation FRF.9 of the Frame Relay Forum provides standards-based compression on Frame Relay, therefore providing multivendor interoperability. FRF.9 uses higher compression ratios, which allows more data to be compressed for faster transmission.

To enable FRF.9 compression on a point-to-point subinterface, use the following command:

```
frame-relay payload-compress frf9 stac
```

For multipoint subinterfaces, the command is as follows:

```
frame-relay map protocol protocol-address dlci payload-compress frf9 stac
```

Frame Relay map Command

Before Inverse ARP was available (prior to 11.2), the most common method to configure Frame Relay was by using **map** statements. Looking at Figure 5-9, the serial interface configuration for Router A is displayed in Example 5-3, and the configuration for Router B is displayed in Example 5-4.

Example 5-3 *Router A Frame Relay Map Configuration Example*

```
interface serial 0
 ip address 172.18.1.5 255.255.255.252
 encapsulation frame-relay
 frame-relay map ip 172.18.1.6 150
```

Figure 5-9 *Frame Relay Map Configuration*

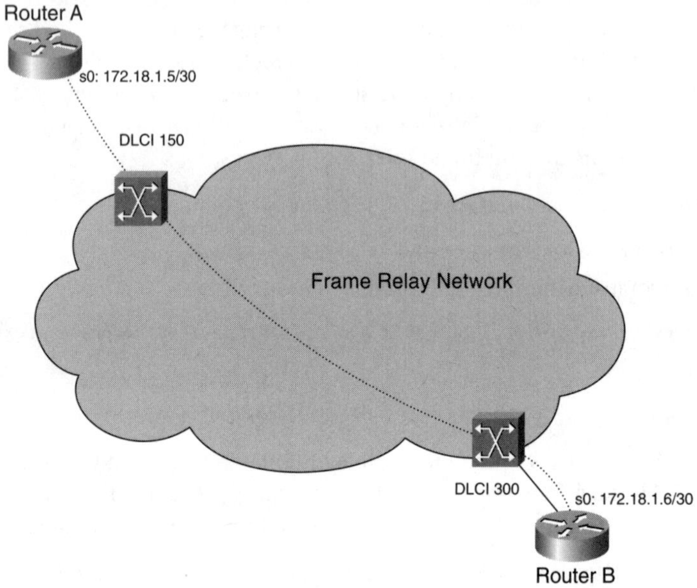

Example 5-4 *Router B Frame Relay Map Configuration Example*

```
interface serial 0
 ip address 172.18.1.6 255.255.255.252
 encapulation frame-relay
 frame-relay map ip 172.18.1.5 300
```

Frame Relay show Commands

The most common commands that observe Frame Relay status and configuration are the following:

- **show frame-relay map**
- **show frame-relay lmi**
- **show frame-relay pvc**

This section shows and explains sample outputs from each of these commands.

Example 5-5 shows output from the **show frame-relay map** command.

Example 5-5 **show frame-relay map** *Command*

```
R5#show frame-relay map
Serial0 (up): ip 172.16.1.3 dlci 103(0x67,0x1870), static,
              broadcast,
              CISCO, status defined, active
Serial0 (up): ip 172.16.1.1 dlci 101(0x65,0x1850), static,
              broadcast,
              CISCO, status defined, active
```

The output from the **show frame-relay map** command shows the current status and relevant information about the mappings. Example 5-5 shows two VCs mapped on serial 0. One has local DLCI 103, IP is the network protocol in use, and the remote IP address associated with DLCI 103 is 172.16.1.3. The numbers in parenthesis display DLCI numbers in two different ways: hexadecimal representation and the value of the 16-bit address field that contains the DLCI, extended address (EA), and congestion control bits. The other mapping shows that IP address 172.16.1.1 is the remote address associated with DLCI 101. Both mappings are statically defined, are configured to broadcast over the VC, use Cisco frame encapsulation, and are active.

The next command, **show frame-relay lmi**, displays the statistics learned through LMI. Example 5-6 shows the output of this command.

Example 5-6 **show frame-relay lmi** *Command*

```
R5#show frame-relay lmi

LMI Statistics for interface Serial0 (Frame Relay DTE) LMI TYPE = ANSI
  Invalid Unnumbered info 0                Invalid Prot Disc 0
  Invalid dummy Call Ref 0                 Invalid Msg Type 0
  Invalid Status Message 0                 Invalid Lock Shift 0
  Invalid Information ID 0                 Invalid Report IE Len 0
  Invalid Report Request 0                 Invalid Keep IE Len 0
  Num Status Enq. Sent 274284              Num Status msgs Rcvd 274285
  Num Update Status Rcvd 0                 Num Status Timeouts 0
```

The output from the command **show frame-relay lmi** displays the LMI statistics on all Frame Relay interfaces. Optionally, you can specify a particular serial interface with the command **show frame-relay lmi** *interface-type interface-number*. Example 5-6 shows that the LMI type on serial 0 is ansi. It also displays the statistics about LMI messages sent and received.

The **show frame-relay pvc** command displays information about each PVC. Optionally, you can specify a particular interface or a particular DLCI, **show frame-relay pvc** [**interface** *interface*] [*dlci*]. Example 5-7 displays information about all the Frame Relay PVCs on the router.

Example 5-7 **show frame-relay pvc** *Command*

```
R5#show frame-relay pvc

PVC Statistics for interface Serial0 (Frame Relay DTE)

              Active     Inactive      Deleted       Static
  Local          4          0             0             0
  Switched       0          0             0             0
  Unused         1          0             0             0

DLCI = 100, DLCI USAGE = LOCAL, PVC STATUS = ACTIVE, INTERFACE = Serial0

  input pkts 296622         output pkts 113774        in bytes 98478504
  out bytes 37772968        dropped pkts 0            in FECN pkts 0
  in BECN pkts 0            out FECN pkts 0           out BECN pkts 0
  in DE pkts 0              out DE pkts 0
  out bcast pkts 113774      out bcast bytes 37772968
  pvc create time 4w3d, last time pvc status changed 2w5d

DLCI = 101, DLCI USAGE = LOCAL, PVC STATUS = ACTIVE, INTERFACE = Serial0

  input pkts 80902          output pkts 59187         in bytes 6773114
  out bytes 4445196         dropped pkts 0            in FECN pkts 0
  in BECN pkts 0            out FECN pkts 0           out BECN pkts 0
  in DE pkts 0              out DE pkts 0
  out bcast pkts 0           out bcast bytes 0
  pvc create time 2w5d, last time pvc status changed 2w5d

DLCI = 103, DLCI USAGE = LOCAL, PVC STATUS = ACTIVE, INTERFACE = Serial0

  input pkts 10             output pkts 10            in bytes 1040
  out bytes 1040            dropped pkts 0            in FECN pkts 0
  in BECN pkts 0            out FECN pkts 0           out BECN pkts 0
  in DE pkts 0              out DE pkts 0
  out bcast pkts 0           out bcast bytes 0
  pvc create time 2w5d, last time pvc status changed 2w5d
```

The command output displayed in Example 5-7 shows that serial 0 has five PVCs. Four are local PVCs, one is unused, and all are active. PVCs are local when the router is a DTE, switched when the router is a DCE, and unused when there is no user-entered configuration information about the PVC. A PVC is marked as inactive when an LMI status report indicates that it is not active. The PVC is marked as deleted when the PVC is not listed at all in the periodic LMI status message. Detailed statistics about three of the PVCs are shown in the example. DLCI 100 is local, active, and associated with serial 0. Statistics about frames sent and received on the PVC are displayed, and you can see that the PVC was created 4 weeks and 3 days ago and that it last changed status 2 weeks and 5 days ago.

ISDN

ISDN services are offered by telephone carriers that provide digital telephony and data-transport services. ISDN links transport voice, video, and data traffic. For the CCIE test, it is important to understand the architecture, interfaces, and protocols in ISDN.

ISDN Architecture

ISDN specifications define component types and reference points for its architecture. The ISDN components are as follows:

- **TA (Terminal Adapter)**—Connects non-ISDN equipment to the ISDN network.
- **TE1 (Terminal Equipment type 1)**—Any terminal equipment, such as a router or telephone, with an ISDN BRI. This device has a four-wire interface and is ISDN compatible.
- **TE2 (Terminal Equipment type 2)**—Any terminal or router that is not ISDN compatible. It connects to the TA through a EIA/TIA-232 or V.35 interface. The TA connects the TE2 device to the ISDN network. Its input is the physical EIA/TIA-232 interface, and the output is the ISDN BRI.
- **NT1 (Network Termination type 1)**—A network termination device responsible for the termination of the ISDN transmission facility at the customer premises. The NT1 connects the 4-wire ISDN interface to the 2-wire phone line. In North America, the customer provides this device. In the rest of the world, the carrier usually provides this device.
- **NT2 (Network Termination type 2)**—Provides switching and concentration of ISDN lines between customer premise equipment, such as digital PBXs. The NT2 provides Layer-2 and Layer-3 protocol and concentration functions. NT2 can be combined with an NT1.
- **LE (Local Exchange)**—The carrier's ISDN central office (CO).

The ISDN architecture defines four reference points that are shown in Figure 5-10. The U (user) reference point is located between the NT1 device and the local exchange. The ISDN local loop in North America is a U reference point, which is a single pair of wires. The T (terminal) reference point is the two pair of wires located between the NT1 and NT2 equipment, if necessary. The S (system) reference point is located between user terminals (TE1 or TA) with BRI interfaces and the NT2. Usually, the S and T points are combined as S/T where the NT1 and NT2 are combined into a single device, sometimes referred to as NT12. And finally, the R (rate) reference point is located between the TE2 (non-ISDN terminals) and the TA.

Figure 5-10 *ISDN Architecture*

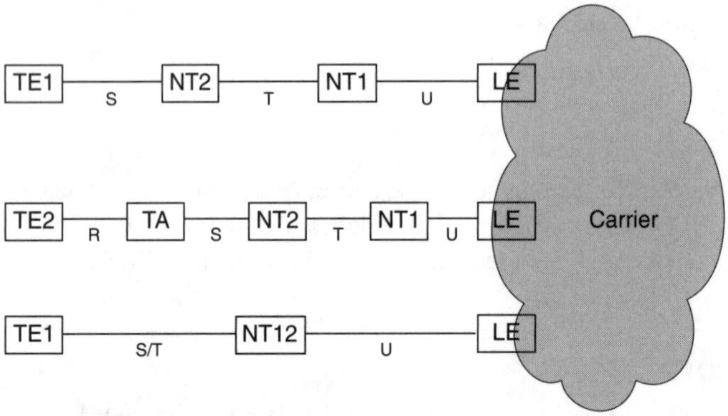

The following summarize the reference points:

- U—Between NT1 and LE, 2-wire
- T—Between NT2 and NT1, 4-wire
- S—Between TE1 or TA and NT2
- R—Between TE1 and TA, usually an EIA/TIA-232

ISDN Interfaces

ISDN interfaces (or services) are provided in two major forms. First, the BRI provides two bearer (B) channels and one data signaling (D) channel. Each B channel operates at 64 kbps and carries data traffic. The D channel operates at 16 kbps and carries signaling and control information. In some instances, you can use the D channel for additional data traffic. BRI interfaces are referred to as 2B+D.

Datagram encapsulation is required on BRI interfaces to provide data connectivity. Usually, you use PPP encapsulation, although HDLC is the default. All the options for datagram encapsulation are shown in Example 5-8. Frame Relay and X.25 are discussed in this chapter. HDLC and PPP are covered in this section. Combinet Proprietary Protocol (CPP) is not covered in this book.

Example 5-8 *ISDN Encapsulation Options*

```
R5(config-if)#encapsulation ?
  cpp          Combinet proprietary protocol
  frame-relay  Frame Relay networks
  hdlc         Serial HDLC synchronous
  lapb         LAPB (X.25 Level 2)
  ppp          Point-to-Point protocol
  x25          X.25
```

The second ISDN interface is the PRI. In North America and Japan, PRIs offer 23 B channels and 1 D channel (23B+D). In other countries, PRIs offer 30 B channels and 1 D channel (30B+D). In PRIs, the D channel has 64 kbps of bandwidth. The 23B+D PRIs run over T1 circuits with 1.522 Mbps of total bandwidth, and 30B+D PRIs run over E-1 circuits with 2.048 Mbps of total bandwidth.

More information on ISDN BRI and PRI is in the ITU-T specifications I.430 (BRI) and I.431 (PRI).

ISDN Layer-1 Frames

ISDN frames are 48 bits in length. There are two formats: one for outbound (toward the ISDN network) and inbound (from the network). Figure 5-11 shows the frame formats.

Figure 5-11 *ISDN Layer-1 Frame Formats*

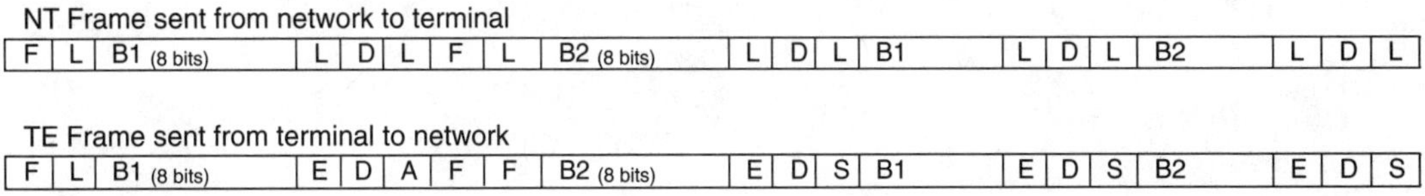

The bits are as follows:

- F—Framing bit for synchronization
- L—Load balancing bit that adjusts the average bit value
- E—Echo of previous D-bit, for contention resolution
- A—Activation bit
- S—Unused
- D—D channel (16 kbps)
- B1—First B channel
- B2—Second B channel

ISDN Layer-2 Protocols

At Layer 2 the ISDN B channels can be encapsulated with X.25, Frame Relay, HDLC, or PPP. The D channel is encapsulated with LAPD or X.25. These protocols are covered in this section.

LAPD

ISDN uses LAPD as the signaling protocol at Layer 2. LAPD is specified in the ITU-T Q.921 standard. You use LAPD on the D channel to ensure proper flow and transmission of the signaling and control information.

The LAPD frame format is shown in Figure 5-12. The address field is similar to the address field in HDLC. The Service Access Point Identifier (SAPI) identifies the LAPD services that are provided to the upper layer (Layer 3). The C/R bit indicates if the frame is a command or response. The terminal endpoint identifier (TEI) identifies single or multiple terminals. If the TEI is all 1s, it indicates a broadcast.

Figure 5-12 *LAPD Frame Format*

Flag	Address	Control	Data	FCS	Flag

Address Field:

SAPI	C/R	EA	TEI	EA

HDLC

HDLC is a leased-line encapsulation method that you commonly use in point-to-point connections. The HDLC standard was developed by the ISO (ISO 3309). Cisco modified the standard by adding a Type field to the frame. Cisco routers use this proprietary version of HDLC. The B channels in ISDN can use HDLC encapsulation. The frame format for HDLC is the same as in LAPD except for some differences in the Address field. On a Cisco router, HDLC encapsulation can only connect with another Cisco router; it is enabled by default.

PPP

PPP is an encapsulation protocol for transporting Layer-3 traffic over point-to-point links. Also, PPP can be configured over other WAN serial lines, including Frame Relay PVCs.

PPP encapsulation can also establish an end-to-end PPP connection over other networks, such as Ethernet (PPPoE). This use of PPP is not discussed in this book.

PPP consists of three major components:

- Encapsulation of packets over serial links using HDLC frame structure as a basis
- Establishment, maintenance, and termination of circuits with the Link Control Program (LCP)
- Multiplexing of upper-layer protocols with Network Control Programs (NCPs)

PPP Frame Format

The PPP frame format is shown in Figure 5-13.

Figure 5-13 *PPP Frame Format*

Bytes:	1	1	1	1	Varies	2 or 4
	Flag	Address	Control	Protocol	Data	FCS

The flag field indicates the start of the frame consisting of binary sequence 01111110.

The address field is set to 11111111; PPP does not assign individual addresses.

The control field contains the binary sequence 00000011, which calls for transmission of user data in an unnumbered frame. A connectionless link service similar to that of Logical Link Control (LLC) Type 1 is provided.

The protocol field identifies the upper-layer protocol.

The data field contains the upper-layer datagram.

FCS handles error detection.

PPP Link Control Protocol (LCP)

The PPP LCP establishes, configures, maintains, and terminates point-to-point links. LCP opens the connection and negotiates configuration parameters before any Layer-3 packets can be exchanged. LCP can be configured to determine if the link quality is sufficient. After this phase is complete, the authentication protocols and NCP take over.

PPP Authentication

Authentication is optional in PPP. The two types of authentication that you can use are the Password Authentication Protocol (PAP) and the Challenge Authentication Protocol (CHAP). PAP was developed earlier and uses cleartext passwords, thus leaving password open to be seen in protocol analyzers.

CHAP, described in RFC 1994, uses encrypted passwords. CHAP uses a three-way challenge-response handshake to authenticate between the ESs. This is done upon initial link establishment and can be repeated anytime after the link has been established. The procedure, as defined in RFC 1994, is as follows:

- After the Link Establishment phase is complete, the authenticator sends a challenge message to the peer.
- The peer responds with a value calculated by using a one-way hash function.

- The authenticator checks the response against its own calculation of the expected hash value. If the values match, the authentication is acknowledged; otherwise, the connection should be terminated.
- At random intervals, the authenticator sends a new challenge to the peer and repeats the previous steps.

PPP Network Control Protocol (NCP)

After LCP link establishment and authentication, NCPs determine and configure the network layer protocols. The NCP uses the IP Control Protocol (IPCP) to negotiate and establish IP peering over a PPP link. Described in RFC 1332, IPCP is responsible for configuring, enabling, and disabling the IP protocol modules on both ends of the point-to-point link. IPCP uses the same packet exchange mechanism as the LCP.

PPP Multilink Protocol (MP)

Described in RFC 1990, the MP provides a means to group or bundle multiple independent links between two systems to aggregate the bandwidth of the individual links. The individual links can be ISDN B channels, async lines, or other PPP links, such as synchronous links, Frame Relay, or X.25. The bundle does not need to be composed of identical link types. Physical links are configured to be part of the MP bundle. A virtual interface represents the bundle. The MP bundle is either configured to be connected indefinitely, as might be the case when multiple T1 circuits make up the bundle, or to be activated as traffic load reaches a predefined threshold, such as when dial-up links provide extra bandwidth between two routers. When the combined load on the active physical links reaches a configured load threshold, additional links are activated. The load threshold can be based on inbound traffic, outbound traffic, or either but cannot be based on the combined total of inbound and outbound traffic.

MP provides packet fragmentation and reassembly, sequencing, multivendor interoperability, and load balancing. Packets are fragmented and sent simultaneously on the individual physical links to the remote destination, which reassembles the packet. MP enables bandwidth on demand and reduces transmission latency across WAN links.

MP links are configured during the LCP link establishment phase. Particular elements that must be negotiated are the Maximum Received Reconstructed Unit (MRRU) and the Endpoint Discriminator (Endpoint Disc). These values must be the same on both ends of each connection. After LCP and authentication is complete, a Virtual Access interface is created for the bundle and NCP operates over the bundle.

ISDN Configuration

ISDN is configured on the router by specifying the ISDN switch type that the router is connecting to and then configuring the interface parameters.

Nine switch types can be configured, as shown in Example 5-9. In the United States, the Lucent 5ESS, Northern Telecom DMS-100, or National ISDN switch types are commonly used.

Example 5-9 *ISDN Switch Types*

```
R5(config)#isdn switch-type ?
  basic-1tr6     1TR6 switch type for Germany
  basic-5ess     Lucent 5ESS switch type for the U.S.
  basic-dms100   Northern Telecom DMS-100 switch type for the U.S.
  basic-net3     NET3 switch type for UK, Europe, Asia and Australia
  basic-ni       National ISDN switch type for the U.S.
  basic-qsig     QSIG switch type
  basic-ts013    TS013 switch type for Australia (obsolete)
  ntt            NTT switch type for Japan
  vn3            VN3 and VN4 switch types for France
```

The BRI interface is configured with PPP encapsulation, optional authentication (PAP or CHAP), and a **dialer map** command. The **dialer map** command maps the next hop IP to the dialed string. Example 5-10 shows a BRI interface configuration.

Example 5-10 *ISDN BRI Configuration*

```
isdn switch-type basic-ni
!
interface BRI0
 ip address 1.1.1.1 255.255.255.252
 encapsulation ppp
 dialer map ip 1.1.1.2 255.255.255.252 name R6 broadcast 2819970300101
 dialer-group 1
 isdn spid1 2816109420101
 isdn spid2 2816109430101
 ppp authentication chap
!
dialer-list 1 protocol ip permit
```

The configuration shows that the carrier's switch type is basic-ni, which is the national switch type for the US. PPP encapsulation is for the ISDN B channels. The dialer map indicates that the next hop IP address, 1.1.1.2 is reached through the ISDN service identifier 2819970300101. The hostname of the next-hop router is R6, and IP broadcasts and directed IP packets are forwarded to this IP address. The dialer group indicates that only IP packets are permitted to activate the ISDN connection. ISDN service profile identifiers (SPID) are local identifiers assigned by the ISDN carrier that are required for DMS-100 and NI switch types only. They have significance at the local ISDN switch only and are required to start ISDN connections.

Dial Backup Configuration

ISDN can back up a primary circuit if it fails or has exceeded a use threshold. If the primary fails, the ISDN circuit is enabled. While the connection is up, IP traffic is passed through the backup interface. Also, the backup BRI can be enabled if the primary circuit reaches a certain load. In Example 5-11, the BRI is enabled if serial 0 reaches 60 percent load or if serial 0 is down for 25 seconds. The BRI is disabled if serial 0 is back up for 60 seconds or if the bandwidth in the primary is below 10 percent.

Example 5-11 *Dial Backup Configuration*

```
interface serial 09
 ip address 10.100.1.101 255.255.255.252
 backup delay 25 60
 backup load 60 10
 backup interface bri 0
!
interface bri 0
 ip address 10.1.1.101 255.255.255.252
 dialer string 2817001111
 dialer-group 1
!
dialer-list 1 protocol ip permit
```

ISDN has many uses and configurations. For more configuration examples, go to the following site:

www.cisco.com/univercd/cc/td/doc/product/software/ios120/12cgcr/dial_c/dcbri.htm#xtocid610022

ATM Architecture

This section uses the ATM reference model to describe the general architecture of ATM.

ATM was developed to meet the need to transport voice, data, and video across enterprise and service provider networks. ATM is a connection-oriented, cell switching, transport technology. ATM supports the ability to adapt to different bandwidths and QoS requirements.

Figure 5-14 ATM Reference Model shows the various functions within the ATM architecture.

The ATM reference model is divided into three areas: user, management, and control. The physical transport functions are part of the control plane.

The user plane is responsible for the transfer of video, voice, and data applications. The user plane is associated with flow control and error recovery.

The management plane is responsible for the interaction between the user plane, control plane, and transport facilities.

Figure 5-14 *ATM Reference Model*

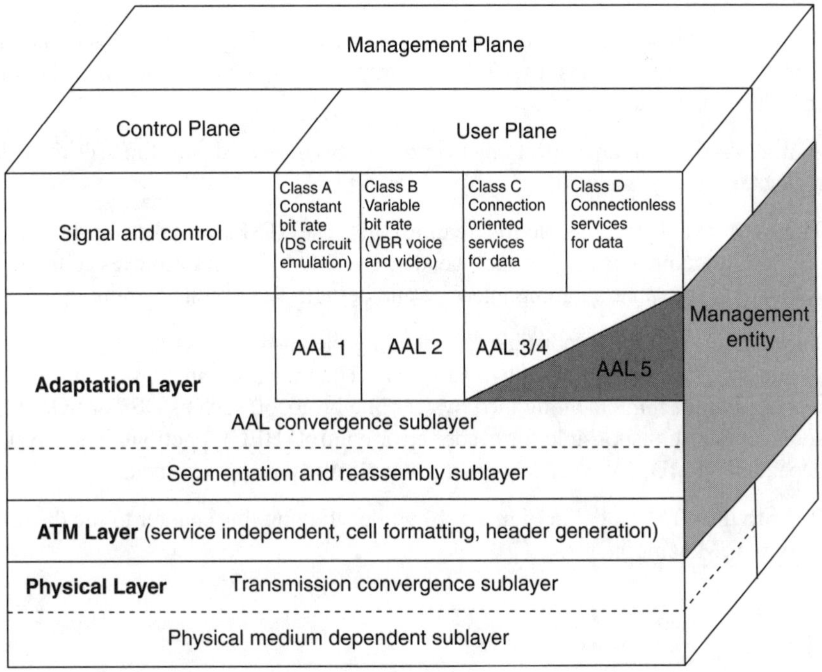

The control plane supports both PVCs and SVCs. The control plane enables the exchange of signaling information between ATM endpoints to establish call setup. It is responsible for call setup, maintenance, and call removal of switched VCs.

AAL

The AAL is responsible for adapting the information provided by the user plane to a form that the ATM layer can use. The AAL identifies five categories of traffic based on the following requirements:

- End-to-end timing relationship
- Bit arrival rate
- Connection requirements

Traffic that is time-sensitive, connection-oriented, and arrives at a constant rate, such as DS1 or DS3 circuit emulation, uses AAL1,which includes a time stamp in the cell.

Traffic that is time-sensitive, connection-oriented, and arrives at a variable rate, such as compressed video, uses AAL2.

Traffic that is connection-oriented, not time-sensitive, and arrives at a variable rate, such as Frame Relay or LAN data, uses AAL5. Compressed video and voice also can use AAL5, with the correct QoS parameters.

AAL 3/4 is defined for connectionless or connection-oriented, non-time-sensitive data. However, it is not often implemented.

The ATM layer is responsible for creating cells. The ATM layer takes the 48-byte payload from the AAL and appends a 5-byte cell header. The ATM layer multiplexes cells from different AALs onto the same outgoing interface and demultiplexes cells coming in from the interface.

The physical layer is responsible for encoding the 53-byte cell on to the physical media. The physical layer is composed of two sublayers. The transmission convergence (TC) sublayer is responsible for implementing the physical line protocol, such as DS3 or SONET. The TC sublayer is also responsible for header error control (HEC) functions. The physical medium dependent (PMD) sublayer implements the electrical or optical media.

Refer to the ATM model in Figure 5-14 while studying this chapter to see the relationships among ATM components.

ATM Cell Format

ATM transports voice, data, or video information in fixed length units called cells. Each cell is 53 bytes long and contains cell header and payload fields. The 5-byte cell header contains addressing, cell type, cell loss priority, and error checking information. The 48-byte cell payload contains a portion of the data, voice, or video information being transported.

The format of the ATM cell header varies depending upon whether the interface being traversed is a UNI or an NNI. The UNI connects the customer premise equipment to the network switch. The NNI is the interface between switches or between networks.

Figure 5-15 shows the format of an ATM cell on a UNI and on an NNI, and Table 5-4 identifies the fields of the cell headers.

Figure 5-15 *ATM Cell Format on UNI and NNI*

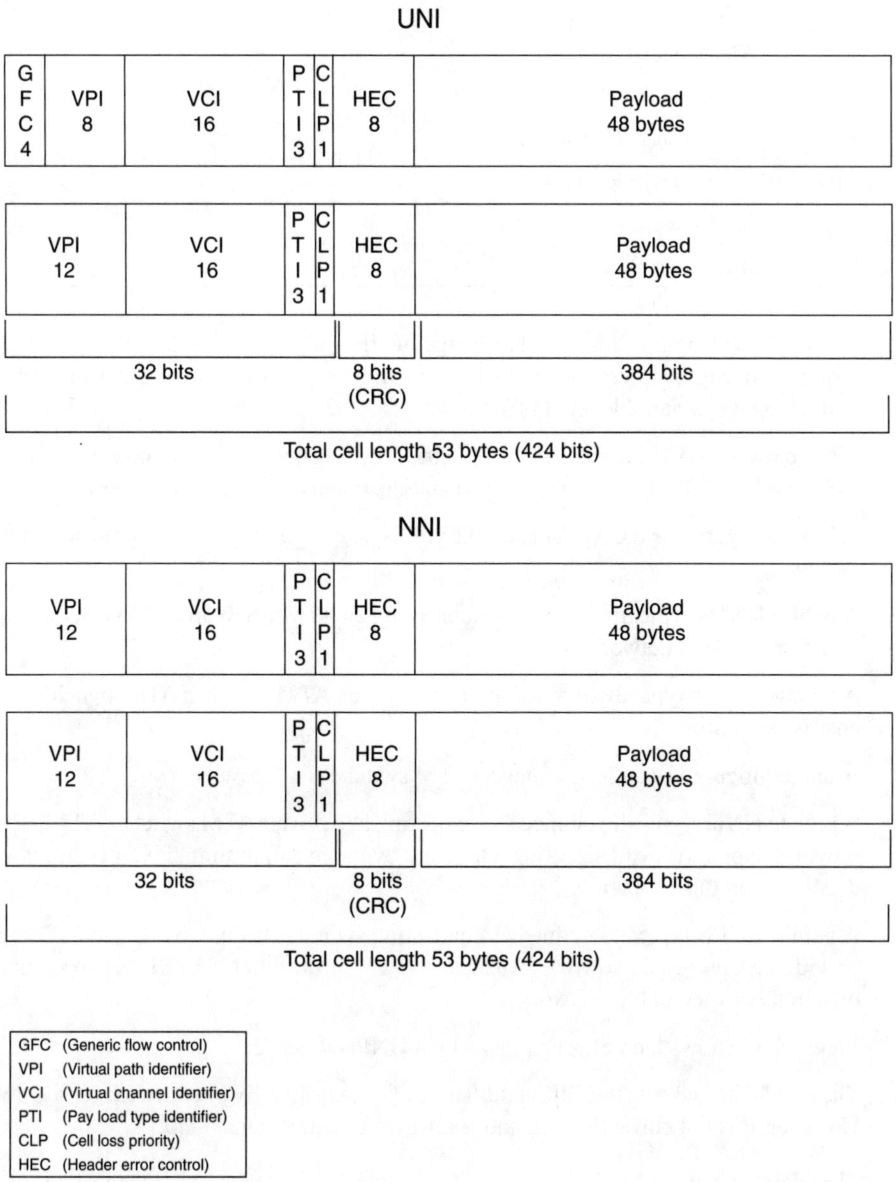

Table 5-4 *ATM Cell Header Fields*

Field	Description
GFC	Generic flow control
VPI	Virtual path identifier
VCI	Virtual channel identifier
PTI	Payload type identifier
CLP	Cell loss priority
HEC	Header error control

Using a fixed length cell has the advantage of allowing the switch to use fixed length buffers. Using fixed length buffers speeds up the switching process as compared to using variable length buffers to switch variable length frames.

Links between ATM devices can be classified as UNI or NNI. The configuration of a link as UNI or NNI affects the cell header type and the connection signaling across the link.

A link configured as a UNI connects ATM ESs, such as routers, hosts, or switches to an ATM switch.

A public UNI is typically defined as connecting an ATM ES to an ATM switch in a public service provider's network.

A private UNI is typically defined as connecting an ATM ES to an ATM switch in a private enterprise network.

A link configured as an NNI connects ATM switches.

A private NNI is typically defined as connecting two private ATM switches. The PNNI protocol provides support for call signaling, QoS, and dynamic call routing. PNNI is discussed in more detail later in this chapter.

A public NNI is typically defined as connecting switches from two different ATM service providers. A protocol known as Broadband Inter-Carrier Interface (BICI) can support services on a link between public networks.

Figure 5-16 shows the fields that make up a UNI cell header.

The first 4 bits make up the GFC field. The GFC was originally intended to provide flow control. However, it is not currently used and is always set to the value 0000.

The next 8 bits make up the VPI. The VPI identifies a virtual path (VP) connection. Conceptually, the VP can be thought of as containing multiple virtual channels (VCs), (also known as virtual circuits). Using eight bits, the VPI can identify 256 VPs.

The next 16 bits make up the VCI. Along with the VPI, the VCI uniquely identifies a cell as belonging to a specific connection. Using 16 bits, the VCI can identify 65,536 VCs.

Figure 5-16 *UNI Cell Header*

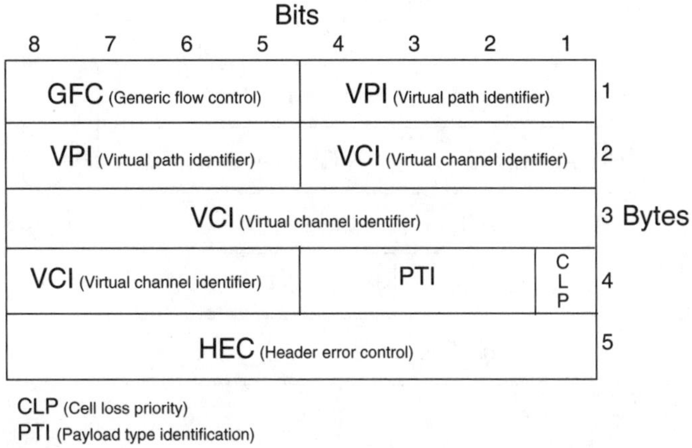

The PTI is made up of three bits. The first bit identifies the cell as user data when set to 0 and as a management cell when set to 1.

The second bit in a user cell is called the EFCI. It indicates that the cell passed through a network component that was experiencing congestion, as described in the ATM Traffic Management section of this chapter.

The third bit in a user cell identifies the last cell that makes up a frame of data. If the third bit is set to 0, the cell is not the last cell in the frame. If the third bit is set to 1, the cell is the last cell in the frame. An example of the use of this bit is to determine if the packet can be discarded because of congestion in the network. A switch might want to discard all but the final cell belonging to a single frame, as described in the ATM Traffic Management section of this chapter.

If the cell is a management cell, the second bit identifies a segment management cell when the bit is set to 0 and an end-to-end management cell when the bit is set to 1. The third bit in a management cell is reserved for future use.

The cell loss priority (CLP) bit identifies the cell as being high or low priority. If the network experiences congestion, the cells with the CLP set to 1 are discarded before any cell with the CLP bit is set to 0. The CLP bit can be set by the end device or as a result of ingress policing, as described in the ATM Traffic Management section of this chapter.

The HEC field is an 8-bit cyclic redundancy check on the cell header.

The payload of a user cell contains the data being transported. The payload of a management cell can contain flow control information or alarm indicators.

Figure 5-17 shows the format of an NNI cell.

Figure 5-17 *NNI Cell Header*

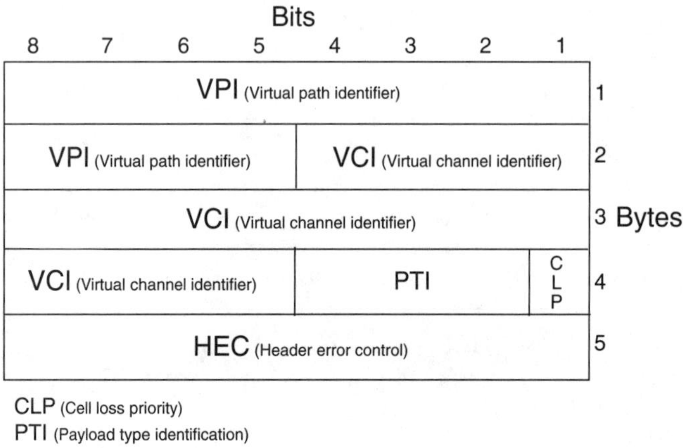

The format of an NNI cell is slightly different than an UNI cell. In an NNI cell, the GFC is replaced with 4 additional VPI bits for a total of 12 VPI bits. Using 12 bits, a NNI cell can identify 4096 unique VPs. The ATM Cell Switching section of this chapter describes the difference between VC and VP switching.

ATM Cell Switching

The header of each cell contains addressing information consisting of a VPI and a VCI. The VPI/VCI address pair is locally significant. For each interface in a switch, the VPI/VCI uniquely identifies the cell as belonging to a particular connection.

When a VC connection is established across a network, each switch involved in the connection creates an entry in its switching table that identifies the incoming VPI/VCI and interface number for the connection. The switching table entry also identifies the outgoing VPI/VCI and interface number for the connection.

When a cell arrives on a particular interface, the switch examines the VPI, VCI, and interface number. The switch then changes the VPI/VCI pair in the header of the cell and switches the cell out the appropriate interface according to the entries in its switching table. Figure 5-18 shows two cells being switched across two VC connections in an ATM network.

Another form of switching is VP switching. When a VP connection is established across a network, the entry in a switch's switching table identifies only the incoming and outgoing VPI and interface number for the connection.

Figure 5-18 *Virtual Circuit Switching*

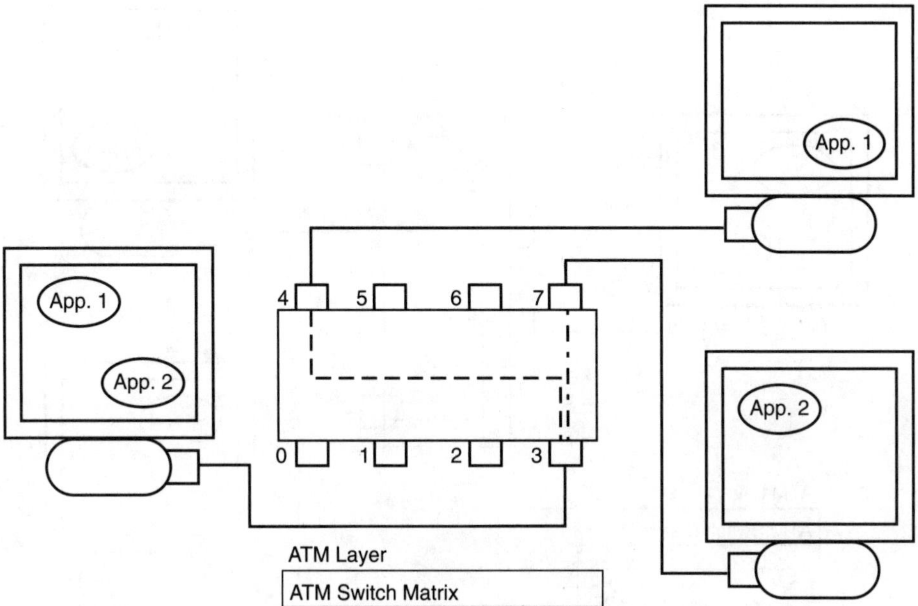

ATM Layer

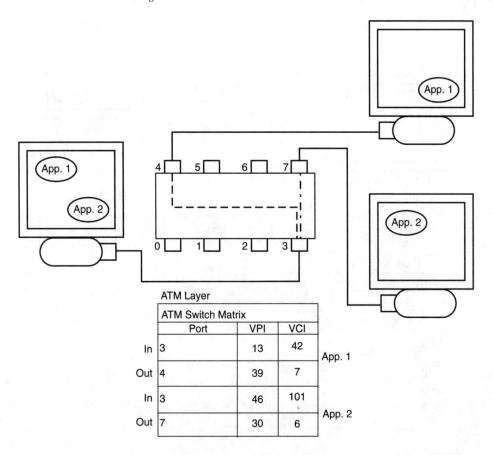

ATM Switch Matrix				
	Port	VPI	VCI	
In	3	13	42	App. 1
Out	4	39	7	
In	3	46	101	App. 2
Out	7	30	6	

When a cell arrives on a particular interface, the switch examines the VPI and interface number. The switch then changes the VPI in the header of the cell and switches the cell out the appropriate interface according to the entries in its switching table. The switch does not examine or modify the cell's VCI.

Figure 5-19 shows two cells being switched across two VP connections in an ATM network.

Conceptually, you can think of the VP as a logical construction that aggregates VCs. Figure 5-20 shows the concept of a VP that contains multiple VCs.

Figure 5-19 *Virtual Path Switching*

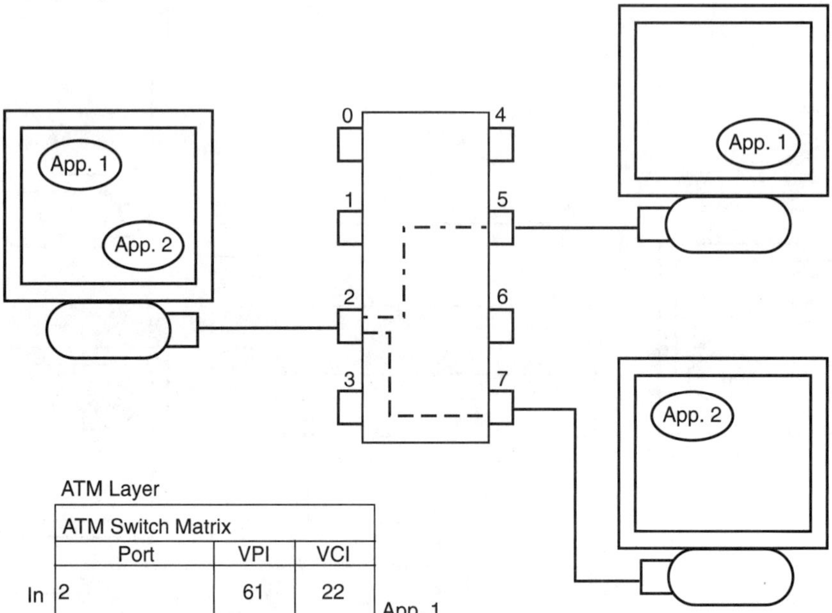

ATM Layer

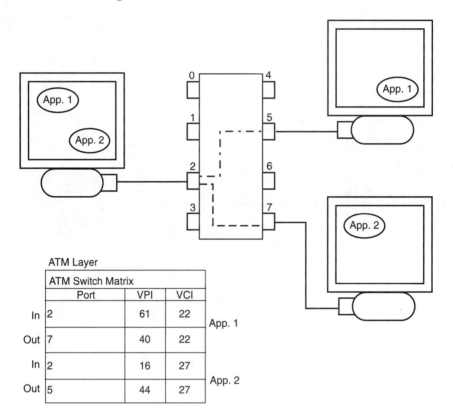

	ATM Switch Matrix			
	Port	VPI	VCI	
In	2	61	22	App. 1
Out	7	40	22	
In	2	16	27	App. 2
Out	5	44	27	

Figure 5-20 *ATM Logical Connection Components*

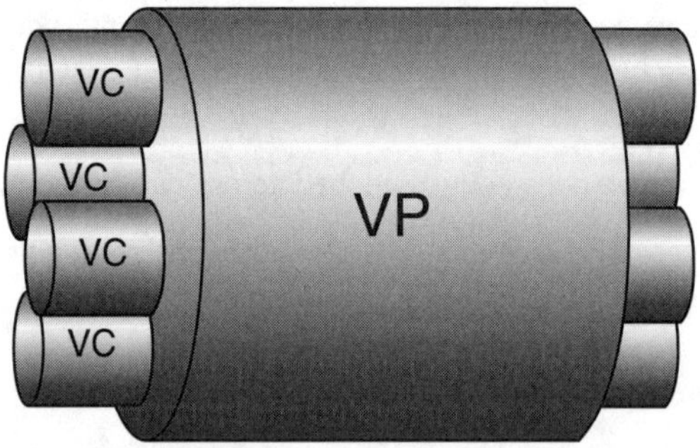

ATM Connections

ATM is a connection-oriented technology. A connection is established between two or more ESs to permit communication. A connection between two end points is called *point-to-point*. A connection between a single originating end point and multiple destination end-points is called *point-to-multipoint*.

ATM uses the concept of virtual connections between ESs rather than physical links. ATM networks support a connection type known as a PVC, which is established manually from a source end-point to a destination end-point. Each switch in the path of a PVC has an entry in the switching tables that identify the VPI/VCI and interface for the ingress and egress of the connection.

A PVC is always connected and is not dynamically rerouted around a link or switch failure; the ESs cannot create or release the connection.

Many switches support a special type of PVC known as a *soft PVC (SPVC)*. A SPVC is established manually by using connection management software and can dynamically reroute around a link or switch failure.

ATM networks also support a connection type known as an *SVC*. An SVC is established by the ES by using signaling. In a SVC, the ES dynamically establishes and releases the connection as needed. SVCs can dynamically reroute around a link or switch failure.

SVCs are established by using UNI signaling. The ATM Forum standard for signaling is UNI 4.0. Most networks support the earlier version, UNI 3.1. UNI signaling is based on the ITU-T Q.2931 specification.

When an end system wants to establish a connection with another end system, it sends a request to the switch that specifies the following:

- Destination ATM ES address
- QoS parameters, such as cell loss ratio, cell transfer delay, and cell delay variance

The switch examines the connection request parameters and determines if it has a routing table entry for the destination ES address and if it can accommodate the requested QoS. If the switch can accept the connection request, it forwards the request to the next switch specified in the connection routing table.

SSCOP

ATM interfaces support a signaling protocol stack and a special signaling ATM adaptation layer (SAAL). The SAAL is composed of the SSCOP and the service specific convergence function (SSCF).

SSCOP provides the reliable transport of signaling messages between peer entities. Signaling requests are encapsulated into SSCOP frames and are carried across the ATM network in AAL5 packets. These signals are carried over a well-known PVC. The ATM Forum PVC for UNI signaling uses the VCI of 5.

Signaling requests support the following message types:

- Call setup
- Call processing
- Status
- Call release

ATM Traffic Management

ATM connections support various service classes. The different service classes in turn support various network services. For example, video transmission uses a constant bit rate (CBR) class of service (CoS). Compressed voice service uses a real-time variable bit rate (RT-VBR). Data might use a non-real-time variable bit rate (NRT-VBR) type of traffic, or if the data device supports flow control, an available bit rate (ABR) traffic type. Low priority data might use an unspecified bit rate (UBR) traffic type to save money.

Each traffic type uses a different set of QoS parameters. These QoS parameters determine how the traffic is treated at the ingress of the network, through the core of the network, and at the egress.

When an ATM cell enters an ATM network, it is subjected to ingress policing. Ingress policing is referred to as *usage parameter control (UPC)*. The purpose of UPC is to prevent the originating device from sending cells faster than the VC is configured to transport them. UPC prevents the network from becoming congested.

Figure 5-21 shows a model that describes how traffic policing works. It is important to note that the leaky bucket is simply a model. The ATM interface does not actually contain tiny little buckets.

When a cell enters an ATM interface where policing is enabled, a token representing the cell is placed into the bucket. The tokens leak out of the bucket at a specified rate. For example, in CBR traffic the leak rate of the bucket is referred to as the *peak cell rate (PCR)*.

As long at the cell arrival rate (AR) is equal to or less than the leak rate of the bucket, it never fills up and all cells are said to be compliant. If the AR is greater than the leak rate, the bucket starts to fill up. The number of tokens the bucket can hold before it is full is specified as a time period, and in a single bucket model, this is referred to as the *cell delay variation tolerance (CDVT)*.

Figure 5-21 *Leaky Bucket Model*

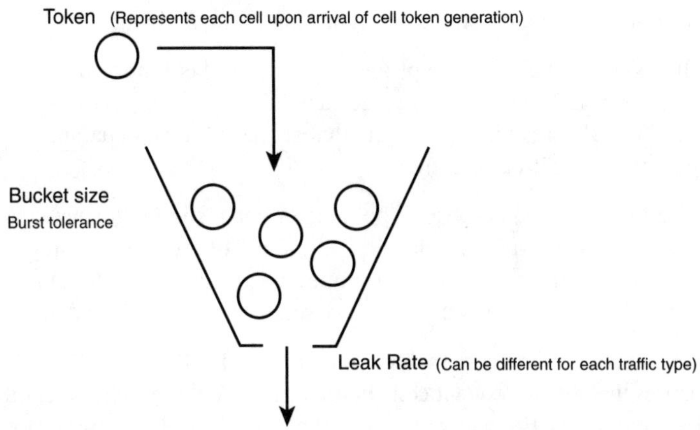

After the bucket is full, any new tokens represent cells that are noncompliant. Also, noncompliant cells can be discarded or they can have their CLP bit set to 1.

In certain types of traffic policing, cells that are compliant in the first bucket are subjected to a second test using a second bucket. Figure 5-22 shows this type of traffic policing.

Figure 5-22 *Dual Leaky Bucket Model*

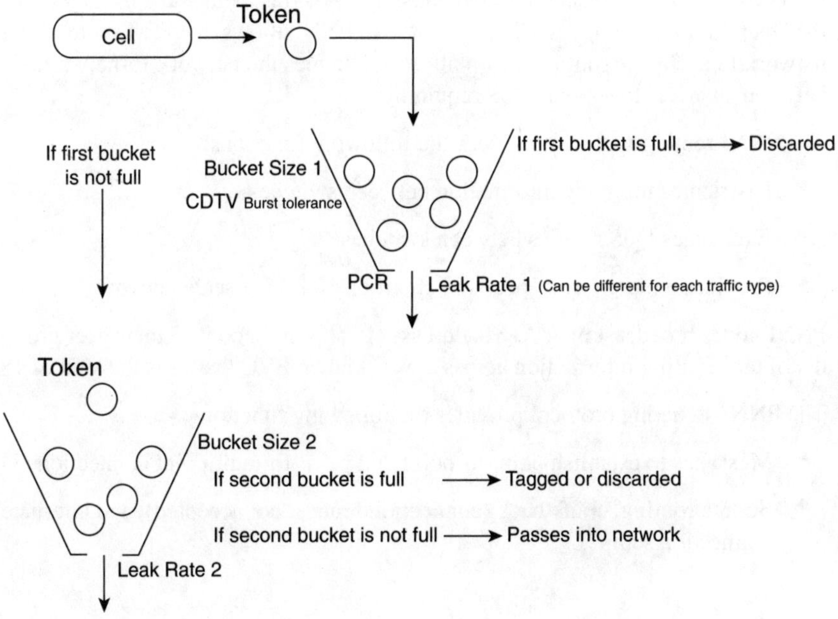

In a dual leaky bucket model, if the cell is compliant in the second bucket, the cell is sent to the network. If the cell is noncompliant in the second bucket, it can be discarded, or it can have its CLP bit set to 1 depending on the configuration of the policing.

As a cell passes through the core of the network, it is held in various buffers. Time sensitive traffic, such as AAL1 traffic, is guaranteed a maximum latency end-to-end through the network. CBR and RT-VBR pass through buffers that are serviced at a guaranteed rate. ABR and UBR traffic pass through different buffers.

When a cell is discarded because of policing or congestion in the network, the traffic type is considered. Video and voice traffic is more tolerant of the loss of a single cell. However, if a discarded AAL5 cell is part of a larger frame of data, the remainder of the frame is useless. For this reason, ATM implements the Frame Based Generic Cell Rate Algorithm (FGCRA).

With FGCRA, the switch can implement partial packet discard (PPD). If a cell is discarded, PPD ensures that all subsequent cells in the frame are discarded, except the last cell. The last cell is required for the ES to recognize that the frame has been sent. The third bit in the PTI field of the cell header indicates if the cell is the last cell in a frame.

With FGCRA, the switch can implement early packet discard (EPD). If the first cell of a frame must be discarded, the entire frame, including the last cell, is discarded when EPD is implemented.

PNNI

When a SVC, and in some cases a SPVC, is established across an ATM network, the PNNI protocol identifies the route for the connection. PNNI is a link-state routing protocol similar to the Open Shortest Path First (OSPF) protocol. PNNI allows the ATM switches within a private network to exchange routing information and defines the network-to-network signaling between switches to support QoS requirements.

The PNNI routing protocol provides the following functions:

- Distributes topology information between switches
- Exchanges QoS metrics between switches
- Provides a hierarchy of peer switch groups for large scale networks

PNNI nodes broadcast their ATM addresses to all other nodes in their peer group. PNNI distributes routing information across a well-known PVC that uses the VCI of 18.

The PNNI signaling protocol provides the following functions:

- Messages to establish point-to-point and point-to-multipoint connections
- Source routing, crank back (connection request not accepted), and alternate routing for connection setup

When a switch receives a request to establish a connection across the network, it creates a designated transit list (DTL) that identifies the route the connection will try to take. The connection request is sent to the next switch in the DTL. That switch has the choice to accept the connection or to reject it based on the connection admission control (CAC) function and the requested QoS. Rejecting a connection request is called *crankback*.

Because PNNI exchanges QoS metrics and topology information between switches, two or more VCs can be established to the same prefix over different paths because the connection requests had different QoS requirements.

Signaling between switches is across an NNI.

If a connection request is rejected, the switch making the request can try a different route. After the connection is accepted, the process repeats until the final ES is reached. If the ES accepts the connection, a signal is sent back to the origination ES, and the connection is established.

In large networks, the PNNI routing protocol tables can become too large for efficient operation. So, PNNI supports a hierarchy of peer switch groups for large networks.

A peer group of ATM switches shares a common peer group ID as part of their ATM address. The peer group level determines the portion of the address that comprises the peer group ID. Figure 5-23 shows an ATM network comprising seven peer groups at three levels.

Figure 5-23 *PNNI Hierarchy*

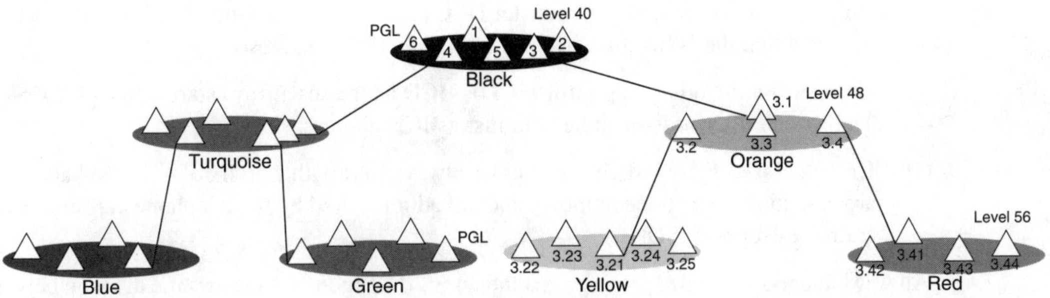

To reduce the amount of routing information being distributed to each switch, PNNI summarizes the information for each group.

Within each group, an elected peer group leader (PGL) sends summarized address prefixes to the PGL in each of the other groups. Prefixes are partial addresses that summarize a group of addresses.

In the example shown in Figure 5-23, the PGL in the turquoise group advertises the summarized ATM address for its group to the green, blue, black, orange, yellow, and red PGLs. (The colors are labeled in Figure 5-23.) When a switch in the green group wants to make a connection to a switch in the red group, it creates a detailed DTL for its own group, plus it identifies the remaining path as the group IDs for the turquoise, black, orange, and red groups. When the receiving switch in the turquoise group receives the connection request, it creates a detailed DTL for its own group. This process repeats until the connection request is routed across all intermediate groups.

Crankback and alternative routing is made more efficient in hierarchical networks. In a non-hierarchical network, a rejected call must go all the way back to the DTL originator before an alternate path can be calculated. With PNNI hierarchy, the call goes back to the entry point node within the current level. Using Figure 5-23, if the call is rejected within the turquoise group because a link within the turquoise group cannot meet the required QoS metrics, crankback is started. The call returns to the entry node within the turquoise group, which then continues the call setup process on a path that avoids the rejecting link.

ATM ES Addresses

To support SVCs and PNNI routing of connections, switches and interfaces must be assigned a 20-byte ATM address. Each ES must have at least one ATM ES address (AESA). The AESA identifies the PNNI peer group, the switch ID, and the ES ID. When the originating end device sends a SVC connection request, it identifies the ATM address of the destination device.

The following three types of addresses are used in private ATM networks:

- **Data Country Code (DCC)**—DCC addresses always start with a prefix of 39. Different authorities in each country administer DCC addresses. In the United States, the American National Standards Institute (ANSI) administers DCC addresses.
- **International Code Designator (ICD)**—ICD addresses always start with a prefix of 47. The British Standards Institute administers ICD addresses.
- **Encapsulated E.164**—E.164 addresses always start with a prefix of 45. E.164 addresses are essentially telephone numbers and are administered by the telephone carriers. E.164 addresses support ISDN.

An ATM address is divided into a prefix and an ES ID. Figure 5-24 shows the division between the prefix and the ES ID.

The AESA and the level identify PNNI peer groups. The PNNI standard supports levels 0 through 104. The level number corresponds to the number of address bits that you use for routing. When selecting a level number, you can use any number between 0 and 104, but it is easier to work with numbers that represent 8-bit boundaries.

For example, level 56 indicates that the first 56 bits (7 bytes) of the ATM address identifies the peer group level. Figure 5-25 shows examples of level 56 ICD addresses.

Figure 5-24 *ATM ES Address*

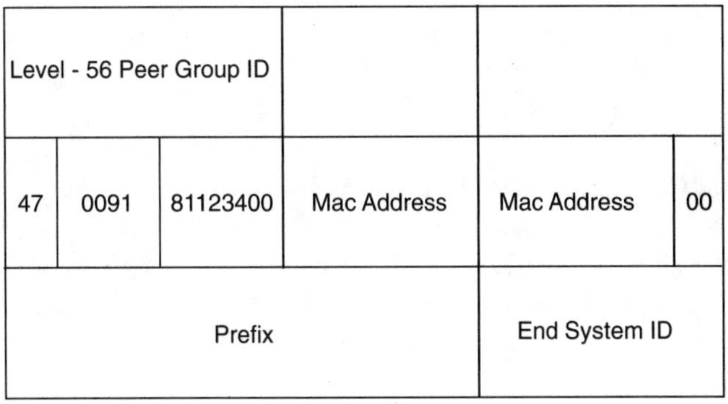

Figure 5-25 *PNNI Peer Group Address Levels*

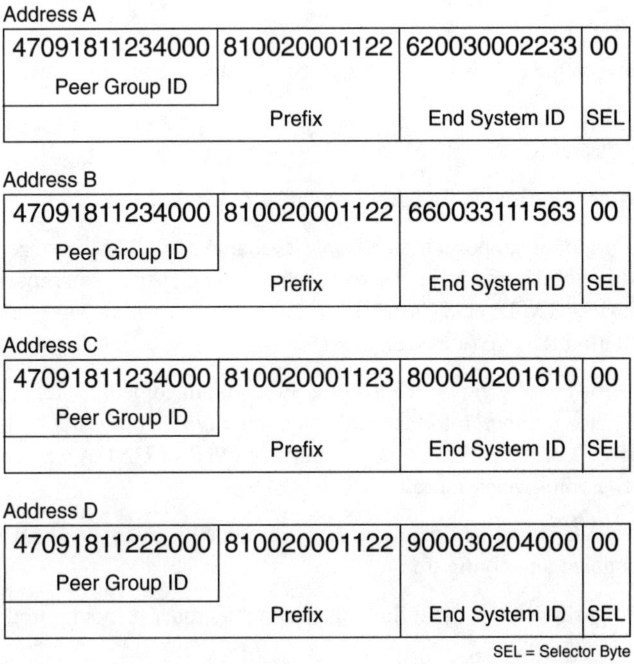

In Figure 5-25, A, B, and C are in the same peer group and D is in a different peer group at the same level. Also, addresses A and B identify different interfaces on the same switch.

A peer group with a level of 48 uses the first 6 bytes of the ATM address for routing and is at a higher level than a peer group at level 56.

Interim Local Management Interface (ILMI)

ILMI is an ATM Forum standard that specifies the use of mechanisms and formats previously defined by the Simple Network Management Protocol (SNMP). Although it is based on SNMP, ILMI communication uses a transport other than IP that traverses only the physical ATM link. ILMI messages are carried over a well-known PVC. The ATM Forum PVC for ILMI uses the VCI 16.

ILMI provides the following:

- Configuration, status, and control information about physical and ATM-layer parameters of the ATM interface
- Interface attributes organized in a standard Management Information Base (MIB) structure
- Access to the adjacent ATM Interface Management Entity (IME) through the ILMI communication protocol
- Address registration across a UNI
- Auto-configuration of a LAN Emulation Client (LEC)

The ILMI protocol supports bidirectional exchanges of ATM interface parameters between IMEs. Using SNMP queries, a network management system can report on the status of the physical layer, ATM layer, VCs or VPs, ES address registration, and service registration such as LAN emulation (LANE) service.

When ILMI is enabled on both ends of a link, a management system can retrieve information on the interface number, interface address, media type, number of VPIs and VCI supported, number of VCs or VPs active, type of interface (NNI or UNI), QoS parameters, adjacent node identification, plus much more.

For PNNI, SVC signaling operation, adjacent node discovery, and LANE registration, ILMI must be enabled and configured.

When configuring ILMI, the following parameters must be configured to the same values at both ends of the link:

- **ILMI VPI/VCI**—The VPI and VCI reserved for ILMI messages; typically 0/16.
- **ILMI Polling**—Enabled or disabled.
- **Trap Enabled**—Enables or disables the sending of unsolicited event and alarm reports.

- **T491 Polling Interval**—The time period between status polls.
- **N491 Error Threshold**—If the number of messages defined by N491 is missing out of a total number of messages defined by N492, a communication failure is reported.
- **N492 Event Threshold**—The number of attempted messages in conjunction with the N491 threshold, to determine a communication failure.

ILMI supports ES address registration. ES address registration allows ESs to automatically be assigned an AESA without operator intervention.

As specified in the UNI 4.0 specification, the Private ATM Address Structure consists of multiple fields. Two of these fields, the end system identifier (ESI) and the selector (SEL) fields form the user part and are supplied by the user-side IME.

All other fields form a network prefix for ATM addresses that typically have the same value for all ATM addresses on the same ATM UNI. The network side of the UNI supplies the value of the network prefix. An ATM address for an ES on the user side of a Private UNI is obtained by appending values for the ESI and SEL fields to the network prefix for that UNI.

IISP

IISP is a static routing protocol for ATM. IISP allows a UNI signaling request to be routed across multiple switches based on static routes. However, IISP does not support QoS. IISP is useful where PNNI is not supported.

IISP requires the configuration of static routes. Use the following rules for configuring IISP:

- IISP static routes must avoid routing loops.
- Each switch is given an ATM address.
- A route can have a primary path and a secondary path.

In each switch a routing table is configured that contains the address prefixes that are reachable through each interface on the switch.

When UNI signaling is enabled, the switch arbitrarily takes the role of a UNI user on the network side.

Figure 5-26 shows an ATM network with UNI signaling enabled for IISP.

When the switch receives a signaling request, the switch matches the destination ATM address with the table entry with the longest prefix match. Each ATM switch that receives the connection setup message selects the next outgoing interface to which to forward the setup message. This process is less efficient than PNNI source routing.

The ability to crank back and compute an alternate route when congestion or connection failure occurs is not inherent in IISP. However, redundant or alternate paths can be configured.

Figure 5-26 *IISP Routing*

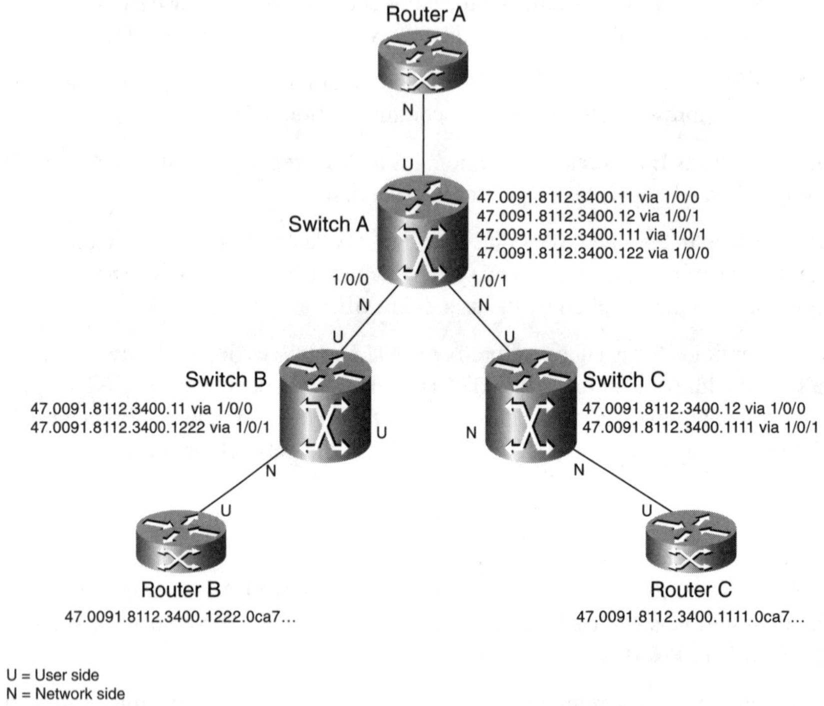

IISP can also provide a route between different PNNI peer groups. This is useful when the PNNI peer groups are administered separately or support different versions of PNNI.

Classical IP over ATM (CIA) (RFC 2225)

CIA is specified in RFC 2225. The purpose of RFC 2225 is to provide a method to send IP packets over ATM. In the RFC 2225 approach, each device that wants to send an IP packet over ATM is directly attached to the ATM network. This device can be a workstation or a router that acts as a proxy for an entire LAN.

For each logical IP subnet (LIS), an ATM ARP server is configured. The job of the ATM ARP server is to map IP addresses to the ATM network service access point (NSAP) or ITU-T E-164 addresses. Figure 5-27 shows how the ATM ARP server learns the addresses of the ARP clients.

Figure 5-27 *CIA Registration*

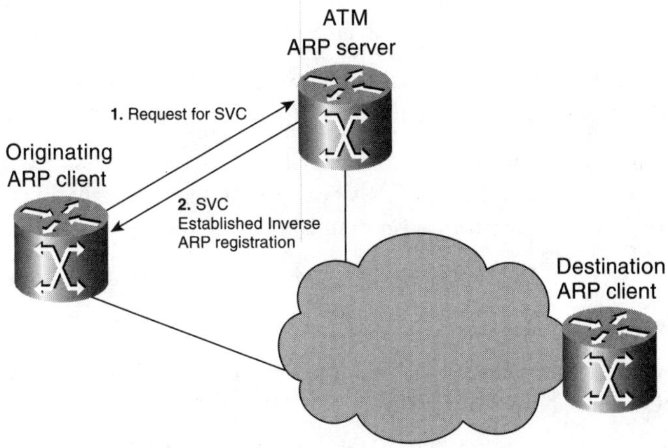

Each device in a LIS is configured with the ATM address of the ATM ARP server and acts as an ARP client. When the ARP client starts up, it sends a request for a SVC over a well-known VC using VCI 5. The ATM ARP server then establishes an SVC with the ARP client. The ATM ARP server uses Inverse ARP to learn the IP and ATM addresses of the client and registers the client. Figure 5-28 shows how the originating ARP client establishes a connection with the destination ARP client.

Figure 5-28 *CIA SVC Establishment*

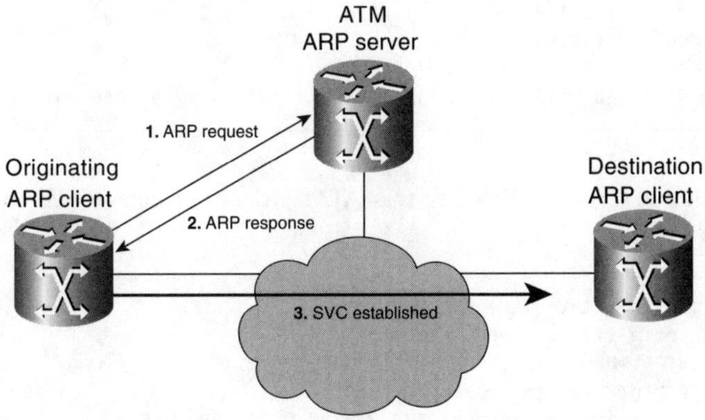

When the device wants to send an IP packet to another device, it sends an ARP request to the ATM ARP server. If the destination device is already registered with the ATM ARP server, the server sends an ARP response to the client. After the originating device has the ATM address of the destination device, it can establish an SVC to the destination using UNI signaling.

If the ATM ARP server does not have an entry for the requested destination device, it sends a negative response to the ARP client.

RFC 2225 uses LLC/Subnetwork Access Protocol (SNAP), as defined in RFC 2684, for encapsulation of IP packets. LLC/SNAP encapsulation allows sharing of VCs. RFC 2225 specifies the use of AAL5 for transport of IP packets.

IP to VC Mapping

The following sections describe configuring an ATM switch router for CIA in an SVC environment using NSAP addressing.

The ATM switch router can be configured as an ATM ARP client to work with an RFC 2225 ATM ARP server. Also, an ATM switch router can be configured to be the ATM ARP server and act as a client.

To configure an ATM switch router as an ATM ARP client, enter the commands in Example 5-12.

Example 5-12 *ATM ARP Client Configuration*

```
router(config)# interface atm 0
router(config-if)# atm nsap-address
47.0091.8100.0000.1122.1123.1111.1111.1111.1111.00
router(config-if)# ip address 123.233.45.1 255.255.255.0
router(config-if)# atm arp-server nsap
47.0091.8100.0000.1122.1123.1111.2222.2222.2222.00
router(config-if)# exit
router(config)# atm route
47.0091.8100.0000.1111.1111.1111.1111.1111.1111 atm 0 internal
```

To configure an ATM switch router as an ATM ARP server, enter the commands in Example 5-13.

Example 5-13 *ATM ARP Server Configuration*

```
router(config)# interface atm 0
router(config-if)# atm nsap-address
47.0091.8100.0000. 1122.1123.1111.1111.1111.1111.00
router(config-if)# atm arp-server self
router(config-if)# ip address 123.233.45.2 255.255.255.0
```

To verify the configuration of the ATM0 interface, use the **show atm arp-server** command.

To verify the mapping of IP addresses to NSAP addresses, use the **show atm map** command.

Multiprotocol Encapsulation over AAL5 (RFC 2684)

Multiprotocol encapsulation over AAL5 is specified in RFC 2684. RFC 2684 routed encapsulation allows IP to run over ATM in native mode, as described previously in CIA (RFC 2225). This method of encapsulation requires separate VCs for each high-level protocol and RFC 2684 routed encapsulation.

In VC-based protocol multiplexing, the carried protocol is identified implicitly by the VC connecting the two ATM stations. Each protocol must be carried over a separate VC. There is no need to include explicit multiplexing information in the payload of the AAL5 common part convergence sublayer protocol data unit (CPCS-PDU). This results in minimal bandwidth and processing overhead.

In routed LLC encapsulation, the protocol of the routed PDU is identified by prefixing the PDU with an IEEE 802.2 LLC header, which might be followed by an IEEE 802.1a SNAP header. The LLC header consists of three octets, the destination subnetwork attachment point (DSAP) address, source subnetwork attachment point (SSAP) address, and the Control field.

In LLC encapsulation for routed protocols, the Control field is always hexadecimal 03. Hexadecimal 03 specifies an unnumbered information command PDU.

RFC 2684 also provides a method for carrying connectionless network traffic as bridged PDUs over ATM. This method of encapsulation allows multiplexing of multiple protocols over a single ATM VC. By prefixing the PDU with an IEEE 802.2 LLC header, the protocol of the PDU is identified. This is the method that you use for LANE.

In LLC encapsulation of bridged PDUs, the type of bridged media is identified in the SNAP header. The SNAP header contains a three-octet Organizationally Unique Identifier (OUI) that identifies the organization, which administers the meaning of the following two octets. For example, the OUI value hexadecimal 00-00-00 specifies that the following Protocol Identifier (PID) contains an Ethernet type field.

The next two octets are the PID. Together, the OUI and the PID identify a distinct bridged protocol. Figure 5-29 shows a bridged Ethernet media LLC/SNAP encapsulation.

Figure 5-29 *Bridged Ethernet LLC/SNAP Encapsulation*

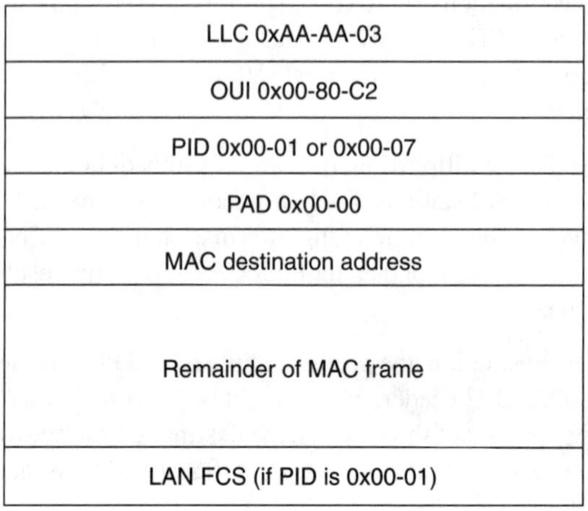

With bridged protocols, the OUI value in the SNAP header is the 802.1 organization code 0x00-80-C2, and the actual type of the bridged media is specified by the two-octet PID.

ATM Interface Configuration

The following sections describe how to configure a router ATM interface for point-to-point and point-to-multipoint connections.

To configure the ATM interface, log in to the router, enter the privileged EXEC mode, and enter the commands in Example 5-14.

Example 5-14 *Base ATM Interface Configuration*

```
router# configure terminal
router(config)# interface atm 4/0
router(config-if)# ip address 172.33.45.1 255.255.255.0
router(config-if)# no shutdown
router(config-if)# exit
router(config)# exit
router# copy running startup
```

In some cases, the router interface identifier is in the form **interface atm** *slot***/***port-adapter***/0** or **interface atm** *number.*

To configure a new ATM PVC, enter interface-ATM-VC configuration mode, and assign a VPI/VCI for the PVC. Optionally, the PVC can be assigned a name. You can also configure ILMI, QSAAL, or Switched Multimegabit Data Service (SMDS) encapsulation for the PVC if it is in an SVC environment.

Example 5-15 assigns VPI 10 and VCI 100 to a PVC named NYtoSF on interface 4/0, going to IP address 172.21.168.5, using the default AAL5 encapsulation.

Example 5-15 *ATM PVC Configuration*

```
router# configure terminal
router(config)# interface atm 4/0
router(config-if)# pvc NYtoSF 10/100
router(config-if-atm-vc)# protocol ip 172.21.168.5 broadcast
router(config-if-atm-pvc)# exit
```

A point-to-multipoint PVC allows the router to send one cell to the ATM switch and have the switch replicate the cell to multiple destinations.

You can configure multipoint signaling on an ATM interface after you have mapped protocol addresses to NSAP addresses and configured one or more protocols for broadcasting.

After multipoint signaling is set, the router uses SVC signaling to establish multipoint calls. The first call is established to the first destination with a Setup signal. Additional parties are added to the call with an AddParty signal. One multipoint call is established for each logical subnet.

Example 5-16 shows how to configure an ATM interface with address 1.4.5.2, create a PVC for qsaal and ilmi signaling, assign an ATM ES address selector field, create a multicast SVC for the IP protocol, and enable multipoint signaling. The **broadcast** keyword enables IP broadcast packets to be duplicated onto the VC. This is important for the function of some routing protocols.

Example 5-16 *ATM Router Configuration with a Multicast SVC*

```
router(config)# interface atm 2/0
router(config-if)# ip address 1.4.5.2 255.255.255.0
router(config-if)# pvc 0/5 qsaal
router(config-if-atm-vc)# exit
!
router(config-if)# pvc 0/16 ilmi
router(config-if-atm-vc)# exit
!
router(config-if)# atm esi-address 3456.7890.1234.12
!
router(config-if)# svc mcast-1 nsap
cd.cdef.01.234566.890a.bcde.f012.3456.7890.1234.12 broadcast
router(config-if-vc)# protocol ip 1.4.5.1 broadcast
router(config-if-vc)# exit
!
router(config-if)# atm multipoint-signalling
router(config-if)# atm maxvc 1024
```

The following commands can verify the ATM VC configuration:

- **show atm interface**
- **show atm pvc**
- **show atm map**
- **show atm traffic**

References Used

The following resources were used to create this chapter:

Internetworking Technologies Handbook, 2nd edition, Cisco Press, 1998

RFC 1990, "The PPP Multilink Protocol (MP)," K. Sklower, B. Lloyd, G. McGregor, D. Carr, T. Coradetti

RFC 2225, "Classical IP and ARP over ATM," M. Laubach, J. Halpern

RFC 2684, "Multiprotocol Encapsulation over ATM Adaptation Layer 5," D. Grossman, J. Heinanen

RFC 2427, "Multiprotocol Interconnect over Frame Relay," C. Brown, A. Malis

RFC 1994, "PPP Challenge Handshake Authentication Protocol (CHAP)," W. Simpson

RFC 1332, "The PPP Internet Protocol Control Protocol (IPCP)," G. McGregor

RFC 2615, "PPP over SONET/SDH," A. Malis, W. Simpson

www.cisco.com/warp/public/cc/techno/wnty/dpty/tech/dptm_wp.htm

www.cisco.com/warp/public/125/21.shtml

www.cisco.com/univercd/cc/td/doc/product/software/ios121/121cgcr/qos_c/qcprt4/qcdfrts.htm#xtocid2189920

www.cisco.com/univercd/cc/td/doc/product/software/ios121/121cgcr/wan_c/wcdfrely.htm#xtocid104

www.cisco.com/univercd/cc/td/doc/cisintwk/ito_doc/isdn.htm

Foundation Summary

The Foundation Summary is a condensed collection of material that provides a convenient review of key concepts in this chapter. If you are already comfortable with the topics in this chapter, this summary will help you recall a few details. If you just read the Foundation Topics section, this review should help solidify some key facts. If you are doing your final preparation before the exam, these materials are a convenient way to review the day before the exam.

Table 5-5 *Frame Relay Concepts*

Item	Description
CIR	Defines the average upper limit of the PVC
DE	Specifies frames that can be discarded
FECN	Notifies the receiving DTE that the frame experienced congestion
BECN	Notifies the sending DTE that frames headed toward the destination are experiencing congestion
FRTS	Receives BECN as input to manage Frame Relay Traffic by specifying parameters for different classes
FRF.9	Standards based Frame Relay compression

Table 5-6 *Frame Relay LAPF Frame Address Field*

Bit	Description
DLCI	10-bit PVC identifier
C/R	Not used
EA	Extended Address; indicates if the containing byte is the last in the addressing field; a mechanism to extend DLCI length beyond 10 bits
FECN	Bit set in frames traveling to the destination, when there is congestion on traffic from source to destination
BECN	Bit set in frames traveling to the source, when there is congestion on traffic from source to destination
DE	Bit set to indicate frame is eligible for discard

Table 5-7 *LMI Fields*

Field	Description
LMI DLCI	The LMI DLCI is 1023 if you use a cisco-type LMI. It is 0 if you use either ANSI or ITU (q333a).
UII	Unnumbered Information Indicator; sets the poll/final bit to zero.
PD	Protocol Discriminator; contains a value indicating the frame is an LMI frame.
Call Ref	Call Reference. This field always contains 0s. It is not currently used.
Message type	Status-inquiry message—Allows a user device to inquire about the status of the network. Status message—Response to an inquiry message.
IE	Information Elements; contains IE identifiers and data.
FCS	Frame Check Sequence; verifies the data.
Flags	Delimits the beginning and end of the frame and is always binary 01111110.

Table 5-8 *FRTS Traffic Shaping Commands*

Command	Description
frame-relay traffic-rate *average* [*peak*]	Defines the traffic rate for the VC.
frame-relay adaptive-shaping {**becn** | **foresight**}}}}	Enables dynamic traffic shaping based on received BECNs or ForeSight. ForeSight is a Cisco proprietary traffic control mechanism. This command replaces **frame-relay becn-response-enable**.
frame-relay custom-queue-list *list-number*	Defines a custom queue list number to apply to the VC.
frame-relay priority-group *list-number*	Defines a priority group number to apply to the VC to enable priority queuing.

Table 5-9 *ISDN Devices*

Device	Description
TE1	Any terminal or router with an ISDN BRI. This device has a 4-wire interface.
TE2	Any terminal or router without a BRI; it connects to the TA through an EIA/TIA-232 or V.35 interface.
TA	Connects the TE2 device to the ISDN network. Its input is the physical EIA/TIA-232 interface and its output is the ISDN BRI.
NT1	Usually the device that connects the 4-wire BRI to the 2-wire phone line.
NT2	NT2 devices provide switching and concentration of ISDN lines on the customer premise.
LE	Carrier's ISDN CO.

ISDN Reference Points

- **U**—Between NT1 and LE, 2-wire
- **T**—Between NT2 and NT1, 2-wire
- **S**—Between TE1 or TA and NT2
- **R**—Between TE1 and TA, usually an EIA/TIA-232
- **S/T**—Between TE1 and NT12 (S and T combined)

SONET Interface Speeds

- OC-1 = 51.85 Mbps
- OC-3 = 155.52 Mbps
- OC-12 = 622.08 Mbps
- OC-24 = 1.244 Gbps
- OC-48 = 2.488 Gbps
- OC-192 = 9.952 Gbps

Table 5-10 *Framing Standards*

Protocol	Frame Type
ISDN D Channel	LAPD
Frame Relay	LAPF
X.25	LAPB
Cisco's HDLC	Proprietary LAP

Table 5-11 *PPP Authentication*

Authentication Protocol	Description
Password Authentication Protocol (PAP)	Uses cleartext passwords
Challenge Authentication protocol (CHAP)	Encrypts passwords and uses three-way handshake

Table 5-12 *ATM Reference Model*

Layer or Plane Name	Description
User	Responsible for the transfer of video, voice, and data applications. The user plane is associated with flow control and error recovery.
Management	Responsible for interaction between the user plane, control plane, and the transport facilities.
Control	Responsible for call setup and maintenance, and call removal for SVCs.
Physical	Responsible for encoding the 53-byte cell on to the physical media. The physical layer is composed of the transmission convergence (TC) sublayer and the physical medium dependent (PMD) sublayer.
ATM	Responsible for creating cells. The ATM layer takes the 48-byte payload from the AAL and appends a 5-byte cell header.
Adaptation	Responsible for adapting the information provided by the user plane to a form that the ATM layer can use.

Table 5-13 *ATM Connection Types*

Layer or Plane Name	Description
VC	Virtual Channel (also known as virtual circuit). A VC switches cells based on the tables in each switch. Connection tables identify the VPI/VCI and interface for incoming and outgoing cells.
VP	Virtual path. A VP switches cells based on the VPI and interface for incoming and outgoing cells.
SVC	A switched virtual circuit is created by UNI signaling from the attached ES, such as a router.
PVC	A permanent virtual circuit is established manually and does not support dynamic rerouting.

Table 5-14 *QoS Components*

Name of Component	Description
AAL	The ATM adaptation layer identifies traffic categories based on end-to-end timing relationships, bit arrival rate, and connection or connectionless operation.
Ingress Policing	Prevents the originating device from sending cells faster than the VC can transport them. UPC prevents the network from becoming congested.
FGCRA	Frame Based Generic Cell Rate Algorithm. If a cell is discarded, PPD ensures that all subsequent cells in the frame are discarded, except the last cell. If the first cell of a frame must be discarded, EPD allows the entire frame, including the last cell, to be discarded.

Table 5-15 *ATM Cell Format*

Name of Field	Description
GFC	The generic flow control field is not currently used and is always set to the value 0000.
VPI	The virtual path identifier identifies a virtual path connection.
VCI	The virtual channel identifier, along with the VPI, uniquely identifies a cell as belonging to a specific virtual connection.
PTI	The payload type identifier identifies the cell as user data or a management cell. The PTI contains the EFCI bit and the end of frame bit.
CLP	The cell loss priority bit identifies the cell as being high or low priority.
HEC	The header error control field does error checking on the cell header.

Table 5-16 *Protocol Definitions*

Name of Protocol	Description
PNNI	The Private Network-Network Interface is a link-state routing protocol similar to OSPF that identifies the route for the ATM SVC.
SSCOP	The Service Specific Connection-Oriented Protocol provides reliable transport of signaling messages between peer entities.
ILMI	Interim Link Management Interface supports bidirectional exchanges of ATM interface parameters by using mechanisms and formats previously defined by the SNMP.
IISP	Interim-Interswitch Signaling Protocol is a static routing protocol for ATM. IISP allows a UNI signaling request to be routed across multiple switches based on static routes.
RFC 2225	Provides a method of sending IP packets over ATM and relies on the use of ATM ARP servers.
RFC 2684	Specifies a method of using routed encapsulation to run native mode protocols across separate ATM VCs. Also specifies a method for encapsulating connectionless bridged network traffic over a single ATM virtual circuit.

Q & A

The Q & A questions are more difficult than what you can expect on the actual exam. The questions do not attempt to cover more breadth or depth than the exam; however, they are designed to make sure that you retain the material. Rather than allowing you to derive the answer from clues hidden inside the question itself, these questions challenge your understanding and recall of the subject. Questions from the "Do I Know This Already?" quiz are repeated here to ensure that you have mastered the chapter's topic areas. A strong understanding of the answers to these questions will help you on the CCIE written exam. As an additional study aide, use the CD-ROM provided with this book to take simulated exams.

Select the best answer. Answers to these questions are in the Appendix, "Answers to Quiz Questions."

1 Which framing standard does X.25 use?

a. HDLC

b. LAPB

c. LAPF

d. LAPD

2 What is the significance of the DE bit?

a. Used in X.25 as a discard error to recover frames

b. Used in ATM to recover from cells with errors

c. Used in Frame Relay to specify discard eligible frames

d. Used in PPP to discard frames

3 What is an NT1 in ISDN architecture?

a. A device that connects the TE2 to the LE

b. Usually lies between the R and S reference points

c. Same as a NT4

d. A device that connects the 4-wire BRI to the 2-wire phone line

4 What is a BECN in Frame Relay?

a. A notification to the destination, indicating congestion in the path from source to destination

b. A notification to the source, indicating congestion in the path from source to destination

c. A notification to the destination, indicating congestion in the path from destination to source

d. A notification to the source, indicating congestion in the path from destination to source

5 Inverse ARP provides what type of address resolution?

a. MAC address to IP address

b. DLCI to IP address

c. X.121 address to IP address

d. ATM address to IP address

6 How many bits are there in a Frame Relay DLCI?

a. 8 bits

b. 10 bits

c. 16 bits

d. 32 bits

7 Which authentication protocol do you use with PPP and encrypted passwords?

a. PPP authentication

b. PAP

c. CHAP

d. SecureID

8 ISDN's D channel uses which framing standard?

a. HDLC

b. LAPB

c. LAPF

d. LAPD

9 For the following configuration, when does the BRI become active?

```
interface serial 0
 ip address 1.1.1.1 255.255.255.252
 backup load 75 10
 backup interface bri 0
```

a. When serial 0 is down for 60 seconds

b. When serial 0 is up for 10 seconds

c. When serial 0 is above 75 percent use

d. When serial 0 is below 10 percent use

10 What does the following command do?

```
x25 map ip 172.18.1.5 12121212 broadcast
```

a. Maps the remote IP address to the remote X.121 address

b. Maps the remote IP address to the local X.121 address

c. Maps the local IP address to the remote X.121 address

d. Maps the local IP address to the local X.121 address

11 Which of the following are layers in the ATM reference model?

a. Physical

b. Datalink

c. ATM

d. Network

e. Transport

f. Presentation

g. Adaptation

h. Session

i. Application

12 How many bytes are in an ATM cell?

a. 21

b. 48

c. 53

d. 128

13 How are ATM payload cells uniquely identified by a switch?

a. By the cell's IP address

b. By the cell's VPI/VCI address

c. By the cell's NSAP address

d. By the cell's AESA address

14 Which ATM class of service is most appropriate for raw video?

a. CBR

b. nrt-VBR

c. ABR

d. UBR

15 In what order do each of the following queues get processed on a DPT ring node?

1. Low-priority transmit queue

2. Low-priority transit queue

3. High-priority transmit queue

4. High-priority transit queue

a. 4,3 2,1

b. 3,4,2,1

c. 4,3,1,2

d. 3,4,1,2

16 Which ATM class of service is most appropriate for Frame Relay data?

a. CBR

b. VBR

c. ABR

d. UBR

17 RFC 2225 provides a method of encapsulating which of the following protocols over ATM?

a. XNS

b. IP

c. IPX

d. SNA

18 Identify the following descriptions as UNI or NNI:

a. Connects an ATM end system to an ATM switch in a public service provider's network

b. Uses eight bits of VPI to identify 256 virtual paths

c. Connects two private ATM switches

d. Connects two switches within the same public ATM service provider

e. Connects an ATM end system to an ATM switch in a private enterprise network

f. Uses 12 bits of VPI to identify 4096 unique virtual paths

19 How is a switched virtual circuit (SVC) established?

a. An SVC is established by the ATM Forum.

b. An SVC is established by manual configuration.

c. An SVC is established by connection management software.

d. An SVC is established by UNI signaling from the attached end device.

20 What is the purpose of ATM end system addresses?

a. To support SVC connection signaling across a PNNI or IISP network

b. To support PVC connection signaling across a PNNI or IISP network

c. To uniquely identify a cell as it enters the switch

d. To uniquely identify a connection in the switching table

21 Match the following well-known VCIs with the protocol that uses them:

a. VCI = 5	1. PNNI
b. VCI = 18	2. ILMI
c. VCI = 16	3. UNI Signaling

22 What does IPCP do in PPP?

a. Establishes IP parameters on a PPP link.

b. Provides communication between the network control program and any Layer-3 protocol.

c. IPCP is not used in PPP; it is a X.25 protocol.

d. IPCP is the frame type used in PPP.

23 Which interface is associated with 30B+D?

a. DS-3

b. ISDN PRI

c. ISDN BRI

d. OC-3

24 Which protocol communicates between a router and the local Frame Relay switch?

a. ILMI

b. MAP

c. NNI

d. LMI

25 Which feature uses BECN bits as input to control the flow of frames into the network?

a. The DE bit

b. Traffic shaping

c. Priority queuing

d. Compression

26 What is Frame Relay's advantage over X.25?

a. Its advanced error checking features.

b. It is connection-oriented.

c. It adds less overhead; therefore, it is available at greater speeds.

d. It is designed to run over bad cable systems.

27 You have a Frame Relay network between Router A and Router B. Host 1 and Router A are on one side, and Host 2 and Router B are on the other. Host 1 transmits a packet to Host 2. The frame is discarded in the wide-area network. Which device is responsible for retransmitting?

a. Host 1

b. Router A

c. Router B

d. The link-layer protocol on the Frame Relay switch

28 You have an X.25 network between Router A and Router B. Host 1 and Router A are on one side, and Host 2 and Router B are on the other. Host 1 transmits a packet to Host 2. Router A forwards the frame into the network, and the frame is discarded. Which device is responsible for retransmitting?

a. Host 1

b. Router A

c. Router B

d. Host 2

29 What does synchronization do?

a. Provides timing information between sender and receiver; used in circuit-switched networks

b. Provides timing information between sender and receiver; used in packet switched networks

c. Provides timing information between sender and receiver; used by IP networks

d. Provides timing information between sender and receiver; used in frame relay networks

30 What is SONET and on which OSI layer is it defined?

a. Symmetric Optical Network, physical layer

b. Synchronous Optical Network, Physical layer

c. Symmetric Optical Network, data-link layer

d. Synchronous Optical Network, data-link Layer

31 What does RFC 2427 define?

a. Multiprotocol connectivity over Frame Relay

b. IP connectivity over ATM

c. Multiprotocol connectivity over ATM

d. IP connectivity over PPP

32 What is the bandwidth capability of an ISDN B channel?

a. 56 kbps

b. 64 kbps

c. 128 kbps

d. 16 kbps

33 Where does the U reference point reside in the ISDN architecture?

a. Between the NT2 and the NT1

b. Between the TA and the TE2

c. Between the NT1 and the LE

d. Between the TE1 and the TA

34 RFC 2225 defines which of the following servers?

a. LAN emulation server

b. Broadcast and unknown server

c. ATM address resolution protocol server

d. LAN emulation configuration server

35 Which of the following protocols provides ATM interface attributes in a standard SNMP MIB structure?

a. PNNI

b. ILMI

c. IISP

d. SSCOP

36 Answer true or false to the following statements:

a. IISP supports dynamic rerouting.

b. An IISP route can have a primary and secondary path.

c. IISP supports QoS.

d. IISP can provide a route between different PNNI peer groups.

e. IISP static routes must avoid routing loops.

f. IISP is less efficient than PNNI source routing.

Scenario

Refer to the following configuration to answer the scenario questions:

```
isdn switch-type basic-ni
!
interface BRI0
 ip address 10.50.1.1 255.255.255.252
 encapsulation ppp
 dialer map ip 10.50.1.2 name R10 broadcast 7139970300101
 dialer-group 1
 isdn spid1 7134691020101
 isdn spid2 7134691030101
 ppp authentication pap
!
dialer-list protocol ip permit
```

1 Which authentication is being used?

a. DES

b. PAP

c. CHAP

d. Clear text

2 What does the **dialer map** command do?

a. Maps the local SPID to 10.50.1.2

b. Maps the remote SPID to 10.50.1.2

c. Defines the local router name as R10

d. Maps the local DLCI to 10.50.1.2

3 What are examples of protocols permitted to start the connection?

a. TCP, UDP, OSPF

b. NLSP, IPX

c. DECNet Phase IV,

d. AURP, NetBEUI

4 The B channel uses which encapsulation?

a. HDLC.

b. PPP.

c. LAPD.

d. Not enough information is given.

5 The D channel uses which frame type?

a. HDLC.

b. LAPB.

c. LAPD.

d. Not enough information is given.

This chapter covers the following topics needed to master the CCIE exam:

- **Transmission Control Protocol/Internet Protocol (TCP/IP) Architecture**—TCP/IP architecture and how it compares to the Open System Interconnection (OSI) model
- **IP Addressing**—Different IP address classes and address subnetting
- **Transport Layer**—TCP and User Datagram Protocol (UDP) transport protocols
- **TCP/IP Protocols, Services, and Applications**—Several TCP/IP protocols and applications, such as Address Resolution Protocol (ARP), Telnet, Internet Control Message Protocol (ICMP), File Transfer Protocol (FTP), Network Address Translation (NAT), Simple Network Management Protocol (SNMP), and (Domain Name System (DNS)
- **IP Version 6 (IPv6)**—Design goals of IPv6 and IPv6 addressing

CHAPTER 6

Internet Protocols

This chapter focuses on the TCP/IP suite of protocols and on IP addressing. The different class types of IP addresses are reviewed. Subnet masks are discussed as the method that subdivides a network. The TCP/IP layers are compared to the OSI model. Finally, some important TCP/IP applications and protocols are discussed. The chapter focuses not only on the theoretical aspects of TCP/IP but also on the implementation in Cisco routers.

"Do I Know This Already?" Quiz

The purpose of this assessment quiz is to help you determine how to spend your limited study time. If you can answer most or all of these questions, you might want to skim the Foundation Topics section and return to it later as necessary. Review the Foundation Summary section and answer the questions at the end of the chapter to ensure that you have a strong grasp of the material covered. If you intend to read the entire chapter, you do not necessarily need to answer these questions now. If you find these assessment questions difficult, read through the entire Foundation Topics section and review it until you feel comfortable with your ability to answer all the Q & A questions at the end of the chapter. These questions are repeated at the end of the chapter with additional questions to test your mastery of the material.

Select the best answer. Answers to these questions are in the Appendix, "Answers to Quiz Questions."

1 Which IP protocol and port does Telnet use?

a. TCP 21

b. Protocol 1, TCP port 23

c. UDP 23

d. IP protocol 6, TCP port 23

2 What is the directed broadcast address for 171.80.32.178/27?

a. 171.80.32.192.

b. 171.80.32.191.

c. 171.80.32.64.

d. There is not sufficient information.

3 When packets are fragmented, where are the fragments reassembled?

a. By the next hop router

b. By the TCP layer in the destination host

c. By the IP layer in the destination host

d. By the router next to the destination host

4 Which type of address class is 190.1.2.0?

a. Class A

b. Class B

c. Class C

d. Class D

5 What does the flag PSH do?

a. Tells the sending TCP process to send the segment immediately

b. Tells the routers to forward the packets with higher priority

c. Tells the destination TCP to push the IP packet to the application layer

d. Tells the IP layer to send immediately

6 Which of the following describes TFTP?

a. A protocol that uses TCP to transfer files with no authentication

b. A protocol for the transfer of files reliably using port 69

c. A protocol for the transfer of files using UDP

d. A protocol to transfer files using TCP 21

7 Which ICMP protocol type does the PING application use?

a. IP protocol 6

b. ICMP echo

c. TCP

d. ARP request

8 What is blocked in the following access list?

```
access-list 105 deny tcp any host 10.1.1.1 eq 23
access-list 105 permit tcp any any
```

a. Packets from host 10.1.1.1 are denied.

b. Packets from any TCP host are denied.

c. Packets from any host sent to host 10.1.1.1 to the Telnet port are denied.

d. Packets to host 10.1.1.1 are permitted; all others are denied.

9 Which methods acquire a default gateway?

a. ARP and RARP

b. BOOTP and DHCP

c. RARP and BOOTP

d. IP address and subnet mask

10 What is the inside global address in NAT?

a. The translated IP address of the device that resides in the internal network

b. The translated IP address of the device that resides in the Global Internet

c. The inside address of the device in the Internet network

d. The translated global address in the internal network that reaches an external device

11 Which of the following is a subnet mask with 27 bits?

a. 255.255.255.192

b. 255.255.255.252

c. 255.255.255.224

d. 255.255.255.240

12 How many hosts are in a Class B network with the default mask?

a. 65,534

b. 16,777,214

c. 254

d. 255

Foundation Topics

TCP/IP Protocol Architecture

TCP/IP protocols are the protocols that you use to run the Internet. Documentation for these protocols is in the form of Request For Comments (RFCs). These documents are published and reviewed by the Internet Engineering Task Force (IETF) working groups. IP RFC 791 (published in September 1981) describes version 4 of the protocol. The next version, IPv6, is described in RFC 2460 (published in 1998).

The TCP/IP protocols were created before and after the OSI reference model was published. There is no TCP/IP model, but the architecture can be compared. Figure 6-1 shows the comparison between the OSI model and the TCP/IP architecture.

Figure 6-1 *TCP/IP Model Compared to the OSI Model*

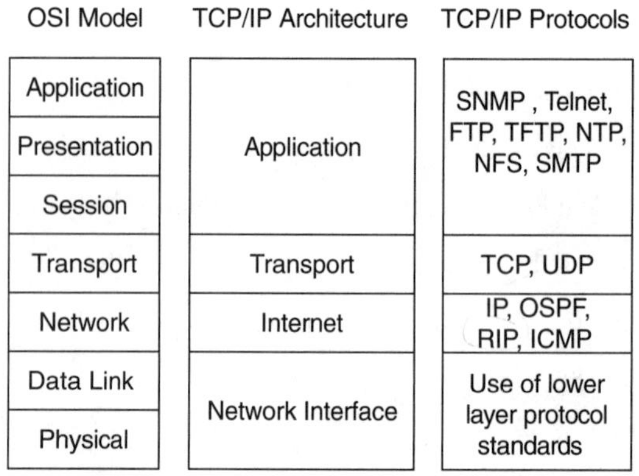

TCP/IP's architecture does not use the presentation and session layers. The application layer protocols use the transport layer services directly. The OSI transport layer provides connection-oriented service; in TCP/IP, this service is provided by TCP. TCP/IP also provides connectionless service in the transport layer with UDP. These protocols are discussed later in the chapter.

The Internet layer of TCP/IP corresponds to the network layer of the OSI model. Although OSI network-layer protocols provide connection-oriented (Connection-Mode Network Service (CMNS), X.25) or Connectionless Network Service (CLNS), IP provides only connectionless network service. The routing protocols are network layer protocols with an IP protocol number. One exception is the Border Gateway Protocol (BGP), which uses a TCP port number. Another is Intermediate System-to-Intermediate System (IS-IS), which resides over the data-link layer. Routing protocols are discussed in Chapter 7, "Static Routing and Distance Vector Routing Protocols," Chapter 8, "IP Link-State Routing Protocols," and Chapter 9, "Border Gateway Protocol."

The data-link and physical layers are not defined by TCP/IP but use the common lower-layer standards as defined by the International Organization for Standardization (ISO), the Institute of Electrical and Electronics Engineers (IEEE), and the International Telecommunication Union (ITU). IP uses protocols such as Integrated Services Digital Network (ISDN), Synchronous Optical Network (SONET), Ethernet, Token Ring, Gigabit Ethernet, Asynchronous Transfer Mode (ATM), Frame Relay, and others for physical transport. The lower-layer protocols are covered in Chapter 4, "Local-Area Networks and LAN Switching," and Chapter 5, "Wide-Area Networks."

Internet Protocol

IP is the network layer protocol that TCP/IP uses, which contains logical addressing and information for the routing of packets throughout the internetwork. IP is described in RFC 791, which was prepared for the Defense Advanced Research Projects Agency (DARPA) in September 1981. It provides for the transmission of blocks of data called *datagrams* (*packets*) from sources to destinations. The sources and destinations are identified by fixed-length IP addresses. The IP protocol provides for the fragmentation and reassembly of long datagrams.

IP Header

The best way to understand IP is to know the IP header. Segments from TCP are passed on to IP, and an IP header is added to the data. Figure 6-2 shows the IP header format.

Figure 6-2 *The IP Header*

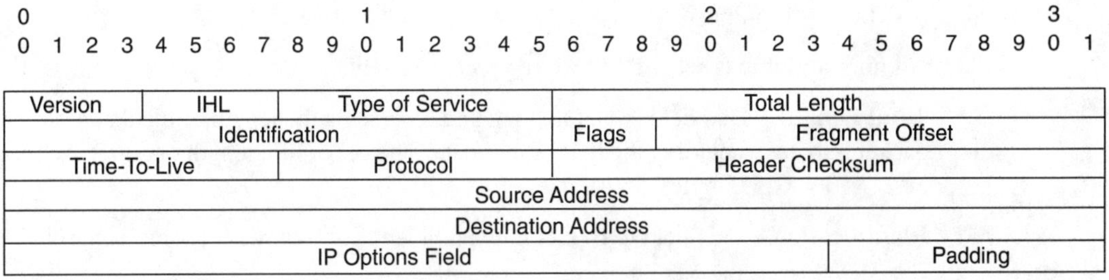

The following is a description of each field in the IP header:

- **Version**—This field is 4 bits long and indicates the format, based on the version number, of the IP header. Version 4 is the current version, so this field is set to 0100.
- **IHL**—This field is 4 bits long and indicates the length of the header in 32-bit words (4 bytes) so that the beginning of the data can be found. The minimum value for a correct header (five 32-bit words) is 5 (0101).

- **Type of Service (ToS)**—This field is 8 bits long and indicates quality of service (QoS) parameters. This field has the format shown in Figure 6-3.

Figure 6-3 *Type of Service Field*

Bit number:	0	1	2	3	4	5	6	7
Description:	Precedence			D	T	R	0	0

The first three (left-most) bits are the precedence bits. These define values that QoS methods use. Bit 3 (D-bit) indicates normal (0) or low (1) delay. Bit 4 (T-bit) indicates normal (0) or high (1) throughput. Bit 5 (R-bit) indicates normal (0) or high (1) reliability. Bits 6 and 7 are reserved for future use.

The RFC describes the precedence bits as follows:

— 111 — Network control

— 110 — Internetwork control

— 101 — Critic

— 100 — Flash override

— 011 — Flash

— 010 — Immediate

— 001 — Priority

— 000 — Routine

All normal traffic is set with 000 in the precedence bits.

- **Total Length**—This field is 16 bits long and represents the length of the datagram or packet in bytes, including the header and data. The maximum length of an IP packet can be $2^{16} - 1 = 65535$ bytes.
- **Identification**—This field is 16 bits long and identifies fragments for reassembly.
- **Flags**—This field is 3 bits long and indicates if the packet can be fragmented and shows more or last fragments. Bit 0 is reserved and set to 0. Bit 1 indicates May Fragment (0) or Do Not Fragment (1). Bit 2 indicates Last Fragment (0) or More Fragments (1) to follow.
- **Time to Live**—This field is 8 bits long and indicates the maximum time the packet is to remain on the network. If this field is zero, the packet must be discarded. This scheme permits undeliverable packets to be discarded.

- **Protocol**—This field is 8 bits long and indicates the upper-layer protocol. Table 6-1 shows some key protocol numbers.

Table 6-1 *IP Protocol Numbers*

Protocol Number	Protocol
1	ICMP
2	IGMP
6	TCP
9	Any IGP, used by Cisco for IGRP
17	UDP
88	EIGRP
89	OSPF
103	PIM

- **Header Checksum**—This field is 16 bits long. The checksum is calculated for the IP header only, without the data. It is recomputed and verified at each point that the IP header is processed.
- **Source Address**—This field is 32 bits long and is the IP address of the sender.
- **Destination Address**—This field is 32 bits long and is the IP address of the receiver.
- **IP Options**—This field is variable in length. Some options are as follows: security, Loose Source Routing, Strict Source Routing, Record Route, and Timestamp.
- **Padding**—This field is variable and ensures that the IP header ends on a 32-bit boundary.

IP Fragmentation

One of the key characteristics of IP is fragmentation and reassembly. Although the maximum length of an IP packet can be over 65,000 bytes, many lower-layer protocols do not support such large maximum transmission units (MTU). For example, the MTU for Ethernet is approximately 1500 bytes. When the IP layer receives a packet to send, it first queries the outgoing interface to get its MTU. If the size of the packet is greater than the MTU of the interface, the packet is fragmented.

When a packet is fragmented, it is not reassembled until it reaches the destination IP layer. The destination IP layer performs the reassembly. Also, any router in the path can fragment a packet, and any router in the path can fragment a fragmented packet again. Each fragmented packet receives its own IP header and is routed independently from other packets.

If one or more fragments are lost, the entire packet must be retransmitted. Retransmission is the responsibility of the higher-layer protocol (such as TCP). Also, the flags field in the IP header might be set to not fragment the packet. If set to not fragment, the packet is discarded if the outgoing MTU is smaller than the packet.

IP Addressing

This section covers the IP address classes, network subnets, and address assignments. The CCIE candidate must be an expert in handling IP addresses.

IP addresses assign a unique logical number to a network device. The number is 32-bits long. To make the number easier to read, you use the dotted decimal format. The bits are combined into four 8-bit groups, each converted into decimal numbers that are separated with dots. The following example shows an IP address in binary and decimal formats:

Binary IP address: 00110000010101011001001000001010
Grouping into four octets: 00110000 01010101 10010010 00001010
Convert each octet into decimal:
00110000 = 48
01010101 = 85
10010010 = 146
00001010 = 10
The IP address is: 48.85.146.10

IP Address Classes

IP addresses are divided into five classes. The most significant bits of the first octet help determine the address class of the IP address. Table 6-2 shows the high-order bits of each IP address class.

Table 6-2 *High-Order Bits of IP Address Classes*

Address Class	High Order Bits
A	0xxxxxxx
B	10xxxxxx
C	110xxxxx
D	1110xxxx
E	1111xxxx

x can be either 1 or 0, regardless of the address class.

The IP Classes A, B, and C are set aside for unicast addresses. Class D is for multicast addresses; Class E is reserved for experimental use.

Class A Addresses

Class A addresses range from 0 (00000000) to 127 (01111111) in the first octet. Network numbers assigned to companies range from 1.0.0.0 to 126.0.0.0, with networks 0 and 127 being reserved. For example, 127.0.0.1 is reserved for the local host. Also, network 10.0.0.0 is reserved for private addresses.

By default, for Class A addresses, the first octet is the network number and the three remaining octets are the host number. In the format N.H.H.H, N is the network part and H the host part. With 24 bits available, there are $2^{24} - 2 = 16,777,214$ IP addresses for host assignment. Two are subtracted for the network number (all 0s) and broadcast address (all 1s). A network with this many hosts attempting to broadcast on the network surely cannot work. This problem is resolved with subnetting, which is discussed in this section.

Class B Addresses

Class B addresses range from 128 (10000000) to 191 (10111111) in the first octet. Network numbers assigned to companies or other organizations range from 128.0.0.0 to 191.255.0.0. There are 16 networks reserved for private use; these are shown later in this section.

By default, for Class B addresses, the first two octets are the network number and the remaining two octets are for the host number. The format is N.N.H.H. With 16 bits available, there are $2^{16} - 2 = 65534$ IP addresses for host assignment. As with Class A addresses, a segment with over 65,000 hosts broadcasting cannot work; this is resolved with subnetting.

Class C Addresses

Class C addresses range from 192 (11000000) to 223 (11011111) in the first octet. Network numbers assigned to companies range from 192.0.0.0 to 223.255.255.0. The format is N.N.N.H. With 8 bits available, there are $2^8 - 2 = 254$ IP addresses for host assignment. H=0 is the network number; H=255 is the broadcast address.

Class D Addresses

Class D addresses range from 224 (11100000) to 239 (11101111) in the first octet. Network numbers are assigned to multicast groups that range from 224.0.0.1 to 239.255.255.255. These addresses do not have a host or network part. Some multicast addresses are already assigned; for example, routers that run EIGRP use 224.0.0.10.

Class E Addresses

Class E addresses range from 240 (11110000) to 254 (11111110) in the first octet. These addresses are reserved for experimental networks. Network 255 is reserved for the broadcast address, such as 255.255.255.255.

Table 6-3 summarizes the IP address classes.

Table 6-3 *IP Address Classes*

Address Class	High Order Bits	Network Numbers
A	0xxxxxxx	1.0.0.0 to 126.0.0.0
B	10xxxxxx	128.0.0.0 to 191.255.0.0
C	110xxxxx	192.0.0.0 to 223.255.255.0
D	1110xxxx	224.0.0.1 to 239.255.255.255
E	1111xxxx	240.0.0.0 to 254.255.255.255

Private Address Space

Some network numbers are reserved for private use. These numbers are not routed on the Internet. Private addresses are explained in RFC 1918, "Address Allocation for Private Internets." Published in 1996, private addresses were one of the first issues addressed with the concern that globally unique address space would become exhausted. Many enterprises use private address space in networks today, combined with accessing the Internet using NAT, which NAT is covered later in this chapter.

The IP address space reserved for private Internets are 10.0.0.0, and 172.16.0.0 to 172.31.0.0, and 192.168.0.0 to 192.168.225.0. This includes 1 Class A network, 16 Class B networks, and 256 Class C networks, respectively. Table 6-4 summarizes private address space.

Table 6-4 *Private Address Space*

Class Type	Start Network	End Network
Class A	10.0.0.0/8	–
Class B	172.16.0.0/16	172.31.0.0/16
Class C	192.168.0.0/24	192.168.255.0/24

IP Address Subnets

Subnetting plays an important part in IP addressing. The subnet mask helps determine the network, subnetwork, and host part of an IP address. The network architect uses subnetting to manipulate the default mask to create subnetworks for LAN and WAN segments. As mentioned earlier, one router interface with 16 million hosts off that interface is not a good thing.

Subnet masks are for Class A, B, and C addresses only. Multicast addresses do not use subnet masks. Subnet masks are a 32-bit number where bits are set to 1 to establish the network portion of the address, and a 0 is the host part of the address. The mask's bits set to 1 are contiguous from the left portion of the mask; the bits set to 0 are also contiguous to the right portion of the mask. Table 6-5 shows the default masks for Class A, B, and C addresses.

Table 6-5 *Default Address Masks*

Class	Binary Mask	Dotted Decimal Mask
A	11111111 00000000 00000000 00000000	255.0.0.0
B	11111111 11111111 00000000 00000000	255.255.0.0
C	11111111 11111111 11111111 00000000	255.255.255.0

Consider, for example, a company with 200 hosts is assigned the Class C network of 200.1.1.0/24. The 200 hosts are in six different LANs. The Class C network can be subnetted by using a mask of 255.255.255.224. Looking at the mask in binary (11111111 11111111 11111111 11100000), the first three bytes are the network part, the first three bits of the fourth byte determine the subnets, and the five remaining 0 bits are for host addressing.

Table 6-6 shows the subnetworks created with a mask of 255.255.255.224. Using this mask, 2^n subnets are created, where n is the number of bits taken from the host part for the subnet mask. In this example, you use 3 bits, so that $2^3 = 8$ subnets. With Cisco routers, the all 1s subnet (LAN 7) can be used for a subnet broadcast. You can use the all 0s subnet with the **ip subnet-zero** command.

Table 6-6 *Subnets for Network 200.1.1.0*

LAN	Fourth Byte	Subnet Number	First Host	Broadcast
LAN 0	**000**00000	200.1.1.0	200.1.1.1	200.1.1.31
LAN 1	**001**00000	200.1.1.32	200.1.1.33	200.1.1.63
LAN 2	**010**00000	200.1.1.64	200.1.1.65	200.1.1.95
LAN 3	**011**00000	200.1.1.96	200.1.1.97	200.1.1.127
LAN 4	**100**00000	200.1.1.128	200.1.1.129	200.1.1.159
LAN 5	**101**00000	200.1.1.160	200.1.1.161	200.1.1.191
LAN 6	**110**00000	200.1.1.192	200.1.1.193	200.1.1.223
LAN 7	**111**00000	200.1.1.224	200.1.1.225	200.1.1.255

In this example, you use a fixed-length subnet mask. The entire network has the same subnet mask, 255.255.255.224. Routing protocols such as Routing Information Protocol version 1 (RIPv1) and IGRP use fixed-length subnet masks. They do not support variable-length subnet masks (VLSM). VLSMs are covered in this chapter.

Mask Nomenclature

IP subnet masks can be represented in several ways. The masks can be represented in binary, hexadecimal, dotted-decimal, or bit mask. The most common way is the dotted decimal format (255.255.255.0). Recently, the number of bits format has become popular. This format represents the mask by using a slash with the number of bits with 1s in the mask. For example, 255.255.0.0 is represented as /16. Table 6-7 shows some mask representations.

Table 6-7 *Subnet Masks*

Dotted Decimal	Bit Mask	Hexadecimal
255.0.0.0	/8	FF-00-00-00
255.192.0.0	/10	FF-C0-00-00
255.255.0.0	/16	FF-FF-00-00
255.255.224.0	/19	FF-FF-E0-00
255.255.240.0	/20	FF-FF-F0-00
255.255.255.0	/24	FF-FF-FF-00
255.255.255.224	/27	FF-FF-FF-E0
255.255.255.240	/28	FF-FF-FF-F0
255.255.255.248	/29	FF-FF-FF-F8
255.255.255.252	/30	FF-FF-FF-FC

Determining the Network Portion of an IP Address

If you have an IP address and subnet mask, you can determine the full classful network, subnetwork, and broadcast number of the subnetwork. This is accomplished by a logical AND operation between the IP address and subnet mask. Table 6-8 shows the AND operation. The AND operation is similar to the multiplication of Bit 1 and Bit 2; if any 0 is present, the result is 0.

Table 6-8 *The AND Logical Operation*

Bit 1	Bit 2	AND
0	0	0
0	1	0
1	0	0
1	1	1

As an example, take the IP address 200.1.1.70 with a subnet mask of 255.255.255.224. The three bolded bits in the subnet mask extend the default Class C mask (/24) to a mask of /27. Perform an AND operation of the IP address with the subnet mask to obtain the subnetwork, as shown in Table 6-9. The broadcast number is obtained by making all the host bits 1.

Table 6-9 *Subnetwork of IP Address 200.1.1.70*

IP Address	11001000 00000001 00000001	010	00110	200.1.1.70
Subnet Mask	11111111 11111111 11111111	111	00000	255.255.255.224
Subnetwork	11001000 00000001 00000001	010	00000	200.1.1.64
	Network	**Subnet**	**Host**	
Broadcast Address	11001000 00000001 00000001	010	11111	200.1.1.95

VLSM

VLSMs further subdivide a network to prevent the wasting of IP addresses. If a Class C network uses 255.255.255.240 as a subnet mask, there are 16 subnets, each with 14 IP addresses. If a point-to-point link needs only 2 IP addresses, 12 IP addresses are wasted. This problem scales further with Class B and Class A address space. With VLSMs, small LANs can use /28 subnets with 14 hosts, whereas larger LANs can use /23 or /22 masks with 510 and 1022 hosts, respectively.

Consider Class B network 172.16.0.0/16 as an example. Using a /20 mask produces 16 subnetworks. Table 6-10 shows the subnetworks. With the /20 subnet masks, the first four bits of the third octet determine the subnets.

Table 6-10 *Subnets with a /20 Mask*

Third Octet	Subnetwork
00000000	172.16.0.0/20
00010000	172.16.16.0/20
00100000	172.16.32.0/20
00110000	172.16.48.0/20
01000000	172.16.64.0/20
01010000	172.16.80.0/20
01100000	172.16.96.0/20
01110000	172.16.112.0/20
10000000	172.16.128.0/20
10010000	172.16.144.0/20

continues

Table 6-10 *Subnets with a /20 Mask (Continued)*

Third Octet	Subnetwork
10100000	172.16.160.0/20
10110000	172.16.176.0/20
11000000	172.16.192.0/20
11010000	172.16.208.0/20
11100000	172.16.224.0/20
11110000	172.16.240.0/20

With fixed-length subnet masks, the network only supports 16 networks. Any LAN or WAN link must use a /20 subnet. This is an inefficient use of address space. With VLSMs, the /20 subnets can be further subnetted.

For example, take 172.16.64.0/20 and subdivide it to support LANs with approximately 500 hosts. Use a /23 mask. This produces the subnetworks shown in Table 6-11.

Table 6-11 *Subnetworks for 172.16.64.0/20*

Third Octet	Subnetwork
0100**000**0	172.16.64.0/23
0100**001**0	172.16.66.0/23
0100**010**0	172.16.68.0/23
0100**011**0	172.16.70.0/23
0100**100**0	172.16.72.0/23
0100**101**0	172.16.74.0/23
0100**110**0	172.16.76.0/23
0100**111**0	172.16.78.0/23

With VLSMs, these subnetworks can be even further subdivided. Take subnetwork 172.16.76.0/23 and use it for two LANs that have fewer than 250 hosts. This produces subnetworks 172.16.76.0/24 and 172.16.77.0/24. Also, subdivide 172.16.78.0/23 for serial links. Because each point-to-point serial link needs only two IP addresses, you can use a /30 mask. The subnetworks that are produced are shown in Table 6-12.

Table 6-12 *Serial Line Subnetworks*

Third Octet	Fourth Octet	Subnetwork
01001110	**000000**00	172.16.78.0/30
01001110	**000001**00	172.16.78.4/30
01001110	**000010**00	172.16.78.8/30
01001110	**000011**00	172.16.78.10/30
...	...	...
01001111	**111101**00	172.16.79.244/30
01001111	**111110**00	172.16.79.248/30
01001111	**111111**00	172.16.79.252/30

Each /30 subnetwork includes the subnetwork number, two IP addresses, and a broadcast address. Table 6-13 shows the bits for 172.16.78.8/30.

Table 6-13 *Addresses Within Subnetwork 172.16.78.8/30*

Binary Address	IP Address	Function
1010110 00010000 01001110 000010**00**	172.16.78.8	Subnetwork
1010110 00010000 01001110 000010**01**	172.16.78.9	IP address #1
1010110 00010000 01001110 000010**10**	172.16.78.10	IP address #2
1010110 00010000 01001110 000010**11**	172.16.78.11	Broadcast address

Classless Interdomain Routing (CIDR) and Address Aggregation

CIDR permits the address aggregation of classful networks. This is accomplished by using the common bits between networks. The networks need to be continuous and have a common bit boundary.

BGP version 4 supports CIDR, which permits the reduction of the size of routing tables by creating aggregated routes that result in supernets. CIDR eliminates the concept of network classes within BGP and supports the advertising of IP prefixes.

With CIDR, ISPs assign groups of Class C networks to enterprise customers. This eliminates the problem of assigning too large of a network (Class B) or needing to assign multiple Class C networks to a customer and needing to route each Class C network, which makes Internet routing tables large. BGP is covered in Chapter 11, "Traffic Management."

Four Class C networks can be summarized at the /22 bit level. For example, networks 200.1.100.0, 200.1.101.0, 200.1.102.0, and 200.1.103.0 share common bits, as shown in Table 6-14. The resulting network is 200.1.100.0/22, which you can use for a 1000 node LAN.

Table 6-14 *Common Bits Within Class C Networks*

Binary Address	IP Address
11001000 00000001 01100100 00000000	200.1.100.0
11001000 00000001 01100101 00000000	200.1.101.0
11001000 00000001 01100110 00000000	200.1.102.0
11001000 00000001 01100111 00000000	200.1.103.0

Network addresses can be summarized by aggregating the networks at a bit boundary. A neighboring router can receive one summarized route, rather than receiving 8, 16, 32, or more routes, depending on the level of summarization. Figure 6-4 shows an example of the route summarization. Router A sends a single route to its upstream router. In Table 6-15, all the Class C networks share a bit boundary with 21 common bits.

Figure 6-4 *Route Summarization*

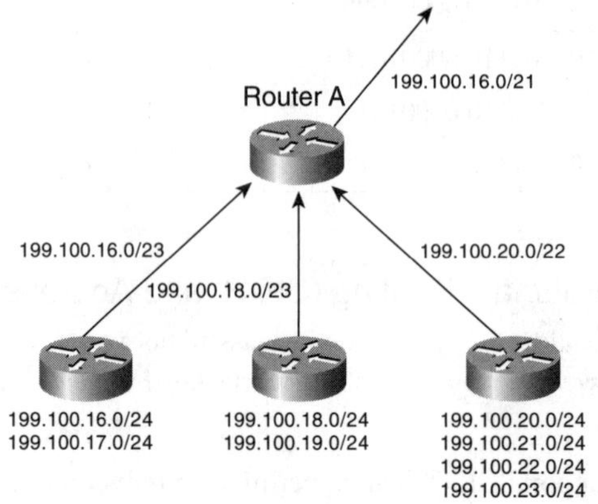

Table 6-15 *Summarization of Networks*

Binary Address	IP Network
11000111 01100100 00010000 00000000	199.100.16.0
11000111 01100100 00010001 00000000	199.100.17.0
11000111 01100100 00010010 00000000	199.100.18.0
11000111 01100100 00010011 00000000	199.100.19.0

Table 6-15 *Summarization of Networks (Continued)*

Binary Address	IP Network
11000111 01100100 00010100 00000000	199.100.20.0
11000111 01100100 00010101 00000000	199.100.21.0
11000111 01100100 00010110 00000000	199.100.22.0
11000111 01100100 00010111 00000000	199.100.23.0

Transport Layer

The transport layer of the TCP/IP architecture provides two services: one connection-oriented with TCP and a connectionless service with UDP. This section covers these protocols.

TCP

TCP is a connection-oriented, end-to-end reliable protocol for the communication between host systems. TCP is specified in RFC 793. TCP assumes unreliable packet delivery service from the lower layers. TCP is accessed by the IP with protocol number 6. TCP accesses upper-layer protocols with port numbers. TCP uses several mechanisms for the reliable delivery of data, including PUSH (PSH) and acknowledgment (ACK) signals, windowing, and multiplexing. Data in TCP is called *segments*.

TCP Mechanics

This section covers some mechanisms that TCP uses for the reliable delivery of data.

PSH Signal

TCP packages bytes into segments for transmission through the network. TCP decides when sufficient data has accumulated to form a segment for transmission. The application that uses TCP can ensure that data is transmitted by indicating that it is pushed to the receiving system. A PSH pointer indicates how much data is to be sent. The PSH causes the TCP to promptly forward and deliver data up to the point indicated in the PSH. The data is sent to the receiver, which is the destination station.

Acknowledgment

TCP must recover damaged, lost, duplicated, or out-of-order data. This is achieved by using (ACKs) from the receiving system. If an ACK is not received within a timeout interval, the data is retransmitted.

Sequence Numbers

Each segment is sent with a sequence number. At the receiving end, the sequence numbers re-order segments that might have been received out of order.

Checksum

Each segment is sent with a checksum number. The checksum is verified at the receiving end. Segments with bad checksum are discarded.

Windowing

TCP uses a window of sequence numbers to implement flow control. The receiver indicates the amount of data to be sent. The receiver sends a window with every ACK that indicates a range of acceptable sequence numbers beyond the last received segment . The window allows the receiver to tell the sender how many bytes to transmit.

Multiplexing

Many processes on a single host can use the TCP protocol. TCP has the capability to multiplex multiple upper-layer applications into a single connection.

To better understand the mechanics of TCP, look at the TCP header.

TCP Header Format

Understanding the format of the TCP header helps comprehend all the functions and mechanics of the protocol. TCP uses port numbers, sequence numbers, a sliding window size, and flags in the header. Figure 6-5 shows the TCP header.

Figure 6-5 *TCP Header*

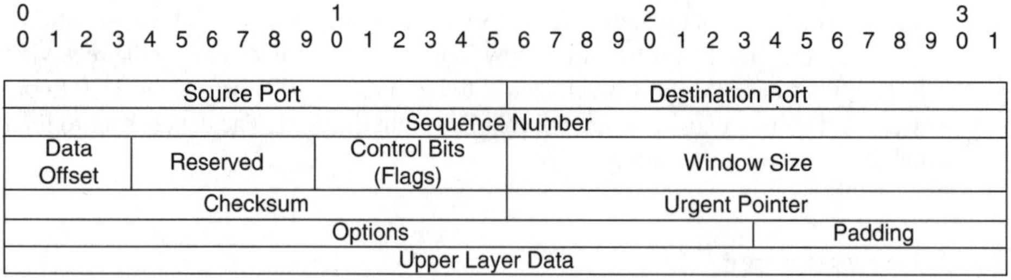

The following is a description of each field of the TCP header in Figure 6-5:

- **Source port**—This field is 16 bits long and indicates the source port number.
- **Destination port**—This field is 16 bits long and indicates the destination port number. Some port numbers are 23 for Telnet, 21 for FTP, and 20 for FTP-Data.
- **Sequence number**—This field is 32 bits long and indicates the sequence number of the first data byte in the segment. One exception is that when synchronize (SYN) is present, it indicates the initial sequence number (ISN) with the first data byte using ISN+1. Sequence numbers use number of bytes and not number of bits.
- **Data Offset**—This field is 4 bits long and indicates the number of 32-bit words in the TCP header. This indicates where the data begins.
- **Reserved**—This field is 6 bits long and is reserved for future use. All bits are set to 0.
- **Control field**—This field is 6 bits long, with each bit representing a flag.

  When the flags are set (1), they have the following meanings:

  — **URG**—Urgent pointer field significant

  — **ACK**—Acknowledgment field significant

  — **PSH**—Push function

  — **RST**—Reset the connection

  — **SYN**—Synchronize the sequence numbers

  — **FIN**—No more data from sender
- **Window Size**—This field is 16 bits long and specifies the number of bytes the sender can accept.
- **Checksum**—This field is 16 bits long and performs a checksum of the header, data, and the TCP pseudo-header. The TCP pseudo-header consists of the source IP address, destination IP address, protocol number, and TCP length. The TCP length is not sent but is calculated for the length of the TCP header and data.
- **Urgent Pointer**—This field is 16 bits long. If the urgent (URG) flag is set, the urgent pointer is added to the sequence number to indicate the end of the urgent data.
- **Options**—This field is variable in length but is always a multiple of 8 bits. One option is the maximum segment size, which indicates the maximum receive segment size the sender can accept.
- **Padding**—The options field is padded to the end of the 32-bit word.

Connection Establishment

TCP connections are established between two systems by synchronizing with each other's initial sequence numbers. This is accomplished by an exchange of connection-establishing segments with the SYN bit set and initial sequence numbers. The TCP connection is full-duplex; each side sends its own initial sequence number and must receive an acknowledgment from the other side.

Figure 6-6 shows the three-way handshake for connection establishment.

Figure 6-6 *Three-Way Handshake for Connection Establishment*

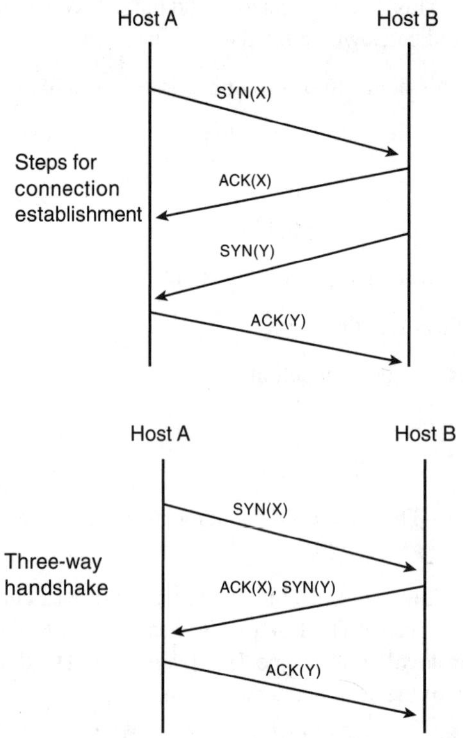

The following steps must occur to have an established connection:

Step 1 Host A sends a SYN with sequence number X to Host B.

Step 2 Host B must ACK that Host A's sequence number is X.

Step 3 Host B sends a SYN with sequence number Y to Host A.

Step 4 Host A must ACK that Host B's sequence number is Y.

This operation is implemented in three steps because Steps 2 and 3 can be sent in one segment. Therefore, this is called a *three-way handshake*.

Connection Flow Control

After a connection is established, the sending TCP sends segments no larger than the received window size. The sender waits for the acknowledgment of sent segments before sending additional data. Each acknowledgment also has the window size, which indicates the amount of data that the receiver is willing to accept. The window can change in size, therefore, the name *sliding window*. Remember, the window size is represented in bytes.

A TCP sender, for example, might have 200 bytes to send to a receiver with a window size of 70 bytes. The sender creates a segment of 70 bytes and sends it, as shown in Figure 6-7. Then, it waits for an ACK. The receiver responds with an ACK value of 71, which indicates that it received bytes 1 through 70. It also indicates that the window size is 90. The sending station then transmits bytes 71 through 160 in the next segment. The next ACK from the receiver is 161, with a window of 80. The sending station finally transmits bytes 161 to 200. The receiving station sends an acknowledgment, expecting sequence number 161 next, with the next window size sliding to 75.

Figure 6-7 *Flow Control*

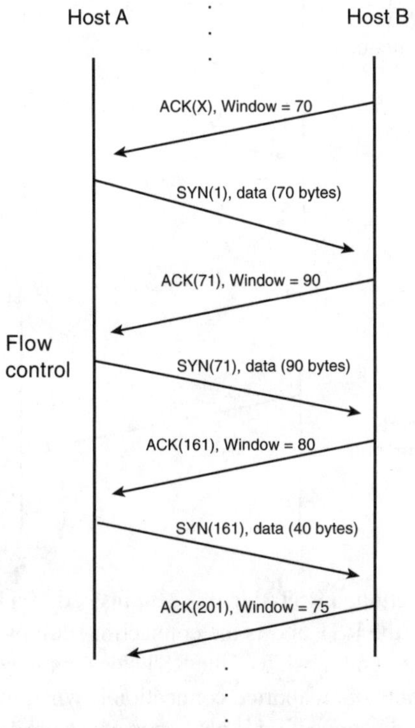

Connection Termination

A connection can terminate in two ways. The first is *graceful termination*, and the second is an *aborted connection*.

For graceful connection termination, both sides must send a finish (FIN) signal and expect an acknowledgment from the other side. It is similar to connection establishment, but in this case, it is a connection termination. It takes four, not three, segments to terminate a connection. Because the connection is full-duplex, each side must shut down independently. Either side can send a FIN to terminate the connection. As shown in Figure 6-8, Host A sends the FIN flag, which is acknowledged by Host B. Host B also sends a FIN flag in a separate segment, which is acknowledged by Host A. At this point, the connection is closed.

Figure 6-8 *Connection Termination*

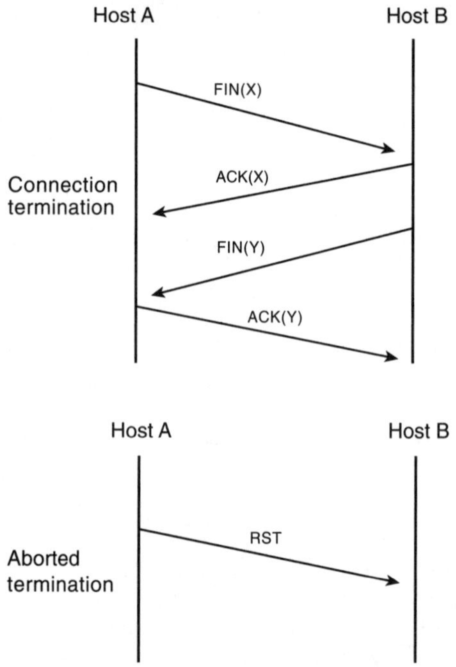

For an aborted connection, a RST signal is sent instead of a FIN, as shown in Figure 6-8. The receiving side of the RST aborts the connection, dumps any data, and does not send an acknowledgment. The sending side of the RST does not have to wait for an ACK to end the connection. An example of an aborted connection is when in a Telnet connection a CTRL-D disconnects. An aborted connection is also known as a hard *close*.

UDP

UDP is a connectionless, best effort transport-layer protocol. UDP uses IP protocol number 17. Because UDP does not spend time setting up and handling connections, it generates less overhead than TCP. UDP's benefit is that with a small header, it can send data with less overhead to the destination. Applications that are time-sensitive, such as voice and video, tend to use UDP transport instead of TCP. There is no need to retransmit a voice conversation.

UDP Header

The UDP header is shown in Figure 6-9.

Figure 6-9 *UDP Header*

0 1 2 3
0 1 2 3 4 5 6 7 8 9 0 1 2 3 4 5 6 7 8 9 0 1 2 3 4 5 6 7 8 9 0 1

Source Port	Destination Port
UDP Length	Checksum

The following is a description of each field of the UDP header in Figure 6-9:

- **Source port**—This field is 16 bits long and indicates the source port number. It is an optional field; a value of zero is inserted if the field is not used.
- **Destination port**—This field is 16 bits long and indicates the destination port number. Some destination ports are 69 (TFTP) and 161 (SNMP).
- **UDP length**—This field is 16 bits long and indicates the length in bytes of the datagram that includes the UDP header and data.
- **Checksum**—This field is 16 bits long. The checksum is performed on the UDP header, UDP data, and IP pseudo-header. The IP pseudo-header consists of the IP source address, IP destination address, protocol, and UDP length. Figure 6-10 shows the pseudo-header.

Figure 6-10 *IP Pseudo-Header for Checksum*

0 1 2 3
0 1 2 3 4 5 6 7 8 9 0 1 2 3 4 5 6 7 8 9 0 1 2 3 4 5 6 7 8 9 0 1

Source IP Address		
Destination IP Address		
00000000	Protocol	UDP Length

TCP/IP Protocols, Services, and Applications

This section covers the different TCP/IP protocols, services, and applications that are required knowledge for the CCIE written exam.

ARP

When an IP packet needs to be sent over an Ethernet network, the sender must find out what 48-bit Media Access Control (MAC) physical address to send the frame to. Given the destination IP, ARP obtains the destination MAC. The destination MAC can be a local host or the gateway router's MAC address if the destination IP is across the routed network. ARP is described in RFC 826 (November 1982). The local host maintains an ARP table with a list of IP addresses to MAC addresses.

ARP operates by having the sender broadcast an ARP Request, as shown in Figure 6-11. In this figure, the workstation with IP address 192.168.1.22 has a packet to send to 192.168.1.17 but does not have a destination MAC address in its ARP table. An ARP request is broadcast to all hosts in a segment, as shown in Step 1 of Figure 6-11. The ARP request contains the sender's IP and MAC address; it also contains the target IP address. All nodes in the broadcast domain receive and process the ARP request. As shown in Step 2, the device with the target IP address sends an ARP reply back to the sender with its MAC address information; the ARP reply is a unicast message that is sent to 192.168.1.22. The sender now has the target MAC address in its ARP; it sends the frame out (Step 3).

Figure 6-11 *ARP Request and Reply*

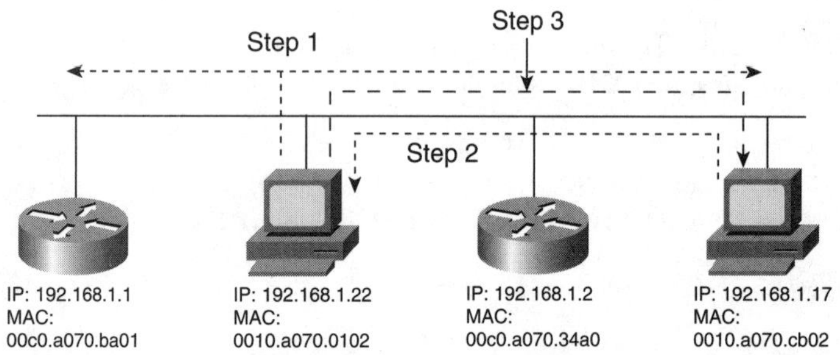

Display the ARP table on Cisco routers with the **show ip arp** command, as shown in Example 6-1.

Example 6-1 *ARP Table*

```
router5#show ip arp
Protocol  Address          Age (min)  Hardware Addr   Type   Interface
Internet  10.1.3.1                 0  0050.3ee4.5859  ARPA   Ethernet0
Internet  10.1.3.2                 0  0010.7b1b.6f9c  ARPA   Ethernet0
Internet  10.1.3.5                 -  0010.7b7e.ccc3  ARPA   Ethernet0
Internet  10.1.3.6                 0  0010.7b7e.cccd  ARPA   Ethernet0
```

You can clear the ARP table by using the global command **clear arp-cache**.

NOTE Ever wondered why sometimes you try to ping a device on the local network and the first ping fails? An ARP request goes out on the first ping and the ping ICMP echo times out as the ARP process goes on. Then, the next four pings are successful. The following shows that when you try the **ping** command for a second time, all five pings work:

```
router3#ping 10.1.3.2
Type escape sequence to abort.
Sending 5, 100-byte ICMP Echos to 10.1.3.2, timeout is 2 seconds:
.!!!!
Success rate is 80 percent (4/5), round-trip min/avg/max = 1/2/4 ms
router3#ping 10.1.3.2
Type escape sequence to abort.
Sending 5, 100-byte ICMP Echos to 10.1.3.2, timeout is 2 seconds:
!!!!!
Success rate is 100 percent (5/5), round-trip min/avg/max = 1/2/4 ms
```

Reverse Address Resolution Protocol (RARP)

RARP, as described in RFC 903, provides a method for workstations to dynamically find their IP protocol address when they only know their hardware (MAC) address. RARP was replaced by the Bootstrap Protocol (BOOTP) and Dynamic Host Configuration Protocol (DHCP) as the primary means to dynamically learn a device IP address.

Proxy ARP

Proxy ARP, as described in RFC 1027, specifies a method for which routers can respond to ARP requests from hosts that do not have a configured gateway, by replying with its local MAC address for destinations on other subnetworks. Cisco routers can reply to ARP requests for destination hosts on different major networks. Also, if the IP prefix is in the routing table, Cisco routers can send the ARP reply even if multiple segments are between the destination host and the router. Figure 6-12 shows an example of the function of proxy-ARP.

Host A does not have a default gateway configured. It has a packet to send to Host B. As shown in Figure 6-12, Host A sends an ARP request (Step 1) to find the MAC address of 192.168.2.20 (Host B). The router is configured for proxy-arp and has Host B's MAC address in its ARP table. The router replies to Host A with an ARP reply (Step 2) by using its own MAC address (00c0.a070.34a0) as the destination MAC, not Host B's MAC address. Host A then proceeds to send the packet with Host B's IP address (192.168.2.20) but with the router's MAC address.

Proxy ARP can be disabled per interface by using the interface configuration command **no ip proxy-arp**.

Figure 6-12 *Proxy-ARP Example*

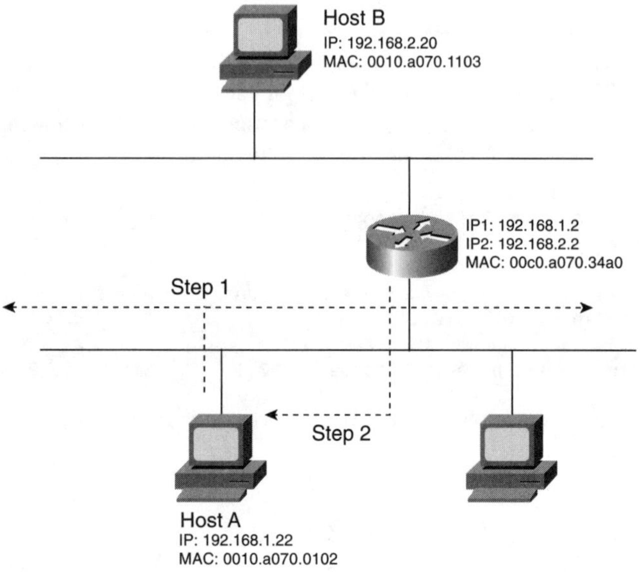

BOOTP

BOOTP was first defined in RFC 951 and has been updated by RFC 1395, RFC 1497, RFC 1532, and RFC 1542. BOOTP is a protocol that allows a booting host to configure itself by dynamically obtaining its IP address, IP gateway, and other information from a remote server. You can use a single server to centrally manage numerous network hosts without having to configure each host independently.

BOOTP is an application layer-based protocol that uses UDP/IP protocols for transport. UDP port 67 sends BOOTP requests to the BOOTP server, and the server uses UDP port 68 to send messages to the UDP client. The destination IP of the BOOTP requests uses the all-hosts (255.255.255.255), which are not forwarded by the router. If the BOOTP server is one or more router hops from the subnet, the local default gateway router must be configured to forward the BOOTP requests.

The interface command **ip helper-address** *x.x.x.x* is configured on interfaces with workstations that acquire their IP address information using BOOTP. The **ip helper-address** command changes the destination IP address of the BOOTP request and forwards it to the configured

IP address. When an IP helper address is configured, UDP forwarding is enabled on default ports. The default ports are as follows:

- TFTP (UDP 69)
- DNS (UDP 53)
- Time Service (UDP 37)
- NetBIOS Name Server (UDP 137)
- NetBIOS Datagram server (UDP 138)
- BOOTP Server and Client (UDP 67 and 68)
- TACACS Service (UDP 49)
- IEN-116 Name Service (UDP 42)

To prevent and control the forwarding of other protocols, you use the **no ip forward-protocol udp** [*port*] command. This is a global command and is not configured on an interface. For example, to forward TFTP, BOOTP, Terminal Access Controller Access Control System (TACACS), and a DNS broadcast, and prevent the other default protocols, you configure the router as displayed in Example 6-2.

Example 6-2 *Helper Address Configuration*

```
router3(config)#int e 0
router3(config-if)#ip helper-address 10.1.1.1
router3(config-if)#exit

router3(config)#no ip forward-protocol udp netbios-dgm
router3(config)#no ip forward-protocol udp netbios-ns
router3(config)#no ip forward-protocol udp nameserver
router3(config)#no ip forward-protocol udp time
```

DHCP

DHCP (defined in RFC 1531) provides a method to dynamically configure hosts on the network. DHCP is based on BOOTP and adds the capability of reusing network addresses and additional configuration options. DHCP server hosts allocate network addresses and deliver configuration parameters dynamically to hosts. In today's networks, most user computers are configured with DHCP. With DHCP, the computer can dynamically obtain its configuration information, such as IP address, subnet mask, IP default-gateway, DNS servers, Windows Internet Naming Service (WINS) servers, and so on. This configuration information is managed centrally on a DHCP server.

DHCP uses BOOTP relay agents (routers) to forward the DHCP requests to the server. Because DHCP is an extension of BOOTP, it uses the message format as defined in RFC 951 for BOOTP.

It uses the same ports as BOOTP: DHCP messages to a server use UDP port 67, and DHCP messages sent to a client use UDP port 68. Because of this, the configuration to support DHCP in the routers is the same as described for BOOTP.

Hot Standby Routing Protocol (HSRP)

HSRP is not a TCP/IP standard defined by an RFC; instead, it is a Cisco protocol that provides automatic router backup. HSRP allows one router to assume the function of a second router if the second router fails. HSRP is useful for critical networks that need a failover router for network reachability. HSRP uses a priority scheme to determine the default active router. The default priority is 100. If you configure a router with a higher priority, it becomes the active router if both routers are configured at the same time. If a second (or third) router is configured after an HSRP router is already active, and that new router is configured with a higher priority, it does not take over the active role unless it's configured with the **preempt** command.

A standards-based protocol similar to HSRP called Virtual Router Redundancy Protocol (VRRP) is defined in the proposed RFC 2338. VRRP is not an exam blueprint and is not covered in this book.

HSRP is supported over Ethernet, Token Ring, and Fiber Distributed Data Interface (FDDI) interfaces. Although each router has its own physical MAC address and logical IP address, with HSRP they share a virtual MAC address and IP address. The active router assumes the virtual IP (VIP). The default gateway of hosts is configured with the VIP address. After a failure, the standby router takes over the active role. HSRP can also be configured to track an outgoing interface (usually a serial interface); if the interface fails, the active router resigns, and the standby router becomes the active router.

HSRP Configuration

Figure 6-13 shows an example for the use of HSRP. Host A is configured with a default gateway of 192.168.1.1. Router A and Router B are configured for HSRP. Router A is configured with a higher priority than Router B, and the default priority is 100. The default timers are hellotime = 3 seconds and holdtime = 10 seconds. Authentication is used for the HSRP group, and the password is "secret." The routers are also configured to preempt, so if Router A fails or the serial interface in Router A fails, Router B becomes active. After Router A becomes available, Router A preempts and becomes the HSRP active router again, even if Router B has not failed.

Figure 6-13 *HSRP Example*

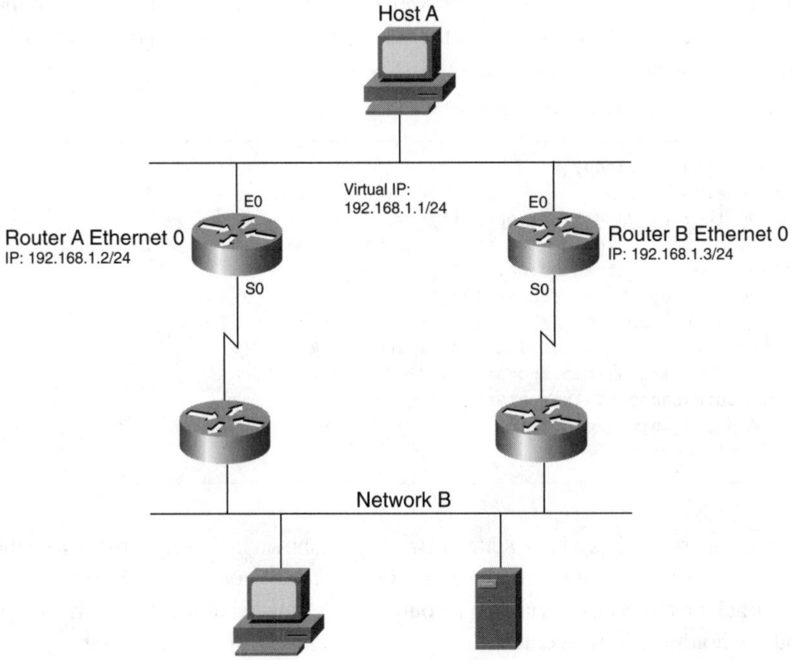

The configuration for Routers A and B for HSRP group #1 are displayed in Example 6-3.

Example 6-3 *Example of HSRP Configuration*

```
hostname RouterA
!
interface ethernet 0
 ip address 192.168.1.2 255.255.255.0
 standby 1 ip 192.168.1.1
 standby 1 preempt
 standby 1 priority 105
 standby 1 authentication secret
 standby 1 track serial 0


hostname RouterB
!
interface ethernet 0
 ip address 192.168.1.3 255.255.255.0
 standby 1 ip 192.168.1.1
 standby 1 preempt
 standby 1 authentication secret
 standby 1 track serial 0
```

To verify HSRP, use the **show standby** command.

The local state is active for the active router, as shown in Example 6-4. From the router output, you can determine that Router A is the active HSRP router with a priority of 105 and that it can preempt. Router A also tracks serial 0.

Example 6-4 **show standby** *Command on Router A*

```
routerA#show standby
Ethernet0 - Group 1
  Local state is Active, priority 105, may preempt
  Hellotime 3 holdtime 10 configured hellotime 3 sec holdtime 10 sec
  Next hello sent in 00:00:02.500
  Hot standby IP address is 192.168.1.1 configured
  Active router is local
  Standby router is 192.168.1.3 expires in 00:00:11
  Standby virtual mac address is 0000.0c07.ac01
  1 state changes, last state change 00:13:10
  Tracking interface states for 1 interface, 1 up:
    Up   Serial0
```

The second router has a local state of standby, as shown in Example 6-5. From the router output, you can determine that Router B is the HSRP standby router with a priority of 100. Router B also tracks its interface serial 0. The output also shows that the default hellotime is 3 seconds and the holdtime is 10 seconds.

Example 6-5 **show standby** *Command on Router B*

```
routerB6#show standby
Ethernet0 - Group 1
  Local state is Standby, priority 100, may preempt
  Hellotime 3 holdtime 10 configured hellotime 3 sec holdtime 10 sec
  Next hello sent in 00:00:00.028
  Hot standby IP address is 192.168.1.1 configured
  Active router is 192.168.1.2 expires in 00:00:12, priority 105
  Standby router is local
  4 state changes, last state change 00:13:32
  Tracking interface states for 1 interface, 1 up:
    Up   Serial0
```

ICMP

ICMP is defined by RFC 792. ICMP operates in the network layer and communicates error messages between hosts and routers. ICMP uses several messages for different situations, for example, when a packet cannot reach a destination, when the router cannot forward the packet, or when the destination host cannot be reached. ICMP uses IP protocol number 1. ICMP returns several message types, each with particular codes. The different message types are described in Table 6-16.

Table 6-16 *ICMP Message Types*

ICMP Type Number	Type Name	Description
0	Echo Reply	Used by the ping application to test connectivity. The station receiving each message replies with an echo reply message.
3	Destination Unreachable	The following codes are used: 0—Destination network unreachable. 1—Destination host unreachable. 2 —Destination protocol unreachable. 3—Destination port unreachable. 4—Fragmentation needed and DF set. 5—Source route failed. Codes 0, 1, 4, and 5 are received from a router. Codes 2 and 3 are received from the destination host.
4	Source Quench	Used if a router discards a packet because it does not have the buffer space needed to queue the packets for output. A source quench message is sent, which is a request to the host to cut back the rate at which it is sending traffic to the destination.
5	Redirect	Tells the sending host to send its traffic for the destination network directly to another gateway.
8	Echo	Used by the ping application to test connectivity. The station testing connectivity sends the echo message.
11	Time Exceeded	The following codes are used: 0—Time to live exceeded in transit 1—Fragment reassembly time exceeded Code 0 can be received from a router. Code 1 is received from the destination host.
12	Parameter Problem	Used if problems are in the header of the IP packet.
13	Timestamp	Contains the original timestamp in the ICMP message.
14	Timestamp Reply	Adds the received timestamp and transmit timestamp in the ICMP message.
15	Information Request	Used by a host to find out what network it is on.
16	Information Reply	Received by the host with information on which network it is on.

Using Ping on Cisco Routers

Ping can verify IP connectivity to a destination address. On Cisco routers, you can verify connectivity by entering in the terminal the command **ping** *ip-address*. Example 6-6 shows that the successful reply destination is represented with exclamation points. By default, five echo messages are sent. The success rate of replies and the time to send and receive the reply is also returned.

Example 6-6 *Example of the Basic Ping Application*

```
router5>ping 10.1.3.1

Type escape sequence to abort.
Sending 5, 100-byte ICMP Echos to 10.1.3.1, timeout is 2 seconds:
!!!!!
Success rate is 100 percent (5/5), round-trip min/avg/max = 4/7/20 ms
```

In router enable mode, you can perform more advanced testing. Enter **ping** and press **Enter**. Here, you can change the number of echos and the size of the datagram. By pressing **y** at the Extended Commands prompt, you can change the ToS, set the Don't fragment bit, record route, and so on. Example 6-7 shows an extended ping where the repeat count is 10, the datagram size is changed to 500 bytes, and the data pattern is all 1s.

Example 6-7 *Advanced Ping Options*

```
router3#ping
Protocol [ip]:
Target IP address: 10.1.3.2
Repeat count [5]: 10
Datagram size [100]: 500
Timeout in seconds [2]:
Extended commands [n]: y
Source address or interface:
Type of service [0]:
Set DF bit in IP header? [no]: y
Validate reply data? [no]: y
Data pattern [0xABCD]: 0xffff
Loose, Strict, Record, Timestamp, Verbose[none]:
Sweep range of sizes [n]:
Type escape sequence to abort.
Sending 10, 500-byte ICMP Echos to 10.1.3.2, timeout is 2 seconds:
Packet has data pattern 0xFFFF
!!!!!!!!!!
Success rate is 100 percent (10/10), round-trip min/avg/max = 4/6/24 ms
```

Although these examples have successful returns, other test characters can be returned. Table 6-17 shows those characters.

Table 6-17 *Ping Test Characters*

Character	Description
!	Receipt of a reply.
.	The network server timed out while waiting for a reply.
U	A destination unreachable error message was received.
Q	Source quench (destination too busy).
M	Could not fragment.
?	Unknown packet type.
&	Packet lifetime exceeded.

Telnet

Telnet is a TCP/IP application-layer protocol that provides remote terminal access. RFC 854 is the current Telnet protocol specification. Telnet runs over TCP, by using TCP port 23 to connect to the Telnet server. The remote terminal is text based; by default, it uses 128 ASCII codes.

FTP

FTP is a TCP/IP application-layer protocol that provides file transfer capabilities. FTP was first specified by RFC 114 and has been updated several times, but the standard RFC is 959. The objectives of the FTP protocol arc to providc sharing of files, shield users from variations in file storage systems among hosts, and transfer data reliably and efficiently.

FTP uses two different connections: One is a control connection between the user and the FTP server, and the second is a data transfer connection. The data connection might not exist until the commands to transfer the files are executed. The FTP control connection is established through a TCP process, and the server port is TCP 21. The data connection uses TCP port 20.

You can use FTP on any Windows system, Unix system, and others.

TFTP

TFTP is a simpler type of FTP. Instead of using TCP as FTP does, it uses UDP as a transport protocol. TFTP does not use a control connection, it cannot list directories, nor does it have user authentication. It reads or writes files from/to a remote TFTP server. TFTP (version 2) is defined in RFC 1350 and uses UDP port 69. An example of the use of TFTP is the transfer of IOS and configuration files to a router. Chapter 3, "Cisco Equipment Operations," covers the methods that you can use to transfer IOS and configuration files from and to a router by using a TFTP server.

DNS

DNS is a method to manage Internet names in a distributed fashion. DNS servers return the destination IP addresses given the domain name. DNS was first specified by RFCs 882 and 883. The current specifications are RFCs 1034 and 1035.

DNS is a distributed database, where separate organizations administer domain name space and can then break the domain into several subdomains. DNS follows a reversed-tree structure for domain name space. The Internet Name Registration Authority manages the root of the tree. The DNS tree is shown in Figure 6-14.

Figure 6-14 *DNS Tree*

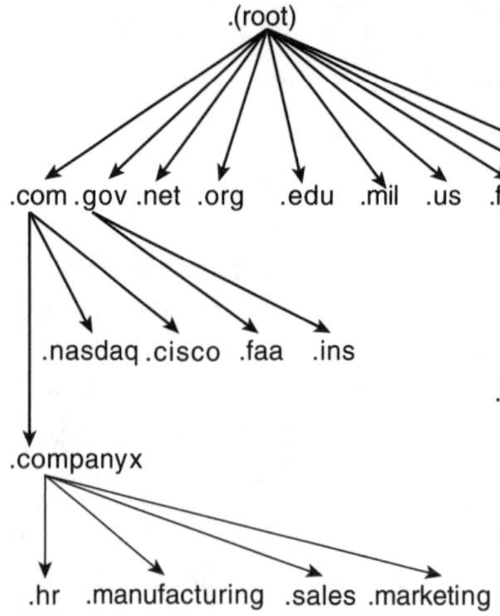

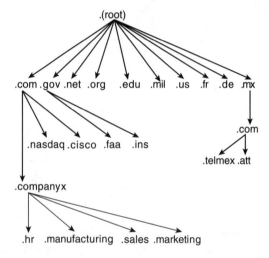

DNS uses TCP and UDP port 53. UDP is the recommended transport protocol for DNS queries. TCP is the recommended protocol for zone transfers between DNS servers. A DNS query searches for the IP address of a Fully Qualified Domain Name (FQDN), such as www.cisco.com.

SNMP

SNMP is a network protocol for the management of network devices. SNMP allows network managers to inspect or change parameters on a device remotely. SNMP was first defined by RFC 1067 (SNMPv1), which was succeeded by RFCs 1155, 1157, and 1212. Version 2 of SNMP is defined by RFC 1442, with other RFCs providing updates. The latest version of SNMP, version 3, is described in RFC 2573.

In SNMP, managed devices (routers, switches, servers) contain an SNMP agent. The agents collect and store management information. The information is made available to the network management system (NMS). NMS uses **read** and **write** commands to query or change information on the SNMP agent. These commands use UDP port 161. Some devices can be configured to send a message to the NMS in the case of an interface failure or other defined event. The message sent to the server is a SNMP trap, which uses UDP port 162.

NAT

NAT devices convert internal IP address space into globally unique IP addresses. NAT is specified by RFC 1631. As shown in Figure 6-15, for outgoing IP packets, the source addresses are converted to globally unique IP addresses. The conversion can be statically done, or you can use a global pool of addresses dynamically.

Figure 6-15 *Network Address Translation (NAT)*

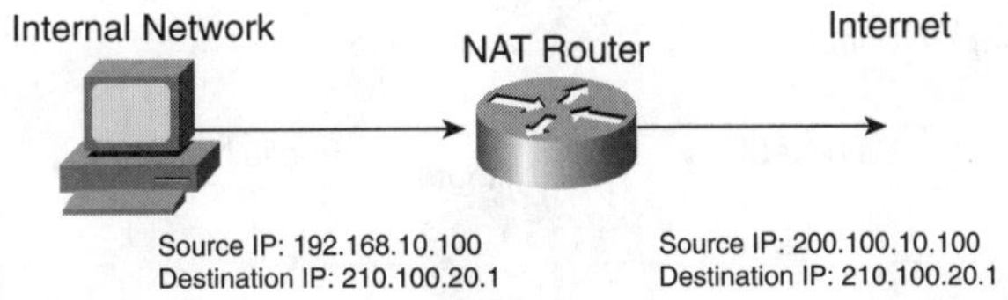

The several forms of NAT follow:

- **Static NAT**—Maps an unregistered IP address to a registered IP address, configured manually.
- **Dynamic NAT**—Dynamically maps an unregistered IP address to a registered IP address from a pool (group) of registered addresses. The two subsets of dynamic NAT are *overloading* and *overlapping*.
- **Overloading**—Maps multiple unregistered IP addresses to a single registered IP address by using different ports. Overloading is also known as Port Address Translation (PAT), single address NAT, or port-level multiplexed NAT.
- **Overlapping**—Maps internal IP addresses to outside IP addresses when the internal addresses are possibly the same as the external addresses. Translates the internal IP addresses to globally unique IP addresses. External addresses can also be mapped to overlapping internal addresses.

Before configuring NAT, you must understand the following terminology:

- **Stub domain**—Internal network that can use private IP addresses.
- **Public network**—Outside the stub domain and resides in the Internet. Addresses in the public network are reachable from the Internet.
- **Inside local address**—Real IP address of the device that resides in the Internal network. The stub domain uses this address.

- **Inside global address**—Translated IP address of the device that resides in the Internal network. The public network uses this address.
- **Outside global address**—Real IP address of a device that resides in the Internet, outside of the stub domain.
- **Outside local address**—Translated IP address of the device that resides in the Internet. The stub domain uses this address.

Figure 6-16 illustrates the previous terms. The real IP address of the host in the stub network is 192.168.10.100, which is the inside local address. The inside local address is translated into the inside global address (200.100.10.100) at the NAT router. Hosts located in the Internet have their real IP address (outside global address) translated. For example, 30.100.2.50 is translated into the outside local address of 192.168.100.50.

Figure 6-16 *NAT Terminology Example*

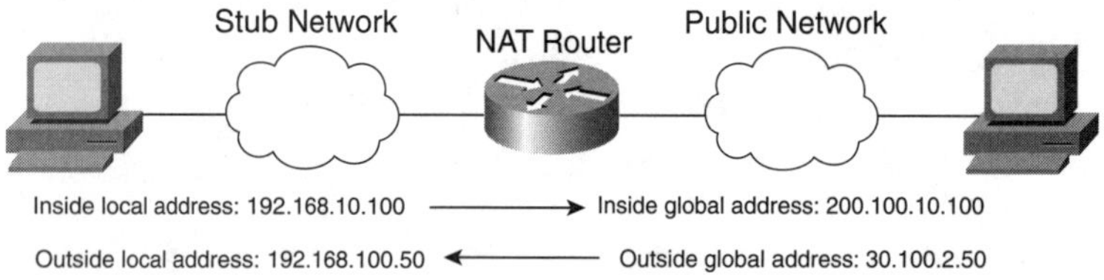

Configuring NAT on Cisco Routers

To configure IP NAT for simple dynamic NAT, performed the following steps:

Step 1 Configure interfaces to be marked as inside or outside. Inside interfaces reside in the stub network, and outside interfaces reside in the public network. Configure inside interfaces with the **ip nat inside** command. Configure outside interfaces with the **ip nat outside** command.

Step 2 Configure an address pool to dynamically assign inside global addresses. You can use a range of IP addresses for dynamic translations that are specified with a starting and ending IP address by using the **ip nat pool** *name start-ip end-ip* **netmask** *netmask* command.

Step 3 Enable the translation of inside local addresses with the **ip nat inside source** [**list** *acl* **pool** *name*] command. The *name* is the same name specified in Step 2. The *acl* access list specifically defines the inside local addresses that are translated.

Example 6-8 shows a sample configuration for Figure 6-17, which translates the inside 192.168.10.0/24 and 192.168.11.0/24 addresses by using a global pool of 200.100.100.0/24. Outside global addresses are not translated.

Figure 6-17 *NAT Example*

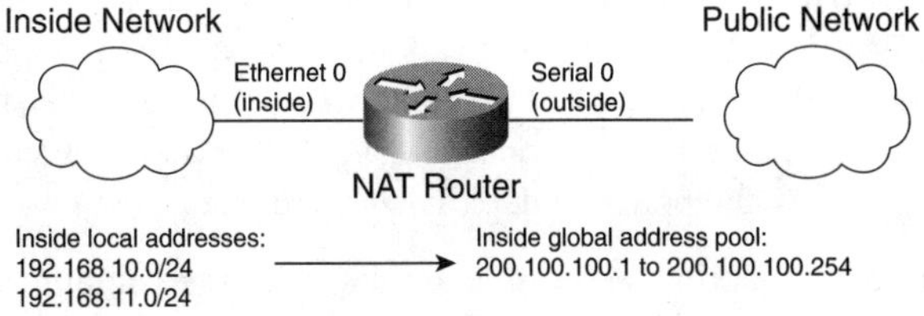

Example 6-8 *NAT Configuration Example*

```
hostname router3
!
ip nat pool ccie 200.100.100.1 200.100.100.254 netmask 255.255.255.0
!
ip nat inside source list 5 pool ccie
!
interface ethernet 0
 description Inside interface
 ip address 192.168.10.1 255.255.255.0
 ip nat inside
!
interface serial 0
 description Outside interface
 ip address 200.100.101.1 255.255.255.252
 ip nat outside
!
access-list 5 permit 192.168.10.0 0.0.0.255
access-list 5 permit 192.168.11.0 0.0.0.255
```

To verify and troubleshoot NAT, use the commands in Table 6-18.

Table 6-18 *NAT Verification Commands*

Command	Description
show ip nat translations	Displays active NAT translations
show ip nat statistics	Displays NAT statistics
clear ip nat translation *	Clears all dynamic translations
debug ip nat [*list*] [**detailed**]	Provides debugging information for NAT

NAT is usually deployed at the edge of the network where there are two separate administrative domains or at the internal network edge with the Internet.

IPv6

Cisco added IPv6 to the CCIE written exam blueprint. You need to become extremely familiar with its specifications. The driving motivation for the adoption of a new version of IP is the limitation imposed by the 32-bit address field in IPv4. In the 1990s, there was concern that the IP address space would be depleted soon. Although CIDR and NAT slowed down the deployment of IPv6, its standards and potential deployments are maturing.

The IPv6 specification provides 128-bits for addressing—a significant increase from 32-bits. The overall specification of IPv6 is in RFC 2460. Other RFCs that describe IPv6 specifications are 2373, 2374, 2461, 2462, and 2463.

IPv6 includes the following enhancements over IPv4:

- **Expanded address space**—IPv6 uses 128-bit addresses instead of the 32-bit addresses in IPv4.
- **Improved option mechanism**—IPv6 options are placed in separate optional headers that are located between the IPv6 header and the transport-layer header.
- **Address autoconfiguration**—This capability provides for the dynamic assignment of IPv6 addresses.
- **Support for resource allocation**—Instead of the ToS field in IPv4, IPv6 enables the labeling of packets that belong to a particular traffic flow, for which the sender requests special handling; this aids in the support of specialized traffic, such as real-time video.
- **Security capabilities**—IPv6 includes features that support authentication and privacy. IPv6 security is discussed in the Security section of this document.

IPv6 Address Representation

RFC 2373 specifies the IPv6 addressing architecture. IPv6 addresses are 128-bits long. IPv6 addresses are represented in hexadecimal, divided into eight 16-bit pieces. This form is represented as follows:

X:X:X:X:X:X:X:X
Each X represents the hexadecimal digits.

An example of a full IPv6 address is FE1A:4CB9:001B:0000:0000:12D0:005B:06B0. All 0 groups can be shortened by using one 0. Multiple groups of 16-bit 0s can be represented with a :: symbol, which can appear only once in the number. Also, leading 0s in a 16-bit piece do not need to be represented. This sample IPv6 address can be shortened to FE1A:4CB9:1B:0:0:12D0:5B:6B0 or FE1A:4CB9:1B::12D0:5B:6B0.

When addresses are in a mixed IPv4 and IPv6 environment, they can be represented by six hexadecimal 16-bit pieces that are concatenated with the dotted-decimal format. This form is represented as follows:

X:X:X:X:X:X:d.d.d.d
Each X represents the hexadecimal digits, and d.d.d.d is the dotted-decimal representation.

An example of a mixed full address is as follows:

0000:0000:0000:0000:0000:0000:100.1.1.1

This example can be shortened to the following:

::100.1.1.1.

IPv6 Prefix Representation

IPv6 prefixes are represented similar to IPv4, as follows:

IPv6 address/prefix

The double-colon is still used only once in the representation. An example of an IPv6 prefix is as follows:

200C:001b:1100:0:0:0:0:0/40 or 200C:1b:1100::/40.

Allocated IPv6 Addresses

The leading bits of an IPv6 address can define the address type. These leading bits are of variable length and are called the *format prefix (FP)*. Table 6-19 shows some initial allocations of some prefixes.

Table 6-19 *IPv6 Initial Prefix Allocations*

Binary Format Prefix	Hexadecimal	Allocation
0000 0000	00	Unspecified, looback, IPv4-compatible
001	2 or 3	Aggregatable global unicast address
1111 1110 10	FE8	Link-local unicast addresses
1111 1110 11	FEC	Site-local unicast addresses
1111 1111	FF	Multicast addresses

References Used

The following resources were used to create this chapter:

Routing TCP/IP, Volume II, Jeff Doyle and Jennifer DeHaven Carroll, Cisco Press, 2001
RFC 791, "INTERNET PROTOCOL," 1981

RFC 793, "TRANSMISSION CONTROL PROTOCOL," September 1981

RFC 951, "BOOTSTRAP PROTOCOL (BOOTP)," W.J.Croft, J.Gilmore, 1985

RFC 768, "User Datagram Protocol," J.Postel, 1980

RFC 1531, "Dynamic Host Configuration Protocol," R. Droms, October 1993

RFC 1542, "Clarifications and Extensions for the Bootstrap Protocol," W. Wilmer, 1993

RFC 1027, "Using ARP to Implement Transparent Subnet Gateways," S. Carl-Mitchell, J.S. Quarterman, 1987

RFC 903, "A Reverse Address Resolution Protocol," R. Finlayson, T. Mann, J.C. Mogul, M. Theimer, June 1984

RFC 826, "An Ethernet Address Resolution Protocol: Or Converting Network Protocol Addresses to 48.bit Ethernet Address for Transmission on Ethernet Hardware," D.C. Plummer

RFC 2338, "Virtual Router Redundancy Protocol," April 1998

RFC 2460, "Internet Protocol, Version 6 (IPv6) Specification." S. Deering, R. Hinden, December 1998

RFC 2373, "IP Version 6 Addressing Architecture," R. Hinden, S. Deering, July 1998

www.cisco.com/univercd/cc/td/doc/cisintwk/ito_doc/ip.htm#xtocid16

www.cisco.com/warp/public/556/nat-cisco.shtml

Foundation Summary

The Foundation Summary is a condensed collection of material that provides a convenient review of key concepts in this chapter. If you are already comfortable with the topics in this chapter, this summary will help you recall a few details. If you just read the Foundation Topics section, this review should help solidify some key facts. If you are doing your final preparation before the exam, these materials are a convenient way to review the day before the exam.

Figure 6-18 *TCP/IP Model Compared to the OSI Model*

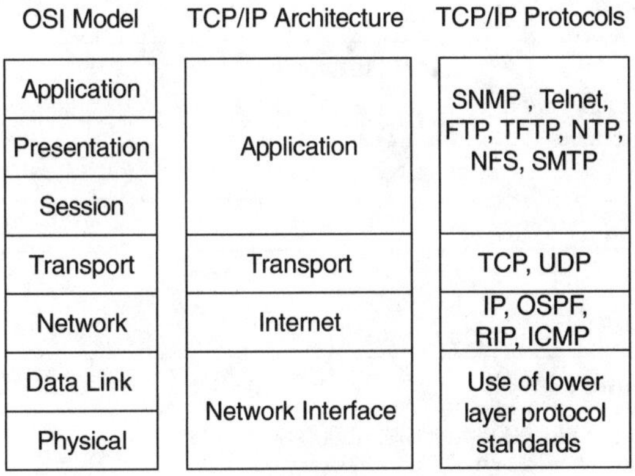

Figure 6-19 *IP Header*

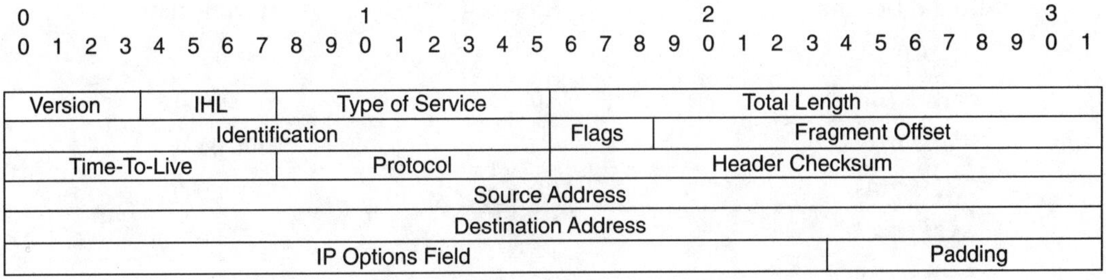

Table 6-20 *IP Address Classes*

Address Class	Address Class Purpose	High Order Bits	Network Numbers
A	For large networks	0xxxxxxx	1.0.0.0 to 126.0.0.0
B	For medium networks	10xxxxxx	128.0.0.0 to 191.255.0.0
C	For small networks	110xxxxx	192.0.0.0 to 223.255.255.0
D	Multicast address	1110xxxx	224.0.0.1 to 239.255.255.255
E	Experimental /reserved	1111xxxx	240.0.0.0 to 254.255.255.255

Table 6-21 *Private Address Space*

Class Type	Start Network	End Network
Class A	10.0.0.0/8	–
Class B	172.16.0.0/16	172.31.0.0/16
Class C	192.168.0.0/24	192.168.255.0/24

Table 6-22 *Default Address Masks*

Class	Binary Mask	Dotted Decimal Mask
A	11111111 00000000 00000000 00000000	255.0.0.0
B	11111111 11111111 00000000 00000000	255.255.0.0
C	11111111 11111111 11111111 00000000	255.255.255.0

Table 6-23 *Subnet Mask Examples*

Dotted Decimal	Bit Mask	Hexadecimal
255.0.0.0	/8	FF000000
255.192.0.0	/10	FFC00000
255.255.0.0	/16	FFFF0000
255.255.224.0	/19	FFFFE000
255.255.240.0	/20	FFFFF000
255.255.255.0	/24	FFFFFF00
255.255.255.224	/27	FFFFFFE0
255.255.255.240	/28	FFFFFFF0
255.255.255.248	/29	FFFFFFF8
255.255.255.252	/30	FFFFFFFC

Table 6-24 *Address Assignment and Summarization*

Term	Description
FLSM	A single subnet mask for the entire IP network number.
VLSM	Permits the use of different subnet masks for a network number.
Summarization	Routing protocols can aggregate subnet routes into one larger route.
CIDR	Implemented in BGP4 to aggregate network routes into a continuous block of address space that is advertised to the rest of the Internet; decreases the number of BGP routes to advertise.

Figure 6-20 *TCP Header*

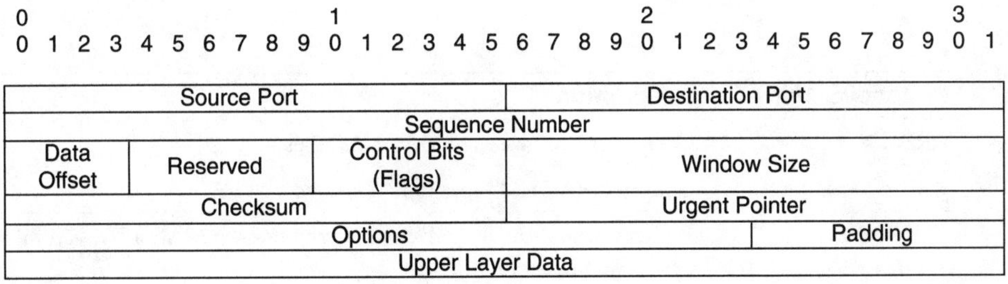

Table 6-25 *TCP Connection Protocol*

Protocol	Description
TCP connection establishment	A three-way handshake is performed as follows: (1) SYN(a) sent (2) ACK(a), SYN(b) received (3) ACK(b) sent
Window size	Number of bytes that the receiver is willing to accept
Session termination	Four signals are sent to terminate the full-duplex connection: (1) FIN(a) sent (2) ACK(a) received (3) FIN(b) received (4) ACK(b) sent

Table 6-26 *TCP Signals*

TCP Signal	Description
URG	Urgent pointer field significant; tells the TCP protocol to look at the urgent pointer field to indicate the length of urgent data.
ACK	Acknowledgement field significant.
PSH	Push function; tells the TCP protocol to send the segment immediately.
RST	Reset the connection; the station receiving a segment with this flag kills the session.
FIN	No more data from sender; indicates the sender wants to end the connection.
SYN	Synchronize the sequence numbers; indicates the first octet sent in the segment.

Table 6-27 *TCP/IP Protocols and Services*

Protocol/Service	Description
ARP	Converts IP addresses to MAC addresses.
RARP	Converts MAC addresses to IP addresses.
Proxy-ARP	Router responds to an ARP request with its own MAC address for a destination in another network.
BOOTP	Allows a booting host to configure itself dynamically by obtaining its IP address, its IP gateway, and other information.
DHCP	DHCP server hosts allocate network addresses and deliver configuration parameters dynamically to hosts.
HSRP	Cisco protocol that provides automatic router backup. HSRP allows one router to assume the function of a second router if the second router fails.
ICMP	ICMP operates in the network layer and communicates error messages between hosts and gateways.
Telnet	TCP/IP application-layer protocol that provides remote terminal access.
FTP	TCP/IP application-layer protocol that provides file transfer services reliably using TCP.
TFTP	TCP/IP application-layer protocol that provides simple file transfer using UDP.
DNS	TCP/IP application-layer protocol that provides a domain name to IP address resolution. DNS is a distributed database of separately administrated domains.
SNMP	SNMP is a network protocol for the management of network devices.
NAT	NAT devices convert internal IP address space into globally unique IP addresses.

Q & A

The Q & A questions are more difficult than what you can expect on the actual exam. The questions do not attempt to cover more breadth or depth than the exam; however, they are designed to make sure that you retain the material. Rather than allowing you to derive the answer from clues hidden inside the question itself, these questions challenge your understanding and recall of the subject. Questions from the "Do I Know This Already?" quiz are repeated here to ensure that you have mastered the chapter's topic areas. A strong understanding of the answers to these questions will help you on the CCIE written exam. As an additional study aide, use the CD-ROM provided with this book to take simulated exams.

Select the best answer. Answers to these questions are in the Appendix, "Answers to Quiz Questions."

1 Which IP protocol and port does Telnet use?

a. TCP 21

b. Protocol 1, TCP port 23

c. UDP 23

d. IP protocol 6, TCP port 23

2 What is the directed broadcast address for 171.80.32.178/27?

a. 171.80.32.192.

b. 171.80.32.191.

c. 171.80.32.64.

d. There is not sufficient information.

3 When packets are fragmented, where are the fragments reassembled?

a. By the next hop router

b. By the TCP layer in the destination host

c. By the IP layer in the destination host

d. By the router next to the destination host

4 Which type of address class is 190.1.2.0?

a. Class A

b. Class B

c. Class C

d. Class D

5 What does the flag PSH do?

a. Tells the sending TCP process to send the segment immediately

b. Tells the routers to forward the packets with higher priority

c. Tells the destination TCP to push the IP packet to the application layer

d. Tells the IP layer to send immediately

6 Which of the following describes TFTP?

a. A protocol that uses TCP to transfer files with no authentication

b. A protocol for the transfer of files reliably using port 69

c. A protocol for the transfer of files using UDP

d. A protocol to transfer files using TCP 21

7 Which ICMP protocol type does the PING application use?

a. IP protocol 6

b. ICMP echo

c. TCP

d. ARP request

8 What is blocked in the following access list?

```
access-list 105 deny tcp any host 10.1.1.1 eq 23
access-list 105 permit tcp any any
```

a. Packets from host 10.1.1.1 are denied.

b. Packets from any TCP host are denied.

c. Packets from any host sent to host 10.1.1.1 to the Telnet port are denied.

d. Packets to host 10.1.1.1 are permitted, all others are denied.

9 Which methods acquire a default gateway?

a. ARP and RARP

b. BOOTP and DHCP

c. RARP and BOOTP

d. IP address and subnet mask

10 What is the inside global address in NAT?

a. The translated IP address of the device that resides in the internal network

b. The translated IP address of the device that resides in the Global Internet

c. The inside address of the device in the Internet network

d. The translated global address in the internal network that reaches an external device

11 Which of the following is a subnet mask with 27 bits?

a. 255.255.255.192

b. 255.255.255.252

c. 255.255.255.224

d. 255.255.255.240

12 How many hosts are in a Class B network with the default mask?

a. 65,534

b. 16,777,214

c. 254

d. 255

13 Which of the following are protocols that are supported by default with the **ip helper-address** command?

a. BOOTP and DHCP

b. RARP, BOOTP, and DHCP

c. ARP and RARP

d. WINS, DNS, and BOOTP

14 How many segments are needed to close a TCP connection?

a. Three

b. Four

c. Two

d. A three-way handshake

15 What is the IHL in the IP header?

a. Internet hop length, indicates the maximum allowed hops

b. Internet header length, measured in octets

c. Internet header length, measured in 32-bit words

d. Internet header length, measured in bits

16 Issuing which of the following IOS commands disables proxy ARP?

a. router#**no ip proxy-arp**

b. router(config-if)#**no ip proxy-arp**

c. router (config-if)#**no proxy-arp**

d. router (config)#**no ip proxy-arp**

17 Which HSRP router becomes active?

a. The router with the higher priority.

b. The router with the lower priority.

c. The router configured with priority 100.

d. The router configured with priority 1.

18 Which protocols are connectionless?

a. Telnet and IP

b. UDP and OSPF

c. UDP and IP

d. FTP and UDP

19 How are connections established in TCP?

a. Two-way full duplex handshake.

b. Three-way handshake.

c. PSH message to send data immediately.

d. URG pointer indicates urgency.

20 How many bits are in the precedence bits field in the IP header?

a. 3

b. 8

c. 5

d. 4

21 The checksum in the IP header is computed for what?

a. The IP header and data

b. The IP header only

c. The pseudo header

d. The UDP header and pseudo header

22 Which is the subnet for 150.100.21.11/22?

a. 150.100.16.0

b. 150.100.18.0

c. 150.100.20.0

d. 150.100.21.0

23 What happens if one IP fragment is lost?

a. The receiving IP protocol requests a retransmit.

b. The TCP layer finds the error and retransmits.

c. The router that fragmented the packet must retransmit.

d. The DF bit must be set to 0.

24 The Internet layer of the TCP/IP architecture corresponds to which OSI layer?

a. Data-link

b. Network

c. Transport

d. Physical and data-link

25 The checksum field in TCP performs a checksum of what?

a. Header only

b. Data only

c. TCP Header, data, and pseudo-header

d. TCP Header and pseudo-header

26 What does the sequence number indicate in TCP?

a. The last byte sent in the segment

b. The first byte sent in the segment

c. The last 32-bit word

d. The number of bytes in the segment

27 Which fields are included in the UDP checksum?

a. UDP header only

b. UDP header, UDP data, source IP, destination IP, port, and UDP length

c. UDP header and UDP data

d. UDP header, UDP data, source IP, destination IP, and port

28 Which command do you use if you want the active HSRP router to resign if a tracked serial interface 0 goes down?

a. standby 1 track serial 0

b. standby 1 serial 0

c. standby 1 track interface serial 0

d. standby 1 interface serial 0 track

29 How many bits are in an IPv6 address?

a. 64

b. 96

c. 128

d. 192

30 Which of the following is a valid IPv6 address?

a. 1070::25:1

b. 1::1::1

c. BGA0::1FAC:2334

d. FED0:0:0:AB10

31 Multicast IPv6 addresses begin with which hexadecimal number(s)?

a. 2

b. FE8

c. FEC

d. FF

32 Which is a valid representation on an IPv4 address in IPv6/IPv4 mixed mode?

a. ::10.10.10.10

b. 10.10.10.10

c. A:A:A:A

d. IPv4 addresses cannot be represented in IPv6.

Scenario

This scenario uses a configuration to review your skills with IP addressing and NAT. Use the following configuration to answer the questions in this section:

```
hostname router
!
ip nat pool local 100.100.1.1 100.100.1.126 netmask 255.255.255.0
!
ip nat inside source list 10 pool local
!
interface ethernet 0
 description outside interface
 ip address 10.1.2.1 255.255.255.0
 ip nat inside
!
interface serial 0
 description inside interface
 ip address 100.100.1.129 255.255.255.252
 ip nat outside
!
access-list 10 permit 10.1.4.0 0.0.3.255
access-list 11 permit 10.1.16.0 0.0.0.255
```

1 Which range of addresses is permitted to access the outside through NAT?

a. From 10.1.4.1 to 10.1.7.255 and from 10.1.16.1 to 10.1.16.255

b. From 10.1.4.1 to 10.1.7.255

c. From 10.1.4.1 to 10.1.16.0

d. From 10.1.4.1 to 10.1.4.255 and from 10.1.16.1 to 10.1.16.255

2 Which type of address is 10.1.4.10?

a. Inside local address

b. Outside global address

c. Inside global address

d. Outside local address

3 Which type of address is 100.100.1.30?

a. Inside local address

b. Outside global address

c. Inside global address

d. Outside local address

4 Which interface is considered a NAT inside interface?

a. Ethernet 0

b. Serial 0

c. Both Ethernet 0 and Serial 0

d. Neither interface

5 Which interface is considered a NAT outside interface?

a. Ethernet 0

b. Serial 0

c. Both Ethernet 0 and Serial 0

d. Neither interface

6 If a packet on the outside has a destination IP of 100.100.1.2 and a source IP of 50.25.10.1, which is the source IP after the packet is inside the stub network?

a. 100.100.1.2

b. 50.25.10.1

c. 100.1.4.2

d. 100.1.16.2

7 If a packet on the inside has a destination IP of 40.1.1.1 and a source IP of 10.1.6.10, which is the destination IP after the packet is outside the stub network?

a. 100.100.1.2

b. 50.25.10.1

c. 100.100.1.50

d. 40.1.1.1

8 If a packet on the inside has a source IP of 10.1.5.100 and a destination IP of 30.1.1.1, which can the source IP address be after the packet is outside the stub network?

a. 100.1.100.5

b. 30.1.1.1

c. 10.1.5.100

d. 100.100.1.50

This chapter covers the following topics needed to master the CCIE Routing and Switching (R&S) written exam:

- **Static routes**—The configuration of static routes
- **Routing Information Protocol version 1**—The first widely used distance vector protocol (RIPv1)
- **Routing Information Protocol version 2**—The second version of RIP (RIPv2)
- **Interior Gateway Routing Protocol**—Cisco's first proprietary distance vector protocol (IGRP)
- **Enhanced Interior Gateway Routing Protocol**—The hybrid routing protocol (EIGRP)

CHAPTER 7

Static Routing and Distance Vector Routing Protocols

This chapter covers static routing, Routing Information Protocol version 1 (RIPv1), RIP version 2 (RIPv2), Interior Gateway Protocol (IGRP), and Enhanced Interior Gateway Protocol (EIGRP). Before reading this chapter, you must be completely familiar with the general networking concepts discussed in Chapter 2, "Networking Concepts Review."

"Do I Know This Already?" Quiz

The purpose of this assessment quiz is to help you determine how to spend your limited study time. If you can answer most or all of these questions, you might want to skim the Foundation Topics section and return to it later as necessary. Review the Foundation Summary section and answer the questions at the end of the chapter to ensure that you have a strong grasp of the material covered. If you intend to read the entire chapter, you do not need to answer these questions now. If you find these assessment questions difficult, read through the entire Foundation Topics section and review it until you feel comfortable with your ability to answer all of the "Q & A" questions at the end of the chapter. The following questions are repeated at the end of the chapter in the Q & A section with additional questions to test your mastery of the material.

Select the best answer. Answers to these questions are in the Appendix, "Answers to Quiz Questions."

1 When will EIGRP and IGRP automatically redistribute routes among themselves?

a. When you use different AS numbers

b. When you use the same AS numbers without the **redistribution** command

c. When you use different AS numbers and the **redistribution** command under EIGRP

d. When you use different AS numbers and the **redistribution** command under IGRP

2 Which command enables RIP?

a. **router rip**

b. **router rip 100**

c. **enable router rip 100**

d. **router rip v1 100**

3 How often does IGRP broadcast routing table updates?

a. Every 30 seconds

b. Every 60 seconds

c. Every 90 seconds

d. Every 180 seconds

4 Which **static route** command is correctly configured?

a. router(config)#**ip route 10.100.0.0 0.0.255.255 192.172.1.1**

b. router(config)#**ip route 10.100.0.0 255.255.0.0 192.172.1.1**

c. router(config)>**ip route 10.100.0.0 255.255.0.0 192.172.1.1**

d. router#**ip route 10.100.0.0 0.0.255.255 192.172.1.1**

5 How long does it take IGRP to remove a possibly down network from the table?

a. 10 minutes

b. 280 seconds

c. 6 minutes

d. 180 seconds

6 RIPv2 improves RIPv1 with which of the following capabilities?

a. Multicast, authentication, hop count

b. Multicast, authentication, VLSM

c. Authentication, VLSM, hop count

d. VLSM, hop count

7 What is the maximum number of routes in a RIP packet?

a. 104

b. 20

c. 25

d. 60

8 Which protocol maintains neighbor adjacencies?

a. RIPv2 and EIGRP

b. IGRP and EIGRP

c. RIPv2

d. EIGRP

9 What does the number in the **router igrp 50** command indicate?

a. The number of processes is 50.

b. The autonomous system number is 50.

c. The arbitrary number 50.

d. IGRP is allowed 50 routes.

10 Which protocols are classful?

a. EIGRP, RIPv1, and IGRP

b. RIPv1, RIPv2, IGRP

c. RIPv1 and IGRP

d. OSPF, RIPv2, and EIGRP

11 Which protocol service interface does EIGRP use?

a. UDP port 520

b. IP protocol 9

c. IP protocol 89

d. IP protocol 88

12 What does the default EIGRP composite metric consist of?

a. Bandwidth

b. Bandwidth and delay

c. Bandwidth, delay, load, and reliability

d. Bandwidth, delay, load, reliability, and hop count

13 For RIP, if route updates are not received for a network, how long before the routes are considered invalid?

a. 180 seconds

b. 90 seconds

c. 60 seconds

d. 240 seconds

14 Which routing protocol implements the DUAL algorithm?

a. IGRP and EIGRP

b. IGRP

c. EIGRP

d. EIGRP and RIPv2

15 Which protocols support VLSM?

a. RIPv2 and IGRP

b. RIPv2, IGRP, and EIGRP

c. RIP and IGRP

d. RIPv2 and EIGRP

Foundation Topics

Static Routes

Before discussing dynamic routing protocols, this section reviews the configuration of static routing protocols.

Static routes are manually configured. For each change in the network topology, an administrator must manually change the static routes as necessary. You can use static routes in hub-and-spoke networks with low bandwidth links so that bandwidth is not used by routing protocols. You can also use static routes in network firewall architectures and at connections with external partners.

Static Route Configuration

Static routes are configured with the **ip route** global command. The format is as follows:

```
ip route destination-network mask destination-IP
```

or

```
ip route destination-IP mask egress-interface
```

The following shows some options for the destination:

```
Router(config)#ip route 10.0.0.0 255.0.0.0 ?
  A.B.C.D    Forwarding router's address
  Ethernet   IEEE 802.3
  Null       Null interface
  Serial     Serial
  TokenRing  IEEE 802.5
```

The following example reaches network 10.100.0.0/16 through IP address 192.172.1.1:

```
router(config)#ip route 10.100.0.0 255.255.0.0 192.172.1.1
```

The following example reaches network 10.100.0.0/16 through Ethernet 0:

```
router(config)#ip route 10.100.0.0 255.255.0.0 ethernet 0
```

You can redistribute static routes into a dynamic routing protocol. Some dynamic routing protocols have the capability to distinguish between local routes and routes that were learned from external resources. Intermediate System-to-Intermediate System (IS-IS), Open Shortest Path First (OSPF), and EIGRP have the further capability to apply separate routing metrics to externally learned routes. EIGRP is covered in this chapter. OSPF and IS-IS are covered in Chapter 8, "IP Link-State Routing Protocols."

RIPv1

RIPv1 was defined in RFC 1058 (June 1988). RIP is a distance vector routing protocol that uses router hop count as a metric. RIP is a classful routing protocol that does not support VLSMs or classless interdomain routing (CIDR). Authentication is not supported in RIPv1. There is no method for authentication of route updates. A RIP router sends a copy of its routing table to its neighbors every 30 seconds. RIP uses split horizon with poison reverse; therefore, route updates are sent out an interface with an infinite metric for routes learned (received) from the same interface. The RIP standard was based on the popular routed program in UNIX systems in the 1980s. Cisco's implementation of RIP adds support for load balancing. RIP loads balance traffic if there are several paths with the same metric (equal-cost load balancing) to a destination RIP. Also, triggered updates are sent when the metric of a route changes. Triggered updates help the network converge faster rather than having to wait for the periodic update. RIP also has an administrative distance of 120; administrative distance is covered in Chapter 10, "Administrative Distance, Access Lists, Route Manipulation, and IP Multicast."

RIP automatically summarizes IP networks at network boundaries. A network boundary occurs on a router that has one or more interfaces without an IP address that is part of the network number. Networks are summarized to their IP class. An IP network that uses 24-bit subnetworks from 180.100.50.0/24 to 180.100.120.0/24 is summarized to 180.100.0.0/16 at a network boundary. You can disable autosummarization with the **no auto-summary** command, as follows:

```
router rip
 no auto-summary
```

RIPv1 Forwarding Information Base

The RIPv1 protocol keeps the following information about each destination:

- **IP address**—IP address of the destination host or network
- **Gateway**—The first gateway along the path to the destination
- **Interface**—The physical network that you must use to reach the destination
- **Metric**—A number that indicates the number of hops to the destination
- **Timer**—The amount of time since the entry was last updated

The database is updated with the route updates received from neighboring routers. As shown in Example 7-1, the **show ip rip database** command shows the RIP database of a router.

Example 7-1 **show ip rip database** *Command*

```
router9#show ip rip database
172.16.0.0/16     auto-summary
172.16.1.0/24     directly connected, Ethernet0
172.16.2.0/24
    [1] via 172.16.4.2, 00:00:06, Serial0
```

Example 7-1 **show ip rip database** *Command (Continued)*

```
172.16.3.0/24
    [1] via 172.16.1.2, 00:00:02, Ethernet0
172.16.4.0/24    directly connected, Serial0
```

RIPv1 Message Format

As described in RFC 1058, the RIPv1 message format is shown in Figure 7-1. The RIP message is appended to a User Datagram Protocol (UDP) header.

Figure 7-1 *IPv1 Message Format*

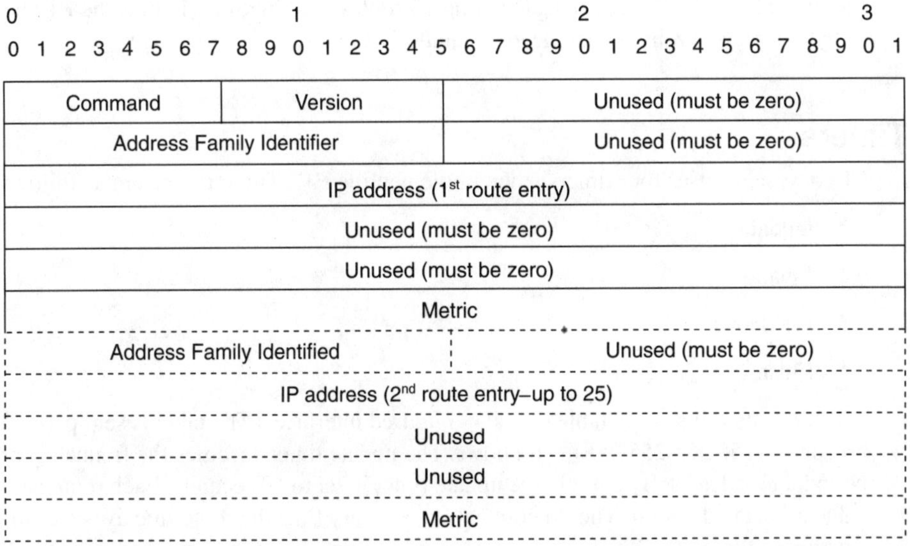

The following is a description of each field:

- **Command**—Describes the purpose of the packet. Five commands are described in the RFC, of which two are obsolete and one is reserved. The two commands that you use are as follows:
  - **request**—Sent to request all or part of the responding router's routing table.
  - **response**—Contains all or part of the sender's routing table. This message can be sent in response to a request, or it can be an update message generated by the sender.
- **Version**—Set to 1 for RIPv1.
- **Address Family Identifier (AFI)**—Set to a value of 2 for IP.

- **IP Address**—This is the destination route; it can be a network address, subnet, or host route. You use special route 0.0.0.0 for the default route.
- **Metric**—The metric field is 32 bits in length. It contains a value between 1 and 15 inclusive, specifying the current metric for the destination. The metric is set to 16 to indicate that a destination is not reachable.

Because RIP has a maximum hop count, it implements counting to infinity. For RIP, infinity is 16 hops. In the RIP message, no subnet masks accompany each route. Five 32-bit words are repeated for each route entry that includes the following: AFI (16-bits), Unused must be zero (16-bits), IP address, two more 32-bit unused fields, and the 32-bit metric. Five 32-bit words equal 20 bytes for each route entry. Up to 25 routes are allowed in each RIP message. The reason that only 25 routes are allowed is that the maximum datagram size is limited to 512 bytes (not including the IP header). Calculating 25 routes × 20 bytes each, plus the RIP header (4 bytes), plus an 8-byte UDP header, equals 512 bytes.

RIPv1 Timers

Cisco Systems uses four timers when implementing RIP. These timers are as follows:

- Update
- Invalid
- Holddown
- Flush

RIP sends its full routing table out all configured interfaces. The table is sent periodically as a broadcast (255.255.255.255) to all hosts. The update timer specifies the frequency of the periodic broadcasts. By default, the update timer is set to 30 seconds. Each route has a timeout value associated with it. The timeout gets reset every time the router receives a routing update containing the route. When the timeout value expires, the route is marked as unreachable by marking it as invalid. The route is marked as invalid by setting the metric to 16. The route is retained in the routing table. By default, the invalid timer is 180 seconds, or six update periods (30 × 6 = 180).

A route entry marked as invalid is retained in the routing table until the flush timer expires. By default, the flush timer is 240 seconds, which is 60 seconds longer than the expiration timer.

Cisco implements an additional timer for RIP—the *holddown* timer. You use the holddown timer to stabilize routes by setting an allowed time for which routing information regarding different paths is suppressed. After the metric for a route entry changes, no updates for the route are accepted until the holddown timer expires. By default, the holddown timer is 180 seconds.

The output of the **show ip protocol** command shows the default timers for RIP, as shown in Example 7-2. The timers can be changed using the **timers basic** *update invalid holddown flush* command.

Example 7-2 *RIP Timers Verified with* **show ip protocol**

```
router9>show ip protocol
Routing Protocol is "rip"
  Sending updates every 30 seconds, next due in 3 seconds
  Invalid after 180 seconds, hold down 180, flushed after 240
  Outgoing update filter list for all interfaces is
  Incoming update filter list for all interfaces is
  Redistributing: rip
  Default version control: send version 1, receive any version
    Interface             Send  Recv  Triggered RIP  Key-chain
    Ethernet0             1     1 2
    Serial0               1     1 2
  Automatic network summarization is in effect
  Routing for Networks:
    172.16.0.0
  Routing Information Sources:
    Gateway         Distance      Last Update
    172.16.4.2           120      00:00:00
    172.16.1.2           120      00:00:07
  Distance: (default is 120)
```

RIPv1 Configuration

The RIPv1 protocol is configured using the global **router rip** command. You enter the routed networks with the **network** command. Figure 7-2 shows a network with three routers. Each router in this section is configured to route the RIPv1 routing protocol.

Figure 7-2 *Routers in a RIP Network*

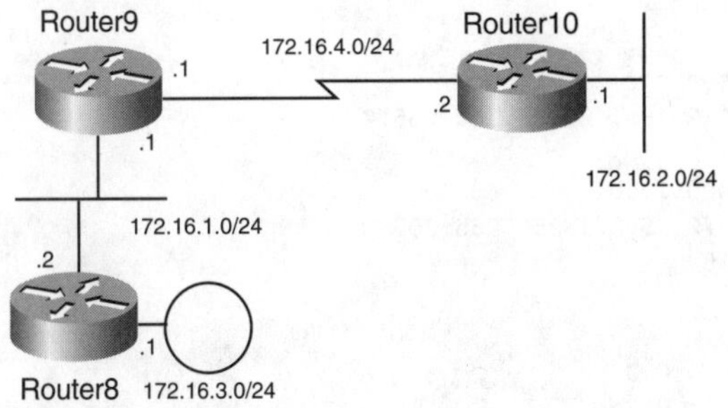

The configuration for Router9 is shown in Example 7-3.

Example 7-3 *Configuration of Router9*

```
hostname router9
!
interface Ethernet0
 ip address 172.16.1.1 255.255.255.0
!
interface Serial0
 ip address 172.16.4.1 255.255.255.0
!
router rip
 network 172.16.0.0
```

The configuration for Router10 is shown in Example 7-4.

Example 7-4 *Configuration of Router10*

```
hostname router10
!
interface Ethernet0
 ip address 172.16.2.1 255.255.255.0
!
interface Serial0
 ip address 172.16.4.2 255.255.255.0
!
router rip
 network 172.16.0.0
```

The configuration for Router8 is shown in Example 7-5.

Example 7-5 *Configuration of Router8*

```
hostname router8
!
interface Ethernet0
 ip address 172.16.1.2 255.255.255.0
!
interface TokenRing0
 ip address 172.16.3.1 255.255.255.0
 ring-speed 16
!
router rip
 network 172.16.0.0
```

After the routers are configured, you can verify the RIP table with the **show ip rip database** command. Example 7-6 shows the output from Router9. Only 172.16.2.0 (Ethernet interface on

Router10) and 172.16.3.0 (Token Ring network) are not directly connected routes learned from RIP.

Example 7-6 **show ip rip database** *Command*

```
router9#show ip rip database
172.16.0.0/16    auto-summary
172.16.1.0/24    directly connected, Ethernet0
172.16.2.0/24
    [1] via 172.16.4.2, 00:00:06, Serial0
172.16.3.0/24
    [1] via 172.16.1.2, 00:00:02, Ethernet0
172.16.4.0/24    directly connected, Serial0
```

You verify the routing table with the **show ip route** command. Example 7-7 shows the output from Router9. All connected interfaces and routes learned from RIP are inserted in the routing table. An R indicates that the route was learned from RIP.

Example 7-7 *Routes Learned from RIP are Marked with an R*

```
router9#show ip route
Codes: C - connected, S - static, I - IGRP, R - RIP, M - mobile, B - BGP
       D - EIGRP, EX - EIGRP external, O - OSPF, IA - OSPF inter area
       N1 - OSPF NSSA external type 1, N2 - OSPF NSSA external type 2
       E1 - OSPF external type 1, E2 - OSPF external type 2, E - EGP
       i - IS-IS, L1 - IS-IS level-1, L2 - IS-IS level-2, ia - IS-IS inter area
       * - candidate default, U - per-user static route, o - ODR
       P - periodic downloaded static route

Gateway of last resort is not set

     172.16.0.0/24 is subnetted, 4 subnets
C       172.16.4.0 is directly connected, Serial0
C       172.16.1.0 is directly connected, Ethernet0
R       172.16.2.0 [120/1] via 172.16.4.2, 00:00:22, Serial0
R       172.16.3.0 [120/1] via 172.16.1.2, 00:00:18, Ethernet0
```

Router10 learns about subnetworks 172.16.1.0 and 172.16.3.0 from Router9. Example 7-8 shows the output of Router10. The shaded routes were learned from RIP.

Example 7-8 *Output for* **show ip rip database** *and* **show ip route** *on Router10*

```
router10>show ip rip database
172.16.0.0/16    auto-summary
172.16.1.0/24
    [1] via 172.16.4.1, 00:00:09, Serial0
172.16.2.0/24    directly connected, Ethernet0
172.16.3.0/24
    [2] via 172.16.4.1, 00:00:09, Serial0
```

continues

Example 7-8 *Output for* **show ip rip database** *and* **show ip route** *on Router10 (Continued)*

```
172.16.4.0/24    directly connected, Serial0
router10>
router10>show ip route
Codes: C - connected, S - static, I - IGRP, R - RIP, M - mobile, B - BGP
       D - EIGRP, EX - EIGRP external, O - OSPF, IA - OSPF inter area
       N1 - OSPF NSSA external type 1, N2 - OSPF NSSA external type 2
       E1 - OSPF external type 1, E2 - OSPF external type 2, E - EGP
       i - IS-IS, L1 - IS-IS level-1, L2 - IS-IS level-2, ia - IS-IS inter area
       * - candidate default, U - per-user static route, o - ODR
       P - periodic downloaded static route

Gateway of last resort is not set

     172.16.0.0/24 is subnetted, 4 subnets
C       172.16.4.0 is directly connected, Serial0
R       172.16.1.0 [120/1] via 172.16.4.1, 00:00:05, Serial0
C       172.16.2.0 is directly connected, Ethernet0
R       172.16.3.0 [120/2] via 172.16.4.1, 00:00:05, Serial0
```

Router8 learns about subnetworks 172.16.4.0 and 172.16.2.0 from Router9. These routes are highlighted in Example 7-9. Example 7-9 shows the output from Router8.

Example 7-9 *Output for* **show ip rip database** *and* **show ip route** *on Router8*

```
router8#show ip rip database
172.16.0.0/16    auto-summary
172.16.1.0/24    directly connected, Ethernet0
172.16.2.0/24
    [2] via 172.16.1.1, 00:00:11, Ethernet0
172.16.3.0/24    directly connected, TokenRing0
172.16.4.0/24
    [1] via 172.16.1.1, 00:00:11, Ethernet0
router8#
router8#show ip route
Codes: C - connected, S - static, I - IGRP, R - RIP, M - mobile, B - BGP
       D - EIGRP, EX - EIGRP external, O - OSPF, IA - OSPF inter area
       N1 - OSPF NSSA external type 1, N2 - OSPF NSSA external type 2
       E1 - OSPF external type 1, E2 - OSPF external type 2, E - EGP
       i - IS-IS, L1 - IS-IS level-1, L2 - IS-IS level-2, ia - IS-IS inter area
       * - candidate default, U - per-user static route, o - ODR
       P - periodic downloaded static route

Gateway of last resort is not set

     172.16.0.0/24 is subnetted, 4 subnets
R       172.16.4.0 [120/1] via 172.16.1.1, 00:00:17, Ethernet0
C       172.16.1.0 is directly connected, Ethernet0
R       172.16.2.0 [120/2] via 172.16.1.1, 00:00:17, Ethernet0
C       172.16.3.0 is directly connected, TokenRing0
```

Example 7-9 *Output for* **show ip rip database** *and* **show ip route** *on Router8 (Continued)*

```
C    192.168.199.0/24 is directly connected, Loopback4
     192.168.1.0/30 is subnetted, 1 subnets
C       192.168.1.0 is directly connected, Serial1
router8#
```

RIPv1 Summary

The characteristics of RIPv1 are summarized as follows:

- Distance vector protocol.
- Uses UDP port 520.
- Classful protocol (no support for VLSM or CIDR).
- Metric is router hop count.
- Maximum hop count is 15; unreachable routes have a metric of 16.
- Periodic route updates broadcast every 30 seconds.
- 25 routes per RIP message.
- Implements split horizon with poison reverse.
- Implements triggered updates.
- No support for authentication.
- Administrative distance for RIP is 120.

RIPv2

RIPv2 was first described in RFC 1388 and RFC 1723 (1994); the current RFC is 2453, written in November 1998. Although current environments use advanced routing protocols, such as OSPF and EIGRP, there still are networks that use RIP. The need for VLSMs and other requirements prompted the definition of RIPv2.

RIPv2 improves upon RIPv1, as it has the capability to use VLSM and supports route authentication and multicasts route updates. RIPv2 also supports CIDR. Updates are still sent every 30 seconds and the 15-hop limit is retained; triggered updates are also still used. RIPv2 uses UDP port 520; the RIP process is responsible for checking the version number. Loop prevention strategies of poison reverse and counting to infinity are retained. On Cisco routes, RIPv2 has the same administrative distance as RIPv1, which is 120. Finally, RIPv2 uses the IP address 224.0.0.9 when multicasting route updates to other RIP routers.

As in RIPv1, RIPv2 also summarizes IP networks at network boundaries. You can disable autosummarization with the **no auto-summary** command, as follows:

```
router rip
 version 2
 no auto-summary
```

You can use RIPv2 in small networks where VLSM is required. You can use authentication to prevent communication with any RIP routers that are not intended to be part of the network, such as UNIX stations running routed. Only those RIP updates with the authentication password are accepted. RFC 1723 defines simple plain text authentication for RIPv2. Besides plain text passwords, Cisco's implementation provides the ability to use MD5 authentication. MD5 is the message-digest algorithm defined in RFC 1321. Its algorithm takes as input a message of arbitrary length and produces as output a 128-bit fingerprint or message digest of the input, making it much more secure than plain text passwords.

RIPv2 Forwarding Information Base

RIPv2 maintains a routing table database, as in version 1. The difference is that the subnet mask information is also kept. The table information of RIPv1 is repeated here as follows:

- **IP address**—IP address of the destination host or network, with subnet mask.
- **Gateway**—The first gateway along the path to the destination.
- **Interface**—The physical network that you must use to reach the destination.
- **Metric**—A number that indicates the number of hops to the destination.
- **Timer**—The amount of time since the route entry was last updated.

RIPv2 Message Format

The RIPv2 message format takes advantage of the unused fields in the RIPv1 message format by adding subnet masks and other information. Figure 7-3 shows the RIPv2 message format.

Figure 7-3 *RIPv2 Message Format*

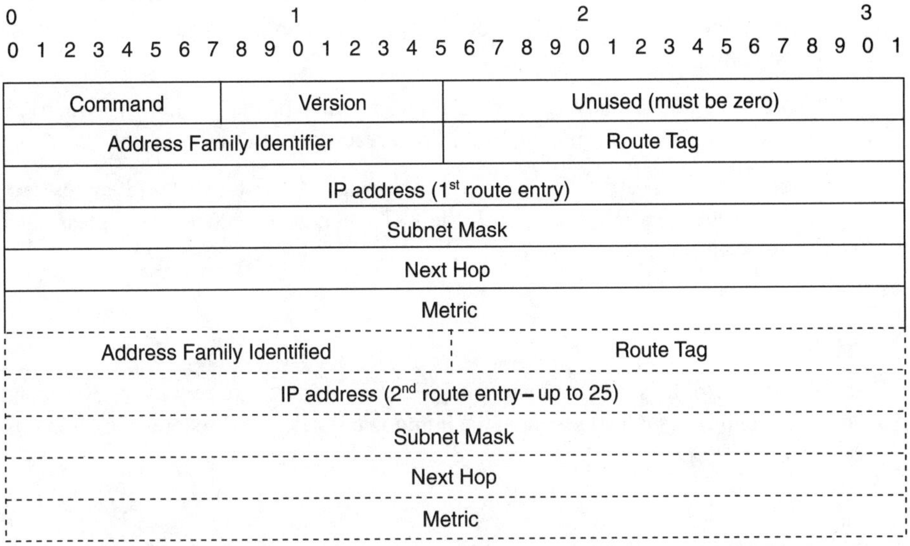

The following is a description of each field:

- **Command**—Indicates whether the packet is a request or a response message. The request message asks that a router send all or part of its routing table. Response messages contain route entries. The response message is set periodically, or as a reply to a request.
- **Version**—Specifies the RIP version. It is set to 2 for RIPv2 and 1 for RIPv1.
- **Address Family Identifier**—Specifies the address family. RIP is designed to carry routing information for several different protocols. Each entry has an address-family identifier to indicate the type of address specified. The address family identifier for IP is 2. The AFI is set to 0xFFF for the first entry to indicate that the remainder of the entry contains authentication information.
- **Route Tag**—Provides a method for distinguishing between internal routes (learned by RIP) and external routes (learned from other protocols). Route tags are covered in Chapter 10.
- **IP address**—Specifies the IP address (network) of the destination.

- **Subnet Mask**—Contains the subnet mask for the destination. If this field is zero, no subnet mask has been specified for the entry.
- **Next Hop**—Indicates the IP address of the next hop where packets are sent to reach the destination.
- **Metric**—Indicates how many router hops to reach the destination. The metric is between 1 and 15 for a valid route, or 16 for an unreachable or infinite route.

Again, as in version 1, up to 25 occurrences of the last five 32-bit words (20 bytes) are permitted for up to 25 routes per RIP message. If the AFI specifies an authenticated message, only 24 routing table entries can be specified.

RIPv2 Timers

RIPv2 timers are the same as in version 1. Periodic updates are sent every 30 seconds. The default invalid timer is 180 seconds, the holddown timer is 180 seconds, and the flush timer is 240 seconds.

RIPv2 Configuration

The RIPv2 protocol is configured just as in RIPv1 by using the global **router rip** command. You use a **version** command to enable use of the RIPv2 protocol. Then, the networks that are routed with RIP are configured with the **network** command. Looking again at Figure 7-2, the routers in this example are configured differently than the example configurations shown for RIPv1. First, you use the **version** command. Second, subnetworks can now have different subnet masks. The serial link is configured with a /30 mask. The Token Ring network is configured with a /28 mask.

The configuration examples in this section are for Router8, Router9, and Router10, as shown in Figure 7-4. In these examples, you use VLSMs and authentication is configured.

Figure 7-4 *Example Network*

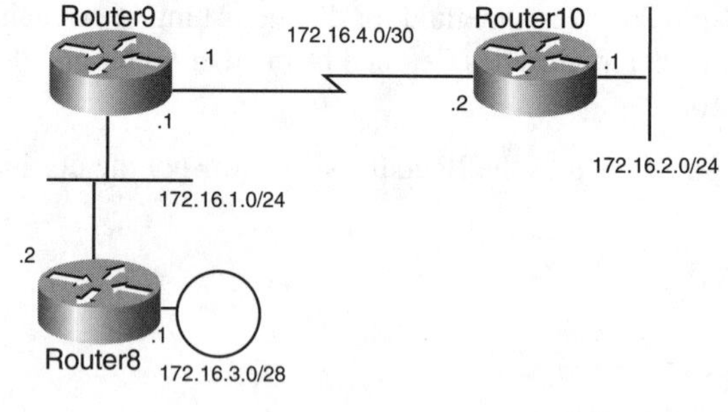

Example 7-10 shows the configuration of Router8 by using RIPv2. You use the **version 2** command to enable RIPv2. Use plain text passwords for route authentication by using the key-chain named ccie. The RIP authentication is configured on Ethernet 0 by using the **ip rip authentication** command.

Example 7-10 *Configuration of Router8*

```
hostname router8
!
key chain ccie
 key 1
  key-string ccie
!
interface Ethernet0
 ip address 172.16.1.2 255.255.255.0
 ip rip authentication key-chain ccie
!
interface TokenRing0
 ip address 172.16.3.1 255.255.255.240
 ring-speed 16
!
router rip
 version 2
 network 172.16.0.0
!
```

Example 7-11 shows the output of the **show ip route** command on Router8. A mask accompanies the learned networks 172.16.4.0/30 and 172.16.2.0/24.

Example 7-11 **show ip route** *Command on Router8*

```
router8#show ip route
Codes: C - connected, S - static, I - IGRP, R - RIP, M - mobile, B - BGP
       D - EIGRP, EX - EIGRP external, O - OSPF, IA - OSPF inter area
       N1 - OSPF NSSA external type 1, N2 - OSPF NSSA external type 2
       E1 - OSPF external type 1, E2 - OSPF external type 2, E - EGP
       i - IS-IS, L1 - IS-IS level-1, L2 - IS-IS level-2, ia - IS-IS inter area
       * - candidate default, U - per-user static route, o - ODR
       P - periodic downloaded static route

Gateway of last resort is not set

     172.16.0.0/16 is variably subnetted, 4 subnets, 3 masks
R       172.16.4.0/30 [120/1] via 172.16.1.1, 00:00:12, Ethernet0
C       172.16.1.0/24 is directly connected, Ethernet0
R       172.16.2.0/24 [120/2] via 172.16.1.1, 00:00:12, Ethernet0
C       172.16.3.0/28 is directly connected, TokenRing0
```

Example 7-12 shows the configuration of Router9. You use the **version 2** command to enable RIPv2. You use a plain text password to communicate with Router8 with authentication by using the key-chain named ccie. The RIP authentication is configured on Ethernet 0 by using the **ip rip authentication** command.

Example 7-12 *Configuration of Router9*

```
hostname router9
!
key chain ccie
 key 1
  key-string ccie
!
interface Ethernet0
 ip address 172.16.1.1 255.255.255.0
 ip rip authentication key-chain ccie
!
interface Serial0
 ip address 172.16.4.1 255.255.255.252

!
router rip
 version 2
 network 172.16.0.0
```

Example 7-13 shows the router output of the **show ip route** command on Router9. The learned routes with variable subnet masks are as follows: 172.16.2.0/24 and 172.16.3.0/28.

Example 7-13 **show ip route** *command on Router9*

```
router9#show ip route
Codes: C - connected, S - static, I - IGRP, R - RIP, M - mobile, B - BGP
       D - EIGRP, EX - EIGRP external, O - OSPF, IA - OSPF inter area
       N1 - OSPF NSSA external type 1, N2 - OSPF NSSA external type 2
       E1 - OSPF external type 1, E2 - OSPF external type 2, E - EGP
       i - IS-IS, L1 - IS-IS level-1, L2 - IS-IS level-2, ia - IS-IS inter area
       * - candidate default, U - per-user static route, o - ODR
       P - periodic downloaded static route

Gateway of last resort is not set

     172.16.0.0/16 is variably subnetted, 4 subnets, 3 masks
C       172.16.4.0/30 is directly connected, Serial0
C       172.16.1.0/24 is directly connected, Ethernet0
R       172.16.2.0/24 [120/1] via 172.16.4.2, 00:00:13, Serial0
R       172.16.3.0/28 [120/1] via 172.16.1.2, 00:00:01, Ethernet0
```

Example 7-14 shows the configuration of Router10.

Example 7-14 *Configuration of Router10*

```
hostname router10
!
interface Ethernet0
 ip address 172.16.2.1 255.255.255.0
!
interface Serial0
 ip address 172.16.4.2 255.255.255.252

!router rip
 version 2

 network 172.16.0.0
```

Example 7-15 shows the output of the **show ip route** command on Router10. Networks 172.16.1.0/24 and 172.16.3.0/28 are learned from Router9 through Serial 0.

Also notice the numbers in brackets: [120/2]. The first number is the administrative distance of RIP (120) and the second number is number of hops to reach the destination (2).

Example 7-15 *Output for* **show ip route** *on Router10*

```
router10#show ip route
Codes: C - connected, S - static, I - IGRP, R - RIP, M - mobile, B - BGP
       D - EIGRP, EX - EIGRP external, O - OSPF, IA - OSPF inter area
       N1 - OSPF NSSA external type 1, N2 - OSPF NSSA external type 2
       E1 - OSPF external type 1, E2 - OSPF external type 2, E - EGP
       i - IS-IS, L1 - IS-IS level-1, L2 - IS-IS level-2, ia - IS-IS inter area
       * - candidate default, U - per-user static route, o - ODR
       P - periodic downloaded static route

Gateway of last resort is not set

     172.16.0.0/16 is variably subnetted, 4 subnets, 3 masks
C       172.16.4.0/30 is directly connected, Serial0
R       172.16.1.0/24 [120/1] via 172.16.4.1, 00:00:08, Serial0
C       172.16.2.0/24 is directly connected, Ethernet0
R       172.16.3.0/28 [120/2] via 172.16.4.1, 00:00:08, Serial0
```

You can verify RIP operation with the **debug ip rip** command. Example 7-16 shows an approximately one-minute sample from Router10. Router10 receives routing updates approximately every 30 seconds: at 23:43, 24:11, and 24:37. Router10 also sends its routing table every 30 seconds: at 23:50 and 24:20.

Example 7-16 *Example of* **debug ip rip** Command

```
router10#debug ip rip
RIP protocol debugging is on
router10#
00:23:43: RIP: received v2 update from 172.16.4.1 on Serial0
00:23:44:      172.16.1.0/24 via 0.0.0.0 in 1 hops
00:23:44:      172.16.3.0/28 via 0.0.0.0 in 2 hops
00:23:50: RIP: sending v2 update to 224.0.0.9 via Serial0 (172.16.4.2)
00:23:50: RIP: build update entries
00:23:50:       172.16.2.0/24 via 0.0.0.0, metric 1, tag 0
00:24:11: RIP: received v2 update from 172.16.4.1 on Serial0
00:24:11:      172.16.1.0/24 via 0.0.0.0 in 1 hops
00:24:11:      172.16.3.0/28 via 0.0.0.0 in 2 hops
00:24:20: RIP: sending v2 update to 224.0.0.9 via Serial0 (172.16.4.2)
00:24:20: RIP: build update entries
00:24:20:       172.16.2.0/24 via 0.0.0.0, metric 1, tag 0
00:24:37: RIP: received v2 update from 172.16.4.1 on Serial0
00:24:37:      172.16.1.0/24 via 0.0.0.0 in 1 hops
00:24:37:      172.16.3.0/28 via 0.0.0.0 in 2 hops
00:24:46: RIP: build update entries
00:24:46:       172.16.2.0/24 via 0.0.0.0, metric 1, tag 0
```

RIPv2 Summary

The characteristics of RIPv2 are summarized as follows:

- Distance vector protocol.
- Uses UDP port 520.
- Classless protocol (support for CIDR).
- Supports VLSM.
- Metric is router hop count.
- Maximum hop count is 15; infinite (unreachable) routes have a metric of 16.
- Periodic route updates sent every 30 seconds to multicast address 224.0.0.9.
- 25 routes per RIP message (24 if you use authentication).
- Supports authentication.
- Implements split horizon with poison reverse.
- Implements triggered updates.
- Subnet mask included in route entry.
- Administrative distance for RIPv2 is 120.

IGRP

IGRP was developed by Cisco Systems to overcome the limitations of RIPv1. IGRP is a distance vector routing protocol that uses bandwidth (and other metrics) instead of hop count as the metric. IGRP is not limited to the 15-hop limit of RIP. Also, faster links that might have a longer hop count are selected as the best path over small hop count routes that might be using slower links.(Note: According to a recent announcement posted on Cisco System's web site, the 351-001 written exam does not test candidates on IGRP. Because the blueprint for the 350-001 exam includes mention of IGRP, the information is included here.)

IGRP is a classful protocol and cannot implement VLSMs or CIDR. IGRP also summarizes at network boundaries. As in RIP, IGRP implements split horizon with poison reverse, triggered updates, and holddown timers for stability and loop prevention. Another benefit of IGRP is that it can load balance over unequal-cost links. As a routing protocol developed by Cisco, IGRP is available only on Cisco routers.

By default, IGRP loads balance traffic if there are several paths with equal-cost to the destination. IGRP does unequal-cost load balancing if configured with the **variance** *n* command. IGRP includes routes that are equal to or less than *n* times the minimum metric route to a destination.

As in RIP, IGRP also summarizes IP networks at network boundaries. Autosummarization can be disabled with the **no auto-summary** command, as follows:

```
router igrp 100
 no auto-summary
```

IGRP Timers

IGRP sends its routing table to its neighbors every 90 seconds. IGRP's update period of 90 seconds is a benefit over RIP, which can overpower bandwidth by sending updates every 30 seconds. IGRP also uses an invalid timer to mark a route as invalid after 270 seconds (3 times the update timer). As with RIP, IGRP also uses a flush timer to remove a route from the routing table; the default flush timer is set to 630 seconds (7 times the update period, over 10 minutes).

If a network goes down or the metric for the network increases, the route is placed in holddown—no new changes are accepted for the route until the holddown timer expires. This is done to prevent routing loops in the network. The default holddown timer is 280 seconds (3 times the update timer plus 10 seconds).

Table 7-1 summarizes the default settings for IGRP timers.

Table 7-1 *IGRP Timers*

IGRP Timer	Default Time
Update	90 seconds
Invalid	270 seconds
Holddown	280 seconds
Flush	630 seconds

The default timers can be changed with the **timers basic** *update invalid holddown flush* command. This is a subcommand under **router igrp**.

IGRP Metrics

IGRP uses a composite metric based on bandwidth, delay, load, and reliability. These metrics are discussed in Chapter 2. By default, bandwidth and delay are used to calculate the composite metric.

The composite metric is calculated as follows:

$$IGRP_{metric} = \{k1 \times BW + [(k2 \times BW)/(256 - load)] + k3 \times delay\} \times \{k5/(reliability + k4)\}$$

In this formula, BW is the lowest interface bandwidth in the path and delay is the sum of all outbound interface delays in the path. Reliability and load are measured dynamically by the router. A 100 percent reliability is expressed as 255/255. Load is expressed as a fraction of 255. An interface with no load is represented as 1/255.

By default, k1 and k3 are set to 1 and k2, k4, and k5 are set to 0. With the default values, the metric becomes the following:

$$IGRP_{metric} = \{1 \times BW + [(0 \times BW)/(256 - load)] + 1 \times delay\} \times \{0/(reliability + 0)\}$$
$$IGRP_{metric} = BW + delay$$

The BW is 10,000,000 divided by the smallest of all the bandwidths (in kbps) from outgoing interfaces to the destination. To find delay, add all the delays (in microseconds) from the outgoing interfaces to the destination and divide by 10. (The delay is in 10s of microsecs.)

Example 7-17 shows the output interfaces to reach network 172.16.2.0 from Router9. The path takes a serial link and the Ethernet interface of Router10. The bandwidths are 10,000 and 1544, and the slowest bandwidth is 1544. The sum of delays is 20,000 + 1000 = 21,000.

Example 7-17 *Output Interfaces to Reach Network 172.16.2.0 from Router9*

```
Router9>show interface serial 0
Serial0 is up, line protocol is up
  Hardware is HD64570
  Internet address is 172.16.4.1/24
  MTU 1500 bytes, BW 1544 Kbit, DLY 20000 usec,
     reliability 255/255, txload 1/255, rxload 1/255
Router10>sh int e 0
Ethernet0 is up, line protocol is up
  Hardware is Lance, address is 0010.7b80.bad5 (bia 0010.7b80.bad5)
  Internet address is 172.16.2.1/24
  MTU 1500 bytes, BW 10000 Kbit, DLY 1000 usec,
     reliability 255/255, txload 1/255, rxload 1/255
```

The IGRP metric is calculated as follows:

$$IGRP_{metric} = (10{,}000{,}000/1544) + (20000 + 1000)/10$$
$$IGRP_{metric} = 6476 + 2100 = 8576$$

The default metrics can be changed by using the **metric weight** *tos k1 k2 k3 k4 k5* subcommand under **router igrp**. Cisco Systems originally intended the *tos* field as a way to implement a specialized service in IGRP; however, it was not implemented and the value of tos is always 0. The *k* arguments are the k values that you use to build the composite metric. If you want to use all metrics, the command is as follows:

```
router igrp n
 metric weight 0 1 1 1 1 1
```

Redistribution into IGRP

When redistributing routes into IGRP, use the **default-metric** command to set the metric of redistributed routes. The values in Table 7-2 are suggested values used for redistribution from Ethernet interfaces. The bandwidth is 10,000 (kbps) and delay is 100 microseconds.

Table 7-2 *Metric Redistribution Values*

Metric	Value
Bandwidth	10,000
Delay	100
Reliability	255
Load	1
MTU	1500

The **default-metric** command that you use to set the default metrics of redistributed routes that are learned from Ethernet interfaces is as follows:

```
router igrp n
 default-metric 10000 100 255 1 1500
```

IGRP Configuration

The configuration commands for IGRP are as simple as for RIPv1. After configuring interfaces, use the **router igrp** command. You use an autonomous system number with the command because multiple instances of IGRP can be configured in a Cisco router. The configuration for the routers in this section is shown in Figure 7-5.

Figure 7-5 *Example Network*

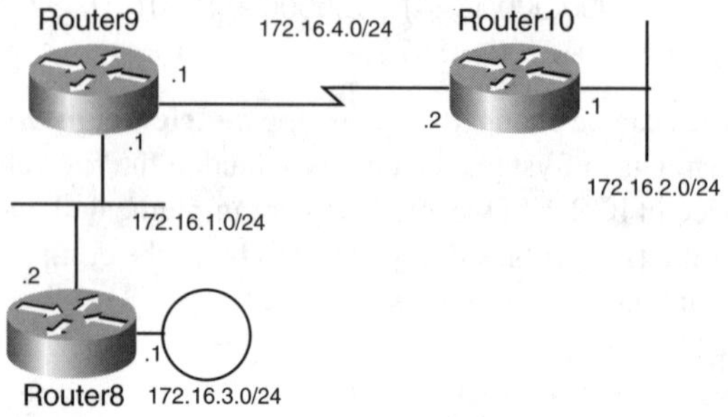

Example 7-18 shows the configuration for Router8. IGRP 100 is enabled with the **router igrp 100** command. The network 172.16.0.0 specifies that all interfaces on this router with an IP address within 172.16.0.0 are part of the IGRP process.

Example 7-18 *IGRP Configuration for Router8*

```
hostname Router8
!
interface Ethernet0
 ip address 172.16.1.2 255.255.255.0
!
interface TokenRing0
 ip address 172.16.3.1 255.255.255.0
 ring-speed 16
!
router igrp 100
 network 172.16.0.0
```

Example 7-19 shows the configuration for Router9. IGRP 100 is enabled with the **router igrp 100** command. The network 172.16.0.0 specifies that all interfaces on this router with an IP address within 172.16.0.0 are part of the IGRP process.

Example 7-19 *IGRP Configuration for Router9*

```
hostname Router9
!
interface Ethernet0
 ip address 172.16.1.1 255.255.255.0
!
interface Serial0
 ip address 172.16.4.1 255.255.255.0
!
router igrp 100
 network 172.16.0.0
```

Example 7-20 shows the configuration for Router10. IGRP 100 is enabled with the **router igrp 100** command. The network 172.16.0.0 specifies that all interfaces on this router with an IP address within 172.16.0.0 are part of the IGRP process.

Example 7-20 *IGRP Configuration for Router10*

```
hostname Router10
!
interface Ethernet0
 ip address 172.16.2.1 255.255.255.0
!
interface Serial0
 ip address 172.16.4.2 255.255.255.0
!
router igrp 100
 network 172.16.0.0
```

You can verify the routes by using the **show ip route** command. In Example 7-21, the IGRP routes are labeled with an I. For Router8, network 172.16.4.0 has an IGRP metric of 8576, and for network 172.16.2.0, the IGRP metric is 8676. The administrative distance for IGRP is 100, which is the number that accompanies the IGRP metric in the brackets.

Example 7-21 *Output for* **show ip route** *on Router8*

```
Router8#show ip route
Codes: C - connected, S - static, I - IGRP, R - RIP, M - mobile, B - BGP
       D - EIGRP, EX - EIGRP external, O - OSPF, IA - OSPF inter area
       N1 - OSPF NSSA external type 1, N2 - OSPF NSSA external type 2
       E1 - OSPF external type 1, E2 - OSPF external type 2, E - EGP
       i - IS-IS, L1 - IS-IS level-1, L2 - IS-IS level-2, ia - IS-IS inter area
       * - candidate default, U - per-user static route, o - ODR
       P - periodic downloaded static route

Gateway of last resort is not set

     172.16.0.0/24 is subnetted, 4 subnets
I       172.16.4.0 [100/8576] via 172.16.1.1, 00:00:32, Ethernet0
C       172.16.1.0 is directly connected, Ethernet0
I       172.16.2.0 [100/8676] via 172.16.1.1, 00:00:32, Ethernet0
C       172.16.3.0 is directly connected, TokenRing0
```

The output of the **show ip route** command from Router9 is shown in Example 7-22. For Router9, network 172.16.2.0 has an IGRP metric of 8576 through the serial interface, and for network 172.16.3.0 the IGRP metric is 1163 through the Ethernet interface.

Example 7-22 *Output for* **show ip route** *on Router9*

```
Router9#show ip route
Codes: C - connected, S - static, I - IGRP, R - RIP, M - mobile, B - BGP
       D - EIGRP, EX - EIGRP external, O - OSPF, IA - OSPF inter area
       N1 - OSPF NSSA external type 1, N2 - OSPF NSSA external type 2
       E1 - OSPF external type 1, E2 - OSPF external type 2, E - EGP
       i - IS-IS, L1 - IS-IS level-1, L2 - IS-IS level-2, ia - IS-IS inter area
       * - candidate default, U - per-user static route, o - ODR
       P - periodic downloaded static route

Gateway of last resort is not set

     172.16.0.0/24 is subnetted, 4 subnets
C       172.16.4.0 is directly connected, Serial0
C       172.16.1.0 is directly connected, Ethernet0
I       172.16.2.0 [100/8576] via 172.16.4.2, 00:00:36, Serial0
I       172.16.3.0 [100/1163] via 172.16.1.2, 00:01:13, Ethernet0
```

The output of the **show ip route** command for Router10 is shown in Example 7-23. For Router10, network 172.16.1.0 has an IGRP metric of 8576 and network 172.16.3.0; the IGRP metric is 8639, through the serial interface.

Example 7-23 *Output for* **show ip route** *on Router10*

```
Router10>show ip route
Codes: C - connected, S - static, I - IGRP, R - RIP, M - mobile, B - BGP
       D - EIGRP, EX - EIGRP external, O - OSPF, IA - OSPF inter area
       N1 - OSPF NSSA external type 1, N2 - OSPF NSSA external type 2
       E1 - OSPF external type 1, E2 - OSPF external type 2, E - EGP
       i - IS-IS, L1 - IS-IS level-1, L2 - IS-IS level-2, ia - IS-IS inter area
       * - candidate default, U - per-user static route, o - ODR
       P - periodic downloaded static route

Gateway of last resort is not set

     172.16.0.0/24 is subnetted, 4 subnets
C       172.16.4.0 is directly connected, Serial0
I       172.16.1.0 [100/8576] via 172.16.4.1, 00:00:04, Serial0
C       172.16.2.0 is directly connected, Ethernet0
I       172.16.3.0 [100/8639] via 172.16.4.1, 00:00:04, Serial0
```

IGRP Summary

The characteristics of IGRP are summarized as follows:

- Distance vector protocol.
- Uses IP protocol 9.

- Classful protocol (no support for CIDR).
- No support for VLSMs.
- Composite metric of bandwidth and delay.
- Load and reliability can be factored into the metric.
- Route updates sent every 90 seconds.
- 104 routes per IGRP message.
- No support for authentication.
- Implements split horizon with poison reverse.
- Implements triggered updates.
- By default, equal-cost load balancing; unequal-cost load balancing with the **variance** command.
- Administrative distance is 100.

EIGRP

EIGRP was released in the early 1990s by Cisco Systems as a evolution of IGRP toward a scalable routing protocol. EIGRP is a classless protocol that permits the use of VLSMs and support for CIDR for scalable allocation of IP addresses. Routing updates are not sent periodically, as in IGRP. EIGRP allows for authentication, with simple passwords or with MD5. EIGRP autosummarizes networks at network borders and can load balance over unequal-cost paths. Packets use IP protocol 88. You can use only EIGRP on Cisco routers.

EIGRP is an advanced distance vector protocol that implements some characteristics similar to link-state protocols. Some of Cisco's documentation might refer to EIGRP as a hybrid protocol. EIGRP advertises its routing table to its neighbors as distance vector protocols do, but it uses hellos and forms neighbor relationships similar to link-state protocols. EIGRP sends partial updates when a metric or the topology changes on the network. Full routing table updates are not sent in periodic fashion, as they are with distance vector protocols. EIGRP uses DUAL to determine loop-free paths to destinations. DUAL is covered in this section.

By default, EIGRP loads balance traffic if there are several paths with equal-cost to the destination. EIGRP does unequal-cost load balancing if configured with the **variance** *n* command. EIGRP includes routes that are equal to or less than *n* times the minimum metric route to a destination.

As in RIP and IGRP, EIGRP also summarizes IP networks at network boundaries. You can disable autosummarization with the **no auto-summary** command as follows:

```
router eigrp 100
 no auto-summary
```

EIGRP internal routes have an administrative distance of 90. EIGRP summary routes have an administrative distance of 5, and EIGRP external routes (from redistribution) have an administrative distance of 170. Administrative distance is covered in Chapter 10.

EIGRP Components

The characteristics of EIGRP are as follows:

- Protocol-dependent modules
- Neighbor discovery and recovery
- Reliable Transport Protocol (RTP)
- DUAL

Protocol-Dependent Modules

EIGRP uses different modules that independently support IP, Internetwork Packet Exchange (IPX), and AppleTalk routable protocols. These modules are the logical interface between DUAL and routing protocols, such as IPX RIP, AppleTalk Routing Table Maintenance Protocol (RTMP), and IGRP. The EIGRP module sends and receives packets but passes received information to DUAL, which makes routing decisions. EIGRP automatically redistributes with IGRP if both protocols are configured with the same autonomous system number. When configured to support IPX, EIGRP communicates with the IPX RIP protocol and forwards the route information to DUAL to select best paths. AppleTalk EIGRP automatically redistributes routes with AppleTalk RTMP to support AppleTalk networks. IPX EIGRP is covered in Chapter 12, "Multiservice Networking, IPX Networking, and Security." AppleTalk is no longer an objective for the Cisco CCIE written test and is not covered in this book.

Neighbor Discovery and Recovery

EIGRP discovers and maintains information about its neighbors. Hello packets are multicast (224.0.0.10) every 5 seconds for most networks. The router builds a table with EIGRP neighbor information. The holdtime to maintain a neighbor is 3 times the hello time: 15 seconds. If a hello is not received in 15 seconds, the neighbor is removed from the table. Hellos are multicast every 60 seconds on multipoint WAN interfaces (X.25, Frame Relay, ATM) with speeds less than 1544 Mbps, inclusive. The neighbor holdtime is 180 second on these types of interfaces.

Example 7-24 shows an EIGRP neighbor database. The table lists the neighbor's IP address, the interface to reach it, the neighbor's holdtime timer, and the uptime.

Example 7-24 *EIGRP Neighbor Database*

```
Router#show ip eigrp neighbor
IP-EIGRP neighbors for process 100
H   Address                 Interface   Hold Uptime    SRTT   RTO  Q   Seq Type
                                        (sec)          (ms)        Cnt Num
1   172.17.1.1              Se0           11 00:11:27   16    200  0   2
0   172.17.2.1              Et0           12 00:16:11   22    200  0   3
```

RTP

RTP manages EIGRP packets, ensures reliable delivery of route updates, and uses sequence numbers to ensure ordered delivery. Update packets are sent using multicast address (224.0.0.10). Updates are acknowledged using unicast hello packets with no data.

DUAL

DUAL selects paths and guarantees freedom from routing loops. DUAL was developed by Dr. J.J. Garcia Luna-Aceves. DUAL was mathematically proven to result in a loop-free topology that provides no need for periodic updates or route holddown mechanisms that make convergence slower.

DUAL selects a best path and a second best path to reach a destination. The best path selected by DUAL is called the *successor*, and the second best path (if available) is the *feasible successor*. The *feasible distance* is the lowest calculated metric of a path to reach the destination. The feasible distance can be viewed in the topology table, as shown in Example 7-25. The example also shows two paths (Ethernet 0 and Ethernet 1) to reach 172.16.4.0/30. Because the paths have different metrics, only one successor is chosen.

Example 7-25 *Feasible Distance as Shown in EIGRP Topology Table*

```
Router8#show ip eigrp topology
IP-EIGRP Topology Table for AS(100)/ID(172.16.3.1)

Codes: P - Passive, A - Active, U - Update, Q - Query, R - Reply,
       r - reply Status, s - sia Status

P 172.16.4.0/30, 1 successors, FD is 2195456
         via 172.16.1.1 (2195456/2169856), Ethernet0
         via 172.16.5.1 (2376193/2348271), Ethernet1
P 172.16.1.0/24, 1 successors, FD is 281600
         via Connected, Ethernet0
```

The topology entries in Example 7-25 are marked P as being in passive state. A destination is in passive state when the router is not performing any recomputations for the entry. If the successor goes down and the route entry has feasible successors, the router does not perform any recomputations, thus the destination does not go into active state.

The route entry for a destination is placed into active state if the successor goes down and no feasible successors exist. EIGRP routers send query packets to neighboring routers to find a feasible successor to the destination. Neighboring routers can send reply packets that indicate they have a feasible successor or they can send a query packet. The query packet indicates that the neighboring router does not havė a feasible successor and that it is participating in the recomputation. A route does not return to passive state until it receives a reply packet from each neighboring router. If the router does not receive all replies before the active-time timer expires, the route is declared as being in the stuck-in-active (SIA) state. The default active timer is three minutes.

EIGRP Timers

EIGRP updates are set only when necessary and are sent only to neighboring routers. There is no periodic update timer.

You use hello packets to learn of neighboring routes. On most networks, the default hello packet interval is 5 seconds. On multipoint networks with link speeds of T1 and slower, hello packets are unicast every 60 seconds.

The holdtime to maintain a neighbor adjacency is three times the hello time: 15 seconds. If a hello is not received in 15 seconds, the neighbor is removed from the table. Hellos are multicast every 60 seconds on multipoint WAN interfaces (X.25, Frame Relay, ATM) with speeds less than 1544 Mbps, inclusive. The neighbor holdtime is 180 seconds on these types of interfaces. If a hello packet is not received within the holdtime, the neighbor is removed from the neighbor table.

NOTE EIGRP updates are not sent using a broadcast address; instead, they are sent to the multicast address 224.0.0.10 (all EIGRP routers).

EIGRP Metrics

EIGRP uses the same composite metric as in IGRP but multiplied by 256 for finer granularity. The composite metric is based on bandwidth, delay, load, and reliability.

The composite metric is calculated with the following formula:

$$EIGRP_{metric} = \{k1 \times BW + [(k2 \times BW)/(256 - load)] + k3 \times delay\} \times \{k5/(reliability + k4)\}$$

In this formula, BW is the lowest interface bandwidth in the path, and delay is the sum of all outbound interface delays in the path. Reliability and load are measured dynamically by the router. A 100 percent reliability is expressed as 255/255. Load is expressed as a fraction of 255. An interface with no load is represented as 1/255.

Bandwidth is inverse minimum bandwidth (in kbps) of the path in bits per second, which is scaled by a factor of 256×10^7.

The formula for bandwidth is as follows: $(256 \times 10^7)/BW_{min}$.

Delay is the sum of the outgoing interface delays (in microseconds) to the destination. A delay of all 1s (that is, a delay of hexadecimal FFFFFFFF) indicates that the network is unreachable.

The formula for delay is as follows: [sum of delays] × 256.

Reliability is specified as a fraction of 255. That is, 255/255 is 100 percent reliability or a perfectly stable link. A value of 229/255 represents 90 percent reliability.

Load is specified as a fraction of 255. A load of 255/255 indicates a completely saturated link. A load of 127/255 represents a 50 percent saturated link.

By default, k1=k3=1 and k2=k4=k5=0. The default composite metric for EIGRP, adjusted for scaling factors, is as follows:

$$EIGRP_{metric} = 256 \times \{ [10^7/BW_{min}] + [sum\_of\_delays] \}$$

BW_{min} is in kbps and the sum of delays are in 10s of microseconds. The bandwidth and delay for an Ethernet interface are 10 Mbps and 1ms, respectively.

The calculated EIGRP BW metric is as follows:

$$\begin{aligned} 256 \times 10^7/BW &= 256 \times 10^7/10{,}000 \\ &= 256 \times 10000 \\ &= 256000 \end{aligned}$$

The calculated EIGRP delay metric is as follows:

$$\begin{aligned} 256 \times \text{sum of delay} &= 256 \times 1\text{ms} \\ &= 256 \times 100 \times 10 \text{ microseconds} \\ &= 25600 \text{ (in tens of microseconds)} \end{aligned}$$

Table 7-3 shows some default values for bandwidth and delay.

Table 7-3 *Default EIGRP Values for Bandwidth and Delay*

Media Type	Delay	Bandwidth
Satellite	5120 (2 seconds)	5120 (500 Mbps)
Ethernet	25,600 (1 ms)	256,000 (10 Mbps)
T-1 (1.544 Mbps)	512,000 (20,000 ms)	1,657,856
64 kbps	512,000	40,000,000
56 kbps	512,000	45,714,176

As with IGRP, the **metric weights** subcommand changes EIGRP metric computation. The k values in the EIGRP composite metric formula can be changed to select EIGRP metrics. The command to change the k values is the **metric weights** *tos k1 k2 k3 k4 k5* subcommand under **router eigrp** *n*. You never use the *tos* value, which is always set to 0. The other arguments are set to 1 or 0 to alter the composite metric. If you want the EIGRP composite metric to use all the parameters, the command is as follows:

```
router eigrp n
 metric weights 0 1 1 1 1 1
```

EIGRP Packet Types

EIGRP uses the following packet types:

- Hello
- Acknowledgment
- Update
- Query
- Reply

Hello packets assist in the discovery of EIGRP neighbors. The packets are multicast to 224.0.0.10. By default, hello packets are sent every 5 seconds (60 seconds on WAN links with 1544 Mbps speeds or less).

An *acknowledgment* packet acknowledges the reception of an update packet. An acknowledgment packet is a hello packet with no data. Acknowledgment packets are sent to the unicast address of the sender of the update packet.

Update packets contain the routing information of destinations. Update packets are unicast to newly discovered neighbors; otherwise, update packets are multicast to 224.0.0.10 when a link or metric changes. Update packets are acknowledged to ensure reliable transmission. *Query* packets are sent to find feasible successors to a destination. *Query* packets are always multicast.

Reply packets are sent to respond to query packets. Reply packets provide a feasible successor to the sender of the query. *Reply* packets are unicast to the sender of the query packet.

EIGRP Configuration

The configuration commands for EIGRP are similar to IGRP. After configuring the interfaces, the **router eigrp** command enables the routing protocol. The networks are defined with the **network** command.

Using the physical network described in Figure 7-6, the configurations for Router8, Router9, and Router10 are presented in this section.

Figure 7-6 *EIGRP Configuration Example*

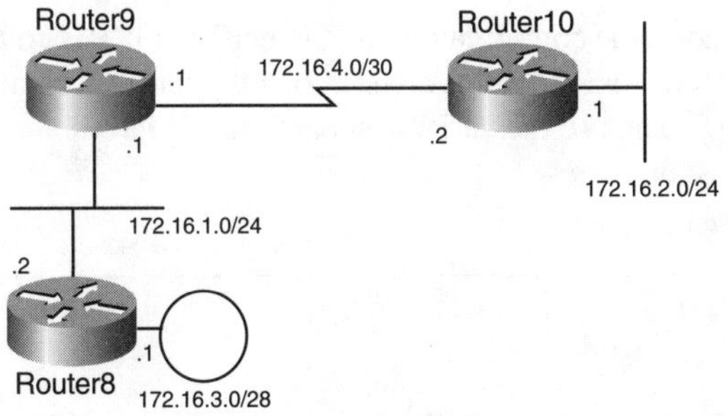

Example 7-26 shows the configuration of Router8. EIGRP is configured with the autonomous system number 100. EIGRP hellos are sent on all interfaces configured with an IP address within 172.16.0.0. You use the variable subnet masks; the subnet mask on Ethernet 0 is /24 and on Token Ring 0 is /28.

Example 7-26 *Configuration of Router8*

```
hostname Router8
!
interface Ethernet0
 ip address 172.16.1.2 255.255.255.0
!
interface TokenRing0
 ip address 172.16.3.1 255.255.255.240
 ring-speed 16
!
router eigrp 100
 network 172.16.0.0
```

Example 7-27 shows the configuration of Router9. EIGRP is configured with the autonomous system number 100. EIGRP hellos are sent on all interfaces configured with an IP address within 172.16.0.0. You use the variable subnet masks; the subnet mask on Ethernet 0 is /24 and on Serial 0 is /30.

Example 7-27 *Configuration of Router9*

```
hostname Router9
!
interface Ethernet0
 ip address 172.16.1.1 255.255.255.0
!
interface Serial0
 ip address 172.16.4.1 255.255.255.252
!
router eigrp 100
 network 172.16.0.0
```

Example 7-28 shows the configuration of Router10. EIGRP is configured with the autonomous system number 100. EIGRP hellos are sent on all interfaces configured with an IP address within 172.16.0.0. You use the variable subnet masks; the subnet mask on Ethernet 0 is /24 and on Serial 0 is /30.

Example 7-28 *Configuration of Router10*

```
hostname Router10
!
interface Ethernet0
 ip address 172.16.2.1 255.255.255.0
!
interface Serial0
 ip address 172.16.4.2 255.255.255.252
!
router eigrp 100
 network 172.16.0.0
```

After the routers are configured, you verify the EIGRP neighbors by using the **show ip eigrp neighbor** command. Example 7-30 shows the output for Router8. From the output, you can determine that the IP address of the neighbor (Router9) is 172.16.1.1, the interface to reach the neighbor is Ethernet 0, the holdtime counter is at 11 seconds (starts at 15 and counts down), and the neighbor uptime is 19 minutes and 42 seconds. Smooth route-trip time (SRTT) is calculated in milliseconds; 11 milliseconds in this example. SRTT is the average time that it takes from when a packet is sent to receive an acknowledgment from a neighbor. Retransmission Timeout (RTO) is the time that the router waits for the acknowledgment on a unicast packet when a multicast fails; 200 milliseconds in this example. The Q count is the number of queued packets, 0, as shown in Example 7-29.

Example 7-29 show ip eigrp neighbor *Command*

```
Router8#show ip eigrp neighbor
IP-EIGRP neighbors for process 100
H   Address          Interface      Hold Uptime     SRTT    RTO  Q   Seq Type
                                    (sec)           (ms)         Cnt Num
0   172.16.1.1       Et0              11 00:19:42    11     200  0   5
```

You verify the EIGRP table with the **show ip eigrp topology** command. Each route has one successor and the feasible distance (FD) is shown. The routes are then placed into the routing table. You can verify all routes with the **show ip route** command. EIGRP routes are labeled with a D. The output for Router8 is shown in Example 7-30.

For the destination network 172.16.4.0/30, you can gather the following information:

- The successor is 172.16.1.1.
- The feasible distance is 2195456.
- The metric used by the neighboring router (Router9) is 2169856.
- The interface to reach network 172.16.4.0 is Ethernet 0.

The EIGRP routes are shaded in the output of the **show ip route** command. EIGRP routes are marked with a D. For destination 172.16.4.0/30, the metric is 2195456 and the administrative distance is 90. The route was last updated 17 minutes and 20 seconds ago. The output interface to reach the destination is through Ethernet 0.

Example 7-30 show ip eigrp topology *and* **show ip route** *Command on Router8*

```
Router8#show ip eigrp topology
IP-EIGRP Topology Table for AS(100)/ID(172.16.3.1)

Codes: P - Passive, A - Active, U - Update, Q - Query, R - Reply,
       r - reply Status, s - sia Status

P 172.16.4.0/30, 1 successors, FD is 2195456
         via 172.16.1.1 (2195456/2169856), Ethernet0
P 172.16.1.0/24, 1 successors, FD is 281600
         via Connected, Ethernet0
P 172.16.2.0/24, 1 successors, FD is 2221056
         via 172.16.1.1 (2221056/2195456), Ethernet0
P 172.16.3.0/28, 1 successors, FD is 176128
         via Connected, TokenRing0
Router8#
Router8#show ip route
Codes: C - connected, S - static, I - IGRP, R - RIP, M - mobile, B - BGP
       D - EIGRP, EX - EIGRP external, O - OSPF, IA - OSPF inter area
       N1 - OSPF NSSA external type 1, N2 - OSPF NSSA external type 2
       E1 - OSPF external type 1, E2 - OSPF external type 2, E - EGP
```

continues

Example 7-30 **show ip eigrp topology** *and* **show ip route** *Command on Router8 (Continued)*

```
       i - IS-IS, L1 - IS-IS level-1, L2 - IS-IS level-2, ia - IS-IS inter area
       * - candidate default, U - per-user static route, o - ODR
       P - periodic downloaded static route

Gateway of last resort is not set

     172.16.0.0/16 is variably subnetted, 4 subnets, 3 masks
D       172.16.4.0/30 [90/2195456] via 172.16.1.1, 00:17:20, Ethernet0
C       172.16.1.0/24 is directly connected, Ethernet0
D       172.16.2.0/24 [90/2221056] via 172.16.1.1, 00:12:40, Ethernet0
C       172.16.3.0/28 is directly connected, TokenRing0
```

The output for Router9 is shown in Example 7-31. The feasible distance (2169856) shown for network 172.16.4.0/30 is the same number shown as the neighbor's metric in Router8's topology table. For the destination network 172.16.2.0/24, you can gather the following information:

- The successor is 172.16.4.2.
- The feasible distance is 2195456.
- The metric used by the neighboring router (Router10) is 281600.
- The interface to reach network 172.16.2.0/24 is serial 0.

Example 7-31 *EIGRP Topology Table of Router9*

```
Router9#show ip eigrp topology
IP-EIGRP Topology Table for AS(100)/ID(172.16.4.1)

Codes: P - Passive, A - Active, U - Update, Q - Query, R - Reply,
       r - reply Status, s - sia Status

P 172.16.4.0/30, 1 successors, FD is 2169856
         via Connected, Serial0
P 172.16.1.0/24, 1 successors, FD is 281600
         via Connected, Ethernet0
P 172.16.2.0/24, 1 successors, FD is 2195456
         via 172.16.4.2 (2195456/281600), Serial0
P 172.16.3.0/28, 1 successors, FD is 297728
         via 172.16.1.2 (297728/176128), Ethernet0
```

The output for Router10 is shown in Example 7-32. The feasible distance (281600) shown for network 172.16.2.0/24 is the same number shown as the neighbor's metric in Router9's topology table.

Example 7-32 *EIGRP Topology Table of Router10*

```
Router10#show ip eigrp topology
IP-EIGRP Topology Table for AS(100)/ID(172.16.4.2)

Codes: P - Passive, A - Active, U - Update, Q - Query, R - Reply,
       r - reply Status, s - sia Status

P 172.16.4.0/30, 1 successors, FD is 2169856
         via Connected, Serial0
P 172.16.1.0/24, 1 successors, FD is 2195456
         via 172.16.4.1 (2195456/281600), Serial0
P 172.16.2.0/24, 1 successors, FD is 281600
         via Connected, Ethernet0
P 172.16.3.0/28, 1 successors, FD is 2211584
         via 172.16.4.1 (2211584/297728), Serial0
```

EIGRP Summary

The characteristics of EIGRP are summarized as follows:

- Hybrid routing protocol (distance vector that has link-state protocol characteristics).
- Uses IP protocol 88.
- Classless protocol (supports VLSMs).
- Default composite metric of bandwidth and delay.
- Load and reliability can be factored into the metric.
- Sends partial route updates only when changes occur.
- Support for authentication.
- Uses DUAL for loop prevention.
- By default, equal-cost load balancing; unequal-cost load balancing with the **variance** command.
- Administrative distance is 90 for EIGRP internal routes, 170 for EIGRP external routes, and 5 for EIGRP summary routes.

References Used

The following resources were used to create this chapter:

Routing TCP/IP, Volume I, Jeff Doyle, Cisco Press, 1998

CCDA Exam Certification Guide, Anthony Bruno and Jacqueline Kim, Cisco Press, 2000

RFC 1058, "Routing Information Protocol," C.L. Hedrick

RFC 2453, "RIP Version 2," G. Malkin

www.cisco.com/univercd/cc/td/doc/cisintwk/ito_doc/en_igrp.htm

www.cisco.com/univercd/cc/td/doc/cisintwk/ito_doc/rip.htm

www.cisco.com/univercd/cc/td/doc/cisintwk/ito_doc/en_igrp.htm

www.cisco.com/warp/public/103/eigrp1.html

www.cisco.com/warp/public/103/19.html

Foundation Summary

The Foundation Summary is a condensed collection of material that provides a convenient review of key concepts in this chapter. If you are already comfortable with the topics in this chapter, this summary will help you recall a few details. If you just read the Foundation Topics section, this review should help solidify some key facts. If you are doing your final preparation before the exam, these materials are a convenient way to review the day before the exam.

RIPv1 Summary

The characteristics of RIPv1 are summarized as follows:

- Distance vector protocol.
- Uses UDP port 520.
- Classful protocol (no support for VLSM or CIDR).
- Metric is router hop count.
- Maximum hop count is 15; unreachable routes have a metric of 16.
- Periodic route updates broadcast every 30 seconds.
- 25 routes per RIP message.
- Implements split horizon with poison reverse.
- Implements triggered updates.
- No support for authentication.
- Administrative distance for RIP is 120.

RIPv2 Summary

The characteristics of RIPv2 are summarized as follows:

- Distance vector protocol.
- Uses UDP port 520.
- Classless protocol (support for CIDR).
- Supports VLSMs.
- Metric is router hop count.
- Maximum hop count is 15; infinite (unreachable) routes have a metric of 16.

- Periodic route updates sent every 30 seconds to multicast address 224.0.0.9.
- 25 routes per RIP message (24 if you use authentication).
- Supports authentication.
- Implements split horizon with poison reverse.
- Implements triggered updates.
- Subnet mask included in route entry.
- Administrative distance for RIPv2 is 120.

IGRP Summary

The characteristics of IGRP are summarized as follows:

- Distance vector protocol.
- Uses IP protocol 9.
- Classfull protocol (no support for CIDR).
- No support for VLSMs.
- Composite metric of bandwidth and delay.
- Load and reliability can be factored into the metric.
- Route updates sent every 90 seconds.
- 104 routes per IGRP message.
- No support for authentication.
- Implements split horizon with poison reverse.
- Implements triggered updates.
- By default, equal-cost load balancing; unequal-cost load balancing with the **variance** command.
- Administrative distance is 100.

EIGRP Summary

The characteristics of EIGRP are summarized as follows:

- Hybrid routing protocol (distance vector that has link-state protocol characteristics).
- Uses IP protocol 88.

- Classless protocol (supports VLSMs).
- Default composite metric of bandwidth and delay.
- Load and reliability can be factored into the metric.
- Sends partial route updates only when changes occur.
- Support for authentication.
- Uses DUAL for loop prevention.
- By default, equal-cost load balancing; unequal-cost load balancing with the **variance** command.
- Administrative distance is 90 for EIGRP internal routes, 170 for EIGRP external routes, and 5 for EIGRP summary routes.

Table 7-4 *Routing Protocols Comparison*

	Routing Protocol			
	RIPv1	RIPv2	IGRP	EIGRP
DistanceVector	yes	yes	yes	hybrid
VLSM	no	yes	no	yes
Authentication	no	yes	no	yes
Update Timer	30	30	90	n/a
Invalid Timer	180	180	270	n/a
Flush Timer	240	240	630	n/a
Protocol/port	UDP 520	UDP 520	IP 9	IP 88
Admin Distance	120	120	100	90

Q & A

The Q & A questions are more difficult than what you can expect on the actual exam. The questions do not attempt to cover more breadth or depth than the exam; however, they are designed to make sure that you retain the material. Rather than allowing you to derive the answer from clues hidden inside the question itself, these questions challenge your understanding and recall of the subject. Questions from the "Do I Know This Already?" quiz are repeated here to ensure that you have mastered the chapter's topic areas. A strong understanding of the answers to these questions will help you on the CCIE written exam. As an additional study aide, use the CD-ROM provided with this book to take simulated exams.

Select the best answer. Answers to these questions are in the Appendix, "Answers to Quiz Questions."

1 When will EIGRP and IGRP automatically redistribute routes among themselves?

a. When you use different AS numbers

b. When you use the same AS numbers without the **redistribution** command

c. When you use different AS numbers and the **redistribution** command under EIGRP

d. When you use different AS numbers and the **redistribution** command under IGRP

2 Which command enables RIP?

a. **router rip**

b. **router rip 100**

c. **enable router rip 100**

d. **router rip v1 100**

3 How often does IGRP broadcast routing table updates?

a. Every 30 seconds

b. Every 60 seconds

c. Every 90 seconds

d. Every 180 seconds

4 Which **static route** command is correctly configured?

a. router(config)#**ip route 10.100.0.0 0.0.255.255 192.172.1.1**

b. router(config)#**ip route 10.100.0.0 255.255.0.0 192.172.1.1**

c. router(config)>**ip route 10.100.0.0 255.255.0.0 192.172.1.1**

d. router#**ip route 10.100.0.0 0.0.255.255 192.172.1.1**

5 How long does it take IGRP to remove a possibly down network from the table?

a. 10 minutes

b. 280 seconds

c. 6 minutes

d. 180 seconds

6 RIPv2 improves RIPv1 with which of the following capabilities?

a. Multicast, authentication, hop count

b. Multicast, authentication, VLSM

c. Authentication, VLSM, hop count

d. VLSM, hop count

7 What is the maximum number of routes in a RIP packet?

a. 104

b. 20

c. 25

d. 60

8 Which protocol maintains neighbor adjacencies?

a. RIPv2 and EIGRP

b. IGRP and EIGRP

c. RIPv2

d. EIGRP

9 What does the number in the **router igrp 50** command indicate?

a. The number of processes is 50.

b. The autonomous system number is 50.

c. The arbitrary number 50.

d. IGRP is allowed 50 routes.

10 Which protocols are classful?

a. EIGRP, RIPv1, and IGRP

b. RIPv1, RIPv2, IGRP

c. RIPv1 and IGRP

d. OSPF, RIPv2, and EIGRP

11 Which protocol service interface does EIGRP use?

a. UDP port 520

b. IP protocol 9

c. IP protocol 89

d. IP protocol 88

12 What does the default EIGRP composite metric consist of?

a. Bandwidth

b. Bandwidth and delay

c. Bandwidth, delay, load, and reliability

d. Bandwidth, delay, load, reliability, and hop count

13 For RIP, if route updates are not received for a network, how long before the routes are considered invalid?

a. 180 seconds

b. 90 seconds

c. 60 seconds

d. 240 seconds

14 Which routing protocol implements the DUAL algorithm?

a. IGRP and EIGRP

b. IGRP

c. EIGRP

d. EIGRP and RIPv2

15 Which protocols support VLSM?

a. RIPv2 and IGRP

b. RIPv2, IGRP, and EIGRP

c. RIP and IGRP

d. RIPv2 and EIGRP

16 How many routes are in an IGRP update packet?

a. 25

b. 50

c. 75

d. 104

17 How does EIGRP summarize routes at network boundaries?

a. By default

b. By configuring no **auto-summary** command

c. If they have the same AS number as IGRP

d. By configuring a static route

18 RIP uses a feature in which routes learned from a neighboring router are sent back to that neighbor with an infinite metric. What is that feature?

a. Simple split horizon

b. DUAL

c. Poison reverse

d. Holddown

19 Which of the following commands do you use to enable RIPv2 for network 192.10.10.0?

a.

```
router rip v2
 network 192.10.10.0
```

b.

```
router rip
 version 2
 network 192.10.10.0
```

c.

```
router rip 50
 version 2
 network 192.10.10.0
```

d.

```
router rip
 send version 2
 network 192.10.10.0
```

20 Which protocol or port does RIP version 2 use?

a. IP protocol 88

b. TCP 88

c. UDP port 520

d. IP protocol 9

21 Which of the following protocols support authentication?

a. RIPv2, IGRP, and EIGRP

b. IGRP and EIGRP

c. RIPv2 and EIGRP

d. RIP and RIPv2

22 If a router with EIGRP configured is performing a recomputation for a network, the route is in which state?

a. Active state

b. Recompute state

c. Update state

d. Passive state

23 To disable automatic summarization for EIGRP 100, which subcommand is used?

a.

```
router eigrp 100
 no summary
```

b.

```
router eigrp 100
 no automatic-summary
```

c.

```
router eigrp 100
 no auto-summary
```

d.

```
router eigrp 1000
 no auto-sum
```

24 When a route is marked as invalid, what prevents the route from being reinstated into the routing table?

a. Invalid timer

b. Flush timer

c. Holddown timer

d. Update timer

25 What is the administrative distance for internal EIGRP routes?

a. 100

b. 110

c. 170

d. 90

26 RIP version 2 packets are identified in the routing table by which letter?

a. I

b. R

c. E

d. R2

27 From the following output, which is the metric to reach network 172.16.4.0/30?

```
Router8#show ip route
Codes: C - connected, S - static, I - IGRP, R - RIP, M - mobile, B - BGP
       D - EIGRP, EX - EIGRP external, O - OSPF, IA - OSPF inter area
       N1 - OSPF NSSA external type 1, N2 - OSPF NSSA external type 2
       E1 - OSPF external type 1, E2 - OSPF external type 2, E - EGP
      i - IS-IS, L1 - IS-IS level-1, L2 - IS-IS level-2, ia - IS-IS inter area
       * - candidate default, U - per-user static route, o - ODR
       P - periodic downloaded static route
```

```
Gateway of last resort is not set

     172.16.0.0/16 is variably subnetted, 4 subnets, 3 masks
D       172.16.4.0/30 [90/2195456] via 172.16.1.1, 00:17:20, Ethernet0
C       172.16.1.0/24 is directly connected, Ethernet0
D       172.16.2.0/24 [90/2221056] via 172.16.1.1, 00:12:40, Ethernet0
C       172.16.3.0/28 is directly connected, TokenRing0
```

a. 90/2221056

b. 90

c. 2195456

d. 2221056

28 Which command is used to check the EIGRP table?

a. **show ip route**

b. **show ip eigrp routes**

c. **show ip eigrp topology**

d. **show ip eigrp table**

29 EIGRP's composite metric scales IGRP's metric by what factor?

a. 256.

b. 256,000.

c. 1000.

d. It uses the same metric.

Scenario

Review Figure 7-7 to answer the following Scenario questions.

Figure 7-7 *Path Selection*

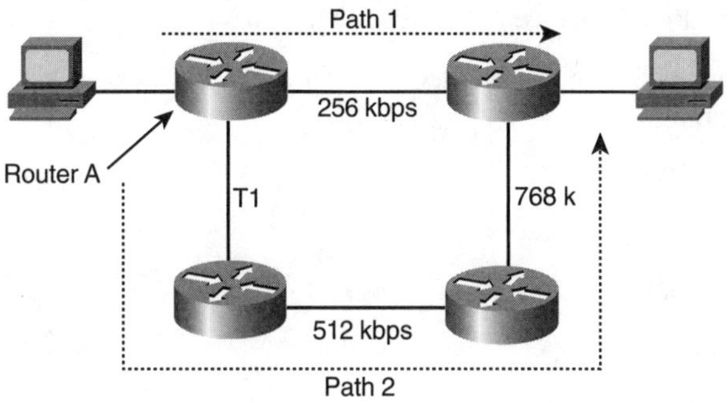

1 By default, if RIPv2 is enabled on all routers, what path is taken?

a. Path 1

b. Path 2

c. Unequal load balance with Path 1 and Path 2

d. Equal load balance with Path 1 and Path 2

2 By default, if IGRP is enabled on all routers, what path is taken?

a. Path 1

b. Path 2

c. Unequal load balance with Path 1 and Path 2

d. Equal load balance with Path 1 and Path 2

3 By default, if EIGRP is enabled on all routers what path is taken?

a. Path 1

b. Path 2

c. Unequal load balance with Path 1 and Path 2

d. Equal load balance with Path 1 and Path 2

4 EIGRP is configured on the routers. If con figured with the variance command, what path is taken?

a. Path 1

b. Path 2

c. Unequal load balance with Path 1 and Path 2

d. Equal load balance with Path 1 and Path 2

5 Which bandwidth does Router A use for the EIGRP calculation of the metric to reach the destination?

a. 256 KB

b. 512 KB

c. 1.544 KB

d. 512 KB + 1.544MB + 768 KB

This chapter covers the following topics needed to master the CCIE Routing and Switching (R&S) written exam:

- **Open Shortest Path First (OSPF)**—Standards-based OSPF routing protocol
- **Intermediate System-to-Intermediate System (IS-IS)**—Open System Interconnection (OSI) IS-IS routing protocol

CHAPTER 8

IP Link-State Routing Protocols

Link-state routing protocols exchange topological information between routers. The information describes information about the routers and the routers' connected links. This information enables each router to understand the topology of the network. After each router understands the network's topology, it can create a routing table based on the topology. This chapter discusses two IP link-state protocols, OSPF and IS-IS. OSPF is the most popular standards-based interior routing protocol. Some service provider networks still use IS-IS, and IS-IS has emerged as an important protocol in Multiprotocol Label Switching (MPLS) architecture. You should understand the general networking concepts discussed in Chapter 2, "Networking Concepts Review," before reading this chapter.

"Do I Know This Already?" Quiz

The purpose of this assessment quiz is to help you determine how to spend your limited study time. If you can answer most or all of these questions, you might want to skim the Foundation Topics section and return to it later as necessary. Review the Foundation Summary section and answer the questions at the end of the chapter to ensure that you have a strong grasp of the material covered. If you intend to read the entire chapter, you do not necessarily need to answer these questions now. If you find these assessment questions difficult, read through the entire Foundation Topics section and review it until you feel comfortable with your ability to answer all of the Q & A questions at the end of the chapter. The following questions are repeated at the end of the chapter in the Q & A section with additional questions to test your mastery of the material.

Select the best answer. Answers to these questions are in the Appendix, "Answers to Quiz Questions."

1 Which type of router always has one or more interfaces connected to Area 0.0.0.0?

a. Level 2 router

b. ASBR

c. Backbone router

d. Autonomous boundary router

2 What is the number in the **router ospf** *number* command?

a. The autonomous system number

b. The process ID

c. The AS number

d. Answer b and c

3 IS-IS has which types of authentication capabilities?

a. Domain, area, and link authentication with cleartext password.

b. Domain, area, and link authentication with md5.

c. Domain, area, and link authentication with cleartext and md5 passwords.

d. There is no authentication in IS-IS.

4 What is the IOS default OSPF cost for a T1 interface?

a. 100

b. 10

c. 290

d. 64

5 What is the default IS-IS metric for a T1 interface?

a. 100

b. 10

c. 290

d. 64

6 What connects an area to the backbone when there is no physical connectivity?

a. T1 link

b. Virtual link

c. Fast Ethernet link

d. Backbone link

7 Which command verifies IS-IS neighbors?

a. **show isis is-neighbors**

b. **show ip isis neighbors**

c. **show clns is-neighbors**

d. **show ip clns isis neighbors**

8 A router that floods external Type-7 LSAs is part of which type of area?

a. Backbone area

b. Stub area

c. Not-so-stubby area

d. Totally stubby area

9 Which LSA type announces reachability to the ASBR?

a. Type 3

b. Type 4

c. Type 5

d. Type 7

10 Which commands add network 10.10.64.0/18 to area 10 in OSPF?

a. **router ospf** and **network 10.10.64.0 0.0.63.255 area 10**

b. **router ospf** and **network 10.10.64.0 255.255.192.0 area 10**

c. **router ospf 99** and **network 10.10.64.0 0.0.63.255 area 10**

d. **router ospf 99** and **network 10.10.64.0 255.255.192.0 area 10**

11 The **ip ospf cost** command is used for what?

a. To change the default cost under **router ospf**

b. To change the default cost on an external link when redistributing into OSPF

c. To change the default cost at the ABR

d. To change the default cost of an interface

12 Which address multicasts to the designated router?

a. 224.0.0.1

b. 224.0.0.5

c. 224.0.0.6

d. 224.0.0.10

13 What is the administrative distance of OSPF routes?

a. 90

b. 100

c. 110

d. 170

14 What is the P-bit used for in NSSA?

a. Set by the ASBR to indicate the priority of routes redistributed into the area

b. Set by the ABR to indicate that the ABR is used as a default route to the rest of the network

c. Set by the ASBR to indicate whether Type 7 LSAs are translated to Type 5 LSAs

d. Set by the ABR in Type 5 LSAs when Type 7 LSAs are translated to Type 5 LSAs; indicates the originating area of a route

15 What is the ATT bit used for in IS-IS?

a. Set by an L1 IS to indicate that it is connected to an external network

b. Set by an L1/L2 IS to indicate to L1 ISs that this L1/L2 IS is available for forwarding traffic destined to routes unknown in the area

c. Set by an L2 IS to indicate that it is connected to an external network

d. Set by an L1/L2 IS to indicate to other L2 ISs that it is connected to multiple L1 areas

Foundation Topics

OSPF

OSPF is defined in RFC 2328. It is a link-state routing protocol that uses Dijkstra's shortest path first (SPF) algorithm to calculate paths to destinations. In OSPF, each router sends link-state advertisements about itself and its links to all its adjacent routers. Each router that receives a link-state advertisement records the information in its topology database and sends a copy of the link-state advertisement to each of its adjacencies (other than the one that originally sent the advertisement). All the link-state advertisements reach all routers in an area, which enables each router in the area to have an identical topology database that describes the routers and links within that area. The router is not sending routing tables but is sending link-state information about its interfaces. When the topology databases are complete, each router individually calculates a loop-free, shortest-path tree to each destination by running the SPF algorithm. The routing table is built from the shortest-path tree. Destinations outside the area are also advertised in link-state advertisements. These, however, do not require that routers run the SPF algorithm before they are added to the routing table.

OSPF is a classless routing protocol that permits the use of variable-length subnet masks (VLSMs). It also supports equal-cost multipath load balancing and neighbor authentication. OSPF uses multicast addresses to communicate between routers. OSPF runs over IP protocol 89.

OSPF Concepts and Design

This section covers OSPF theory and design concepts. OSPF link-state advertisements, area types, and router types are discussed.

OSPF Metric

OSPF uses the cost metric, which is an unsigned 16-bit integer in the range of 1 to 65,535. The default cost for interfaces is calculated based on the bandwidth in the formula 10^8 / BW, with BW being the bandwidth of the interface expressed as a full integer of bps. If the result is smaller than 1, the cost is set to 1. A 10BaseT (10Mbps = 10^7 bps) interface has a cost of $10^8 / 10^7 = 10$. OSPF performs a summation of the costs to reach a destination; the lowest cost is the preferred path. Some sample interface metrics are shown in Table 8-1.

Table 8-1 *OSPF Interface Costs*

Interface Type	OSPF Cost
Gigabit Ethernet	.1 → 1
OC-3 (155 Mbps)	.64516 → 1
Fast Ethernet	$10^8 / 10^8 = 1$
DS-3 (45 Mbps)	2
Ethernet	$10^8 / 10^7 = 10$
T1	64
512 KB	195
256 KB	390

In Layer-2 technologies, which support speeds greater than 100 Mbps, the default metric is set to 1 without regard to the different capabilities (speed) of the network.

The default reference bandwidth that calculates OSPF costs is 10^8 (Cost = 10^8 / BW). You can change the reference bandwidth by using the following command:

```
ospf auto-cost reference-bandwidth ref-bw
```

The *ref-bw* is the reference bandwidth, in megabits per second. To change the reference bandwidth to 1 Gbps, use the following commands:

```
router ospf 10
 ospf auto-cost reference-bandwidth 1000
```

Change the interface cost by using the interface command **ip ospf cost** *value*. The value specified with this command overrides the cost resulting from the **ospf auto-cost** command. You can change the default cost for a T1 serial interface from the default (64) to 50 by using the following commands:

```
interface serial 0
 ip ospf cost 50
```

OSPF Adjacencies and Hello Timers

OSPF uses Hello packets for neighbor discovery. The default Hello interval is 10 seconds (30 seconds for nonbroadcast multiaccess (NBMA) networks). Hellos are multicasted to 224.0.0.5 (ALLSPFROuters). OSPF neighboring routers become adjacent when the parameters in their Hello packets match, the routers see their own address listed in a Hello packet from their neighbor (indicating bidirectional communication), they exchange link-state advertisements (LSAs), and their databases are synchronized.

For point-to-point (p2p) networks, valid neighbors always become adjacent and communicate by using multicast 224.0.0.5. For broadcast (such as Ethernet) and NBMA (such as Frame

Relay) networks, all routers become adjacent to the designated and backup designated router (DR and BDR) but not to each other. The DR concept is discussed later in this chapter, in the "Designated Router" section.

On OSPF point-to-multipoint (p2mp) networks, it might be necessary to configure the set of neighbors that are directly reachable over the p2mp network. Each neighbor is identified by its IP address on the p2mp network. DRs are not elected on p2mp networks, so the DR eligibility of configured neighbors is undefined. Communication is similar to p2p networks that use multicast 224.0.0.5.

For OSPF virtual links, OSPF packets are unicast. Virtual links are discussed in this chapter.

Certain parameters in the Hello packets that are exchanged between neighbors must match before the neighbors can become adjacent. The interface that receives the Hello packets checks the network mask, the Hello interval, and the router dead timer to determine if they match its own values. Interfaces on p2p links or virtual links ignore the value of the network mask. If these values don't match, the Hello packet is dropped.

Another parameter that must match is indicated by an option bit, which identifies how the area handles the external routes. This is the E-bit. An interface belongs to a single OSPF area. The E-bit in a Hello packet that is received by an interface must match the receiving area's external route capabilities. If external routes are not flooded into and throughout this area (this is a stub area), the E-bit must not be set in the received Hello packets; otherwise, the E-bit must be set. Stub areas are discussed later in this chapter, in the "OSPF Stub Area Types" section.

LSA Types

OSPF routers generate LSAs that are flooded throughout an area or the entire autonomous system (AS). OSPF defines different LSA types for router, network, summary, external, and so on. Understanding of the LSA types help with other OSPF concepts. Table 8-2 describes the major LSA types.

Table 8-2 *Major LSA Types*

Type Code	Type	Description
1	Router LSA	Produced by every router and includes all the router links, interfaces, state of links, and cost. This LSA type is flooded within a single area.
2	Network LSA	Produced by every DR on every broadcast or NBMA network. It lists all the routers in the multiaccess network. This LSA type is contained within an area.
3	Summary LSA for ABRs	Produced by area border routers (ABRs). It is sent into an area to advertise destinations outside the area.

continues

Table 8-2 *Major LSA Types (Continued)*

Type Code	Type	Description
4	Summary LSA for ASBRs	Originated by ABRs. Sent into an area by the ABR to advertise the AS boundary routers (ASBRs).
5	AS External LSA	Originated by ASBRs. Advertises destinations external to the OSPF AS, flooded throughout the entire OSPF AS.
7	Not-so-stubby area External LSA	Originated by ASBRs in a not-so-stubby area (NSSA). It is not flooded throughout the OSPF AS, only to the NSSA.

External Path Types

Two types of External paths exist. External paths can be Type 1 or Type 2. Do not confuse these with the router and network LSAs. By default, external routes Type 2. The metric of Type 2 external routes is the metric of the route at the point of redistribution into the OSPF network. Type 1 external routes have a metric that is the sum of the redistribution cost plus the cost of the path to reach the ASBR. To set the external metric type for external routes, use the **metric-type** keyword in the **redistribution** statement, as shown in Example 8-1.

Example 8-1 *Setting the External Route Metric Type*

```
Router9(config)#router ospf 100
Router9(config-router)#redistribute static metric-type 1
```

The keyword **metric-type 1** causes the redistributed routes to be external Type-1 routes. The keyword **metric-type 2** makes the routes external Type-2 routes.

OSPF Areas

As a network grows, the initial flooding and database maintenance of LSAs can burden the CPU of a router. OSPF uses areas to reduce these effects. An area is a logical grouping of routers and links that divides the network. Routers share link-state information with only those routers in their area. This reduces the size of the database.

Each area is assigned a 32-bit integer number. Area 0 (or 0.0.0.0) is reserved for the backbone area. The backbone area is responsible for distributing routing information between areas. If more than one area exists in a network, one of the areas must be a backbone area. Every other area must have at least one connection to the backbone. As you can see in Figure 8-1, communication between area 1 and area 2 must flow through area 0, or at least flow through a router that is directly connected to area 0.

Figure 8-1 *OSPF Areas*

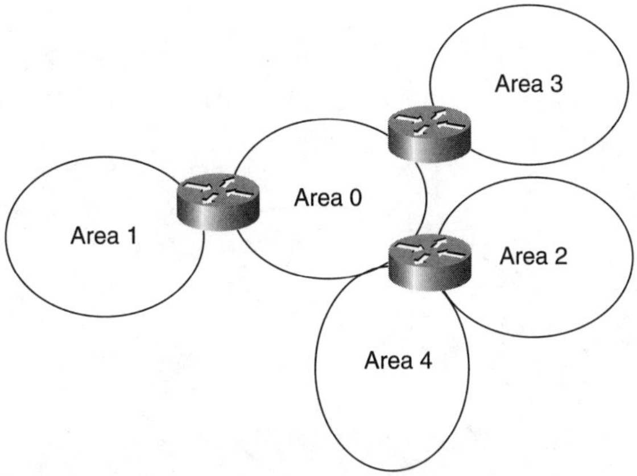

Intra-area traffic consists of packets that are passed between routers in a single area. Intra-area traffic is routed within an area based on the routing table that is built from information learned through Type-1 and Type-2 LSAs. Interarea traffic is passed between routers in different areas. Type-3 and Type-5 LSAs are flooded throughout all areas, and advertise IP network addresses that are located in other areas and autonomous systems. These addresses are added directly to each router's routing table, without forcing the router to run the SPF algorithm first.

OSPF Router Types

OSPF defines several router types that are related to their place and function in the area architecture. Figure 8-2 shows a diagram of OSPF router types.

The following is a list of explanations for each router type in Figure 8-2:

- **Internal router**—Interface belongs to the same OSPF area and keeps only one link-state database.
- **Area border router (ABR)**—Connects to more than one area; maintains a link-state database for each area that it belongs to and generates summary LSAs.
- **Autonomous system boundary router (ASBR)**—Inject external LSAs into the OSPF database. External routes are learned either through other routing protocols or static routes.
- **Backbone router**—Has at least one interface attached to area 0.

A router can be an ABR, ASBR, and backbone router at the same time.

Figure 8-2 *OSPF Router Types*

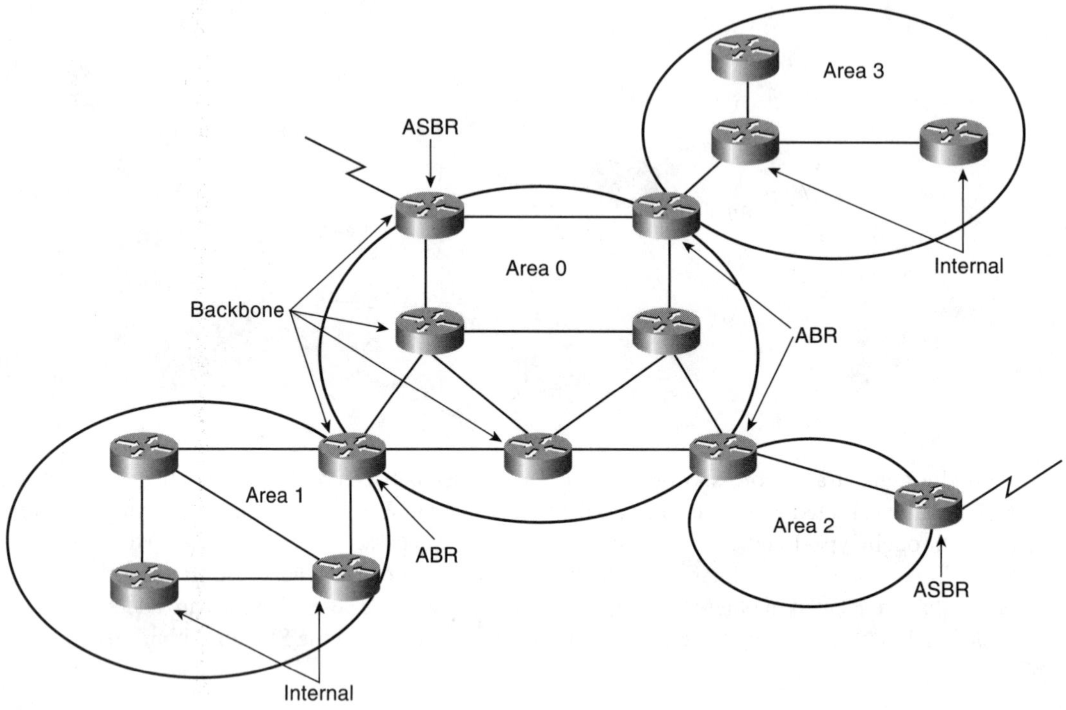

Designated Routers

Although not an OSPF router type, some routers on multiaccess networks (such as Ethernet or multipoint Frame Relay) are selected as DRs. The purpose of the DR is to collect all LSAs for the multiaccess network and to forward the LSA to all non-DR routers. This reduces the amount of LSA traffic generated on an Ethernet network. A router can be the DR for one multiaccess network and not the DR in another attached multiaccess network.

The DR also floods the Network LSA (Type 2) to the rest of the area. A BDR is also selected, which takes over the function of the DR if the DR fails. Both the DR and BDR become adjacent to all routers in the multiaccess network. All routers that are not DR and BDR are classified Drothers, and these routers are adjacent only to the DR and BDR. DRothers multicast packets to the DR and BDR by using the multicast address 224.0.0.6 (AllDRouters). The DR floods updates by using ALLSPFRouters (224.0.0.5).

DR and BDR selection is based on an OSPF DR interface priority. The default value is 1 and the highest priority determines the DR. If there is a tie, it uses the numerically highest router ID (RID). Routers with a priority of 0 are not considered for DR/BDR selection.

Looking at Figure 8-3, Router A is configured with a priority of 10, and Router B is configured with a priority of 5. Assuming that these routers are turned on simultaneously, Router A becomes the DR for the Ethernet network. Router C has a lower priority and becomes adjacent to Router A and Router B but not to Router D. Router D has a priority of 0 and is not a candidate to become a DR or BDR. The dotted lines in Figure 8-3 show the adjacencies in the network.

Figure 8-3 *Designated Routers (DRs)*

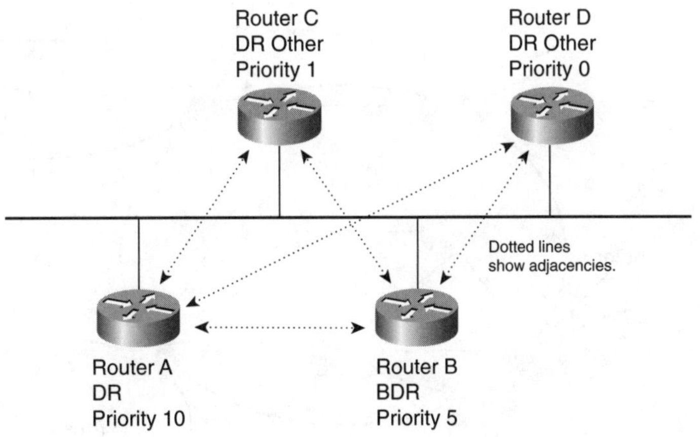

If a new router is introduced to the network with a higher priority than the current DR and BDR, it does not become the selected DR unless both the DR and BDR fail. If the DR fails, the current BDR becomes the DR.

The OSPF interface priority can be changed with the following interface command:

```
ip ospf priority value
```

The *value* argument is the priority assigned to the router for that interface. The range is from 0 to 255; 0 means that the router is not a DR or BDR candidate.

OSPF Stub Area Types

OSPF provides support for stub areas. The concept is to reduce the number of interarea or external LSAs that are flooded into a stub area. RFC 2328 defines OSPF stub areas. RFC 1587 defines support for NSSA. Totally stubby areas are not defined in an RFC, but Cisco and other vendors' routers do use them.

Stub Areas

Consider area 3 in Figure 8-4. Its only path to the external networks is through Router C. All external routes are flooded to all areas in the OSPF AS. An area can be configured as a stub area to prevent OSPF external LSAs (Type 5) from being flooded into that area. The ABR injects a default route into the stub area rather than flooding the external routes into the area.

Figure 8-4 *OSPF Network with Areas*

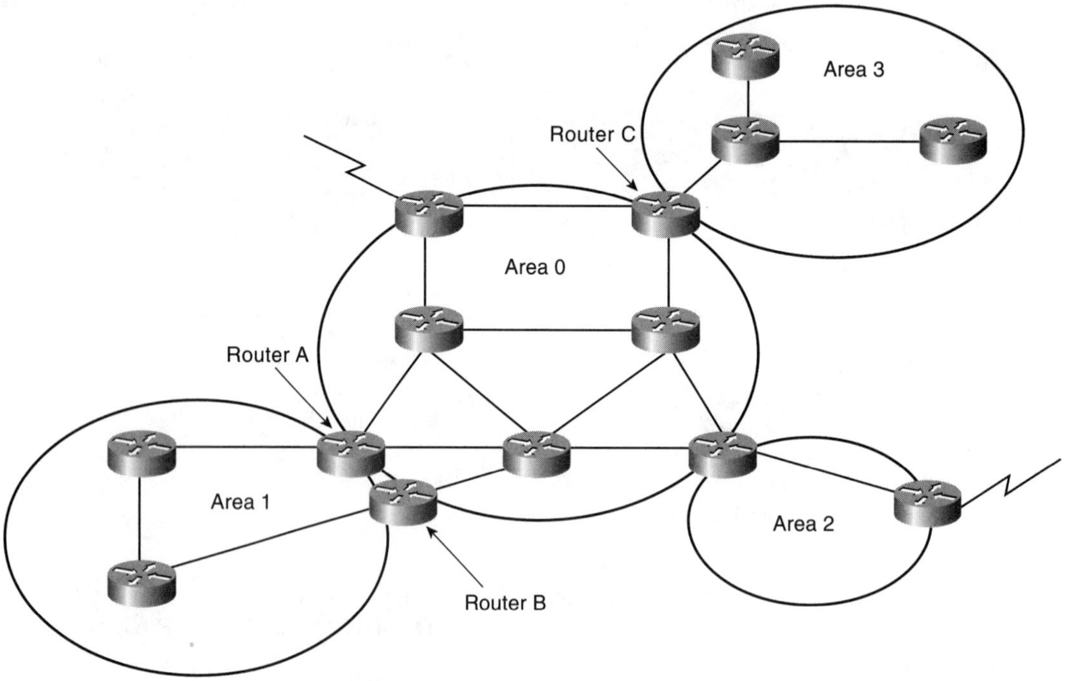

Consider area 1 in Figure 8-4. It has two ABRs connecting it to the backbone. Area 1 can also be configured as a stub area. Both Router A and Router B inject default routes into the area. Area 1 routers forward traffic destined to external routes (or any other unknown route) to the closest (based on the metric of the default route) ABR.

Network summary LSAs (Type 3) from other areas are still flooded into area 1.

To configure area 1 as a stub area, all routers must be configured with the following OSPF command:

```
area 1 stub
```

Totally Stubby Areas

Take the area 3 case in Figure 8-4 one step further. The only path for routers in area 3 to get to destinations in area 0 and other areas is through Router C. In a totally stubby area, neither OSPF external LSAs (Type 5) nor network summary LSAs (Type 3) are flooded into the area. A single LSA is sent for the default route. Stub areas with multiple ABRs can also be configured as totally stubby.

To configure area 3 as a totally stubby area, all routers in the area must be configured with the **area 3 stub** command, and the ABRs for the area must be configured with the following OSPF command:

```
area 3 stub no-summary
```

To configure the cost of the injected default route, use the command **area** *area-number* **default-cost** *cost*. The default cost is 1. The specified cost can be any 24-bit number.

NSSA

Area 2 in Figure 8-4 has an ASBR. If this area is configured as an NSSA, it allows the external LSAs (Type 7) into the OSPF system, while retaining the characteristics of a stub area to the rest of the AS. The ABR for area 2 can translate the NSSA External LSAs (Type 7) to AS External LSAs (Type 5) and flood the rest of the internetwork. The Type 7 LSA generated by the NSSA ASBR sets a bit (the P-bit) to dictate whether the LSA is translated from a Type 7 to a Type 5 LSA by the ABR. If the bit is set to 1, the translation occurs and the Type 5 LSA is flooded to the rest of the internetwork. If the bit is set to 0, the translation does not occur.

To configure area 2 as a NSSA, all routers in the area must be configured with the following OSPF router command:

```
area 2 nssa
```

Virtual Links

OSPF requires that all areas be connected to a backbone router. Sometimes, wide-area network (WAN) link provisioning or sudden failures can prevent an OSPF area from being directly connected to a backbone router. Virtual links can temporarily connect (virtually) the area to the backbone.

As shown in Figure 8-5, Area 4 is not directly connected to the backbone. A virtual link is configured between Router A and Router B. Area 2 becomes the transit area, through which the virtual link is configured. Router A and Router B are configured with the following command:

```
area transit-area virtual-link ip-address
```

Figure 8-5 *OSPF Network with a Virtual Link Connecting an Area to the Backbone*

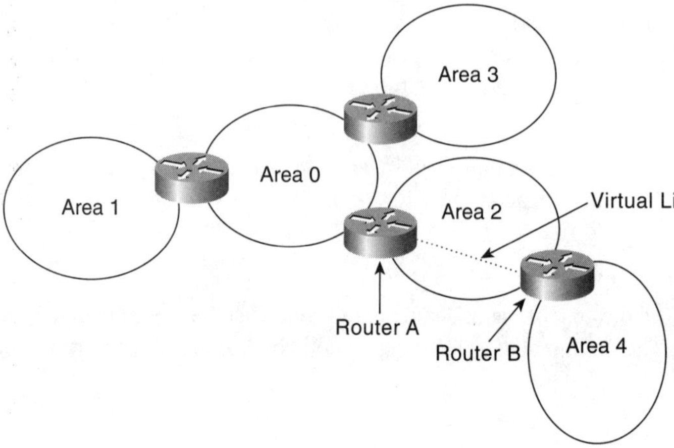

In this command, *ip-address* is the RID of the remote router of the virtual link. The virtual link can be verified with the **show ip ospf virtual-link** command.

OSPF Router Authentication

OSPF supports the authentication of routes using 64-bit simple password or cryptographic Message Digest 5 (MD5) authentication. MD5 authentication provides higher security than plain text authentication. The same type of authentication must be configured on all routers within an area. Authentication passwords do not need to be the same for the routers throughout the area, but they must be the same between neighbors.

To enable authentication with MD5, use the following command under **router ospf**:

```
area area-id authentication message-digest
```

Then configure the interfaces with the MD5 keys by using the following interface command:

```
ip ospf message-digest-key 1 md5 key
```

OSPF Summarization

OSPF ABRs can be configured to summarize networks using the **area range** command. For example, if a router has two Ethernet interfaces with the networks 200.100.100.0/24 and 200.100.101.0/24, and these networks are in the same area, ABR can be configured to summarize as follows:

```
area 10 range 200.100.100.0 255.255.254.0
```

Routes can also be summarized by an ASBR when routes are redistributed into OSPF. Rather than advertising routes individually in an external LSA, a summarized route can be advertised.

The ASBR uses the **summary-address** command to summarize redistributed routes. For example, if networks 200.100.0.0/24 through 200.100.255.0/24 are redistributed into OSPF at the same ASBR, you can configure the ASBR with the following command:

```
summary-address 200.100.0.0 255.255.0.0
```

The external LSA includes the summary address of 200.100.0.0 rather than each individual network number, 200.100.0.0, 200.100.1.0, 200.100.2.0, and so on.

The following section shows a summarization example.

OSPF Configuration

This section covers the configuration of OSPF routers and the commands that you use to verify OSPF routes.

Use Figure 8-6 as a reference, where four routers are configured to run OSPF using area 0 and three other areas. Area 10 is configured to do authentication and has a Frame Relay link. Area 30 is connected to area 0 through a virtual link. Area 20 is a transit area with a p2p link. Router 3 is configured with a higher priority so that it is elected as the DR for the Ethernet segment. The interface IP addresses and OSPF area numbers are shown in Figure 8-6.

Figure 8-6 *OSPF Configuration Diagram*

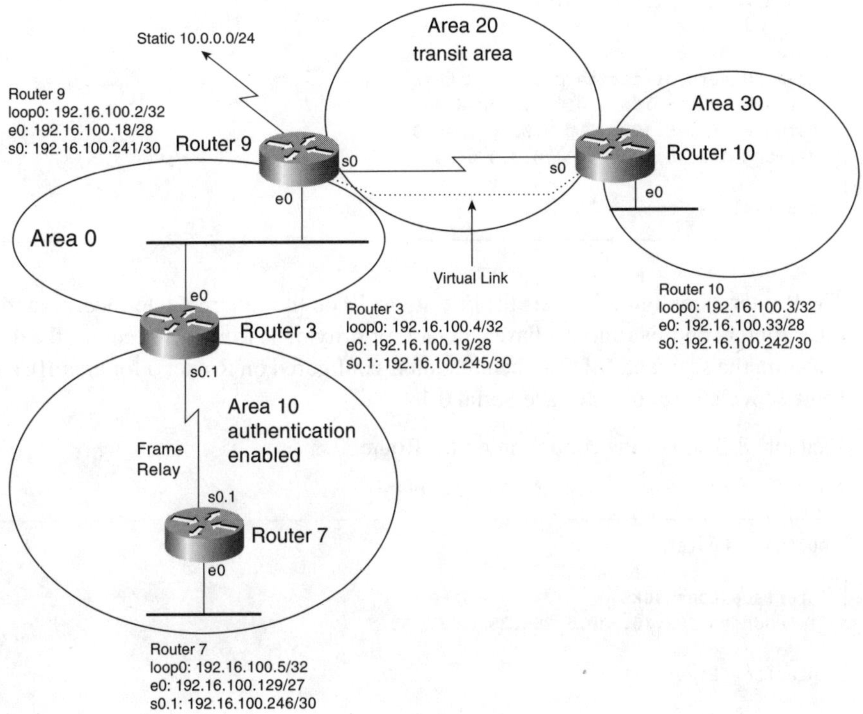

The router configurations based on the information provided in Figure 8-6 follow.

Example 8-2 shows the configuration for Router 3.

Example 8-2 *OSPF Router Configuration for Router 3 in Figure 8-6*

```
hostname router3
!
interface Loopback0
 ip address 192.16.100.4 255.255.255.255
!
interface Ethernet0
 ip address 192.16.100.19 255.255.255.240
 no ip directed-broadcast
 ip ospf priority 10
!
interface Serial0
 no ip address
 no ip directed-broadcast
 encapsulation frame-relay
 frame-relay lmi-type ansi
!
interface Serial0.1 point-to-point
 ip address 192.16.100.245 255.255.255.252
 no ip directed-broadcast
 ip ospf message-digest-key 1 md5 ciscoccie
 frame-relay interface-dlci 104
!
router ospf 100
 area 10 authentication message-digest
 network 192.16.100.4 0.0.0.0 area 0
 network 192.16.100.16 0.0.0.15 area 0
 network 192.16.100.244 0.0.0.3 area 10
!
ip classless
```

The Router 3 configuration sets the priority to 10 on the Ethernet interface. Assuming that all other routers on this Ethernet have a default priority of 1, Router 3 becomes the designated router on the segment. MD5 authentication is configured on Router 3 for area 10, and the MD5 key **ciscoccie** is set on interface Serial 0.1.

Example 8-3 shows the configuration for Router 7.

Example 8-3 *OSPF Router Configuration for Router 7 in Figure 8-6*

```
hostname Router7
!
interface Loopback0
 ip address 192.16.100.5 255.255.255.255
!
interface Ethernet0
```

Example 8-3 *OSPF Router Configuration for Router 7 in Figure 8-6 (Continued)*

```
 ip address 192.16.100.129 255.255.255.224
!
interface Serial0
 no ip address
 encapsulation frame-relay
 frame-relay lmi-type ansi
!
interface Serial0.1 point-to-point
 ip address 192.16.100.246 255.255.255.252
 ip ospf message-digest-key 1 md5 ciscoccie
 frame-relay interface-dlci 101
!
router ospf 100
 log-adjacency-changes
 area 10 authentication message-digest
 passive-interface Ethernet0
 network 192.16.100.0 0.0.0.255 area 10
!
ip classless
```

Router 7, which is also in area 10 and connected to Router 3's Serial 0.1 interface, is required to have the same authentication type and key configured. MD5 authentication is configured for area 10, and the key defined on the interface that connects to Router 3, Serial 0.1, is configured with the correct MD5 key **ciscoccie**.

Example 8-4 shows the configuration for Router 9.

Example 8-4 *OSPF Router Configuration for Router 9 in Figure 8-6*

```
hostname Router9
!
interface Loopback0
 ip address 192.16.100.2 255.255.255.255
!
interface Ethernet0
 ip address 192.16.100.18 255.255.255.240
!
interface Serial0
 ip address 192.16.100.241 255.255.255.252
!
router ospf 100
 log-adjacency-changes
 area 20 virtual-link 192.16.100.3
 redistribute static metric 1000
 network 192.16.100.2 0.0.0.0 area 0
 network 192.16.100.16 0.0.0.15 area 0
 network 192.16.100.240 0.0.0.3 area 20
!
ip classless
ip route 10.0.0.0 255.0.0.0 Null0
```

Router 9 is part of area 20, which is the transit area for the virtual link to area 30. The Router 10 RID, 192.16.100.3, is configured as the remote end of the virtual link that transits area 20. Router 9 is also on the same Ethernet segment as Router 3. You can see that the OSPF priority is not modified on Router 9.

Example 8-5 shows the configuration for Router 10.

Example 8-5 *OSPF Router Configuration for Router 10 in Figure 8-6*

```
hostname Router10
!
interface Loopback0
 ip address 192.16.100.3 255.255.255.255
!
interface Ethernet0
 ip address 192.16.100.33 255.255.255.240
!
interface Serial0
 ip address 192.16.100.242 255.255.255.252
!
router ospf 100
 log-adjacency-changes
 area 20 virtual-link 192.16.100.2
 passive-interface Ethernet0
 network 192.16.100.3 0.0.0.0 area 20
 network 192.16.100.32 0.0.0.15 area 30
 network 192.16.100.240 0.0.0.3 area 20
!
ip classless
```

Router 10 connects to area 30 and area 20 but not to area 0, so a virtual link is configured that transits area 20. the Router 9 RID is configured as the remote end of the virtual link.

Monitoring OSPF Elements

OSPF elements, such as neighbors, databases, and routing tables, can be monitored by using **show** commands. The available **show** commands enable the administrator to view OSPF neighbor states, statistics, databases, and routing tables.

After all routers are configured, the OSPF adjacencies can be verified. The **show ip ospf neighbor** command verifies the OSPF neighbors for each router. Example 8-6 displays the output for all the routers in Figure 8-6. A fully adjacent router is labeled with a FULL state. For Ethernet networks, the neighbor is labeled as a DR, BDR, or other. The Neighbor ID is the loopback address. OSPF uses the loopback address as the RID if a loopback interface is configured.

Example 8-6 *Output of* **show ip ospf neighbor** *on All Routers in Figure 8-6*

```
router3#show ip ospf neighbor

Neighbor ID     Pri   State           Dead Time   Address         Interface
192.16.100.2      1   FULL/BDR        00:00:33    192.16.100.18   Ethernet0
192.16.100.5      1   FULL/  -        00:00:34    192.16.100.246  Serial0.1

Router7#show ip ospf neighbor

Neighbor ID     Pri   State           Dead Time   Address         Interface
192.16.100.4      1   FULL/  -        00:00:38    192.16.100.245  Serial0.1
Router7#

Router9#show ip ospf neighbor

Neighbor ID     Pri   State           Dead Time   Address         Interface
192.16.100.4     10   FULL/DR         00:00:32    192.16.100.19   Ethernet0
192.16.100.3      1   FULL/  -        00:00:36    192.16.100.242  Serial0

Router10#show ip ospf neighbor

Neighbor ID     Pri   State           Dead Time   Address         Interface
192.16.100.2      1   FULL/  -        00:00:38    192.16.100.241  Serial0
```

Router 9, Ethernet 0, with a priority of 1, is the BDR for the segment. Router 3, Ethernet 0, with a priority of 10, is the DR on the segment. All neighbors have synchronized databases and are, therefore, in the FULL operating state.

To inspect OSPF database information, use the **show ip ospf database** command. All LSA types for each OSPF area to which the router connects are listed in the database. The **show ip route** command verifies the routes entered into the master routing table.

NOTE OSPF routers maintain three databases. One table lists the OSPF neighbors, the second is the OSPF topology table, and the third is the master routing table (**show ip route**).

Example 8-7 shows the output from the **show ip ospf database** command on Router 3 in Figure 8-6.

Example 8-7 *Output of* **show ip ospf database** *Command on Router 3 from Figure 8-6*

```
router3#show ip ospf database

       OSPF Router with ID (192.16.100.4) (Process ID 100)


                Router Link States (Area 0)

Link ID         ADV Router      Age         Seq#       Checksum Link count
192.16.100.2    192.16.100.2    63          0x80000004 0xFA32   3
192.16.100.3    192.16.100.3    2     (DNA) 0x80000003 0x37E7   1
192.16.100.4    192.16.100.4    871         0x8000000A 0xC111   2

                Net Link States (Area 0)

Link ID         ADV Router      Age         Seq#       Checksum
192.16.100.19   192.16.100.4    871         0x80000001 0x4116

                Summary Net Link States (Area 0)

Link ID         ADV Router      Age         Seq#       Checksum
192.16.100.3    192.16.100.2    873         0x80000001 0xB81
192.16.100.3    192.16.100.3    3     (DNA) 0x80000001 0x8249
192.16.100.5    192.16.100.4    1315        0x80000001 0xEA9D
192.16.100.32   192.16.100.3    3     (DNA) 0x80000001 0x5F55
192.16.100.128  192.16.100.4    1315        0x80000001 0xB76B
192.16.100.240  192.16.100.2    60          0x80000004 0x9D02
192.16.100.240  192.16.100.3    3     (DNA) 0x80000001 0x9D04
192.16.100.240  192.16.100.241  2744        0x80000005 0xFBB2
192.16.100.244  192.16.100.4    1058        0x80000004 0x6930

                Summary ASB Link States (Area 0)

Link ID         ADV Router      Age         Seq#       Checksum
192.16.100.2    192.16.100.3    2     (DNA) 0x80000001 0xF695


                Router Link States (Area 10)

Link ID         ADV Router      Age         Seq#       Checksum Link count
192.16.100.4    192.16.100.4    1334        0x8000000E 0xADE9   2
192.16.100.5    192.16.100.5    1336        0x80000007 0xB5EB   4

                Summary Net Link States (Area 10)

Link ID         ADV Router      Age         Seq#       Checksum
192.16.100.2    192.16.100.4    864         0x80000001 0xEAD6
192.16.100.3    192.16.100.4    867         0x80000001 0x631D
192.16.100.4    192.16.100.4    1825        0x80000003 0x6E59
192.16.100.16   192.16.100.4    882         0x8000000B 0xE5D3
```

Example 8-7 *Output of* **show ip ospf database** *Command on Router 3 from Figure 8-6 (Continued)*

```
192.16.100.32   192.16.100.4    585         0x80000001 0x4029
192.16.100.240  192.16.100.4    67          0x80000003 0xF79C

                Summary ASB Link States (Area 10)

Link ID         ADV Router      Age         Seq#       Checksum
192.16.100.2    192.16.100.4    67          0x80000001 0xD2EE

                Type-5 AS External Link States

Link ID         ADV Router      Age         Seq#       Checksum Tag
10.0.0.0        192.16.100.2    73          0x80000001 0xBEC8   0
```

Router 3, which is an ABR, has LSAs for area 0 and area 10. Router 3 also lists the external route for network 10.0.0.0. The output shows three routers in the Router Link State section for area 0, and lists each router in area 0. Router 10 is listed, even though it is connected to area 0 through a virtual link.

The Router 3 **show ip route** output shows all OSPF and connected routes, as shown in Example 8-8. Intra-area routes are labeled with O. Interarea routes are labeled with O IA; OSPF external Type-2 routes are labeled with O E2.

Example 8-8 *Output of* **show ip route** *on Router 3 in Figure 8-6*

```
router3#show ip route
Codes: C - connected, S - static, I - IGRP, R - RIP, M - mobile, B - BGP
       D - EIGRP, EX - EIGRP external, O - OSPF, IA - OSPF inter area
       N1 - OSPF NSSA external type 1, N2 - OSPF NSSA external type 2
       E1 - OSPF external type 1, E2 - OSPF external type 2, E - EGP
       i - IS-IS, L1 - IS-IS level-1, L2 - IS-IS level-2, * - candidate default
       U - per-user static route, o - ODR

Gateway of last resort is not set

O E2 10.0.0.0/8 [110/1000] via 192.16.100.18, 00:00:01, Ethernet0
     192.16.100.0/24 is variably subnetted, 9 subnets, 4 masks
O       192.16.100.128/27 [110/74] via 192.16.100.246, 00:21:09, Serial0.1
C       192.16.100.244/30 is directly connected, Serial0.1
O IA    192.16.100.240/30 [110/74] via 192.16.100.18, 00:00:01, Ethernet0
O IA    192.16.100.32/28 [110/84] via 192.16.100.18, 00:00:01, Ethernet0
C       192.16.100.16/28 is directly connected, Ethernet0
C       192.16.100.4/32 is directly connected, Loopback0
O       192.16.100.5/32 [110/65] via 192.16.100.246, 00:21:09, Serial0.1
O       192.16.100.2/32 [110/11] via 192.16.100.18, 00:00:12, Ethernet0
O IA    192.16.100.3/32 [110/75] via 192.16.100.18, 00:00:02, Ethernet0
```

Example 8-9 shows the output of the **show ip ospf database** command and the **show ip route** command, as executed on Router 7 from Figure 8-6. There is only a database for Area 10. ABRs maintain a database for each connected area, as shown in Router 3 output. A router connected to the backbone with a virtual link, such as Router 10 in Figure 8-6, maintains databases for its physically connected areas, and for area 0, which is connected only through the virtual link. The Router 7 routing table includes all routes, as does the Router 3 routing table. Later in this chapter, area 10 is configured as a stub area and the number of routes are significantly reduced.

Example 8-9 *Output from* **show ip ospf database** *and* **show ip route** *on Router 7 in Figure 8-6*

```
Router7#show ip ospf database

       OSPF Router with ID (192.16.100.5) (Process ID 100)


                Router Link States (Area 10)

Link ID         ADV Router      Age         Seq#       Checksum Link count
192.16.100.4    192.16.100.4    1594        0x8000000E 0xADE9   2
192.16.100.5    192.16.100.5    1593        0x80000007 0xB5EB   4

                Summary Net Link States (Area 10)

Link ID         ADV Router      Age         Seq#       Checksum
192.16.100.2    192.16.100.4    1122        0x80000001 0xEAD6
192.16.100.3    192.16.100.4    1122        0x80000001 0x631D
192.16.100.4    192.16.100.4    56          0x80000004 0x6C5A
192.16.100.16   192.16.100.4    1137        0x8000000B 0xE5D3
192.16.100.32   192.16.100.4    840         0x80000001 0x4029
192.16.100.240  192.16.100.4    322         0x80000003 0xF79C

                Summary ASB Link States (Area 10)

Link ID         ADV Router      Age         Seq#       Checksum
192.16.100.2    192.16.100.4    322         0x80000001 0xD2EE

                Type-5 AS External Link States

Link ID         ADV Router      Age         Seq#       Checksum Tag
10.0.0.0        192.16.100.2    329         0x80000001 0xBEC8   0


Router7#show ip route
Codes: C - connected, S - static, I - IGRP, R - RIP, M - mobile, B - BGP
       D - EIGRP, EX - EIGRP external, O - OSPF, IA - OSPF inter area
       N1 - OSPF NSSA external type 1, N2 - OSPF NSSA external type 2
       E1 - OSPF external type 1, E2 - OSPF external type 2, E - EGP
       i - IS-IS, L1 - IS-IS level-1, L2 - IS-IS level-2, ia - IS-IS inter area
       * - candidate default, U - per-user static route, o - ODR
       P - periodic downloaded static route
```

Example 8-9 *Output from* **show ip ospf database** *and* **show ip route** *on Router 7 in Figure 8-6 (Continued)*

```
Gateway of last resort is not set

O E2 10.0.0.0/8 [110/1000] via 192.16.100.245, 00:05:31, Serial0.1
     192.16.100.0/24 is variably subnetted, 9 subnets, 4 masks
C       192.16.100.128/27 is directly connected, Ethernet0
C       192.16.100.244/30 is directly connected, Serial0.1
O IA    192.16.100.240/30 [110/138] via 192.16.100.245, 00:05:32, Serial0.1
O IA    192.16.100.32/28 [110/148] via 192.16.100.245, 00:05:32, Serial0.1
O IA    192.16.100.16/28 [110/74] via 192.16.100.245, 00:05:32, Serial0.1
O IA    192.16.100.4/32 [110/65] via 192.16.100.245, 00:05:33, Serial0.1
C       192.16.100.5/32 is directly connected, Loopback0
O IA    192.16.100.2/32 [110/75] via 192.16.100.245, 00:05:33, Serial0.1
O IA    192.16.100.3/32 [110/139] via 192.16.100.245, 00:05:33, Serial0.1
```

The routers performing the functions of ASBR or ABR can be verified by using the **show ip ospf border-routers**, as shown in Example 8-10.

Example 8-10 *Output from* **show ip ospf border-routers**

```
Router7#show ip ospf border-routers

OSPF Process 100 internal Routing Table

Codes: i - Intra-area route, I - Inter-area route

I 192.16.100.2 [74] via 192.16.100.245, Serial0.1, ASBR, Area 10, SPF 6
i 192.16.100.4 [64] via 192.16.100.245, Serial0.1, ABR, Area 10, SPF 6
```

Only the ABRs in the same area as the router are displayed with this command, while all ASBRs within the OSPF internetwork are displayed. 192.16.100.2 has a metric of 74. Remember that the default OSPF cost for a T1 is 64 and the cost for Ethernet is 10. These are the links in the path from Router 7 to the ASBR.

The OSPF virtual link is verified by using the **show ip ospf virtual links** command. Example 8-11 displays the output of the command issued on Router 9.

Example 8-11 *Output of* **show ip ospf virtual-links** *Command*

```
Router9#show ip ospf virtual-links
Virtual Link OSPF_VL3 to router 192.16.100.3 is up
  Run as demand circuit
  DoNotAge LSA allowed.
  Transit area 20, via interface Serial0, Cost of using 64
  Transmit Delay is 1 sec, State POINT_TO_POINT,
  Timer intervals configured, Hello 10, Dead 40, Wait 40, Retransmit 5
    Hello due in 00:00:06
    Adjacency State FULL (Hello suppressed)
```

continues

Example 8-11 *Output of* **show ip ospf virtual-links** *Command (Continued)*

```
    Index 2/3, retransmission queue length 0, number of retransmission 1
    First 0x0(0)/0x0(0) Next 0x0(0)/0x0(0)
    Last retransmission scan length is 1, maximum is 1
    Last retransmission scan time is 0 msec, maximum is 0 msec
```

The remote end of the virtual link is 192.16.100.3. The transit area is area 20 through Serial 0. The OSPF cost of the virtual link is 64.

OSPF interfaces can be verified by using the **show ip ospf interface** command, as shown in Example 8-12. For Router 3, the Ethernet interface is labeled as a BROADCAST Type with a cost of 10. The Frame Relay interface is POINT_TO_POINT with a cost of 64 (for a T1). The default Hello interval is 10 seconds and the dead time interval is 40 seconds. The priority for the Ethernet interface is 10, and Router 3 is the DR router.

Example 8-12 *Output from* **show ip ospf interface**

```
router3#show ip ospf interface
Ethernet0 is up, line protocol is up
  Internet Address 192.16.100.19/28, Area 0
  Process ID 100, Router ID 192.16.100.4, Network Type BROADCAST, Cost: 10
  Transmit Delay is 1 sec, State DR, Priority 10
  Designated Router (ID) 192.16.100.4, Interface address 192.16.100.19
  Backup Designated router (ID) 192.16.100.2, Interface address 192.16.100.18
  Timer intervals configured, Hello 10, Dead 40, Wait 40, Retransmit 5
    Hello due in 00:00:00
  Neighbor Count is 1, Adjacent neighbor count is 1
    Adjacent with neighbor 192.16.100.2  (Backup Designated Router)
  Suppress hello for 0 neighbor(s)
Loopback0 is up, line protocol is up
  Internet Address 192.16.100.4/32, Area 0
  Process ID 100, Router ID 192.16.100.4, Network Type LOOPBACK, Cost: 1
  Loopback interface is treated as a stub Host
Serial0.1 is up, line protocol is up
  Internet Address 192.16.100.245/30, Area 10
  Process ID 100, Router ID 192.16.100.4, Network Type POINT_TO_POINT, Cost: 64
  Transmit Delay is 1 sec, State POINT_TO_POINT,
  Timer intervals configured, Hello 10, Dead 40, Wait 40, Retransmit 5
    Hello due in 00:00:01
  Neighbor Count is 1, Adjacent neighbor count is 1
    Adjacent with neighbor 192.16.100.5
  Suppress hello for 0 neighbor(s)
  Message digest authentication enabled
    Youngest key id is 1
```

Ethernet 0 is in area 0 and is the DR for the segment, with a priority of 10. The BDR is 192.16.100.2. There is only one neighbor on the Ethernet and it is adjacent.

A loopback interface is configured, so the router uses the loopback interface IP address as its RID. The loopback interface is in area 0.

Interface Serial 0.1 is a Frame Relay link in area 10. MD5 is enabled on this interface.

Summarizing OSPF Routes

The internetwork from Figure 8-6 in the previous examples is modified by adding a new interface to Router 10, which has another router and several new IP subnets connected to it, as shown in Figure 8-7. Tokenring0 is enabled on Router 10 and is part of area 20. The new subnetwork is 192.16.100.64/29.

Figure 8-7 *OSPF Network Shown in Figure 8-6 with the Addition of a New Network on Router 10*

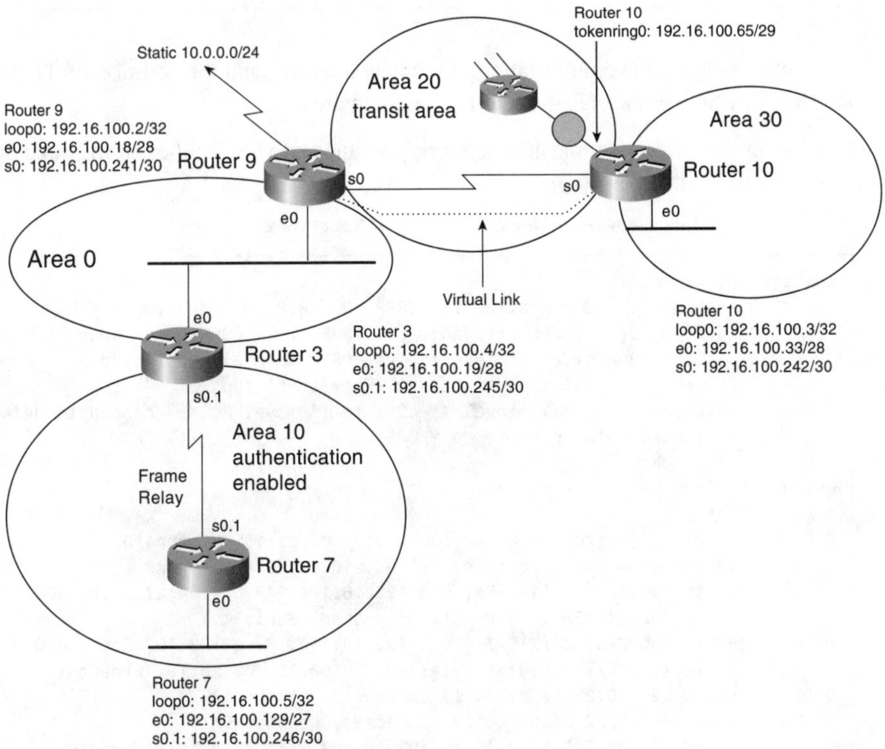

The configuration changes for Router 10 are displayed in Example 8-13.

Example 8-13 *Router 10 Configuration Changes for Adding a New Network*

```
interface TokenRing0
 ip address 192.16.100.65 255.255.255.248
 ring-speed 16
!
router ospf 100
 log-adjacency-changes
 area 20 virtual-link 192.16.100.2
 passive-interface Ethernet0
 network 192.16.100.3 0.0.0.0 area 20
 network 192.16.100.32 0.0.0.15 area 30
 network 192.16.100.64 0.0.0.7 area 20
 network 192.16.100.240 0.0.0.3 area 20
```

The only change is the configuration of the new interface and the addition of the **network** command, which associates the interface with an area.

The successful addition of the new network is verified by viewing the routing table on Router 3, as shown in Example 8-14.

Example 8-14 *Verification of a New Network Added to the OSPF Internetwork*

```
router3>show ip route
Codes: C - connected, S - static, I - IGRP, R - RIP, M - mobile, B - BGP
       D - EIGRP, EX - EIGRP external, O - OSPF, IA - OSPF inter area
       N1 - OSPF NSSA external type 1, N2 - OSPF NSSA external type 2
       E1 - OSPF external type 1, E2 - OSPF external type 2, E - EGP
       i - IS-IS, L1 - IS-IS level-1, L2 - IS-IS level-2, * - candidate default
       U - per-user static route, o - ODR

Gateway of last resort is not set

O E2 10.0.0.0/8 [110/1000] via 192.16.100.18, 00:23:18, Ethernet0
     192.16.100.0/24 is variably subnetted, 10 subnets, 5 masks
O       192.16.100.128/27 [110/74] via 192.16.100.246, 00:44:27, Serial0.1
C       192.16.100.244/30 is directly connected, Serial0.1
O IA    192.16.100.240/30 [110/74] via 192.16.100.18, 00:23:19, Ethernet0
O IA    192.16.100.32/28 [110/84] via 192.16.100.18, 00:23:19, Ethernet0
C       192.16.100.16/28 is directly connected, Ethernet0
C       192.16.100.4/32 is directly connected, Loopback0
O       192.16.100.5/32 [110/65] via 192.16.100.246, 00:44:27, Serial0.1
O       192.16.100.2/32 [110/11] via 192.16.100.18, 00:23:30, Ethernet0
O IA    192.16.100.3/32 [110/75] via 192.16.100.18, 00:23:20, Ethernet0
O IA    192.16.100.64/29 [110/80] via 192.16.100.18, 00:01:17, Ethernet0
O IA    192.16.100.72/29 [110/86] via 192.16.100.18, 00:01:17, Ethernet0
O IA    192.16.100.80/29 [110/86] via 192.16.100.18, 00:01:17, Ethernet0
O IA    192.16.100.88/29 [110/86] via 192.16.100.18, 00:01:17, Ethernet0
```

Now, summarize networks 192.16.100.64/29, 192.16.100.72/29, 192.16.100.80/29, and 192.16.100.88/29 by using the OSPF **area range** command. The networks are summarized in the ABR for the area Router 9. The configuration change for Router 9 is shown in Example 8-15.

Example 8-15 *Route Summarization using* **area range**

```
router ospf 100
 area 20 range 192.16.100.64 255.255.255.224
```

The range of addresses 192.16.100.64 255.255.255.224 includes the four new routes. Now ,the route is summarized and added to Router 3's table, as shown in Example 8-16.

Example 8-16 *Routing Table Displaying the Summarized Route*

```
router3#sh ip route
Codes: C - connected, S - static, I - IGRP, R - RIP, M - mobile, B - BGP
       D - EIGRP, EX - EIGRP external, O - OSPF, IA - OSPF inter area
       N1 - OSPF NSSA external type 1, N2 - OSPF NSSA external type 2
       E1 - OSPF external type 1, E2 - OSPF external type 2, E - EGP
       i - IS-IS, L1 - IS-IS level-1, L2 - IS-IS level-2, * - candidate default
       U - per-user static route, o - ODR

Gateway of last resort is not set

O E2 10.0.0.0/8 [110/1000] via 192.16.100.18, 00:27:45, Ethernet0
     192.16.100.0/24 is variably subnetted, 11 subnets, 5 masks
O       192.16.100.128/27 [110/74] via 192.16.100.246, 00:48:54, Serial0.1
C       192.16.100.244/30 is directly connected, Serial0.1
O IA    192.16.100.240/30 [110/74] via 192.16.100.18, 00:27:46, Ethernet0
O IA    192.16.100.32/28 [110/84] via 192.16.100.18, 00:27:46, Ethernet0
C       192.16.100.16/28 is directly connected, Ethernet0
C       192.16.100.4/32 is directly connected, Loopback0
O       192.16.100.5/32 [110/65] via 192.16.100.246, 00:48:54, Serial0.1
O       192.16.100.2/32 [110/11] via 192.16.100.18, 00:27:56, Ethernet0
O IA    192.16.100.3/32 [110/75] via 192.16.100.18, 00:27:46, Ethernet0
O IA    192.16.100.64/27 [110/80] via 192.16.100.18, 00:03:13, Ethernet0
```

Only the summary route is now displayed in the routing table.

Totally Stubby Area Configuration

In this section, you see what happens when you configure area 10 as a totally stubby area.

First, area 10 is configured as a stub area, and the link-state database and routing tables of a router in the stub area are displayed. Next, area 10 is made a totally stubby area, with the same tables displayed.

The following commands are added to all routers in area 10 to make the area a stub area.

```
router ospf 100
  area 10 stub
```

The link-state database and routing table on Router 7 had six summary network addresses and one external address before area 10 became a stub network. It still has the six summary network addresses plus an additional one for the injected default route. The databases no longer list the external route. This is not much of an improvement. Example 8-17 displays the new link-state database and routing table on Router 7 in Figure 8-7. Nonrelevant entries have been removed from the link-state database.

Example 8-17 *Link-State Database and Routing Table for Stub Area*

```
Router7#show ip ospf database
       OSPF Router with ID (192.16.100.5) (Process ID 100)
...
                Summary Net Link States (Area 10)

Link ID         ADV Router      Age         Seq#       Checksum
192.16.100.2    192.16.100.4    1122        0x80000001 0xEAD6
192.16.100.3    192.16.100.4    1122        0x80000001 0x631D
192.16.100.4    192.16.100.4    56          0x80000004 0x6C5A
192.16.100.16   192.16.100.4    1137        0x8000000B 0xE5D3
192.16.100.32   192.16.100.4    840         0x80000001 0x4029
192.16.100.240  192.16.100.4    322         0x80000003 0xF79C
0.0.0.0         192.16.100.4    460         0x80000001 0x9371
...

Router7#show ip route

Gateway of last resort is 192.16.100.245 to network 0.0.0.0

     192.16.100.0/24 is variably subnetted, 9 subnets, 4 masks
C       192.16.100.128/27 is directly connected, Ethernet0
C       192.16.100.244/30 is directly connected, Serial0.1
O IA    192.16.100.240/30 [110/138] via 192.16.100.245, 00:05:32, Serial0.1
O IA    192.16.100.32/28 [110/148] via 192.16.100.245, 00:05:32, Serial0.1
O IA    192.16.100.16/28 [110/74] via 192.16.100.245, 00:05:32, Serial0.1
O IA    192.16.100.4/32 [110/65] via 192.16.100.245, 00:05:33, Serial0.1
C       192.16.100.5/32 is directly connected, Loopback0
O IA    192.16.100.2/32 [110/75] via 192.16.100.245, 00:05:33, Serial0.1
O IA    192.16.100.3/32 [110/139] via 192.16.100.245, 00:05:33, Serial0.1
O*IA 0.0.0.0/0 [110/65] via 192.16.100.245, 00:00:09, Serial0.1
```

The **no-summary** keyword makes the area totally stubby versus a regular stub area. It is added to the area 10 ABR routers as follows:

```
router ospf 100
  area 10 stub no-summary
```

Now, the OSPF database and routing table are significantly reduced in Router 7, from seven OSPF routes to one OSPF route in the **show ip route** output. Also, the default gateway has only one summary network LSA. Example 8-18 displays the link-state database and routing table.

Example 8-18 *Link-State Database and Routing Table for a Totally Stubby Area*

```
Router7#sh ip ospf database
       OSPF Router with ID (192.16.100.5) (Process ID 100)


                Summary Net Link States (Area 10)

Link ID         ADV Router      Age         Seq#       Checksum
0.0.0.0         192.16.100.4    460         0x80000001 0x9371

Router7#sh ip ro
Codes: C - connected, S - static, I - IGRP, R - RIP, M - mobile, B - BGP
       D - EIGRP, EX - EIGRP external, O - OSPF, IA - OSPF inter area
       N1 - OSPF NSSA external type 1, N2 - OSPF NSSA external type 2
       E1 - OSPF external type 1, E2 - OSPF external type 2, E - EGP
       i - IS-IS, L1 - IS-IS level-1, L2 - IS-IS level-2, ia - IS-IS inter area
       * - candidate default, U - per-user static route, o - ODR
       P - periodic downloaded static route

Gateway of last resort is 192.16.100.245 to network 0.0.0.0

     192.16.100.0/24 is variably subnetted, 3 subnets, 3 masks
C       192.16.100.128/27 is directly connected, Ethernet0
C       192.16.100.244/30 is directly connected, Serial0.1
C       192.16.100.5/32 is directly connected, Loopback0
O*IA 0.0.0.0/0 [110/65] via 192.16.100.245, 00:00:09, Serial0.1
```

Depending upon the configuration of the network and the number of external routes injected into the OSPF AS, stub areas might not add much benefit to the configuration, although totally stubby areas can have a large effect.

OSPF Summary

The characteristics of OSPF are summarized as follows:

- Link-state routing protocol.
- Uses IP protocol 89.
- Classless Protocol (supports VLSMs).
- Metric is cost (based on interface bandwidth) by default.
- Sends partial route updates only when there are changes.

- Routes labeled as intra-area, interarea, external Type 1, or external Type 2.
- Supports authentication.
- Uses Dijkstra algorithm to calculate SPF tree.
- Default administrative distance is 110.
- Uses multicast 224.0.0.5 (ALLSPFrouters).
- Uses multicast 224.0.0.6 (ALLDRrouters).

IS-IS

IS-IS is an International Organization for Standardization (ISO) dynamic routing specification. IS-IS is described in ISO/IEC 10589. IS-IS is a link-state routing protocol that floods link-state information throughout the network to build a picture of network topology. IS-IS was primarily intended for routing OSI Connectionless Network Protocol (CNLP) packets but has the capability to route IP packets. When routing IP packets, Integrated IS-IS provides the ability to route protocols outside of the OSI family, such as IP.

Similar to OSPF, IS-IS establishes a hierarchical architecture of the network. IS-IS creates two levels of hierarchy, with Level 1 (L1) for intra-area and Level 2 (L2) for interarea routing.

IS-IS distinguishes between L1 and L2 routers. (A router is called an IS in IS-IS.) L1 ISs communicate with other L1 ISs in the same area. L2 ISs route between L1 areas and form an intradomain routing backbone. Hierarchical routing simplifies backbone design because L1 ISs only need to know how to get to the nearest L2 IS.

NOTE In IS-IS, a router is usually the intermediate system (IS) and personal computers, workstations, and servers are end systems (ES).

IS-IS Metrics

IS-IS uses a single required default metric with a maximum path value of 1023. The metric is arbitrary and typically is assigned by a network administrator. Any single link can have a maximum value of 64, unless the wide metric extension is implemented. IS-IS extensions enable a three- and four-byte default metric value. Path links are calculated by summing link values. Maximum metric values were set at these levels to provide the granularity to support various link types, while at the same time ensuring that the SPF algorithm for route computation is reasonably efficient. In Cisco routers, all interfaces have the default metric of 10. The administrator must configure the interface metric if a different value is required.

IS-IS also defines three optional metrics (costs): delay, expense, and error. The delay cost metric reflects the amount of delay on the link. The expense cost metric reflects the communications cost associated with using the link. The error cost metric reflects the error rate of the link. IS-IS maintains a mapping of these four metrics to the *quality-of-service* (QoS) option in the CLNP packet header. IS-IS uses these mappings to compute routes through the internetwork. Cisco routers do not support the three optional metrics.

IS-IS Operation

This section discusses IS-IS areas, designated ISs, authentication, and the network entity title.

Network Entity Title (NET)

To configure the IS-IS routing protocol, a NET must be configured on every IS. Although IS-IS can be configured to route IP, the communication between ISs uses OSI protocol data units (PDUs), not IP packets, and runs directly over the data-link layer. The NET is the OSI address that each IS uses to communicate, by using OSI PDUs. NET addresses range from 8 to 20 bytes. The NET is made up of two major fields, the initial domain part (IDP) and the domain specific part (DSP). The IDP consists of a 1-byte authority and format identifier (AFI) and an initial domain identifier (IDI). The value of the AFI determines the length of the IDI and the specific encoding format of the DSP. The DSP is composed of a High-Order DSP (HO-DSP), an Area ID, a System ID and a selector (SEL). All ISs within the routing domain have the same IDP and HO-DSP value.

IS-IS divides the NET into an area address and a system address, as shown in Figure 8-8.

Figure 8-8 *Network Entity Title*

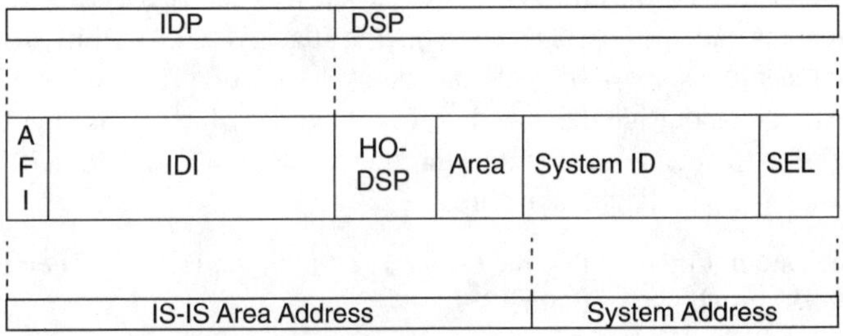

L2 ISs use the Area ID. The area address is composed of all bits from the AFI to the HO-DSP. The System ID must be the same length for all ISs in an area, and for Cisco routers, they must be 6 bytes in length. Usually, an IS MAC address identifies each unique IS. The SEL is configured as 00. The NET is configured under the **router isis** command. In this example, the AFI is 49, the area is 0001, the System ID is 00aa.0101.0001, and the SEL is 00:

```
router isis
 net 49.0001.00aa.0101.0001.00
```

Designated IS (DIS)

As with OSPF, IS-IS selects DISs on multiaccess networks. There is no backup DIS as in OSPF. If the DIS fails, a new DIS is elected. L1 and L2 DISs are selected separately and might or might not be the same IS. One difference between OSPF and IS-IS in multiaccess subnetworks is that all IS-IS ISs establish adjacencies with all others in the subnetwork, not just with the DIS.

The IS with the highest priority becomes the DIS. By default, the priority value is 64. The priority value can be changed to a value from 0 to 127. If the priority is set to 0, the IS is not eligible to become a DIS for that network. The highest System ID selects the DIS if there is a tie with the priorities. If a new IS is added to a network with an existing DIS, and the new IS has a higher priority or an equal priority and a higher System ID, the new IS becomes the DIS. On p2p networks, the priority is set to 0 because no DIS is elected. The interface **isis priority** command changes the priority.

IS-IS Areas

IS-IS uses a two-level hierarchy that is similar to the OSPF areas. ISs are configured to route L1, L2, or both L1 and L2 routes (L1/L2). L1 ISs are similar to OSPF internal routers. An L2 IS is similar to an OSPF backbone router. An IS that has both L1 and L2 routes is similar to an OSPF ABR.

Each L1 IS in an area has an identical link-state database. The L1/L2 ISs maintain a separate link-state database for the L1 routes and L2 routes. The L1/L2 ISs do not advertise L2 routes to the L1 area. Instead, the L1/L2 IS sets a bit, the attached bit (ATT bit), in the L1 advertisements, to indicate that it has knowledge of other areas. L1 ISs do not have specific routing information about destinations outside the area, but they do know which IS has the knowledge. L1 ISs forward traffic to outside destinations through the nearest L1/L2 IS. L1 ISs are similar to OSPF internal routers in a totally stubby area.

IS-IS areas are not bounded by the L1/L2 ISs but by the links between L1/L2 ISs and L2 backbone ISs, as shown in Figure 8-9.

Figure 8-9 *IS-IS Areas and IS Types*

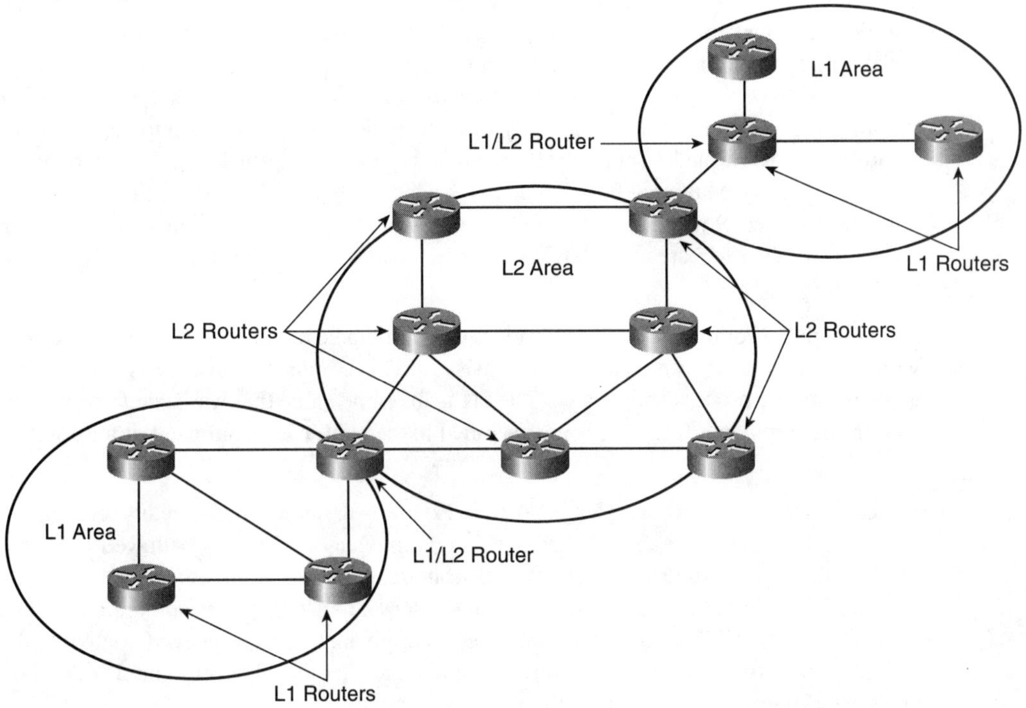

IS-IS Authentication

IS-IS supports three types of authentication: link authentication, area authentication, and domain authentication. For all these types, only cleartext password authentication is supported.

You use link authentication between ISs in a common subnetwork (such as Ethernet, private line). The cleartext password must be common only between the ISs on the link. The password is configured with the interface command **isis password** *password* [**level-1** | **level-2**] command. The optional **level-1** or **level-2** keywords specify which routes, L1 or L2, use the password. You must use a separate command for each level; **level-1** is the default.

If you use area authentication, all ISs in the area must use authentication and must have the same password. The IS-IS area password is configured with the **router isis** sub-command **area-password** *password*.

Use domain authentication on L2 and L1/L2 ISs only. All L2 and L1/L2 ISs must be configured for authentication and must use the same password. The IS-IS domain password is configured with the **router isis** sub-command **domain-password** *password*.

IS-IS Configuration

Configuration for IS-IS is relatively simple. An IS-IS process is created by using the **router isis** *tag* command. Only one IS-IS process performing L2 routing is allowed per IS, and that process can also perform L1 routing. However, multiple L1-only IS-IS routing processes can be configured (up to 29 additional L1-only processes). If the *tag* value is not specified, a null tag is assumed. If multiple L1 routing processes are configured, each is labeled with a tag to facilitate area identification. Multiple L1 routing processes can be configured if the L1/L2 IS is connected to multiple L1 areas. Multiarea functionality was added in IOS 12.0(5). Prior to that IOS level, only one area per IS was allowed. Then, the **net** *network-entity-title* command specifies area addresses for the IS-IS area. The NET address is not an IP address; instead, it is an OSI network layer address.

After the global configuration, the interfaces that participate in the IS-IS process are configured with the interface subcommand **ip router isis** *tag*. This command associates an interface with an IS-IS routing process and an area. The tag is the same value that was specified under the **router isis** command. If the tag is not specified in the **router isis** command, it must not be specified here.

The configurations for Routers 8, 9, and 10 in Figure 8-10 are displayed in this section. Router 8 is an L2 IS. Router 9 is an L1/L2 IS, which communicates L2 routes with Router 8, and L1 and L2 routes with Router 10. Router 9 redistributes an external static route to network 10.0.0.0/8 as an IS-IS external L1 and L2 route. Both Router 8 and Router 9 are configured with a link password of ciscopass. Router 9 is configured to originate a default-gateway route (0.0.0.0) with the **default-information originate** command. Router 8 is also configured with a DIS priority of 70 to make it the DIS for the Ethernet network.

Figure 8-10 *Simple IS-IS Network*

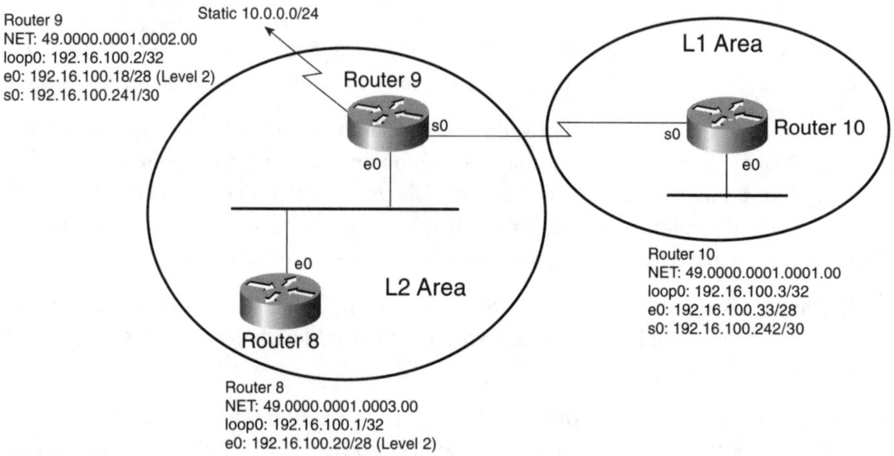

The configuration for Router 8 is shown in Example 8-19.

Example 8-19 *IS-IS Configuration for Router 8*

```
hostname Router8
!
interface Loopback0
 ip address 192.16.100.1 255.255.255.255
 ip router isis cisco
 isis metric 5 level-2
!
interface Ethernet0
 ip address 192.16.100.20 255.255.255.240
 ip router isis cisco
 isis circuit-type level-2-only
 isis password ciscopass level-2
 isis priority 70 level-2
!
router isis cisco
 net 49.0000.0001.0003.00
!
ip classless
```

Use the tag value of **cisco** for both the **router isis** command and the **ip router isis** command. The Ethernet interface is configured to establish adjacencies only with other L2 ISs. Because Router 8 is an L2 IS, another way to make sure that only L2 adjacencies are formed with other ISs is to configure the command **is-type level-2-only** under the **router isis** process. The L2 password and priority are also configured on the Ethernet interface.

The configuration for Router 9 is shown in Example 8-20.

Example 8-20 *IS-IS Configuration for Router 9*

```
hostname Router9
!
interface Loopback0
 ip address 192.16.100.2 255.255.255.255
 ip router isis cisco
 isis circuit-type level-2-only
 isis metric 5 level-2
!
interface Ethernet0
 ip address 192.16.100.18 255.255.255.240
 ip router isis cisco
 isis circuit-type level-2-only
 isis password ciscopass level-2
!
interface Serial0
 ip address 192.16.100.241 255.255.255.252
 ip router isis cisco
 isis metric 40 level-1
```

continues

Example 8-20 *IS-IS Configuration for Router 9 (Continued)*

```
!
router isis cisco
 redistribute static ip metric 60 metric-type external level-1-2
 default-information originate
 net 49.0000.0001.0002.00
!
ip classless
ip route 10.0.0.0 255.0.0.0 Null0
```

Ethernet 0 has the same L2 password as the Router 8 Ethernet. These passwords must be the same for an adjacency to be formed. No priority is set on Ethernet 0, so the default value, 64, is used. Router 9 is an L1/L2 IS. It forms an L2 adjacency with Router 8. Because Serial 0 has no circuit-type defined, L1 and L2 adjacencies can be formed. If Router 10 is an L1-only IS, or if the serial interface on Router 10 is configured with the **isis circuit-type level-1-only** command, only L1 adjacencies are formed. Otherwise, both L1 and L2 adjacencies are formed. The **isis metric** command changes the default metric from 10 to 40 for L1 routes on Serial 0. The static IP address is redistributed into IS-IS as an L1 and an L2 external route with a metric of 60. A default route is originated by this IS and advertised to IS-IS L2 ISs.

The configuration for Router 10 is shown in Example 8-21.

Example 8-21 *IS-IS Configuration for Router 10*

```
hostname Router10
!
interface Loopback0
 ip address 192.16.100.3 255.255.255.255
 ip router isis cisco
!
interface Ethernet0
 ip address 192.16.100.33 255.255.255.240
 ip router isis cisco
 isis circuit-type level-1
!
interface Serial0
 ip address 192.16.100.242 255.255.255.252
 ip router isis cisco
 no fair-queue
 isis metric 40 level-1
!
router isis cisco
 net 49.0000.0001.0001.00
!
ip classless
```

Router 10 is not defined as an L1-only IS, nor is Serial 0. L1 and L2 adjacencies are, therefore, established with Router 9.

IS-IS **show** Commands

After all ISs are configured, several **show** commands can verify connectivity when using IS-IS. These commands are as follows:

- **show isis database**
- **show isis topology**
- **show clns is-neighbors**
- **show ip route**
- **show ip protocols**

All the configurations in this section refer to Figure 8-10.

The output of these commands is displayed throughout this section. IS-IS routes are marked with an i. L1 and L2 mark L1 and L2 routes. IS-IS routes use 115 as an administrative distance in Cisco routers. Example 8-22 displays the routing table on Router 8.

Example 8-22 *Router 8 Routing Table*

```
Router8#show ip route
Codes: C - connected, S - static, I - IGRP, R - RIP, M - mobile, B - BGP
       D - EIGRP, EX - EIGRP external, O - OSPF, IA - OSPF inter area
       N1 - OSPF NSSA external type 1, N2 - OSPF NSSA external type 2
       E1 - OSPF external type 1, E2 - OSPF external type 2, E - EGP
       i - IS-IS, L1 - IS-IS level-1, L2 - IS-IS level-2, ia - IS-IS inter area
       * - candidate default, U - per-user static route, o - ODR
       P - periodic downloaded static route

Gateway of last resort is 192.16.100.18 to network 0.0.0.0

     172.16.0.0/28 is subnetted, 1 subnets
C       172.16.3.0 is directly connected, TokenRing0
i L2 10.0.0.0/8 [115/134] via 192.16.100.18, Ethernet0
     192.16.100.0/24 is variably subnetted, 6 subnets, 3 masks
i L2    192.16.100.240/30 [115/20] via 192.16.100.18, Ethernet0
i L2    192.16.100.32/28 [115/60] via 192.16.100.18, Ethernet0
C       192.16.100.16/28 is directly connected, Ethernet0
C       192.16.100.1/32 is directly connected, Loopback0
i L2    192.16.100.2/32 [115/15] via 192.16.100.18, Ethernet0
i L2    192.16.100.3/32 [115/60] via 192.16.100.18, Ethernet0
i*L2 0.0.0.0/0 [115/10] via 192.16.100.18, Ethernet0
```

Router 8's only connection to another IS is through an L2-only circuit, so only L2 routes are in the table. The redistributed route, 10.0.0.0, is shown as a L2 route, and the default route that was originated on Router 9 is also shown.

The **show isis database** command shows the L1 and L2 ISs listed in the database, as displayed in Example 8-23.

Example 8-23 *Router 8 IS-IS Database*

```
Router8#show isis database

IS-IS Level-1 Link State Database:
LSPID                 LSP Seq Num  LSP Checksum  LSP Holdtime      ATT/P/OL
Router8.00-00       * 0x00000004   0x0DB6        1076              0/0/0
IS-IS Level-2 Link State Database:
LSPID                 LSP Seq Num  LSP Checksum  LSP Holdtime      ATT/P/OL
Router10.00-00        0x00000004   0x2F63        782               0/0/0
Router9.00-00         0x000000DE   0xDBD2        784               0/0/0
Router8.00-00       * 0x000000D5   0xA508        835               0/0/0
Router8.01-00       * 0x000000D3   0xA060        620               0/0/0
```

Router 8 is listed as an L1 and an L2 IS. The Router 8 loopback has the default circuit type of L1 and L2. Therefore, the IS is both an L1 and L2 IS.

Two entries for Router 8 are in the L2 link-state database. This is because Router 8 is the DIS for the Ethernet network. The entry, Router8.00-00, represents the actual IS, while the entry, Router8.01-00, represents the pseudonode that is created by the DIS for the multiaccess network.

The **show isis topology** command lists the metric to reach other ISs in the network. Example 8-24 shows the output of the command issued on Router 8.

Example 8-24 *Router 8 IS-IS Topology Table*

```
Router8#show isis topology

IS-IS paths to level-1 routers
System Id       Metric  Next-Hop        Interface       SNPA
Router8         --

IS-IS paths to level-2 routers
System Id       Metric  Next-Hop        Interface       SNPA
Router10        20      Router9         Et0             00e0.b064.6e47
Router9         10      Router9         Et0             00e0.b064.6e47
Router8         --
```

The metric to reach Router 10 is 20. The metric on the serial link between Router 9 and Router 10 was changed for L1 routes only; therefore, the default metric, 10, is still used for L2 routes for a total path cost from Router 8 to Router 10 of 20.

For Router 9, the **show clns is-neighbors** command shows the adjacent ISs, the IS type, priority, and state, as displayed in Example 8-25.

Example 8-25 *IS Neighbor Display on Router 9*

```
Router9>show clns is-neighbors

System Id      Interface    State  Type Priority  Circuit Id          Format
Router10       Se0          Up     L1L2 0 /0      00                  Phase V
Router8        Et0          Up     L2   64        Router8.01          Phase V
```

Router 9 is adjacent to two ISs, Router 10 and Router 8. Both L1 and L2 adjacencies have been formed on the link between Router 9 and Router 10. The link between Router 9 and Router 8 is L2 only. The Router 9 priority on the Ethernet interface is 64. The Circuit ID is a single-byte numerical identifier that uniquely identifies the IS-IS interface. The Circuit Id associated with Router 8 is Router8.01. This is the pseudonode identifier, which consists of the DIS system name concatenated with the Circuit Id.

For Router 9, the **show ip route** command shows all L1 and L2 routes for the network. The **show ip protocols** command displays the protocol configuration on Router 9. Example 8-26 displays the results of the commands **show ip route**, **show ip protocols**, **show isis topology**, and **show isis database** on Router 9.

Example 8-26 *Router 9 Routing Table, Protocol Configuration, Topology, and Database*

```
Router9#show ip route
Codes: C - connected, S - static, I - IGRP, R - RIP, M - mobile, B - BGP
       D - EIGRP, EX - EIGRP external, O - OSPF, IA - OSPF inter area
       N1 - OSPF NSSA external type 1, N2 - OSPF NSSA external type 2
       E1 - OSPF external type 1, E2 - OSPF external type 2, E - EGP
       i - IS-IS, L1 - IS-IS level-1, L2 - IS-IS level-2, ia - IS-IS inter area
       * - candidate default, U - per-user static route, o - ODR
       P - periodic downloaded static route

Gateway of last resort is not set

S    10.0.0.0/8 is directly connected, Null0
     192.16.100.0/24 is variably subnetted, 6 subnets, 3 masks
C       192.16.100.240/30 is directly connected, Serial0
i L1    192.16.100.32/28 [115/50] via 192.16.100.242, Serial0
C       192.16.100.16/28 is directly connected, Ethernet0
i L2    192.16.100.1/32 [115/15] via 192.16.100.20, Ethernet0
C       192.16.100.2/32 is directly connected, Loopback0
i L1    192.16.100.3/32 [115/50] via 192.16.100.242, Serial0

Router9#show ip protocols
Routing Protocol is "isis cisco"
  Invalid after 0 seconds, hold down 0, flushed after 0
```

continues

Example 8-26 *Router 9 Routing Table, Protocol Configuration, Topology, and Database (Continued)*

```
  Outgoing update filter list for all interfaces is
  Incoming update filter list for all interfaces is
  Redistributing: static, isis
  Address Summarization:
    None
  Routing for Networks:
    Loopback0
    Serial0
    Ethernet0
  Routing Information Sources:
    Gateway         Distance      Last Update
    192.16.100.1         115      00:04:02
    192.16.100.3         115      00:04:02
  Distance: (default is 115)

Router9#show isis topology

IS-IS paths to level-1 routers
System Id       Metric  Next-Hop        Interface       SNPA
Router10        40      Router10        Se0             *HDLC*
Router9         --

IS-IS paths to level-2 routers
System Id       Metric  Next-Hop        Interface       SNPA
Router10        10      Router10        Se0             *HDLC*
Router9         --
Router8         10      Router8         Et0             00e0.b064.6e49
Router9#

Router9#show isis database

IS-IS Level-1 Link State Database:
LSPID                 LSP Seq Num  LSP Checksum  LSP Holdtime      ATT/P/OL
Router10.00-00        0x000000D6   0x4E0C        820               0/0/0
Router9.00-00       * 0x000000DE   0xF943        1017              0/0/0
IS-IS Level-2 Link State Database:
LSPID                 LSP Seq Num  LSP Checksum  LSP Holdtime      ATT/P/OL
Router10.00-00        0x00000004   0x2F63        1012              0/0/0
Router9.00-00       * 0x000000DE   0xDBD2        1014              0/0/0
Router8.00-00         0x000000D5   0xA508        1062              0/0/0
Router8.01-00         0x000000D3   0xA060        848               0/0/0
```

The routing table for Router 9 shows L1 routes learned from Router 10 and L2 routes learned from Router 8.

The output from the **show ip protocols** command displays information about the configured IS-IS protocol and its tag value, cisco. The process redistributes static routes and runs on interfaces Loopback 0, Ethernet 0, and Serial 0. The IS is learning routes from 192.16.100.1 (Router 8) and 192.16.100.3 (Router 10).

The topology table shows the L1 and L2 metrics to Router 10. The L1 metric is 40, as configured on the IS. The L2 metric is the default value of 10.

The IS-IS database shows that Router 9 and Router 10 are L1/L2 ISs.

The Router 10 IP routing table is displayed in Example 8-27.

Example 8-27 *Router 10 IP Routing Table*

```
Router10#show ip route
Codes: C - connected, S - static, I - IGRP, R - RIP, M - mobile, B - BGP
       D - EIGRP, EX - EIGRP external, O - OSPF, IA - OSPF inter area
       N1 - OSPF NSSA external type 1, N2 - OSPF NSSA external type 2
       E1 - OSPF external type 1, E2 - OSPF external type 2, E - EGP
       i - IS-IS, L1 - IS-IS level-1, L2 - IS-IS level-2, ia - IS-IS inter area
       * - candidate default, U - per-user static route, o - ODR
       P - periodic downloaded static route

Gateway of last resort is 192.16.100.241 to network 0.0.0.0

i L1 10.0.0.0/8 [115/164] via 192.16.100.241, Serial0
     192.16.100.0/24 is variably subnetted, 6 subnets, 3 masks
C       192.16.100.240/30 is directly connected, Serial0
C       192.16.100.32/28 is directly connected, Ethernet0
i L2    192.16.100.16/28 [115/20] via 192.16.100.241, Serial0
i L2    192.16.100.1/32 [115/25] via 192.16.100.241, Serial0
i L2    192.16.100.2/32 [115/15] via 192.16.100.241, Serial0
C       192.16.100.3/32 is directly connected, Loopback0
i*L2 0.0.0.0/0 [115/10] via 192.16.100.241, Serial0
```

The entry for the redistributed route 10.0.0.0 is redistributed as both L1 and L2. Router 8 displayed the route as an L2 route. Here, it is an L1 route even though Router 9 advertises both L1 routes and L2 routes. If multiple paths exist to the same destination, as with 10.0.0.0 (path 1 is L1, path 2 is L2), the L1 path is preferred over the L2 path.

IS-IS Summary

The characteristics of IS-IS are summarized as follows:

- Link-state protocol
- Uses OSI PDUs between ISs
- Classless Protocol (supports VLSMs)
- Default metric is set to 10 for all interfaces
- Arbitrary metric: single link max = 64, path max = 1024

- Sends partial route updates only when there are changes
- Authentication with cleartext passwords
- Administrative distance is 115

References Used

The following resources were used to create this chapter:

Routing TCP/IP, Volume I, Jeff Doyle, Cisco Press, 1998

CCDA Exam Certification Guide, Anthony Bruno/Jacqueline Kim, Cisco Press, 2000

RFC 2328, "OSPF Version 2," J. Moy

www.cisco.com/univercd/cc/td/doc/cisintwk/idg4/nd2003.htm#xtocid22

www.cisco.com/univercd/cc/td/doc/cisintwk/ito_doc/ospf.htm

www.cisco.com/univercd/cc/td/doc/product/software/ios120/12cgcr/np1_c/1cprt1/1cospf.htm

www.cisco.com/univercd/cc/td/doc/cisintwk/ito_doc/osi_rout.htm#xtocid7

Foundation Summary

The Foundation Summary is a condensed collection of material that provides a convenient review of key concepts in this chapter. If you are already comfortable with the topics in this chapter, this summary will help you recall a few details. If you just read the Foundation Topics section, this review should help solidify some key facts. If you are doing your final preparation before the exam, these materials are a convenient way to review the day before the exam.

Table 8-3 *OSPF Major LSA Types*

Type Code	Type	Description
1	Router LSA	Produced by every router and includes all the router's links, interfaces, state of links, and cost; flooded within a single area
2	Network LSA	Produced by every DR on every broadcast or nonbroadcast multiaccess (NBMA) network; lists all the routers in the multiaccess network; contained within an area
3	Summary LSA for ABRs	Produced by area border routers (ABRs); sent into an area to advertise destinations outside the area
4	Summary LSA for ASBRs	Originated by area border routers (ABRs); sent into an area by the ABR to advertise the AS boundary routers (ASBRs)
5	AS External LSA	Originated by ASBRs; advertises destinations external to the OSPF AS; flooded throughout the entire OSPF AS
7	Not-so-stubby area External LSA	Originated by ASBRs in a not-so-stubby area (NSSA); not flooded throughout the OSPF AS, only to the NSSA

Table 8-4 *OSPF Router Types*

OSPF Router Type	Description
Internal router	Interfaces belong to the same OSPF area
Area Border Router (ABR)	Connects to more than one area; generates summary LSAs
ASBR	Injects external routes into the OSPF protocol
Backbone router	At least one interface connects to area 0

Table 8-5 *OSPF Stub Network Types*

OSPF Area Stub Type	Description	LSA Type Not Permitted
Stub area	No OSPF External LSA	Type 5
Totally stubby	No OSPF External and Summary LSA	Type 3 and Type 5
NSSA	No OSPF External, Type 7 produced by NSSA	Type 5

OSPF Summary

The characteristics of OSPF are summarized as follows:

- Link-state routing protocol.
- Uses IP protocol 89.
- Classless Protocol (supports VLSMs).
- Metric is cost (based on interface bandwidth).
- Sends partial route updates only when there are changes.
- Routes labeled as intra-area, interarea, external type-1, or external type-2.
- Support for authentication (cleartext and md5).
- Uses Dijkstra algorithm to calculate SPF tree.
- Default administrative distance is 110.
- Uses multicast 224.0.0.5 (ALLSPFrouters).
- Uses multicast 224.0.0.6 (ALLDRrouters.

IS-IS Summary

The characteristics of IS-IS are summarized as follows:

- Link-state protocol.
- Uses OSI PDUs between ISs.
- Classless Protocol (supports VLSMs).
- Default metric is set to 10 for all interfaces.
- Arbitrary metric: single link max = 64, path max = 1024.

- Routes labeled as L1 or L2.
- Sends partial route updates only when there are changes.
- Authentication with cleartext passwords.
- Administrative distance is 115.

Q & A

The Q & A questions are more difficult than what you can expect on the actual exam. The questions do not attempt to cover more breadth or depth than the exam; however, they are designed to make sure that you retain the material. Rather than allowing you to derive the answer from clues hidden inside the question itself, these questions challenge your understanding and recall of the subject. Questions from the "Do I Know This Already?" quiz are repeated here to ensure that you have mastered the chapter's topic areas. A strong understanding of the answers to these questions will help you on the CCIE written exam. As an additional study aide, use the CD-ROM provided with this book to take simulated exams.

Select the best answer. Answers to these questions are in the Appendix, "Answers to Quiz Questions."

1 Which type of router always has one or more interfaces connected to Area 0.0.0.0?

   a. Level 2 router

   b. ASBR

   c. Backbone router

   d. Autonomous boundary router

2 What is the number in the **router ospf** *number* command?

   a. The autonomous system number

   b. The process ID

   c. The AS number

   d. Answer b and c

3 IS-IS has which types of authentication capabilities?

   a. Domain, area, and link authentication with cleartext password.

   b. Domain, area, and link authentication with md5.

   c. Domain, area, and link authentication with cleartext and md5 passwords.

   d. There is no authentication in IS-IS.

4 What is the IOS default OSPF cost for a T1 interface?

   a. 100

   b. 10

   c. 290

   d. 64

5 What is the default IS-IS metric for a T1 interface?

a. 100

b. 10

c. 290

d. 64

6 What connects an area to the backbone when there is no physical connectivity?

a. T1 link

b. Virtual link

c. Fast Ethernet link

d. Backbone link

7 Which command verifies IS-IS neighbors?

a. **show isis is-neighbors**

b. **show ip isis neighbors**

c. **show clns is-neighbors**

d. **show ip clns isis neighbors**

8 A router that floods external Type-7 LSAs is part of which type of area?

a. Backbone area

b. Stub area

c. Not-so-stubby area

d. Totally stubby area

9 Which LSA type announces reachability to the ASBR?

a. Type 3

b. Type 4

c. Type 5

d. Type 7

10 Which commands add network 10.10.64.0/18 to area 10 in OSPF?

a. **router ospf** and **network 10.10.64.0 0.0.63.255 area 10**

b. **router ospf** and **network 10.10.64.0 255.255.192.0 area 10**

c. **router ospf 99** and **network 10.10.64.0 0.0.63.255 area 10**

d. **router ospf 99** and **network 10.10.64.0 255.255.192.0 area 10**

11 The **ip ospf cost** command is used for what?

a. To change the default cost under **router ospf**

b. To change the default cost on an external link when redistributing into OSPF

c. To change the default cost at the ABR

d. To change the default cost of an interface

12 Which address multicasts to the designated router?

a. 224.0.0.1

b. 224.0.0.5

c. 224.0.0.6

d. 224.0.0.10

13 What is the administrative distance of OSPF routes?

a. 90

b. 100

c. 110

d. 170

14 What is the P-bit used for in NSSA?

a. Set by the ASBR to indicate the priority of routes redistributed into the area

b. Set by the ABR to indicate that the ABR is used as a default route to the rest of the network

c. Set by the ASBR to indicate whether or not Type 7 LSAs are translated to Type 5 LSAs

d. Set by the ABR in Type 5 LSAs when Type 7 LSAs are translated to Type 5 LSAs; indicates the originating area of a route

15 What is the ATT bit used for in IS-IS?

a. Set by an L1 IS to indicate that it is connected to an external network

b. Set by an L1/L2 IS to indicate to L1 ISs that this L1/L2 IS is available for forwarding traffic destined to routes unknown in the area

c. Set by an L2 IS to indicate that it is connected to an external network

d. Set by an L1/L2 IS to indicate to other L2 ISs that it is connected to multiple L1 areas

16 To where are OSPF Type 1 LSAs flooded?

a. The OSPF area

b. The OSPF domain

c. From the area to the OSPF backbone

d. Through the virtual link

17 The DR forms adjacencies to which routers?

a. Only to the BDR.

b. The BDR is adjacent to all, not the DR.

c. The DR forwards all LSAs.

d. To all routers in the multiaccess network.

18 In IS-IS, the BDIS forms adjacencies to which routers?

a. Only to the DIS.

b. To all routers.

c. The BDIS only becomes adjacent when the DIS is down.

d. There is no BDIS in IS-IS.

19 What produces Type 2 LSAs?

a. ABR

b. ASBR

c. DR

d. NSSA ASBR

20 In the following command, what is area 50?

```
area 50 virtual-link 1.1.1.1
```

a. Backbone area

b. Virtual area

c. Transit area

d. Nonconnected area

21 Which of the following are link-state protocols?

a. RIPv2 and OSPF

b. IGRP and EIGRP

c. OSPF and IS-IS

d. RIPv1 and IGRP

22 OSPF has two equal-cost paths to a destination. What does OSPF do?

a. Uses the router ID to select one path

b. Uses both paths to load-balance

c. Uses the highest IP to select one path

d. Uses both paths to load-balance even if the costs are different

23 OSPF has two nonequal-cost paths to a destination. What does OSPF do?

a. Uses the router ID to select one path

b. Uses both paths to load-balance

c. Uses the lowest cost to select one path

d. Uses both paths to load-balance even if the costs are different

24 OSPF routers use which IP protocol or port?

a. IP protocol 89.

b. TCP port 89.

c. UDP port 89.

d. It does not use IP for transport.

25 IS-IS routers use which IP protocol or port?

a. IP protocol 89.

b. TCP port 89.

c. UDP port 89.

d. IS-IS uses the data-link layer.

26 What are OSPF Type 3 LSAs?

a. Router LSAs with interface state information produced by all routers

b. ASBR summary LSAs produced by ABRs

c. Summary LSAs produced by ABRs

d. External LSAs produced by ABRs

27 The following router output is produced by which command?

```
Neighbor ID     Pri   State           Dead Time   Address         Interface
112.20.150.6      1   FULL/DR         00:00:33    112.20.150.111  Ethernet0
112.20.150.7      1   FULL/  -        00:00:34    112.20.150.236  Serial0.1
```

a. **show clns is-neighbors**

b. **show ip eigrp neighbors**

c. **show ip ospf neighbors**

d. **show isis neighbors**

28 What happens if an L1/L2 router can reach a destination through two different paths: one an L1 path, the other an L2 path?

a. If the L1 and L2 path costs are equal, both routes are added to the routing table and load balancing occurs.

b. The path with the lowest cost is used.

c. The L2 path is always used, regardless of the path costs.

d. The L1 path is always used, regardless of the path costs.

29 What does O E2 mean in the following router output?

```
O E2 1.0.0.0/8 [110/1000] via 1.1.1.1, 00:00:01, Ethernet0
```

a. The route is an OSPF internal Type 2 route.

b. The route has a metric of 110.

c. The route is an OSPF external Type 2 route.

d. The route is an OSPF interarea route.

30 What does a set E-bit indicate in OSPF Hello messages?

a. The sending router has a connected external interface and is redistributing routes into OSPF.

b. The area is a not-so-stubby area (NSSA).

c. The area is not a stub area.

d. The interface sending the Hello message is not capable of becoming the DR for the network.

31 What is the metric in the following router output?

```
O IA    1.1.1.1/28 [110/100] via 2.2.2.2, 00:05:32, Serial0.1
```

a. 110

b. 100

c. 0

d. 28

Scenarios

Scenario 8-1

Use the following configuration to answer the scenario questions:

```
hostname RouterA
!
interface Loopback0
 ip address 1.1.1.1 255.255.255.255
!
interface Ethernet0
 ip address 1.1.1.18 255.255.255.240
!
interface Serial0
 ip address 2.2.2.241 255.255.255.252
!
router ospf 50
 log-adjacency-changes
 area 20 virtual-link 2.2.2.250
 redistribute static metric 500
 network 1.1.1.1 0.0.0.0 area 0
 network 1.1.1.16 0.0.0.15 area 0
 network 2.2.2.240 0.0.0.3 area 20
!
ip classless
ip route 10.0.0.0 255.0.0.0 Null0
```

1 From Router A's configuration, which interfaces are in area 0?

a. Ethernet 0 and Serial 0

b. Serial 0 and Loopback 0

c. Ethernet 0 and Loopback 0

d. Ethernet 0 only

2 What is the OSPF cost for Ethernet 0?

a. 1.

b. 10.

c. 100.

d. Not enough information is given.

3 What is the number of the area that uses the virtual link to connect to area 0?

a. 0.

b. 10.

c. 20.

d. Not enough information is given.

4 What is the router ID of Router A?

a. 1.1.1.18

b. 1.1.1.1

c. 2.2.2.241

d. 2.2.2.250

Scenario 8-2

Use the following router command output to answer the scenario questions:

```
Router9>show clns is-neighbors

System Id      Interface    State  Type Priority  Circuit Id         Format
Router10       Se0          Up     L1L2 0 /0      00                 Phase V
Router8        Et0          Up     L2   64        Router8.01         Phase V


Router9#show isis database

IS-IS Level-1 Link State Database:
LSPID                  LSP Seq Num  LSP Checksum  LSP Holdtime       ATT/P/OL
Router10.00-00         0x000000D6   0x4E0C        820                0/0/0
Router9.00-00        * 0x000000DE   0xF943        1017               0/0/0
IS-IS Level-2 Link State Database:
LSPID                  LSP Seq Num  LSP Checksum  LSP Holdtime       ATT/P/OL
Router10.00-00         0x00000004   0x2F63        1012               0/0/0
Router9.00-00        * 0x000000DE   0xDBD2        1014               0/0/0
Router8.00-00          0x000000D5   0xA508        1062               0/0/0
Router8.01-00          0x000000D3   0xA060        848                0/0/0
```

1 What router is the DIS?

a. Router 10.

b. Router 8.

c. Router 9.

d. Not enough information is given.

2 What is the IS-IS interface priority on Router 8?

a. 64

b. Less than 64.

c. Greater than 64.

d. Not enough information is given.

3 How many ISs exist in the routing domain?

a. 6

b. 5

c. 4

d. 3

This chapter covers the following topics needed to master the CCIE Routing and Switching (R&S) written exam:

- **Border Gateway Protocol (BGP) review**—BGP concepts: internal BGP (iBGP), also known as Interior BGP (IBGP), versus external BGP (eBGP), also known as Exterior BGP (EBGP), BGP filters, BGP neighbors, and the different methods to advertise networks
- **BGP attributes, weight, and the BGP decision process**—The process that BGP uses to select a best path to a destination and the BGP attributes in the decision process
- **BGP route dampening, peer groups, route reflectors, and confederations**—Peer groups, route reflectors, and BGP confederations
- **BGP show commands**—Reviews some commands that you can use with BGP, which are important to review for the exam

CHAPTER 9

Border Gateway Protocol

This chapter covers BGP concepts listed in the CCIE blueprint for the written test. The BGP design concepts include the following: neighbors, decision algorithm, iBGP, eBGP, peer groups, route reflectors, confederations, attributes, autonomous systems, route maps, and filters.

"Do I Know This Already?" Quiz

The purpose of this assessment quiz is to help you determine how to spend your limited study time. If you can answer most or all of these questions, you might want to skim the Foundation Topics section and return to it later as necessary. Review the Foundation Summary section and answer the questions at the end of the chapter to ensure that you have a strong grasp of the material covered. If you intend to read the entire chapter, you do not necessarily need to answer these questions now. If you find these assessment questions difficult, read through the entire Foundation Topics section and review it until you feel comfortable with your ability to answer all the "Q & A" questions at the end of the chapter. The following questions are repeated at the end of the chapter in the Q & A section with additional questions to test your mastery of the material.

Select the best answer. Answers to these questions are in the Appendix, "Answers to Quiz Questions."

1 A router has the following configuration. Which routing protocol are you using?

```
router bgp 10
 neighbor 1.1.1.1 remote-as 10
```

a. OBGP with an external neighbor

b. BGP with an internal neighbor

c. BGP with an external neighbor

d. EIGRP with an internal neighbor

2 MED is used for which of the following functions?

a. To give a hint to the routers on what outbound path to take

b. To give a hint to the confederation routers on what outbound path to take

c. To give a hint to the external BGP peers on what inbound path to take

d. To give a hint to local BGP peers on what inbound path to take

3 Which of the following best describes the BGP weight attribute?

a. Determines a path; not locally significant.

b. Determines a path; lowest value is preferred.

c. Locally significant; lowest value is preferred.

d. Locally significant; highest value is preferred.

4 What is the process by which BGP speakers in a transit AS do not advertise a route until all routers have learned about the route through an IGP?

a. Redistribution

b. BGP synchronization

c. OSPF redistribution

d. OSPF synchronization

5 What does the number represent in the following router command?

```
router bgp 200
```

a. ASN.

b. Process ID.

c. Autonomous process ID.

d. The number is incorrect; it must be 65,000 or higher.

6 Which service access point does BGP use?

a. UDP port 179

b. IP protocol 179

c. TCP port 179

d. None of the above

7 Which of the following shows the correct order that BGP uses to select a best path?

a. Origin, lowest IP, AS Path, Weight, Local Preference

b. Weight, Local Preference, AS Path, Origin, MED, lowest IP

c. Lowest IP, AS Path, Origin, Weight, MED, Local Preference

d. Weight, Origin, Local Preference, AS Path, MED, lowest IP

8 BGP communities apply common policy to what?

a. Routers

b. A group of destinations

c. Dampened routes

d. Autonomous systems

9 What does the > symbol mean in the output of **show ip bgp**?

a. Compares a route as less than another

b. Indicates an internal BGP route

c. Compares a route as greater than another

d. Indicates the selected route

10 Which of the following is the administrative distance of an external BGP route?

a. 1

b. 20

c. 50

d. 200

11 Which mechanism penalizes flapping BGP routes by suppressing them?

a. Route reflectors

b. Route dampening

c. Route suppression

d. Route filtering

12 Which feature was implemented in BGPv4 to provide forwarding of packets based on IP prefixes?

a. MED

b. VLSM

c. CIDR

d. AS path

Foundation Topics

BGP Review

This section covers BGP theory and design concepts.

The current version of BGP, version 4 (BGP4), is defined in RFC 1771 (March 1995). BGP is an interdomain routing protocol. The primary function of BGP is to provide and exchange network reachability information between domains or autonomous systems. BGP uses TCP port 179 as its transport protocol between BGP peers or neighbors. BGP4 was created to provide classless interdomain routing (CIDR), a feature that was not present in the earlier versions.

NOTE CIDR is described in RFC 1519. CIDR provides the capability of forwarding packets that are based on IP prefixes with no distinction of IP address class. CIDR was created as a solution to the scaling problem of IP addressing in the Internet that was imminent in the early 1990s. At that time, there was an increased growth of the Internet routing tables and a reduction of Class B address space. CIDR provides a way for service provider's to assign address blocks smaller than a Class B network but larger than a Class C network.

BGP Neighbors

BGP is usually configured between two directly connected routers that belong to different autonomous systems. Each AS is under different technical administration: Usually, one is the enterprise company and the other is the service provider, or between different service providers, as shown in Figure 9-1.

Figure 9-1 *BGP Neighbors*

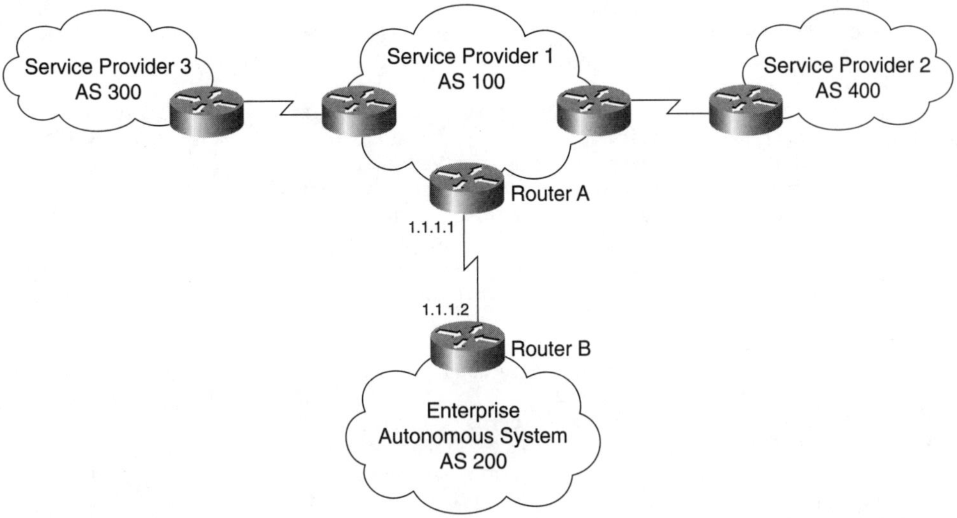

Before routing updates can be exchanged between two BGP routers, the routers must become established neighbors. After BGP routers establish a TCP connection, exchange information, and accept the information, they become established neighbors and start exchanging routing updates. If the neighbors do not reach an established state, BGP updates are not exchanged. The information exchanged before the neighbors are established includes the following: BGP version number, AS number, and the BGP router ID (RID).

The configuration to establish BGP neighbors between Router A and Router B in Figure 9-1 is as follows:

The Router A configuration that establishes BGP neighbors between Router A and Router B is

```
router bgp 100
 neighbor 1.1.1.2 remote-as 200
```

The Router B configuration that establishes BGP neighbors between Router A and Router B is

```
router bgp 200
 neighbor 1.1.1.1 remote-as 100
```

To verify BGP neighbors, use the **show ip bgp neighbors** command, as shown in Example 9-1. The external BGP neighbor is 1.1.1.2 with a remote AS of 200. The BGP state is established. The router ID of the neighbor is 10.10.10.10. The external port is 179, the TCP port for BGP. The keepalive is 60 seconds and the holdtime is 180 seconds.

Example 9-1 *Display of BGP Neighbors*

```
Router A#show ip bgp neighbors
BGP neighbor is 1.1.1.2,  remote AS 200, external link
  BGP version 4, remote router ID 10.10.10.10
  BGP state = Established, up for 00:00:22
  Last read 00:00:21, hold time is 180, keepalive interval is 60 seconds
  Neighbor capabilities:
    Route refresh: advertised and received(new)
    Address family IPv4 Unicast: advertised and received
  Received 3 messages, 0 notifications, 0 in queue
  Sent 3 messages, 0 notifications, 0 in queue
  Route refresh request: received 0, sent 0
  Default minimum time between advertisement runs is 30 seconds

 For address family: IPv4 Unicast
  BGP table version 1, neighbor version 1
  Index 1, Offset 0, Mask 0x2
  0 accepted prefixes consume 0 bytes
  Prefix advertised 0, suppressed 0, withdrawn 0
  Number of NLRIs in the update sent: max 0, min 0

  Connections established 1; dropped 0
  Last reset never
Connection state is ESTAB, I/O status: 1, unread input bytes: 0
Local host: 1.1.1.1, Local port: 11007
Foreign host: 1.1.1.2, Foreign port: 179
```

BGP Forms of Peering Relationships

BGP can establish two kinds of peering relationships: iBGP and eBGP.

iBGP

iBGP describes the peering between BGP neighbors in the same autonomous system(AS). You use iBGP in transit autonomous systems. Transit autonomous systems forward traffic from one AS to another AS. If you do not use iBGP in transit autonomous systems, the eBGP learned routes are redistributed into an IGP and then redistributed into the BGP process in another eBGP router. iBGP provides a better way to control the routes for the transit AS. With iBGP, the external route information (attributes) are forwarded. iBGP is preferred over redistribution with an IGP because the IGP does not understand AS paths and other BGP attributes.

Another use for iBGP is in large corporations where the IGP networks are too large to be supported by an IGP, such as Open Shortest Path First (OSPF). Three independent IGPs are in Figure 9-2: one for the Americas; one for Asia and Australia; and one for Europe, the Middle East, and Africa. Routes are redistributed into an iBGP core.

Figure 9-2 *iBGP in a Large Corporation*

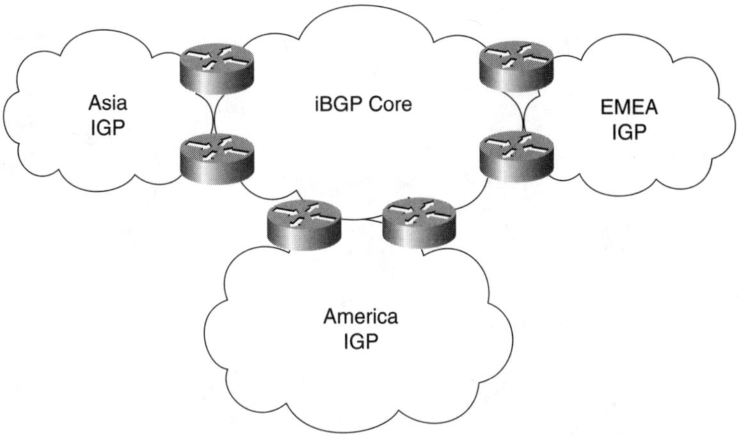

It is important to configure a full mesh between iBGP speakers within an AS to prevent routing loops. When a BGP speaker receives an update from other BGP speakers in its own AS (iBGP), the receiving BGP speaker does not redistribute that information to other iBGP peers. The receiving BGP speaker redistributes that information to other BGP speakers outside of its AS.

External BGP

eBGP describes BGP peering between neighbors in different autonomous systems. As required by the RFC, the eBGP peers share a common subnet. In Figure 9-3, all routers within AS 500 speak iBGP among each other, and they speak eBGP with the routers in other autonomous systems.

eBGP Multihop

Although it is an exception to the norm, eBGP peers can be configured over several intervening subnets by configuring eBGP multihop. eBGP Multihop is also used to peer with the loopback address of a BGP neighbor that shares the same physical data-link segment. This is a proprietary Cisco IOS feature. Static routing or an IGP protocol must provide connectivity between the eBGP peers by using multihop. You only use multihop with eBGP peers; you do not use it with iBGP. Figure 9-4 shows eBGP multihop peers.

Figure 9-3 *eBGP versus iBGP*

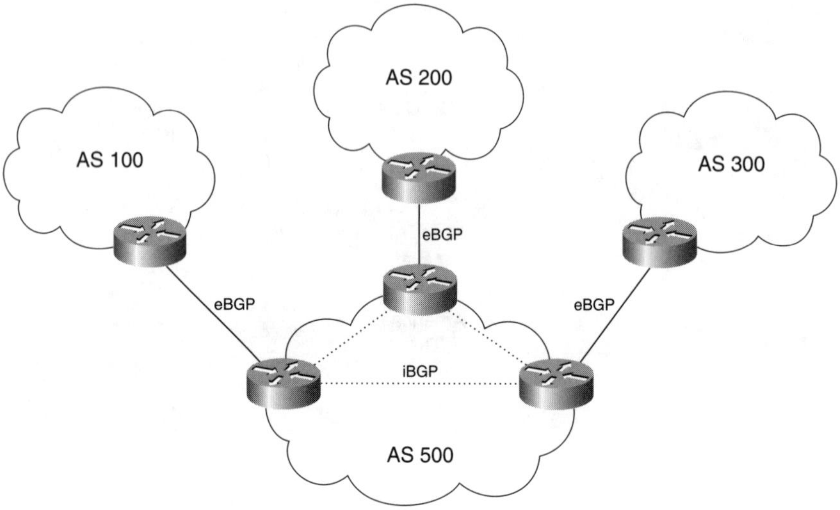

Figure 9-4 *eBGP Multihop Peers*

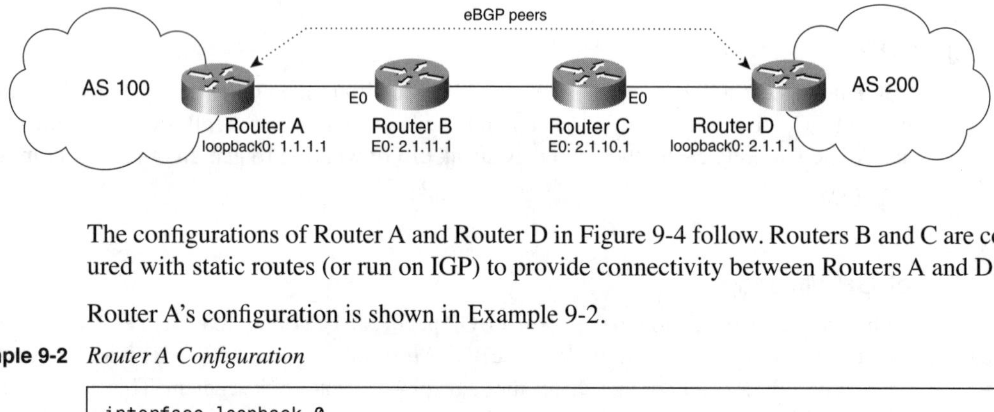

The configurations of Router A and Router D in Figure 9-4 follow. Routers B and C are configured with static routes (or run on IGP) to provide connectivity between Routers A and D.

Router A's configuration is shown in Example 9-2.

Example 9-2 *Router A Configuration*

```
interface loopback 0
 ip address 1.1.1.1 255.255.255.255
!
router bgp 100
 neighbor 2.1.1.1 remote-as 200
 neighbor 2.1.1.1 ebgp-multihop
 neighbor 2.1.1.1 update-source loopback0
!
ip route 2.1.1.1 0.0.0.0 2.1.11.1
```

Router D's configuration is shown in Example 9-3.

Example 9-3 *Router D Configuration*

```
interface loopback 0
 ip address 2.1.1.1 255.255.255.255
!
router bgp 200
 neighbor 1.1.1.1 remote-as 100
 neighbor 1.1.1.1 ebgp-multihop
 neighbor 1.1.1.1 update-source loopback0
!
 ip route 1.1.1.1 0.0.0.0 2.1.10.1
```

Advertising Networks

You can configure BGP in three ways to advertise networks to other peers:

1. **network** command
2. **aggregate-address** command
3. Redistribution of IGPs

network Command

The **network** command specifies which routes in the local IP routing table are added to the BGP table. By default, auto-summary is enabled on Cisco routers. This enables the router to summarize subnets into the classful network boundaries. With auto-summary enabled, and the **network** command used without a mask or with a classful mask, at least one subnet for that network must be present in the IP routing table and the specified network will be added to the BGP table. If auto-summary is disabled, no classful summary route is created. The network specified in the **network** statement must exactly match an entry in the local routing table before the network is added to the BGP table.

If the specified network does not coincide with classful network boundaries, a mask must be specified. The **network** command with a mask causes a route to be announced if there is an exact match for the prefix in the routing table. If the network is not present in the routing table, BGP does not announce it, even if the **network** command is configured. The following is a configuration example to advertise network 4.0.0.0/8 and 5.0.0.0/16 from AS 100:

```
router bgp 100
 network 4.0.0.0
 network 5.0.0.0 mask 255.255.0.0
```

The default auto-summary is enabled. At least one subnet from network 4.0.0.0 must be present in the routing table before network 4.0.0.0/8 is added to the BGP table. Network 5.0.0.0/16, not a different subnet of 5.0.0.0, must be in the routing table before 5.0.0.0/16 is added to the BGP table.

aggregate-address Command

The **aggregate-address** command advertises an aggregate (summary) network if any more-specific prefixes are present in the BGP table. A **summary-only** keyword suppresses advertisements of the more-specific prefixes.

For example, if the BGP table has networks 100.100.4.0/24, 100.100.5.0/24, 100.100.6.0/24, and 100.100.7.0/24, you can configure it to advertise an aggregate network of 100.100.4.0/22 and suppress the more specific networks. The commands are as follows:

```
router bgp 100
 aggregate-address 100.100.4.0 255.255.252.0 summary-only
```

BGP Redistribution

Another method to advertise BGP routes is to import them into the BGP routing table through redistribution of an IGP (such as OSPF and EIGRP). Both the **network** command and redistribution from an IGP add routes that are already in the IP table into the BGP table. You commonly use this method in large enterprise internetworks with iBGP cores. Filtering selects the redistributed prefixes and properly sets their attributes (especially origin). In Example 9-4, a route map specifies attributes to some of the redistributed networks (on access list 40). Other redistributed networks are specified in access list 50. You use the route map eigrp-to-bgp in the **redistribute** command. The first **route-map** statement sets local preference, origin, and weight to redistributed routes that match access list 40. The second **route-map** statement permits routes that match access list 50 for redistribution.

Example 9-4 *Redistribution of an IGP into BGP*

```
router eigrp 111
 network 15.0.0.0
!
router bgp 65511
 no synchronization
 redistribute eigrp 111 route-map eigrp-to-bgp
!
route-map eigrp-to-bgp permit 5
 match ip address 40
 set local-preference 200
 set weight 10
 set origin igp
!
route-map eigrp-to-bgp permit 10
 match ip address 50
!
!
access-list 40 permit 15.186.0.0
access-list 40 permit 15.168.0.0
```

Example 9-4 *Redistribution of an IGP into BGP (Continued)*

```
access-list 40 permit 15.124.0.0
access-list 40 permit 15.24.0.0 0.7.0.0
!
access-list 50 permit 15.202.208.0
access-list 50 permit 15.238.200.0
```

BGP Administrative Distance

The IOS assigns an administrative distance to eBGP and iBGP routes, as it does with other routing protocols. For the same prefix, the route with the lowest administrative distance is selected for inclusion in the IP forwarding table. Because iBGP learned routes do not have metrics associated with the route as IGPs (OSPF and EIGRP) do, iBGP learned routes are less trusted. The following are the administrative distances for BGP:

- eBGP routes—20
- iBGP routes—200

BGP Filters

Several methods filter BGP updates, including community lists, prefix filters, distribute lists, and AS path filters. Route maps also create route filters that are based on detailed parameters. (Route maps are covered in Chapter 10, "Administrative Distance, Access Lists, Route Manipulation, and IP Multicast.")

BGP Communities

A group of policies can be applied to a community of networks or destinations with community filters. Each destination can belong to multiple communities. Communities provide a method to control distribution and filter routing information.

The **communities** attribute is an optional, transitive, global attribute that is in the numerical range from 1 to 4,294,967,200. BGP communities are optional because BGP has the option to support the attribute. Transitive attributes are passed along to other BGP routers. A few predefined, well-known communities follow:

- **internet**—Advertises this route to the Internet community. All routers belong to it.
- **no-export**—Does not advertise this route to other eBGP peers.
- **no-advertise**—Does not advertise this route to any peer (internal or external).
- **local-as**—Sends this route to peers in other sub-autonomous systems within the local confederation; does not advertise this route to a peer outside the confederation.

Example 9-5 shows a BGP community configuration that does not advertise network 2.0.0.0/8 to the external BGP neighbor 1.1.2.5. The community commnolocal does not change or set the attribute of other networks.

Example 9-5 *BGP Community Configuration Example*

```
router bgp 100
 neighbor 1.1.2.5 remote-as 300
 neighbor 1.1.2.5 send-community
 neighbor 1.1.2.5 route-map commnolocal out
!
route-map commnolocal permit 10
 match ip address 10
 set community no-export
!
route-map commnolocal permit 20
 match ip address 11
!
access-list 10 permit 2.0.0.0
access-list 11 permit 3.0.0.0
access-list 11 permit 4.0.0.0
```

BGP Prefix Filter

BGP prefix lists filter routes inbound or outbound to a neighbor. The list filters the routes that are sent to, or received from, a BGP neighbor. When the route in an update matches an entry in the prefix list, the router does not need to continue trying to match entries in the list. The result is that if there are multiple entries in the list that will match a given route, the entries in the top of the list, which are the entries with the lowest sequence numbers, will be used. An implicit deny appears at the end of the list for any networks that do not have a match. Example 9-6 shows a prefix list that filters what routes are included in the route updates to BGP neighbor 1.1.1.1.

Example 9-6 *BGP Prefix Filter Configuration Example*

```
router bgp 100
 neighbor 1.1.1.1 prefix-list ccie out
!
ip prefix-list ccie seq 1 permit 2.0.0.0/8
ip prefix-list ccie seq 2 permit 3.0.0.0/8
```

BGP Neighbor Distribute Lists

Distribute lists also filter routes inbound or outbound to a neighbor. The list number is specified in the **neighbor** command, and access lists specify the networks to filter. Example 9-7 shows a distribute list that permits two networks from neighbor 1.1.1.1.

Example 9-7 *BGP Distribute List Configuration Example*

```
router bgp 100
 neighbor 1.1.1.1 distribute-list 99 in
!
access-list 99 permit 2.0.0.0 0.0.0.0 log
access-list 99 permit 3.0.0.0 0.0.0.0 log
```

BGP AS Path Filters

Instead of filtering network routes, AS path filters filter BGP AS numbers (paths) by using regular expressions. You can use path filters on a nontransit network to prevent passing external routes from one service provider to another. Example 9-8 denies any BGP route that begins with AS 111 or AS 222 to be advertised back to BGP neighbor 111.11.19.17. The ^ (caret) indicates a match of the beginning of the AS path. Filter 20 denies local routes to be advertised to the iBGP neighbor 27.18.9.21 by using ^$. The expression .* indicates any AS path.

Example 9-8 *AS Path Filter Configuration Example*

```
router bgp 100
 neighbor 111.11.19.17 remote-as 111
 neighbor 111.11.19.17 filter-list 10 out
 neighbor 27.18.9.21 remote-as 100
 neighbor 27.18.9.21 filter-list 20 out
 neighbor 27.18.9.21 next-hop-self
!
ip as-path access-list 10 deny ^111_
ip as-path access-list 10 deny ^222_
ip as-path access-list 10 permit .*
!
ip as-path access-list 20 deny ^$
ip as-path access-list 20 permit .*
```

Some regular expression examples are shown in Table 9-1.

Table 9-1 *Meanings of Regular Expressions*

Expression	Meaning
.	Any single character
^	Matches beginning of any input string
$	Matches the end of any input string
_	Matches a comma (,), left brace ({), right brace (}), left parenthesis, right parenthesis, the beginning of the input string, the end of the input string, or a space
*	Matches 0 or any sequence in a pattern

continues

Table 9-1 *Meanings of Regular Expressions (Continued)*

^222_	Any AS path that begins with AS 222
.*	All (any AS path)
^$	Matches an empty string (no path info), which indicates a local route

More information on regular expressions is at the following site:

www.cisco.com/univercd/cc/td/doc/product/atm/c8540/12_0/13_19/cmd_ref/appc.htm#xtocid68796

BGP Synchronization

By default, BGP synchronization is enabled on Cisco routers. If enabled, there must be a match for the network prefix in the routing table (from an IGP) for an iBGP path to be considered a valid path. If disabled, the router does not wait to check if the network prefix is in the routing table to advertise it to an external peer, or offer it to the IOS as a potential path. The purpose of synchronization is that if an AS provides transit service to another, BGP must not advertise a route for the network until all routers within the AS have learn the route through an IGP. This is to prevent packets from being lost by routers in the transit network, which do not have a route for the advertised network.

As shown in Figure 9-5, the BGP synchronization rule states that Router B cannot advertise network 1.0.0.0/8 to Router E until there is a match for the network in its IGP. This is to ensure that all routers in the IGP (Routers A, B, C, and D) know of network 1.0.0.0/8 so that packets are not lost in transit AS 20. An IGP is running on routers within the transit AS 20; BGP is not running on all routers. In order for the routers within AS 20 to forward traffic to 1.0.0.0, the IGP must have an entry for 1.0.0.0 in the IP routing table. Router B does not advertise network 1.0.0.0 to Router E until all other routers in the AS know how to forward a packet with a destination to network 1.0.0.0.

Figure 9-5 *BGP Synchronization*

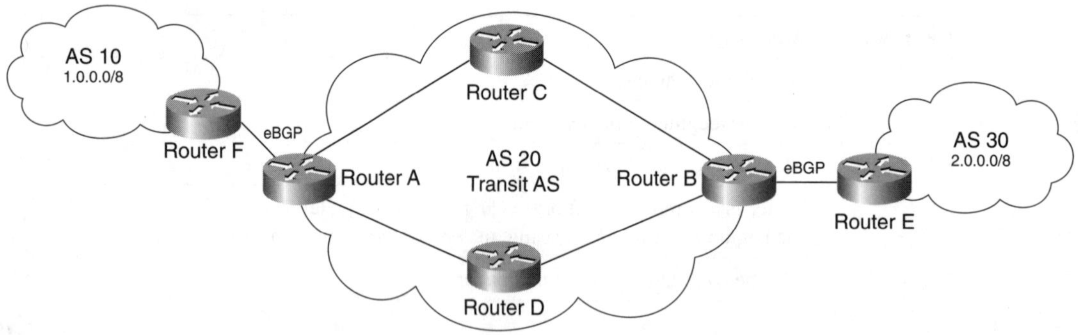

Usually, BGP synchronization is disabled, which allows BGP to converge more quickly because BGP does not have to wait for the IGP to converge. It can be disabled if the AS is not a transit AS, or if all transit routers run BGP. You can disable BGP synchronization with the following command:

```
no bgp synchronization
```

BGP Attributes, Weight, and the BGP Decision Process

BGP is a simple protocol that uses route attributes to make a selection for the best path to a destination. This section describes BGP attributes, the use of weight to influence path selection, and the BGP decision process.

BGP Path Attributes

BGP uses several attributes for the path selection process. BGP uses path attributes to communicate routing policies. BGP path attributes include the following: next hop, local preference, number of AS path hops, origin, Multi-Exit Discriminator (MED), atomic aggregate, and aggregator.

BGP attributes can be categorized as *well-known* or *optional*. Well-known attributes are recognized by all BGP implementations. Optional attributes do not need to be supported by the BGP process.

Well-known attributes can be further subcategorized as mandatory or discretionary. Mandatory attributes are always included in BGP update messages. Discretionary attributes might or might not be included in the BGP update message.

Optional attributes can be further subcategorized as *transitive* or *nontransitive*. Routers must advertise the route with transitive attributes to its peers even if is does not support the attribute locally. If the path attribute is nontransitive, the router does not need to advertise the route to its peers.

Each attribute category is covered in the sections that follow. Know the category of each attribute for the exam.

Next-Hop Attribute

The next-hop attribute is simply the IP address of the next eBGP hop that you use to reach the destination. The next-hop attribute is a well-known, mandatory attribute. With eBGP, the next hop is set by the eBGP peer when it announces the route. The next-hop attribute is used on multiaccess networks where there is more than one BGP speaker. With iBGP, routers advertise the next hop as the external (eBGP) peer instead of itself. In fully meshed multiaccess networks, you might want to minimize routing hops taken by having iBGP speakers advertise themselves as the next hop instead of the IP address of eBGP speaker. To specify the next hop as itself, use the BGP **next-hop-self** command. An example of the command is as follows:

```
router bgp 100
 neighbor 1.1.1.1 remote-as 100
 neighbor 1.1.1.1 next-hop-self
```

Local Preference Attribute

The local preference attribute indicates which path to use to exit the AS. It is a well-known discretionary attribute used between iBGP peers and not passed on to external BGP peers. In the IOS, the default local preference is 100; the higher local preference is preferred.

The default local preference is configured on the BGP router with an external path. It then advertises its local preference to iBGP peers. An example of the local preference attribute where Routers B and C are configured with different local preference is shown in Figure 9-6. Router A prefers using Router C to route Internet packets because it has a higher local preference (400) than router B (300).

Figure 9-6 *BGP Local Preference*

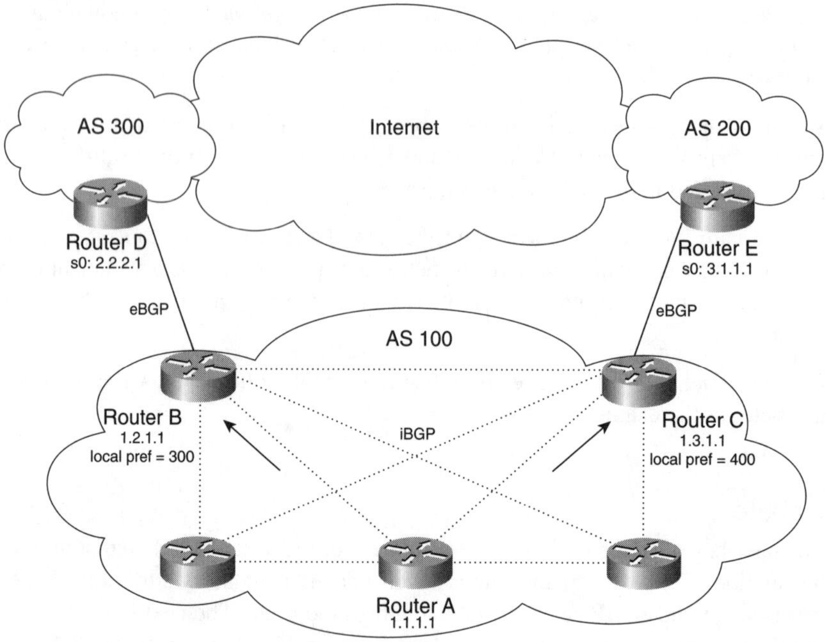

The configuration for Router A in Figure 9-6 is as follows:

```
router bgp 100
 neighbor 1.2.1.1 remote-as 100
 neighbor 1.3.1.1 remote-as 100
```

The configuration for Router B in Figure 9-6 is as follows:

```
router bgp 100
 neighbor 2.2.2.1 remote-as 300
 neighbor 1.1.1.1 remote-as 100
 neighbor 1.3.1.1 remote-as 100
 bgp default local-preference 300
```

The configuration for Router C in Figure 9-6 is as follows:

```
router bgp 100
 neighbor 3.1.1.1 remote-as 200
 neighbor 1.1.1.1 remote-as 100
 neighbor 1.2.1.1 remote-as 100
 bgp default local-preference 400
```

Origin Attribute

Origin is a well-known, mandatory attribute that defines the source of the path information. Do not confuse defining the origin with comparing if the route is eBGP or iBGP. The origin attribute is received from the source BGP speaker. The three types of origin attributes follow:

- IGP—Indicated by an **i** in the BGP table; present when the route is learned by way of the **network** statement
- EGP—Indicated by an **e** in the BGP table; learned from exterior gateway protocol (EGP)
- Incomplete—Indicated by a **?** in the BGP table; learned from redistribution of the route

In terms of choosing a route based on origin, BGP prefers routes that have been verified by the IGP over routes that have been learned from EGP peers, and BGP prefers routes learned from eBGP peers over incomplete paths.

AS Path Length Attribute

The AS Path is a well-known, mandatory attribute that contains a list of AS numbers in the path to the destination. Each AS prepends its own AS number to the AS Path. The AS Path describes all the autonomous systems that a packet must travel to reach the destination IP network; it ensures that the path is loop free. When the AS Path attribute selects a path, the route with the least number of AS hops is preferred. In the case of a tie, other attributes, such as MED, decide. Example 9-9 shows the AS Path for network 200.50.32.0/19. To reach the destination, a packet must pass autonomous systems 3561, 7004, and 7418. The command **show ip bgp 200.50.32.0** displays the AS Path information.

Example 9-9 *The* **show ip bgp 200.50.32.0** Output

```
Router# show ip bgp 200.50.32.0
BGP routing table entry for 200.50.32.0/19, version 93313535
Paths: (1 available, best #1)
  Not advertised to any peer
  3561 7004 7418
    206.24.241.181 (metric 490201) from 165.117.1.219 (165.117.1.219)
      Origin IGP, metric 4294967294, localpref 100, valid, internal, best
      Community: 2548:182 2548:337 2548:666 3706:153
```

MED

The MED attribute, also known as the metric, tells external BGP peers the preferred path into the AS when there are multiple paths into the AS. In other words, MED influences which one of many paths a neighboring AS uses to reach destinations within the AS. It is an optional, nontransitive attribute carried in eBGP updates. You do not use the MED attribute with iBGP peers. The lowest MED value is preferred and the default value is 0. The MED is not compared for paths received from two separated autonomous systems.

Consider the diagram in Figure 9-7. With all attributes considered equal, Router C selects Router A as its best path into AS 100, which is based on Router A's lower RID. The configurations below assign a higher MED to Router A to make Router C select Router B as the best path to AS 100. No additional configuration is required on Router B because the default MED is 0.

Figure 9-7 *MED Attribute*

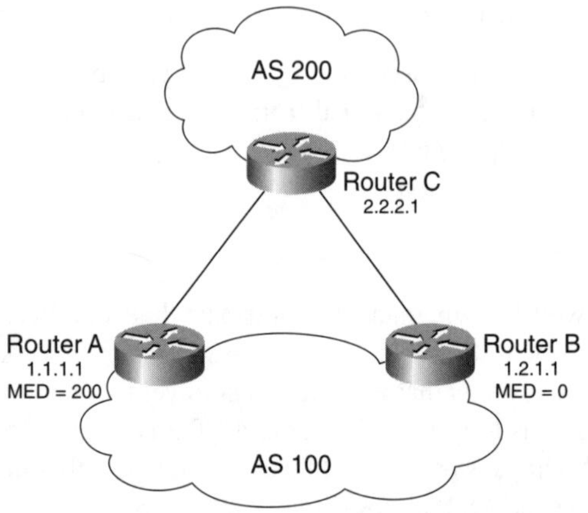

The configuration of Router A from Figure 9-7 is shown in Example 9-10. A route map is configured on Router A for neighbor 2.1.1.1 (Router C) to set the metric to 200 for advertised routes.

Example 9-10 *Configuration of Router A*

```
interface loopback 0
 ip address 1.1.1.1 255.255.255.255
!
router bgp 100
 neighbor 1.2.1.1 remote-as 100
 neighbor 1.2.1.1 update-source loopback 0
 neighbor 2.1.1.1 remote-as 200
 neighbor 2.1.1.1 ebgp-multihop
 neighbor 2.1.1.1 update-source loopback 0
 neighbor 2.1.1.1 route-map setmed out
!
route-map setmed permit 10
 set metric 200
```

The configuration of Router B from Figure 9-7 is shown in Example 9-11. There are no additional commands in Router B; therefore, advertised routes have a default metric of 0.

Example 9-11 *Configuration of Router B*

```
interface loopback 0
 ip address 1.2.1.1 255.255.255.255
!
router bgp 100
 neighbor 1.1.1.1 remote-as 100
 neighbor 1.1.1.1 update-source loopback 0
 neighbor 2.1.1.1 remote-as 200
 neighbor 2.1.1.1 ebgp-multihop
 neighbor 2.1.1.1 update-source loopback 0
```

The configuration of Router C from Figure 9-7 is shown in Example 9-12.

Example 9-12 *Configuration of Router C*

```
interface loopback 0
 ip address 2.1.1.1 255.255.255.255
!
router bgp 200
 neighbor 1.1.1.1 remote-as 100
 neighbor 1.1.1.1 ebgp-multihop
 neighbor 1.1.1.1 update-source loopback 0
 neighbor 1.2.1.1.remote-as 100
 neighbor 1.2.1.1 ebgp-multihop
 neighbor 1.2.1.1 update-source loopback 0
```

Cisco added two BGP configuration commands that might influence MED best path selection. The first, **bgp deterministic-med**, ensures the comparison of MED values when choosing routes advertised by different peers in the same autonomous system. The second, **bgp always-compare-med**, enables the comparison of the MED values from neighbors in different autonomous systems. The **bgp always-compare-med** command compares the MED attribute from different autonomous systems to select a preferred path.

Community Attribute

Although not an attribute in the routing decision process, the community attribute group routes and applies policies or decisions (accept, prefer) to those routes.

Atomic Aggregate and Aggregator Attributes

The Atomic Aggregate attribute informs BGP peers that the local router is using a less specific (aggregated) route to a destination.

If a BGP speaker selects a less specific route, when a more specific route is available, it must attach the Atomic Aggregate attribute when propagating the route. The Atomic Aggregate attribute lets the BGP peers know that the BGP speaker used an aggregated route.

When you use the Atomic Aggregate attribute, the BGP speaker has the option to send the Aggregator attribute. The Aggregator attribute includes the AS number and the IP address of the router that originated the aggregated route. In Cisco routers, the IP address is the RID of the router that performs the route aggregation. Atomic Aggregate is a well-known attribute and Aggregator is an optional, transitive attribute.

Weight

Weight is assigned locally on a router to specify a preferred path if multiple paths exist out of a router for a destination. Weights can be applied to individual routes or to all routes that are received from a peer. Weight is specific to Cisco routers and is not propagated to other routers. The weight value ranges from 0 to 65,535. Routes with a higher weight are preferred when multiple routes exist to a destination. Routes that are originated by the local router have a default weight of 32,768.

Weight can be used instead of local preference to influence the selected path to external BGP peers. The difference is that weight is configured locally and not exchanged in BGP updates. However, the local preference attribute is exchanged between iBGP peers and configured at the gateway router.

Figure 9-8 shows an example of the use of weight to influence the preferred route.

Figure 9-8 *BGP Weight*

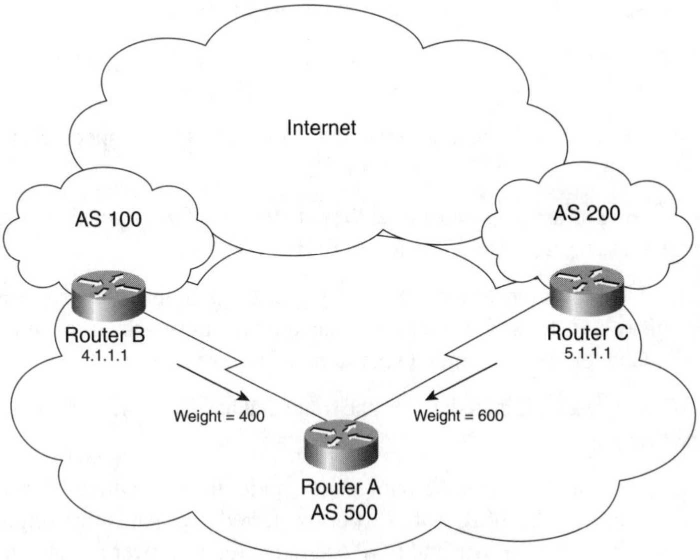

When the same destinations are advertised from both Router B and Router C in Figure 9-8, Router A prefers the routes from Router C over Router B because the routes received from Router C have a larger weight (600).

The configuration for Router A is shown in Example 9-13.

Example 9-13 *Configuration of Weight*

```
router bgp 500
 neighbor 4.1.1.1 remote-as 100
 neighbor 4.1.1.1 weight 400
 neighbor 5.1.1.1 remote-as 200
 neighbor 5.1.1.1 weight 600
```

BGP Decision Process

By default, BGP selects only a single path to reach a specific destination (unless you specify maximum paths). Cisco's implementation of BGP uses a simple decision process. When the path is selected, BGP puts the selected path in its routing table and propagates the path to its neighbors.

To select the best path to a destination, Cisco routers running BGP use the following algorithm:

1. If the specified next hop is inaccessible, drop the path.
2. If the path is internal, synchronization is enabled, and the path is not in the IGP; drop the path.
3. Prefer the path with the largest weight. (This step is Cisco specific and weight is localized to the router.)
4. If the weights are the same, prefer the path with the largest local preference. Used by iBGP only to reach the preferred external BGP router.
5. If the local preferences are the same, prefer the path that was originated by BGP running on this router. These are routes originated by the **network** command, **aggregate-address** command, or redistribution. (This step is Cisco specific.)
6. If no route was originated, prefer the route that has the shortest AS path. (This step is Cisco specific.)
7. If all paths have the same AS path length, prefer the path with the lowest origin type. Paths with an origin type of IGP are (lower) preferred over paths that originated from exterior gateway protocol (EGP), and EGP origin is preferred over a route with an incomplete origin. (This step is Cisco specific.)
8. If the origin codes are the same, prefer the path with the lowest MED attribute. Used by an eBGP peer to select a best path to AS. (This step is a tiebreaker, as described in the RFC.)
9. If the paths have the same MED, prefer the eBGP over the iBGP path. (This step is Cisco specific.)
10. If the paths are still the same, prefer the path through the closest IGP neighbor. (This step is a tiebreaker, as described in the RFC.)
11. Prefer the path with the BGP neighbor with the lowest RID (described in the RFC).

After BGP has decided on a best path, it marks it with a > sign in the **show ip bgp** table and adds it to the IP routing table.

BGP Route Dampening, Peer Groups, Route Reflectors, and Confederations

This section covers route dampening, which is a method to reduce the network instability that results from oscillating routes. Also, peer groups are covered, which apply a common set of policies to a group of BGP peers. Route reflectors and confederations are covered, which reduce the amount of BGP neighbor meshing that is required in iBGP networks.

Route Dampening

Route dampening minimizes the instability caused by oscillating or flapping routes. Route flaps occur when a valid route is considered invalid and then valid again. Route dampening is a method to stop unstable routes from being propagated throughout an internetwork. The BGP dampening process assigns a penalty to a route for each flap. The penalty carries a value of 1000. Penalties are cumulative. The route is suppressed if the penalty reaches the suppress limit, which is 2000 by default.

The penalty value decreases by half when the configured half-life time is reached (15 minutes by default). When the value reaches the reuse value, it becomes active. The maximum time a route can be suppressed is 60 minutes by default. The *maximum-suppress-time* field in the command changes the maximum time the route can be suppressed.

The command syntax to enable BGP route dampening is the following:

```
router bgp as-number
 bgp dampening half-life-time reuse-value suppress-limit maximum-suppress-time
```

The *half-life-time* is the number of minutes for half-life time for the penalty and is a number between 1 to 45, inclusive. The default *half-life-time* is 15 minutes. The *reuse-value* identifies the value to which the penalty needs to fall before the route can be re-advertised to the network and is a number from 1 to 20,000. The default *reuse-value* is 750. The *suppress-limit* indicates the value the penalty needs to reach before the route is suppressed; it is a number from 1 to 20,000. The default *suppress-limit* is 2000. The *maximum-suppress-time* is the maximum duration to suppress a stable route; values are from 1 to 255. The default *maximum-suppress-time* is four times the half-life or 60 minutes.

BGP Peer Groups

Peer groups are a grouping of BGP neighbors that are applied to the same policies. The policies can be the following: distribution list, route maps, next hop, update source, and so on. Peer groups can be assigned to iBGP peers or eBGP peers, but a peer group cannot contain both types of peers. The major benefit of a peer group is that it reduces the amount of CPU and memory resources on the router because it allows the routing table to be looked up once for update generation for all routers in the peer group. For large tables with a large number of prefixes, this can significantly reduce the load. Another benefit is that it simplifies the configuration of BGP neighbors because each command policy can be configured for the peer group without having to configure the policy for each BGP peer. For example, 15 BGP neighbors with 5 command policies are configured with approximately 75 commands. If all BGP neighbors are assigned to a peer group, the number of commands is reduced to approximately 20.

Example 9-14 shows the configuration of the iBGP peer group globalnet. All peers in the group share the same **neighbor globalnet** commands. The globalnet peer group is defined with the **neighbor** *globalnet* **peer-group** command. The shared commands are configured for the peer group; in this example, the remote AS is 65500, the update-source is loopback 0 of each router, each router announces itself as the next hop of its advertised routers, the BGP version is 4, and inbound soft-reconfiguration is enabled. Each neighbor is assigned to the peer group with the **neighbor** *ip-address* **peer-group** *group-name* command.

Example 9-14 *Example of Peer Group Configuration*

```
router bgp 65500
 no synchronization
 neighbor globalnet peer-group
 neighbor globalnet remote-as 65500
 neighbor globalnet update-source Loopback0
 neighbor globalnet next-hop-self
 neighbor globalnet version 4
 neighbor globalnet soft-reconfiguration inbound
 neighbor 1.25.1.160 peer-group globalnet
 neighbor 1.25.1.161 peer-group globalnet
 neighbor 1.25.1.164 peer-group globalnet
 neighbor 1.25.1.165 peer-group globalnet
 neighbor 1.25.1.166 peer-group globalnet
 neighbor 1.25.1.167 peer-group globalnet
 neighbor 1.25.1.168 peer-group globalnet
 neighbor 1.25.1.169 peer-group globalnet
 neighbor 1.25.1.170 peer-group globalnet
 neighbor 1.25.1.171 peer-group globalnet
 neighbor 1.25.1.172 peer-group globalnet
 neighbor 1.25.1.173 peer-group globalnet
 neighbor 1.25.1.174 peer-group globalnet
```

Route Reflectors

Network administrators can use route reflectors to reduce the number of required mesh links between iBGP peers. Some routers are selected to become the route reflectors to serve several other routers that act as clients. Route reflectors allow a router to advertise or reflect routes to clients. The route reflector and its clients form a cluster. All client routers in the cluster peer with the route reflectors within the cluster. The route reflectors also peer with all other route reflectors in the internetwork. A cluster can have more than one route reflector.

In Figure 9-9, without route reflectors, all iBGP routers are configured in an iBGP mesh, as required by the protocol. When Routers A and G become route reflectors, they peer with Routers C and D. Router B becomes a route reflector for Routers E and F. Router A, B, and G peer among each other.

Figure 9-9 *Route Reflectors*

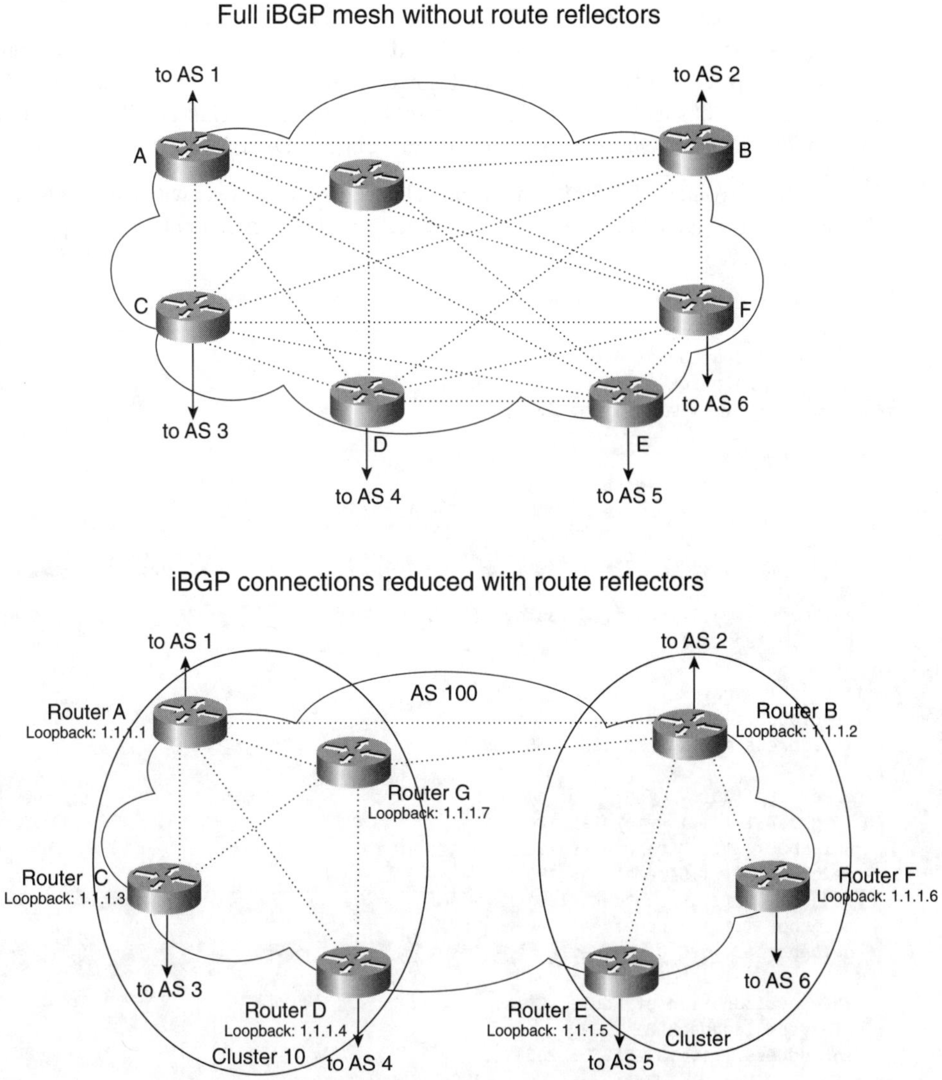

NOTE The combination of the route reflector and its clients is called a cluster. In Figure 9-9, Routers A, G, C, and D form a cluster. Routers B, E, and F form another cluster.

The configuration for route reflectors in Figure 9-9 is shown in Example 9-15. This example shows two clusters that are configured to reduce the iBGP mesh. Routers A and G are configured as route reflectors by defining route-reflector clients with the **neighbor** *ip-address* **route-reflector-client** command. Routers A and G are configured to peer with each other, and with Routers B, C, and D. Routers C and D are configured to peer with Routers A and G only. Because the first cluster has two route reflectors, you use the **bgp cluster-id** command. All route reflectors in the same cluster must have the same cluster ID number.

Router B is the router reflector for the second cluster. Router B peers with Routers A and G, and with Routers E and F in its cluster. Routers E and F are route-reflector clients and peer only with Router B.

Example 9-15 *Route Reflector Configuration Example*

```
!The configuration of Router A is:
interface loopback 0
 ip address 1.1.1.1 255.255.255.255
!
router bgp 100
 neighbor 1.1.1.2 remote-as 100
 neighbor 1.1.1.7 remote-as 100
 neighbor 1.1.1.3 remote-as 100
 neighbor 1.1.1.3 route-reflector-client
 neighbor 1.1.1.4 remote-as 100
 neighbor 1.1.1.4 route-reflector-client
 bgp cluster-id 10

!The configuration of Router B is:
interface loopback 0
 ip address 1.1.1.2 255.255.255.255
!
router bgp 100
 neighbor 1.1.1.1 remote-as 100
 neighbor 1.1.1.7 remote-as 100
 neighbor 1.1.1.5 remote-as 100
 neighbor 1.1.1.5 route-reflector-client
 neighbor 1.1.1.6 remote-as 100
 neighbor 1.1.1.6 route-reflector-client

!The configuration of Router C is:
interface loopback 0
 ip address 1.1.1.3 255.255.255.255
!
router bgp 100
 neighbor 1.1.1.1 remote-as 100
 neighbor 1.1.1.7 remote-as 100

!The configuration of Router D is:
interface loopback 0
 ip address 1.1.1.4 255.255.255.255
```

Example 9-15 *Route Reflector Configuration Example (Continued)*

```
!
router bgp 100
 neighbor 1.1.1.1 remote-as 100
 neighbor 1.1.1.7 remote-as 100

!The configuration of Router E is:
interface loopback 0
 ip address 1.1.1.5 255.255.255.255
!
router bgp 100
 neighbor 1.1.1.2 remote-as 100

!The configuration of Router F is:
interface loopback 0
 ip address 1.1.1.6 255.255.255.255
!
router bgp 100
 neighbor 1.1.1.2 remote-as 100

!The configuration of Router G is:
interface loopback 0
 ip address 1.1.1.7 255.255.255.255
!
router bgp 100
 neighbor 1.1.1.1 remote-as 100
 neighbor 1.1.1.2 remote-as 100
 neighbor 1.1.1.3 remote-as 100
 neighbor 1.1.1.3 route-reflector-client
 neighbor 1.1.1.4 remote-as 100
 neighbor 1.1.1.4 route-reflector-client
 bgp cluster-id 10
```

Confederations

Another method to reduce the iBGP mesh within an AS is to use BGP confederations. With confederations, the AS is divided into smaller, private autonomous systems, and the entire group is assigned a confederation ID. The routers within each private AS are configured with the full iBGP mesh. Each private AS is configured with eBGP to communicate with other semi-autonomous systems in the confederation. Only the AS number of the confederation is seen by external autonomous systems, and this number is configured with the **bgp confederation identifier** command.

In Figure 9-10, a confederation divides the AS into two.

Figure 9-10 *BGP Confederations*

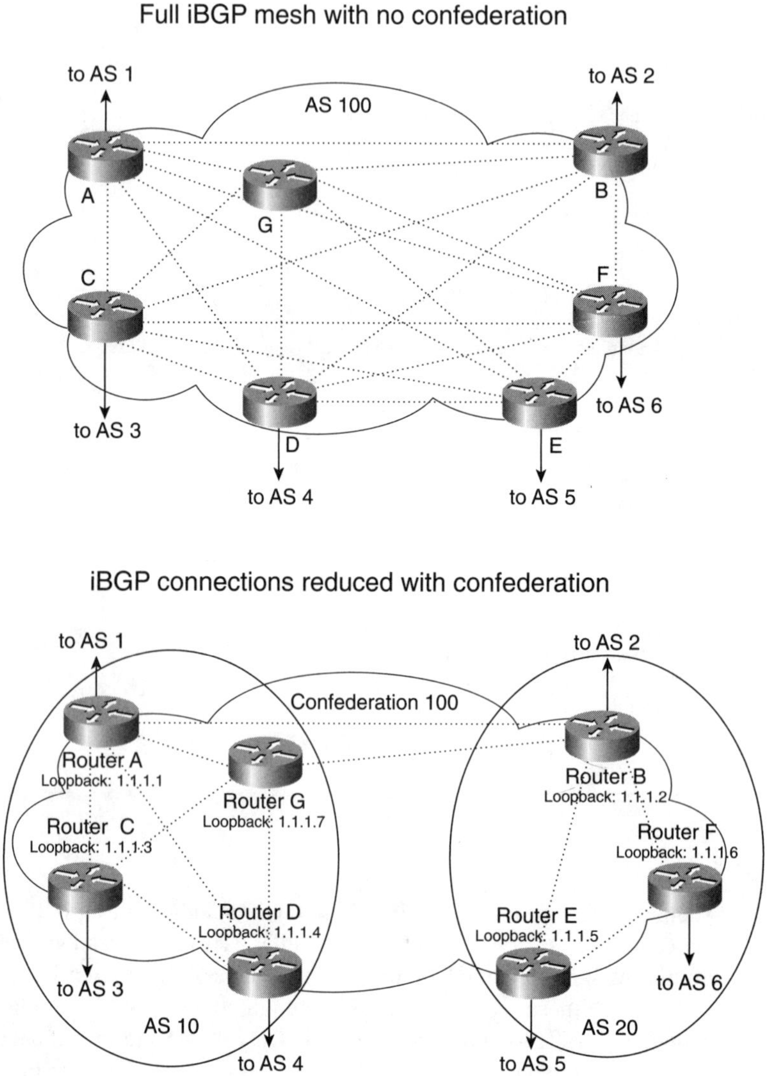

The configuration for all routers from Figure 9-10 is shown in Example 9-16. Routers A, B, and G are configured for eBGP between the private autonomous systems. These routers are configured with the **bgp confederation identifier** command. The confederation identifier number is the same for all routers in the network. The **bgp confederation** command identifies the AS number of other private autonomous systems in the confederation. Because Router A and G are in AS 10, the peer confederation is AS 20. Router B is in AS 20 and its peer confederation is AS 10, as shown in Example 9-16.

Routers C and D are part of AS 10 and peer with each other and with routers A and G. Routers E and F are part of AS 20 and peer with each other and with Router B.

Example 9-16 *BGP Confederation Example*

```
!The configuration of Router A is:
interface loopback 0
 ip address 1.1.1.1 255.255.255.255
!
router bgp 10
 bgp confederation identifier 100
 bgp confederation peers 20
 neighbor 1.1.1.2 remote-as 20
 neighbor 1.1.1.7 remote-as 10
 neighbor 1.1.1.3 remote-as 10
 neighbor 1.1.1.4 remote-as 10

!The configuration of Router B is:
interface loopback 0
 ip address 1.1.1.2 255.255.255.255
!
router bgp 20
 bgp confederation identifier 100
 bgp confederation peers 10
 neighbor 1.1.1.1 remote-as 10
 neighbor 1.1.1.5 remote-as 20
 neighbor 1.1.1.6 remote-as 20

!The configuration of Router C is:
interface loopback 0
 ip address 1.1.1.3 255.255.255.255
!
router bgp 10
 neighbor 1.1.1.1 remote-as 10
 neighbor 1.1.1.7 remote-as 10
 neighbor 1.1.1.4 remote-as 10

!The configuration of Router D is:
interface loopback 0
 ip address 1.1.1.4 255.255.255.255
!
router bgp 10
 neighbor 1.1.1.1 remote-as 10
 neighbor 1.1.1.7 remote-as 10
 neighbor 1.1.1.3 remote-as 10

!The configuration of Router E is:
interface loopback 0
 ip address 1.1.1.5 255.255.255.255
```

continues

Example 9-16 *BGP Confederation Example (Continued)*

```
!
router bgp 20
 neighbor 1.1.1.2 remote-as 20
 neighbor 1.1.1.6 remote-as 20

!The configuration of Router F is:
interface loopback 0
 ip address 1.1.1.6 255.255.255.255
!
router bgp 20
 neighbor 1.1.1.2 remote-as 20
 neighbor 1.1.1.5 remote-as 20

!The configuration of Router G is:
interface loopback 0
 ip address 1.1.1.7 255.255.255.255
!
router bgp 10
 bgp confederation identifier 100
 bgp confederation peers 20
 neighbor 1.1.1.2 remote-as 20
 neighbor 1.1.1.1 remote-as 10
 neighbor 1.1.1.3 remote-as 10
 neighbor 1.1.1.4 remote-as 10
```

BGP show Commands

This section briefly reviews some **show** commands that you can use with BGP. For the CCIE written exam, know how to read the fields in the output of these commands.

The first command is **show ip bgp neighbors**, as shown in Example 9-17. Use this command to check if a TCP connection has been established with the neighbor. The BGP neighbor is the IP address of the peer. The remote AS number is provided. The remote RID is the BGP RID of the peer. The BGP state is Established. Notifications are the number of error messages sent or received from the peer. NLRI means Network Layer Reachability Information, which are destination IP networks. The local router IP address and port is 1.1.1.1 and 11007. The remote IP address is 1.1.1.2 and the TCP port is 179 (for BGP).

Example 9-17 **show ip bgp neighbors** *Command*

```
R9#show ip bgp neighbors 1.1.1.2
BGP neighbor is 1.1.1.2,  remote AS 200, external link
  BGP version 4, remote router ID 10.10.10.10
  BGP state = Established, up for 00:00:22
  Last read 00:00:21, hold time is 180, keepalive interval is 60 seconds
  Neighbor capabilities:
    Route refresh: advertised and received(new)
```

Example 9-17 show ip bgp neighbors *Command (Continued)*

```
    Address family IPv4 Unicast: advertised and received
  Received 3 messages, 0 notifications, 0 in queue
  Sent 3 messages, 0 notifications, 0 in queue
  Route refresh request: received 0, sent 0
  Default minimum time between advertisement runs is 30 seconds

 For address family: IPv4 Unicast
  BGP table version 1, neighbor version 1
  Index 1, Offset 0, Mask 0x2
  0 accepted prefixes consume 0 bytes
  Prefix advertised 0, suppressed 0, withdrawn 0
  Number of NLRIs in the update sent: max 0, min 0

  Connections established 1; dropped 0
  Last reset never
Connection state is ESTAB, I/O status: 1, unread input bytes: 0
Local host: 1.1.1.1, Local port: 11007
Foreign host: 1.1.1.2, Foreign port: 179
```

The command **show ip bgp** lists the networks in the BGP table, as shown in Example 9-18. The next hop, metric, preference, weight, AS path, and origin attributes are listed in this command's output. The status codes are on the left; origin codes are on the right.

Status codes are as follows:

- s indicates suppressed routes; the route is suppressed when its penalty exceeds the limit.
- d indicates dampened routes; the route has flapped so often that the router does not advertise this route to BGP neighbors.
- h indicates a history state; after a route flaps once, it is assigned a penalty and put into history state, meaning the router does not have the best path, based on historical information.
- * indicates a valid route.
- > indicates the best route.
- i indicates an internal route.

Origin codes are as follows:

- i indicates entry originated from an IGP advertised with the **network** command.
- e indicates entry originated from EGP.
- ? indicates origin is unknown, usually from redistribution.

Example 9-18 show ip bgp *Command*

```
R7#show ip bgp
BGP table version is 14, local router ID is 7.7.7.7
Status codes: s suppressed, d damped, h history, * valid, > best, i - internal
Origin codes: i - IGP, e - EGP, ? - incomplete

   Network          Next Hop            Metric LocPrf Weight Path
*> 18.88.88.0/24    78.1.1.8                 0             0 128 i
* i                 172.16.64.1                   100      0 128 i
*>i79.7.7.0/24      9.9.9.9                  0    100      0 i
*>i109.1.1.0/24     10.10.10.10              0    100      0 i
*>i155.55.55.0/24   172.16.64.1                   100      0 128 i
*> 172.16.1.0/24    78.1.1.8                               0 128 i
* i                 172.16.64.1              0    100      0 128 i
*>i199.99.99.0      9.9.9.9                  0    100      0 i
*>i222.222.222.0    172.16.64.1
```

You can use several keywords to clear BGP sessions. Example 9-19 shows the possible keywords. To reset all of BGP, use **clear ip bgp ***. To clear peers within an AS, use **clear ip bgp** *as-number*. To clear a BGP neighbor, use **clear ip bgp** *ip-address*. To clear all BGP external peers, use **clear ip bgp external**.

Example 9-19 *Clearing the BGP Table*

```
R7#clear ip bgp ?
  *                 Clear all peers
  <1-65535>         Clear peers with the AS number
  A.B.C.D           BGP neighbor address to clear
  dampening         Clear route flap dampening information
  external          Clear all external peers
  flap-statistics   Clear route flap statistics
  ipv4              Address family
  peer-group        Clear all members of peer-group
  vpnv4             Address family
```

The router enters BGP table entries into the routing table. To verify BGP routes, use the **show ip routes** command, as shown in Example 9-20. By default, eBGP routes have an administrative distance of 20, and iBGP routes have an administrative distance of 200. In the example, network 222.222.222.0/24 was learned from BGP with an administrative distance of 200 (iBGP). Network 18.88.88.0/24 is an eBGP route, and the next hop is 78.1.1.8. Network 172.16.1.0/24 was learned from an external BGP peer because its administrative distance is 20. Network 199.99.99.0/24 was learned from an internal BGP peer because the administrative distance is 200.

Example 9-20 *BGP Routes Marked in the Routing Table*

```
R7#sh ip route
Codes: C - connected, S - static, I - IGRP, R - RIP, M - mobile, B - BGP
       D - EIGRP, EX - EIGRP external, O - OSPF, IA - OSPF inter area
       N1 - OSPF NSSA external type 1, N2 - OSPF NSSA external type 2
       E1 - OSPF external type 1, E2 - OSPF external type 2, E - EGP
       i - IS-IS, L1 - IS-IS level-1, L2 - IS-IS level-2, ia - IS-IS inter area
       * - candidate default, U - per-user static route, o - ODR
       P - periodic downloaded static route

Gateway of last resort is not set

B    222.222.222.0/24 [200/0] via 172.16.64.1, 1d03h
     155.55.0.0/24 is subnetted, 1 subnets
B       155.55.55.0 [200/0] via 172.16.64.1, 1d03h
     18.0.0.0/24 is subnetted, 1 subnets
B       18.88.88.0 [20/0] via 78.1.1.8, 1d22h
     172.16.0.0/16 is variably subnetted, 2 subnets, 2 masks
B       172.16.1.0/24 [20/0] via 78.1.1.8, 1d22h
R       172.16.64.0/25 [120/2] via 79.7.7.9, 00:00:01, Ethernet0
     7.0.0.0/32 is subnetted, 1 subnets
C       78.1.1.0 is directly connected, Serial1
     109.0.0.0/24 is subnetted, 1 subnets
R       109.1.1.0 [120/1] via 79.7.7.9, 00:00:04, Ethernet0
     79.0.0.0/24 is subnetted, 1 subnets
C       79.7.7.0 is directly connected, Ethernet0
B    199.99.99.0/24 [200/0] via 9.9.9.9, 1d22h
```

References Used

The following resources were used to create this chapter:

Routing TCP/IP, Volume II, Jeff Doyle/Jennifer DeHaven Carroll, Cisco Press, 2001

RFC 1771, "A Border Gateway Protocol 4." Y. Rekhter, T. Li, March 1995

RFC 1519, "Classless Inter-Domain Routing (CIDR): an Address Assignment and Aggregation Strategy." V. Fuller, T. Li, J. Yu, K. Varadhan, September 1993

RFC 1997, "BGP Communities Attribute." R. Chandra, P. Traina, T. Li, August 1996

www.cisco.com/univercd/cc/td/doc/cisintwk/ito_doc/bgp.htm

www.cisco.com/univercd/cc/td/doc/product/software/ios121/121cgcr/ip_c/ipcprt2/1cdbgp.htm

Foundation Summary

The Foundation Summary is a condensed collection of material that provides a convenient review of key concepts in this chapter. If you are already comfortable with the topics in this chapter, this summary will help you recall a few details. If you just read the Foundation Topics section, this review should help solidify some key facts. If you are doing your final preparation before the exam, these materials are a convenient way to review the day before the exam.

BGP Summary

The characteristics of BGP are summarized as follows:

- Interdomain routing protocol.
- Uses TCP port 179 to establish connections with neighbors.
- BGP4 implements CIDR.
- eBGP for external neighbors.
- iBGP for internal neighbors.
- Uses several attributes for decision algorithm.
- Uses confederations and route reflectors to reduce BGP peering.
- Peer Groups apply policies to a group of routers; Communities apply policies to a group of networks.
- MED (metric) attribute between autonomous systems to influence inbound traffic.
- Weight attribute influences the path of outbound traffic from a single router, configured locally.
- Local preference attribute influences the path of outbound traffic from an AS.
- Administrative Distance is 20 for eBGP and 200 for iBGP.

BGP Decision Algorithm

The BGP decision algorithm can be summarized as follows:

1. If no next hop, drop the path.
2. For internal path with synchronization, and the route is not in the IGP, drop the path.
3. Highest weight.
4. Highest local preference.

5. Locally originated route.
6. Shortest AS Path.
7. Lowest origin type (IGP < EGP < Incomplete).
8. Lowest MED (metric).
9. External path over Internal path.
10. Nearest eBGP neighbor (best IGP path to eBGP neighbor).
11. Path with Lowest RID.

Table 9-2 *BGP Attributes*

Attribute	Class	Description
Next-Hop	Well-known, mandatory	IP address that reaches the destination
Weight	n/a	Configured on the router to assign a preference of routes from different sources (not an RFC attribute)
Local Preference	Well-known, discretionary	Indicates a path for exiting the AS
Origin	Well-known, mandatory	I (IGP), e (EGP), ? (incomplete)
AS Path	Well-known, mandatory	Number of autonomous systems to reach the destination, list of AS numbers
MED (metric)	Optional, transitive	Tells the eBGP peers the preferred path into the AS
Community	Optional, transitive	Groups networks for policy assignment

Q & A

The Q & A questions are more difficult than what you can expect on the actual exam. The questions do not attempt to cover more breadth or depth than the exam; however, they are designed to make sure that you retain the material. Rather than allowing you to derive the answer from clues hidden inside the question itself, these questions challenge your understanding and recall of the subject. In addition to new questions, questions from the "Do I Know This Already?" quiz are repeated here to ensure that you have mastered the chapter's topic areas. A strong understanding of the answers to these questions will help you on the CCIE written exam. As an additional study aide, use the CD-ROM provided with this book to take simulated exams.

Select the best answer. Answers to these questions are in the Appendix, "Answers to Quiz Questions."

1 A router has the following configuration. Which routing protocol are you using?

```
router bgp 10
 neighbor 1.1.1.1 remote-as 10
```

a. OBGP with an external neighbor

b. BGP with an internal neighbor

c. BGP with an external neighbor

d. EIGRP with an internal neighbor

2 MED is used for which of the following functions?

a. To give a hint to the routers on what outbound path to take

b. To give a hint to the confederation routers on what outbound path to take

c. To give a hint to the external BGP peers on what inbound path to take

d. To give a hint to local BGP peers on what inbound path to take

3 Which of the following best describes the BGP weight attribute?

a. Determines a path; not locally significant.

b. Determines a path; lowest value is preferred.

c. Locally significant; lowest value is preferred.

d. Locally significant; highest value is preferred.

4 What is the process by which BGP speakers in a transit AS do not advertise a route until all routers have learned about the route through an IGP?

a. Redistribution

b. BGP synchronization

c. OSPF redistribution

d. OSPF synchronization

5 What does the number represent in the following router command?

```
router bgp 200
```

a. ASN.

b. Process ID.

c. Autonomous process ID.

d. The number is incorrect; it must be 65,000 or higher.

6 Which service access point does BGP use?

a. UDP port 179

b. IP protocol 179

c. TCP port 179

d. None of the above

7 Which of the following shows the correct order that BGP uses to select a best path?

a. Origin, lowest IP, AS Path, Weight, Local Preference

b. Weight, Local Preference, AS Path, Origin, MED, lowest IP

c. Lowest IP, AS Path, Origin, Weight, MED, Local Preference

d. Weight, Origin, Local Preference, AS Path, MED, lowest IP

8 BGP communities apply common policy to what?

a. Routers

b. A group of destinations

c. Dampened routes

d. Autonomous systems

9 What does the > symbol mean in the output of **show ip bgp**?

a. Compares a route as less than another

b. Indicates an internal BGP route

c. Compares a route as greater than another

d. Indicates the selected route

10 Which of the following is the administrative distance of an external BGP route?

a. 1

b. 20

c. 50

d. 200

11 Which mechanism penalizes flapping BGP routes by suppressing them?

a. Route reflectors

b. Route dampening

c. Route suppression

d. Route filtering

12 Which feature was implemented in BGPv4 to provide forwarding of packets based on IP prefixes?

a. MED

b. VLSM

c. CIDR

d. AS path

13 What is configured if an external BGP neighbor does not share a common subnet?

a. BGP confederation, with iBGP only

b. BGP multihop, with eBGP only

c. BGP multihop, with iBGP only

d. BGP confederation, with eBGP only

14 Which of the following is the best definition of an autonomous system?

a. Group of routers running iBGP

b. Group of routers running OSPF

c. Group of routers running eBGP

d. Group of routers under single administration

15 Which mechanism applies the same policies to a group of neighbors?

a. Peer group

b. Confederation group

c. Community group

d. Route-reflector group

16 Router A and Router B are in AS 50. Router A has two BGP peers (Router C and Router D) to AS 100. Routers C and D announce the same destination. Router C announces a MED of 200. Router D announces a MED of 300. Which path does Router A take to reach AS 100?

a. Router A

b. Router B

c. Router C

d. Router D

17 Router A has three BGP peers: Router B, Router C, and Router D. Routers B, C, and D announce the same destinations. Router B announces the default local preference. Router C announces a local preference of 200. Router D announces a local preference of 300. Which path does Router A take?

a. Router A

b. Router B

c. Router C

d. Router D

18 Which network prefix is more specific?

a. 100.1.0.0/16

b. 100.1.1.0/24

c. 100.1.0.0/28

d. 100.1.1.0/26

19 Which command resets all BGP connections?

a. **reset ip bgp ***

b. **show ip bgp ***

c. **clear ip bgp ***

d. **disc ip bgp ***

20 Which of the following BGP routes is selected?

a. AS path = 23 50 801, MED = 10, routerID = 1.1.1.1

b. AS path = 24 51 801, MED = 0, routerID = 2.2.2.2

c. AS path = 100 24 51 801, MED = 10, routerID = 3.3.3.3

d. AS path = 23 50 801, MED = 0, routerID = 4.4.4.4

21 BGP has two routes for a network. One has an origin code of i; the second has an origin code of e. Which one is chosen?

a. The route marked with i as the origin type.

b. The route marked with e as the origin type.

c. The route is invalid.

d. Not enough information given.

22 How many route reflectors are allowed in a cluster?

a. Only one.

b. More than one.

c. Route reflectors are used in confederations.

d. None.

23 A router announces several networks through redistribution in BGP. If you use the **aggregate-address 100.64.0.0 255.252.0.0** command, which networks are announced?

Announced networks: 100.64.224.0/24 through 100.65.10.0/24

a. Network 100.64.0.0/14 only

b. Network 100.64.0.0/16 only

c. Network 100.64.0.0/14 and announced networks

d. Network 100.64.0.0/16 and announced networks

Scenarios

Scenario 9-1

Use the following router output to answer the questions in this scenario:

```
R1>show ip bgp
BGP table version is 66, local router ID is 172.16.99.1
Status codes: s suppressed, d damped, h history, * valid, > best, i - internal
Origin codes: i - IGP, e - EGP, ? - incomplete

   Network          Next Hop            Metric LocPrf Weight Path
*>i18.88.88.0/24    8.8.8.8                  0    100      0 i
* i79.7.7.0/24      78.1.1.7                      100      0 7910 i
*>                  172.16.64.10                           0 7910 i
* i109.1.1.0/24     78.1.1.7                      100      0 7910 i
*>                  172.16.64.10             0             0 7910 i
*>i155.55.55.0/24   2.2.2.2                  0    100      0 i
*> 172.16.1.0/24    0.0.0.0                  0         32768 i
* i199.99.99.0      78.1.1.7                      100      0 7910 i
*>                  172.16.64.10                           0 7910 i
*>i222.222.222.0    2.2.2.2                  0    100      0 i
```

1 Which of the following is the selected route for network 109.1.1.0/24?

a. 78.1.1.7

b. 172.16.64.10

c. 172.16.99.1

d. 2.2.2.2

2 Why is 172.16.64.10 the best next hop for network 199.99.99.0?

a. It is an internal route.

b. There is no local preference.

c. The weight is 0.

d. The route is external.

3 Which of the following is the router identifier of the local router?

a. 172.16.63.10

b. 172.16.99.1

c. 78.1.1.7

d. 2.2.2.2

Scenario 9-2

Use the following router output to answer the questions in this scenario:

```
router# show ip bgp neighbors 100.10.10.2
BGP neighbor is 100.10.10.2,  remote AS 500, external link
  BGP version 4, remote router ID 100.10.10.10
  BGP state = Established, up for 00:00:22
  Last read 00:00:21, hold time is 180, keepalive interval is 60 seconds
  Neighbor capabilities:
    Route refresh: advertised and received(new)
    Address family IPv4 Unicast: advertised and received
  Received 4 messages, 0 notifications, 0 in queue
  Sent 4 messages, 0 notifications, 0 in queue
  Route refresh request: received 0, sent 0
  Default minimum time between advertisement runs is 30 seconds

 For address family: IPv4 Unicast
  BGP table version 1, neighbor version 1
  Index 1, Offset 0, Mask 0x2
  0 accepted prefixes consume 0 bytes
  Prefix advertised 0, suppressed 0, withdrawn 0
  Number of NLRIs in the update sent: max 0, min 0

  Connections established 1; dropped 0
  Last reset never
Connection state is ESTAB, I/O status: 1, unread input bytes: 0
Local host: 100.10.10.1, Local port: 11007
Foreign host: 100.10.10.2, Foreign port: 179
```

1 Which of the following is the router ID of the remote peer?

a. 100.10.10.2

b. 100.10.10.1

c. 100.10.10.10

d. 100.10.10.255

2 What is NLRI?

a. Network Layer Reachability Information

b. Network Link Reachability Information

c. Network Link Route Information

d. Network Local Reachability Information

3 Which of the following is the remote AS number?

a. 100.

b. 200.

c. 500.

d. Not enough information is given.

4 What is the state of the TCP connection?

a. TCP 179

b. TCP 11079

c. Established

d. Idle

Scenario 9-3

Use the following configuration to answer the questions in this scenario:

```
interface loopback 0
 ip address 1.1.1.1 255.255.255.255
!
router bgp 200
 network 1.0.0.0 mask 255.240.0.0
 neighbor 2.2.2.1 remote-as 300
 neighbor 2.2.2.1 route-map ccie out
 neighbor 1.1.1.3 remote-as 200
 neighbor 1.1.1.3 route-reflector-client
 neighbor 1.1.1.4 remote-as 200
 neighbor 1.1.1.4 route-reflector-client
 neighbor 1.1.1.5 remote-as 200
 bgp cluster-id 5
!
route-map ccie permit 10
 set metric 100
```

1 Which of the following is the local AS number?

a. 100

b. 200

c. 300

d. Not specified

2 Which router is a route reflector? (There might be more than one.)

a. 1.1.1.1 only

b. 1.1.1.3 only

c. 2.2.2.1 only

d. 1.1.1.3 and 1.1.1.4

3 Which of the following is the router ID of the router with this configuration?

a. 1.1.1.1

b. 1.1.1.3

c. 1.1.1.4

d. 2.2.2.1

4 Which of the following is the external peer's AS number?

a. 100

b. 200

c. 300

d. Not specified

5 Which attribute is configured in the route map?

a. Origin

b. Local Preference

c. MED

d. AS Hop metric

This chapter covers the following topics needed to master the CCIE Routing and Switching (R&S) written exam:

- **Administrative distance**—The Cisco administrative distance, which is applied to all routing protocols, static routes, and connected interfaces
- **IP access lists**—IP standard and extended access lists and their format
- **Route manipulation**—Route maps, distribution lists, policy routing, and redistribution
- **IP multicast protocols**—Multicast protocols, such as Internet Group Management Protocol (IGMP), Cisco Group Management Protocol (CGMP), Protocol Independent Multicast (PIM), and Distance Vector Multicast Routing Protocol (DVMRP)

CHAPTER 10

Administrative Distance, Access Lists, Route Manipulation, and IP Multicast

This chapter covers routing topics that might not pertain to any one routing protocol. These items include redistribution, access lists, distribute lists, and route maps. Administrative distance and IP multicast protocols are also covered in this chapter.

"Do I Know This Already?" Quiz

The purpose of this assessment quiz is to help you determine how to spend your limited study time. If you can answer most or all of these questions, you might want to skim the Foundation Topics section and return to it later as necessary. Review the Foundation Summary section and answer the questions at the end of the chapter to ensure that you have a strong grasp of the material covered. If you intend to read the entire chapter, you do not need to answer these questions now. If you find these assessment questions difficult, read through the entire Foundation Topics section and review it until you feel comfortable with your ability to answer all of the "Q & A" questions at the end of the chapter. These questions are repeated at the end of the chapter with additional questions to test your mastery of the material.

Select the best answer. Answers to these questions are in the Appendix, "Answers to Quiz Questions."

1 What is the administrative distance of EIGRP external routes?

a. 90

b. 100

c. 110

d. 170

2 Which protocol do hosts use to join a multicast group?

a. CGMP

b. DVMRP

c. PIM-SM

d. IGMP

3 When redistributing EIGRP routes into RIP, how do the bandwidth and delay metrics get converted?

a. RIP assigns the bandwidth and delay metrics with the **default-metric** command.

b. EIGRP metrics do not get converted; RIP assigns a default hop count metric as configured by the **default- metric** command.

c. RIP uses the bandwidth metric and discards the delay.

d. RIP uses the delay metric and discards the bandwidth.

4 What does the multicast address 224.0.0.2 represent?

a. All hosts on the subnet

b. All routers on the subnet

c. All OSPF routers on the network

d. All PIM routers on the network

5 When an EIGRP route is redistributed into OSPF, what is the default administrative distance of the resulting OSPF route in the IP routing table?

a. 90

b. 100

c. 110

d. 170

6 A router is running two routing protocols: OSPF and EIGRP. Both protocols internally learn of the route 10.1.1.4/24. Which route is added to the routing table?

a. The EIGRP route.

b. The OSPF route.

c. Both are added with equal load balancing.

d. Both are added with unequal load balancing.

7 Which access list denies Telnet and ping and permits everything else?

a.

```
access-list 99 deny tcp any  any eq echo log
access-list 99 deny tcp any any telnet eq telnet
access-list 99 permit ip any any
```

b.

```
access-list 100 deny icmp any any echo log
access-list 100 deny tcp any any telnet
```

c.

```
access-list 100 deny icmp any any echo log
access-list 100 deny icmp any any echo-reply
access-list 100 deny tcp any any eq telnet
access-list 100 permit ip any any
```

d.

```
access-list 99 deny icmp any any echo log
access-list 99 deny icmp any any echo-reply
access-list 99 deny tcp any any eq telnet
access-list 99 permit ip any any
```

8 In an internetwork of 50 routers running EIGRP, you need to filter the networks received by one spoke router. What can you use?

a. Use an access list and apply it to the inbound interface with the **ip access-group** command.

b. Redistribute the routes into OSPF with a route map.

c. Use a distribute list under the EIGRP process with an access list to filter the networks.

d. Change the administrative distance of the router.

9 Which access list permits all hosts in network 192.172.100.0/28?

a. access-list 100 permit 192.172.100.0 0.0.0.31.

b. access-list 10 permit 192.172.100.0 255.255.255.240.

c. access-list 10 permit 192.172.100.0 0.0.0.31.

d. access-list 10 permit ip 192.172.100.0 0.0.0.31.

10 What does PIM stand for?

a. Protocol Inbound Multicast

b. Protocol Independent Multicast

c. Protocol Independent Management

d. Password Independent Multicast

Foundation Topics

Administrative Distance

On routers running several IP routing protocols, two different routing protocols might have a route to the same destination. Cisco routers assign each routing protocol an administrative distance. The default values are shown in Table 10-1. In the event that two or more routing protocols offer the same route for inclusion in the routing table, the Cisco IOS selects the route from the routing protocol with the lowest administrative distance.

Table 10-1 *Default Administrative Distances for IP Routes*

IP Route	Administrative Distance
Connected interface	0
Static route directed to a connected interface	0
Static route directed to an IP address	1
Enhanced Interior Gateway Protocol (EIGRP) summary route	5
External BGP route	20
Internal EIGRP route	90
Interior Gateway Protocol (IGRP) route	100
Open Shortest Path First (OSPF) route	110
Intermediate System-to Intermediate System (IS-IS) route	115
Routing Information Protocol (RIP) route	120
Exterior gateway protocol (EGP) route	140
External EIGRP route	170
Internal BGP route	200
Route of unknown origin	255

The administrative distance establishes a precedence among routing algorithms. A router has an internal EIGRP route to network 172.20.10.0/24 with the best path out Ethernet 0 and an OSPF route for the same network out Ethernet 1. Because EIGRP has an administrative distance of 90 and OSPF has an administrative distance of 110, you enter the EIGRP route in the routing table, and packets with destinations of 172.20.10.0/24 are sent out Ethernet 0.

Administrative Distance Configuration

To change the administrative distance for routing protocols, use the **distance** *number* command. The *number* value ranges from 0 to 255. For OSPF, separate distances are configured for external, intra-area, and internal routes. The command examples in Table 10-2 change the administrative distances of routing protocols to a number between 40 and 50. (Don't do this on a real internetwork!)

Table 10-2 *Use of the* **distance** *Command for Routing Protocols*

Protocol	Commands
RIP	`router rip` ` distance 49`
IGRP	`router igrp 100` ` distance 48`
EIGRP	`router eigrp 100` ` distance 41`
IS-IS	`router isis` ` distance 42`

OSPF	`router ospf 100`
	` distance external 45`
	` distance inter-area 46`
	` distance intra-area 44`

BGP	`router bgp 6000` ` distance 47`

Static routes have a default administrative distance of 1. There is one exception. If the static route points to a connected interface, it inherits the administrative distance of connected interfaces, which is 0. Static routes can be configured with a different distance by appending the distance value to the end of the command. The following command gives an administrative distance of 250 to the static route:

```
ip route 1.0.0.0 255.0.0.0 3.3.3.3 250
```

IP Access Lists

Many uses exist for IP access lists on Cisco routers and switches. You use access lists to control access to networks and virtual local-area networks (VLANS), to redistribute or filter routes in route maps, and so on. An access list defines a set of criteria that can be applied to every packet processed by the router or switch.

When applied to an interface, an access list can block or permit traffic forwarding. The access list can be applied at the ingress (inbound) or at the egress (outbound) of a network. If the list is applied inbound, the system checks the access list's statements for a match when the router receives a packet. If the packet is permitted, the system continues processing the packet (checking the routing table and so on). If the packet is denied, it is discarded.

A packet is received and routed to the outbound interface before being processed for an outbound access list. If the packet is applied outbound, the system checks the access list's statements for a match. If the packet is permitted, the system transmits the packet. If the packet is denied, it is discarded.

IP Access List Configuration

Cisco IOS contains two types of access lists for IP. The first is the standard access list; the second is the extended access list. Each access list is configured using an access list number. Standard access lists are configured with numbers from 1 to 99. Extended access lists are configured from 100 to 199. The access list is a sequential list of permit or deny conditions. The router tests the packets' IP addresses and port numbers against each condition in the list one by one. The first match determines if the packet is forwarded or discarded. After a match is made in the list for the packet, the statements that follow in the list are ignored; therefore, order of conditions in the access list is important. Also, if no conditions match, the router rejects the packet with an implicit deny all at the end of the list. An expanded range of access list numbers exist. The expanded range permits the configuration of IP standard or IP extended access lists by using these numbers, which are highlighted in the following example:

```
ag1.hstttx.lab(config)#access-list ?
<1-99> IP standard access list
<100-199> IP extended access list
<1100-1199> Extended 48-bit MAC address access list
<1300-1999> IP standard access list (expanded range)
<200-299> Protocol type-code access list
<2000-2699> IP extended access list (expanded range)
<700-799> 48-bit MAC address access list
```

NOTE Remember the access list numbers. For IP, standard access lists use 1 to 99. For IP, extended access lists use 100 to 199.

IP Standard Access List Configuration

You can configure standard access lists by using the following global command:

```
access-list list {permit | deny} address wildcard-mask log
```

The argument *list* is the access list number (1–99 or 1300–1999). The *address* is the source IP address of the packet. A network or network range can be defined with *wildcard-mask*. The wildcard mask is an inverse mask; if the bit is a 1, the address bit is variable. An inverse mask of 0.0.0.0 means that the specific host specified in the address field, and an inverse mask of 255.255.255.255, is any host. The *address* can be replaced with the keyword **any**, which matches any packet that did not have a match in earlier conditions in the list. After the access list is built, it can be applied to an interface with the following interface command:

```
ip access-group list {in | out}
```

The default is inbound if you do not use the **in** or **out** keyword.

In Example 10-1, an access list is applied on an interface to deny packets from IP address 192.168.10.100, to permit all other devices in subnet 192.168.10.0/24, and to deny all other packets.

Example 10-1 *Access List to Deny Host 192.168.10.100*

```
access-list 99 deny host 192.168.10.100
access-list 99 permit 192.168.10.0 0.0.0.255
!
interface ethernet 0
 ip access-group 99
!
```

The access list can be verified by using the **show access-list** command, as shown in Example 10-2.

Example 10-2 *The* **show access-list** *Command*

```
router3#show access-list 99
Standard IP access list 99
    deny   192.168.10.100
    permit 192.168.10.0, wildcard bits 0.0.0.255
```

The limitation of standard lists is that the only criteria for denying or permitting packets is a source IP address. For advance filtering, IP-extended access lists are necessary.

IP Extended Access List Configuration

Extended access lists allow filtering based on both source and destination address and some protocol and port number specifications. The access list is configured by using the following global commands:

```
access-list list {permit | deny} protocol source source-mask destination
    destination-mask [operator operand] [established]
```

The argument *list* is an access list number from 100 to 199 or 2000 to 2699 in the expanded range. The argument *protocol* can be **ip**, **tcp**, **udp**, or **icmp**. The argument *source* is the source IP address. The **ip** and **icmp** values do not allow port distinctions. The source IP and mask can be replaced with the keyword **any** if the source can be from any IP address; it replaces 0.0.0.0 255.255.255.255. The argument *destination* is the destination IP address. The source mask and destination mask define the IP address range; they are inverse masks.

Table 10-3 shows all the protocols that can be selected for filtering.

Table 10-3 *Extended Access List IP Protocols*

Keyword	Protocol
0–255	IP protocol number
ahp	Authentication Header Protocol
eigrp	Cisco's EIGRP
esp	Encapsulation Security Protocol
gre	Cisco's GRE tunneling
icmp	Internet Control Message Protocol (ICMP)
igmp	Internet Group Message Protocol (IGMP)
igrp	Cisco's IGRP
ip	Any IP
ipinip	IP in IP tunneling
nos	KA9Q NOS IP over IP tunneling
ospf	OSPF routing protocol
pcp	Payload Compression Protocol (PCP)
pim	PIM
tcp	Transmission Control Protocol (TCP)
udp	User Datagram Protocol (UDP)

With the **tcp** and **udp** keywords, the argument *operator* can be one of the following keywords, within others:

- **lt**—For ports less than the specified number
- **gt**—For ports greater than the specified number
- **eq**—For ports equal to the specified number
- **neq**—For ports not equal to the specified number
- **range**—For all ports within the specified range

The argument *operand* is the decimal number for the specified port. You use the number **161** for Simple Network Management Protocol (SNMP). Some ports have been predefined with keywords. For the TCP protocol, the keyword **established** allows TCP segments with the ACK and RST bits set. For the TCP protocol, the keyword **pop3** allows the Post Office Protocol (POP) on TCP port 110.

In Example 10-3, the router interface is configured outbound to allow Telnet connections to 192.168.1.1 from any source port above 1024, to allow pings, and to deny all other packets. A deny statement does not need to be configured because any access list ends with an implicit deny all.

Example 10-3 *Access List to Permit Telnet and Pings*

```
access-list 100 permit tcp any gt 1024 host 192.168.1.1 eq telnet log
access-list 100 permit icmp any any echo log
access-list 100 permit icmp any any echo-reply log
!
interface ethernet 0
 ip access-group 100 out
!
```

The access list is verified with the **show access-list** command, as shown in Example 10-4.

Example 10-4 show access-list 100 *Command*

```
router3#show access-list 100
Extended IP access list 100
    permit tcp any gt 1024 host 192.168.1.1 eq telnet log
    permit icmp any any echo log
    permit icmp any any echo-reply log
```

IP Named Access List Configuration

Named access lists can be configured to identify a standard or extended access list with a name instead of a number. All functions of IP standard and extended access lists remain the same when using named access lists. Named access lists reduce the confusion of identifying access lists and permit the editing of the access list instead of having to re-create the list when changes are necessary.

Example 10-5 configures the router to perform the same functions as Example 10-3, but uses named access lists. The **ip access-group** *name* {**in** | **out**} command is used on the interface. The named list in Example 10-5 is CCIE. The IP extended named access list is created with the **ip access-list extended** *name* command. The name must match the name configured with the **ip access-group** command.

The named access list in Example 10-5 configures the router to allow Telnet connections to 192.168.1.1 from any source port above 1024, to allow pings, and to deny all other packets outbound on Ethernet 0.

Example 10-5 *IP Named Access List Configuration Example*

```
interface Ethernet0
 ip access-group CCIE out
!
ip access-list extended CCIE
 permit tcp any gt 1024 host 192.168.1.1 eq telnet log
 permit icmp any any echo log
 permit icmp any any echo-reply log
```

The named access list is verified with the **show access-list** command, as shown in Example 10-6; the named access list is called CCIE.

Example 10-6 *Named Access List as Displayed with the* **show access-list** *Command*

```
Router#show access-list
Extended IP access list CCIE
    permit tcp any gt 1024 host 192.168.1.1 eq telnet log
    permit icmp any any echo log
    permit icmp any any echo-reply log
```

Route Manipulation

Several mechanisms exist for manipulating the distribution of routing information within and among routing protocols. This section reviews the methods that control routes.

Route Maps

Route maps are script-like procedures that can filter and modify routing information passed between BGP peers or policy routing, or that are learned through route redistribution. Route maps provide for flexibility, which simplifies access lists. A route map instance consists of MATCH statements that identify routes or their attributes, and SET statements that modify route attributes. A route map name is referenced when applied to a scheme. Example 10-7 shows the options for the **route-map ccie** command. You can use several BGP parameters to match. IP matches also include the route address, next-hop address, or source address.

A route map can consist of multiple instances. When configuring route maps, it is advisable to start with an instance number greater than 1. If a route map has multiple statements (instances), it is advisable to number them with some gaps. Start with number 10, the next instance is 15, then 20, and so on. This allows you to insert new instances (additional route-map statements) without having to reconfigure all instances.

Example 10-7 *Route Map Match Options*

```
ag1.hstttx.lab(config)#route-map ccie permit 10
ag1.hstttx.(config-route-map)#?
Route Map configuration commands:
default         Set a command to its defaults
description     Route-map comment
exit            Exit from route-map configuration mode
help            Description of the interactive help system
match           Match values from routing table
no              Negate a command or set its defaults
set             Set values in destination routing protocol


ag1.hstttx.(config-route-map)#match ?
as-path          Match BGP AS path list
clns             CLNS information
community        Match BGP community list
extcommunity     Match BGP/VPN extended community list
interface        Match first hop interface of route
ip               IP specific information
length           Packet length
metric           Match metric of route
route-type       Match route-type of route
tag              Match tag of route

ag1.hstttx.(config-route-map)#match ip ?
address          Match address of route or match packet
next-hop         Match next-hop address of route
route-source     Match advertising source address of route
```

Example 10-8 shows the **set** options and specific **set ip** options.

Example 10-8 *Route Map Set Options*

```
ag1.hstttx.(config-route-map)#set ?
as-path            Prepend string for a BGP AS-path attribute
automatic-tag      Automatically compute TAG value
clns               OSI summary address
comm-list          set BGP community list (for deletion)
community          BGP community attribute
dampening          Set BGP route flap dampening parameters
default            Set default information
extcommunity       BGP extended community attribute
interface          Output interface
ip                 IP specific information
level              Where to import route
```

continues

Example 10-8 *Route Map Set Options (Continued)*

```
local-preference  BGP local preference path attribute
metric            Metric value for destination routing protocol
metric-type       Type of metric for destination routing protocol
origin            BGP origin code
tag               Tag value for destination routing protocol
traffic-index     BGP traffic classification number for accounting
weight            BGP weight for routing table

ag1.hstttx.(config-route-map)#set ip ?
default          Set default information
df               Set DF bit
next-hop         Next hop address
precedence       Set precedence field
qos-group        Set QOS Group ID
tos              Set type of service field
```

This section does not cover every combination or permutation of route maps but does provide some examples to familiarize you with route maps. Besides examples shown in the Policy-Based Routing (PBR) and Redistribution sections, two examples follow in this section.

Route Map Example 1

Example 10-9 shows a route map that modifies the BGP weight of any route originating in AS 555 from neighbor 1.1.1.1.

Example 10-9 *Route Map to Match as-path 1 and Set Weight to 200*

```
router bgp 100
 neighbor 1.1.1.1 remote-as 200
 neighbor 1.1.1.1 route-map bgpwin in
!
ip as-path access-list 1 permit 555$_
!
route-map bgpwin permit 10
 match as-path 1
 set weight 200
!
route-map bgpwin permit 20
```

Route Map Example 2

Example 10-10 shows a route map that uses access list 50 to filter the networks that are redistributed into EIGRP from RIP, except networks 3.0.0.0 and 4.0.0.0. The implicit deny discards all routes that don't meet the criteria in the first route map statement.

Example 10-10 *Route Map to Filter Routes for Redistribution*

```
router eigrp 100
 redistribute rip route-map rip-to-eigrp
!
access-list 50 permit 3.0.0.0
access-list 50 permit 4.0.0.0
!
route-map rip-to-eigrp permit 10
 match ip address 50
```

PBR

Policy routing can modify the next-hop address or mark packets to receive differential service. Routing is based on destination addresses; PBR is commonly used to modify the next-hop IP address, which is based on the source address. More recently, PBR has been implemented to mark the IP precedence bits in outbound IP packets so that they comply with Quality of Service (QoS) policies.

PBR is configured using route maps. In Example 10-11, the next-hop IP address is modified for all inbound packets on Ethernet 0 that match access list 10 or 20. The next hop is modified to 192.168.100.1 for any packet from network 192.168.1.0/24. The next hop is modified to 192.168.100.2 for any packet from network 192.168.2.0/24. Packets from other sources use the next hop, which is determined by the routing protocol.

Example 10-11 *Policy-Based Routing Configuration Example*

```
access-list 10 permit 192.168.1.0
access-list 20 permit 192.168.2.0
!
interface ethernet 0
 ip policy route-map nexthop
!
route-map nexthop permit 10
 match ip address 10
 set ip next-hop 192.168.100.1
!
route-map nexthop permit 20
 match ip address 20
 set ip next-hop 192.168.100.2
!
route-map nexthop permit 30
```

Distribute Lists

Distribute lists filter the contents, inbound or outbound, of routing updates. They can control which network updates are accepted into the routing table or which network updates are advertised. Two examples follow.

Distribute List Example 1

In Example 10-12, any inbound EIGRP route is checked against access list 1. Any match for 140.175.x.x and 140.176.x.x is placed in the routing table.

Example 10-12 *Distribute List to Filter Inbound Routing Updates*

```
router eigrp 100
 distribute-list 1 in
!
access-list 1 permit 140.175.0.0 0.0.255.255
access-list 1 permit 140.176.0.0 0.0.255.255
```

Distribute List Example 2

In Example 10-13, to prevent any routing loops, only networks 150.175.1.0 and 150.175.2.0 are redistributed into OSPF from EIGRP.

Example 10-13 *Distribute List to Filter Routes for Redistribution*

```
router eigrp 100
 redistribute ospf 200
 distribute-list 1 out ospf 200
!
access-list 1 permit 150.175.1.0 0.0.0.255
access-list 1 permit 150.175.2.0 0.0.0.255
!
router ospf 200
 redistribute eigrp 100
```

Redistribution

The redistribution between routing protocols must be configured carefully to prevent routing loops. Access lists, distribution lists, and route maps can affect redistribute routes; these methods specify (select) routes for redistribution, for setting metrics, or for setting other policies to the routes.

Default Metric

When redistributing routes into RIP, IGRP, and EIGRP, you must also configure the metric of the redistributed routes. The metric can be configured in the redistribution statement or a default metric can be configured. You can also use the command in OSPF. IS-IS does not use the **default-metric** command. The **default-metric** command has the following syntax for IGRP and EIGRP:

```
default-metric bandwidth delay reliability load mtu
```

The possible values for the arguments in the preceding syntax are listed in Table 10-4.

Table 10-4 *Value Ranges for* **default-metric** *Arguments*

Argument	Value Range
bandwidth (in kbps)	1—4,294,967,295
delay (in 10 microsecond units)	0–4,294,967,295
reliability	0–255
load	1–255
mtu	1–4,294,967,295

Example 10-14 shows a simple redistribution of RIP into EIGRP.

Example 10-14 *Default Metric*

```
router eigrp 100
 default-metric 10000 1000 255 1 1500
 redistribute rip
```

EIGRP Redistribution

The CCIE candidate needs to know several things regarding EIGRP redistribution. First, routes redistributed into EIGRP have an administrative distance of 170. Second, if the autonomous systems numbers are the same when redistributing between IGRP and EIGRP, the **redistribution** command is not necessary. In Figure 10-1, Router B is redistributing between EIGRP 100 and IGRP 100.

Figure 10-1 *EIGRP-IGRP Redistribution*

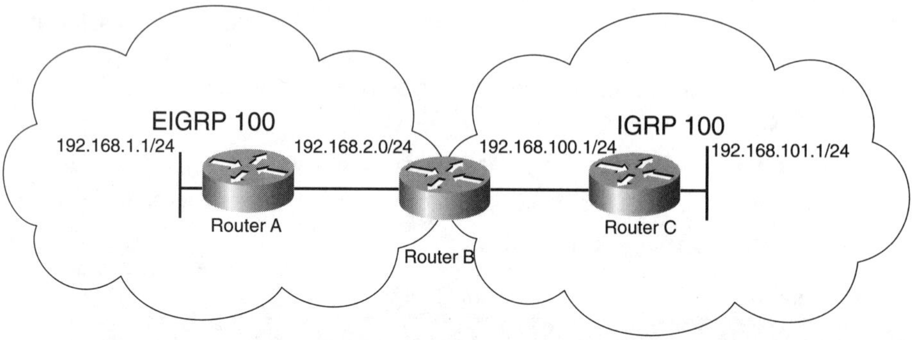

The configuration for the routers in Figure 10-1 is shown in Example 10-15.

Example 10-15 *Configuration of Routers with EIGRP and IGRP Redistribution*

```
hostname routerA
router eigrp 100
 network 192.168.1.0
 network 192.168.2.0

hostname routerB
router eigrp 100
 network 192.168.2.0
!
router igrp 100
 network 192.168.100.0

hostname routerC
router igrp 100
 network 192.168.100.0
 network 192.168.101.0
```

OSPF Redistribution

This section reviews several things that you need to remember when redistributing with OSPF.

When redistributing routes into OSPF, use the **subnets** keyword to permit subnetted routes to be received. If you do not use the keyword, only the major network route is redistributed without any sub-networks. In other words, OSPF performs automatic summarization.

By default, redistributed routes are classified as external Type 2 (E2) in OSPF. The **metric-type** keyword changes the external route to an external Type 1 (E1). For more information on this see Chapter 8, "IP Link-State Routing Protocols."

In Figure 10-2, Router B is configured to perform mutual redistribution between EIGRP and OSPF. In this example, route maps and access lists prevent routing loops. The **subnets** keyword permits any subnetwork to be redistributed into OSPF. This example also shows another use of route maps in redistribution.

Figure 10-2 *OSPF and EIGRP Redistribution*

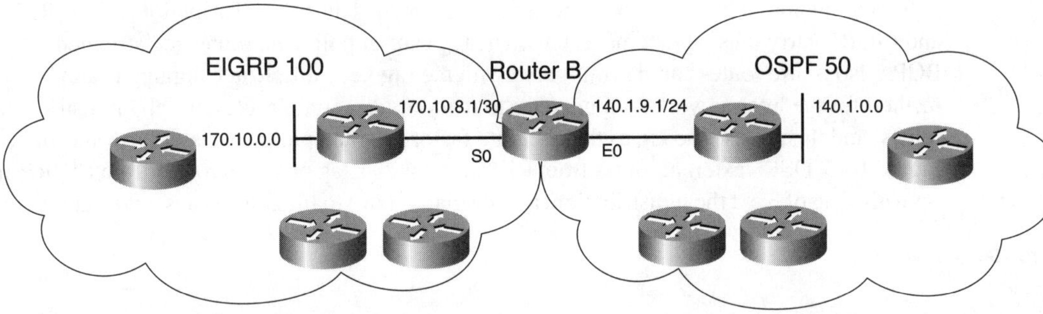

The configuration for Router B is shown in Example 10-16.

Example 10-16 *Redistribution Between OSPF and EIGRP*

```
 hostname routerB
!
interface Ethernet0
 ip address 140.1.9.1 255.255.255.0
!
interface Serial1
 ip address 170.10.8.1 255.255.255.252
!
router eigrp 100
 redistribute ospf 50 route-map OSPFtoEIGRP
 network 170.10.0.0
 default-metric 10000 1000 255 1 1500
!
router ospf 50
 redistribute eigrp 100 subnets route-map EIGRPtoOSPF
 network 140.1.9.0 0.0.0.255 area 0
!
access-list 1 permit 170.10.0.0 0.0.255.255
access-list 2 permit 140.1.0.0 0.0.255.255
!
route-map OSPFtoEIGRP permit 10
 match ip address 2
!
route-map EIGRPtoOSPF permit 10
 match ip address 1
```

Route Tagging

Routes can be configured with an administrative tag that identifies their origination. Routes originated from one external source can be set with a tag of 1, and routes from another external source can be set with a tag of 2. This is useful in identifying routes to be filtered when redistributing into other networks. The tag can be matched during redistribution. OSPF, RIPv2, and EIGRP carry tags on external routes. The tag can set policy on routes redistributed into BGP. Also, static routes can be configured with the **tag** keyword. Route tagging is another method for the internetwork administrator to mark or tag certain routes, usually redistributed routes, and then to use the tag as the deciding factor on route policy decisions. As shown in Figure 10-3, OSPF external routes from RIP are set with a tag of 5, and routes from EIGRP are set with a tag of 3. At the redistribution, a route map is built to filter the routes with a tag set to 5.

Figure 10-3 *Route Tags*

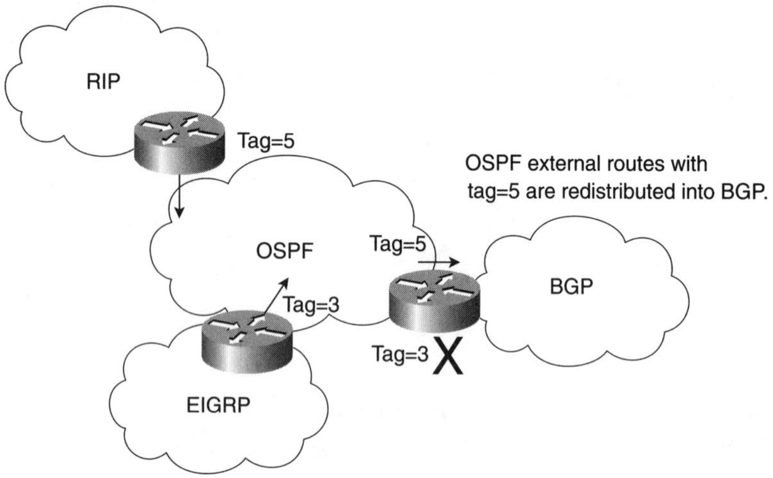

The following commands set a tag value of 5 to routes redistributed from EIGRP into OSPF:

```
router ospf 100
 redistribute eigrp 50 tag 5
```

The following command sets a tag value of 10 to a static route:

```
ip route 1.1.1.1 0.0.0.0 2.2.2.2 200 tag 10
```

The following commands redistribute OSPF routes that have a tag value of 10 and set the BGP local preference to 200:

```
router bgp 1000
 redistribute ospf 100 route-map ospftag2bgp
!
route-map ospftag2bgp permit 10
 match tag 10
 set local-preference 200
route-map ospftag2bgp permit 20
```

IP Multicast Protocols

This section reviews the multicast protocols that are of interest in the CCIE written test.

Multicast Review

With multicast, packets are sent to a multicast group, which is identified with an IP multicast address. Multicast supports the transmission of IP packets from one source to multiple hosts. Packets with unicast addresses are sent to one device and broadcast addresses are sent to all hosts; packets with multicast addresses are sent to a group of hosts.

Multicast Addresses

You use class D addresses from the IPv4 protocol for multicast addressing.

Routing protocols (RIPv2, IS-IS, EIGRP and OSPF) use multicast addresses to speak to their neighbors. For example, OSPF routers use 224.0.0.6 to speak to the designated router (DR) in a multiaccess network. Class D multicast addresses range from 224.0.0.0 to 239.255.255.255. Multicast addresses in the range of 224.0.0.1 to 224.255.255.255 are reserved for network protocols on a multiaccess link. Table 10-5 contains some well-known addresses.

Table 10-5 *Multicast Addresses*

Multicast Address	Description
224.0.0.1	All hosts or all systems on this subnet
224.0.0.2	All multicast routers
224.0.0.4	DVMRP routers
224.0.0.5	All OSPF routers
224.0.0.6	All OSPF DR routers
224.0.0.9	RIPv2 routers
224.0.0.10	EIGRP routers
224.0.0.13	All PIM routers
224.0.0.39	Route Processor (RP)-Announce
224.0.0.40	RP-Discovery

Administrative Scoped Multicast Addresses

Per RFC 2365, multicast addresses 239.000.000.000–239.255.255.255 are reserved for administratively scoped functions. This RFC defines administrative group addresses for IPv4 that source and receivers for multicast applications do not use. Also, the administrative scoped addresses do not cross administrative boundaries of multicast networks.

Layer-3 to Layer-2 Mapping

Multicast-aware Ethernet, Token Ring, and Fiber Distributed Data Interface (FDDI) network interface cards use the reserved IEEE 802 address 0100.5e00.0000 for multicast addresses at the MAC layer. In the high order byte, 0x01, the low order bit set to 1. This is the I/G bit and signifies whether the address is an individual address (0) or a group address (1). This bit is set to 1 for multicast addresses.

Ethernet interfaces map the lower 23 bits of the IP multicast address to the lower 23 bits of the MAC 0100.5e00.0000. As an example, the IP multicast address 224.0.0.2 is mapped to the MAC layer as 0100.5e00.0002. Figure 10-4 shows another example that looks at the bits of multicast IP 236.130.44.56. The IP address in hexadecimal is EC:82:2C:38. The lower 23 bits are mapped into the lower 23 bits of the base Multicast MAC to produce the multicast MAC address of 01:00:5E:02:2C:38.

Figure 10-4 *Mapping of Multicast IP Addressing to MAC Addresses*

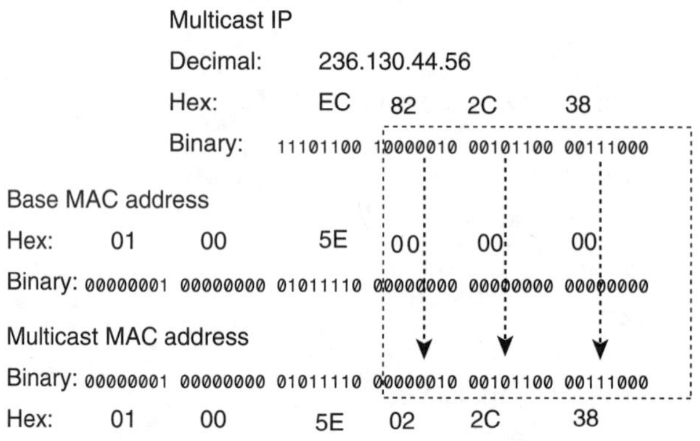

IGMP

IGMP is the protocol that multicast implementations use between end hosts and the local router. IGMP version 2 (IGMPv2) is described in RFC 2236. The first version of IGMP is described in RFC 1112.

IP hosts use IGMP to report their multicast group memberships to routers. IGMP messages use IP protocol number 2. IGMP messages are limited to the local interface and are not routed.

IGMPv1

The first RFC describing IGMP (RFC 1112) was written in 1989. It describes the host extension of multicasting. IGMPv1 protocol provides simple message types for communication between hosts and routers. These messages are as follows:

- **Membership query—**Sent by the host to request to join a multicast group
- **Membership report—**Sent by the router to check if hosts are still in multicast groups in the segment

The problem with IGMPv1 is the latency involved with a host leaving a group. With IGMPv1, the router periodically sends out membership reports, and a host waits for the membership report message to leave a group.

IGMPv2

IGMPv2 provides improvement over IGMPv1 by allowing faster termination or leaving of multicast groups.

IGMPv2 includes the following three message types, plus one for backward compatibility:

- **Membership query**—Sent to indicate that a host wants to join a group.
- **Version 2 membership report**—Message sent to the group address with the multicast group members (IP addresses). The message is sent to verify that hosts are still in multicast groups on the segment.
- **Leave group**—Sent by the hosts to indicate that a host is leaving a group, sent to destination 224.0.0.2. The message is sent without having to wait for the IGMPv2 membership report message.
- **Version 1 membership report**—For backward compatibility with IGMPv1 hosts.

IGMP is enabled on an interface when the multicast routing protocol is enabled, such as PIM. The version of IGMP can be configured for the interface with the **ip igmp version** [**1** | **2**] command. The known multicast groups on a router can be queried with the **show ip igmp groups** command.

IGMPv2 Designated Querier

Multicast querier routers send host membership query messages to discover which multicast groups have members on the router's attached networks. Hosts respond with IGMP report messages that indicate that the host wants to become a member of the group. Host-query messages are addressed to the all-hosts multicast group, which has the address 224.0.0.1, and have an IP TTL value of 1.

On segments with more than one multicast routers, normally one becomes the designated querier. The designated querier sends the IGMP membership query messages on the segment. The designated querier is the router with the lowest IP address on the segment that is running a multicast routing protocol.

CGMP

CGMP is a Cisco proprietary protocol that controls multicast traffic at Layer 2. Because a Layer-2 switch is not aware of Layer-3 IGMP messages, it cannot restrain multicast packets from being sent to all ports.

As shown in Figure 10-5, with CGMP, the LAN switch can speak with the IGMP router to find out the MAC addresses of the hosts that want to receive the multicast packets. With CGMP, switches distribute multicast sessions to the switch ports that have group members.

Figure 10-5 *CGMP*

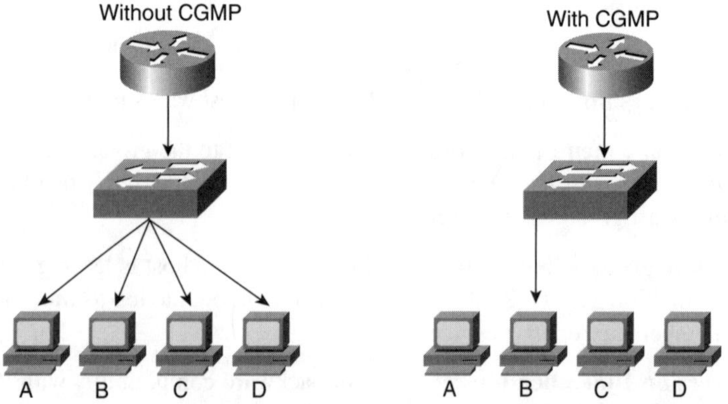

When a router receives an IGMP report, it processes the report and then sends a CGMP message to the switch. The switch can then forward the multicast messages to the port with the host that is receiving the multicast traffic. CGMP Fast-Leave Processing allows the switch to detect IGMPv2 leave messages that are sent by hosts on any of the supervisor engine module ports. When the IGMPv2 leave message is sent, the switch can then disable multicast for the port.

You enable CGMP on the router with the **ip cgmp** command. On the switch, you use the **set cgmp enable** command.

IGMP Snooping

IGMP Snooping is another method for switches to control multicast traffic at Layer 2. It listens to IGMP messages between the hosts and routers. If a host sends an IGMP query message to the router, the switch adds the host to the multicast group and permits that port to receive multicast traffic. The port is removed from multicast traffic if an IGMP leave message is sent from the host to the router. The disadvantage of IGMP Snooping is that it must listen to every IGMP control message, which can impact the switch's CPU use.

The command to enable IGMP Snooping on a router interface is **ip igmp snooping**. You enable IGMP Snooping on a switch with the **set igmp enable** command.

Sparse Versus Dense Multicast Routing Protocols

IP multicast traffic for a particular (source, destination group) pair is transmitted from the source to the receivers through a spanning tree that connects all the hosts in the group. Each host can register as a particular member of selected multicast groups through the use of IGMP. Routers keep track of these groups dynamically and build distribution trees that chart paths from each sender to all receivers. IP multicast routing protocols follow two approaches.

The first approach is based on the assumption that the multicast group members are densely distributed throughout the network, (many of the subnets contain at least one group member) and that bandwidth is plentiful. The approach with dense multicast routing protocols is to flood the traffic throughout the network, and then, at the request of receiving routers, stop the flow of traffic on branches of the network that have no members of the multicast group. Multicast routing protocols that follow this technique of flooding the network include DVMRP, Multicast Open Shortest Path First (MOSPF), and Protocol Independent Multicast-Dense Mode (PIM-DM). MOSPF is not a CCIE written test topic and is not discussed in this guide.

The second approach to multicast routing assumes that multicast group members are sparsely distributed throughout the network and that bandwidth is not necessarily widely available. Sparse mode does not imply that the group has few members—just that they are widely dispersed. The approach with sparse multicast routing protocols is to not send traffic until it is requested by the receiving routers or hosts. Multicast routing protocols of this type are Core Based Trees (CBT) and Protocol Independent Multicast-Sparse Mode (PIM-SM). CBT is not a CCIE written test topic and is not discussed in this guide.

Multicast Source and Shared Trees

Multicast distribution trees control the path multicast packets take to the destination hosts. Two types of distribution trees exist: source and shared.

With source trees, the tree roots from the source of the multicast group and then expands throughout the network in spanning-tree fashion to the destination hosts. Source trees are also called shortest path trees (SPT) because they create best paths without having to go through a rendezvous point. The drawback is that all routers through the path must use memory resources to maintain a list of all multicast groups. PIM-Dense Mode uses a source tree. Its multicast entries are in the (S,G) format, where S is the IP address of the source, and G is the IP address of the multicast group.

Shared trees create the root of the distribution tree somewhere between the source and the receivers of the network. The root is called the rendezvous point (RP). The tree is created from the RP in spanning-tree fashion with no loops. The advantage of shared trees is that they reduce the memory requirements of routers in the multicast network. The drawback is that the multicast packets might not take the best paths to the receivers because they need to pass through the RP. The RP router also has high memory requirements to implement its functions. PIM-Sparse mode (PIM-SM) uses a RP. Its multicast entries are in the (*,G) format. You do not use the S (source) because the distribution tree is not from the source.

PIM

PIM comes in *sparse mode (PIM-SM)* and *dense mode (PIM-DM)*. As the names imply, the first operates in sparse mode and the second in dense mode.

PIM-DM uses a technique known as *reverse path forwarding (RPF)*. When the router receives a packet, it forwards it out all other interfaces, which allows the data stream to reach all segments. If no hosts are members of a multicast group on any of the router's attached or downstream subnets, the router sends a prune message up the distribution tree to inform the upstream router to not send packets for the multicast group. So, the analogy for PIM-DM is the push method for sending junk mail, and you have to tell them to stop sending it.

Dense Mode Configuration

Cisco recommends configuring PIM with the **sparse-dense-mode** keyword. If the multicast group is in dense mode, the interface is treated as dense. Example 10-17 shows the simple configuration of PIM.

Example 10-17 *Configuration of PIM*

```
ip multicast-routing
!
interface ethernet 0
 ip address x
 ip pim sparse-dense-mode
!
interface ethernet 1
 ip address y
 ip pim sparse-dense-mode
```

If the requirement exists to strictly run in dense mode, the configuration is as shown in Example 10-18. The only difference is that you use the **dense-mode** keyword instead of **sparse-dense-mode**.

Example 10-18 *Configuration of PIM in Dense Mode*

```
ip multicast-routing
!
interface ethernet 0
 ip address x
 ip pim dense-mode
!
interface ethernet 1
 ip address y
 ip pim dense-mode
```

PIM Sparse Mode

PIM-SM is defined in RFC 2362 (experimental). PIM-SM assumes that no hosts want to receive multicast traffic unless specifically requested. In PIM-SM, a router is selected as the *rendezvous point (RP)*. The RP has the task of gathering the information of senders and making the information available to receivers. Routers with receivers have to register with the RP. Routers register as traffic receivers, not end host systems. The end host systems still request multicast group membership by using IGMP with their local routers.

Joining PIM-SM

With PIM-SM, designated routers (DR) on end segments receive IGMP query messages from hosts wanting to join a multicast group (*,G). The router checks to see if it is already receiving the group for another interface. If it is receiving the group, the new interface is added to the table and membership reports are sent periodically on the new interface.

If the multicast (*,G) group is not in the multicast table, the interface is added to the multicast table and the router sends a join message to the RP with multicast address 224.0.0.13 requesting the multicast group.

Pruning PIM-SM

When a PIM-SM does not have any more multicast receiving hosts or receiving routers out any of its interfaces, it sends a prune message to the RP. The prune message includes the (*,G) group to be pruned or removed.

PIM Designated Router

A designated router is selected in multiaccess segments running PIM. The PIM DR is responsible for sending join, prune, and register messages to the RP. The PIM router with the highest IP address is selected as the DR.

Multicast Routing Table

The multicast routing (Mroute) table is shown with the **show ip mroute** command. It lists the multicast (*,G) groups for PIM-SM, the RP, and the incoming and outgoing interfaces for the group. Example 10-19 shows the output for the command.

Example 10-19 **show ip mroute** *Command*

```
router# show ip mroute 237.44.55.100
IP Multicast Routing Table
Flags: D - Dense, S - Sparse, C - Connected, L - Local, P - Pruned
       R - RP-bit set, F - Register flag, T - SPT-bit set
Timers: Uptime/Expires

(*, 237.44.55.100), 00:07:40/0:01:43, RP 198.168.75.1, flags: S
   Incoming interface: Serial0.2, RPF neighbor 198.168.2.10
   Outgoing interface list:
     Serial0.3, Forward state, Sparse mode, uptime 00:07:40, expires 0:01:04
```

Sparse Mode Configuration

As mentioned in the Dense Mode Configuration section, Cisco recommends using the **sparse-dense-mode** keyword when running PIM. If the multicast group is running in sparse-mode (that is, an RP is known), the interface is treated as sparse-mode. Example 10-20 shows a simple configuration that you can use on all routers running PIM. The **ip pim rp-address** command uses the IP address of the RP to tell the router who the RP is.

Example 10-20 *Configuration of PIM for Sparse Mode*

```
ip multicast-routing
!
interface ethernet 0
 ip address x
 ip pim sparse-dense-mode
!
interface ethernet 1
 ip address y
 ip pim sparse-dense-mode
!
ip pim rp-address address-of-RP
```

Auto-RP

Another method of configuring the RP for the network is to have the RP announce its services to the PIM network. This is called *Auto-RP*. Candidate RPs send their announcements to RP mapping agents with multicast address 224.0.1.39. RP mapping agents are also configured. In smaller networks, the RP can be the mapping agent. Configured RP mapping agents listen to the announcements. The RP mapping agent then selects the RP for a group, based on the highest

IP address of all the candidate-RPs. The RP mapping agents then send RP-discovery messages to the rest of the PIM-SM routers in the internetwork, with the selected RP to group mappings.

The configuration of a router as the RP and RP mapping agent is shown in Example 10-21. Candidate RPs are configured with the **ip pim send-rp-announce** command. Mapping agents are configured with the **ip pim send-rp-discovery** command.

Example 10-21 *Configuration of the RP in PIM-SM*

```
ip multicast-routing
ip pim send-rp-announce ethernet0 scope 3
ip pim send-rp-discovery scope 3
!
interface ethernet 0
 ip address x
 ip pim sparse-dense-mode
!
interface ethernet 1
 ip address y
 ip pim sparse-dense-mode
```

All other routers use the simple configuration, as shown in Example 10-22.

Example 10-22 *Configuration of Non-RP Routers*

```
ip multicast-routing
!
interface ethernet 0
 ip address x
 ip pim sparse-dense-mode
!
interface ethernet 1
 ip address y
 ip pim sparse-dense-mode
```

PIMv2 Bootstrap Router (BSR)

Instead of Auto-RP, a PIMv2 Bootstrap Router (BSR) can be configured to automatically select an RP for the network. BSR is described in the RFC for PIM version 2, RFC 2362. With BSR, you configure BSR candidates (C-BSRs) with priorities from 0 to 255 and a BSR address. C-BSRs exchange bootstrap messages. Bootstrap messages are sent to multicast IP 224.0.0.13 (All PIM routers). If a C-BSR receives a bootstrap message, it compares it with its own. The largest priority C-BSR is selected as the BSR.

Candidate BSRs are configured with the following command:

ip pim *bsr-candidate interface hash-mask-len pref*

After the BSR is selected for the network, it collects a list of candidate RPs. The BSR selects RP to group mappings, which is called the RP-set, and distributes the selected RPs using bootstrap messages sent to 224.0.0.13.

DVMRP

DVMRP is described in RFC 1075. It is the primary multicast routing protocol in the Multicast Backbone (MBONE). The research community uses MBONE.

DVMRP operates in dense mode by having routers send a copy of a multicast packet out all paths. Routers that receive the multicast packets send prune messages back to their upstream neighbor router to stop a data stream if no downstream receivers of the multicast group exist (either receiving routers or hosts on connected segments). DVMRP implements its own unicast routing protocol, similar to RIP, based on hop counts. DVMRP has been known not to scale well. Cisco's support of DVMRP is partial; usually DVMRP networks are implemented on UNIX machines that are running the mrouted process. You usually configure a DVMRP tunnel to connect to the DVMRP network.

(Distance Vector Multicast Routing Protocol)

DVMRP Tunnel Configuration

The commands to create a DVMRP tunnel to a DVMRP router are as follows:

```
interface tunnel 0
 ip unnumbered any pim interface
 tunnel source address
 tunnel destination address
 tunnel mode dvmrp
 ip pim sparse-dense-mode
```

References Used

The following resources were used to create this chapter:

Routing TCP/IP, Volume II, Jeff Doyle, Cisco Press, 2001, (ISBN 1-57870-089-2)

RFC 1112, "Host Extensions for IP Multicasting," S.E. Deering

RFC 2362 (Experimental), "Protocol Independent Multicast-Sparse Mode (PIM-SM): Protocol Specification," D. Estrin, D. Farinacci, A. Helmy, D. Thaler, S. Deering, M. Handley, V. Jacobson, C. Liu, P. Sharma, L. Wei

RFC 2365, "Administratively Scoped IP Multicast," D. Meyer
Internet Protocol (IP) Multicast Technology Overview www.cisco.com/warp/public/cc/pd/iosw/tech/ipmu_ov.htm

Foundation Summary

The Foundation Summary is a condensed collection of material that provides a convenient review of key concepts in this chapter. If you are already comfortable with the topics in this chapter, this summary will help you recall a few details. If you just read the Foundation Topics section, this review should help solidify some key facts. If you are doing your final preparation before the exam, these materials are a convenient way to review the day before the exam.

Table 10-6 *Administrative Distances*

IP Route	Administrative Distance
Connected interface	0
Static route directed to a connected interface	0
Static route directed to an IP address	1
EIGRP summary route	5
External BGP route	20
Internal EIGRP route	90
IGRP route	100
OSPF route	110
IS-IS route	115
RIP route	120
EGP route	140
External EIGRP route	170
Internal BGP route	200
Route of unknown origin	255

Table 10-7 *Route Manipulation*

Method	Description
Route maps	Sets parameters for the matched items.
Policy routing	Changes the next-hop route based on source address.
Distribution list	Filters the routes in or out from a routing process.
Redistribution	Brings in routes from one routing protocol to another; access lists and route maps filter the routes.
Route tag	Marker configured at redistribution that can filter routes.

Table 10-8 *Reserved Multicast Addresses*

Multicast Address	Description
224.0.0.1	All hosts or all systems on this subnet
224.0.0.2	All multicast routers
224.0.0.4	DVMRP routers
224.0.0.5	All OSPF routers
224.0.0.6	All OSPF DR routers
224.0.0.9	RIPv2 routers
224.0.0.10	EIGRP routers
224.0.0.13	All PIM routers
224.0.0.39	RP-Announce
224.0.0.40	RP-Discovery

Table 10-9 *Multicast Protocols*

Protocol	Description
IGMP	Internet Group Management Protocol—IP hosts use to report their multicast group memberships to routers
CGMP	Cisco Group Management Protocol—Switches use to prune ports that do not have multicast members
PIM-SM	Protocol Independent Multicast-Sparse Mode—Uses an RP to determine how to distribute multicast streams
PIM-DM	Protocol Independent Multicast-Dense Mode—Sends packets out all interfaces
DVMRP	Distance Vector Multicast Routing Protocol —Multicast protocol that MBONE uses

Q & A

The Q & A questions are more difficult than what you can expect on the actual exam. The questions do not attempt to cover more breadth or depth than the exam; however, they are designed to make sure that you retain the material. Rather than allowing you to derive the answer from clues hidden inside the question itself, these questions challenge your understanding and recall of the subject. Questions from the "Do I Know This Already?" quiz are repeated here to ensure that you have mastered the chapter's topic areas. A strong understanding of the answers to these questions will help you on the CCIE written exam. As an additional study aide, use the CD-ROM provided with this book to take simulated exams.

Select the best answer. Answers to these questions are in the Appendix, "Answers to Quiz Questions."

1 What is the administrative distance of EIGRP external routes?

a. 90

b. 100

c. 110

d. 170

2 Which protocol do hosts use to join a multicast group?

a. CGMP

b. DVMRP

c. PIM-SM

d. IGMP

3 When redistributing EIGRP routes into RIP, how do the bandwidth and delay metrics get converted?

a. RIP assigns the bandwidth and delay metrics with the **default-metric** command.

b. The EIGRP metrics do not get converted; RIP assigns a default hop count metric as configured by the **default-metric** command.

c. RIP uses the bandwidth metric and discards the delay.

d. RIP uses the delay metric and discards the bandwidth.

4 What does the multicast address 224.0.0.2 represent?

a. All hosts on the subnet

b. All routers on the subnet

c. All OSPF routers on the network

d. All PIM routers on the network

5 When an EIGRP route is redistributed into OSPF, what is the default administrative distance of the resulting OSPF route in the IP routing table?

a. 90

b. 100

c. 110

d. 170

6 A router is running two routing protocols: OSPF and EIGRP. Both protocols internally learn of the route 10.1.1.4/24. Which route is added to the routing table?

a. The EIGRP route.

b. The OSPF route.

c. Both added with equal load balancing.

d. Both added with unequal load balancing.

7 Which access list denies Telnet and ping and permits everything else?

a.

```
access-list 99 deny tcp any  any eq echo log
access-list 99 deny tcp any any telnet eq telnet
access-list 99 permit ip any any
```

b.

```
access-list 100 deny icmp any any echo log
access-list 100 deny tcp any any telnet
```

c.

```
access-list 100 deny icmp any any echo log
access-list 100 deny icmp any any echo-reply
access-list 100 deny tcp any any eq telnet
access-list 100 permit ip any any
```

d.

```
access-list 99 deny icmp any any echo log
access-list 99 deny icmp any any echo-reply
access-list 99 deny tcp any any eq telnet
access-list 99 permit ip any any
```

8 In an internetwork of 50 routers running EIGRP, you need to filter the networks received by one spoke router. What can you use?

a. Use an access list and apply it to the inbound interface with the **ip access-group** command.

b. Redistribute the routes into OSPF with a route map.

c. Use a distribute list under the EIGRP process with an access list to filter the networks.

d. Change the administrative distance of the router.

9 Which access list permits all hosts in network 192.172.100.0/28?

a. access-list 100 permit 192.172.100.0 0.0.0.31.

b. access-list 10 permit 192.172.100.0 255.255.255.240.

c. access-list 10 permit 192.172.100.0 0.0.0.0.

d. access-list 10 permit ip 192.172.100.0 0.0.0.31.

10 What does PIM stand for?

a. Protocol Inbound Multicast

b. Protocol Independent Multicast

c. Protocol Independent Management

d. Password Independent Multicast

11 In an access list command, the keyword **any** replaces which network/mask pair?

a. 0.0.0.0 0.0.0.0

b. 0.0.0.0 255.255.255.255

c. 255.255.255.255 255.255.255.255

d. 255.255.255.255 0.0.0.0

12 OSPF external routes can be assigned an administrative distance of 120 with which OSPF subcommand?

a. **distance 120**

b. **distance external 120**

c. **ospf distance 120**

d. **distance ospf-external 120**

13 When redistributing between EIGRP and IGRP on the same router, which statement is correct?

a. If the AS numbers are the same, you use the **redistribute** command.

b. If the AS numbers are the same, you do not use the **redistribute** command.

c. If the AS numbers are different, you use the **redistribute** command.

d. Both b and c are correct.

14 A router has network 140.175.0.0/16 in its RIP database table and an IBGP learned route in its BGP table. Which one does the router include in the IP routing table?

a. The RIP route

b. The IBGP route

c. Both with equal load balancing because the metrics are the same

d. Both with unequal load balancing because the metrics are different

15 What is the default administrative distance of OSPF?

a. 90

b. 110

c. 115

d. 120

16 If applied to an interface, what does the following access list permit?

```
access-list 101 permit udp any host 10.10.10.10 eq snmp log
```

a. Permits host 10.10.10.10 to access any network with SNMP

b. Permits any host to access host 10.10.10.10 with SNMP, and logs every match; denies all other traffic

c. Permits the SNMP server to access all devices through UDP

d. Permits SNMP traps to be sent to 10.10.10.10 from any host; denies all other traffic

17 In multicast routing (PIM-SM), which device has the task of gathering the information of senders and making the information available to other PIM routers?

a. Sending host

b. Router using IGMP

c. RP

d. Mapping agent

18 What happens to the metrics when redistributing from IGRP to EIGRP?

a. They do not change.

b. They change by a factor of 100.

c. They change by a factor of 256.

d. They change to hop count.

19 Which protocol controls multicast traffic in a switched LAN environment?

a. IGMP

b. CGMP

c. IGMP Snooping

d. b and c

20 Which issues must be addressed when redistributing OSPF into IGRP at multiple locations?

a. Default metric

b. Variable length subnet masks

c. Route loops

d. All of the above

21 Which route manipulation method changes the IP next hop based on the source address of a packet?

a. Distribution list

b. Policy routing

c. Static routing

d. Redistribution

22 Which commands change the next hop for hosts in subnetwork 10.1.1.128/28?

a.

```
interface e 0
 ip policy route-map gonext
!
route-map gonext permit 20
 match ip address 50
 set ip next-hop 1.1.1.1
!
route-map gonext permit 25
!
access-list 20 permit 10.1.1.128 0.0.0.15
```

b.

```
interface e 0
 ip policy route-map gonext
!
route-map gonext permit 20
 match ip address 50
 set ip next-hop 1.1.1.1
!
route-map gonext permit 30
!
access-list 30 permit 10.1.1.128 0.0.0.15
```

c.

```
interface e 0
 ip policy route-map gonext
!
route-map gonext permit 20
 match ip address 50
 set ip next-hop 1.1.1.1
!
route-map gonext permit 25
!
access-list 50 permit 10.1.1.128 0.0.0.15
```

d.

```
interface e 0
 ip policy route-map gonext
!
route-map gonext permit 20
 match ip address 50
 set ip next-hop 1.1.1.1
!
route-map gonext permit 25
!
access-list 50 permit 10.1.1.128 0.0.0.255
```

23 Which configuration redistributes all subnetworks from EIGRP into OSPF?

a.

```
router ospf 100
 redistribute eigrp 100 route-map eigrp2ospf
!
route-map eigrp2ospf permit 20
 match ip address 1
 set permit subnets
!
access-list 1 permit 0.0.0.0 255.255.255.255
```

```
router ospf 100
 redistribute eigrp 100 subnets
```

b.

```
router ospf 100
 redistribute eigrp 100 route-map eigrp2ospf subnets
!
route-map eigrp2ospf deny 20
 match ip address 1
 set permit subnets
!
access-list 1 permit 0.0.0.0 255.255.255.255
```

c.

```
router ospf 100
 redistribute eigrp 100 route-map eigrp2ospf
!
route-map eigrp2ospf permit 20
 match ip address 1
 set permit subnets
!
access-list 1 deny 0.0.0.0 255.255.255.255
```

24 What methods allow a PIM network to automatically determine the RP for multicast groups?

a. Auto-RP

b. BSR

c. Both a and b

d. None of the above

25 What is the MAC address of multicast IP 224.0.0.5?

a. 0100.5e00.2242.

b. 0100.5e00.0005.

c. 0c00.5e00.0005.

d. Not enough information is given.

Scenario

Use the following configuration to answer the scenario questions:

```
router bgp 200
 redistribute ospf 100 route-map bgpospf
!
route-map bgpospf permit 10
 match tag 5
 set metric 100
!
route-map bgpospf permit 15
 match tag 6
 set metric 200
```

1 How are the routes being manipulated?

a. OSPF 100 routes are redistributed into BGP 200; OSPF routes with a tag of 5 or 6 are set with a MED of 100 and 200, respectively.

b. OSPF 100 routes are redistributed into BGP 200; a tag of 5 or 6 and metrics are set for the BGP routes.

c. BGP is redistributed into OSPF; tag values and metrics are set.

d. b and c.

2 What happens to OSPF routes with a tag of 7?

a. They are redistributed.

b. They are not redistributed.

c. A metric of 100 is set.

d. A tag of 5 is set.

This chapter covers the following topics needed to master the CCIE Routing and Switching (R&S) written exam:

- **Queuing algorithms**—First-in, first-out (FIFO), priority queuing (PQ), custom queuing (CQ), and weighted fair queuing (WFQ)
- **Other Quality of Service (QoS) and traffic management mechanisms**—Generic and Frame Relay traffic shaping, compression, Resource Reservation Protocol (RSVP), Multiprotocol Label Switching (MPLS), weighted random early detection (WRED), Weighted Round Robin (WRR), and load balancing

CHAPTER 11

Traffic Management

This chapter covers methods that manage the performance and QoS of traffic.

"Do I Know This Already?" Quiz

The purpose of this assessment quiz is to help you determine how to spend your limited study time. If you can answer most or all of these questions, you might want to skim the Foundation Topics section and return to it later as necessary. Review the Foundation Summary section and answer the questions at the end of the chapter to ensure that you have a strong grasp of the material covered. If you intend to read the entire chapter, you do not need to answer these questions now. If you find these assessment questions difficult, read through the entire Foundation Topics section and review it until you feel comfortable with your ability to answer all of the "Q & A" questions at the end of the chapter. These questions are repeated at the end of the chapter with additional questions to test your mastery of the material.

Select the best answer. Answers to these questions are in the Appendix, "Answers to Quiz Questions."

1 Which queuing scheme can be used to SNA traffic before servicing other traffic types?

a. FIFO

b. CQ

c. PQ

d. CBWFQ

2 Which protocol permits hosts to request quality of service parameters from network resources?

a. MPLS

b. RSVP

c. CAR

d. RTP

3 Which mechanism drops packets to prevent congestion?

a. CQ

b. WRED

c. WFQ

d. DPack

4 Which scheme is configured with the **traffic-shape** IOS command?

a. MPLS

b. CAR

c. CRTP

d. GTS

5 Which routing protocol permits load balancing over unequal-cost paths?

a. EIGRP

b. OSPF

c. RIP

d. IS-IS

6 If EIGRP has ten paths to a destination, how many can be used by default?

a. Four

b. Six

c. Eight, if all are equal-cost paths

d. Ten, if all are unequal-cost paths

7 What is the standards-based Frame Relay compression method?

a. FRF.5

b. FRF.9

c. FRF.11

d. FRF.12

8 Which mechanism inserts a 32-bit field between the Layer-2 header and Layer-3 header to provide high-speed switching?

a. RSVP

b. FRTS

c. MPLS

d. Tunnel switching

9 After the priority queues have been defined, which command enables priority queuing on an interface?

a. **priority-group**

b. **priority-list**

c. **ip priority-group**

d. **priority-list 1 queue-byte 1000**

10 Stacker is based on which compression algorithm?

a. Ford-Fergerson

b. Lempel-Ziv

c. Bruno-Cicala

d. SPF

Foundation Topics

Queuing Algorithms

A CCIE candidate must be familiar with Cisco router interface queuing methods. Queuing mechanisms help to prioritize traffic when interfaces become congested. This section covers FIFO, PQ, CQ, and WFQ.

FIFO

This queuing method does not implement any sophisticated schemes. With FIFO, packets are sent out in the order that they are received. No prioritization occurs for any traffic. To check an interface's queuing method, use the **show interface** command. Next, check the queuing strategy output. The router output in Example 11-1 shows an Ethernet interface using FIFO.

Example 11-1 *Interface Using FIFO Queuing*

```
R4#show interface
Ethernet0 is up, line protocol is up
  Hardware is PQUICC Ethernet, address is 0010.7b1b.6f9c (bia 0010.7b1b.6f9c)
  MTU 1500 bytes, BW 10000 Kbit, DLY 1000 usec,
     reliability 255/255, txload 1/255, rxload 1/255
  Encapsulation ARPA, loopback not set
  ARP type: ARPA, ARP Timeout 04:00:00
  Last input 00:00:03, output 00:00:05, output hang never
  Last clearing of "show interface" counters never
  Queueing strategy: fifo
  Output queue 0/40, 0 drops; input queue 0/75, 0 drops
  5 minute input rate 0 bits/sec, 0 packets/sec
  5 minute output rate 0 bits/sec, 0 packets/sec
     21536 packets input, 5601684 bytes, 0 no buffer
     Received 21536 broadcasts, 0 runts, 0 giants, 0 throttles
     0 input errors, 0 CRC, 0 frame, 0 overrun, 0 ignored
     0 input packets with dribble condition detected
     16262 packets output, 3818070 bytes, 0 underruns
     0 output errors, 0 collisions, 1 interface resets
     0 babbles, 0 late collision, 1 deferred
     0 lost carrier, 0 no carrier
     0 output buffer failures, 0 output buffers swapped out
```

PQ

PQ provides a mechanism to prioritize traffic by using four queues. The four queues are designated as high, medium, normal, and low, as shown in Figure 11-1. Traffic can be assigned to the queues based on protocol, port number, or other criteria. As traffic arrives to the router, it is assigned to one of the four output queues. Packets with a higher priority are transmitted first. If there is traffic in the high and normal queues, the high priority traffic is transmitted first and then the normal queue traffic. Traffic in the medium, normal, and low queues is not transmitted until all traffic in the high queue is sent. PQ gives mission-critical traffic the highest priority. One drawback is the potential for queue starvation as lower priority traffic waits to be serviced.

Figure 11-1 *PQs*

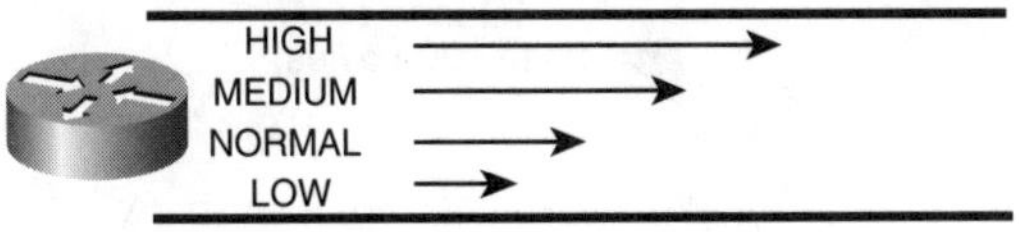

Configuring PQ

PQ is configured by specifying the priority queue levels for different protocols by using the **priority-list** command. A default priority level is also configured for those protocols or ports that do not match access-list statements. The priority list is then applied to an interface with the **priority-group** command. Example 11-2 shows a sample configuration of PQ.

Example 11-2 *Configuration of PQ*

```
interfaces serial 0
 priority-group 1
!
priority-list 1 protocol dlsw high
priority-list 1 protocol ip medium list 99
priority-list 1 default normal
priority-list 1 protocol cdp low
!
access-list 99 permit 192.168.1.0 0.0.0.255
```

CQ

CQ uses a different approach than PQ for prioritizing traffic. Similar to PQ, traffic can be assigned to various queues based on protocol, port number, or other criteria. However, CQ allows traffic to be assigned to one of 16 queues that are dequeued in a round-robin fashion. Priority is established by defining how many bytes can be transmitted from each queue in turn. This is equivalent to allocating bandwidth to a protocol. Up to 16 queues can be configured. The transmission size of each queue is specified in bytes. After the configured byte-count of a queue is transmitted, the router sends the current packet and moves on to the next queue.

When the transmission window size is reached by transmitting the appropriate number of frames from a queue, the next queue is dequeued, as shown in Figure 11-2. Traffic assigned to queue 1 is sent (up to 2000 bytes), then traffic assigned to queue 2 (up to 700 bytes), then traffic assigned to queue 3 (up to 1200 bytes), and then it round-robins to queue 1. CQ is fairer than PQ, although PQ is more powerful for prioritizing mission-critical protocol.

Figure 11-2 *CQs*

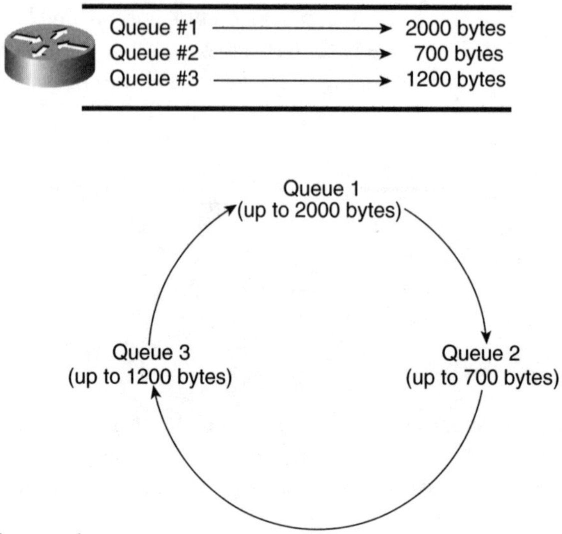

Configuring CQ

CQ is configured by assigning protocols or port numbers to a queue in the queue list by using the **queue-list** command. A byte count is applied to each queue. Configure the queue list for the interface by using the **custom-queue-list** command.

The syntax of the **queue-list** command to assign a protocol to a queue number is as follows:

```
queue-list list-number protocol protocol-name queue-number
    queue-keyword keyword-value
```

The list number is from 1 to 16. The queue number is from 0 to 16.

The syntax of the **queue-list** command to configure the number of bytes per queue is as follows:

```
queue-list list-number queue queue-number byte-count num-bytes
```

The *num-bytes* is the size of bytes from 1 to 16777215.

Example 11-3 shows a sample configuration of CQ by using four queues.

Example 11-3 *Configuration of CQ*

```
interface s 0
 custom-queue-list 1
!
queue-list 1 protocol dlsw 1
queue-list 1 protocol ip 2 list 99
queue-list 1 protocol cdp 3
queue-list 1 default 4
```

Example 11-3 *Configuration of CQ (Continued)*

```
!
queue-list 1 queue 1 byte-count 3000
queue-list 1 queue 2 byte-count 2000
queue-list 1 queue 3 byte-count 300
queue-list 1 queue 4 byte-count 1500
!
access-list 99 permit 192.168.1.0 0.0.0.255
```

WFQ

WFQ classifies packets into conversations by flow. Packets with the same source Internet Protocol (IP) address, destination IP address, source Transmission Control Protocol (TCP) or User Datagram Protocol (UDP) port, destination TCP or UDP port, protocol, and type of service (ToS) field belong to the same flow. Each flow corresponds to a separate output queue. When a packet is assigned to a flow, it is placed in the queue for that flow. During periods of congestion, WFQ allocates an equal share of the bandwidth to each active queue. WFQ is also called flow-based WFQ.

WFQ is fairer than either PQ or CQ because it handles the problems inherent in queuing schemes that are essentially first-come, first-serve.

The main problem with first-come, first-serve algorithms is that sessions using large packets can impede sessions using small packets. FTP can negatively affect the performance of Telnet when they are competing for bandwidth because a small Telnet packet can get stuck behind a larger FTP packet. The WFQ implementation looks at sizes of messages and ensures that high-volume senders do not crowd out low-volume senders. WFQ removes packets from the queues based on the arrival time of the last bit rather than the first bit, which ensures that applications that use large packets cannot unfairly monopolize the bandwidth. If the last bit of a small packet is received, it is sent because the router is still waiting for the last bit of a larger packet.

Configuring WFQ

WFQ is enabled by default on serial interfaces at E1 (2.048 Mbps) or lower speeds. If disabled, WFQ is enabled by using the **fair-queue** command as follows:

```
interface serial 0
  fair-queue
```

Class-Based Weighted Fair Queuing (CBWFQ)

CBWFQ is an extension of WFQ. It allows packets to be assigned to different queues that are based on input interfaces, IP addresses, or protocols. CBWFQ allows network managers to configure class of services (CoS) for different traffic types. With CBWFQ, up to 64 classes can be configured, providing different service policies for each flow. For more information on CBWFQ, consult Cisco's web site at www.cisco.com/univercd/cc/td/doc/product/software/ios120/120newft/120t/120t5/cbwfq.htm.

Other QoS and Traffic Management Mechanisms

This section covers Generic Traffic Shaping (GTS), Frame Relay Traffic Shaping (FRTS), IEEE 802.1P, and compression.

GTS

GTS uses queuing on an Asynchronous Transfer Mode (ATM), Frame Relay, or other type of network to limit traffic bursts, which can cause congestion. GTS is a way to control the flow of traffic on a particular interface or for specific traffic. It reduces the outbound traffic flow by limiting traffic to a specified rate.

The idea is to shape the traffic to a specified rate to avoid congestion. It is important to understand that this is not a policing scheme, just a shaping mechanism. A policing mechanism, Committed Access Rate (CAR), is discussed in the following section. Traffic shaping is supported on all media and encapsulation types on the router. Traffic shaping can also be applied to a specific access list on an interface.

The interface configuration command for GTS is as follows:

```
traffic-shape rate bit-rate [burst-size [excess-burst-size]]
```

The *bit-rate* is the specified maximum rate for traffic on the interface. The *burst-size* is the sustained number of bits that can be sent per burst interval. The *excess-burst-size* is the number of bits that can be sent beyond the burst size. By default, the *excess-burst-size* is equal to the *burst-size*.

Another format of the command that uses access lists to configure traffic flow limits to specified traffic is as follows:

```
traffic-shape group group-num bit-rate [burst-size [excess-burst-size]]
```

The *group-num* is the access-list number.

In Example 11-4, Ethernet 0 is configured to limit FTP traffic to 2 Mbps, and Ethernet 1 is configured to limit all output to 7 Mbps.

Example 11-4 *Traffic-Shaping Configuration*

```
access-list 100 permit tcp any any eq ftp
access-list 100 permit tcp any any eq ftp-data
!
interface Ethernet0
 traffic-shape group 100 2000000 250000 250000
!
interface Ethernet1
 traffic-shape rate 7000000 875000 755000
```

Verify the traffic-shaping configuration with the **show traffic-shape** command, as shown in Example 11-5.

Example 11-5 *Router Output for* **show traffic-shape** *Command*

```
R4#show traffic-shape

Interface   Et0
       Access Target    Byte   Sustain   Excess    Interval  Increment Adapt
VC     List   Rate      Limit  bits/int  bits/int  (ms)      (bytes)   Active
-      100    2000000   62500  250000    250000    125       31250     -

Interface   Et1
       Access Target    Byte   Sustain   Excess    Interval  Increment Adapt
VC     List   Rate      Limit  bits/int  bits/int  (ms)      (bytes)   Active
-             7000000   218750 875000    775000    125       109375    -
```

FRTS

FRTS allows for the management of traffic congestion in Frame Relay networks. FRTS-enabled routers use received Backward Explicit Congestion Notification (BECN) information as input to manage the outbound traffic. If the number of BECN notifications increases, FRTS scales back the amount of outbound traffic. FRTS is enabled on the major interface, and traffic classes are defined in the global configuration. A traffic class is configured on each subinterface for the specified speeds.

FRTS can be configured in several ways; one method is shown in Example 11-6. The FRTS class named 128kb is configured for an average rate of 128 kbps (equal to the committed information rate (CIR)) and a peak rate of 256 kbps. The FRTS class named 512kb is configured with an average rate of 512 kbps (equal to the CIR) and a peak rate of 1024 kbps.

Example 11-6 *Configuring FRTS*

```
interface serial 0
 encapsulation frame-relay
 frame-relay traffic-shaping
!
interface serial 0.1 point-to-point
 ip address 192.168.100.5 255.255.255.252
 frame-relay interface-dlci 100
 frame-relay class 128kb
!
interface serial 0.2 point-to-point
 ip address 192.168.100.9 255.255.255.252
 frame-relay interface-dlci 200
 frame-relay class 512kb
!
map-class frame-relay 128kb
 frame-relay traffic-rate 128000 256000
 frame-relay adaptive-shaping becn
!
map-class frame-relay 512kb
 frame-relay traffic-rate 512000 1024000
frame-relay adaptive-shaping becn
```

RSVP

For the written test, you must be familiar with RSVP, which is covered in this section.

RSVP is one of the first significant protocols to set up end-to-end QoS over IP. RSVP is a signaling protocol that enables stations to obtain special qualities of service for their application data flows. RSVP reserves bandwidth for the network application. RSVP works in conjunction with routing protocols and installs the equivalent of dynamic access lists along the routes that routing protocols calculate. RSVP operates in the transport layer of the OSI model. RSVP is also known as Resource Reservation Setup Protocol. The IETF charter is at the following site: www.ietf.org/html.charters/rsvp-charter.html. The first standards version of the protocol is in RFC 2205.

Configuring RSVP

RSVP is enabled with the **ip rsvp bandwidth** [*interface-kbps*] [*single-flow-kbps*] interface command. This command starts RSVP and sets the bandwidth and single-flow limits. The default maximum bandwidth is up to 75 percent of the bandwidth available on the interface. By default, the amount reservable for a flow can be up to the entire reservable bandwidth of the interface.

On subinterfaces, the amount reservable for a flow is the most restrictive available bandwidth, which is the one assigned to the subinterface. A T1 interface that is using Frame Relay has 1.536 Mbps of bandwidth. If a subinterface is used, with 128 kbps of bandwidth, the default maximum bandwidth for a data flow in the subinterface is 75 percent of 128 kbps, which is 96 kbps.

In Example 11-7, RSVP uses 7500 kbps and the largest reservable bandwidth that a flow can reserve is 5000 kbps of bandwidth.

Example 11-7 *Configuring RSVP*

```
interface FastEthernet4/1
 ip address 10.100.50.1 255.255.255.252
 ip rsvp bandwidth 7500 5000
```

The **show ip rsvp interface** command shows the RSVP information, as shown in Example 11-8.

Example 11-8 **show ip rsvp interface** *Command*

```
R4-HOU#show ip rsvp interface
interface    allocate i/f max  flow max per/255 UDP  IP   UDP_IP   UDP M/C
Et0          0M        7500K   5M         0  /255 0   0    0        0
```

The configuration in Example 11-9 configures RSVP on Frame Relay, and the **show** command in Example 11-10 verifies the configuration.

Example 11-9 *RSVP on a Frame Relay Interface*

```
interface Serial0
 no ip address
 encapsulation frame-relay
 frame-relay lmi-type ansi
 ip rsvp bandwidth 1158 1158
 ip rsvp signalling dscp 0
!
interface Serial0.1 point-to-point
 ip address 192.168.1.150 255.255.255.252
 frame-relay interface-dlci 100
 ip rsvp bandwidth 500 250
```

Example 11-10 **show ip rsvp interface** *Command*

```
R6-HOU#show ip rsvp interface
interface    allocated  i/f max  flow max pct UDP  IP   UDP_IP   UDP M/C
Se0          0M         1158K    1158K    0   0    0    0        0
Se0.1        0M         500K     250K     0   0    0    0        0
```

Controlling Neighbors

By default, any neighbor can make an RSVP request. To control which RSVP neighbors make requests, you use the **ip rsvp neighbor** *access-list-number* command.

Example 11-11 shows how to configure the router to accept only RSVP requests from 192.168.1.1 on the Ethernet interface.

Example 11-11 *Configuration to Control RSVP Neighbors*

```
access-list 50 permit 192.168.1.1
!
interface ethernet 0
 ip address 192.168.1.4 255.255.255.0
 ip rsvp bandwidth
 ip rsvp neighbor 50
```

RSVP **show** Commands

Several commands can monitor RSVP. Table 11-1 describes each command.

Table 11-1 *Commands to Monitor RSVP*

Command	Description
show ip rsvp interface [*type number*]	Displays RSVP-related interface information
show ip rsvp installed [*type number*]	Displays RSVP filters and bandwidth information
show ip rsvp neighbor	Displays current RSVP neighbors
show ip rsvp sender	Displays RSVP sender information
show ip rsvp request	Displays RSVP request information
show ip rsvp reservation	Displays RSVP receiver information

Multiprotocol Label Switching (MPLS)

MPLS provides ways to perform traffic engineering, to guarantee bandwidth or set paths, and to enable Virtual Private Networks (VPNs). It specifies ways that Layer-3 traffic can be mapped to connection-oriented Layer-2 transport protocols, such as ATM. It adds a label containing specific routing information to each IP packet that directs traffic through explicitly defined paths, and it allows managers to implement policies that assign labels to various CoS. This enables the managers to offer different CoS to different traffic types or from different customers. The policies could send traffic over a path that is not necessarily the path with the lowest routing metric. With MPLS, service providers can provide VPN services and scale those services for many customers.

In a MPLS environment, forwarding is based on the lookup of the MLPS label and not the Layer-3 IP address. Labels are inserted at the edge of the MPLS network and removed when the packet leaves the MPLS network. The MPLS network applies services and forwards packets that are based on the information contained in the label.

MPLS Label

In a packet environment, the MPLS label is inserted between the Layer-2 header and the Layer-3 header in a Layer-2 frame. This applies for Packet over Synchronous Optical Network (SONET) (PoS), Ethernet, Frame Relay, and label over ATM. In ATM networks with label switching, the label is mapped into the virtual path identifier/virtual channel identifier (VPI/VCI) fields of the ATM header. The MPLS label field is 32 bits in length, with the actual label (tag) being 20 bits.

MPLS Label Switch Routers (LSRs)

All routers within a MPLS network are LSRs, which forward based on the label and not based on routing protocols. If the MPLS network uses ATM, the LSRs are called ATM LSRs. The Edge Label Switch Router (Edge LSR) is responsible for adding or removing the label to the packet.

Figure 11-3 shows a diagram of these routers.

Figure 11-3 *MPLS LSRs*

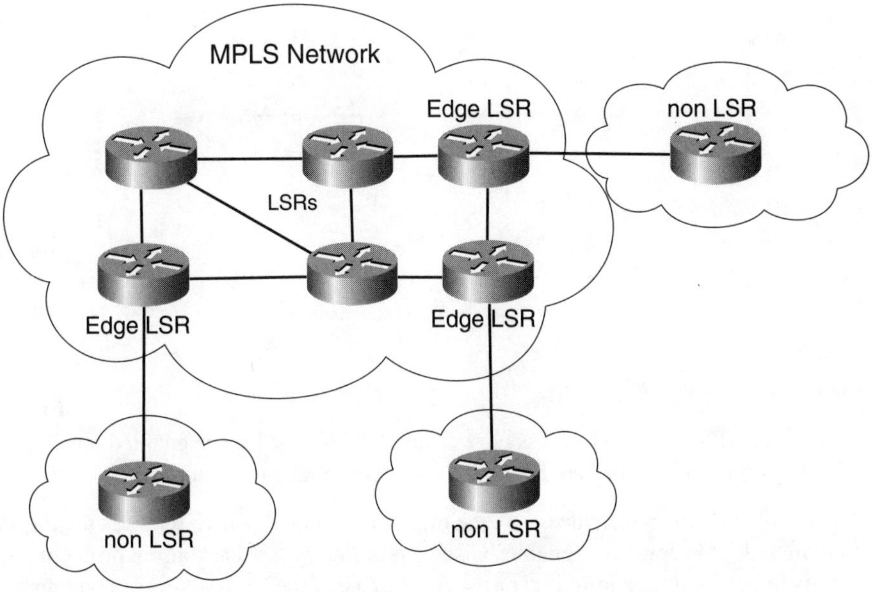

MPLS VPN Router Types

MPLS VPN architectures use the following four router types:

- **P router**—The service provider's internal core routers. These routers do not need to maintain VPN routes.
- **C router**—The customer's internal routers. They do not connect to the provider. These routers do not maintain VPN routes.
- **CE router**—The edge routers on the customer side that connect to the service provider. These routers do not maintain VPN routes.
- **PE router**—The edge routers on the service provider side that connect with the customer's CE routers. PE routers maintain VPN routes for the VPNs associated with the connected interfaces.

Figure 11-4 shows a diagram of these routers in an MPLS VPN network.

Figure 11-4 *MPLS VPN Routers*

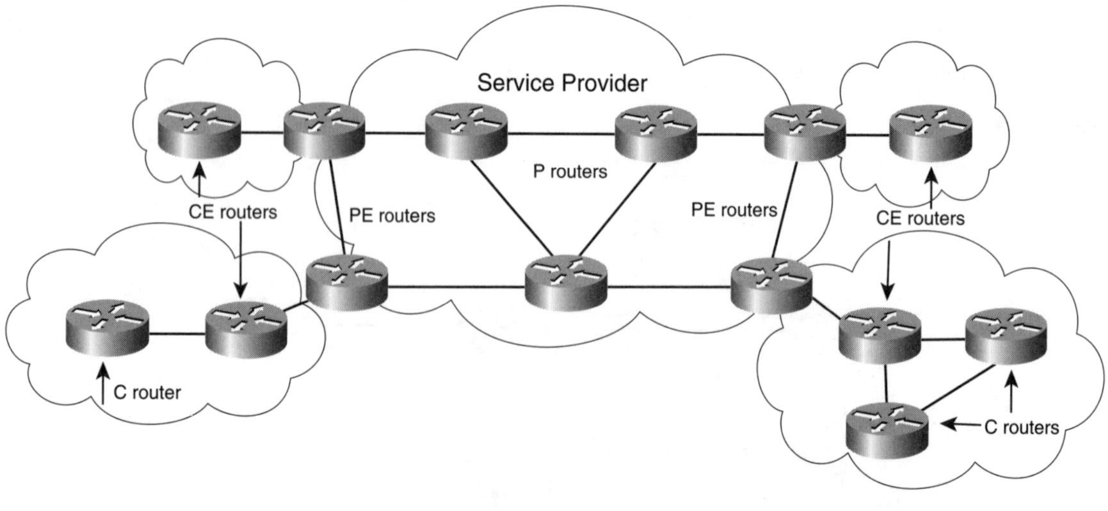

Enabling MPLS

To enable MPLS, Cisco Express Forwarding (CEF) must first be enabled on all routers running MPLS. You can accomplish this with the **ip cef** global command.

To enable MPLS on interfaces, use the **mpls ip** command, which replaces the **tag-switching ip** command. This command enables Cisco's proprietary tag distribution protocol (TDP). The **mpls ip** command is configured on every interface of the LSR. A simple configuration of a LSR in a MPLS network is shown in Example 11-12.

Example 11-12 *Simple MPLS Router Configuration*

```
hostname mplsrouter1
 !
 ip cef
 !
 interface Loopback0
  ip address 192.168.16.1 255.255.255.255
 !
 interface Serial0/0
  encapsulation frame-relay
 !
 interface Serial0/0.1 point-to-point
  ip address 192.168.20.5 255.255.255.252
  mpls ip
  frame-relay interface-dlci 123
 !
 interface Serial0/0.2 point-to-point
  ip address 192.168.20.9 255.255.255.252
  mpls ip
  frame-relay interface-dlci 124
 !
 interface Serial0/0.3 point-to-point
  ip address 192.168.20.14 255.255.255.252
  mpls ip
  frame-relay interface-dlci 125
 !
 router ospf
    network 192.168.16.0 0.0.0.255 area 1
    network 192.168.20.0 0.0.0.255 area 1
 !
 ip classless
 !
 end
```

This book covers MPLS at a high level. For more information, consult Cisco's web site at www.cisco.com/warp/public/732/Tech/mpls/mpls_learnabout.shtml, RFC #2547, or the Cisco Press publication *MPLS and VPN Architectures*.

CAR

CAR provides the means to limit the input or output transmission rate on an interface or subinterface based on traffic sources and destinations, while specifying policies for handling traffic that exceeds bandwidth allocations. Rate policies can be set based on IP access lists, IP Precedence, Media Access Control (MAC) addresses, or a QoS group. The difference between CAR and traffic shaping is that CAR is a policing scheme. CAR sets maximum limits on traffic but does not shape traffic to a specified rate. CAR typically drops traffic that exceeds the rate; in contrast, traffic shaping delays traffic in a buffer to delay packets to shape the flow of traffic.

CAR is configured with the interface **rate-limit** command. The command has the following syntax:

```
rate-limit {input | output} [access-group [rate-limit]
    acl-index | qos-group number] bps burst-normal burst-max
    conform-action action exceed-action action
```

Example 11-13 configures CAR on a High-Speed Serial Interface (HSSI) to limit the bandwidth to 25 Mbps, in and out. The interface is also configured to allow bursts up to 30,000 bytes, with all exceeded packets being dropped.

Example 11-13 *CAR Configuration*

```
interface Hssi0/0/0
  description 45Mbps Link with CAR
  ip address 1.1.1.1 255.255.255.252
  rate-limit input 25000000 30000 30000 conform-action transmit
      exceed-action drop
  rate-limit output 25000000 30000 30000 conform-action transmit
      exceed-action drop
```

To verify the configuration and monitor CAR statistics, use the **show interfaces rate-limit** command, as shown in Example 11-14.

Example 11-14 **show interfaces rate-limit** *Command*

```
R4# show interfaces hssi 0/0/0 rate-limit
Hssi0/0/0 45Mbps Link with CAR
  Input
    matches: all traffic
      params: 25000000 bps, 30000 limit, 30000 extended limit
      conformed 14 packets, 828 bytes; action: transmit
      exceeded 0 packets, 0 bytes; action: drop
      last packet: 110ms ago, current burst: 0 bytes
      last cleared 00:05:31 ago, conformed 0 bps, exceeded 0 bps
  Output
    matches: all traffic
      params: 25000000 bps, 30000 limit, 30000 extended limit
      conformed 0 packets, 0 bytes; action: transmit
      exceeded 0 packets, 0 bytes; action: drop
      last packet: 110ms ago, current burst: 0 bytes
      last cleared 00:05:31 ago, conformed 0 bps, exceeded 0 bps
```

IEEE 802.1p

The IEEE 802.1p signaling technique is an OSI Layer-2 standard for prioritizing network traffic at the data link/MAC sub-layer. It can be characterized as a best-effort service at Layer 2. IEEE 802.1p traffic is simply classified (using 3 priority bits) and sent to the destination; no special bandwidth services are established for the prioritized frames.

IEEE 802.1p is a subset of the 802.1q virtual local-area network (VLAN) trunking standard. The 802.1q standard specifies a tag that is appended to a MAC frame just after the MAC address, or just after the Routing Information Field (RIF), if a RIF is present. The VLAN tag carries VLAN information. The VLAN tag has two parts: VLAN ID (12 bits) and prioritization (3 bits). The 802.1p implementation defines this prioritization field.

802.1p establishes eight levels (3 bits) of priority, which is similar to IP Precedence. Network adapters and switches can route traffic based on the priority level. Using Layer-3 switches allows you to map 802.1p prioritization to IP Precedence before forwarding to routers. Because 802.1p is defined at Layer 2, it supports network layer protocols, such as IPX, SNA, and AppleTalk, in addition to IP.

Load Balancing

The Cisco blueprint lists load balancing as a performance management topic. Load balancing support for each routing protocol is covered in Chapter 7, "Static Routing and Distance Vector Routing Protocols," Chapter 8, "IP Link-State Routing Protocols," and Chapter 9, "Border Gateway Protocol." For easy reference, Table 11-2 lists the load balancing capabilities covered on each routing protocol.

Table 11-2 *Load Balancing Support*

Protocol	Load Balancing Support
Enhanced Interior Gateway Protocol (EIGRP)	Unequal-cost load balancing up to six paths
Open Shortest Path First (OSPF)	Equal-cost load balancing up to six paths
Intermediate System-to-Intermediate System (IS-IS)	Equal-cost load balancing up to six paths
(Interior Gateway Routing Protocol (IGRP)	Unequal-cost load balancing up to six paths
RIP version 1 (v1) and RIPv2	Equal-cost load balancing
Border Gateway Protocol (BGP)	By default, selects only one path, but supports load balancing with BGP Multipath to the same autonomous system (AS)

WRR

WRR is enabled by default on Cisco Layer-3 switches (Cisco 8500 or 6500 switches) egress ports. With WRR, the administrator uses IP Precedence bits to configure policies for traffic. IP Precedence bits are set at a device other than the switch that is using WRR. As packets enter the Layer-3 switch, WRR maps packets that are using IP Precedence bits to one of four outbound WRR queues. This is also known as *WRR scheduling*. Each WRR queue has a queue weight and delay priority. More bandwidth is given to packets with higher weight. Table 11-3 shows IP Precedence to WRR queue assignments.

Table 11-3 *IP Precedence to WRR Queue Assignments*

IP Precedence	WRR Queue Assigned	WRR Queue Weight	WRR Delay Priority
0,1	0	1	0
2,3	1	2	1
4,5	2	4	2
6,7	3	8	3

RED and WRED

RED is a congestion avoidance mechanism that randomly drops packets before congestion can occur. RED uses TCP's congestion control mechanisms by dropping packets and letting TCP reduce the source host's window size. RED is typically implemented in the core of the network on IP networks. The disadvantage of RED is that dropped packets can affect UDP or Novell Internetwork Packet Exchange (IPX) transmissions that do not implement a windowing flow control mechanism.

WRED is a Cisco implementation of RED that implements a preferential treatment of packets when determining which packets to drop when congestion occurs. WRED uses the IP Precedence bits to determine which packets to drop. The higher the IP Precedence is in a packet, the less likely the packet might be dropped. Up to six CoS can be configured.

WRED can also be configured to use other factors. WRED drops packets that are not part of an RSVP flow on interfaces that are configured for RSVP. WRED can also be configured to use Differentiated Services Code Point (DSCP) values as the decision factor of packets to be dropped. DSCP is explained in the following subsection.

WRED is configured with the following interface command, which uses default parameters:

```
interface interface num
   random-detect
```

Where *interface num* is the interface name and number (such as serial 0).

Differentiated Services Code Point

DSCP

DSCP, which is defined in RFC 2474, provides for 64 values (2^6) for prioritization by using the six most-significant bits of the IP ToS field. DSCP replaces the ToS field with the DSCP field, as shown in Figure 11-5. You can use DSCP for packet classification for later policing. With DSCP, service providers can classify packets into more service levels (CoS) than the eight levels possible with the IP Precedence bits.

Figure 11-5 *DSCP Field Replaces the ToS Field*

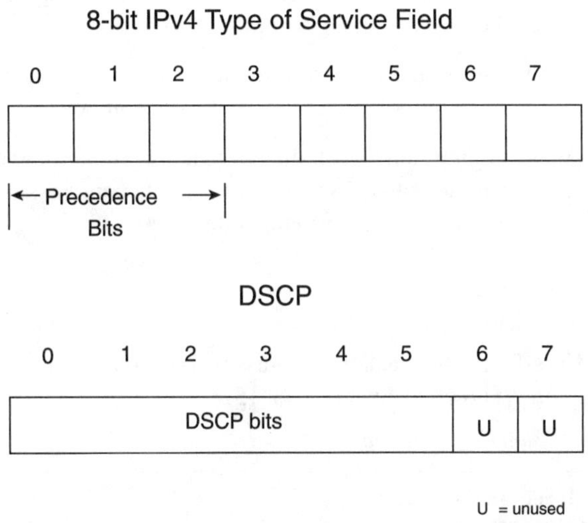

Consult RFC 2474, "Definition of the Differentiated Services Field (DS Field) in the IPv4 and IPv6 Headers," for more information on DSCP.

Network-Based Application Recognition (NBAR)

NBAR is a Cisco IOS feature that provides classification of network applications. NBAR marks packets in the ToS or DSCP field so that other QoS mechanisms can prioritize traffic. The advantage of NBAR is that it is preconfigured with network applications so that the network can automatically classify (mark) packets.

For more information and configuration examples, go to the following site: www.cisco.com/warp/public/cc/so/neso/ienesv/cxne/nbar_ov.htm.

PoS and IP Precedence

POS/Synchronous Digital Hierarchy (SDH) technology removes the ATM layer (IP/ATM/SONET) between IP and SONET. This permits the ability to configure IP QoS mechanisms on

PoS interfaces. Packets in PoS interfaces can be marked by setting IP Precedence bits. IP Precedence bits enable mechanisms such as CAR, RED, and WRED on the network.

Compression

Cisco internetworking devices use the Stacker and Predictor data compression algorithms. Stacker is based on the Lempel-Ziv (LZS) compression algorithm. LZS is available in Cisco's Link Access Procedure, Balanced (LAPB), high-level data link control (HDLC), X.25, and Frame Relay data compression solutions. FRF.9 and IP Payload Compression (IPComp) protocol use the LZS compression algorithm.

The Predictor compression algorithm tries to predict the next sequence of characters in the data stream by using an index to look up a sequence in the compression dictionary.

The Predictor data compression algorithm makes more efficient use of CPU cycles but requires more memory. You can use both LZS and Predictor data compression algorithms with Point-to-Point Protocol (PPP) or LAPB encapsulated interfaces.

HDLC Interface Compression

Under HDLC interfaces, the Stacker compression is the only method available for compression. The configuration is shown in Example 11-15.

Example 11-15 *Stacker Compression Configuration*

```
R5(config)#interface serial 1
R5(config-if)#compress ?
  stac  stac compression algorithm

R5(config-if)#compress stac
```

TCP Header Compression

Another compression method is TCP header compression, which is described in RFC 1144, "Compressing TCP/IP Headers for Low-Speed Serial Links." Because of the processing overhead, you generally use TCP header compression on links with speeds of 64 kbps or less. You must use only this form of compression to gain advantage for interactive traffic with small payloads, such as Telnet. Header compression can produce varying throughput improvements across low-speed lines depending on line rate. Header compression is enabled on an interface as follows:

```
R5(config-if)#ip tcp header-compression
```

Real-Time Protocol (RTP) Header Compression

RTP headers can be compressed on serial links by enabling Compressed RTP (CRTP). For HDLC and PPP interfaces, you use the **ip rtp header-compression** [**passive**] command. On Frame Relay interfaces, use the **frame-relay ip rtp header-compression** [**passive**] command. Use CRTP on interfaces with Voice over IP (VoIP) traffic.

Frame Relay Compression

With Cisco routers, you can configure payload compression on point-to-point or multipoint interfaces.

For point-to-point subinterfaces, you use the following command:

```
frame-relay payload-compress packet-by-packet
```

For multipoint subinterfaces, the command is as follows:

```
frame-relay map protocol protocol-address dlci
   payload-compress packet-by-packet
```

FRF.9 Compression

Implementation FRF.9 of the Frame Relay Forum provides standards-based compression on Frame Relay, therefore providing multivendor interoperability. FRF.9 specified per virtual circuit compression for Frame Relay permanent virtual circuits (PVCs) or switched virtual circuits (SVCs). The payload is compressed at the entry DLCI and decompressed at the termination of the virtual circuit.

To enable FRF.9 compression on a point-to-point subinterface, use the following command:

```
frame-relay payload-compress frf9 stac
```

References Used

The following resources were used to create this chapter:

MLPS and VPN Architectures, Ivan Pepelnjak and Jim Guichard, Cisco Press, 2001

CCDA Exam Certification Guide, Anthony Bruno and Jacqueline Kim, Cisco Press, 2000

www.cisco.com/univercd/cc/td/doc/product/software/ios122/122cgcr/fqos_c/qcfintro.htm

www.cisco.com/univercd/cc/td/doc/product/software/ios120/12cgcr/qos_c/qcpart2/qcwfq.htm

www.cisco.com/univercd/cc/td/doc/cisintwk/ito_doc/rsvp.htm

www.cisco.com/warp/public/732/Tech/mpls/mpls_techdoc.shtml

www.cisco.com/univercd/cc/td/doc/cisintwk/ito_doc/mpls_tsw.htm#xtocid1

www.cisco.com/univercd/cc/td/doc/product/software/ios122/122cgcr/fqos_c/fqcprt4/qcfpolsh.htm

www.cisco.com/warp/public/cc/pd/iosw/tech/compr_wp.htm

www.cisco.com/univercd/cc/td/doc/product/rtrmgmt/ciscoasu/class/qpm1_1/using_qo/c1plan.htm#31947

www.cisco.com/warp/public/732/Tech/qos/nbar/

www.cisco.com/univercd/cc/td/doc/product/software/ios120/12cgcr/qos_c/qcpart3/qcconavd.htm

Foundation Summary

The Foundation Summary is a condensed collection of material that provides a convenient review of key concepts in this chapter. If you are already comfortable with the topics in this chapter, this summary will help you recall a few details. If you just read the Foundation Topics section, this review should help solidify some key facts. If you are doing your final preparation before the exam, these materials are a convenient way to review the day before the exam.

Table 11-4 *Queuing Strategies*

Queuing Strategies	Description
FIFO	First packet in, first packet out
PQ	Prioritizes traffic into high, medium, normal, or low queues
CQ	Prioritizes traffic with up to 16 queues, each queue is assigned a byte count limitation
WFQ	Queues packets based on the arrival time of the last bit rather than the first bit, which ensures that applications that use large packets cannot unfairly monopolize the bandwidth
CBWFQ	Uses IP Precedence bits in the ToS field or configured QoS groups to prioritize traffic

QoS and Traffic Mechanisms Summary

- A host uses the RSVP protocol to request specific qualities of service from the network for particular application data streams or flows.
- MPLS fuses the intelligence of Layer-3 routing protocols with the speed of Layer-2 switching protocols. MPLS provides methods to perform traffic engineering, to guarantee bandwidth, and to further enable Virtual Private Networks (VPNs).
- GTS reduces outbound traffic flow to avoid congestion by constraining specified traffic to a particular bit rate. It is configured with the following command:

```
traffic-shape rate bit-rate [burst-size [excess-burst-size]]
```

- FRTS-enabled routers use received BECN information as input to manage the outbound traffic. Traffic is shaped to the specified rate, not limited. It is configured by creating classes of traffic and applying them to the interface with the **frame-relay class** command.
- CAR provides the means to limit the input or output transmission rate on an interface or subinterface based on traffic sources and destinations, while specifying policies for handling traffic that exceeds bandwidth allocations. It is configured with the following command:

```
rate-limit {input | output} [access-group [rate-limit]
    acl-index | qos-group number] bps burst-normal burst-max
    conform-action action exceed-action action
```

- IEEE 802.1p establishes eight levels (3 bits) of priority for frames; it uses a 3-bit field in the 802.1q VLAN tagging protocol.
- WRR Scheduling maps packets by using IP Precedence bits to one of four outbound WRR queues. Each WRR queue has a different weight. More bandwidth is given to packets with higher weights.
- WRED is a congestion avoidance mechanism that implements a preferential treatment of packets by determining which packets to drop when congestion might occur. WRED uses the IP Precedence bits to determine which packets to drop. The higher the IP Precedence is in a packet, the less likely the packet is dropped.

Table 11-5 *Compression Techniques*

Compression	Description
Stacker	Can use in HDLC interfaces; configure with **compress stac**
TCP header compression	Compresses TCP header, described in RFC 1144
FRF.9	Frame Relay Forum standards-based compression method on Frame Relay; provides multivendor interoperability
RTP header compression	Compresses RTP header

Q & A

The Q & A questions are more difficult than what you can expect on the actual exam. The questions do not attempt to cover more breadth or depth than the exam; however, they are designed to make sure that you retain the material. Rather than allowing you to derive the answer from clues hidden inside the question itself, these questions challenge your understanding and recall of the subject. Questions from the "Do I Know This Already?" quiz are repeated here to ensure that you have mastered the chapter's topic areas. A strong understanding of the answers to these questions will help you on the CCIE written exam. As an additional study aide, use the CD-ROM provided with this book to take simulated exams.

Select the best answer. Answers to these questions are in the Appendix, "Answers to Quiz Questions."

1 Which queuing scheme can be used to SNA traffic before servicing other traffic types?

a. FIFO

b. CQ

c. PQ

d. CBWFQ

2 Which protocol permits hosts to request quality of service parameters from network resources?

a. MPLS

b. RSVP

c. CAR

d. RTP

3 Which mechanism drops packets to prevent congestion?

a. CQ

b. WRED

c. WFQ

d. DPack

4 Which scheme is configured with the **traffic-shape** IOS command?

a. MPLS

b. CAR

c. CRTP

d. GTS

5 Which routing protocol permits load balancing over unequal-cost paths?

a. EIGRP

b. OSPF

c. RIP

d. IS-IS

6 If EIGRP has ten paths to a destination, how many can you use by default?

a. Four

b. Six

c. Eight, if all are equal-cost paths

d. Ten, if all are unequal-cost paths

7 What is the standards-based Frame Relay compression method?

a. FRF.5

b. FRF.9

c. FRF.11

d. FRF.12

8 Which mechanism inserts a 32-bit field between the Layer-2 header and Layer-3 header to provide high-speed switching?

a. RSVP

b. FRTS

c. MPLS

d. Tunnel switching

9 After the priority queues have been defined, which command enables priority queuing on an interface?

a. **priority-group**

b. **priority-list**

c. **ip priority-group**

d. **priority-list 1 queue-byte 1000**

10 Stacker is based on which compression algorithm?

a. Ford-Fergerson

b. Lempel-Ziv

c. Bruno-Cicala

d. SPF

11 Which queuing scheme can explicitly prioritize traffic into ten different size queues?

a. FIFO

b. CQ

c. PQ

d. WFQ

12 Which scheme is configured with the **rate-limit** command?

a. MPLS

b. CAR

c. CRTP

d. GTS

13 If OSPF has ten equal-cost paths to a destination, how many paths can you use?

a. Four

b. Six

c. Eight

d. Ten

14 EIGRP has ten paths to a destination. How many can you use if the maximum is configured?

a. Four

b. Six

c. Eight, if all are equal-cost paths

d. Ten, if all are unequal-cost paths

15 Which command configures custom queuing on an interface?

a. **priority-list**

b. **custom-group**

c. **custom-list**

d. **custom-queue-list**

16 Priority queuing uses how many queues?

a. Three

b. Four

c. Six

d. Eight

17 Which queuing strategy forwards frames based on the order that they are received?

a. FIFO

b. CQ

c. WFQ

d. PQ

18 Which queuing strategy forwards frames based on the last bit of the frame received?

a. FIFO

b. CQ

c. WFQ

d. PQ

19 The following command is configured on an interface. What happens when the output transmission rate exceeds 30 Mbps?

```
rate-limit output 30000000 31000 31000 conform-action transmit
    exceed-action drop
```

a. Bursts to 31,000 bytes, then dropped

b. Dropped

c. Bursts to 31,000 bytes, then dropped

d. None of the above

20 Which interface command enables FIFO queuing?

a. **fifo**

b. **no fair-queue**

c. **enable fifo**

d. **queue fifo**

21 What does WRR do?

a. Drops packets based on IP Precedence

b. Assigns packets with different IP Precedence into one of 4 queues

c. Configures 16 queues

d. Uses 4 queues called high, normal, slow, and default

22 IP prioritization with DSCP uses how many bits?

a. 3

b. 6

c. 8

d. 64

Scenario

Use the following configuration to answer the scenario questions:

```
interface s 0
 custom-queue-list 1
!
queue-list 1 protocol dlsw 1
queue-list 1 protocol ip 2 list 10
queue-list 1 protocol cdp 3
queue-list 1 default 4
!
queue-list 1 queue 1 byte-count 2000
queue-list 1 queue 2 byte-count 3000
queue-list 1 queue 3 byte-count 500
queue-list 1 queue 4 byte-count 3500
!
access-list 10 permit 200.1.1.0 0.0.0.255
```

1 Which queuing strategy is configured?

a. PQ

b. CQ

c. CBWFQ

d. FIFO

2 Approximately what percent of the bandwidth is queued for DLSW bandwidth?

a. 33 percent

b. 22 percent

c. 10 percent

d. 39 percent

3 Approximately what percent of the bandwidth do you use for IP networks not in access list 10?

a. 33 percent

b. 22 percent

c. 10 percent

d. 39 percent

This chapter covers the following topics needed to master the CCIE exam:

- **Multiservice Networks**—Multiservice technologies that support voice and data integration, such as coder-decoders (codecs), H.323, Signaling System (SS7), and Real-Time Transfer Protocol (RTP)
- **Security**—Authentication-authorization-accounting (AAA), Terminal Access Controller Access Control System Plus (TACACS+), Remote Authentication Dial-In User Service (RADIUS), PIX Firewalls, and encryption
- **Desktop Protocols**—Legacy Novell Internetwork Packet Exchange (IPX) and Windows NT

CHAPTER 12

Multiservice Networking, IPX Networking, and Security

"Do I Know This Already?" Quiz

The purpose of this assessment quiz is to help you determine how to spend your limited study time. If you can answer most or all of these questions, you might want to skim the Foundation Topics section and return to it later as necessary. Review the Foundation Summary section and answer the questions at the end of the chapter to ensure that you have a strong grasp of the material covered. If you intend to read the entire chapter, you do not necessarily need to answer these questions now. If you find these assessment questions difficult, read through the entire Foundation Topics section and review it until you feel comfortable with your ability to answer all the "Q & A" questions at the end of the chapter. The following questions are repeated at the end of the chapter in the Q & A section with additional questions to test your mastery of the material.

Select the best answer. Answers to these questions are in the Appendix, "Answers to Quiz Questions."

1 Which ITU standard provides a framework for multimedia protocols for the transport of voice, video, and data over packet-switched networks?

a. RTP/RCTP

b. VoIP

c. H.323

d. WFQ

2 Which of the following is the default codec that you use with VoIP dial peers?

a. G.711

b. G.723

c. G.728

d. G.729

3 Which authentication protocol uses TCP?

a. Kerberos

b. TACACS

c. RADIUS

d. AAA

4 Which encryption method uses a 168-bit key?

a. DES

b. PGP

c. 3DES

d. IPSec

5 What is AAA?

a. Automation, authentication, and accounting

b. Authentication, abomination, and accounting

c. Automation, authorization, and accounting

d. Authentication, authorization, and accounting

6 RTP operates in which layer of the OSI model?

a. Application

b. Session

c. Transport

d. Network

7 Which H.323 protocol is responsible for call setup and signaling?

a. H.245

b. Q.931

c. H.225

d. RTCP

8 Which unit measures the number of voice calls in one hour?

a. Kbps

b. Erlangs

c. DS0

d. FXS

9 Which feature does not transmit packets when there is silence?

a. E&M

b. VAD

c. Dial-Peer

d. DSS

10 What does CRTP compresses?

a. The RTP header

b. The RTP, TCP, and IP headers

c. The RTP, UDP, and IP headers

d. The RTCP header

11 Which protocol(s) reduce broadcasts in an IPX internetwork?

a. IPX RIP

b. NLSP

c. IPX EIGRP

d. Answers b and c

12 How many bits are in an IPX address?

a. 32 bits

b. 48 bits

c. 60 bits

d. 80 bits

13 Which is not a valid IPX network number?

a. DEAD

b. 0FFFFFF0

c. DEAGF0

d. 10

14 Which method is preferred for transporting NetBIOS?

a. NetBEUI

b. NBT

c. ATP

d. Ethernet

Foundation Topics

Multiservice Networks

This section discusses several concepts related to the support of multiservice networks, which are networks that run integrated voice, video, and data traffic. This section covers the following written exam blueprint topics:

- H.323
- Codecs
- SS7
- RTP
- RTP Control Protocol (RTCP)
- Session initiation protocol (SIP)

Packet Voice

With the converging data and voice networks, the introduction of packet-voice technology provides the ability for companies to save toll charges on voice telephone calls. Voice is digitized (coded) into packets, cells, or frames; sent as data throughout the networks, and converted back to analog voice. Coding for this is covered in the Codecs section.

An example of packetized voice is when calls are placed on phones that are attached to routers, as shown in Figure 12-1. The routers digitize the voice and then forward calls on the wide-area network (WAN) links. If the router determines that bandwidth is not available on the data network, the call can be forwarded over the public switched telephone network (PSTN). Calls placed outside the company's intranet are forwarded to the PSTN.

With Voice over IP (VoIP) technology, voice is digitized (coded) into IP packets. A dial plan is created to list the IP destinations of VoIP phones and outbound phones. When a number is dialed on phones attached to a router, it looks at the digits and routes the calls to the appropriate destination. Phones are attached to Foreign Exchange Station (FXS) ports.

For example, in Figure 12-1, if a call to 8-1234 is placed from phone 6-1234, Router A forwards the packets with voice data to Router B. Router B converts the digitized voice into analog signals out its voice interface to phone 8-1234.

Figure 12-1 *Packet Voice Example*

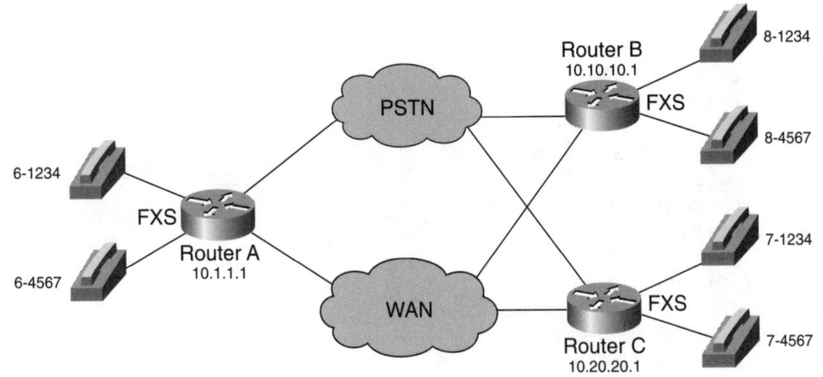

The dial plan for Router A from Figure 12-1 is shown in Table 12-1.

Table 12-1 *Dial Plan for Router A*

Phone Number	Destination
Calls to 8xxxx	Forward to IP: 10.10.10.1
Calls to 7xxxx	Forward to IP: 10.20.20.1
Outside calls	Forward to PSTN
6-1234	Voice FXS port 1/1
6-4567	Voice FXS port 1/2

Router A is configured for VoIP, as shown in Example 12-1. Dial peers are created and they map dialed digits to a destination. Dial peer 6000 maps digits 61234 to the FXS port 1/1. Dial peer 6001 maps digits 64567 to port 1/2. Dial peers 8000 and 8001 configure VoIP destinations. Dial peer 8000 maps digit 8 followed by any 4 digits to the IP destination 10.10.10.1 and sets the IP precedence bits to 101 for VoIP packets. Dial peer 8001 maps digit 7 followed by any 4 digits to the IP destination 10.20.20.1 and sets the VoIP packet's IP precedence bits to 101. Compressed RTP is also configured on the serial interface.

Example 12-1 *VoIP Configuration Example*

```
dial-peer voice 6000 pots
 destination-pattern 61234
 port 1/1
!
dial-peer voice 6001 pots
 destination-pattern 64567
 port 1/2
```

continues

Example 12-1 *VoIP Configuration Example (Continued)*

```
!
dial-peer voice 8000 voip
 destination-pattern 8....
 session target ipv4:10.10.10.1
 ip precedence 5
!
dial-peer voice 8001 voip
 destination-pattern 7....
 session target ipv4:10.20.20.1
 ip precedence 5
!
interface serial 0
 ip address 10.1.1.1 255.255.255.0
 ip rtp header-compression
 ip rtp compression-connections 25
!
voice-port 1/1
!
voice-port 1/2
```

Ports

Several ports can connect to voice end stations (phones) and voice switches:

- **Foreign Exchange Station (FXS)**—Connects to an analog phone and fax machines; provides dial tone and ring voltage.
- **Foreign Exchange Office (FXO)**—An RJ-11 connector that allows an analog connection to be directed at the PSTN's central office (CO) or to a station interface on a private branch exchange (PBX). The FXO sits on the switch end of the connection and plugs directly into the line side of the switch, so the switch thinks that the FXO interface is a telephone.
- **Ear and mouth (E&M)**—An analog trunk that connects to a voice switch; supports tie-line facilities or signaling between phone switches.
- **Channelized T1 (or E1)**—A digital trunk line that connects to a phone switch where each digital service zero (DS0) supports an active phone call connection.

Erlangs

An *Erlang* is a unit of telecommunications traffic measurement that represents the continuous use of one voice path. In practice, it describes the total traffic volume of one hour. Erlangs determine voice call usage for bandwidth requirements for voice network designs, including VoIP.

If a group of users make 20 calls in an hour, and each call lasts 10 minutes, the erlangs are calculated as follows:

$$20 \text{ calls/hour} \times 10 \text{ minutes/call} = 200 \text{ minutes/hour}$$
$$\text{Traffic volume} = (200 \text{ minute/hour}) / (60 \text{ minutes/hour})$$
$$= 3.33 \text{ erlangs}$$

Voice Activity Detection (VAD)

Because you listen and pause between sentences, typical voice conversations can contain up to 60 percent of silence. In plain telephone networks, all voice calls use fixed-bandwidth, 64-kbps links, regardless of how much of the conversation is speech and how much is silence. In multiservice networks, all conversation and silence is packetized. Using VAD, packets of silence spurs can be suppressed. Instead of sending VoIP packets of silence, VoIP gateways can interweave data traffic with VoIP conversations to more effectively utilize network bandwidth. Bandwidth savings are at least 35 percent in conservative estimates.

VAD is enabled by default for all VoIP calls. Although VAD reduces the silence in VoIP conversations, it also provides Comfort-Noise-Generation (CNG). Because you can mistake silence for a disconnected call, CNG provides locally generated white noise so that the call appears normally connected to both parties.

If VAD is not active, it can be enabled by using the **vad** command under the **dial-peer** statement. Example 12-2 shows the **vad** command enabling VAD for the VoIP dial peer 100.

Example 12-2 *Enabling VAD for a VoIP Dial Peer*

```
dial-peer voice 100 voip
 destination-pattern +12817810300
 vad
 session target ipv4:1.1.1.1
```

RTP

In VoIP, RTP transports audio streams. RTP is defined in RFC 1889. RTP runs over User Datagram Protocol (UDP), which has a lower delay than TCP. Because of the time sensitivity of voice traffic and the delay incurred in retransmissions, you use UDP instead of TCP. Real-time traffic is carried over UDP ports that range from 16384 to 16624. The only requirement is that the RTP data is transported on an even port and RTCP is carried on the next odd port. RTCP is also defined in RFC 1889. RTCP monitors the delivery of data and provides control and identification functions.

Because voice applications are sensitive to the delay of packets, any quality of service (QoS) techniques on the network need to prioritize these RTP/UDP IP packets over other traffic, such as File Transfer Protocol (FTP) and Hypertext Transfer Protocol (HTTP). You can use the **ip precedence** *number* subcommand under the **dial-peer** command to mark VoIP packets with a particular IP precedence. You can also use RTP header compression on WAN links to reduce the size of voice packets. It is also referred as Compressed RTP (CRTP). RTP header compression is enabled in serial interfaces with the **ip rtp header-compression** command. The maximum number of compression sessions is controlled with the **ip rtp compression-connections** *number* command. As shown in Figure 12-2, CRTP reduces the IP/UDP/RTP header from 40 bytes to up to 4 bytes in length—a significant decrease in overhead. CRTP is done on a hop-by-hop basis with compression and decompression occurring on every link.

Figure 12-2 *Compressed RTP (CRTP)*

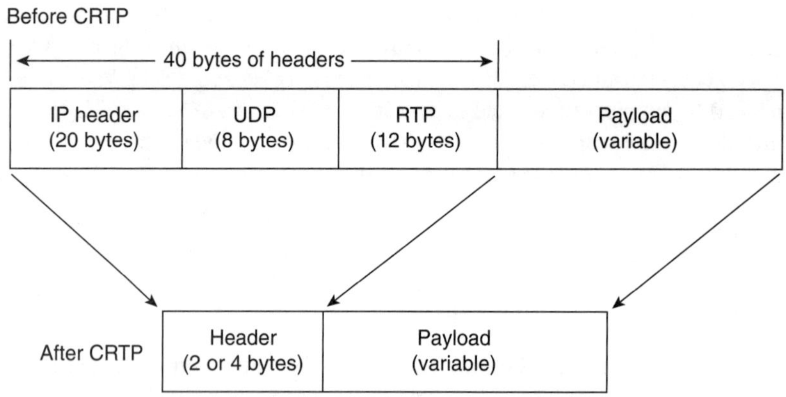

Codecs

Codecs transform analog signals into a digital bit stream and digital signals back into analog signals. In this case, it specifies the voice coder rate of speech for a dial peer. Figure 12-3 shows an analog signal that is digitized with a coder for digital transport. The decoder converts the digital signal into analog form. Codecs are presentation layer protocols.

Figure 12-3 *Codec*

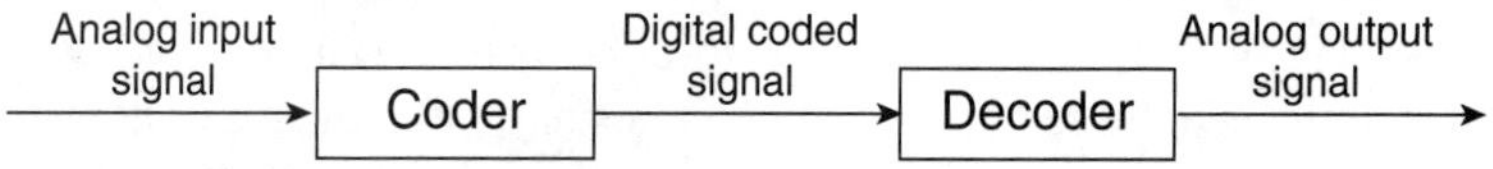

The default codec setting for VoIP is G.729 (**g729r8**). Some other codec standards are listed in Table 12-2.

Table 12-2 *Codec Standards*

Codec	Bit Rate	Description
G.711u	64 kbps	Pulse code modulation (PCM); mu-law version in North America and Japan; samples speech 8000 times per second, represented in 8 bytes
G.711a	64 kbps	PCM; a-law in Europe and in international routes
G.723.1	6.3 kbps	MPE-MLQ (Multi-Pulse Excitation-Maximum Likelihood Quantization)
G.723.1	5.3 kbps	ACELP (algebraic code excited linear prediction)
G.726	16/24/ 32/40 kbps	Adaptive differential pulse code modulation (AD-PCM)
G.729	8 kbps	CS-ACELP (Conjugate Structure ACELP)

H.323

H.323 is a standard that is published by the International Telecommunication Union (ITU) that works as a framework document for multimedia protocols, which includes voice, video, and data conferencing for use over packet-switched networks. H.323 describes terminals and other entities (such as gatekeepers) that provide multimedia applications.

H.323 includes the following elements:

- **Terminals**—Telephones, video phones, and voice mail systems
- **Multipoint Control Units (MCU)**—Responsible for managing multipoint conferences
- **Gateways**—Composed of a Media Gateway Controller for call signaling and a Media Gateway to handle media
- **Gatekeeper**—Optional component for admission control and address resolution
- **Border Elements**—Collocated with the gatekeepers; provides addressing resolution and participates in call authorization

H.323 terminals must support the following standards:

- H.245
- Q.931
- H.225
- RTP/RTCP

H.245 specifies messages for opening and closing channels for media streams, other commands, requests, and indications. It is a conferencing control protocol.

Q.931 is a standard for call signaling and setup.

H.225 specifies messages for call control that includes signaling between end point, registration, admissions, and packetization/synchronization of media streams.

RTP is the transport layer protocol that transports VoIP packets. RCTP is a session layer protocol.

H.323 includes a series of protocols for multimedia that are listed in Table 12-3.

Table 12-3 *H.323 Protocols*

	Video	Audio	Data	Transport
H.323 Protocol	H.261	G.711	T.122	RTP
	H.263	G.722	T.124	H.225
		G.723.1	T.125	H.235
		G.728	T.126	H.245
		G.729	T.127	H.450.1
				H.450.2
				H.450.3
				X.224.0

SIP

SIP is defined by the Internet Engineering Task Force (IETF) and is specified in RFC 2543. It is an alternative multimedia framework to H.323, developed specifically for IP telephony.

SIP is an application layer control (signaling) protocol for creating, modifying, and terminating Internet multimedia conferences, Internet telephone calls, and multimedia distribution. Communication between members in a session can be through a multicast, unicast mesh, or a combination of these.

SIP is designed as part of the overall IETF multimedia data and control architecture that incorporates protocols such as the following:

- Resource Reservation Protocol (RSVP) (RFC 2205) for reserving network resources
- RTP (RFC 1889) for transporting real-time data and providing QoS feedback
- RTSP (RFC 2326) for controlling delivery of streaming media
- Session Announcement Protocol (SAP) for advertising multimedia sessions through multicast
- Session Description Protocol (SDP) (RFC 2327) for describing multimedia sessions.

SIP supports user mobility by using proxy and redirect servers to redirect requests to the user's current location. Users can register their current location and SIP location services, which provide the location of user agents.

SIP uses a modular architecture that includes the following components:

- **SIP user agent**—Endpoints that create and terminate sessions, SIP phones, SIP PC clients, or gateways
- **SIP proxy server**—Routes messages between SIP user agents
- **SIP redirect server**—Call control device that provides routing information to user agents
- **SIP registrar server**—Stores the location of all user agents in the domain or subdomain
- **SIP location services**—Provides the logical location of user agents; used by proxy, redirect, and registrar servers
- **Back-to-back user agent**—Call-control device that allows centralized control of network call flows

Signaling System 7 (SS7)

SS7 is a global ITU standard for telecommunications that allows voice network calls to be routed and controlled by central call-control centers. SS7 implements call setup, routing, and control, which ensure that intermediate and far-end switches are available when a call is placed. With SS7, telephone companies can implement modern consumer telephone services, such as caller ID, toll-free numbers, call forwarding, and so on.

SS7 provides mechanisms for exchanging control, status, and routing messages on public telephone networks. SS7 messages pass over a separate channel that is reserved for voice communication. This technique is commonly referred to as *out of band signaling*. SS7 is the network that controls call signaling, routing, and connections between the CO, inter-exchange carrier, and competitive local exchange carrier (LEC) switches. Figure 12-4 shows the connectivity between SS7 components, which are described in this section.

As shown in Figure 12-4, SS7 has the following system components:

- **SCP (Signaling Control Point)**—Databases that provide the necessary information for special call processing and routing, including 800 and 900 call services, credit card calls, local number portability, cellular roaming services, and advanced call center applications.
- **STP (Signaling Transfer Point)**—Receives and routes incoming signaling messages toward their destinations. STPs are deployed in mated pairs and share the traffic between them.
- **SSP (Signaling Switching Point)**—Telephone switches equipped with SS7 software and signaling links. Each SSP is connected to both STPs in a mated pair.

Figure 12-4 *SS7 Components*

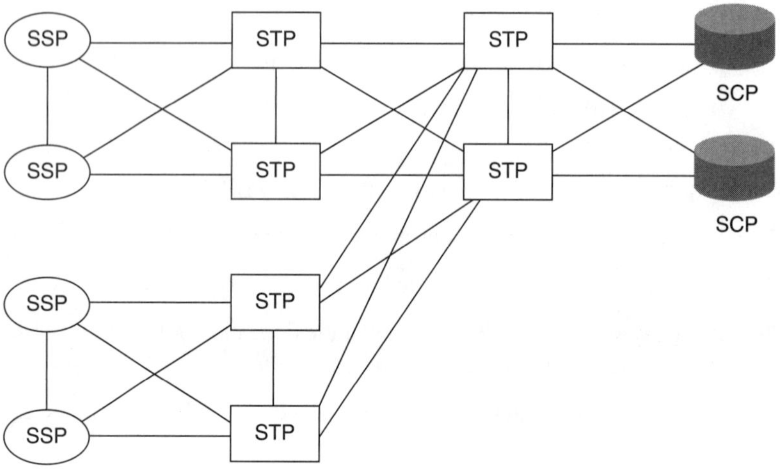

Tools for Better Bandwidth Utilization in VoIP Networks

Cisco provides different QoS tools that you must use on edge and backbone routers to support VoIP networks. Edge routers are concerned with packet classification, admission control, bandwidth management, and queuing. Backbone routers perform high-speed switching and transport, congestion management, and queue management.

The following tools are valuable for VoIP networks:

- **Multilink PPP with Interleaving**—Allows large packets to be multilink-encapsulated and fragmented into smaller packets.
- **RTP Header Compression**—Compresses IP/UDP/RTP headers from 40 bytes to 2/4 bytes.
- **Weighted Fair Queuing (WFQ)**—Queues packets based on the arrival time of the last bit rather than the first bit, which ensures that applications that use large packets cannot unfairly monopolize the bandwidth. Class Based-WFQ (CB-WFQ) can be configured to look at the IP precedence bits of IP packets.

Security

This section covers the following exam security blueprint topics:

- Authentication, authorization, and accounting (AAA)
- TACACS

- RADIUS
- PIX Firewalls
- Encryption

These security topics go beyond the simple line and enable passwords on the routers by providing additional methods to authenticate, authorize, and secure network resources.

AAA

AAA (triple A) provides a modular framework for configuring three security functions. The three functions are as follows:

- **Authentication**—Who is the user?
- **Authorization**—What resources can be accessed?
- **Accounting**—When was the device accessed, by whom, and what commands were used?

Authentication allows the identification of the user that is accessing the device. Authentication can include login and password dialogs, challenge and response, and encryption.

Authorization specifies the level of access that the user can have on the system. For example, a user might be given *exec* router privileges but denied access to enable mode.

Accounting tracks users and stores the information in an off-line server. It also tracks the amount of network resources (bytes) used. Examples of parameters that are stored in the accounting server are device failed and successful login attempts, commands used, and time and date of event.

AAA router commands provide additional security over exec and enable level passwords. AAA uses protocols such as RADIUS, TACACS+, and Kerberos to administer its security functions. AAA is the means through which you establish communication between the router and the RADIUS, TACACS+, or Kerberos security server. The Cisco Secure ACS server software can act as a RADIUS or TACACS+ server.

AAA Configuration

AAA is enabled with the command **aaa new-model**. After AAA is enabled, security protocol parameters (TACACS/RADIUS) can be configured. Authentication, authorization, and accounting are configured with the following commands:

- **aaa authentication** *keywords*
- **aaa authorization** *keywords*
- **aaa accounting** *keywords*

This guide does not cover every AAA configuration option. The following are configurations that use TACACS+ and RADIUS.

Example 12-3 shows AAA with TACACS+. The first command enables AAA. The second command configures the router to use the TACACS+ server for authentication. The following commands configure parameters for authorization and accounting by using the TACACS+ server. The **tacacs-server** command provides the IP address of the TACACS+ server and the key. The commands under **line con 0** disable AAA on the console.

Example 12-3 *Router Configuration Example for AAA Using TACACS+*

```
aaa new-model
aaa authentication login default group tacacs+ local
aaa authentication login NO_AUTHEN none
aaa authentication ppp default if-needed group tacacs+ local
aaa authorization exec default group tacacs+ if-authenticated
aaa authorization exec NO_AUTHOR none
aaa authorization commands 15 default group tacacs+
aaa authorization commands 15 NO_AUTHOR none
aaa accounting exec default stop-only group tacacs+
aaa accounting commands 15 default stop-only group tacacs+
aaa accounting network default start-stop group tacacs+
!
username admin privilege 15 password 7 xxxxxxxxxxxx
username diallocal access-class 110 password 7 xxxxxxxxxxx
username diallocal autocommand ppp
!
tacacs-server host 172.22.53.204
tacacs-server key ciscorules
!
line con 0
 authorization commands 15 NO_AUTHOR
 authorization exec NO_AUTHOR
 login authentication NO_AUTHEN
 transport input none
```

Example 12-4 shows AAA with RADIUS. The first command enables AAA. The second command configures the router to use the RADIUS server for authentication. The following commands configure parameters for authorization and accounting by using the RADIUS server. The **radius-server host** command provides the IP address and RADIUS key. The commands under **line con 0** disable AAA on the console.

Example 12-4 *Router Configuration Example for AAA Using RADIUS*

```
aaa new-model
aaa authentication login default group radius local
aaa authentication login NO_AUTHEN none
aaa authentication ppp default if-needed group radius local
aaa authorization exec default group radius if-authenticated
aaa authorization exec NO_AUTHOR none
```

Example 12-4 *Router Configuration Example for AAA Using RADIUS (Continued)*

```
aaa authorization commands 15 NO_AUTHOR none
aaa accounting exec default stop-only group radius
aaa accounting network default start-stop group radius
!
username admin privilege 15 password 7 xxxxxxxxxxxxx
username diallocal access-class 110 password 7 xxxxxxxxxxx
username diallocal autocommand ppp
!
radius-server host 172.22.53.204 auth-port 1645 acct-port 1646 key ciscorules
!
line con 0
 authorization commands 15 NO_AUTHOR
 authorization exec NO_AUTHOR
 login authentication NO_AUTHEN
 transport input none
```

Kerberos

Kerberos is a network authentication protocol that is designed to provide authentication for client/server applications by using secret-key cryptography. The Kerberos protocol uses strong cryptography so that a client can prove its identity to a server (and vice versa) across an insecure network connection. After a client and server use Kerberos to prove their identity, they can also encrypt all their communications to ensure privacy and data integrity as they conduct their business.

Kerberos is not a test topic; therefore, it is not covered further in this book. TACACS and RADIUS are AAA protocols that are definitely in the test; these are covered here.

TACACS

TACACS was first discussed in RFC 1492, "An Access Control Protocol, Sometimes Called TACACS." Cisco has three versions of the protocol:

- TACACS
- Extended TACACS
- TACACS+

TACACS is the first standards-based implementation of the protocol. Extended TACACS (XTACACS) is an extension of the protocol that provides additional router information. Both of these versions are deprecated and are no longer supported by Cisco.

TACACS+ is the supported version of the protocol, which provides detailed accounting information and flexible administrative control over authentication and authorization processes. It is supported in the Cisco ACS server. TACACS+ is facilitated through AAA and can be enabled only through AAA commands.

Key TACACS+ features are as follows:

- TACACS+ separates AAA into three distinct functions (authentication, authorization and accounting).
- TACACS+ supports router command authorization integration with advanced authentication mechanisms, such as Data Encryption Standard (DES) and One-Time Password (OTP) key.
- TACACS+ supports 16 different privilege levels (0 to 15).
- TACACS+ permits the control of services, such as Point-to-Point Protocol (PPP), shell, standard log in, enable, AppleTalk Remote Access (ARA) protocol, Novell Asynchronous Services Interface (NASI), remote command (RCMD), and firewall proxy.
- TACACS+ permits the blocking of services to a specific port, such as a TTY or VTY interface on a router.

The most common services supported by TACACS+ are PPP for IP and router EXEC shell access by using console or VTY ports. The EXEC shell allows users to connect to router shells and select services (such as PPP, Telnet, TN3270) or to manage the router itself.

RADIUS

RADIUS was initially created by Livingston Enterprises and is defined by the draft standard RFC 2865, "Remote Authentication Dial In User Service (RADIUS)," and RFC 2866, "RADIUS Accounting."

Internet service providers (ISPs) often use RADIUS with remote access servers. With RADIUS, a router or network access server (NAS) operates as a client of RADIUS. The client is responsible for passing user information to the designated RADIUS servers and then acting on the response, which is returned. RADIUS servers are responsible for receiving user connection requests, authenticating the user, and then returning all configuration information necessary for the client to deliver service to the user.

A RADIUS server can act as a proxy client to other RADIUS servers or other kinds of authentication servers. In this function, the router or NAS sends RADIUS requests to the RADIUS-proxy-server, which, in turn, sends it to another RADIUS server. The response is sent back to the NAS. Service provider wholesaling services use this method.

Transactions between the client and RADIUS server are authenticated through the use of a shared secret, which is never sent over the network. Any user passwords are sent encrypted between the client and RADIUS server to eliminate the possibility that someone snooping on an unsecured network can determine a user's password.

TACACS+ and RADIUS Compared

As a CCIE candidate, you need to know the differences between TACACS+ and RADIUS for the exam. Table 12-4 describes the differences between these protocols.

Table 12-4 *RADIUS Versus TACACS+*

	RADIUS	TACACS+
Transport Protocol	Newer RADIUS implementations use UDP port 1812. Earlier versions used UDP port 1645, plus 1646 for accounting.	Uses TCP
Encryption	Encrypts only the password in the access-request packet and is less secure.	Encrypts the entire body of the packet and is more secure
AAA	Combines authentication and authorization.	Uses the AAA architecture, which separates authentication, authorization, and accounting
Standard	Industry standard.	Cisco proprietary
Multiprotocol Support	Does not support AppleTalk Remote Access, NetBIOS Frame Protocol Control protocol, Novell NASI, and X.25 PAD connections.	Offers multiprotocol support
Authorization support	Does not allow users to control which commands can be executed on a router.	Provides two ways to control the authorization of router commands: on a per-user or per-group basis

Firewalls

Firewalls prevent unauthorized access to resources. Firewalls can be a single specialized device or a group of devices that filter addresses, ports, and applications.

Demilitarized Zone (DMZ) Architecture

A *firewall* is a system of devices and applications that protect one network from an untrusted network, such as the Internet. Usually, it is implemented with a three-layered design. On the outside is a filtering router that implements access lists to permit access to only hosts in the Isolation local-area network (LAN). In the center, the DMZ is implemented by using specialized hosts to permit services such as web server, DNS, FTP servers, e-mail relays, and Telnet. These hosts are usually referred to as bastion hosts. Most of the time, the DMZ resides on a third leg (interface) of a firewall.

An inside router permits access from the internal network to the Isolation LAN. There should be no devices communicating directly from the inside network to the outside router (no backdoors).

Figure 12-5 shows a diagram of a three-part firewall system. The outside filtering router restricts Telnet access to itself, uses static routing, and encrypts passwords. It permits access to the bastion hosts based on specific TCP/UDP port numbers. Use the **established** keyword to allow inbound TCP packets from established TCP sessions. The inside filtering router also allows inbound TCP packets from established TCP sessions. It permits access to bastion hosts in the Isolation LAN, such as proxy services, Domain Name System (DNS), and web servers.

Figure 12-5 *Firewall System*

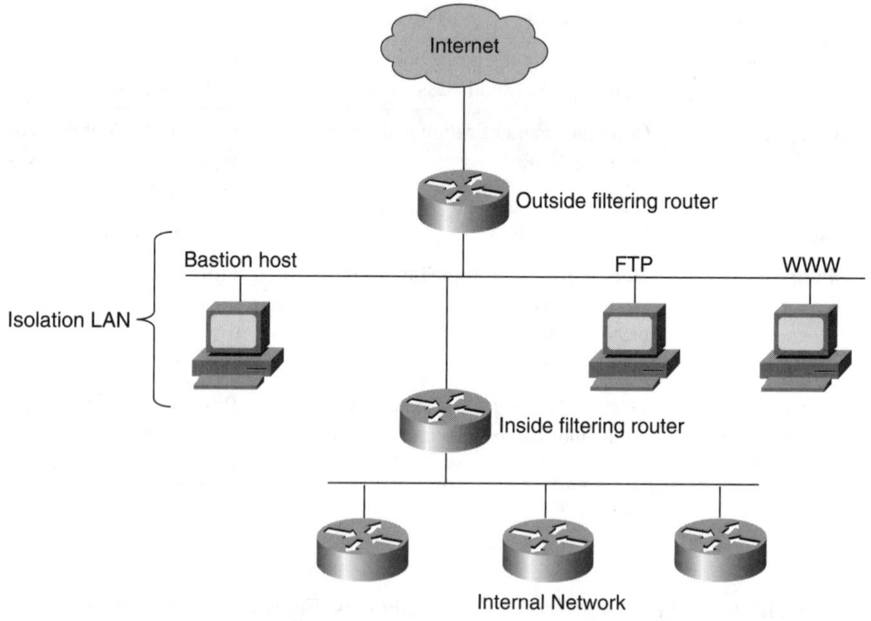

Access Lists in Firewall Implementations

The filtering routers are configured with access lists to restrict access to hosts. Extended IP access lists (100 to 199) filter IP networks and transport ports. Chapter 10, "Administrative Distance, Access Lists, Route Manipulation, and IP Multicast," discusses IP access lists.

Cisco PIX Firewall

Sites that require strong security can use the Cisco Firewall in addition to or instead of packet-filtering routers. Cisco's PIX Firewall is a hardware device that offers more robust security than packet-filtering routers, provides Network Address Translation (NAT), and verifies inbound traffic state information. NAT translations can be static or dynamic, and are verified on the command line interface.

The Cisco Secure PIX Firewall provides security with a protection scheme that is based on the Adaptive Security Algorithm (ASA), which offers stateful connection-oriented firewalling. Stateful security is less complex and more robust than packet filtering. It also offers higher performance and is more scalable than application-level proxy firewalls. ASA tracks the source and destination address, TCP sequence numbers, port numbers, and additional TCP flags of each packet.

An example of architecture with a PIX Firewall is shown in Figure 12-6. The PIX controls access between the outside and isolation network and between the isolation network and the inside. NAT can translate inside node IP addresses to an outside IP address pool.

Figure 12-6 *DMZ with PIX Firewall*

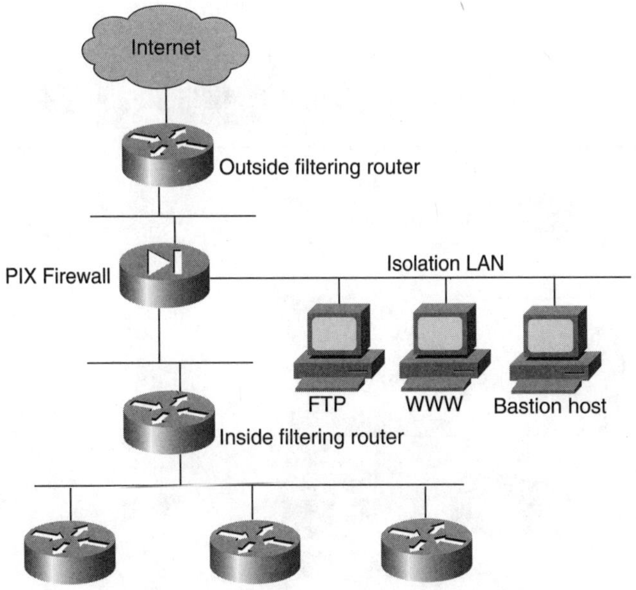

Some enterprises implement a multilayered firewall system, as shown in Figure 12-7. In this system, a PIX Firewall filters between the Internet and the DMZ. Another firewall filters between the DMZ and inside hosts. Hosts are connected to the Isolation LAN to provide services to Internet clients and connected to the inside Isolation LAN to provide service or for administrator access.

Figure 12-7 *Multilayered Firewall System*

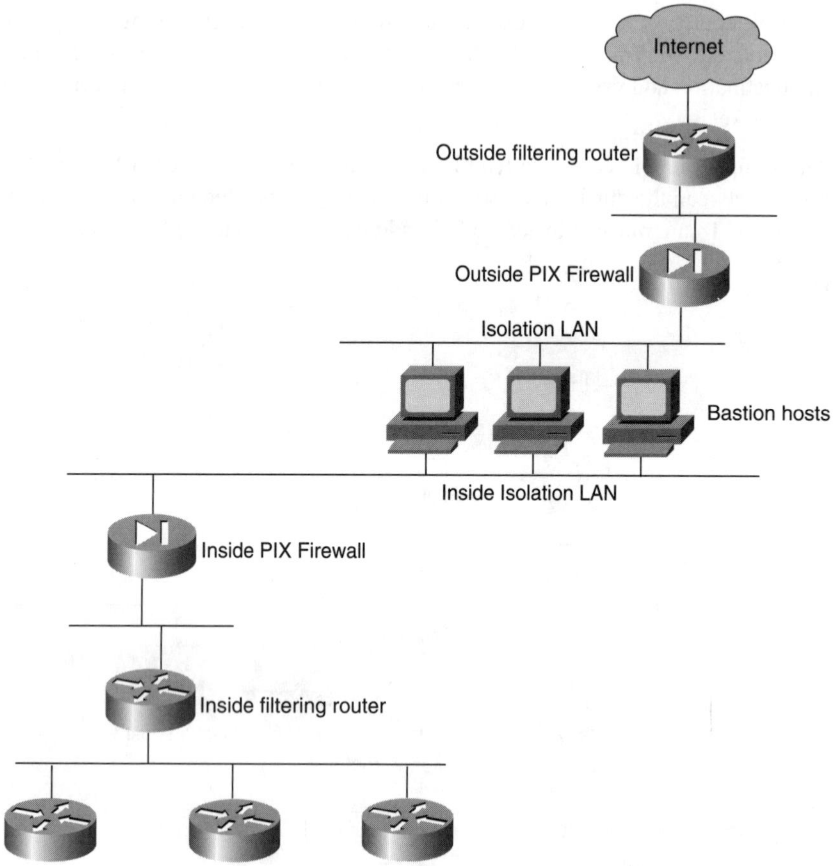

PIX Firewall Configuration

This section contains a simple PIX Firewall configuration. The PIX Firewall has exec and enable modes that are similar to a router. Set the exec password with the **passwd** command. Set the enable password with the **enable password** command. Configure outside and inside IP addresses with the **ip address** command. Configure static routes for outbound and inbound packets with the **route inside** and **route outside** commands.

Use the **nat** and **global** commands together to configure outbound translations. The **nat** command specifies which inside hosts are translated. The **global** command configures the outside addresses to which translations occur. The outside global addresses are Internet routable, globally unique addresses.

Use the **static** and **conduit** commands together to configure inbound connections, such as web server access. The **static** command configures the static outside to inside translation. The **conduit** command configures the allowed IP or ports that can be accessed inbound.

In Example 12-5, the inside 10.0.0.0 address is dynamically translated to 200.200.100.0/24. When NAT addresses run out, port address translation (PAT) translates them to 200.200.100.251. Inbound access is allowed to the web server with the global address of 200.200.200.1 with an inside address of 10.1.1.1.

Example 12-5 *Simple PIX Firewall Configuration*

```
enable password Yxxxxxxxx2 encrypted
passwd 8xxxxxxxxxK encrypted
hostname Pix1
ip address outside 200.200.1.5 255.255.255.224
ip address inside 10.10.1.1 255.255.255.0
global (outside) 1 200.200.100.1-200.200.100.250 netmask 255.255.255.0
global (outside) 1 200.200.100.251 netmask 255.255.255.0
nat (inside) 1 10.0.0.0 255.0.0.0 0 0
static (inside,outside) 200.200.200.1 10.1.1.1 netmask 255.255.255.255 0 0
conduit permit tcp host 200.200.200.1 eq www any
route outside 0.0.0.0 0.0.0.0 200.200.1.2 1
route inside 10.0.0.0 255.0.0.0 10.10.1.65 1
```

PIX Firewall Models

Several models of the PIX Firewall exist, as described in Table 12-5.

Table 12-5 *PIX Firewall Models*

Model	Description	Number of Sessions Supported
PIX 535	Processor: 1.0-GHz Intel Pentium III Random-access memory (RAM): 512 MB, or 1 GB of Synchronous Dynamic RAM (SDRAM) (Registered PC133) Flash Memory: 16 MB Cache: 256 KB Level 2 at 1 GHz System BUS: Dual 64-bit, 66-MHz PCI; Single 32-bit, 33-MHz PCI	500,000

continues

Table 12-5 *PIX Firewall Models (Continued)*

Model	Description	Number of Sessions Supported
PIX 525	Processor: 600 MHz Intel Pentium III RAM: Up to 256 MB Flash Memory: 16 MB Interfaces: Dual integrated 10/100 Base-T Fast Ethernet (FE), RJ-45 PCI Slots: 3	280,000
PIX 515 (515-R and 515-UR)	Processor: 200-MHz processor RAM: 32 MB (515-R), 64 MB (515-UR) Interfaces: Dual integrated 10/100 Base-T FE, RJ-45	50,000 (515-R) 100,000 (515-UR)
PIX 506E	Processor: 300 MHz Intel Celeron RAM: 32 MB Flash Memory: 8 MB Interfaces: Dual integrated 10 Base-T ports, RJ-45	Simultaneous VPN peers: up to 25
PIX 501	For small office or teleworkers For broadband (DSL and cable modem) environments *Processor:* 133 MHz AMD SC520 Processor *RAM:* 16 MB of SDRAM *Flash memory:* 8 MB *System bus:* Single 32-bit, 33-MHz PCI	Concurrent connections: 3500 Simultaneous VPN Peers: up to 5

Encryption

Encryption is the process of taking cleartext data and encoding it in such a way that only the system with a certain key can decode it. The data is encoded by the sender, transmitted over unsecured lines, and decoded by the receiver. Data is encrypted for various reasons, such as to protect data privacy and provide data integrity.

Public/Private Key Encryption

Keys are a sequence of digits that encrypt and decrypt data. The longer the key length, the less likely an unauthorized person or system can decrypt the data.

Public-key encryption uses a *private* key and a *public* key. The private key is known only to the source system. The public key is given to the receiver or any system that wants to communicate securely with it. To decode an encrypted message, a system must use the public key, which is provided by the originating system, and its own private key. All systems keep their private key secret but share the public key with everyone who might want to communicate with them.

Cisco Encryption Technology (CET)

Encryption can occur in one of three places in the Open System Interconnection (OSI) layered model:

- Physical/data-link (1–2)
- Network/transport (3–4)
- Application layers (5–7)

Physical encryption occurs in specialized hardware to encrypt data in links. Application layer encryption occurs between end hosts. Network layer encryption is routable. Cisco implements network layer encryption with its CET.

CET uses the following technologies:

- **Digital Signature Standard (DSS)**—A public/private key system to verify the identity of another party and also to prove a user's own identity when communicating through electronic means.
- **Diffie-Hellman**—For key exchange, but it does not exchange the keys.
- **Digital Encryption Standard (DES)**—Encrypts and decrypts data.

DES

DES is a U.S. Government standard that is widely used for encryption. DES uses a 56-bit key to scramble and unscramble messages. A 40-bit bit version exists for exported DES. The latest DES standard uses a 3 × 56 bit key (168 bit-key called Triple DES), where the input is encrypted three times. When you use it for communication, both sender and receiver must know the same secret key, which can encrypt and decrypt the message, or generate and verify a message authentication code.

Desktop Protocols

This section covers desktop protocols that are still included in the new CCIE Routing and Switching (R&S) written exam blueprint. Cisco removed AppleTalk and DECnet from the blueprint. This section discusses Novell IPX addressing and protocols and Windows NT protocols.

Novell IPX

Although newer implementations of Novell operating systems use TCP/IP, the Novell IPX protocols are still required knowledge for the written test. This section discusses the IPX protocols.

IPX Protocols

Figure 12-8 shows the NetWare protocol suite and the relationship with the OSI reference model from the network layer and up. IPX runs over the commonly implemented Layer-2 protocols, such as Ethernet, Token Ring, PPP, and so on.

Figure 12-8 *NetWare Protocols*

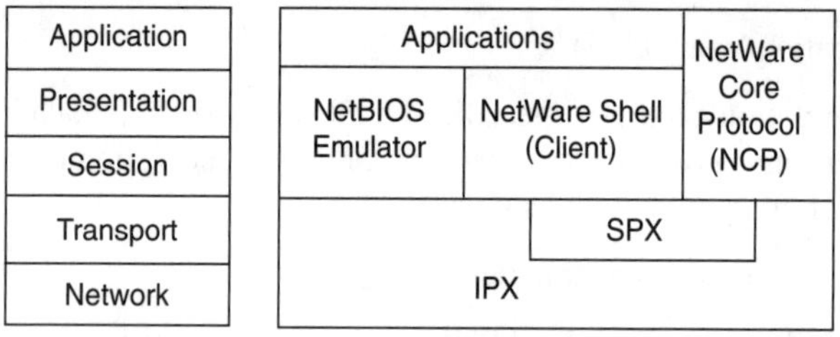

IPX

IPX is the network layer protocol that legacy Novell systems use (especially in version 3.x). IPX is a connectionless packet-based protocol, which is similar to IP. IPX uses IPX Routing Information Protocol (RIP) or *NetWare Link Services Protocol* (NLSP) for routing.

SPX (Sequenced Packet Exchange)

SPX protocol is the NetWare connection-oriented transport protocol. SPX is a reliable, connection-oriented protocol that supplements the datagram service provided by the IPX, NetWare's network layer (Layer 3) protocol.

NetWare Core Protocol (NCP)

NCP is a series of server routines designed to satisfy application requests coming from, for example, the NetWare shell. The services provided by NCP include file access, printer access, name management, accounting, security, and file synchronization.

Network Basic Input/Output System (NetBIOS)

NetWare also supports the (NetBIOS) session layer interface specification from Sytek. Novell's NetBIOS emulation software allows programs written to the industry-standard NetBIOS interface to run within NetWare system.

The NetWare shell runs clients (often called workstations in the NetWare community) and intercepts application input/output (I/O) calls to determine whether they require network access for completion. If the application request requires network access, the NetWare shell packages the request and sends it to lower-layer software for processing and network transmission. If the application request does not require network access, the request is passed to the local I/O resources. Client applications are unaware of any network access required for completion of application calls.

Get Nearest Server (GNS)

Clients learn their network number by sending a GNS broadcast. Servers on the local segment respond to the broadcast and the client selects a server. If no servers are on the local segment, the router responds to the GNS.

On the router, a GNS request for a file server chooses the server at the top of its respective type portion of the table if all servers have the same metric and hop count. Whenever a file server is taken out of service and then put back in service sometime later, it is put back in the Service Advertising Protocol (SAP) table at the top of the list for its respective type/metric.

NetWare Directory Services (NDS)

NDS is a distributed information database that stores information about all Internet, intranet, and network resources on a network. NDS is a directory service that can store and manage millions of objects, such as users, applications, network devices, and data. NDS natively supports the directory standard Lightweight Directory Access Protocol (LDAP) version 3 over Secure Socket Layer (SSL).

The NDS directory is a list of objects that represent network resources, such as network users, groups, servers, printers, print queues, and applications. It provides a single, global, and logical view of all network resources and services. The NDS directory also provides single logon applications.

NDS organizes resources or objects in a hierarchical tree structure. The organization can arrange resources in the directory tree according to the policies and procedures unique to the company.

IPX Addressing

An IPX address is an 80-bit value that consists of a 32-bit network number and a 48-bit host number. The 32-bit network address is represented in hexadecimal format and is configured by the network administrator. The host part of the IPX address is the 48-bit Media Access Control (MAC) address of the network node. The host part is not configured by the network administrator; although, it can be changed on some devices, such as routers. Novell's strict definition of the address also includes a 16-bit socket number that makes the address 96 bits in length.

Table 12-6 shows an IPX network number in binary and hexadecimal format. Every 4 bits of the binary number is converted to hexadecimal, and vice versa.

Table 12-6 *IPX Network Number in Binary and Hexadecimal*

Binary	0000	0001	0011	1111	1100	0101	0010	1110
Hexadecimal	0	1	3	F	C	5	2	E

A host in the 013FC52E network can have the IPX address of 013FC52E.00c0.02a2.04bc. Some valid network addresses include 00000001, 0000dead, 00035a8, dadadada, 0abcdef0, 00badbad, and 00addbed.

IPX RIP and SAP

IPX RIP is a legacy distance vector routing protocol for the Novell operating system when using IPX. IPX RIP sends periodic updates every 60 seconds and flushes routes in 180 seconds. IPX RIP uses tick as the distance vector metric. A *tick* is a delay assigned to interfaces of a router. One tick is $1/18^{th}$ of a second. LAN media has by default 1 tick, and any WAN media has a 6-tick metric. In the case of two paths with equal tick counts, hop count is the tiebreaker. As with IP RIP, IPX RIP has a maximum hop count limit of 15 hops. IPX RIP updates include 50 routes per packet.

IPX SAP advertises the addresses and service capabilities of network resources, such as file and print servers. SAP is a companion protocol to IPX RIP. RIP takes care of network advertising, and SAP takes care of service advertising. AS with IPX RIP updates, SAP advertisements are sent every 60 seconds. Routers gather SAP advertisements, add them to the local SAP table, and broadcast their SAP table every 60 seconds. IPX SAP includes 7 SAP entries per packet.

Configuring IPX RIP

IPX networks are enabled by configuring interfaces with IPX network numbers and enabling IPX RIP on routers. Example 12-6 shows a configuration example of IPX. First, IPX routing is enabled with the **ipx routing** command. Interfaces are configured with the 32-bit IPX network number with the **ipx network** command. In Example 12-6, Ethernet 0 is configured with IPX network 0x10. IPX RIP is enabled with the **ipx router rip** command.

Example 12-6 *Configuration of IPX RIP*

```
hostname RouterA
!
ipx routing
!
interface ethernet 0
 ipx network 10
!
interface ethernet 1
 ipx network 11
!
interface serial 0
 ipx network aa
!
interface serial 1
 ipx network a0
!
ipx router rip
```

NLSP

IPX RIP and SAP each produce periodic broadcasts every 60 seconds, which adds significant traffic to the network. NLSP is a link-state protocol that is designed to overcome the limitations of IPX RIP/SAP. NLSP has characteristics similar to other link-state protocols. Link-state PDUs (LSPs) are generated by routers and are flooded throughout the network. Each router receives the LSPs and independently computes best paths to destinations. Updates are sent only when changes occur. NLSP is based on the OSI Intermediate System-to-Intermediate System (IS-IS) routing protocol.

NLSP also supports up to 127 hops and permits hierarchical routing with area, domain, and global internetwork components. An *area* is a collection of connected networks with the same area address, and a *domain* is a collection of areas. A *global internetwork* is a collection of domains.

Novell's NLSP specification defines Level 1, Level 2, and Level 3 routers. Level 1 routers connect networked systems within a given routing area. Areas connect to each other by Level 2 routers, and domains connect by Level 3 routers. A Level 2 router also acts as a Level 1 router within its own area; likewise, a Level 3 router also acts as a Level 2 router within its own domain. Cisco's implementation of NLSP implements only Level 1 routing.

NLSP supports hierarchical addressing, in which each area is identified by a 32-bit address and a 32-bit mask. This is similar to the masking in IP addressing. The mask helps identify the network address for an area. For example, consider the address of 00705A00 with a mask of FFFFFF00. With this mask, the first 24 bits of the address identify the area. For this example, the area is 00705A and the remaining 8 bits are set aside for networks within this area.

NLSP Configuration

NLSP is enabled by the **ipx router nlsp** command. An **area-address** command sets network numbers of the current NLSP area. Each interface is also configured to use NLSP with the **ipx nlsp enable** command.

Example 12-7 shows an example of NLSP configuration. An internal network address is assigned to the router with the **ipx internal-network** command. Each interface is enabled for NLSP routing with the **ipx nlsp enable** command. In Example 12-7, IPX RIP is disabled with the **no ipx router rip** command. An area address is assigned to the router with the **area-address** command.

Example 12-7 *NLSP Configuration Example*

```
ipx routing
ipx internal-network a100
!
interface ethernet 0
 ipx network a101
 ipx nlsp enable
!
interface ethernet 1
 ipx network a102
 ipx nlsp enable
!
interface serial 0
 ipx network a10a
 ipx nlsp enable
!
no ipx router rip
!
ipx router nlsp
 area-address aaaaa000 ffff0000
```

IPX EIGRP

Using Enhanced Interior Gateway Routing Protocol (EIGRP) on IPX networks provides fast rerouting and partial update capabilities that IPX RIP does not provide. EIGRP has several capabilities that are designed to facilitate large Novell networks that use IPX:

- Supports incremental SAP updates and route updates only when changes occur
- Increases the network to 224 hops, from the IPX RIP limit of 15 hops
- Provides for optimal path selection by using EIGRP metrics versus the IPX RIP ticks and hop count metric

IPX EIGRP is usually configured on serial links with IPX RIP over the local LAN. IPX RIP is configured to not broadcast on the interfaces running IPX EIGRP. Example 12-8 shows an example of the configuration of IPX EIGRP. Each interface is configured with the **ipx network** command. IPX EIGRP is enabled with the **ipx router eigrp** command. In the example, the IPX networks of the serial interfaces are configured for IPX EIGRP with the **network aa** and **network a0** commands. Networks AA and A0 are disabled for IPX RIP.

Example 12-8 *IPX EIGRP Configuration*

```
hostname RouterA
!
ipx routing
!
interface ethernet 0
 ipx network 10
!
interface ethernet 1
 ipx network 11
!
interface serial 0
 ipx network aa
!
interface serial 1
 ipx network a0
!
ipx router eigrp 10
 network aa
 network a0
!
ipx router rip
 no network aa
 no network a0
```

Routes are verified with the **show ipx route** command. Routes learned from EIGRP are marked with an (E), as shown in Example 12-9.

Example 12-9 *Output for the* **show ipx route** *Command*

```
C  Net 20 (HDLC), is directly connected, 66 uses, Serial0
C  Net 30 (HDLC), is directly connected, 73 uses, Serial1
E  Net 45 [2195456/0] via 30.0000.0c00.c47e, age 0:01:23, 1 uses, Serial1
C  Net AA (NOVELL-ETHER), is directly connected, 3 uses, Ethernet0
R  Net BB [1/1] via AA.0000.0c03.8b25,  48 sec, 87 uses, Ethernet0
```

IPXWAN

IPXWAN is a connection startup protocol that establishes link configuration information prior to sending traffic over WAN dialup links. IPXWAN allows a Cisco router to connect to other vendor routers by using the IPXWAN protocol. One of the primary advantages of IPXWAN is the ability to define unnumbered IPX point-to-point (p2p) links. You use PPP encapsulation when connecting a Cisco router with a Novell Server with IPXWAN. You can use high-level data link control (HDLC) encapsulation when connecting two Cisco routers with IPXWAN.

IPX Access Lists

IPX access lists filter the routes broadcasted by IPX RIP. The standard IPX access list numbers range from 800 to 899. The extended IPX access list numbers range from 900 to 999.

The command syntax for a standard access list is as follows:

```
access-list access-list-number [permit | deny] source-net destination-net
```

The command syntax for an extended access list is as follows:

```
access-list access-list-number [protocol] source-net source-socket
    destination-net destination-socket
```

The *protocol* field can be a number from 0 to 255 or one of the following keywords: **any**, **ncp**, **netbios**, **rip**, **sap**, **spx**.

The access list is applied on interfaces with the **ipx input-network-filter** or **ipx output-network-filter** commands.

Example 12-10 filters network 10 outbound on serial 0. The first line in access list 800 denies IPX network 10. The second line permits all other IPX networks.

Example 12-10 *IPX Network Access List*

```
interface e0
 ipx network a0
interface e1
 ipx network 10
interface s0
 ipx network aa
 ipx output-network-filter 800
!
ipx routing
!
access-list 800 deny 10
access-list 800 permit -1
```

SAP Access Lists

SAP access lists can be configured to filter SAP updates that are based on the source network address, the SAP number, and the name of the server that is generating the SAP service. SAP numbers are 16 bits in length. Some SAP numbers are 0x0004 for file server, 0x0007 for print server, and 0x0047 for advertising the print server. A list of Novell SAP numbers can be found at the following site:

www.iana.org/assignments/novell-sap-numbers

SAP access lists on Cisco routers use list numbers 1000 to 1099. The format is as follows:

```
access-list access-list-number [deny | permit] network[.node]
    [service-type [server-name]]
```

The *access-list numbers* range from 1000 to 1099. The *network* number is a valid 32-bit IPX network number. A network number of -1 indicates any network. The *service-type* is a valid 16-bit SAP number. The access list can be applied as an **output-sap-filter** or **input-sap-filter**. Example 12-11 shows an example of a SAP access list. An input SAP filter is configured on Ethernet 0 by using access list 1000.

Example 12-11 *SAP Access List*

```
interface ethernet 0
 ipx network 8CAF3C00
 ipx input-sap-filter 1000
!
access-list 1000 permit 8CAF3C00.00aa.0056.3527 3FC
access-list 1000 permit -1 4
access-list 1000 permit -1 47 PRINTSVER
access-list 1000 deny -1
```

Windows NT

Although newer implementations of NT (2000) implement TCP/IP protocols and move away from WINS and NetBIOS, the CCIE candidate must still have knowledge of the legacy protocols in NT.

Windows NT organizes clients and servers into NT domains. Each domain has a Primary Domain Controller (PDC) and one or more Backup Domain Controllers (BDC). Resources are given names that clients use to reach them. The four methods for a device to resolve friendly device names to IP addresses follow:

- LMHOSTS configuration file
- NetBIOS broadcast
- NetBIOS local cache
- Windows Internet Naming Service (WINS)

The LMHOSTS file is statically configured on the local computer.

NetBIOS

NT uses the session layer NetBIOS protocol for file and print sharing, messaging, and name resolution. By default, Windows computers send NAME_QUERY broadcasts to all devices on a segment. The device with the NetBIOS name that is being requested responds with its IP address. This produces broadcast traffic on the network. The device might also keep a table of NetBIOS names and corresponding IP addressing in its local cache.

NetBIOS runs over NetBIOS Extended User Interface (NetBEUI). With this method, the broadcasts are not routable and are only bridged. NetBIOS can also run over IPX; in NT environments, this is called NWLink. It uses IPX socket type 20. The most scalable solutions run NetBIOS over TCP/IP (NBT). With NBT, NetBIOS broadcasts still exist, but they run over TCP port 137. This provides the ability to filter NetBIOS with access lists.

WINS

WINS a service that provides a dynamic NetBIOS name registration database, which is similar to the service DNS provides for Internet names. The IP address of the WINS server can be automatically given to the clients through Dynamic Host Configuration Protocol (DHCP).

Windows clients register their NetBIOS names with the WINS server upon startup and then send unicast requests directly to the WINS server to resolve NetBIOS names to IP addresses, which virtually eliminates NAME_QUERY broadcasts. The stations use the WINS server to get name resolution, which reduces the NBT traffic, as shown in Figure 12-9.

Figure 12-9 *WINS*

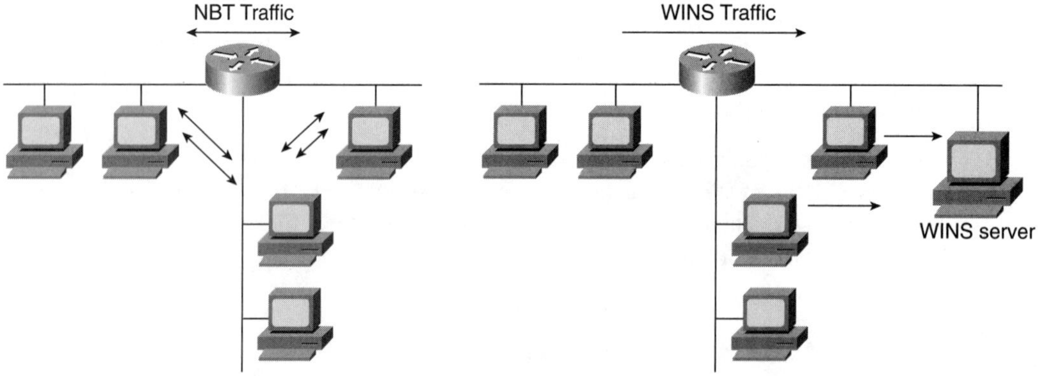

Filtering NetBIOS with Access Lists

If required, IP-extended access lists can filter NBT packets. NetBIOS name service uses UDP and TCP port 137; NetBIOS datagram service uses UDP and TCP port 138; and the NetBIOS session service uses UDP and TCP port 139.

The following is an example:

```
access-list 101 deny udp any any eq netbios-ns
access-list 101 deny tcp any any eq 137
access-list 101 permit ip any any
```

References Used

The following resources were used to create this chapter:

Internetworking Technologies Handbook, Second Edition, Cisco Press, 1998

Cisco IP Telephony, David Lovell, Cisco Press, 2002

CCDA Exam Certification Guide, Anthony Bruno/Jacqueline Kim, Cisco Press, 2000

RFC 1889, "RTP: A Transport Protocol for Real-Time Applications, Audio-Video Transport Working Group," H. Schulzrinne, S. Casner, R. Frederick, V. Jacobson

RFC 1890," RTP Profile for Audio and Video Conferences with Minimal Control, Audio-Video Transport Working Group," H. Schulzrinne

RFC 2543, "SIP: Session Initiation Protocol," M. Handley, H. Schulzrinne, E. Schooler, J. Rosenberg

RFC 2865, "Remote Authentication Dial In User Service (RADIUS)," C. Rigney, S. Willens, A. Rubens, W. Simpson

www.cisco.com/warp/public/cc/pd/rt/mc3810/prodlit/pvnet_in.htm

www.cisco.com/warp/public/788/pkt-voice-general/bwidth_consume.htm

www.cisco.com/univercd/cc/td/doc/product/software/ios113ed/113ed_cr/secur_c/scprt1/scaaa.htm

www.cisco.com/univercd/cc/td/doc/cisintwk/ito_doc/netwarep.htm

www.cisco.com/warp/public/cc/pd/iosw/ioft/mmcm/tech/h323_wp.htm

www.cisco.com/warp/public/cc/so/neso/sqso/eqso/encrp_wp.htm

www.cisco.com/univercd/cc/td/doc/cisintwk/ito_doc/netwarep.htm

Foundation Summary

The Foundation Summary is a condensed collection of material that provides a convenient review of key concepts in this chapter. If you are already comfortable with the topics in this chapter, this summary will help you recall a few details. If you just read the Foundation Topics section, this review should help solidify some key facts. If you are doing your final preparation before the exam, these materials are a convenient way to review the day before the exam.

Table 12-7 *Multiservice Technologies*

Technology	Description
FXS	Foreign Exchange Station
FXO	Foreign Exchange Office
E&M	Ear and Mouth—analog Trunk
Erlang	Total voice traffic volume in one hour
VAD	Voice activity detection
RTP	Real-Time Transport Protocol—carries coded voice; runs over UDP
RTCP	RTP Control Protocol
Codec	Coder-decoder—transforms analog signals into digital bit streams
H.323	ITU framework for multimedia protocols
SIP	Session initiation protocol—IETF framework for multimedia protocols
SS7	Allows voice and network calls to be routed and controlled by central call controllers; permits modern consumer telephone services

Table 12-8 *Codec Standards*

Codec	Bit Rate	Description
G.711u	64 kbps	Pulse code modulation (PCM); mu-law version in North America and Japan. Samples speech 8000 times per second represented in 8 bytes.
G.711a	64 kbps	PCM; a-law in Europe and in international routes.
G.723.1	6.3 kbps	MPE-MLQ (Multi-Pulse Excitation-Maximum Likelihood Quantization)
G.723.1	5.3 kbps	ACELP (algebraic code-excited linear prediction).
G.726	16/24/ 32/ 40 kbps	Adaptive differential pulse code modulation (AD-PCM).
G.729	8 kbps	CS-ACELP (Conjugate Structure ACELP).

AAA

AAA (triple A) provides a modular framework for configuring three security functions. The three functions are as follows:

- **Authentication**—Who is the user?
- **Authorization**—What resources can be accessed?
- **Accounting**—When was the device accessed, by whom, and what commands were used?

Table 12-9 *Security Protocols and Concepts*

Protocol	Description
Kerberos	A network authentication protocol
TACACS+	Terminal Access Controller Access Control System Plus; separates AAA, supports 16 privileges; encrypts full body of packet
RADIUS	Remote Authentication Dial-In User Service; only encrypts password; combines authentication with authorization
DMZ	Demilitarized Zone
PIX	Cisco Firewall that implements Adaptive Security Algorithm (ASA) for stateful security
CET	Cisco Encryption Technology; implements DSS, Diffie-Hellman, and DES
DES	56-bit key and 168-bit key with 3DES
DSS	Digital Signature Standard (DSS); uses a public/private key system to verify the identity of another party and also to prove a user's own identity when communicating through electronic means
Diffie-Hellman	For key exchange but it does not exchange the keys

Table 12-10 *Distance Vector Protocol Comparison*

Routing Protocol	Default Update Time (sec)	Routes Per Packet
IP RIP	30	25
IP IGRP	90	104
IPX RIP	60	50
IPX SAP	60	7

Q & A

The Q & A questions are more difficult than what you can expect on the actual exam. The questions do not attempt to cover more breadth or depth than the exam; however, they are designed to make sure that you retain the material. Rather than allowing you to derive the answer from clues hidden inside the question itself, these questions challenge your understanding and recall of the subject. Questions from the "Do I Know This Already?" quiz are repeated here to ensure that you have mastered the chapter's topic areas. A strong understanding of the answers to these questions will help you on the CCIE written exam. As an additional study aide, use the CD-ROM provided with this book to take simulated exams.

Select the best answer. Answers to these questions are in the Appendix, "Answers to Quiz Questions."

1 Which ITU standard provides a framework for multimedia protocols for the transport of voice, video, and data over packet-switched networks?

a. RTP/RCTP

b. VoIP

c. H.323

d. WFQ

2 Which of the following is the default codec that you use with VoIP dial peers?

a. G.711

b. G.723

c. G.728

d. G.729

3 Which authentication protocol uses TCP?

a. Kerberos

b. TACACS

c. RADIUS

d. AAA

4 Which encryption method uses a 168-bit key?

a. DES

b. PGP

c. 3DES

d. IPSec

5 What is AAA?

a. Automation, authentication, and accounting

b. Authentication, abomination, and accounting

c. Automation, authorization, and accounting

d. Authentication, authorization, and accounting

6 RTP operates in which layer of the OSI model?

a. Application

b. Session

c. Transport

d. Network

7 Which H.323 protocol is responsible for call setup and signaling?

a. H.245

b. Q.931

c. H.225

d. RTCP

8 Which unit measures the number of voice calls in one hour?

a. Kbps

b. Erlangs

c. DS0

d. FXS

9 Which feature does not transmit packets when there is silence?

a. E&M

b. VAD

c. Dial-Peer

d. DSS

10 What does CRTP compresses?

a. The RTP header

b. The RTP, TCP, and IP headers

c. The RTP, UDP, and IP headers

d. The RTCP header

11 Which protocol(s) reduce broadcasts in an IPX internetwork?

a. IPX RIP

b. NLSP

c. IPX EIGRP

d. Answers b and c

12 How many bits are in an IPX address?

a. 32 bits

b. 48 bits

c. 60 bits

d. 80 bits

13 Which is not a valid IPX network number?

a. DEAD

b. 0FFFFFF0

c. DEAGF0

d. 10

14 Which method is preferred for transporting NetBIOS?

a. NetBEUI

b. NBT

c. ATP

d. Ethernet

15 Which IETF standard provides a framework for multimedia protocols for the transport of voice, video, and data over packet-switched networks?

a. RTP/RCTP

b. VoIP

c. H.323

d. SIP

16 Which authentication protocol uses UDP?

a. Kerberos

b. TACACS

c. RADIUS

d. AAA

17 What is FXS?

a. Feeder Exchange Station

b. Foreign Exchange Source

c. Foreign Exchange Station

d. Federal Exchange Station

18 Which codec produces 64 kbps of bandwidth?

a. G.711

b. G.723

c. G.726

d. G.729

19 Which SS7 component is a database?

a. SCP

b. STP

c. SSP

d. Billing

20 Which AAA function determines which resources are accessed?

a. Accounting

b. Authorization

c. Authentication

d. TACACS

21 Which authentication protocol separates each AAA function into separate modules?

a. Kerberos

b. RADIUS

c. TACACS+

d. AAA

22 Which AAA function identifies the user?

a. Accounting

b. Authorization

c. Authentication

d. TACACS

23 Which algorithm does the Cisco PIX Firewall use?

a. Adaptive Security Algorithm

b. Authoritative Security Algorithm

c. Authenticating Security Algorithm

d. Access Security algorithm

24 Which of the following are QoS tools that you can use for VoIP networks?

a. CQ and TCP compression

b. CRTP and WFQ

c. DES and CRTP

d. ATM and UDP header compression

25 An IPX address consists of what?

a. 32-bit network and 8-bit host part

b. 24-bit network part and 8-bit host part

c. 24-bit network part and 48-bit host part

d. 32-bit network part and 48-bit host part

26 Which service can reduce NetBIOS traffic?

a. DNS

b. WINS

c. GNS

d. SAP

27 Which access list number can filter IPX SAP traffic?

a. 850

b. 101

c. 989

d. 1099

28 NLSP is which type of protocol?

a. Hybrid

b. Distance vector

c. Link-state

d. Broadcast

29 Which protocol do you use in a routed TCP/IP network for Network Neighborhood browsing?

a. NetBEUI

b. NWlink

c. NBT

d. Internet Explorer

30 How often does IPX RIP broadcast its routing table?

a. Every 30 seconds

b. Every 60 seconds

c. Every 90 seconds

d. None of the above

31 How often does IPX EIGRP broadcast its routing table?

a. Every 30 seconds

b. Every 60 seconds

c. Every 90 seconds

d. None of the above

Scenarios

Scenario 12-1

Use the following configuration to answer the questions in this scenario:

```
dial-peer voice 100 pots
 destination-pattern 1111
 port 1/1
!
dial-peer voice 200 pots
 destination-pattern 1112
 port 1/2
!
dial-peer voice 8000 voip
 destination-pattern 2...
 session target ipv4:1.1.1.1
 vad
 ip precedence 4
!
dial-peer voice 8001 voip
 destination-pattern 3...
 session target ipv4:2.2.2.2
 vad
 ip precedence 4
!
interface serial 0
 ip address 3.1.1.1 255.255.255.252
 ip rtp header-compression
 ip rtp compression-connections 10
```

1 To which IP address are calls to 3111 sent?

a. 3.1.1.1

b. 1.1.1.1

c. 2.2.2.2

d. 255.255.255.252

2 What are the precedence bits set to for VoIP packets?

a. 010

b. 011

c. 100

d. 101

3 Are packets sent during silent spurs?

a. No, the IP precedence bit is set to 4.

b. No, VAD is disabled.

c. Yes, the dial-peer is over 8000.

d. No, VAD is enabled.

4 Where are calls to 1112 sent?

a. 2.2.2.2

b. Port 1/1

c. Port 1/2

d. 3.1.1.1

5 Which of the following is the default codec that you use in dial peer 8000?

a. G.711.

b. G.726.

c. G.729.

d. Not enough information is given.

Scenario 12-2

Use the following configuration to answer the questions in this scenario:

```
hostname router
!
ipx routing
!
interface ethernet 0
 ipx network 15
 ipx input-network-filter 850
!
interface ethernet 1
 ipx network 16
 ipx input-sap-filter 1050
!
interface serial 0
 ipx network 2a
!
interface serial 1
 ipx network 2b
!
ipx router eigrp 50
 network 2a
 network 2b
!
ipx router rip
 no network 2a
 no network 2b
```

```
!
access-list 850 deny 10
access-list 850 deny 11
access-list 850 deny a0
access-list 850 permit -1
!
access-list 1050 permit -1 4
access-list 1050 deny -1
```

1 What is the IPX network for Ethernet 0?

   a. 15

   b. 0x15

   c. 850

   d. 16

2 What does the filter configured for Ethernet 0 do?

   a. Filters IP networks 10, 11, and a0

   b. Filters SAP number 4

   c. Filters IPX networks 10, 11, and a0

   d. Denies all other IPX networks

3 What does the filter configured for Ethernet 1 do?

   a. Filters IP networks 10, 11, and a0

   b. Filters SAP number 4

   c. Filters IPX networks 10, 11, and a0

   d. Denies all other IPX networks

4 Which routing protocol do you use in the WAN interfaces?

   a. IPX RIP

   b. IPX NLSP

   c. IPX EIGRP

   d. IPX OSPF

5 Which routing protocol do you use in the Ethernet interfaces?

   a. IPX RIP

   b. IPX NLSP

   c. IPX EIGRP

   d. IPX OSPF

APPENDIX

Answers to Quiz Questions

This appendix contains answers to the Q & A questions from each chapter. In each chapter, the Q & A questions repeat the "Do I Know This Already" questions for assessment purposes, so you will also find the answers to those questions here as well. (The "Do I Know This Already" questions are always the first questions in each chapter's Q & A.) For your convenience, the questions are repeated here with the answers, so you can also use this appendix as a study tool.

Chapter 2 Answers to Q & A Section

1 Routers limit network traffic by controlling what?

a. DNS domain

b. Broadcast domain

c. Microsoft broadcast domains

d. Novell SAP broadcasts

Answer: b

Routers operate on the network layer. Routers limit the broadcast domain.

2 Which layer of the OSI model is responsible for converting frames into bits and bits into frames?

a. Network layer

b. Physical layer

c. Data-link layer

d. LLC layer

Answer: c

The data-link layer is responsible for converting frames into bits and vice versa.

3 Which scheme suppresses a route announcement out an interface from which the route was learned?

a. Holddowns

b. Split horizon

c. Poison reverse

d. Passive interface

Answer: b

Split horizon does not announce routes out the interface from which the route was learned.

4 Convert the following IP address into dotted decimal format:

10100010001011010001100111000000

a. 162.46.24.128

b. 162.45.25.92

c. 161.45.25.192

d. 162.45.25.192

Answer: d

Convert every 8 bits into decimal: 10100010 = 162, 00101101 = 45, 00011001 = 25, 11000000 = 192. The answer is 162.45.25.192.

5 List the routing protocols that support VLSM.

a. IGRP, EIGRP, OSPF, IS-IS

b. RIPv2, EIGRP, OSPF, IS-IS

c. EIGRP, OSPF, IS-IS, IGRP

d. EIGRP, OSPF, RIPv2, IGRP

Answer: b

EIGRP, OSPF, IS-IS, and RIPv2 support VLSM. RIPv1 and IGRP do not support VLSM.

6 When you have configured your router for EIGRP routing, how do you configure the gateway of last resort?

a. Use the **ip default-gateway** command.

b. Use the **ip-default gateway** command.

c. Use the **ip default-network** command.

d. Use the **ip default-gateway-network** command.

Answer: c

You use the ip default-network command to configure the gateway of last resort. You use the ip default-gateway command when routing is disabled.

7 If a Token Ring has been configured with ring number 24, what is its hexadecimal equivalent?

a. 0x18

b. 0x24

c. 0x16

d. 0x10

Answer: a

The hexadecimal equivalent of decimal 24 is 0x18.

8 Which layer of the hierarchical design model implements access lists, distribution lists, route summarization, VLAN routing, security policy, and address aggregation?

a. Session layer

b. Distribution layer

c. Transport layer

d. Core layer

Answer: b

The hierarchical design model consists of core, distribution, and access layers. The distribution layer implements access lists, distribution lists, route summarization, VLAN routing, security policy, and address aggregation.

9 Which routing protocol periodically sends its routing table to its neighbors?

a. A hierarchical routing protocol

b. A hybrid routing protocol

c. A link-state routing protocol

d. A distance vector routing protocol.

Answer: d

Distance vector routing protocols periodically send a copy of the full routing table to neighboring routers.

10 The switch functions of blocking and forwarding, which are based on a MAC address, operates in which layer of the OSI model?

a. Layer 3

b. Network layer

c. Data-link layer

d. Layer 1

Answer: c

Switches that implement these functions are essentially bridges that operate in the data-link layer (Layer 2).

11 Which is the best measurement of reliability and load of an interface?

a. Rely 255/255, load 1/255

b. Rely 255/255, load 255/255

c. Rely 1/255, load 1/255

d. Rely 1/255, load 255/255

Answer: a

The preferred reading for reliability is 100 percent or 255/255. The preferred reading for load is the nearest 0 percent or 1/255.

12 Which OSI layer deals with frames?

a. Physical layer

b. Layer 4

c. Network layer

d. Data-link layer

Answer: d

The data-link layer of the OSI model deals with frames, the physical layer deals with bits, the network layer deals with packets, and the transport layer (Layer 4) deals with segments.

13 Which type of routing protocol do you use between autonomous systems?

a. Interior Gateway Protocol

b. Exterior gateway protocol

c. Interior Gateway Routing Protocol

d. Nonrouting exterior gateway protocol

Answer: b

You use Interior Gateway Protocols (IGPs) within an autonomous system. Some IGPs are as follows: RIP, OSPF, IS-IS, and EIGRP. You use exterior gateway protocols (EGPs) between autonomous systems. BGPv4 is the commonly used EGP.

14 Which layer of the OSI model is concerned with data representation, data compression schemes, encryption, and voice coding?

a. Session layer

b. Presentation layer

c. Data-link layer

d. Physical layer

Answer: b

The presentation layer implements data representation with ASCII and EBCDIC. MPEG is a coding and compression example at the presentation layer. In VoIP, you use codecs in the presentation layer.

15 Which metric is concerned with the time a packet takes to travel from one end to another in the internetwork?

a. Cost

b. Reliability

c. Delay

d. Load

Answer: c

The delay metric measures the time it takes for a packet to travel.

16 Which summary route aggregates the following networks: 192.168.33.0/24, 192.168.32.0/25, 192.168.32.128/25, 192.168.34.0/23?

a. 192.168.33.0/22

b. 192.168.32.0/22

c. 192.168.30.0/22

d. 192.168.32.0/21

Answer: b

Network 192.168.32.0, with a mask of 255.255.252.0, summarizes from 192.168.32.0 to 192.168.35.255.

17 Which device controls collision domains but does not control broadcast domains?

a. Bridges

b. Hubs with Ethernet ports

c. Routers

d. Forwarding gateways

Answer: a

Bridges define the collision domain. Routers define the broadcast domain.

18 Which routing protocol requires a hierarchical topology?

a. IGRP

b. RIP

c. EIGRP

d. OSPF

Answer: d

OSPF requires a two-layer topology with all areas connecting to the backbone.

19 Which layer of the OSI model does TCP operate in?

a. Layer 3

b. Layer 4

c. Layer 5

d. Layer 6

Answer: b

TCP operates in the transport layer (Layer 4).

20 Convert 11011011 to decimal.

a. 199

b. 215

c. 219

d. 217

Answer: c

11011011 is 128+64+16+8+2+1 = 219.

21 Which OSI layer operates with packets?

a. Physical layer

b. Core layer

c. Network layer

d. Distribution layer

Answer: c

The physical layer deals with bits. The data-link layer deals with frames. The network layer deals with packets. The transport layer deals with segments.

22 For what metric is the value for a 10 Mbps Ethernet interface calculated as $10^8/10^7 = 10$?

a. Cost

b. Hop count

c. Bandwidth

d. Load

Answer: a

The OSPF cost metric is calculated as 10^8/BW.

23 In which type of routing protocol does each router advertise its status to all routers in the network, and each router calculates the best routes in the network?

a. Hop count

b. Link-state

c. Distance vector

d. Hybrid state

Answer: b

With link-state routing protocols the status of each router in the network is propagated to all other routers in the network, and each router calculates the best routes in the network.

24 Which command can be used to configure the default route out interface serial 0?

a. **ip default-gateway serial0**

b. **ip default 0.0.0.0 0.0.0.0 serial 0**

c. **ip default-network serial 0**

d. **ip route 0.0.0.0 0.0.0.0 serial 0**

Answer: d

The correct format is ip route 0.0.0.0 0.0.0.0 serial 0.

25 What is 0xFC in decimal?

a. 240

b. 248

c. 253

d. 252

Answer: d

0xFC is 11111100 in binary, which is 128+64+32+16+8+4 = 252.

26 A routing protocol that sends out routes with an unreachable metric is using what?

a. Metric holddowns

b. Poison reverse

c. Route updates

d. Simple split horizon

Answer: b

Split horizon with poison reverse sends a route with an infinite metric out the interface from which it learned the route.

27 Which hierarchical design model layer has high-speed backbone ATM switches with redundant connections?

a. Data-link layer

b. Core layer

c. Network layer

d. Transport layer

Answer: b

The core layer of the hierarchical design model uses high-speed connections.

28 Convert the mask 255.255.255.224 into binary.

a. 11111111 11111111 11111111 11000000

b. 11111111 11111111 11111111 11110000

c. 11111111 11111111 11111111 11100000

d. 00000000 00000000 00000000 00111111

Answer: c

11111111 = 255 and 11100000 = 224.

29 What does OSI stand for?

a. Operation System Interconnection

b. Open System Interconnection

c. Open Systems Interconnect

d. Operation Systems Interconnect

Answer: b

30 Which of the following routing protocols is classful?

a. IGRP

b. RIPv2

c. EIGRP

d. OSPF

Answer: a

Chapter 2 Answers to Scenario Section

Answer the following questions based on Figure 2-11. Each question tests your knowledge of how different metrics affect the chosen route to a destination.

Figure 2-11 *Scenario Diagram*

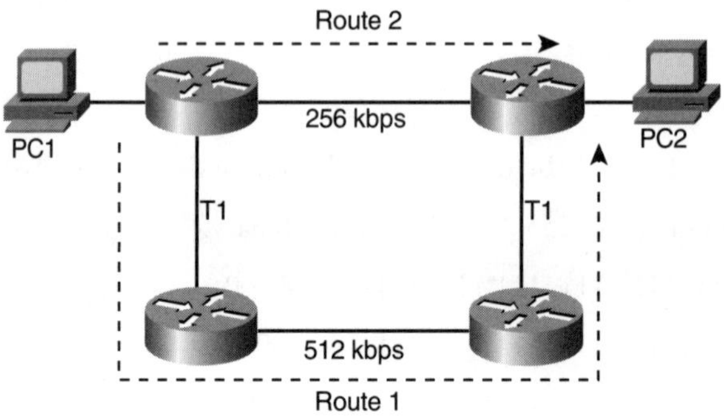

1 A user performs a Telnet from PC 1 to PC 2. If the metric that the configured routing protocol uses is bandwidth, which route will the packets take?

a. Route 1.

b. Route 2.

c. Neither, there is not sufficient information.

d. One packet takes Route 1, the following packet takes Route 2, and so on.

Answer: a

The maximum bandwidth through Route 1 is 512 kbps. The maximum bandwidth through Route 2 is 256 kbps. The route with the highest bandwidth is preferred, Route 1.

2 A user performs a Telnet from PC 1 to PC 2. If the metric that the configured routing protocol uses is hop count, which route will the packets take?

a. Route 1.

b. Route 2.

c. Neither, there is not sufficient information.

d. One packet takes Route 1, the following packet takes Route 2, and so on.

Answer: b

Route 2 has fewer router hops than Route 1.

3 A user performs a Telnet from PC 1 to PC 2. If the metric that the configured routing protocol uses is cost, which route will the packets take?

a. Route 1.

b. Route 2.

c. Neither, there is not sufficient information.

d. One packet takes Route 1, the following packet takes Route 2, and so on.

Answer: a

Route 2 has a higher cost than Route 1.

Chapter 3 Answers to Q & A Section

1 If the configuration register is set to 0x2101, where is the IOS image booted from?

a. Flash

b. Slot0:

c. ROM

d. NVRAM

Answer: c

The least significant number of the configuration register (ox2101) determines which image is loaded. If set to 0x1 (0001 binary), the router boots the ROM image.

2 Which command copies the IOS image file from a UNIX server into flash?

a. **config net**

b. **copy tftp flash**

c. **copy unix flash**

d. **copy tftp startup-config**

Answer: b

3 Which switch command's output is similar to the output of the router **show ip interface brief** command?

a. **show vlan interface brief**

b. **show port status**

c. **show port interface**

d. **show ip vlan**

Answer: b

The switch show port status command provides a summary table of interfaces with port number, VLAN, and Status information. The show ip interface brief command provides a summary table of interfaces with interface name and number, IP address, and status information.

4 When booting a router, you reach the following message:

```
         --- System Configuration Dialog ---
Would you like to enter the initial configuration dialog? [yes/no]:
```

What might have caused this to occur?

a. The router's configuration register was set to 0x2142.

b. A **write erase** command was performed prior to reboot.

c. The running configuration was deleted from NVRAM.

d. Answer a or b.

Answer: d

Either answer a or answer b could have occurred. If the second right-most digit (0x2142) is set to 4, the router ignores the configuration in NVRAM and enters the Initial Configuration Dialog. Answer b is correct if the startup configuration is erased from NVRAM with the write erase command. If there is no configuration in NVRAM at router boot up, the router enters the Initial Configuration Dialog.

5 After entering the **debug ip rip** command, no messages appear on your Telnet screen. What is one likely cause?

a. OSPF is also running.

b. The console port is disabled.

c. The **terminal monitor** command needs to be configured.

d. RIP broadcasts every 30 seconds.

Answer: c

When accessing the router through Telnet, the terminal monitor command needs to be configured to view debug output.

6 Which command verifies the configuration register setting for the next reload?

a. **show hardw**

b. **show version**

c. **show config-reg**

d. Answer a or b

Answer: d

The configuration register setting can be verified with the show hardware or show version command.

7 Where is the startup configuration usually stored?

a. slot0 of the flash card

b. NVRAM

c. Active RAM after bootup

d. ROM

Answer: b

The startup configuration is in NVRAM.

8 Which statement is correct?

a. The **enable secret** command overrides the **password** *password* command.

b. The **enable secret** command overrides the **enable password** command.

c. The **enable secret** command overrides the **service password-encryption** command.

d. The **enable secret** command sets the console password.

Answer: b

The password configured with the enable secret command overrides the password configured with the enable password command.

9 What does the **o/r 0x2142** command do?

a. Configures the router to ignore the contents in flash

b. Configures the router to ignore the boot system commands

c. Configures the router to enter into rommon mode

d. Configures the router to ignore the contents in NVRAM

Answer: d

The o/r 0x2142 command is usually configured during a password recovery procedure. It modifies the configure register by telling the router to ignore the configuration in NVRAM.

10 Which command configures the enable password on a Catalyst switch?

a. **set enablepass**

b. **set password**

c. **set enable secret**

d. **set pass**

Answer: a

11 The configuration register is set to 0x2101 and the **boot** commands are as follows:

```
boot system tftp mc3810-a2isv5-mz.120-7.XK1.bin 1.1.1.1
boot system flash
```

Which IOS is used?

a. IOS on the TFTP server

b. IOS in flash

c. IOS in ROM

d. IOS in NVRAM

Answer: c

The boot field is set to 0001, which tells the router to boot from ROM. The boot system commands are ignored.

12 What is the purpose of the bootstrap?

a. Initializes the CPU and starts the bootloader

b. Links the IOS in flash to the boot ROM

c. Initializes the CPU and starts the routing processes

d. Copies the startup configuration to the running configuration

Answer: a

The system bootstrap initializes the CPU and starts the bootloader.

13 Which command configures the router from the network?

a. **copy startup-config running-config**

b. **copy tftp running**

c. **copy running-config tftp**

d. **write network**

Answer: b

The copy tftp running-config command configures the router from a network TFTP server.

14 Which command allows the NMS server to make changes on the router?

a. **snmp enable ccie rw**

b. **snmp community ccie ro**

c. **snmp community ccie rw**

d. **enable snmp-secret ccie rw**

Answer: c

The snmp community ccie rw command allows the network management server to write changes on the router. Answer b permits only read access.

15 If you Telnet to a router that has the **login** command configured for all vtys but cannot log in, what is missing?

a. The enable password

b. The **password** command

c. The **login** command

d. The auxiliary port configuration

Answer: b

If the login command is configured for all vtys but not the password command, the router prompts with password not set and disconnects the Telnet session.

16 Which command sets the configuration register to 0x2102?

a. router(config-in)#**configure-register 0x2102**

b. router(config)#**configure-register 0x2102**

c. router(config)#**conf-reg 0x2102**

d. router(config)#**config-register 0x2102**

Answer: d

17 Which command shows the five second, one minute, and five minute CPU use time for each process on the router?

a. **show process**

b. **show process cpu**

c. **show process memory**

d. **show cpu**

Answer: b

The show process cpu command shows the five second, one minute, and five minute CPU use time for each process on the router.

18 Which command shows the memory (allocated/freed/holding) used per process?

a. **show process**

b. **show process cpu**

c. **show process memory**

d. **show ram**

Answer: c

The show process memory command shows the memory used per process.

19 Where is the IOS image stored?

a. Flash

b. NVRAM

c. ROM

d. Answers a and c

Answer: d

IOS is not stored in NVRAM.

20 A user telnets to a router that has the **password** command configured for all vty lines. If the user is granted access with no password, what is missing?

a. The console password

b. The enable password

c. The **login** command

d. The **enable secret** command

Answer: c

If the login command is not configured on vty lines, users are granted access without having to enter a password.

21 Which prompt indicates that the router is in ROM monitor mode?

a. `>`

b. `router>`

c. `router#`

d. `router(config)#`

Answer: a

A router is in ROM monitor mode if it has one of the following two prompts:

```
>
rommon >
```

22 What is the procedure for password recovery?

a. Break, reboot, set ignore NVRAM, copy password

b. Reboot, break, set 0x2142, reboot, copy password, disable ignore NVRAM, reboot

c. Reboot, break, set 0x2142, reboot, copy password, ignore NVRAM, reboot, enter password

d. Set 0x2142, reboot, copy password

Answer: b

Answer b best describes the password recovery procedure. Answer a is wrong because you do not break first. Answer c is wrong because after you copy the password, you do not ignore NVRAM. Answer d is wrong because you cannot set the configuration register to 0x2142 without access and before rebooting and breaking.

23 You have deleted two files in the flash, but when you try to copy a new image into flash, an error occurs. What is the reason for the error?

a. You deleted the files but did not format the flash card.

b. If the files still show when a **dir** command is issued, it means that you have not deleted the files.

c. When the **dir** command is issued, the files show up with a "D"; perform a squeeze.

d. Reboot the router; that fixes everything.

Answer: c

Chapter 3 Answers to Scenario Section

This scenario tests your understanding of the configuration register, **boot system** commands, and passwords used in Cisco routers. Use the following configuration to answer the Scenario questions.

```
hostname router1
!
boot system flash mc3810-a2isv5-mz.120-7.XK1.bin
boot system tftp mc3810-a2isv5-mz.120-6.XK1.bin 1.1.1.1
boot system rom
!
enable secret 5 1$yfrZ$TWjcS4u2GVh/FbH3zK  (encrypted ccie2)
enable password ccie1
!
interface ethernet 0
 ip address 1.1.1.2 255.255.255.0
!
line con 0
 password ccie3
 login
!
line vty 0 4
 password ccie4
!
```

1 If the configuration register is set to 0x2102, which IOS is loaded?

a. mc3810-a2isv5-mz.120-7.XK1.bin

b. mc3810-a2isv5-mz.120-6.XK1.bin

c. IOS in ROM

d. ROM monitor

Answer: a

If the boot field is set to 0010, the boot system commands load in the order that they appear.

2 If the configuration register is set to 0x2100, which IOS is loaded?

a. mc3810-a2isv5-mz.120-7.XK1.bin

b. mc3810-a2isv5-mz.120-6.XK1.bin

c. IOS in ROM

d. ROM monitor

Answer: d

If the boot field is set to 0000, the router loads the ROM monitor.

3 If the configuration register is set to 0x2101, which IOS is loaded?

a. mc3810-a2isv5-mz.120-7.XK1.bin

b. mc3810-a2isv5-mz.120-6.XK1.bin

c. IOS in ROM

d. ROM monitor

Answer: c

If the boot field is set to 0001, the router loads from ROM.

4 If the configuration register is set to 0x2102, and there is no IOS image file in flash, which IOS is loaded?

a. mc3810-a2isv5-mz.120-7.XK1.bin

b. mc3810-a2isv5-mz.120-6.XK1.bin

c. IOS in ROM

d. ROM monitor

Answer: b

Following the boot system commands, if there is no IOS in flash, the router attempts to boot the IOS from the TFTP server.

5 If the configuration register is set to 0x2102, and there is no IOS image file in flash and the TFTP server is down, which IOS is loaded?

a. mc3810-a2isv5-mz.120-7.XK1.bin

b. mc3810-a2isv5-mz.120-6.XK1.bin

c. IOS in ROM

d. ROM monitor

Answer: c

Following the boot system commands, if there is no IOS in flash, the router attempts to boot the IOS from the TFTP server. If the attempt to boot from the TFTP server fails, the router boots the IOS in ROM.

6 If the configuration register is set to 0x2142, which IOS is loaded?

a. 3810-a2isv5-mz.120-7.XK1.bin

b. 3810-a2isv5-mz.120-6.XK1.bin

c. IOS in ROM

d. ROM monitor

Answer: c

The boot field is 0002. Following the boot system commands, if there is no IOS in flash, the router attempts to boot the IOS from the TFTP server. If the attempt to boot from the TFTP server fails, the router boots the IOS in ROM.

7 What password is entered to reach privileged exec mode?

a. ccie1

b. ccie2

c. ccie3

d. ccie4

Answer: b

You use the password configured with the enable secret command.

8 What password accesses the router through Telnet to the router?

a. ccie2.

b. ccie3.

c. ccie4.

d. No password is used.

Answer: b

Because the login command is not configured on the vty line, the user is not prompted for a password.

Chapter 4 Answers to Q & A Section

1 What bit of each byte does an Ethernet NIC expect to read first off the wire?

a. The least significant bit first; this is the noncanonical format.

b. The most significant bit first; this is the noncanonical format.

c. The least significant bit first; this is the canonical format.

d. The most significant bit first; this is the canonical format.

Answer: c

Ethernet is canonical; it expects the least significant bit first. Token Ring is noncanonical; it expects the most significant bit first.

2 Which access method listens to the wire before transmitting?

a. Token access

b. CSMA/CD

c. Token bus

d. 4B/5B

Answer: b

Carrier sense multiple access with collision detection (CSMA/CD) is the access method that listens to the wire before transmitting.

3 Which IEEE frame format includes a type field?

a. IEEE 802.3

b. IEEE 802.5

c. IEEE 802.3 SNAP

d. IEEE 802.1q

Answer: c

The IEEE 802.3 SNAP frame contains an Ethernet type field in the SNAP field.

4 Which bridging method associates a MAC address with its ports?

a. Transparent

b. SRB

c. SR/TLB

d. RSRB

Answer: a

Transparent bridges create a table that associates learned MAC address with its ports.

5 What does the following command do?

```
source-bridge transparent 10 5 1 6
```

a. Configures DLSw

b. Configures transparent bridging

c. Configures source-route bridging

d. Configures translational bridging from an Ethernet bridge group

Answer: d

The source-bridge transparent command configures translational bridging. In the example in this question bridge group 6 is associated with pseudo ring 5, which is bridged into ring group 10.

6 What is the RIF in hexadecimal for a source route frame if it is to route from Token Ring 4, through bridge 12, ending on Token Ring 15?

a. 0630.004c.0015

b. 0630.0412.0015

c. 0630.040c.0150

d. 0630.004c.00f0

Answer: d

The Routing Information Field consists of a 2-byte RIF header followed by 2-byte route descriptors. The route descriptor includes the 12-bit ring number and 4-bits for the bridge number. The last route descriptor ends with the bridge number set to 0x0. Numbers need to be converted to hexadecimal. The first route descriptor is 0x004c (Ring 4, bridge 12). The final route descriptor is 0x00f0 (Ring 15, bridge 0).

7 Which access list denies 00c0.00a0.0010 but permits other MAC addresses?

a.

```
access-list 700 deny 00c0.00a0.0010 ffff.ffff.ffff
access-list 700 permit 0000.0000.0000 ffff.ffff.ffff
```

b.

```
access-list 700 deny 00c0.00a0.0010 0000.0000.0000
access-list 700 permit 0000.0000.0000 ffff.ffff.ffff
```

c.

```
access-list 200 deny 00c0.00a0.0010 ffff.ffff.ffff
access-list 200 permit 0000.0000.0000 ffff.ffff.ffff
```

d.

```
access-list 200 deny 00c0.00a0.0010 0000.0000.0000
access-list 200 permit 0000.0000.0000 ffff.ffff.ffff
```

Answer: b

MAC address lists range from 700 to 799. Answer a is incorrect because it denies all MAC address by using a mask of ffff.ffff.ffff. Answer b is correct because it specifically denies 00c0.00a0.0010 and permits all other addresses.

8 Which trunking method places an internal tag to identify the VLAN number?

a. ISL

b. 802.1q

c. 802.1p

d. VTP pruning

Answer: b

IEEE 802.1q identifies the VLAN by using an internal tag. ISL uses an external tag.

9 Which answer best describes the VTP client?

a. Stores VLAN information in NVRAM

b. Adds and deletes VLANs in the VTP domain

c. Maintains a full list of VLANs

d. Does not participate in VTP

Answer: c

The VTP client participates in VTP by maintaining a list of VLANs but does not store the information in NVRAM, nor can it add, delete, or rename VLANs.

10 What is the BID?

a. BLAN ID number

b. Bridge identifier used in STP

c. Border identifier used in SRB

d. Bridged identifier used in VTP

Answer: b

The bridge identifier (BID) is used in the Spanning-Tree Protocol. The BID is 8 bytes long and contains a bridge priority (2 bytes) along with one of the bridge's MAC addresses (6 bytes).

11 What is the transparent bridge port state sequence from a disabled port to a forwarding port?

a. Disabled, listening, learning, forwarding, blocked

b. Disabled, enabled, listening, learning, forwarding

c. Disabled, blocking, listening, learning, forwarding

d. Disabled, blocking, learning, listening, forwarding

Answer: c

Answer c lists the correct sequence.

12 What is a BVI?

a. Bridged VLAN identifier

b. Bridge virtual interface, used in IRB

c. Bridge ID, in RIFs

d. When set, indicates to use SRB

Answer: b

Bridge virtual interfaces configure integrated routing and bridging (IRB).

13 Which type of bridge removes the RIF, checks the MTU, and reorders bits before sending the frame on?

a. Transparent

b. DLSw

c. SRT

d. SR/TLB

e. SRB

f. RSRB

Answer: d

Source-route translational bridging (SR/TLB) performs these steps when passing frames from a Token Ring network to an Ethernet network.

14 What is the RIF in the following?

```
source-bridge ring-group 5
!
dlsw local-peer peer-id 1.1.1.1 promiscuous
dlsw remote-peer 0 tcp 2.2.2.1
!
interface tokenring 0
 source-bridge 1 2 5
```

a. 0630.0012.0050.

b. 0830.0125.

c. 0830.0012.0051.

d. Not enough information is given.

Answer: a

If RIF Passthru is not configured for DLSW the RIF terminates at the local ring group. The RIF includes ring 1, bridge 2, and ring-group 5.

15 What is the maximum segment length of 10Base2 media?

a. 100 m

b. 185 m

c. 200 feet

d. 500 feet

Answer: b

The maximum segment length for 10Base2 is 185 m.

16 At what speed does Gigabit Ethernet transmit data?

a. 1000 kbps

b. 100 Mbps

c. 1000 Mbps

d. 1250 kbps

Answer: c 1 Gbps = 1000 Mbps

17 What is the IEEE standard for Fast Ethernet?

a. IEEE 802.3a

b. IEEE 802.3ab

c. IEEE 802.3u

d. IEEE 802.3z

Answer: c

18 What is a BPDU?

a. Bridge packet descriptor unit

b. Bridge protocol data unit

c. Basic protocol descriptor unit

d. None of the above

Answer: b

BPDU means Bridge Protocol Data Unit.

19 If the DSAP and SSAP have the value 0xAAAA, what does it indicate?

a. a.That a SNAP field follows

b. That a NSAP field follows

c. That a V2 frame follows

d. That a FDDI frame follows

Answer: a

If the DSAP and SSAP fields are set to 0xAA, it indicates that a Subnetwork Access Protocol (SNAP) field follows.

20 What bit of each byte does a Token Ring NIC expect to read first off the wire?

a. The least significant bit first; this is the noncanonical format.

b. The most significant bit first; this is the noncanonical format.

c. The least significant bit first; this is the canonical format.

d. The most significant bit first; this is the canonical format.

Answer: b

Token Ring is noncanonical; the most significant bit is expected first. Ethernet is canonical; the least significant bit is expected first.

21 Which bridging method permits source-route frames over non-Token Ring media?

a. Transparent

b. SRT

c. SR/TLB

d. RSRB

Answer: d

Remote Source Route Bridging (RSRB) permits sending SRB frames over non-Token Ring media.

22 Which bridging method runs STP?

a. Transparent

b. SRT

c. SR/TLB

d. RSRB

Answer: a

Transparent bridges run the spanning-tree protocol (STP) algorithm.

23 What is the RIF in hexadecimal for a source-route frame if it is to route from Token Ring 4, through Bridge 12, to Token Ring 0x11, through Bridge 8, ending on Token Ring 22?

a. 0830.4c11.8220

b. 0830.0412.0011.8220

c. 0830.004c.0118.0160

d. 0630.0412.0011.8220

Answer: c

24 Which answer best describes the VTP server?

a. Stores VLAN information in NVRAM

b. Adds and deletes VLANs in the VTP domain

c. Maintains a full list of VLANs

d. Does not participate in VTP

e. Answers a, b, and c

Answer: e

VTP servers maintain a full list of VLANs, adds and deletes VLANs, and stores VLAN information in NVRAM.

25 Which answer best describes the VTP transparent switch?

a. Stores VTP learned VLAN info in NVRAM

b. Adds and deletes VLANs in the VTP domain

c. Maintains a full list of VLANs

d. Does not participate in VTP

e. Answers b and c

Answer: d

Switches in VTP transparent mode do not participate in VTP.

26 What is the sequence for Token Ring insertion?

a. Physical insertion, lobe check, address verification, initialize, ring poll

b. Lobe check, physical insertion, address verification, ring poll, initialize

c. Physical insertion, lobe check, address verification, initialize, ring poll

d. Physical insertion, ring poll, lobe check, initialize, address verification

Answer: b

Answer b is the correct sequence from phase 0 to phase 4 of Token Ring Insertion.

27 What command is used to enable IEEE 802.1q trunking on port 2/1?

a. **set trunk 2/1 on 802.1q**

b. **set trunk 2/1 on isl1q**

c. **set trunk 2/1 on dot1q**

d. **set trunk 2/1 on isl**

Answer: c

You use the dot1q keyword to enable IEEE 802.1q trunking in the set truck command.

28 How many instances of STP are running on a Catalyst running 802.1q with 3 VLANs configured?

a. 1

b. 2

c. 3

d. None

Answer: c

IEEE 802.1q implements one instance of STP for each VLAN allowed on the trunks.

29 What are the functions of a transparent bridge?

a. Disabled, listening, learning, filtering, forwarding

b. Learn, filter, and forward

c. Listen, learn, filter, block, and forward

d. Enabled, listen, forward, flood

Answer: b

Transparent bridges learn MAC addresses, filter frames with destination MAC addresses located on the same incoming port, and forward frames to the port associated with the destination MAC address.

30 Which Layer-2 protocol changes blocked interfaces to the forwarding state in the case of bridge failure?

a. HSRP

b. VTP

c. STP

d. EIGRP

Answer: c

Spanning-Tree Protocol enables blocked interfaces if the primary link or bridge fails.

31 What is the path cost in STP?

a. Sum of segment costs to reach the root bridge

b. OSPF interface costs for the STP algorithm

c. The cost of Gigabit Ethernet is 1000

d. None of the above

Answer: a

The path cost is the addition of segment costs to reach the root bridge.

32 Which access list denies Ethernet type 0x6006?

a.

```
access-list 101 deny ipv2 any any 0x6006 eq type
access-list 101 permit ip any any
```

b.

```
access-list 700 deny 0x6006 0x0000
access-list 700 permit 0x0000 0xffff
```

c.

```
access-list 200 deny 0x6006 0x0000
access-list 200 permit 0x0000 0xffff
```

d.

```
access-list 200 deny 0x6006 any eq type
access-list 200 permit any any eq type
```

Answer: c

Ethernet type access lists numbers are from 200 to 299. Answer c specifically denies 0x6006 and allows all other Ethernet types.

33 What is the default STP priority?

a. 0

b. 1

c. 32,768

d. 56,535

Answer: c

34 From the following configuration, what is the RIF from Ring 1 to Ring 2?

```
source-bridge ring-group 7
!
interface tokenring 0
 source-bridge 1 10 7
 source-bridge spanning
!
interface tokenring 1
 source-bridge 2 11 7
 source-bridge spanning
```

a. 0830.0110.0711.0200

b. 0630.1A7b.0200

c. 0630.1011.0201

d. 0830.001a.007b.0020

Answer: d

From ring 1, to bridge 10, to ring 7, to bridge 11, and then ring 2. Answer d has the RIF that represents this path.

35 What is CDP?

a. Control Description Protocol

b. Control data packet

c. Cisco Discovery Protocol

d. Cisco Description Protocol

Answer: c

Cisco Discovery Protocol is the correct answer.

36 What information can be gathered from neighbors using CDP?

a. Device name, management IP address, platform type, and OS version

b. Device name and IP address only

c. Answer a, plus running routing protocol

d. Device name, management IP address, platform type, and all enabled interface IP addresses

Answer: a

With CDP, the neighbor's device name, management IP address, platform type, and OS version can be gathered.

37 Which command produced the following router output?

```
Capability Codes: R - Router, T - Trans Bridge, B - Source Route Bridge
                  S - Switch, H - Host, I - IGMP, r - Repeater

Port     Device-ID                 Port-ID            Platform      Capability
-------- ------------------------  -----------------  ----------------- --
 2/14     Router13                 Ethernet0          Cisco MC3810         R
 2/15     Router10                 Ethernet0          cisco 2500           R
```

a. **show ip ospf neighbor**

b. **show ip bgp neighbor**

c. **show ip cdp neighbor**

d. **show cdp neighbor**

Answer: d

The Catalyst switch output was obtained using show cdp neighbor.

38 What standard specifies 11 Mbps wireless LANs at a frequency of 2.4 GHz?

a. IEEE 802.11

b. IEEE 802.11a

c. IEEE 802.11b

d. IEEE 802.11g

Answer: c

IEEE 802.11b provides specifications for WLANs using frequencies of the ISM 2.4 GHz.

39 What standard specifies 54 Mbps Wireless LANs at a frequency of 5 GHz?

a. IEEE 802.11

b. IEEE 802.11a

c. IEEE 802.11b

d. IEEE 802.11g

Answer: b

IEEE 802.11a provides specifications for WLANs using frequency bands of the UNII 5 GHz.

40 Which standard provides port-based authentication?

a. IEEE 802.11x

b. IEEE 802.11i

c. IEEE 802.1x

d. IEEE 802.1u

Answer: c

IEEE 802.1x specifies a port-based authentication mechanism that uses EAP and RADIUS.

41 Which Wireless LAN mode uses one Access Point?

a. BSS

b. IBSS

c. ESS

d. Ad-hoc

Answer: a

The Basic Service Set mode uses one Access Point for clients to access the wired LAN. BSS is also referred to as Infrastructure mode.

42 Which ATM LANE component is contacted first by a joining client?

a. LEC

b. LES

c. LECS

d. BUS

Answer: c

The LAN Emulation Configuration Server (LECS) is contacted first by joining LECs. The LECS provides the ATM address of the LES to the client.

43 Which protocol provides LES/BUS replication in an ATM LANE environment?

a. LE-ARP

b. SSRP

c. BUS

d. PNNI

Answer: b

The Simple Server Replication Protocol (SSRP) provides replication of LES/BUS and LECS services in ATM LANE environments.

44 What does LE-ARP translates?

a. IP addresses to MAC addresses

b. IP addresses to ATM addresses

c. MAC addresses to ATM addresses

d. Ethernet MAC addresses to Token Ring addresses

Answer: c

LE-ARP translates MAC addresses to ATM addresses.

Chapter 4 Answers to Scenario Section

Scenario 4-1

This scenario reviews your knowledge of RSRB. Knowledge of RSRB configurations and RIF constructs in RSRB environments is essential for the CCIE written test. Use Figure 4-34 to answer the following questions.

Figure 4-34 *RSRB*

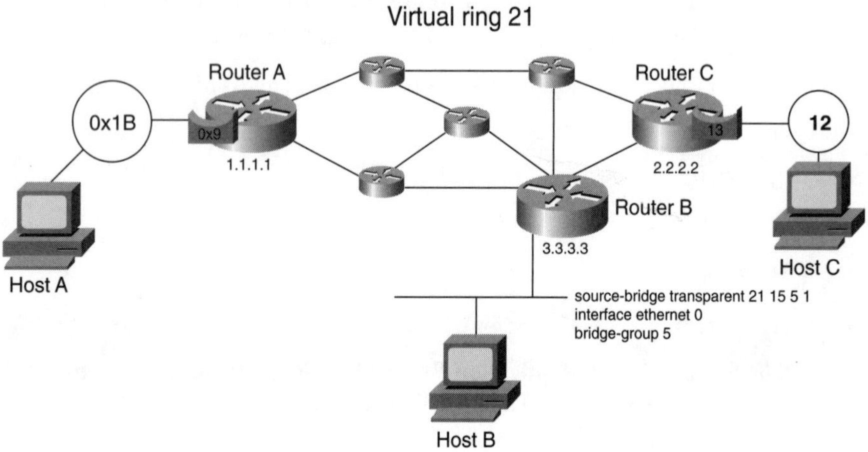

1 What is the RIF from Host A to Host C?

a. 0830.01b9.021d.0120

b. 0830.01b9.015d.00c0

c. 0830.01b9.0151.20c0

d. 0630.01b9.121d.0120

Answer: b

From Host A to Host C, a frame travels from Ring 0x01b, Bridge 0x9, Ring 21 (0x015), Bridge 13 (0xd), Ring 12 (0xc).

2 What is the RIF from Host A to Host B?

a. 0630.01b9.01f5

b. 0830.01b0.0210

c. 0630.01b9.0150

d. 0830.01b9.0155.00f0

Answer: d

From Host A to Host B, a frame travels from Ring 0x01b, Bridge 0x9, Ring 21 (0x015), Bridge 5, Pseudo-ring 15 (0x00f).

3 What is the correct configuration for Router A?

a.

```
source-bridge ring-group 21
source-bridge remote-peer 21 tcp 1.1.1.1
source-bridge remote-peer 21 tcp 2.2.2.2 local-ack
source-bridge remote-peer 21 tcp 3.3.3.3 local-ack
!
interface loopback 0
 ip address 1.1.1.1 255.255.255.255
!
interface tokenring 0
  source-bridge 1b 9 10
  source-bridge spanning
```

b.

```
source-bridge ring-group 15
source-bridge transparent 15 6 2 5
source-bridge remote-peer 15 tcp 1.1.1.1
source-bridge remote-peer 15 tcp 2.2.2.2 local-ack
source-bridge remote-peer 15 tcp 3.3.3.3 local-ack
!
interface loopback 0
 ip address 1.1.1.1 255.255.255.255
!
interface tokenring 0
  source-bridge 1b 9 15
  source-bridge spanning
```

c.

```
source-bridge ring-group 21
source-bridge remote-peer 21 tcp 1.1.1.1
source-bridge remote-peer 21 tcp 2.2.2.2 local-ack
source-bridge remote-peer 21 tcp 3.3.3.3 local-ack
!
interface loopback 0
 ip address 1.1.1.1 255.255.255.255
!
interface tokenring 0
  source-bridge 27 9 21
  source-bridge spanning
```

d.

```
source-bridge ring-group 15
source-bridge remote-peer 15 tcp 1.1.1.1
source-bridge remote-peer 15 tcp 2.2.2.2 local-ack
source-bridge remote-peer 15 tcp 3.3.3.3 local-ack
!
interface loopback 0
 ip address 1.1.1.1 255.255.255.255
!
interface tokenring 0
  source-bridge 1b 9 15
  source-bridge spanning
```

Answer: c

Ring and bridge numbers are configured in decimal. Answers a, b, and d have hexadecimal numbers in the source-bridge commands.

4 What is the correct configuration for Router C?

a.

```
source-bridge ring-group 21
source-bridge remote-peer 21 tcp 1.1.1.1 local-ack
source-bridge remote-peer 21 tcp 2.2.2.2
source-bridge remote-peer 21 tcp 3.3.3.3 local-ack
!
interface loopback 0
 ip address 2.2.2.2 255.255.255.255
!
interface tokenring 0
  source-bridge c d f
  source-bridge spanning
```

b.

```
source-bridge ring-group 21
source-bridge remote-peer 21 tcp 2.2.2.2
source-bridge remote-peer 21 tcp 1.1.1.1 local-ack
source-bridge remote-peer 21 tcp 3.3.3.3 local-ack
!
interface loopback 0
 ip address 2.2.2.2 255.255.255.255
!
interface tokenring 0
  source-bridge 12 13 15
  source-bridge spanning
```

c.

```
source-bridge ring-group 15
source-bridge remote-peer 15 tcp 2.2.2.2
source-bridge remote-peer 15 tcp 2.2.2.2 local-ack
source-bridge remote-peer 15 tcp 3.3.3.3 local-ack
!
interface loopback 0
 ip address 2.2.2.2 255.255.255.255
!
interface tokenring 0
  source-bridge 12 13 15
  source-bridge spanning
```

d.

```
source-bridge ring-group 15
source-bridge remote-peer 15 tcp 1.1.1.1
source-bridge remote-peer 15 tcp 2.2.2.2 local-ack
source-bridge remote-peer 15 tcp 3.3.3.3 local-ack
```

```
!
interface loopback 0
 ip address 2.2.2.2 255.255.255.255
!
interface tokenring 0
   source-bridge c d f
  source-bridge spanning
```

Answer: b

Answers a and d are incorrect because you do not use hexadecimal numbers in the source-bridge commands. Answer c is incorrect because the virtual ring is configured with decimal 21, not hexadecimal 0x15.

5 What is the bridge number of the bridge between the virtual ring and the pseudo-ring on Router B?

a. 21

b. 0x6

c. 0x2

d. 0x5

Answer: c

From the source-bridge transparent 21 6 2 5 command, the virtual ring is 0x15, the pseudo-ring number is 0x5, and bridge number is 0x2; the transparent bridge group is 0x5.

Scenario 4-2

This scenario reviews your knowledge of DLSw. Knowledge of DLSw configuration and RIF construct in DLSw environment is essential for the CCIE written test. Use Figure 4-35 to answer the following questions.

Figure 4-35 *DLSw*

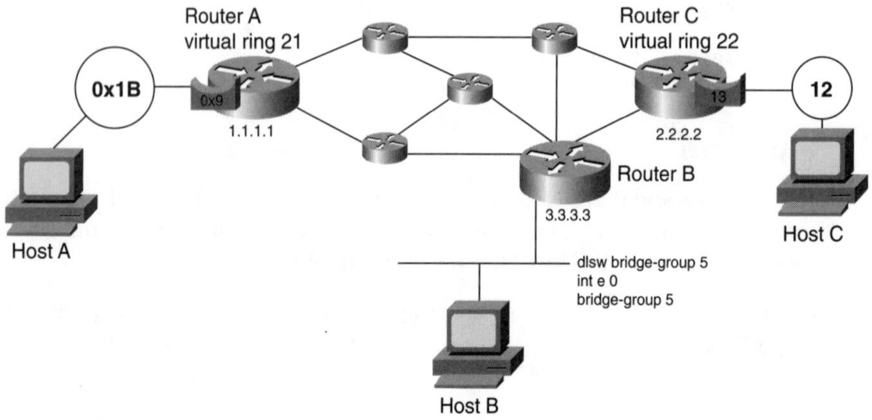

1 What is the RIF from Host A to Host C?

a. 0830.01b9.021d.0120

b. 0830.01b9.015d.00c0

c. 0630.01b9.0210

d. 0630.01b9.0150

Answer: d

With DLSw, the RIF terminates at the local virtual ring. Frame travels from ring 0x01b, bridge 0x9, and ring 21 (0x015).

2 What is the RIF from Host A to Host B?

a. 0830.01b9.021d.0120

b. 0830.01b9.0152.0060

c. 0630.01b9.0210

d. 0630.01b9.0150

Answer: d

With DLSw, the RIF terminates at the local virtual ring. Frame travels from ring 0x01b, bridge 0x9, and ring 21 (0x015).

3 What is the correct configuration of Router A?

a.

```
interface loopback 0
 ip address 1.1.1.1 255.255.255.255
!
source-bridge ring-group 21
!
dlsw local-peer peer-id 1.1.1.1
dlsw remote-peer 0 tcp 2.2.2.2
dlsw remote-peer 0 tcp 3.3.3.3
!
interface tokenring 0
 source-bridge 27 9 21
```

b.

```
interface loopback 0
 ip address 1.1.1.1 255.255.255.255
!
source-bridge ring-group 21
!
dlsw local-peer peer-id 1.1.1.1
dlsw remote-peer 0 tcp 2.2.2.2 ring 22
dlsw remote-peer 0 tcp 3.3.3.3 ring 23
!
interface tokenring 0
 source-bridge 27 9 21
```

c.

```
interface loopback 0
 ip address 1.1.1.1 255.255.255.255
!
source-bridge ring-group 21
!
dlsw local-peer peer-id 10.1.1.1
dlsw remote-peer 22 tcp 2.2.2.2
dlsw remote-peer 23 tcp 3.3.3.3
!
interface tokenring 0
 source-bridge 27 9 21
```

d.

```
interface loopback 0
 ip address 1.1.1.1 255.255.255.255
!
source-bridge ring-group 27
!
dlsw local-peer peer-id 11.1.1.1
dlsw remote-peer 0 tcp 2.2.2.2
dlsw remote-peer 0 tcp 3.3.3.3
!
interface tokenring 0
 source-bridge 27 9 21
```

Answer: a

Answer b is incorrect because no ring keywords are in the dlsw remote-peer statements. Answer c has incorrect dlsw remote-peer statements. Answer d is incorrect because the ring group is 21, not 27.

4 What is the pseudo-ring number on Router B?

a. 21.

b. 6.

c. 1.

d. There is no pseudo-ring.

Answer: d

Pseudo-rings are used in translational bridging (SR/TLB) configuration. DLSw does not require the configuration of SR/TLB for Ethernet networks.

5 Routers A and C are reconfigured as follows:

Router A changes the following:

```
dlsw remote-peer 0 tcp 2.2.2.2 rif-passthru
```

Router C changes the following:

```
source-bridge ring-group 21
dlsw remote-peer 0 tcp 1.1.1.1 rif-passthru
```

What is the RIF from Host A to Host C?

a. 0830.01b9.021d.0120

b. 0830.01b9.015d.00c0

c. 0830.01b9.0151.20c0

d. 0630.01b9.121d.0120

Answer: b

With rif-passthru, the RIF field is built from ring 0x01b to the token ring Router C. The path is ring 0x01b, bridge 0x9, ring 21 (0x15), bridge 13 (0xd), ring 12 (0x00c).

6 What is the correct configuration of Router B?

a.

```
interface loopback 0
 ip address 3.3.3.3 255.255.255.255
!
dlsw bridge-group 4
!
dlsw local-peer peer-id 3.3.3.3
```

```
dlsw remote-peer 0 tcp 1.1.1.1
dlsw remote-peer 0 tcp 2.2.2.2
!
interface ethernet 0
 bridge-group 5
```

b.

```
interface loopback 0
 ip address 3.3.3.3 255.255.255.255
!
source-bridge ring-group 21
source-bridge transparent 21 15 6 5
!
dlsw local-peer peer-id 3.3.3.3
dlsw remote-peer 0 tcp 1.1.1.1
dlsw remote-peer 0 tcp 2.2.2.2
!
interface ethernet 0
 bridge-group 5
interface loopback 0
 ip address 3.3.3.3 255.255.255.255
!
source-bridge ring-group 21
source-bridge transparent 21 15 6 1
dlsw transparent bridge-group 1
!
dlsw local-peer peer-id 3.3.3.3
dlsw remote-peer 0 tcp 1.1.1.1
dlsw remote-peer 0 tcp 2.2.2.2
!
interface ethernet 0
 bridge-group 5
```

c.

```
interface loopback 0
 ip address 3.3.3.3 255.255.255.255
!
dlsw transparent bridge-group 5
!
dlsw local-peer peer-id 3.3.3.3
dlsw remote-peer 0 tcp 1.1.1.1
dlsw remote-peer 0 tcp 2.2.2.2
!
interface ethernet 0
 bridge-group 5
```

Answer: a

Answer b is incorrect because the dlsw bridge-group command is required. Answer c is incorrect because source-bridge commands are not used; no transparent keyword is in the dlsw bridge-group command, and the bridge group number is 5, not 1. Answer d is incorrect because no transparent keyword is in the dlsw bridge-group command.

Chapter 5 Answers to Q & A Section

1 Which framing standard does X.25 use?

a. HDLC

b. LAPB

c. LAPF

d. LAPD

Answer: b

X.25 uses LAPB, a variant of HDLC, for Layer-2 framing.

2 What is the significance of the DE bit?

a. Used in X.25 as a discard error to recover frames

b. Used in ATM to recover from cells with errors

c. Used in Frame Relay to specify discard eligible frames

d. Used in PPP to discard frames

Answer: c

Discard Eligible bit is set on frames exceeding the Committed Information Rate (CIR), which is the contracted traffic rate by Frame Relay network switches or is set by the Frame Relay DTE (router) on relatively low priority frames. Frames with the DE bit set are discarded in a congested network before frames without the DE bit set.

3 What is an NT1 in ISDN architecture?

a. A device that connects the TE2 to the LE

b. Usually lies between the R and S reference points

c. Same as a NT4

d. A device that connects the 4-wire BRI to the 2-wire phone line

Answer: d

NT1 is a physical layer device that connects the 4-wire BRI from ISDN equipment to the 2-wire phone line provided by the telephone company.

4 What is a BECN in Frame Relay?

a. A notification to the destination, indicating congestion in the path from source to destination

b. A notification to the source, indicating congestion in the path from source to destination

c. A notification to the destination, indicating congestion in the path from destination to source

d. A notification to the source, indicating congestion in the path from destination to source

Answer: b

The BECN bit is set in frames traveling from the destination to the source, when congestion occurs in the Frame Relay network on the path from the source to the destination. A BECN attempts to throttle the rate of traffic being sent by the source DTE.

5 Inverse ARP provides what type of address resolution?

a. MAC address to IP address

b. DLCI to IP address

c. X.121 address to IP address

d. ATM address to IP address

Answer: b

Routers on Frame Relay networks learn local DLCIs by using LMI. Then, they learn the remote IP address associated with the local DLCI through the inverse-arp process.

6 How many bits are there in a Frame Relay DLCI?

a. 8 bits

b. 10 bits

c. 16 bits

d. 32 bits

Answer: b

There are 10 bits in a Frame Relay DLCI without extended addressing.

7 Which authentication protocol do you use with PPP and encrypted passwords?

a. PPP authentication

b. PAP

c. CHAP

d. SecureID

Answer: c

PPP supports PAP and CHAP authentication. PAP uses clear text passwords; CHAP uses encrypted passwords.

8 ISDN's D channel uses which framing standard?

a. HDLC

b. LAPB

c. LAPF

d. LAPD

Answer: d

ISDN D channels use the LAPD framing standard.

9 For the following configuration, when does the BRI become active?

```
interface serial 0
 ip address 1.1.1.1 255.255.255.252
 backup load 75 10
 backup interface bri 0
```

a. When serial 0 is down for 60 seconds

b. When serial 0 is up for 10 seconds

c. When serial 0 is above 75 percent use

d. When serial 0 is below 10 percent use

Answer: c

The command backup load *enable-threshold disable-threshold* indicates that the BRI becomes active when the load on serial 0 exceeds 75 percent use.

10 What does the following command do?

```
x25 map ip 172.18.1.5 12121212 broadcast
```

a. Maps the remote IP address to the remote X.121 address

b. Maps the remote IP address to the local X.121 address

c. Maps the local IP address to the remote X.121 address

d. Maps the local IP address to the local X.121 address

Answer: a

The X.25 command maps the next hop IP address 172.18.1.5 to the remote X.121 address 12121212.

11 Which of the following are layers in the ATM reference model?

a. Physical

b. Datalink

c. ATM

d. Network

e. Transport

f. Presentation

g. Adaptation

h. Session

i. Application

Answers: a, c, g

The ATM reference model contains the physical, ATM, and adaptation layers.

12 How many bytes are in an ATM cell?

a. 21

b. 48

c. 53

d. 128

Answer: c

The ATM header is 5 bytes, the payload is 48 bytes, and the entire cell is 53 bytes.

13 How are ATM payload cells uniquely identified by a switch?

a. By the cell's IP address

b. By the cell's VPI/VCI address

c. By the cell's NSAP address

d. By the cell's AESA address

Answer: b

ATM payload cells are identified by the VPI/VCI pair.

14 Which ATM class of service is most appropriate for raw video?

a. CBR

b. nrt-VBR

c. ABR

d. UBR

Answer: a

Video requires minimal delay variation, which is obtained by requesting a static amount of bandwidth for the life of the connection.

CBR: The network guarantees the negotiated ATM layer QoS to all cells that are at or below the negotiated peak cell rate.

nrt-VBR: Because this is for non-real-time traffic, no delay bounds associated with nrt-VBR. Used for bursty traffic, it is characterized by peak cell rate (PCR), sustainable cell rate (SCR) and maximum burst size (MBS). A low cell loss ratio is expected by the application that uses this class of service for cells transmitted within the negotiated traffic contract (PCR, SCR, and MBS).

ABR: Provides flow control mechanisms to alter the source rate of the traffic during a connection.

UBR: As is nrt-VBR, this is for non-real-time traffic; traffic that does not require consistent and minimal delay. UBR does not guarantee any quality of service. It is best effort.

15 In what order do each of the following queues get processed on a DPT ring node?

1. Low-priority transmit queue
2. Low-priority transit queue
3. High-priority transmit queue
4. High-priority transit queue

a. 4,3 2,1

b. 3,4,2,1

c. 4,3,1,2

d. 3,4,1,2

Answer: c

High-priority transit packets first, high-priority transmit packets, and low-priority transmit packets, then low-priority transit packets. The threshold is configured for the length of the low-priority transit packets to ensure that it eventually gets served.

16 Which ATM class of service is most appropriate for Frame Relay data?

a. CBR

b. VBR

c. ABR

d. UBR

Answer: c

Frame-relay supports flow control. ABR provides flow control mechanisms to alter source rate.

17 RFC 2225 provides a method of encapsulating which of the following protocols over ATM?

a. XNS

b. IP

c. IPX

d. SNA

Answer: b

RFC 2225 defines classical IP over ATM.

18 Identify the following descriptions as UNI or NNI:

a. Connects an ATM end system to an ATM switch in a public service provider's network

b. Uses eight bits of VPI to identify 256 virtual paths

c. Connects two private ATM switches

d. Connects two switches within the same public ATM service provider

e. Connects an ATM end system to an ATM switch in a private enterprise network

f. Uses 12 bits of VPI to identify 4096 unique virtual paths

Answer: a = UNI, b = UNI, c = NNI, d = NNI, e = UNI, f = NNI

The interface that connects an ATM switch to an ATM end system is UNI. The interface that connects two ATM switches is NNI. UNI uses 8 bits in the cell header for VPI. NNI uses 12 bits for VPI.

19 How is a switched virtual circuit (SVC) established?

a. An SVC is established by the ATM Forum.

b. An SVC is established by manual configuration.

c. An SVC is established by connection management software.

d. An SVC is established by UNI signaling from the attached end device.

Answer: d

An ATM DTE uses UNI signaling to establish an SVC when a connection is desired.

20 What is the purpose of ATM end system addresses?

a. To support SVC connection signaling across a PNNI or IISP network

b. To support PVC connection signaling across a PNNI or IISP network

c. To uniquely identify a cell as it enters the switch

d. To uniquely identify a connection in the switching table

Answer: a

SVC connections are established based on the PNNI or IISP ATM routing tables. The destination ATM end system address helps to choose a path through the network for the SVC.

21 Match the following well-known VCIs with the protocol that uses them:

a. VCI = 5	1. PNNI
b. VCI = 18	2. ILMI
c. VCI = 16	3. UNI Signaling

Answer: a = 3, b = 1, c = 2

UNI signaling uses VCI 5, PNNI uses VCI 18, and ILMI uses VCI 16.

22 What does IPCP do in PPP?

a. Establishes IP parameters on a PPP link.

b. Provides communication between the network control program and any Layer-3 protocol.

c. IPCP is not used in PPP; it is a X.25 protocol.

d. IPCP is the frame type used in PPP.

Answer: a

The NCP uses the IP Control Protocol (IPCP) to negotiate and establish IP peering over a PPP link.

23 Which interface is associated with 30B+D?

a. DS-3

b. ISDN PRI

c. ISDN BRI

d. OC-3

Answer: b

In locations other then North America and Japan, the ISDN PRI runs over E1 circuits, providing 30 B channels and 1 D channel (30B+D).

24 Which protocol communicates between a router and the local Frame Relay switch?

a. ILMI

b. MAP

c. NNI

d. LMI

Answer: d

ATM uses ILMI. MAP is not a protocol. NNI is the network-network interface in ATM. LMI is the local management interface protocol that communicates between the router and the local Frame Relay switch.

25 Which feature uses BECN bits as input to control the flow of frames into the network?

a. The DE bit

b. Traffic shaping

c. Priority queuing

d. Compression

Answer: b

BECN bits are sent to the source end station in an attempt to throttle the sending traffic rate. If traffic shaping is enabled, the router uses these BECN bits to control the flow of frames into the network.

26 What is Frame Relay's advantage over X.25?

a. Its advanced error checking features.

b. It is connection-oriented.

c. It adds less overhead; therefore, it is available at greater speeds.

d. It is designed to run over bad cable systems.

Answer: c

Frame Relay has fewer error checking features than X.25; therefore, it is not designed to run over bad cable systems. Both X.25 and Frame Relay are connection-oriented. Frame Relay adds less overhead; therefore, it is available at greater speeds.

27 You have a Frame Relay network between Router A and Router B. Host 1 and Router A are on one side, and Host 2 and Router B are on the other. Host 1 transmits a packet to Host 2. The frame is discarded in the wide-area network. Which device is responsible for retransmitting?

a. Host 1

b. Router A

c. Router B

d. The link-layer protocol on the Frame Relay switch

Answer: a

Frame Relay networks drop frames when there is congestion in the network and do not retransmit them. The sending host must retransmit any dropped frames.

28 You have an X.25 network between Router A and Router B. Host 1 and Router A are on one side, and Host 2 and Router B are on the other. Host 1 transmits a packet to Host 2. Router A forwards the frame into the network, and the frame is discarded. Which device is responsible for retransmitting?

a. Host 1

b. Router A

c. Router B

d. Host 2

Answer: b

X.25 runs LAPB link-layer protocol between the DTE (router) and DCE (X.25 switch), which performs error detection and recovery. If the DTE transmits the frame but does not receive an acknowledgment within a specified period of time, the DTE retransmits the frame.

29 What does synchronization do?

a. Provides timing information between sender and receiver; used in circuit-switched networks

b. Provides timing information between sender and receiver; used in packet switched networks

c. Provides timing information between sender and receiver; used by IP networks

d. Provides timing information between sender and receiver; used in frame relay networks

Answer: a

Circuit-switched networks use synchronization, where synchronous circuits are dependent on having the same clock so that the receiving side knows exactly when each frame bit is received.

30 What is SONET and on which OSI layer is it defined?

a. Symmetric Optical Network, physical layer

b. Synchronous Optical Network, Physical layer

c. Symmetric Optical Network, data-link layer

d. Synchronous Optical Network, data-link Layer

Answer: b

SONET: Synchronous Optical Network operates at the physical layer.

31 What does RFC 2427 define?

a. Multiprotocol connectivity over Frame Relay

b. IP connectivity over ATM

c. Multiprotocol connectivity over ATM

d. IP connectivity over PPP

Answer: a

RFC 2427 defines multiprotocol interconnect over Frame Relay.

32 What is the bandwidth capability of an ISDN B channel?

a. 56 kbps

b. 64 kbps

c. 128 kbps

d. 16 kbps

Answer: b

Each B channel has the bandwidth capacity of 64 kbps.

33 Where does the U reference point reside in the ISDN architecture?

a. Between the NT2 and the NT1

b. Between the TA and the TE2

c. Between the NT1 and the LE

d. Between the TE1 and the TA

Answer: c

The U reference point is between the NT1 and the Local Exchange. TE1s do not connect to TAs. The R reference point is between the TA and TE2. The T reference point is between the NT2 and the NT1.

34 RFC 2225 defines which of the following servers?

a. LAN emulation server

b. Broadcast and unknown server

c. ATM address resolution protocol server

d. LAN emulation configuration server

Answer: c

RFC 2225 defines classical IP and ARP (address resolution protocol) over ATM.

35 Which of the following protocols provides ATM interface attributes in a standard SNMP MIB structure?

a. PNNI

b. ILMI

c. IISP

d. SSCOP

Answer: b

Integrated Local Management Interface provides the ATM interface attributes in an SNMP MIB structure.

36 Answer true or false to the following statements:

a. IISP supports dynamic rerouting.

b. An IISP route can have a primary and secondary path.

c. IISP supports QoS.

d. IISP can provide a route between different PNNI peer groups.

e. IISP static routes must avoid routing loops.

f. IISP is less efficient than PNNI source routing.

Answer: a = F, b = T, c = F, d = T, e = T, f = T.

IISP supports static routing only and can have both a primary and a secondary route, but it must avoid routing loops. IISP does not support QoS metrics. IISP can provide a route between different PNNI peer groups. The static nature of IISP is less efficient than PNNI source routing.

Chapter 5 Answers to Scenario Section

Refer to the following configuration to answer the scenario questions:

```
isdn switch-type basic-ni
!
interface BRI0
 ip address 10.50.1.1 255.255.255.252
 encapsulation ppp
 dialer map ip 10.50.1.2 name R10 broadcast 7139970300101
 dialer-group 1
 isdn spid1 7134691020101
 isdn spid2 7134691030101
 ppp authentication pap
!
dialer-list protocol ip permit
```

1 Which authentication is being used?

a. DES

b. PAP

c. CHAP

d. Clear text

Answer: b

PAP authentication is being used (ppp authentication *authentication-type*).

2 What does the **dialer map** command do?

a. Maps the local SPID to 10.50.1.2

b. Maps the remote SPID to 10.50.1.2

c. Defines the local router name as R10

d. Maps the local DLCI to 10.50.1.2

Answer: b

The dialer map maps the remote SPID to 10.50.1.2. The local SPIDs are defined in the isdn spid1 and isdn spid2 commands.

3 What are examples of protocols permitted to start the connection?

a. TCP, UDP, OSPF

b. NLSP, IPX

c. DECNet Phase IV,

d. AURP, NetBEUI

Answer: a

Only IP is permitted to start the connection. TCP, UDP, and OSPF are all IP protocols.

4 The B channel uses which encapsulation?

a. HDLC.

b. PPP.

c. LAPD.

d. Not enough information is given.

Answer: b

The encapsulation type defined under the BRI is PPP.

5 The D channel uses which frame type?

a. HDLC.

b. LAPB.

c. LAPD.

d. Not enough information is given.

Answer: c

LAPD is the default frame type on the D channel.

Chapter 6 Answers to Q & A Section

1 Which IP protocol and port does Telnet use?

a. TCP 21

b. Protocol 1, TCP port 23

c. UDP 23

d. IP protocol 6, TCP port 23

Answer: d

Telnet uses IP protocol 6, which is TCP. TCP uses port 23 for Telnet.

2 What is the directed broadcast address for 171.80.32.178/27?

a. 171.80.32.192.

b. 171.80.32.191.

c. 171.80.32.64.

d. There is not sufficient information.

Answer: b

The subnet address is 171.80.32.160/27, with host addresses from 172.80.32.161/27 to 172.80.32.190/27. The broadcast address for the subnet is 172.80.32.191.

3 When packets are fragmented, where are the fragments reassembled?

a. By the next hop router

b. By the TCP layer in the destination host

c. By the IP layer in the destination host

d. By the router next to the destination host

Answer: c

The IP protocol layer at the destination host is responsible for reassembling any IP fragments before sending the packet up to TCP.

4 Which type of address class is 190.1.2.0?

a. Class A

b. Class B

c. Class C

d. Class D

Answer: b

Network 190.1.2.0 is an IP class B address. Class B addresses range from 128.0.0.0 to 191.255.0.0.

5 What does the flag PSH do?

a. Tells the sending TCP process to send the segment immediately

b. Tells the routers to forward the packets with higher priority

c. Tells the destination TCP to push the IP packet to the application layer

d. Tells the IP layer to send immediately

Answer: a

TCP waits for data to accumulate before forming a segment. The PSH pointer indicates to promptly send the data.

6 Which of the following describes TFTP?

a. A protocol that uses TCP to transfer files with no authentication

b. A protocol for the transfer of files reliably using port 69

c. A protocol for the transfer of files using UDP

d. A protocol to transfer files using TCP 21

Answer: c

The Trivial File Transfer Protocol (TFTP) uses UDP for file transfer.

7 Which ICMP protocol type does the PING application use?

a. IP protocol 6

b. ICMP echo

c. TCP

d. ARP request

Answer: b

The PING application uses the Internet Control Message Protocol (ICMP) echo type.

8 What is blocked in the following access list?

```
access-list 105 deny tcp any host 10.1.1.1 eq 23
access-list 105 permit tcp any any
```

a. Packets from host 10.1.1.1 are denied.

b. Packets from any TCP host are denied.

c. Packets from any host sent to host 10.1.1.1 to the Telnet port are denied.

d. Packets to host 10.1.1.1 are permitted, all others are denied.

Answer: c

The access list denies any host to access host 10.1.1.1 on TCP port 23, which is the Telnet port.

9 Which methods acquire a default gateway?

a. ARP and RARP

b. BOOTP and DHCP

c. RARP and BOOTP

d. IP address and subnet mask

Answer: b

The Bootstrap protocol (BOOTP) and the Dynamic Host Configuration Protocol (DHCP) are methods to provide an IP address, mask, and a default gateway to a host.

10 What is the inside global address in NAT?

a. The translated IP address of the device that resides in the internal network

b. The translated IP address of the device that resides in the Global Internet

c. The inside address of the device in the Internet network

d. The translated global address in the internal network that reaches an external device

Answer: a

The real IP address of a device in the internal network is translated to a globally unique address, which is the Inside Local Address.

11 Which of the following is a subnet mask with 27 bits?

a. 255.255.255.192

b. 255.255.255.252

c. 255.255.255.224

d. 255.255.255.240

Answer: c

Mask 255.255.255.224 has 27 bits that are set to 1 and 5 that are set to 0.

12 How many hosts are in a Class B network with the default mask?

a. 65,534

b. 16,777,214

c. 254

d. 255

Answer: a

The default mask for a Class B network is 255.255.0.0, which provides 2^{16}-2 hosts.

13 Which of the following are protocols that are supported by default with the **ip helper-address** command?

a. BOOTP and DHCP

b. RARP, BOOTP, and DHCP

c. ARP and RARP

d. WINS, DNS, and BOOTP

Answer: a

The ip helper-address supports BOOTP, DHCP, NETBIOS, TFTP, DNS, TACACS, Time service, and IEN-116 name service by default.

14 How many segments are needed to close a TCP connection?

a. Three

b. Four

c. Two

d. A three-way handshake

Answer: b

Four segments close a TCP connection.

15 What is the IHL in the IP header?

a. Internet hop length, indicates the maximum allowed hops

b. Internet header length, measured in octets

c. Internet header length, measured in 32-bit words

d. Internet header length, measured in bits

Answer: c

The Internet header length (IHL) is measured in 32-bit words.

16 Issuing which of the following IOS commands disables proxy ARP?

a. router#**no ip proxy-arp**

b. router(config-if)#**no ip proxy-arp**

c. router (config-if)#**no proxy-arp**

d. router (config)#**no ip proxy-arp**

Answer: b

Answers a and d are incorrect because proxy-arp is configured on an interface. Answer c is incorrect because it has a wrong command structure.

17 Which HSRP router becomes active?

a. The router with the higher priority.

b. The router with the lower priority.

c. The router configured with priority 100.

d. The router configured with priority 1.

Answer: a

The router with the highest HSRP priority becomes the active router. The default HSRP priority is 100.

18 Which protocols are connectionless?

a. Telnet and IP

b. UDP and OSPF

c. UDP and IP

d. FTP and UDP

Answer: c

Telnet uses TCP, which is connection oriented. FTP uses TCP, which is connection oriented. UDP and IP are not connection oriented.

19 How are connections established in TCP?

a. Two-way full duplex handshake.

b. Three-way handshake.

c. PSH message to send data immediately.

d. URG pointer indicates urgency.

Answer: b

TCP connections are established with a three-way handshake.

20 How many bits are in the precedence bits field in the IP header?

a. 3

b. 8

c. 5

d. 4

Answer: a

There are 3 bits in the precedence bits field.

21 The checksum in the IP header is computed for what?

a. The IP header and data

b. The IP header only

c. The pseudo header

d. The UDP header and pseudo header

Answer: b

The IP checksum is computed for the IP header only.

22 Which is the subnet for 150.100.21.11/22?

a. 150.100.16.0

b. 150.100.18.0

c. 150.100.20.0

d. 150.100.21.0

Answer: c

The major Class B network is 150.100.0.0. The subnet is 150.100.20.0/22, with addresses from 150.100.20.1 to 150.100.23.254. The broadcast address for the subnet is 150.100.23.255.

23 What happens if one IP fragment is lost?

a. The receiving IP protocol requests a retransmit.

b. The TCP layer finds the error and retransmits.

c. The router that fragmented the packet must retransmit.

d. The DF bit must be set to 0.

Answer: b

IP provides best-effort delivery. If a fragment is lost, the upper layer is responsible for detecting missing data and for requesting a retransmission.

24 The Internet layer of the TCP/IP architecture corresponds to which OSI layer?

a. Data-link

b. Network

c. Transport

d. Physical and data-link

Answer: b

The TCP/IP Internet layer corresponds to the network layer of the OSI model.

25 The checksum field in TCP performs a checksum of what?

a. Header only

b. Data only

c. TCP Header, data, and pseudo-header

d. TCP Header and pseudo-header

Answer: c

The checksum is performed on the TCP header, data, and psuedo-header.

26 What does the sequence number indicate in TCP?

a. The last byte sent in the segment

b. The first byte sent in the segment

c. The last 32-bit word

d. The number of bytes in the segment

Answer: b

The sequence number indicates the first byte in the segment.

27 Which fields are included in the UDP checksum?

a. UDP header only

b. UDP header, UDP data, source IP, destination IP, port, and UDP length

c. UDP header and UDP data

d. UDP header, UDP data, source IP, destination IP, and port

Answer: b

All fields in answer b calculate the checksum.

28 Which command do you use if you want the active HSRP router to resign if a tracked serial interface 0 goes down?

a. standby 1 track serial 0

b. standby 1 serial 0

c. standby 1 track interface serial 0

d. standby 1 interface serial 0 track

Answer: a

Answer a has the correct command structure.

29 How many bits are in an IPv6 address?

a. 64

b. 96

c. 128

d. 192

Answer: c

An IPv6 address is 128 bits in length.

30 Which of the following is a valid IPv6 address?

a. 1070::25:1

b. 1::1::1

c. BGA0::1FAC:2334

d. FED0:0:0:AB10

Answer: a

Answer b is incorrect because you can only use the :: symbol once. Answer c is incorrect because G is not a hexadecimal number. Answer d is incorrect because the address is not a valid length.

31 Multicast IPv6 addresses begin with which hexadecimal number(s)?

a. 2

b. FE8

c. FEC

d. FF

Answer: d

Multicast IPv6 addresses begin with FF. Aggregatable global unicast addressees begin with 2 or 3. Link-local unicast addresses begin with FE8. Site-local unicast addresses begin with FEC.

32 Which is a valid representation on an IPv4 address in IPv6/IPv4 mixed mode?

a. ::10.10.10.10

b. 10.10.10.10

c. A:A:A:A

d. IPv4 addresses cannot be represented in IPv6.

Answer: a

Answer a has the correct mixed mode representation.

Chapter 6 Answers to Scenario Section

This scenario uses a configuration to review your skills with IP addressing and NAT. Use the following configuration to answer the questions in this section:

```
hostname router
!
ip nat pool local 100.100.1.1 100.100.1.126 netmask 255.255.255.0
!
ip nat inside source list 10 pool local
!
interface ethernet 0
 description outside interface
 ip address 10.1.2.1 255.255.255.0
 ip nat inside
!
interface serial 0
 description inside interface
 ip address 100.100.1.129 255.255.255.252
 ip nat outside
!
access-list 10 permit 10.1.4.0 0.0.3.255
access-list 11 permit 10.1.16.0 0.0.0.255
```

1 Which range of addresses is permitted to access the outside through NAT?

a. From 10.1.4.1 to 10.1.7.255 and from 10.1.16.1 to 10.1.16.255

b. From 10.1.4.1 to 10.1.7.255

c. From 10.1.4.1 to 10.1.16.0

d. From 10.1.4.1 to 10.1.4.255 and from 10.1.16.1 to 10.1.16.255

Answer: b

Addresses in access list 10 are permitted. Addresses in access list 11 are not permitted because the source list only references list 10.

2 Which type of address is 10.1.4.10?

a. Inside local address

b. Outside global address

c. Inside global address

d. Outside local address

Answer: a

The addresses in access list 10 are inside local addresses.

3 Which type of address is 100.100.1.30?

a. Inside local address

b. Outside global address

c. Inside global address

d. Outside local address

Answer: c

The addresses listed in the ip nat pool local command are inside global addresses, which you use for dynamic translation.

4 Which interface is considered a NAT inside interface?

a. Ethernet 0

b. Serial 0

c. Both Ethernet 0 and Serial 0

d. Neither interface

Answer: a

Ethernet 0 has the ip nat inside command. The interface description is incorrect.

5 Which interface is considered a NAT outside interface?

a. Ethernet 0

b. Serial 0

c. Both Ethernet 0 and Serial 0

d. Neither interface

Answer: b

Serial 0 has the ip nat outside command. The interface description is incorrect.

6 If a packet on the outside has a destination IP of 100.100.1.2 and a source IP of 50.25.10.1, which is the source IP after the packet is inside the stub network?

a. 100.100.1.2

b. 50.25.10.1

c. 100.1.4.2

d. 100.1.16.2

Answer: b

Outside global addresses are not translated; therefore, the address remains the same after the packet passes through the NAT router.

7 If a packet on the inside has a destination IP of 40.1.1.1 and a source IP of 10.1.6.10, which is the destination IP after the packet is outside the stub network?

a. 100.100.1.2

b. 50.25.10.1

c. 100.100.1.50

d. 40.1.1.1

Answer: d

The router configuration shown does not translate a destination address.

8 If a packet on the inside has a source IP of 10.1.5.100 and a destination IP of 30.1.1.1, which can the source IP address be after the packet is outside the stub network?

a. 100.1.100.5

b. 30.1.1.1

c. 10.1.5.100

d. 100.100.1.50

Answer: d

The source address is translated to an address between 100.100.1.1 and 100.100.1.126, inclusive.

Chapter 7 Answers to Q & A Section

1 When will EIGRP and IGRP automatically redistribute routes among themselves?

a. When you use different AS numbers

b. When you use the same AS numbers without the **redistribution** command

c. When you use different AS numbers and the **redistribution** command under EIGRP

d. When you use different AS numbers and the **redistribution** command under IGRP

Answer: b

If EIGRP and IGRP are configured with the same AS number in a router, they automatically redistribute routes without having to use the redistribution command.

2 Which command enables RIP?

a. **router rip**

b. **router rip 100**

c. **enable router rip 100**

d. **router rip v1 100**

Answer: a

Answer a has the correct format of the command. You do not use an AS or process number when enabling RIP.

3 How often does IGRP broadcast routing table updates?

a. Every 30 seconds

b. Every 60 seconds

c. Every 90 seconds

d. Every 180 seconds

Answer: c

IGRP sends periodic updates every 90 seconds.

4 Which **static route** command is correctly configured?

a. router(config)#**ip route 10.100.0.0 0.0.255.255 192.172.1.1**

b. router(config)#**ip route 10.100.0.0 255.255.0.0 192.172.1.1**

c. router(config)>**ip route 10.100.0.0 255.255.0.0 192.172.1.1**

d. router#**ip route 10.100.0.0 0.0.255.255 192.172.1.1**

Answer: b

Answer b has the correct format. Answer a has the incorrect mask. Answer c has the wrong router prompt. Answer d has an incorrect mask and router prompt.

5 How long does it take IGRP to remove a possibly down network from the table?

a. 10 minutes

b. 280 seconds

c. 6 minutes

d. 180 seconds

Answer: a

The default flush timer for IGRP is 7 times the update period (7 × 90 seconds = 630 seconds), which is over 10 minutes (600 seconds).

6 RIPv2 improves RIPv1 with which of the following capabilities?

a. Multicast, authentication, hop count

b. Multicast, authentication, VLSM

c. Authentication, VLSM, hop count

d. VLSM, hop count

Answer: b

RIPv2 implements support for variable length subnet masks (VLSM) and an authentication mechanism for route updates, and can multicast updates instead of being broadcast.

7 What is the maximum number of routes in a RIP packet?

a. 104

b. 20

c. 25

d. 60

Answer: c

There can be up to 25 routes in a RIP update packet.

8 Which protocol maintains neighbor adjacencies?

a. RIPv2 and EIGRP

b. IGRP and EIGRP

c. RIPv2

d. EIGRP

Answer: d

EIGRP routers maintain adjacencies with their neighboring routers.

9 What does the number in the **router igrp 50** command indicate?

a. The number of processes is 50.

b. The autonomous system number is 50.

c. The arbitrary number 50.

d. IGRP is allowed 50 routes.

Answer: b

The format of the command to enable IGRP is router igrp *autonomous-system.*

10 Which protocols are classful?

a. EIGRP, RIPv1, and IGRP

b. RIPv1, RIPv2, IGRP

c. RIPv1 and IGRP

d. OSPF, RIPv2, and EIGRP

Answer: c

Only RIPv1 and IGRP are classful routing protocols. RIPv2, EIGRP, OSPF, and IS-IS are classless routing protocols.

11 Which protocol service interface does EIGRP use?

a. UDP port 520

b. IP protocol 9

c. IP protocol 89

d. IP protocol 88

Answer: d

EIGRP uses IP protocol 88.

12 What does the default EIGRP composite metric consist of?

a. Bandwidth

b. Bandwidth and delay

c. Bandwidth, delay, load, and reliability

d. Bandwidth, delay, load, reliability, and hop count

Answer: b

By default, EIGRP uses bandwidth and delay in its composite metric.

13 For RIP, if route updates are not received for a network, how long before the routes are considered invalid?

a. 180 seconds

b. 90 seconds

c. 60 seconds

d. 240 seconds

Answer: a

The invalid timer for RIP is 6 times the update timer (6 × 30 seconds), which is 180 seconds.

14 Which routing protocol implements the DUAL algorithm?

a. IGRP and EIGRP

b. IGRP

c. EIGRP

d. EIGRP and RIPv2

Answer: c

EIGRP implements a Diffusing Update Algorithm (DUAL). DUAL selects best path and second best paths to a destination.

15 Which protocols support VLSM?

a. RIPv2 and IGRP

b. RIPv2, IGRP, and EIGRP

c. RIP and IGRP

d. RIPv2 and EIGRP

Answer: d

RIPv2, EIGRP, OSPF, and IS-IS support Variable Length Subnet Masks.

16 How many routes are in an IGRP update packet?

a. 25

b. 50

c. 75

d. 104

Answer: d

Up to 104 routes are listed in an IGRP packet. Up to 25 routes are listed in a RIP packet.

17 How does EIGRP summarize routes at network boundaries?

a. By default

b. By configuring no **auto-summary** command

c. If they have the same AS number as IGRP

d. By configuring a static route

Answer: a

By default, EIGRP summarizes routes at network boundaries.

18 RIP uses a feature in which routes learned from a neighboring router are sent back to that neighbor with an infinite metric. What is that feature?

a. Simple split horizon

b. DUAL

c. Poison reverse

d. Holddown

Answer: c

RIP uses split horizon with poison reverse to prevent routing loops.

19 Which of the following commands do you use to enable RIPv2 for network 192.10.10.0?

a.

```
router rip v2
 network 192.10.10.0
```

b.

```
router rip
 version 2
 network 192.10.10.0
```

c.

```
router rip 50
 version 2
 network 192.10.10.0
```

d.

```
router rip
 send version 2
 network 192.10.10.0
```

Answer: b

20 Which protocol or port does RIP version 2 use?

a. IP protocol 88

b. TCP 88

c. UDP port 520

d. IP protocol 9

Answer: c

RIP version 1 and version 2 uses UDP port 520.

21 Which of the following protocols support authentication?

a. RIPv2, IGRP, and EIGRP

b. IGRP and EIGRP

c. RIPv2 and EIGRP

d. RIP and RIPv2

Answer: c

RIPv2 and EIGRP support route authentications. RIPv1 has no authentication mechanism.

22 If a router with EIGRP configured is performing a recomputation for a network, the route is in which state?

a. Active state

b. Recompute state

c. Update state

d. Passive state

Answer: a

EIGRP places a route into active state when performing a recomputation for the route.

23 To disable automatic summarization for EIGRP 100, which subcommand is used?

a.

```
router eigrp 100
 no summary
```

b.

```
router eigrp 100
 no automatic-summary
```

c.

```
router eigrp 100
 no auto-summary
```

d.

```
router eigrp 1000
 no auto-sum
```

Answer: c

Only answer c has the correct format for the commands.

24 When a route is marked as invalid, what prevents the route from being reinstated into the routing table?

a. Invalid timer

b. Flush timer

c. Holddown timer

d. Update timer

Answer: c

If a route is removed, no new updates for the route are accepted until the holddown timer expires. The holddown timer for RIP is 180 and for IGRP is 280.

25 What is the administrative distance for internal EIGRP routes?

a. 100

b. 110

c. 170

d. 90

Answer: d

The administrative distance of internal EIGRP routes is 90.

26 RIP version 2 packets are identified in the routing table by which letter?

a. I

b. R

c. E

d. R2

Answer: b

RIP routes (version 1 or version 2) are identified with an R.

27 From the following output, which is the metric to reach network 172.16.4.0/30?

```
Router8#show ip route
Codes: C - connected, S - static, I - IGRP, R - RIP, M - mobile, B - BGP
       D - EIGRP, EX - EIGRP external, O - OSPF, IA - OSPF inter area
       N1 - OSPF NSSA external type 1, N2 - OSPF NSSA external type 2
       E1 - OSPF external type 1, E2 - OSPF external type 2, E - EGP
       i - IS-IS, L1 - IS-IS level-1, L2 - IS-IS level-2, ia - IS-IS inter area
       * - candidate default, U - per-user static route, o - ODR
       P - periodic downloaded static route

Gateway of last resort is not set

     172.16.0.0/16 is variably subnetted, 4 subnets, 3 masks
D       172.16.4.0/30 [90/2195456] via 172.16.1.1, 00:17:20, Ethernet0
C       172.16.1.0/24 is directly connected, Ethernet0
D       172.16.2.0/24 [90/2221056] via 172.16.1.1, 00:12:40, Ethernet0
C       172.16.3.0/28 is directly connected, TokenRing0
```

a. 90/2221056

b. 90

c. 2195456

d. 2221056

Answer: c

The metric is 2195456; the route was learned from EIGRP.

28 Which command is used to check the EIGRP table?

a. **show ip route**

b. **show ip eigrp routes**

c. **show ip eigrp topology**

d. **show ip eigrp table**

Answer: c

The EIGRP topology table is checked with the show ip eigrp topology command.

29 EIGRP's composite metric scales IGRP's metric by what factor?

a. 256.

b. 256,000.

c. 1000.

d. It uses the same metric.

Answer: a

EIGRP scales the metric by 256.

Chapter 7 Answers to Scenario Section

Review Figure 7-7 to answer the following Scenario questions.

Figure 7-7 *Path Selection*

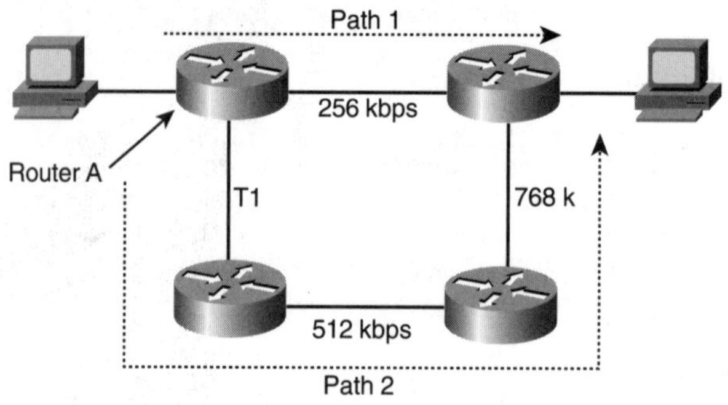

1 By default, if RIPv2 is enabled on all routers, what path is taken?

a. Path 1

b. Path 2

c. Unequal load balance with Path 1 and Path 2

d. Equal load balance with Path 1 and Path 2

Answer: a

From Router A, path 1 is one router hop; path 2 is three router hops. RIP selects path 1 because of the lower metric.

2 By default, if IGRP is enabled on all routers, what path is taken?

a. Path 1

b. Path 2

c. Unequal load balance with Path 1 and Path 2

d. Equal load balance with Path 1 and Path 2

Answer: b

From Router A, the lowest bandwidth in Path 1 is 256 KB, the lowest bandwidth in Path 2 is 512 KB. IGRP selects the path with the best bandwidth, which is Path 2.

3 By default, if EIGRP is enabled on all routers what path is taken?

a. Path 1

b. Path 2

c. Unequal load balance with Path 1 and Path 2

d. Equal load balance with Path 1 and Path 2

Answer: b

From Router A, the lowest bandwidth (BW_{min1}) in path 1 is 256 KB; the lowest bandwidth in path 2 (BW_{min2}) is 512 KB. IGRP selects the highest BW_{min}, which is path 2.

4 EIGRP is configured on the routers. If configured with the variance command, what path is taken?

a. Path 1

b. Path 2

c. Unequal load balance with Path 1 and Path 2

d. Equal load balance with Path 1 and Path 2

Answer: c

By default, EIGRP loads balance using equal-cost paths. EIGRP does unequal load balancing when you use the variance command.

5 Which bandwidth does Router A use for the EIGRP calculation of the metric to reach the destination?

a. 256 KB

b. 512 KB

c. 1.544 KB

d. 512 KB + 1.544MB + 768 KB

Answer: b

The lowest bandwidth in Path 2 (BW_{min}) is used for the EIGRP metric calculation.

Chapter 8 Answers to Q & A Section

1 Which type of router always has one or more interfaces connected to Area 0.0.0.0?

a. Level 2 router

b. ASBR

c. Backbone router

d. Autonomous boundary router

Answer: c

An OSPF backbone router always has one or more interfaces connected to the backbone. An ASBR can have one or more interfaces connected to the backbone, but it isn't a requirement.

2 What is the number in the **router ospf** *number* command?

a. The autonomous system number

b. The process ID

c. The AS number

d. Answer b and c

Answer: b

The *number* in the router ospf *number* command is the process ID. Multiple instances of OSPF can run on a single router. The process number identifies each running process.

3 IS-IS has which types of authentication capabilities?

a. Domain, area, and link authentication with cleartext password.

b. Domain, area, and link authentication with md5.

c. Domain, area, and link authentication with cleartext and md5 passwords.

d. There is no authentication in IS-IS.

Answer: a

IS-IS supports cleartext password authentication only.

4 What is the IOS default OSPF cost for a T1 interface?

a. 100

b. 10

c. 290

d. 64

Answer: d

IOS default OSPF cost is calculated by using the formula 10^8 / BW. 10^8 / 1544000 = 64.

5 What is the default IS-IS metric for a T1 interface?

a. 100

b. 10

c. 290

d. 64

Answer: b

In Cisco routers, all IS-IS interfaces have a default metric of 10.

6 What connects an area to the backbone when there is no physical connectivity?

a. T1 link

b. Virtual link

c. Fast Ethernet link

d. Backbone link

Answer: b

All areas are required to connect to the OSPF backbone. If an area does not have physical connectivity to the backbone, but it does connect to another area that connects to the backbone, a virtual link can provide the required area to the backbone connection.

7 Which command verifies IS-IS neighbors?

a. **show isis is-neighbors**

b. **show ip isis neighbors**

c. **show clns is-neighbors**

d. **show ip clns isis neighbors**

Answer: c

8 A router that floods external Type-7 LSAs is part of which type of area?

a. Backbone area

b. Stub area

c. Not-so-stubby area

d. Totally stubby area

Answer: c

External routes advertised in a not-so-stubby area are flooded within the area with Type-7 LSAs.

9 Which LSA type announces reachability to the ASBR?

a. Type 3

b. Type 4

c. Type 5

d. Type 7

Answer: b

Type 3 LSAs are summary LSAs. Type 4 LSAs announce reachability to the ASBR. Type 5 LSAs announce AS external routes. Type 7 LSAs announce external routes within an NSSA.

10 Which commands add network 10.10.64.0/18 to area 10 in OSPF?

a. **router ospf** and **network 10.10.64.0 0.0.63.255 area 10**

b. **router ospf** and **network 10.10.64.0 255.255.192.0 area 10**

c. **router ospf 99** and **network 10.10.64.0 0.0.63.255 area 10**

d. **router ospf 99** and **network 10.10.64.0 255.255.192.0 area 10**

Answer: c

The router ospf *process-ID* is the correct syntax for the router ospf command. The network 10.10.64.0 0.0.63.255 area 10 adds interfaces with addresses 10.10.64.0/18 to area 10. The network 10.10.64.0 255.255.192.0 area 10 adds interfaces addressed with 0.0.0.0 through 255.255.192.0 to area 10.

11 The **ip ospf cost** command is used for what?

a. To change the default cost under **router ospf**

b. To change the default cost on an external link when redistributing into OSPF

c. To change the default cost at the ABR

d. To change the default cost of an interface

Answer: d

Costs are associated with interfaces. The ip ospf cost command changes the default cost of an interface.

12 Which address multicasts to the designated router?

a. 224.0.0.1

b. 224.0.0.5

c. 224.0.0.6

d. 224.0.0.10

Answer: c

224.0.0.1 is the all systems on this subnet multicast address. 224.0.0.5 is the all OSPF router multicast address. 224.0.0.6 is the all OSPF designated router multicast address. 224.0.0.10 is the all IGRP routers multicast address.

13 What is the administrative distance of OSPF routes?

a. 90

b. 100

c. 110

d. 170

Answer: c

OSPF default administrative distance is 110.

14 What is the P-bit used for in NSSA?

a. Set by the ASBR to indicate the priority of routes redistributed into the area

b. Set by the ABR to indicate that the ABR is used as a default route to the rest of the network

c. Set by the ASBR to indicate whether or not Type 7 LSAs are translated to Type 5 LSAs

d. Set by the ABR in Type 5 LSAs when Type 7 LSAs are translated to Type 5 LSAs; indicates the originating area of a route

Answer: c

ASBRs set the P-bit in Type 7 LSAs. An ABR receiving the LSA translates the Type 7 LSA to a Type 5 LSA if the P-bit is set to 1.

15 What is the ATT bit used for in IS-IS?

a. Set by an L1 IS to indicate that it is connected to an external network

b. Set by an L1/L2 IS to indicate to L1 ISs that this L1/L2 IS is available for forwarding traffic destined to routes unknown in the area

c. Set by an L2 IS to indicate that it is connected to an external network

d. Set by an L1/L2 IS to indicate to other L2 ISs that it is connected to multiple L1 areas

Answer: b

The attached (ATT) bit is set by a L1/L2 IS to indicate that it is attached to an L2 area and is, therefore, available to forward traffic outside of the L1 area.

16 To where are OSPF Type 1 LSAs flooded?

a. The OSPF area

b. The OSPF domain

c. From the area to the OSPF backbone

d. Through the virtual link

Answer: a

Type 1 LSAs are flooded within an area only. These enable all routers within an area to create identical link-state databases.

17 The DR forms adjacencies to which routers?

a. Only to the BDR.

b. The BDR is adjacent to all, not the DR.

c. The DR forwards all LSAs.

d. To all routers in the multiaccess network.

Answer: d

The DR forms adjacencies with all routers in a multiaccess network.

18 In IS-IS, the BDIS forms adjacencies to which routers?

a. Only to the DIS.

b. To all routers.

c. The BDIS only becomes adjacent when the DIS is down.

d. There is no BDIS in IS-IS.

Answer: d

IS-IS multiaccess networks have designated ISs only, no backup designated IS (BDIS) exists.

19 What produces Type 2 LSAs?

a. ABR

b. ASBR

c. DR

d. NSSA ASBR

Answer: c.

Type 2 LSAs are produced by the DR.

20 In the following command, what is area 50?

```
area 50 virtual-link 1.1.1.1
```

a. Backbone area

b. Virtual area

c. Transit area

d. Nonconnected area

Answer: c

The format of the command is area *transit-area* virtual-link *remote-ip-address*.

21 Which of the following are link-state protocols?

a. RIPv2 and OSPF

b. IGRP and EIGRP

c. OSPF and IS-IS

d. RIPv1 and IGRP

Answer: c

Of those listed, only OSPF and IS-IS are link-state protocols.

22 OSPF has two equal-cost paths to a destination. What does OSPF do?

a. Uses the router ID to select one path

b. Uses both paths to load-balance

c. Uses the highest IP to select one path

d. Uses both paths to load-balance even if the costs are different

Answer: b.

OSPF does equal-cost, multipath load balancing.

23 OSPF has two nonequal-cost paths to a destination. What does OSPF do?

a. Uses the router ID to select one path

b. Uses both paths to load-balance

c. Uses the lowest cost to select one path

d. Uses both paths to load-balance even if the costs are different

Answer: c

OSPF does not do unequal-cost, multipath load balancing. If two paths exist to the same destination, OSPF chooses the path with the lowest cost.

24 OSPF routers use which IP protocol or port?

a. IP protocol 89.

b. TCP port 89.

c. UDP port 89.

d. It does not use IP for transport.

Answer: a

25 IS-IS routers use which IP protocol or port?

a. IP protocol 89.

b. TCP port 89.

c. UDP port 89.

d. IS-IS uses the data-link layer.

Answer: d

IS-IS does not run over IP.

26 What are OSPF Type 3 LSAs?

a. Router LSAs with interface state information produced by all routers

b. ASBR summary LSAs produced by ABRs

c. Summary LSAs produced by ABRs

d. External LSAs produced by ABRs

Answer: c

Type 3 LSAs are Summary LSAs and are produced by ABRs. They are flooded into areas to advertise destinations outside the area.

27 The following router output is produced by which command?

```
Neighbor ID      Pri   State           Dead Time   Address         Interface
112.20.150.6       1   FULL/DR         00:00:33    112.20.150.111  Ethernet0
112.20.150.7       1   FULL/  -        00:00:34    112.20.150.236  Serial0.1
```

a. **show clns is-neighbors**

b. **show ip eigrp neighbors**

c. **show ip ospf neighbors**

d. **show isis neighbors**

Answer: c

This is OSPF output and displays the state of OSPF neighbors.

28 What happens if an L1/L2 router can reach a destination through two different paths: one an L1 path, the other an L2 path?

a. If the L1 and L2 path costs are equal, both routes are added to the routing table and load balancing occurs.

b. The path with the lowest cost is used.

c. The L2 path is always used, regardless of the path costs.

d. The L1 path is always used, regardless of the path costs.

Answer: d

If two paths exist to a single destination, the L1 path takes precedence, regardless of the cost.

29 What does O E2 mean in the following router output?

```
O E2 1.0.0.0/8 [110/1000] via 1.1.1.1, 00:00:01, Ethernet0
```

a. The route is an OSPF internal Type 2 route.

b. The route has a metric of 110.

c. The route is an OSPF external Type 2 route.

d. The route is an OSPF interarea route.

Answer: c

O means it is an OSPF derived route; E2 means that it is an external Type 2 route.

30 What does a set E-bit indicate in OSPF Hello messages?

a. The sending router has a connected external interface and is redistributing routes into OSPF.

b. The area is a not-so-stubby area (NSSA).

c. The area is not a stub area.

d. The interface sending the Hello message is not capable of becoming the DR for the network.

Answer: c

The E-bit specifies whether an area supports external routes. If the area does not support the flooding of external routes, the area is a stub area and the E-bit must be cleared in Hello packets on all interfaces in the area. If the area does support external routes, the area is not a stub area and the E-bit must be set.

31 What is the metric in the following router output?

```
O IA    1.1.1.1/28 [110/100] via 2.2.2.2, 00:05:32, Serial0.1
```

a. 110

b. 100

c. 0

d. 28

Answer: b

The metric is the second value in the parenthesis. The first value, 110, is the administrative distance.

Chapter 8 Answers to Scenario Section

Scenario 8-1

Use the following configuration to answer the scenario questions:

```
hostname RouterA
!
interface Loopback0
 ip address 1.1.1.1 255.255.255.255
!
interface Ethernet0
 ip address 1.1.1.18 255.255.255.240
!
interface Serial0
 ip address 2.2.2.241 255.255.255.252
```

```
!
router ospf 50
 log-adjacency-changes
 area 20 virtual-link 2.2.2.250
 redistribute static metric 500
 network 1.1.1.1 0.0.0.0 area 0
 network 1.1.1.16 0.0.0.15 area 0
 network 2.2.2.240 0.0.0.3 area 20
!
ip classless
ip route 10.0.0.0 255.0.0.0 Null0
```

1 From Router A's configuration, which interfaces are in area 0?

a. Ethernet 0 and Serial 0

b. Serial 0 and Loopback 0

c. Ethernet 0 and Loopback 0

d. Ethernet 0 only

Answer: c

The network commands define the range of IP addresses in a specific area. The interface addresses are then compared to the ranges to determine which area an interface is in.

Network 1.1.1.1 0.0.0.0 area 0 indicates that any interface with the exact IP address 1.1.1.1 is in area 0. This specifies the loopback interface.

Network 1.1.1.16 0.0.0.15 area 0 indicates that any interface with an IP address from 1.1.1.16 through 1.1.1.31 is in area 0. Ethernet 0 falls in this range.

2 What is the OSPF cost for Ethernet 0?

a. 1.

b. 10.

c. 100.

d. Not enough information is given.

Answer: b

Because no cost is configured, you use the default value. The default formula on Cisco routers for calculating the cost of a link is 10^8 / BW, so 10^8 / 10000000 is 10.

3 What is the number of the area that uses the virtual link to connect to area 0?

a. 0.

b. 10.

c. 20.

d. Not enough information is given.

Answer: d

Because Router A is connected to area 0, the area in question must be the area on the other side of the virtual link. The virtual link configuration command specifies the transit area, not the remote area. Area 20 is the transit area.

4 What is the router ID of Router A?

a. 1.1.1.18

b. 1.1.1.1

c. 2.2.2.241

d. 2.2.2.250

Answer: b

If a loopback interface exists, its IP address becomes the router ID.

Scenario 8-2

Use the following router command output to answer the scenario questions:

```
Router9>show clns is-neighbors

System Id      Interface   State  Type Priority  Circuit Id         Format
Router10       Se0         Up     L1L2 0 /0      00                 Phase V
Router8        Et0         Up     L2   64        Router8.01         Phase V


Router9#show isis database

IS-IS Level-1 Link State Database:
LSPID                 LSP Seq Num  LSP Checksum  LSP Holdtime      ATT/P/OL
Router10.00-00        0x000000D6   0x4E0C        820               0/0/0
Router9.00-00       * 0x000000DE   0xF943        1017              0/0/0
IS-IS Level-2 Link State Database:
LSPID                 LSP Seq Num  LSP Checksum  LSP Holdtime      ATT/P/OL
Router10.00-00        0x00000004   0x2F63        1012              0/0/0
Router9.00-00       * 0x000000DE   0xDBD2        1014              0/0/0
Router8.00-00         0x000000D5   0xA508        1062              0/0/0
Router8.01-00         0x000000D3   0xA060        848               0/0/0
```

1 What router is the DIS?

a. Router 10.

b. Router 8.

c. Router 9.

d. Not enough information is given.

Answer: b

The DIS's system name is concatenated with the circuit ID to form the pseudonode name on multiaccess networks.

2 What is the IS-IS interface priority on Router 8?

a. 64

b. Less than 64.

c. Greater than 64.

d. Not enough information is given.

Answer: d

The priority shown in the show clns is-neighbors command on the line showing Router 8 is that of Router 9, the router on which the command was entered. Because Router 8 is the DIS on Ethernet 0, its priority must be greater than 64; or if it is equal to 64, it must have a higher system ID than Router 9. Because you don't know the system IDs, you can't determine if the priority is 64 or greater than 64.

3 How many ISs exist in the routing domain?

a. 6

b. 5

c. 4

d. 3

Answer: d

Three ISs are in the routing domain: Router 8, Router 9, and Router 10. Router 9 and Router 10 are listed twice, once in the L1 section and once in the L2 section. Router 8 is the DIS, so there is an entry for the pseudonode with the pseudonode name of Router8.01.

Chapter 9 Answers to Q & A Section

1 A router has the following configuration. Which routing protocol are you using?

```
router bgp 10
 neighbor 1.1.1.1 remote-as 10
```

a. OBGP with an external neighbor

b. BGP with an internal neighbor

c. BGP with an external neighbor

d. EIGRP with an internal neighbor

Answer: b

The router's BGP AS number is 10 and the BGP neighbor's AS is 10.

2 MED is used for which of the following functions?

a. To give a hint to the routers on what outbound path to take

b. To give a hint to the confederation routers on what outbound path to take

c. To give a hint to the external BGP peers on what inbound path to take

d. To give a hint to local BGP peers on what inbound path to take

Answer: c

Multi-Exit Discriminator (MED) is used when an AS has multiple connections to another AS. It is an attempt by an AS to influence the selected route a neighboring AS should select.

3 Which of the following best describes the BGP weight attribute?

a. Determines a path; not locally significant.

b. Determines a path; lowest value is preferred.

c. Locally significant; lowest value is preferred.

d. Locally significant; highest value is preferred.

Answer: d

The Weight attribute selects a best outbound route, it is not advertised to peers, and it is locally significant. The highest Weight is selected.

4 What is the process by which BGP speakers in a transit AS do not advertise a route until all routers have learned about the route through an IGP?

a. Redistribution

b. BGP synchronization

c. OSPF redistribution

d. OSPF synchronization

Answer: b

BGP synchronization requires that BGP speakers in a transit AS not advertise routes until all routers within that AS have learned about the route through an IGP.

5 What does the number represent in the following router command?

```
router bgp 200
```

a. ASN.

b. Process ID.

c. Autonomous process ID.

d. The number is incorrect; it must be 65,000 or higher.

Answer: a

The number is the autonomous system number.

6 Which service access point does BGP use?

a. UDP port 179

b. IP protocol 179

c. TCP port 179

d. None of the above

Answer: c

BGP uses TCP port 179.

7 Which of the following shows the correct order that BGP uses to select a best path?

a. Origin, lowest IP, AS Path, Weight, Local Preference

b. Weight, Local Preference, AS Path, Origin, MED, lowest IP

c. Lowest IP, AS Path, Origin, Weight, MED, Local Preference

d. Weight, Origin, Local Preference, AS Path, MED, lowest IP

Answer: b

Only answer b has the correct order of BGP path selection.

8 BGP communities apply common policy to what?

a. Routers

b. A group of destinations

c. Dampened routes

d. Autonomous systems

Answer: b

BGP communities apply a common policy or properties to a group of destinations.

9 What does the > symbol mean in the output of **show ip bgp**?

a. Compares a route as less than another

b. Indicates an internal BGP route

c. Compares a route as greater than another

d. Indicates the selected route

Answer: d

The selected route is marked with the > symbol.

10 Which of the following is the administrative distance of an external BGP route?

a. 1

b. 20

c. 50

d. 200

Answer: b

External BGP routes have an administrative distance of 20. Internal BGP routes have an administrative distance of 200.

11 Which mechanism penalizes flapping BGP routes by suppressing them?

a. Route reflectors

b. Route dampening

c. Route suppression

d. Route filtering

Answer: b

Route dampening suppresses flapping BGP routes.

12 Which feature was implemented in BGPv4 to provide forwarding of packets based on IP prefixes?

a. MED

b. VLSM

c. CIDR

d. AS path

Answer: c

Classless Interdomain routing (CIDR) was first implemented in BGPv4.

13 What is configured if an external BGP neighbor does not share a common subnet?

a. BGP confederation, with iBGP only

b. BGP multihop, with eBGP only

c. BGP multihop, with iBGP only

d. BGP confederation, with eBGP only

Answer: b

BGP Multihop is configured to peer with an external BGP neighbor that is not in a local subnet.

14 Which of the following is the best definition of an autonomous system?

a. Group of routers running iBGP

b. Group of routers running OSPF

c. Group of routers running eBGP

d. Group of routers under single administration

Answer: d

15 Which mechanism applies the same policies to a group of neighbors?

a. Peer group

b. Confederation group

c. Community group

d. Route-reflector group

Answer: a

BGP peer groups apply a common set of policies to a group of BGP neighbors.

16 Router A and Router B are in AS 50. Router A has two BGP peers (Router C and Router D) to AS 100. Routers C and D announce the same destination. Router C announces a MED of 200. Router D announces a MED of 300. Which path does Router A take to reach AS 100?

a. Router A

b. Router B

c. Router C

d. Router D

Answer: c

The lowest BGP MED is selected.

17 Router A has three BGP peers: Router B, Router C, and Router D. Routers B, C, and D announce the same destinations. Router B announces the default local preference. Router C announces a local preference of 200. Router D announces a local preference of 300. Which path does Router A take?

a. Router A

b. Router B

c. Router C

d. Router D

Answer: d

The highest local preference is selected, Router D. The default local preference is 100, which is announced by Router B.

18 Which network prefix is more specific?

a. 100.1.0.0/16

b. 100.1.1.0/24

c. 100.1.0.0/28

d. 100.1.1.0/26

Answer: c

The highest bit mask is more specific.

19 Which command resets all BGP connections?

a. **reset ip bgp ***

b. **show ip bgp ***

c. **clear ip bgp ***

d. **disc ip bgp ***

Answer: c

The clear ip bgp * command resets all BGP connections.

20 Which of the following BGP routes is selected?

a. AS path = 23 50 801, MED = 10, routerID = 1.1.1.1

b. AS path = 24 51 801, MED = 0, routerID = 2.2.2.2

c. AS path = 100 24 51 801, MED = 10, routerID = 3.3.3.3

d. AS path = 23 50 801, MED = 0, routerID = 4.4.4.4

Answer: b

Following the BGP decision process, check AS Path length, then lowest MED, and then lowest Router ID IP address. Answers b and d both have the same AS Path length and a MED of 0. Because 2.2.2.2 is lower than 4.4.4.4, answer b is selected.

21 BGP has two routes for a network. One has an origin code of i; the second has an origin code of e. Which one is chosen?

a. The route marked with i as the origin type.

b. The route marked with e as the origin type.

c. The route is invalid.

d. Not enough information given.

Answer: a

Based on origin type, routes originated by an IGP (i) are preferred over routes originated by an EGP (e).

22 How many route reflectors are allowed in a cluster?

a. Only one.

b. More than one.

c. Route reflectors are used in confederations.

d. None.

Answer: b

One or more route reflectors are allowed in a cluster.

23 A router announces several networks through redistribution in BGP. If you use the **aggregate-address 100.64.0.0 255.252.0.0** command, which networks are announced?

Announced networks: 100.64.224.0/24 through 100.65.10.0/24

a. Network 100.64.0.0/14 only

b. Network 100.64.0.0/16 only

c. Network 100.64.0.0/14 and announced networks

d. Network 100.64.0.0/16 and announced networks

Answer: c

Because the summary-only keyword was not in the command, all announced networks are announced with the aggregate network.

Chapter 9 Answers to Scenario Section

Scenario 9-1

Use the following router output to answer the questions in this scenario:

```
R1>show ip bgp
BGP table version is 66, local router ID is 172.16.99.1
Status codes: s suppressed, d damped, h history, * valid, > best, i - internal
Origin codes: i - IGP, e - EGP, ? - incomplete

   Network          Next Hop            Metric LocPrf Weight Path
*>i18.88.88.0/24    8.8.8.8                  0    100      0 i
* i79.7.7.0/24      78.1.1.7                      100      0 7910 i
*>                  172.16.64.10                           0 7910 i
* i109.1.1.0/24     78.1.1.7                      100      0 7910 i
*>                  172.16.64.10             0             0 7910 i
*>i155.55.55.0/24   2.2.2.2                  0    100      0 i
*> 172.16.1.0/24    0.0.0.0                  0         32768 i
* i199.99.99.0      78.1.1.7                      100      0 7910 i
*>                  172.16.64.10                           0 7910 i
*>i222.222.222.0    2.2.2.2                  0    100      0 i
```

1 Which of the following is the selected route for network 109.1.1.0/24?

a. 78.1.1.7

b. 172.16.64.10

c. 172.16.99.1

d. 2.2.2.2

Answer: b

The selected route is indicated by >. There are two valid routes for network 109.1.1.0/24 with next hops of 78.1.1.7 and 172.16.64.10. Next hop 172.16.64.10 is selected with the > code.

2 Why is 172.16.64.10 the best next hop for network 199.99.99.0?

a. It is an internal route.

b. There is no local preference.

c. The weight is 0.

d. The route is external.

Answer: d

External paths are preferred over internal paths.

3 Which of the following is the router identifier of the local router?

a. 172.16.63.10

b. 172.16.99.1

c. 78.1.1.7

d. 2.2.2.2

Answer: b

The local Router ID is indicated in the first line, the BGP table version is 66, and the local router ID is 172.16.99.1.

Scenario 9-2

Use the following router output to answer the questions in this scenario:

```
router# show ip bgp neighbors 100.10.10.2
BGP neighbor is 100.10.10.2,  remote AS 500, external link
  BGP version 4, remote router ID 100.10.10.10
  BGP state = Established, up for 00:00:22
  Last read 00:00:21, hold time is 180, keepalive interval is 60 seconds
  Neighbor capabilities:
    Route refresh: advertised and received(new)
    Address family IPv4 Unicast: advertised and received
  Received 4 messages, 0 notifications, 0 in queue
  Sent 4 messages, 0 notifications, 0 in queue
  Route refresh request: received 0, sent 0
  Default minimum time between advertisement runs is 30 seconds

 For address family: IPv4 Unicast
  BGP table version 1, neighbor version 1
  Index 1, Offset 0, Mask 0x2
  0 accepted prefixes consume 0 bytes
  Prefix advertised 0, suppressed 0, withdrawn 0
  Number of NLRIs in the update sent: max 0, min 0

  Connections established 1; dropped 0
  Last reset never
Connection state is ESTAB, I/O status: 1, unread input bytes: 0
Local host: 100.10.10.1, Local port: 11007
Foreign host: 100.10.10.2, Foreign port: 179
```

1 Which of the following is the router ID of the remote peer?

a. 100.10.10.2

b. 100.10.10.1

c. 100.10.10.10

d. 100.10.10.255

Answer: c

The peer router ID is indicated in the second line: BGP version 4, remote router ID 100.10.10.10.

2 What is NLRI?

a. Network Layer Reachability Information

b. Network Link Reachability Information

c. Network Link Route Information

d. Network Local Reachability Information

Answer: a

NLRI is Network Layer Reachability Information, which are destination IP networks.

3 Which of the following is the remote AS number?

a. 100.

b. 200.

c. 500.

d. Not enough information is given.

Answer: c.

The remote AS number is indicated in the first line: BGP neighbor 100.10.10.2, remote AS 500, external link.

4 What is the state of the TCP connection?

a. TCP 179

b. TCP 11079

c. Established

d. Idle

Answer: c

The BGP state is indicated in the third line: BGP state = Established, up for 00:00:22

Scenario 9-3

Use the following configuration to answer the questions in this scenario:

```
interface loopback 0
 ip address 1.1.1.1 255.255.255.255
!
router bgp 200
 network 1.0.0.0 mask 255.240.0.0
 neighbor 2.2.2.1 remote-as 300
```

```
 neighbor 2.2.2.1 route-map ccie out
 neighbor 1.1.1.3 remote-as 200
 neighbor 1.1.1.3 route-reflector-client
 neighbor 1.1.1.4 remote-as 200
 neighbor 1.1.1.4 route-reflector-client
 neighbor 1.1.1.5 remote-as 200
 bgp cluster-id 5
!
route-map ccie permit 10
 set metric 100
```

1 Which of the following is the local AS number?

a. 100

b. 200

c. 300

d. Not specified

Answer: b

The local AS number is indicated by router bgp 200.

2 Which router is a route reflector? (There might be more than one.)

a. 1.1.1.1 only

b. 1.1.1.3 only

c. 2.2.2.1 only

d. 1.1.1.3 and 1.1.1.4

Answer: a

Route-reflector clients are configured on the route reflector, which is the local router. The loopback address of the local router is 1.1.1.1.

3 Which of the following is the router ID of the router with this configuration?

a. 1.1.1.1

b. 1.1.1.3

c. 1.1.1.4

d. 2.2.2.1

Answer: a

The loopback interface IP address: 1.1.1.1.

4 Which of the following is the external peer's AS number?

a. 100

b. 200

c. 300

d. Not specified

Answer: c

There is one external peer (2.2.2.1), which is configured with AS 300.

5 Which attribute is configured in the route map?

a. Origin

b. Local Preference

c. MED

d. AS Hop metric

Answer: c

The Multi-Exit Discriminator is configured with the set metric command.

Chapter 10 Answers to Q & A Section

1 What is the administrative distance of EIGRP external routes?

a. 90

b. 100

c. 110

d. 170

Answer: d

The administrative distance for internal EIGRP routes is 90. The administrative distance for external EIGRP routes is 170.

2 Which protocol do hosts use to join a multicast group?

a. CGMP

b. DVMRP

c. PIM-SM

d. IGMP

Answer: d

Hosts use Internet Group Management Protocol (IGMP) to join a multicast group. IGMP operates between the host and the local router.

3 When redistributing EIGRP routes into RIP, how do the bandwidth and delay metrics get converted?

a. RIP assigns the bandwidth and delay metrics with the **default-metric** command.

b. The EIGRP metrics do not get converted; RIP assigns a default hop count metric as configured by the **default-metric** command.

c. RIP uses the bandwidth metric and discards the delay.

d. RIP uses the delay metric and discards the bandwidth.

Answer: b

You use the default-metric *hop count* command under router RIP to configure the metric of redistributed routes.

4 What does the multicast address 224.0.0.2 represent?

a. All hosts on the subnet

b. All routers on the subnet

c. All OSPF routers on the network

d. All PIM routers on the network

Answer: b

The IANA has reserved addresses in the range from 224.0.0.0 through 224.0.0.255 that network protocols use on a local network segment. The address 224.0.0.1 means "all systems on this subnet," 224.0.0.2 means "all routers on this subnet," and 224.0.0.5 is for OSPF routers.

5 When an EIGRP route is redistributed into OSPF, what is the default administrative distance of the resulting OSPF route in the IP routing table?

a. 90

b. 100

c. 110

d. 170

Answer: c

On Cisco routers, OSPF external routes have an administrative distance of 110. The distance of OSPF external routes can be changed by using the distance external command.

6 A router is running two routing protocols: OSPF and EIGRP. Both protocols internally learn of the route 10.1.1.4/24. Which route is added to the routing table?

a. The EIGRP route.

b. The OSPF route.

c. Both added with equal load balancing.

d. Both added with unequal load balancing.

Answer: a

The EIGRP route has the lowest administrative distance (90), versus the distance of OSPF (110).

7 Which access list denies Telnet and ping and permits everything else?

a.

```
access-list 99 deny tcp any  any eq echo log
access-list 99 deny tcp any any telnet eq telnet
access-list 99 permit ip any any
```

b.

```
access-list 100 deny icmp any any echo log
access-list 100 deny tcp any any telnet
```

c.

```
access-list 100 deny icmp any any echo log
access-list 100 deny icmp any any echo-reply
access-list 100 deny tcp any any eq telnet
access-list 100 permit ip any any
```

d.

```
access-list 99 deny icmp any any echo log
access-list 99 deny icmp any any echo-reply
access-list 99 deny tcp any any eq telnet
access-list 99 permit ip any any
```

Answer: c

Extended access lists range from 100 to 199. Answer c uses the correct format.

8 In an internetwork of 50 routers running EIGRP, you need to filter the networks received by one spoke router. What can you use?

a. Use an access list and apply it to the inbound interface with the **ip access-group** command.

b. Redistribute the routes into OSPF with a route map.

c. Use a distribute list under the EIGRP process with an access list to filter the networks.

d. Change the administrative distance of the router.

Answer: c

Distribute lists filter the contents, inbound or outbound, of routing updates.

9 Which access list permits all hosts in network 192.172.100.0/28?

a. access-list 100 permit 192.172.100.0 0.0.0.31.

b. access-list 10 permit 192.172.100.0 255.255.255.240.

c. access-list 10 permit 192.172.100.0 0.0.0.31.

d. access-list 10 permit ip 192.172.100.0 0.0.0.31.

Answer: c

10 What does PIM stand for?

a. Protocol Inbound Multicast

b. Protocol Independent Multicast

c. Protocol Independent Management

d. Password Independent Multicast

Answer: b

Protocol Independent Multicast is a multicast routing protocol. The two flavors of PIM are sparse mode and dense mode.

11 In an access list command, the keyword **any** replaces which network/mask pair?

a. 0.0.0.0 0.0.0.0

b. 0.0.0.0 255.255.255.255

c. 255.255.255.255 255.255.255.255

d. 255.255.255.255 0.0.0.0

Answer: b

The network mask pair 0.0.0.0 255.255.255.255 signifies any network.

12 OSPF external routes can be assigned an administrative distance of 120 with which OSPF subcommand?

a. **distance 120**

b. **distance external 120**

c. **ospf distance 120**

d. **distance ospf-external 120**

Answer: b

The distance external command can assign an administrative distance, which is different than the default (110), to OSPF external routes.

13 When redistributing between EIGRP and IGRP on the same router, which statement is correct?

a. If the AS numbers are the same, you use the **redistribute** command.

b. If the AS numbers are the same, you do not use the **redistribute** command.

c. If the AS numbers are different, you use the **redistribute** command.

d. Both b and c are correct.

Answer: d

If EIGRP and IGRP are configured with the same AS number, the router redistributes automatically without the redistribute command. If the AS numbers are different, the redistribute command needs to be configured for redistribution.

14 A router has network 140.175.0.0/16 in its RIP database table and an IBGP learned route in its BGP table. Which one does the router include in the IP routing table?

a. The RIP route

b. The IBGP route

c. Both with equal load balancing because the metrics are the same

d. Both with unequal load balancing because the metrics are different

Answer: a

The RIP route is entered in the routing table because the administrative distance of RIP is 120 and the administrative distance of IBGP is 200.

15 What is the default administrative distance of OSPF?

a. 90

b. 110

c. 115

d. 120

Answer: b

The default administrative distance of OSPF is 110.

16 If applied to an interface, what does the following access list permits?

```
access-list 101 permit udp any host 10.10.10.10 eq snmp log
```

a. Permits host 10.10.10.10 to access any network with SNMP

b. Permits any host to access host 10.10.10.10 with SNMP, and logs every match; denies all other traffic

c. Permits the SNMP server to access all devices through UDP

d. Permits SNMP traps to be sent to 10.10.10.10 from any host; denies all other traffic

Answer: b

The access list permits any host to send UDP packets to host 10.10.10.10 on UDP port 161, which is SNMP.

17 In multicast routing (PIM-SM), which device has the task of gathering the information of senders and making the information available to other PIM routers?

a. Sending host

b. Router using IGMP

c. RP

d. Mapping agent

Answer: c

The rendezvous point (RP). The RP is charged with the task to gather the information of senders and make the information available to other PIM routers.

18 What happens to the metrics when redistributing from IGRP to EIGRP?

a. They do not change.

b. They change by a factor of 100.

c. They change by a factor of 256.

d. They change to hop count.

Answer: c

Metrics are converted by a factor of 256 between EIGRP and IGRP.

19 Which protocol controls multicast traffic in a switched LAN environment?

a. IGMP

b. CGMP

c. IGMP Snooping

d. b and c

Answer: d

Cisco Group Management Protocol (CGMP) and IGMP Snooping are both methods to control multicast traffic in a switched LAN environment.

20 Which issues must be addressed when redistributing OSPF into IGRP at multiple locations?

a. Default metric

b. Variable length subnet masks

c. Route loops

d. All of the above

Answer: d

All the answers are issues when redistributing between OSPF and IGRP.

21 Which route manipulation method changes the IP next hop based on the source address of a packet?

a. Distribution list

b. Policy routing

c. Static routing

d. Redistribution

Answer: b

Policy-based routing can change the next-hop address based on the source IP address of the packet.

22 Which commands change the next hop for hosts in subnetwork 10.1.1.128/28?

a.

```
interface e 0
ip policy route-map gonext
!
route-map gonext permit 20
match ip address 50
set ip next-hop 1.1.1.1
!
route-map gonext permit 25
!
access-list 20 permit 10.1.1.128 0.0.0.15
```

b.

```
interface e 0
 ip policy route-map gonext
!
route-map gonext permit 20
 match ip address 50
 set ip next-hop 1.1.1.1
!
route-map gonext permit 30
!
access-list 30 permit 10.1.1.128 0.0.0.15
```

c.

```
interface e 0
 ip policy route-map gonext
!
route-map gonext permit 20
 match ip address 50
 set ip next-hop 1.1.1.1
!
route-map gonext permit 25
!
access-list 50 permit 10.1.1.128 0.0.0.15
```

d.

```
interface e 0
 ip policy route-map gonext
!
route-map gonext permit 20
 match ip address 50
 set ip next-hop 1.1.1.1
!
route-map gonext permit 25
!
access-list 50 permit 10.1.1.128 0.0.0.255
```

Answer: c

Answer c has the correct command structure. Answers a and b have the wrong access list number. Answer d has the wrong reverse mask in access-list 50.

23 Which configuration redistributes all subnetworks from EIGRP into OSPF?

a.

```
router ospf 100
 redistribute eigrp 100 route-map eigrp2ospf
!
route-map eigrp2ospf permit 20
 match ip address 1
 set permit subnets
!
access-list 1 permit 0.0.0.0 255.255.255.255
```

b.

```
router ospf 100
 redistribute eigrp 100 subnets
```

c.

```
router ospf 100
 redistribute eigrp 100 route-map eigrp2ospf subnets
!
route-map eigrp2ospf deny 20
 match ip address 1
 set permit subnets
!
access-list 1 permit 0.0.0.0 255.255.255.255
```

d.

```
router ospf 100
 redistribute eigrp 100 route-map eigrp2ospf
!
route-map eigrp2ospf permit 20
 match ip address 1
 set permit subnets
!
access-list 1 deny 0.0.0.0 255.255.255.255
```

Answer: b

Answer b is the only correct answer. You use the subnets keyword in this instance.

24 What methods allow a PIM network to automatically determine the RP for multicast groups?

a. Auto-RP

b. BSR

c. Both a and b

d. None of the above

Answer: c

Auto-RP and PIM Bootstrap Router (BSR) are methods for PIM networks to configure the RP automatically for multicast groups.

25 What is the MAC address of multicast IP 224.0.0.5?

a. 0100.5e00.2242

b. 0100.5e00.0005

c. 0c00.5e00.0005

d. Not enough information is given.

Answer: b

The lower 23 bits of the multicast IP address merges with the lower 23 bits of 0100.5e00.0000, thus producing 0100.5e00.0005.

Chapter 10 Answers to Scenario Section

Use the following configuration to answer the scenario questions:

```
router bgp 200
 redistribute ospf 100 route-map bgpospf
!
route-map bgpospf permit 10
 match tag 5
 set metric 100
!
route-map bgpospf permit 15
 match tag 6
 set metric 200
```

1 How are the routes being manipulated?

a. OSPF 100 routes are redistributed into BGP 200; OSPF routes with a tag of 5 or 6 are set with a MED of 100 and 200, respectively.

b. OSPF 100 routes are redistributed into BGP 200; a tag of 5 or 6 and metrics are set for the BGP routes.

c. BGP is redistributed into OSPF; tag values and metrics are set.

d. b and c.

Answer: a

Answer a is the only correct answer. Answer b is incorrect because tags are not being set. Answer c is incorrect because the configuration does not show BGP being redistributed into OSPF. Answer d is incorrect because answer b and c are incorrect.

2 What happens to OSPF routes with a tag of 7?

a. They are redistributed.

b. They are not redistributed.

c. A metric of 100 is set.

d. A tag of 5 is set.

Answer: b

Answer b is correct because the route-map bgpospf has permit statements for OSPF routes with tag 5 and tag 6. There is not a permit statement for other routes; therefore, they fail to get redistributed.

Chapter 11 Answers to Q & A Section

1 Which queuing scheme can be used to SNA traffic before servicing other traffic types?

a. FIFO

b. CQ

c. PQ

d. CBWFQ

Answer: c

Priority queuing (PQ) always empties the high queue before servicing the lower priority queues.

2 Which protocol permits hosts to request quality of service parameters from network resources?

a. MPLS

b. RSVP

c. CAR

d. RTP

Answer: b

The Resource Reservation Protocol (RSVP) is a signaling protocol that enables hosts to obtain special qualities of service for data traffic.

3 Which mechanism drops packets to prevent congestion?

a. CQ

b. WRED

c. WFQ

d. DPack

Answer: b

Weighted random early detection (WRED) drops packets to prevent congestion. WRED expects TCP to reduce its window size as packets are dropped and, therefore, to transmit fewer packets.

4 Which scheme is configured with the **traffic-shape** IOS command?

a. MPLS

b. CAR

c. CRTP

d. GTS

Answer: d

Generic Traffic Shaping (GTS) is configured with the traffic-shape command. This command controls the traffic flow on an interface.

5 Which routing protocol permits load balancing over unequal-cost paths?

a. EIGRP

b. OSPF

c. RIP

d. IS-IS

Answer: a

EIGRP and IGRP can load balance over unequal-cost paths. Cisco's implementation of OSPF, ISIS, and RIP can load balance over equal-cost paths.

6 If EIGRP has ten paths to a destination, how many can you use by default?

a. Four

b. Six

c. Eight, if all are equal-cost paths

d. Ten, if all are unequal-cost paths

Answer: a

By default, EIGRP uses four paths for load balancing to a destination. EIGRP can be configured to load balance up to six paths. The paths do not need to have equal costs.

7 What is the standards-based Frame Relay compression method?

a. FRF.5

b. FRF.9

c. FRF.11

d. FRF.12

Answer: b

Implementation FRF.9 of the Frame Relay Forum defines compression on Frame Relay networks. FRF.5 is the Frame Relay/ATM Network Interworking Implementation. FRF.11 is the Voice over Frame Relay Implementation Agreement. FRF.12 is the Frame Relay Fragmentation Agreement.

8 Which mechanism inserts a 32-bit field between the Layer-2 header and Layer-3 header to provide high-speed switching?

a. RSVP

b. FRTS

c. MPLS

d. Tunnel switching

Answer: c

Multi-Protocol Label Switching inserts a 32-bit field, which includes a 20-bit tag, between the Layer-2 header and the Layer-3 header.

9 After the priority queues have been defined, which command enables priority queuing on an interface?

a. **priority-group**

b. **priority-list**

c. **ip priority-group**

d. **priority-list 1 queue-byte 1000**

Answer: a

10 Stacker is based on which compression algorithm?

a. Ford-Fergerson

b. Lempel-Ziv

c. Bruno-Cicala

d. SPF

Answer: b

Stacker is a Cisco enhanced version of the Lempel-Ziv (LZS) compression algorithm.

11 Which queuing scheme can explicitly prioritize traffic into ten different size queues?

a. FIFO

b. CQ

c. PQ

d. WFQ

Answer: b

Custom queuing (CQ) can configure up to 16 queues to prioritize traffic.

12 Which scheme is configured with the **rate-limit** command?

a. MPLS

b. CAR

c. CRTP

d. GTS

Answer: b

Only Committed Access Rate (CAR) uses the rate-limit command.

13 If OSPF has ten equal-cost paths to a destination, how many paths can you use?

a. Four

b. Six

c. Eight

d. Ten

Answer: b

OSPF can be configured to use up to six equal-cost paths.

14 EIGRP has ten paths to a destination. How many can you use if the maximum is configured?

a. Four

b. Six

c. Eight, if all are equal-cost paths

d. Ten, if all are unequal-cost paths

Answer: b

EIGRP can be configured to use up to six equal-cost paths.

15 Which command configures custom queuing on an interface?

a. **priority-list**

b. **custom-group**

c. **custom-list**

d. **custom-queue-list**

Answer: d

Custom queuing is configured by creating queues with the queue-list protocol command, assigning byte counts to the queues with the queue-list queue byte-count command, and then configuring the interface with the custom-queue-list command.

16 Priority queuing uses how many queues?

a. Three

b. Four

c. Six

d. Eight

Answer: b

Priority queuing uses four queues: high, medium, normal, and low.

17 Which queuing strategy forwards frames based on the order that they are received?

a. FIFO

b. CQ

c. WFQ

d. PQ

Answer: a

First-in, first out forwards frames in the order that they were received. You use no special mechanisms to prioritize traffic.

18 Which queuing strategy forwards frames based on the last bit of the frame received?

a. FIFO

b. CQ

c. WFQ

d. PQ

Answer: c

Weighted Fair Queuing (WFQ) ensures that applications that use large packets cannot unfairly monopolize the bandwidth for smaller packets by looking at the arrival time of the last bit of the packets.

19 The following command is configured on an interface. What happens when the output transmission rate exceeds 30 Mbps?

```
rate-limit output 30000000 31000 31000 conform-action transmit
    exceed-action drop
```

a. Bursts to 31,000 bytes, then dropped

b. Dropped

c. Bursts to 31,000 bytes, then dropped

d. None of the above

Answer: c

This is a CAR configuration. The exceed-action is to drop the packets after the exceed rate is met.

20 Which interface command enables FIFO queuing?

a. fifo

b. no fair-queue

c. enable fifo

d. queue fifo

Answer: b

Answer b is the correct command to enable FIFO.

21 What does WRR do?

a. Drops packets based on IP Precedence

b. Assigns packets with different IP Precedence into one of 4 queues

c. Configures 16 queues

d. Uses 4 queues called high, normal, slow, and default

Answer: b

WRR maps packets by using IP Precedence bits to one of four outbound WRR queues. This is also known as WRR scheduling. Each WRR queue has a queue weight and a delay priority. More bandwidth is given to packets with higher weight.

22 IP prioritization with DSCP uses how many bits?

a. 3

b. 6

c. 8

d. 64

Answer: b

DSCP uses 6 bits, which produce 64 values for packet classification.

Chapter 11 Answers to Scenario Section

Use the following configuration to answer the scenario questions:

```
interface s 0
 custom-queue-list 1
!
queue-list 1 protocol dlsw 1
queue-list 1 protocol ip 2 list 10
queue-list 1 protocol cdp 3
queue-list 1 default 4
!
queue-list 1 queue 1 byte-count 2000
queue-list 1 queue 2 byte-count 3000
queue-list 1 queue 3 byte-count 500
queue-list 1 queue 4 byte-count 3500
!
access-list 10 permit 200.1.1.0 0.0.0.255
```

1 Which queuing strategy is configured?

a. PQ

b. CQ

c. CBWFQ

d. FIFO

Answer: b

The configuration enables Custom Queuing on serial 0.

2 Approximately what percent of the bandwidth is queued for DLSW bandwidth?

a. 33 percent

b. 22 percent

c. 10 percent

d. 39 percent

Answer: b

DLSW uses queue 1. Queue 1 has 2000/(2000+3000+500+3500) = 2000/9000 = .222 = 22 percent of the bandwidth.

3 Approximately what percent of the bandwidth do you use for IP networks not in access list 10?

a. 33 percent

b. 22 percent

c. 10 percent

d. 39 percent

Answer: d

IP networks not in access list 10 use queue 4, the default queue. Queue 4 has 3500/(2000+3000+500+3500) = 3500/9000 = .3889 = 39 percent of the bandwidth.

Chapter 12 Answers to Q & A Section

1 Which ITU standard provides a framework for multimedia protocols for the transport of voice, video, and data over packet-switched networks?

a. RTP/RCTP

b. VoIP

c. H.323

d. WFQ

Answer: c

H.323 is the ITU standard that provides a framework for the transport of voice, video, and data over packet-switched networks.

2 Which of the following is the default codec that you use with VoIP dial peers?

a. G.711

b. G.723

c. G.728

d. G.729

Answer: d

The default codec in Cisco VoIP dial peers is G.729, which has an 8 kbps bit rate.

3 Which authentication protocol uses TCP?

a. Kerberos

b. TACACS

c. RADIUS

d. AAA

Answer: b

4 Which encryption method uses a 168-bit key?

a. DES

b. PGP

c. 3DES

d. IPSec

Answer: c

The triple DES (3DES) key is 3 × 56 bits = 168 bits.

5 What is AAA?

a. Automation, authentication, and accounting

b. Authentication, abomination, and accounting

c. Automation, authorization, and accounting

d. Authentication, authorization, and accounting

Answer: d

6 RTP operates in which layer of the OSI model?

a. Application

b. Session

c. Transport

d. Network

Answer: c

Real-Time Transport Protocol (RTP) operates in the transport layer of the OSI model.

7 Which H.323 protocol is responsible for call setup and signaling?

a. H.245

b. Q.931

c. H.225

d. RTCP

Answer: b

The Q.931 standard defines the procedures responsible for call setup and signaling.

8 Which unit measures the number of voice calls in one hour?

a. Kbps

b. Erlangs

c. DS0

d. FXS

Answer: b

Erlangs is the unit that describes the number of calls in one hour.

9 Which feature does not transmit packets when there is silence?

a. E&M

b. VAD

c. Dial-Peer

d. DSS

Answer: b

Voice Activity Detection reduces traffic by not transmitting packets when there is silence in voice conversations.

10 What does CRTP compresses?

a. The RTP header

b. The RTP, TCP, and IP headers

c. The RTP, UDP, and IP headers

d. The RTCP header

Answer: c

Compressed Real-Time Transport Protocol (CRTP) compresses the RTP, UDP, and IP headers.

11 Which protocol(s) reduce broadcasts in an IPX internetwork?

a. IPX RIP

b. NLSP

c. IPX EIGRP

d. Answers b and c

Answer: d

NLSP and IPX EIGRP routing protocols reduce IPX broadcast traffic.

12 How many bits are in an IPX address?

a. 32 bits

b. 48 bits

c. 60 bits

d. 80 bits

Answer: d

The 80-bit IPX address consists of the 32-bit network number plus a 48-bit MAC address.

13 Which is not a valid IPX network number?

a. DEAD

b. 0FFFFFF0

c. DEAGF0

d. 10

Answer: c

Answer c is not valid because G is not a hexadecimal digit. All other answers are valid network numbers.

14 Which method is preferred for transporting NetBIOS?

a. NetBEUI

b. NBT

c. ATP

d. Ethernet

Answer: b

NetBIOS over TCP/IP (NBT) is the preferred method for transporting NetBIOS traffic over routed internetworks.

15 Which IETF standard provides a framework for multimedia protocols for the transport of voice, video, and data over packet-switched networks?

a. RTP/RCTP

b. VoIP

c. H.323

d. SIP

Answer: d

Session initiation protocol (SIP) is the IETF standard for the transport of voice, video, and data over packet-switched networks. H.323 is the ITU standard.

16 Which authentication protocol uses UDP?

a. Kerberos

b. TACACS

c. RADIUS

d. AAA

Answer: c

RADIUS uses UDP port 1812 or UDP 1645 and UDP 1646. TACACS uses TCP.

17 What is FXS?

a. Feeder Exchange Station

b. Foreign Exchange Source

c. Foreign Exchange Station

d. Federal Exchange Station

Answer: c

Foreign Exchange Station (FXS) ports provide dial time and ring voltage.

18 Which codec produces 64 kbps of bandwidth?

a. G.711

b. G.723

c. G.726

d. G.729

Answer: a

The G.711 codec produces a 64 kbps bit rate.

19 Which SS7 component is a database?

a. SCP

b. STP

c. SSP

d. Billing

Answer: a

The Signaling Control Point (SCP) is a database for special call processing and routing.

20 Which AAA function determines which resources are accessed?

a. Accounting

b. Authorization

c. Authentication

d. TACACS

Answer: b

Authorization determines which resources are accessed. Authentication determines who is the user. Accounting keeps track of what resources were accessed, by whom and when.

21 Which authentication protocol separates each AAA function into separate modules?

a. Kerberos

b. RADIUS

c. TACACS+

d. AAA

Answer: c

TACACS+ separates AAA functions into separate modules. RADIUS combines authentication and authorization.

22 Which AAA function identifies the user?

a. Accounting

b. Authorization

c. Authentication

d. TACACS

Answer: c

Authentication determines the user. Authorization determines which resources are accessed. Accounting keeps track of which resources were accessed, by whom and when.

23 Which algorithm does the Cisco PIX Firewall use?

a. Adaptive Security Algorithm

b. Authoritative Security Algorithm

c. Authenticating Security Algorithm

d. Access Security algorithm

Answer: a

The PIX Firewall uses the Adaptive Security Algorithm (ASA) for stateful, connection-oriented security.

24 Which of the following are QoS tools that you can use for VoIP networks?

a. CQ and TCP compression

b. CRTP and WFQ

c. DES and CRTP

d. ATM and UDP header compression

Answer: b

Compressed RTP (CRTP) and Weighted Fair Queuing (WFQ) are used in VoIP networks.

25 An IPX address consists of what?

a. 32-bit network and 8-bit host part

b. 24-bit network part and 8-bit host part

c. 24-bit network part and 48-bit host part

d. 32-bit network part and 48-bit host part

Answer: d

The IPX address is 80 bits in length, consisting of a 32-bit network part and a 48-bit host part.

26 Which service can reduce NetBIOS traffic?

a. DNS

b. WINS

c. GNS

d. SAP

Answer: b

The Windows Internet Naming System (WINS) provides dynamic NetBIOS name registration services that reduce NAME_Query broadcasts.

27 Which access list number can filter IPX SAP traffic?

a. 850

b. 101

c. 989

d. 1099

Answer: d

IPX SAP filter access list numbers range from 1000 to 1099.

28 NLSP is which type of protocol?

a. Hybrid

b. Distance vector

c. Link-state

d. Broadcast

Answer: c

NetWare Link Services Protocol (NLSP) is a link-state protocol that is based on IS-IS.

29 Which protocol do you use in a routed TCP/IP network for Network Neighborhood browsing?

a. NetBEUI

b. NWlink

c. NBT

d. Internet Explorer

Answer: c

You use NetBIOS over TCP/IP (NBT) in IP networks.

30 How often does IPX RIP broadcast its routing table?

a. Every 30 seconds

b. Every 60 seconds

c. Every 90 seconds

d. None of the above

Answer: b

IPX RIP broadcasts every 60 seconds.

31 How often does IPX EIGRP broadcast its routing table?

a. Every 30 seconds

b. Every 60 seconds

c. Every 90 seconds

d. None of the above

Answer: d

IPX EIGRP does not broadcast the routing table periodically.

Chapter 12 Answers to Scenario Section

Scenario 12-1

Use the following configuration to answer the questions in this scenario:

```
dial-peer voice 100 pots
 destination-pattern 1111
 port 1/1
!
dial-peer voice 200 pots
 destination-pattern 1112
 port 1/2
!
dial-peer voice 8000 voip
 destination-pattern 2...
 session target ipv4:1.1.1.1
 vad
 ip precedence 4
!
dial-peer voice 8001 voip
 destination-pattern 3...
```

```
 session target ipv4:2.2.2.2
 vad
 ip precedence 4
!
interface serial 0
 ip address 3.1.1.1 255.255.255.252
 ip rtp header-compression
 ip rtp compression-connections 10
```

1 To which IP address are calls to 3111 sent?

a. 3.1.1.1

b. 1.1.1.1

c. 2.2.2.2

d. 255.255.255.252

Answer: c

All calls with a destination pattern of 3... are sent to IP address 2.2.2.2.

2 What are the precedence bits set to for VoIP packets?

a. 010

b. 011

c. 100

d. 101

Answer: c

Precedence bits are set to the binary value of 4.

3 Are packets sent during silent spurs?

a. No, the IP precedence bit is set to 4.

b. No, VAD is disabled.

c. Yes, the dial-peer is over 8000.

d. No, VAD is enabled.

Answer: d

Voice activity detection (VAD) is enabled on VoIP dial peers 8000 and 8001.

4 Where are calls to 1112 sent?

a. 2.2.2.2

b. Port 1/1

c. Port 1/2

d. 3.1.1.1

Answer: c

Destination pattern 1112 is sent to the POTS port 1/2.

5 Which of the following is the default codec that you use in dial peer 8000?

a. G.711.

b. G.726.

c. G.729.

d. Not enough information is given.

Answer: c.

The default CODEC used in VoIP dial peers is G.729.

Scenario 12-2

Use the following configuration to answer the questions in this scenario:

```
hostname router
!
ipx routing
!
interface ethernet 0
 ipx network 15
 ipx input-network-filter 850
!
interface ethernet 1
 ipx network 16
 ipx input-sap-filter 1050
!
interface serial 0
 ipx network 2a
!
interface serial 1
 ipx network 2b
!
ipx router eigrp 50
 network 2a
 network 2b
!
ipx router rip
 no network 2a
 no network 2b
!
access-list 850 deny 10
access-list 850 deny 11
access-list 850 deny a0
access-list 850 permit -1
!
access-list 1050 permit -1 4
access-list 1050 deny -1
```

1 What is the IPX network for Ethernet 0?

a. 15

b. 0x15

c. 850

d. 16

Answer: b

The IPX network number is hexadecimal 0x15.

2 What does the filter configured for Ethernet 0 do?

a. Filters IP networks 10, 11, and a0

b. Filters SAP number 4

c. Filters IPX networks 10, 11, and a0

d. Denies all other IPX networks

Answer: c

Access list 850 is applied to the input network filter in Ethernet 0. List 850 denies IPX networks 10, 11, and a0 and permits all other IPX networks.

3 What does the filter configured for Ethernet 1 do?

a. Filters IP networks 10, 11, and a0

b. Filters SAP number 4

c. Filters IPX networks 10, 11, and a0

d. Denies all other IPX networks

Answer: b

Access list 1050 is applied to the input SAP filter in Ethernet 1. List 1050 permits SAP number 4 and denies all other SAPs.

4 Which routing protocol do you use in the WAN interfaces?

a. IPX RIP

b. IPX NLSP

c. IPX EIGRP

d. IPX OSPF

Answer: c

IPX EIGRP is configured for networks 2A and 2B, which are the IPX network numbers of serial 0 and serial 1, respectively.

5 Which routing protocol do you use in the Ethernet interfaces?

a. IPX RIP

b. IPX NLSP

c. IPX EIGRP

d. IPX OSPF

Answer: a

IPX RIP is configured for all networks except for 2A and 2B.

INDEX

Numerics

A

B

C

D

E

F

G

H

I

J-K

L

M

N

O

P

Q

R

S

U

V

W

X

Cisco Press
Learning is serious business.
Invest wisely.